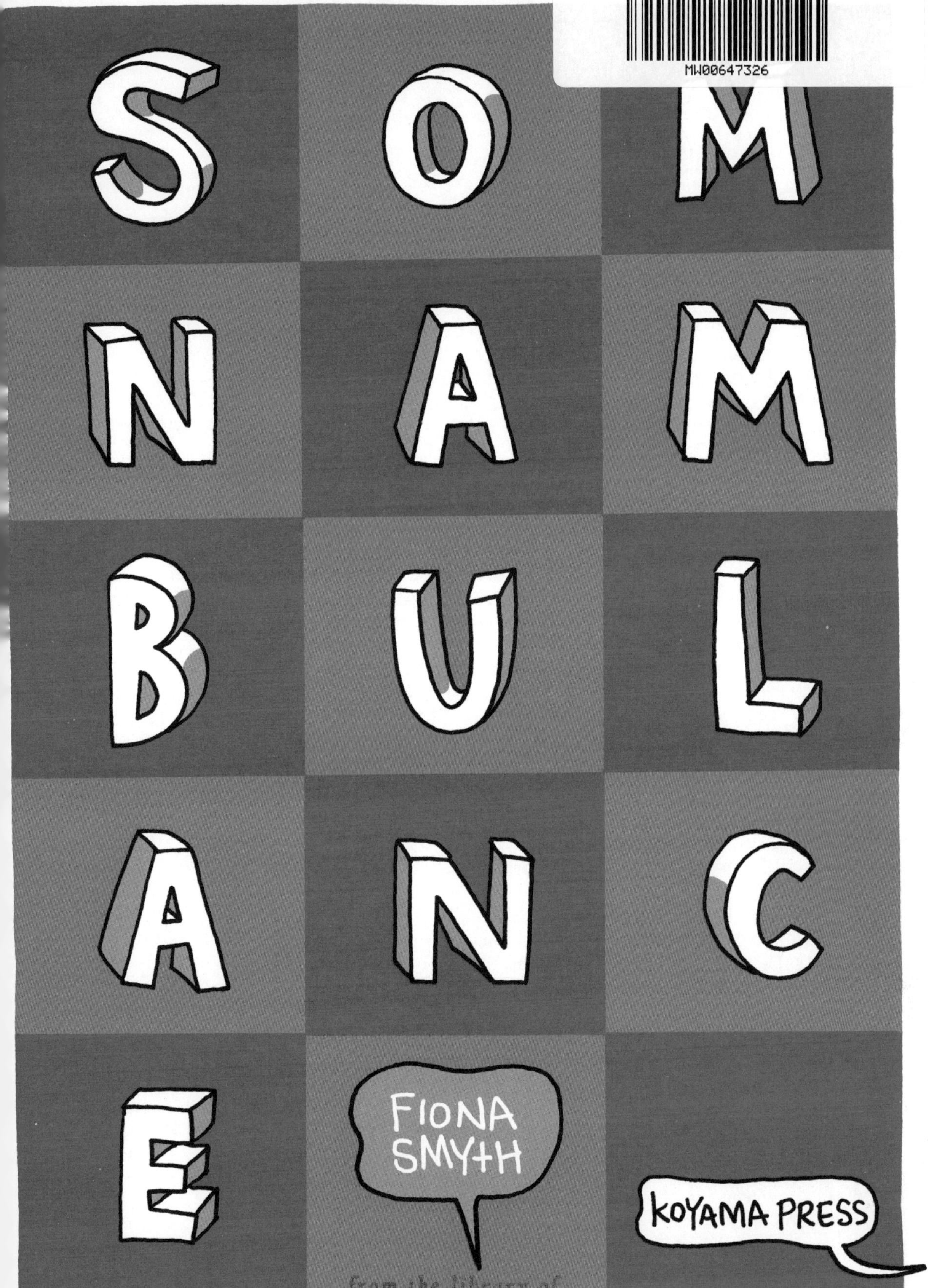
SOM
NAM
BUL
ANC
E
FIONA SMYtH
KOYAMA PRESS

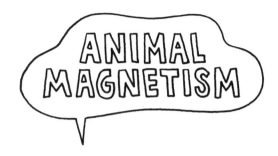

ANIMAL MAGNETISM

THIS IS ONE HELL OF A BOOK: AN ABUNDANCE OF FIONA SMYTH DELIGHTS, ALL IN ONE VOLUME. WELCOME, FRIEND. SIT DOWN AND REVEL. THE ONLY THING THAT MATCHES THE GENEROSITY OF SMYTH'S WORK ITSELF IS THIS PLENTIFUL, JOYOUS SELECTION. FROM HER EARLY COMICS AND HER LONG-RUNNING SERIES TO STAND-ALONE WORKS, THERE'S ENOUGH HERE TO FILL ANY TREASURE TROLL'S MAGIC CAVE. LET'S BE GREEDY AND EAT ALL THE CANDY AT ONCE.

AS A LONG-TIME FIONA FAN, I SEE WORKS INCLUDED HERE THAT I INSTANTLY RECOGNIZE AND AM GLAD TO MEET AGAIN, AND ALSO A NUMBER OF NEW (TO ME) POTS OF GOLD. WHAT WE HAVE IN THIS ASSEMBLAGE IS A KIND OF HISTORY OF FIONA'S WORK AS WELL AS AN (OVERDUE) CELEBRATION OF HER LONG AND VARIED CAREER. HOWEVER, I WRITE "KIND OF HISTORY", AS OPPOSED TO JUST "HISTORY," BECAUSE I KNOW THAT FIONA IS A MAXIMALIST AND MAXIMALISTS PRODUCE AND PRODUCE AND PRODUCE. IT WOULD TAKE ANOTHER WHOLE VOLUME SUCH AS THIS, AND THEN PERHAPS YET ANOTHER, TO COMPLETELY CHRONICLE ALL THE MANY OBJECTS, DRAWINGS, PAINTINGS, COMIX, SCULPTURES, ZINES, POSTERS, PRINTS, TEXTS, TEXTILES, BOOKLETS... PHEW..., ALL THE QUICKIES AND FUNSIES AND GLEEFUL OUTBURSTS OF PURE CREATIVE FORCE THAT COMBINE TO MAKE UP THE FIONA CANON, TO PORTRAY WHAT WE SO STUPIDLY NOW CALL AN ARTIST'S CAREER.

FIONA SMYTH DOES NOT HAVE A "CAREER" ANY MORE THAN A FORCE OF NATURE COULD BE SAID TO DO SO. FIONA MAKES THINGS BECAUSE MAKING THINGS IS AS NECESSARY TO HER AS HER OWN BLOOD.

IT'S NOT EVERY DAY YOU GET TO LOOK INTO THE MIND OF AN ARTIST. AND WHAT DO WE LEARN FROM COMBING THROUGH (AND LOITERING OVER, DREAMILY) THREE DECADES OF FIONA'S ART?

WE FIND IN FIONA AN ARTIST KEENLY ALERT TO THE MIND'S WONDROUS (AND AT TIMES TERRIFYING) ABILITY TO SEE THROUGH THE APPARENT AND ON TO THE SUBLIME, HOWEVER GOOEY AND STRANGE THAT SUBLIME MIGHT BE.

WE FIND AN ARTIST LESS INTERESTED IN DOCUMENTING THE WORLD AROUND HER THAN IN MAKING THE WORLD AROUND HER BEND, LIKE RUBBER. FIONA CATCHES THE EMOTIONAL AND PSYCHOLOGICAL VIBRATIONS THAT SURROUND A SETTING, AN OBJECT, OR A CREATURE.

SHE IS ATTUNED TO THE ANIMAL MAGNETISM THAT FLOWS BETWEEN
PEOPLE AND ANIMALS AND THINGS. TO WIT, LOOK AT FIONA'S MANY
DRAWINGS AND PAINTINGS OF CHAIRS. WHO THINKS ABOUT CHAIRS AS
ANYTHING MORE THAN BASIC TOOLS? IN FIONA'S WORLD, A CHAIR
PRANCES ABOUT WITH ITS LEGS CURLED UP, AS IF OUT FOR A JAUNT,
AND THUS REMINDS US THAT NOTHING IS CONFINEABLE, NOTHING
NEED BE KEPT TO OR LIMITED BY ITS FIRST FUNCTION (A MESSAGE
I FIND DEEPLY LIBERATING).

WE FIND AN ARTIST NOT ONLY AWARE OF REALITY'S INNATE FLUIDITY,
INDEED INSTABILITY, BUT ONE WHO REVELS IN SAME. FIONA IS NOT
A SURREALIST, AS HER WORK IS HARDLY BURDENED BY NIHILISM
OR THE GENRE'S TWIN TOXIC OBSESSIONS WITH SHOCK AND GUILT.
RATHER, SHE IS AN ARTIST GROUNDED IN THE FIGURATIVE WHO
REALIZES HOW UNRELIABLE FIGURATION OFTEN IS, WHICH BEGS
A SIMPLE QUESTION: WHICH REALITY DO YOU PREFER? I LIKE MY
CHAIRS LEGGY, THANKS, WITH LOTS OF KICK.

MOST CONTEMPORARY ART LEAVES ME COLD. I SUSPECT MOST
CONTEMPORARY ART FEELS THE SAME WAY ABOUT ME.
FIONA SMYTH IS A SINGULAR ARTIST IN A WORLD FULL OF TREND-
CHASERS, CYNICAL ACADEMICS, BUZZKILLERS AND ALL AROUND
YAWNFEST-INDUCERS. IN AN ART SCENE OVERRUN BY CON(NIVING)
ARTISTS, FIONA SMYTH JUST WANTS TO SHARE: SHARE HER JOY,
SHARE THE VISUAL WEALTH, AND SHARE THE OPEN INVITATION
THAT IS HER WORK.
FIONA'S ART BRINGS THE VIEWER IN. FIONA IS THE HOST AND WE
ARE THE LUCKY GUESTS. BEING OPEN AND WELCOMING, THE ART
CONTAINED HERE PERFORMS THE HAPPY OPPOSITE OF WHAT
PASSES FOR CULTURAL ENGAGEMENT TODAY.
AS I NOTED ABOVE, THERE IS A MAGNANIMITY IN THESE
WORKS THAT HAS, AT ITS HEART, ONE FUNCTION - TO BRING
MORE TO EVERY VIEWER'S TABLE (WOBBLY LEGS AND ALL).

RM VAUGHAN

THE BAROMETER OF HIP...

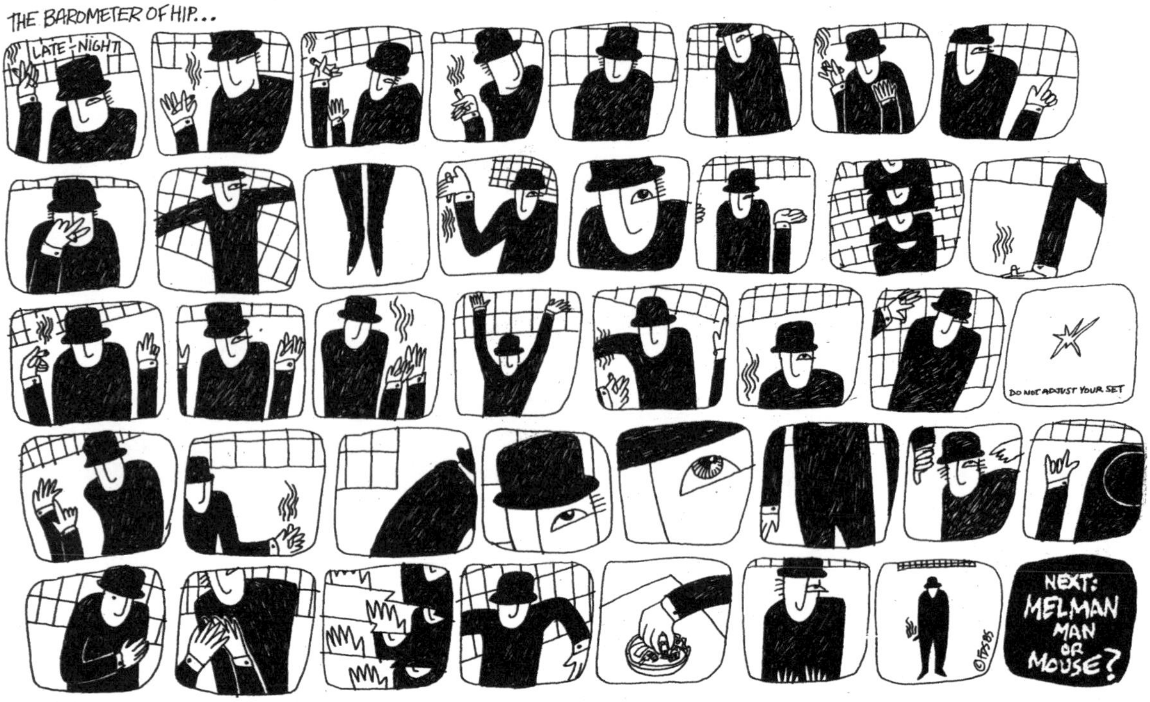
LATE-NIGHT
DO NOT ADJUST YOUR SET
©FDS85
NEXT: MELMAN MAN OR MOUSE?

ATTACK OF THE INHUMAN SPONGE STARRING NASTY KINKY AND L.B. MELMAN ©FDS85

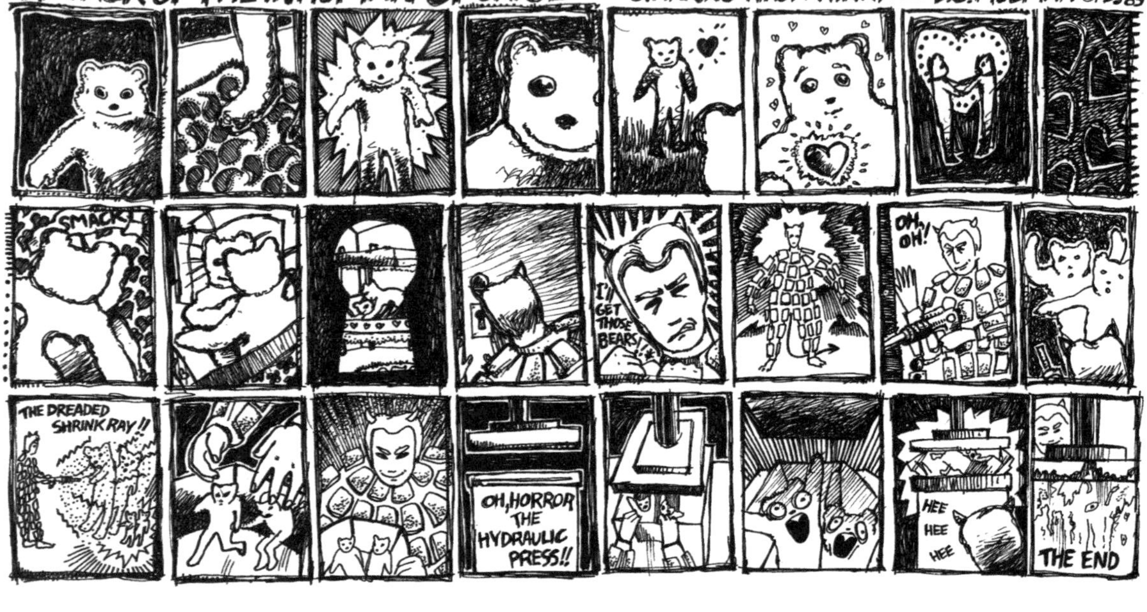
SMACK!
I'LL GET THOSE BEARS
OH, OH!
THE DREADED SHRINK RAY!!
OH, HORROR THE HYDRAULIC PRESS!!
HEE HEE HEE
THE END

JUGGS THE MILKMAN AND DICK THE DETECTIVE

FIONA SMYTH 1985©

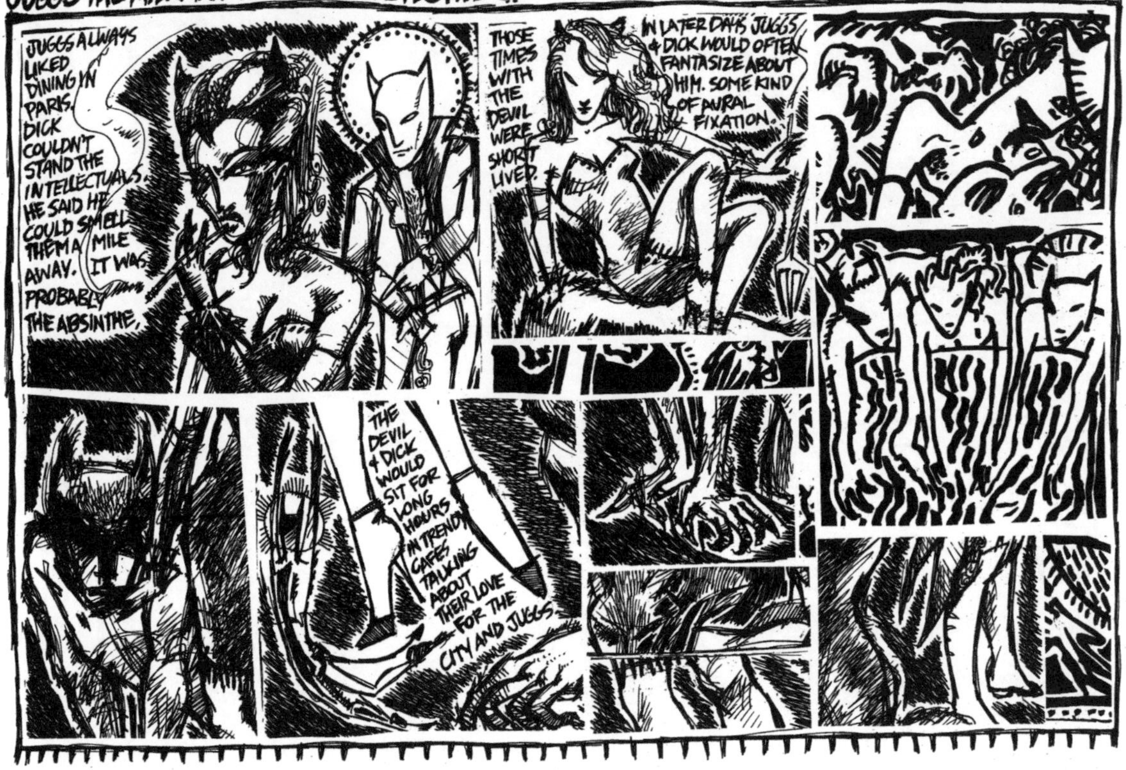
JUGGS ALWAYS LIKED DINING IN PARIS. DICK COULDN'T STAND THE INTELLECTUALS. HE SAID HE COULD SMELL THEM A MILE AWAY. IT WAS PROBABLY THE ABSINTHE.
THOSE TIMES WITH THE DEVIL WERE SHORT LIVED.
IN LATER DAYS JUGGS & DICK WOULD OFTEN FANTASIZE ABOUT HIM. SOME KIND OF AURAL FIXATION.
THE DEVIL & DICK WOULD SIT FOR LONG HOURS IN TRENDY CAFES TALKING ABOUT THEIR LOVE FOR THE CITY AND JUGGS.

MANHOLE LAMENTS THE DEATH OF HIS LOVE, BOOBTUBE.

FIONA SMYTH '85©

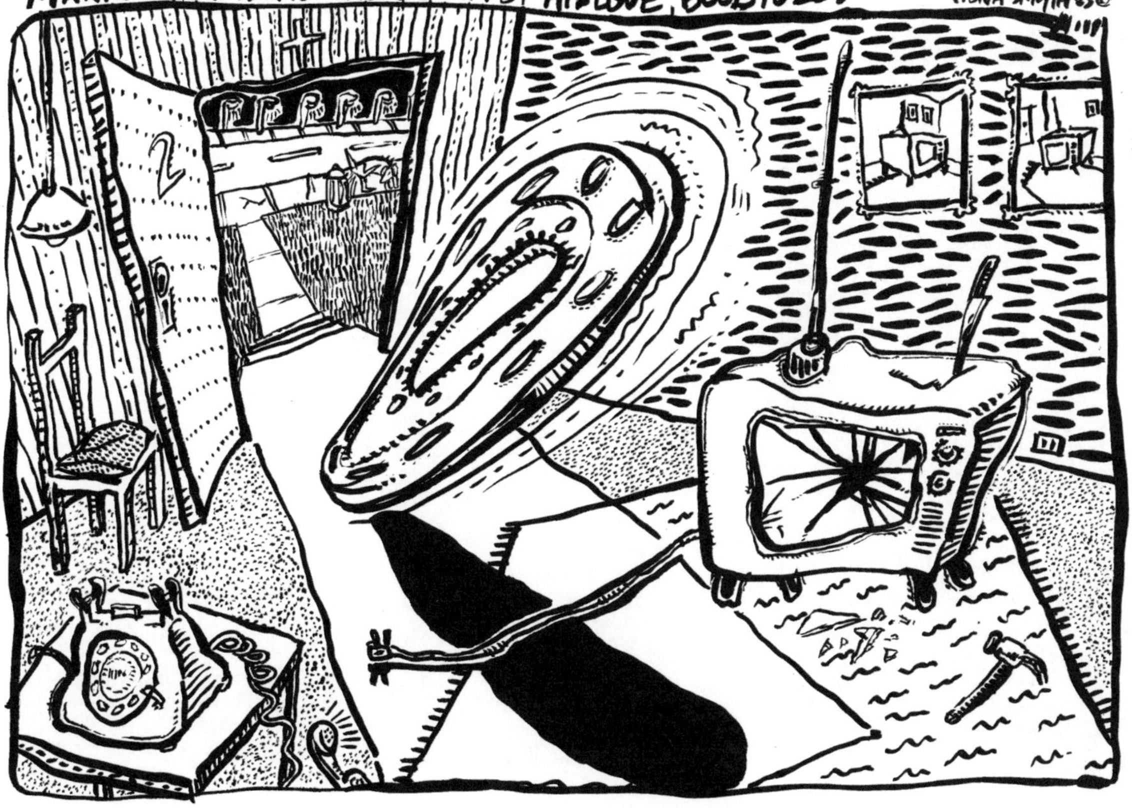

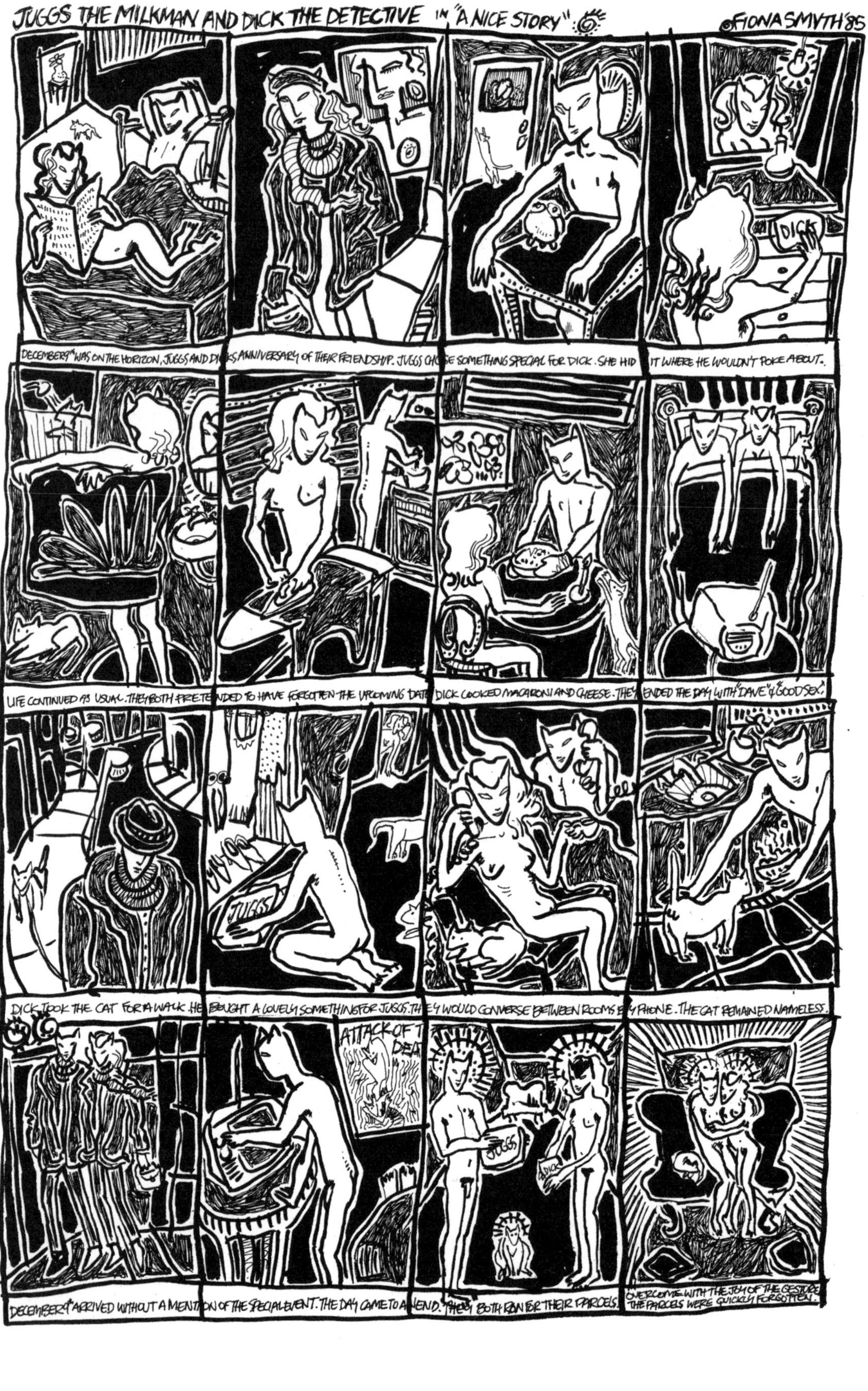

JUGGS THE MILKMAN AND DICK THE DETECTIVE IN "A NICE STORY"
©FIONA SMYTH '85
DICK
DECEMBER 9TH WAS ON THE HORIZON, JUGGS AND DICKS ANNIVERSARY OF THEIR FRIENDSHIP. JUGGS CHOSE SOMETHING SPECIAL FOR DICK. SHE HID IT WHERE HE WOULDN'T POKE ABOUT.
LIFE CONTINUED AS USUAL. THEY BOTH PRETENDED TO HAVE FORGOTTEN THE UPCOMING DATE. DICK COOKED MACARONI AND CHEESE. THEY ENDED THE DAY WITH "DAVE" & "GOOD SEX."
JUGGS
DICK TOOK THE CAT FOR A WALK. HE BOUGHT A LOVELY SOMETHING FOR JUGGS. THEY WOULD CONVERSE BETWEEN ROOMS BY PHONE. THE CAT REMAINED NAMELESS.
ATTACK OF T
DEA
JUGGS
DICK
DECEMBER 9TH ARRIVED WITHOUT A MENTION OF THE SPECIAL EVENT. THE DAY CAME TO AN END. THEY BOTH RAN FOR THEIR PARCELS.
OVERCOME WITH THE JOY OF THE GESTURE THE PARCELS WERE QUICKLY FORGOTTEN.

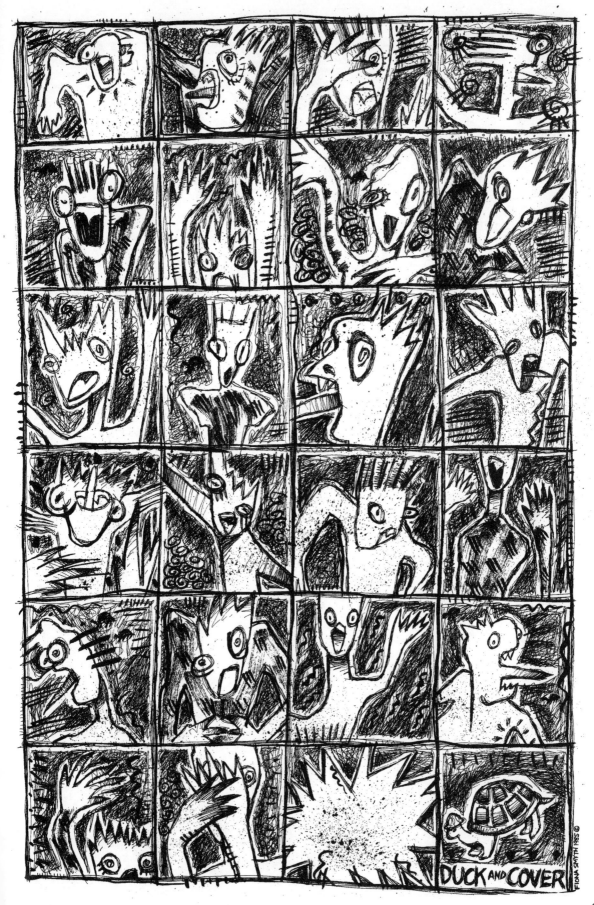

DUCK AND COVER

FIONA SMYTH 1985 ©

7

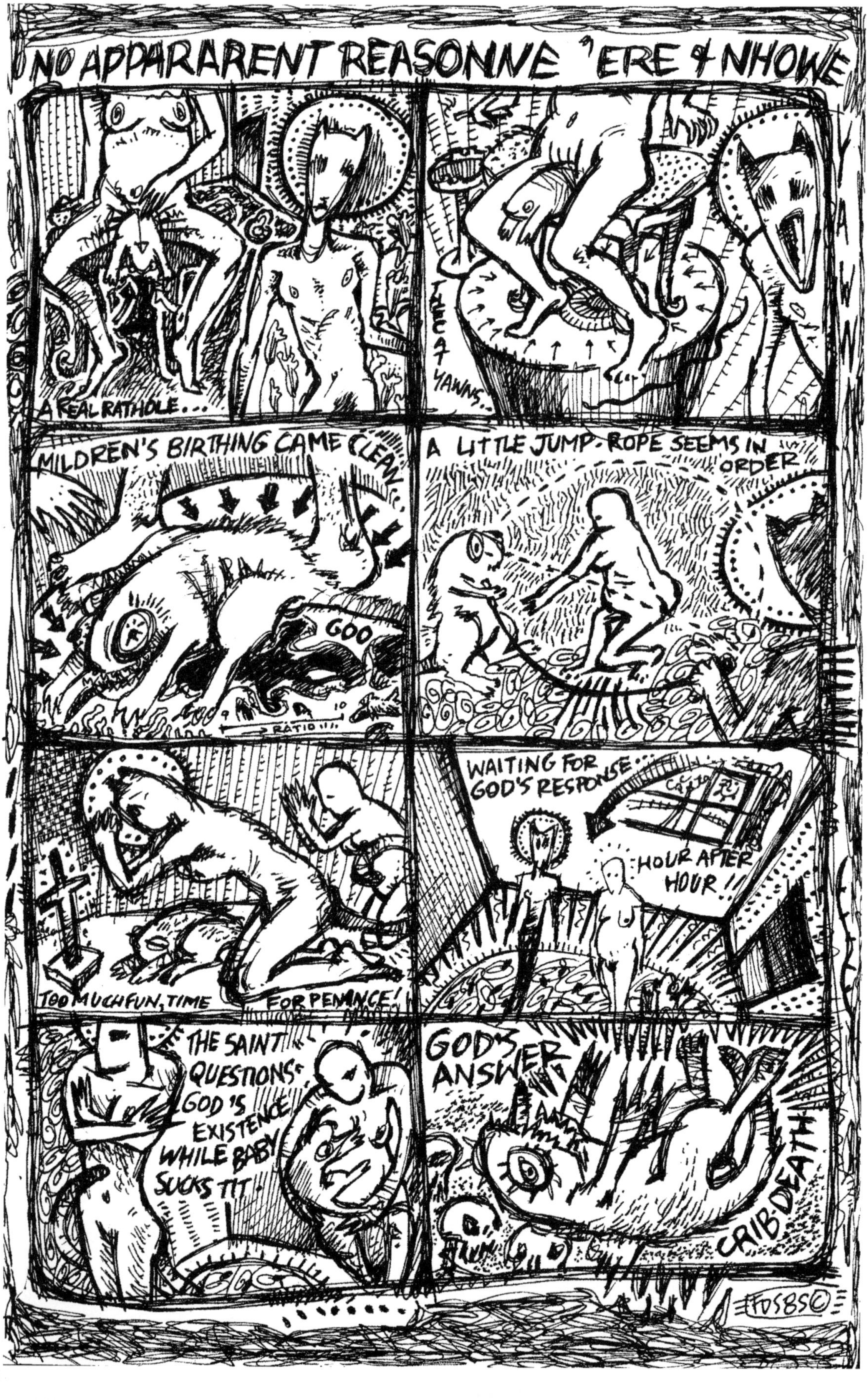
NO APPARARENT REASONINNE 'ERE & NHOWE
A REAL RATHOLE...
THE CAT YAWNS
YAWN
MILDREN'S BIRTHING CAME CLEAN
GOO
RATIO
A LITTLE JUMP-ROPE SEEMS IN ORDER
TOO MUCH FUN, TIME FOR PENANCE!
WAITING FOR GOD'S RESPONSE
HOUR AFTER HOUR!
THE SAINT QUESTIONS GOD'S EXISTENCE WHILE BABY SUCKS TIT
GOD'S ANSWER
CRIB-DEATH
FDS85©

JUGGS THE MILKMAN AND DICK THE DETECTIVE

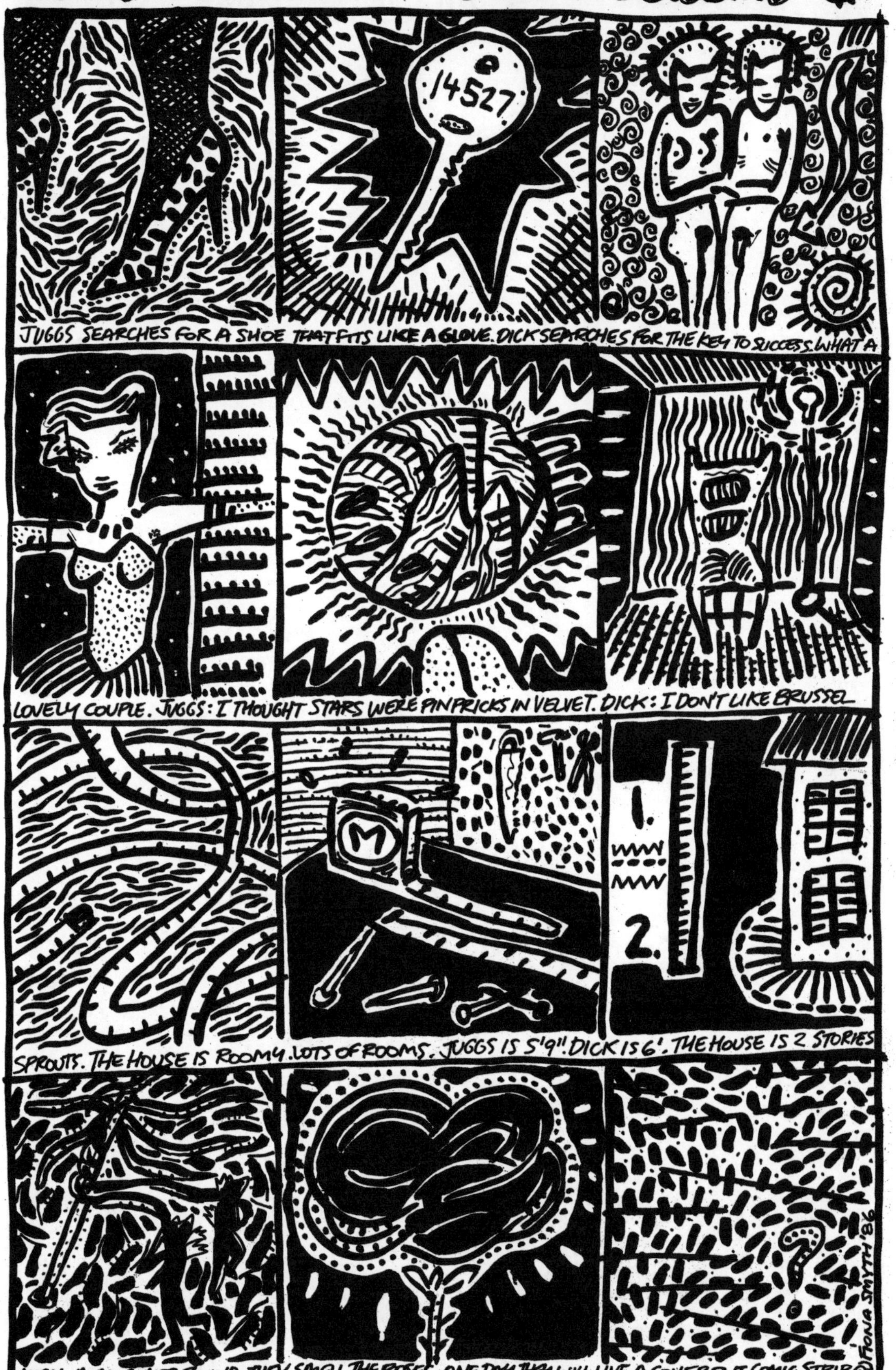
14527
JUGGS SEARCHES FOR A SHOE THAT FITS LIKE A GLOVE. DICK SEARCHES FOR THE KEY TO SUCCESS. WHAT A
LOVELY COUPLE. JUGGS: I THOUGHT STARS WERE PINPRICKS IN VELVET. DICK: I DON'T LIKE BRUSSEL
M
1.
2.
SPROUTS. THE HOUSE IS ROOMY. LOTS OF ROOMS. JUGGS IS 5'9". DICK IS 6'. THE HOUSE IS 2 STORIES
HIGH. MAY COMES ROUND. THEY SMELL THE ROSES. ONE DAY THEY WILL LIVE A COHERENT COMIC STRIP
© FIONA SMYTH '86

JUGGS THE MILKMAN & DICK THE DETECTIVE IN "SWEET STUFF"

EDS © 86

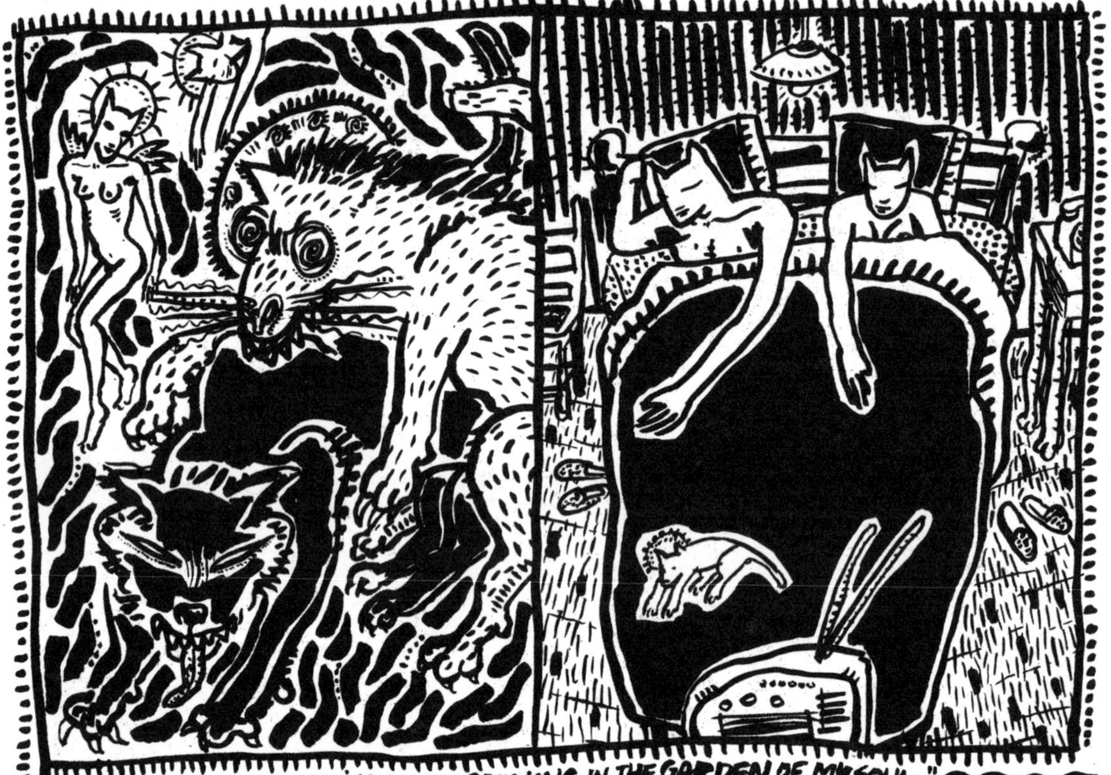

"JUGGS, YOU ARE THE MORNING GLORY GROWING IN THE GARDEN OF MY SOUL."

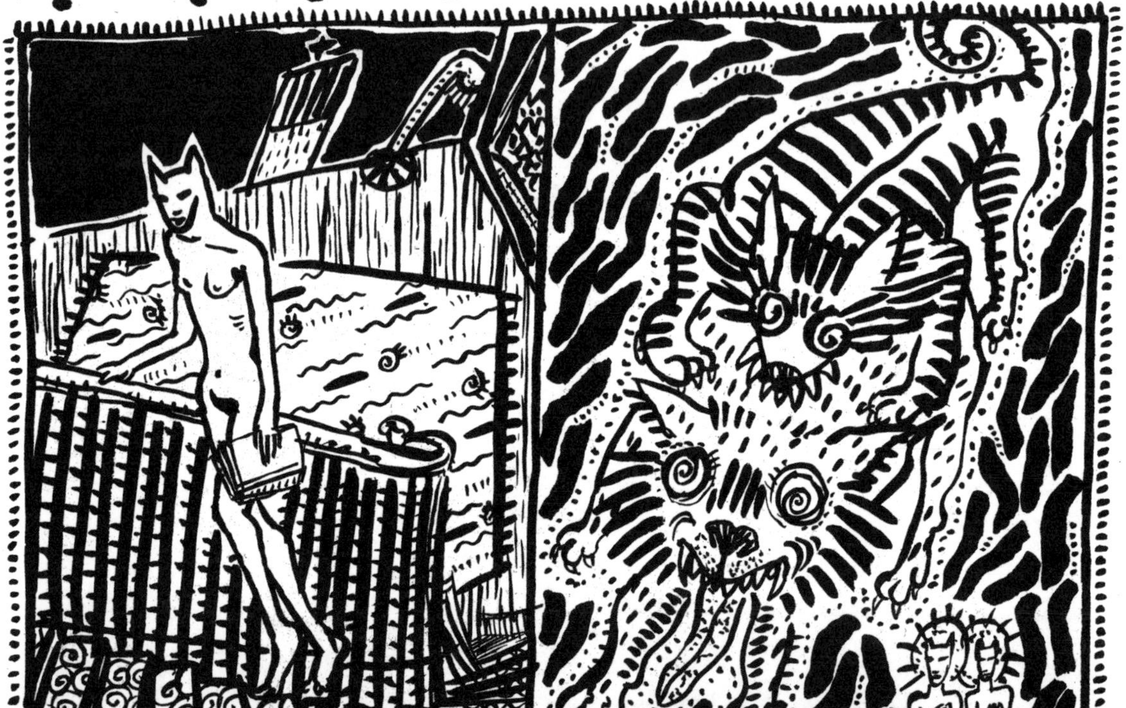

"DICK, YOU INSPIRE ME A LITTLE BIT HIGHER."

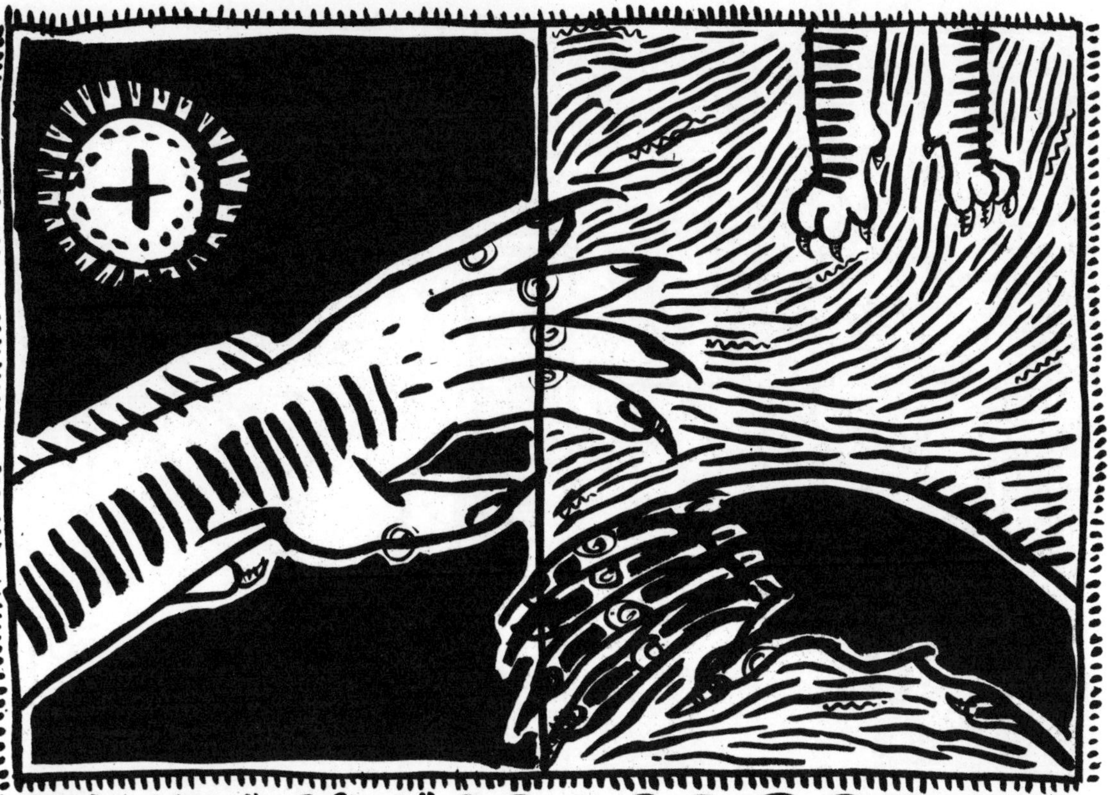

"JUBOS, YOU ARE MY LIFEBLOOD."

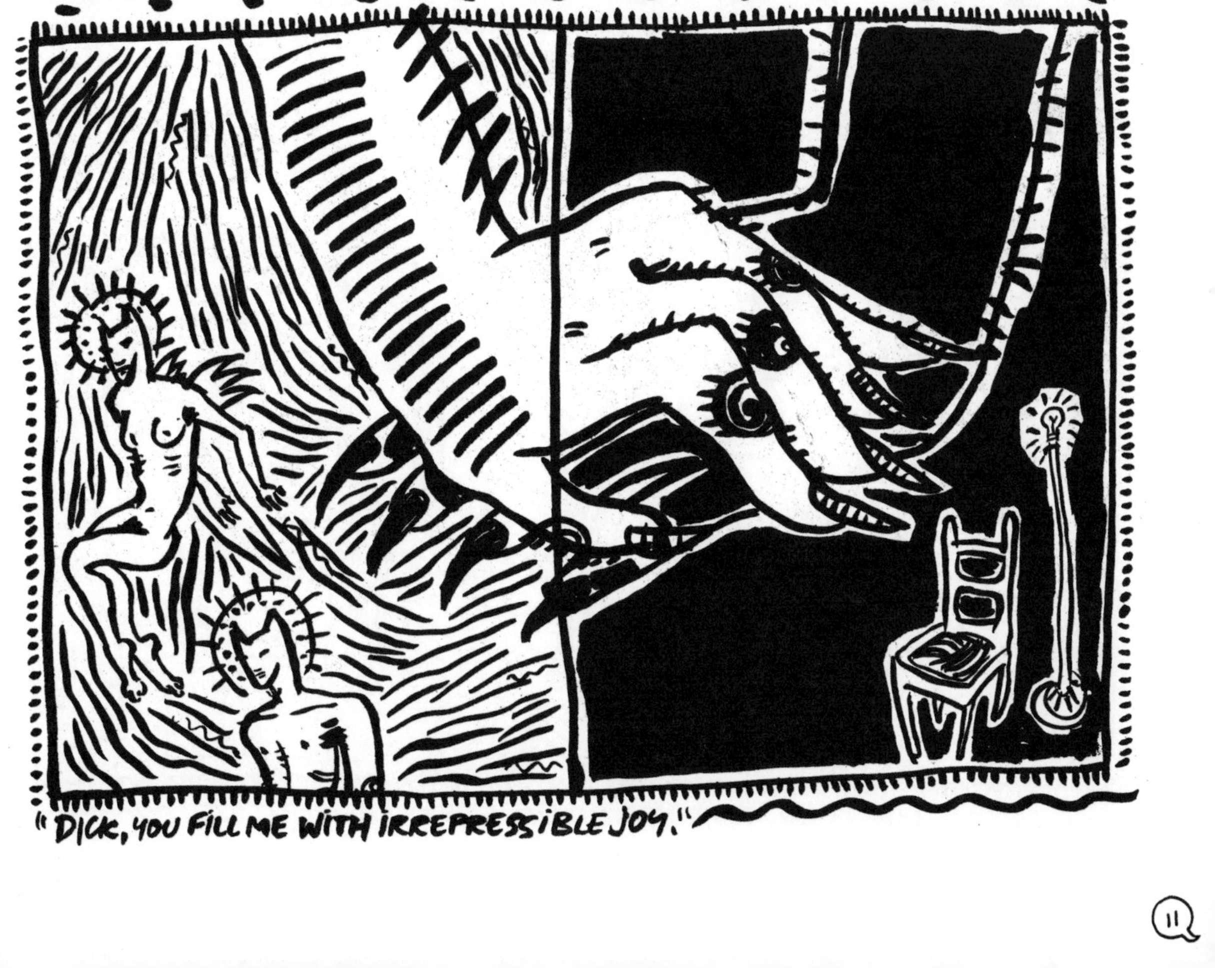

"DICK, YOU FILL ME WITH IRREPRESSIBLE JOY."

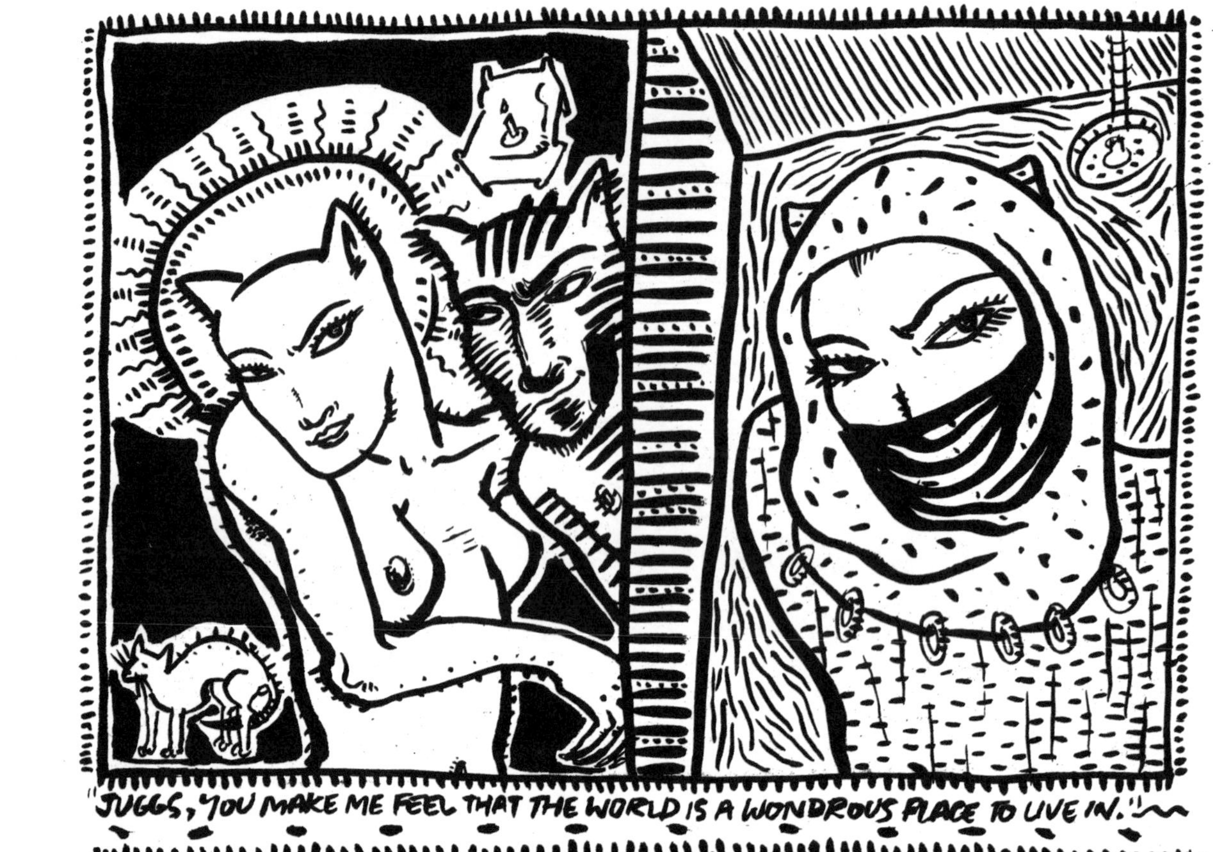

"JUGGS, YOU MAKE ME FEEL THAT THE WORLD IS A WONDROUS PLACE TO LIVE IN."

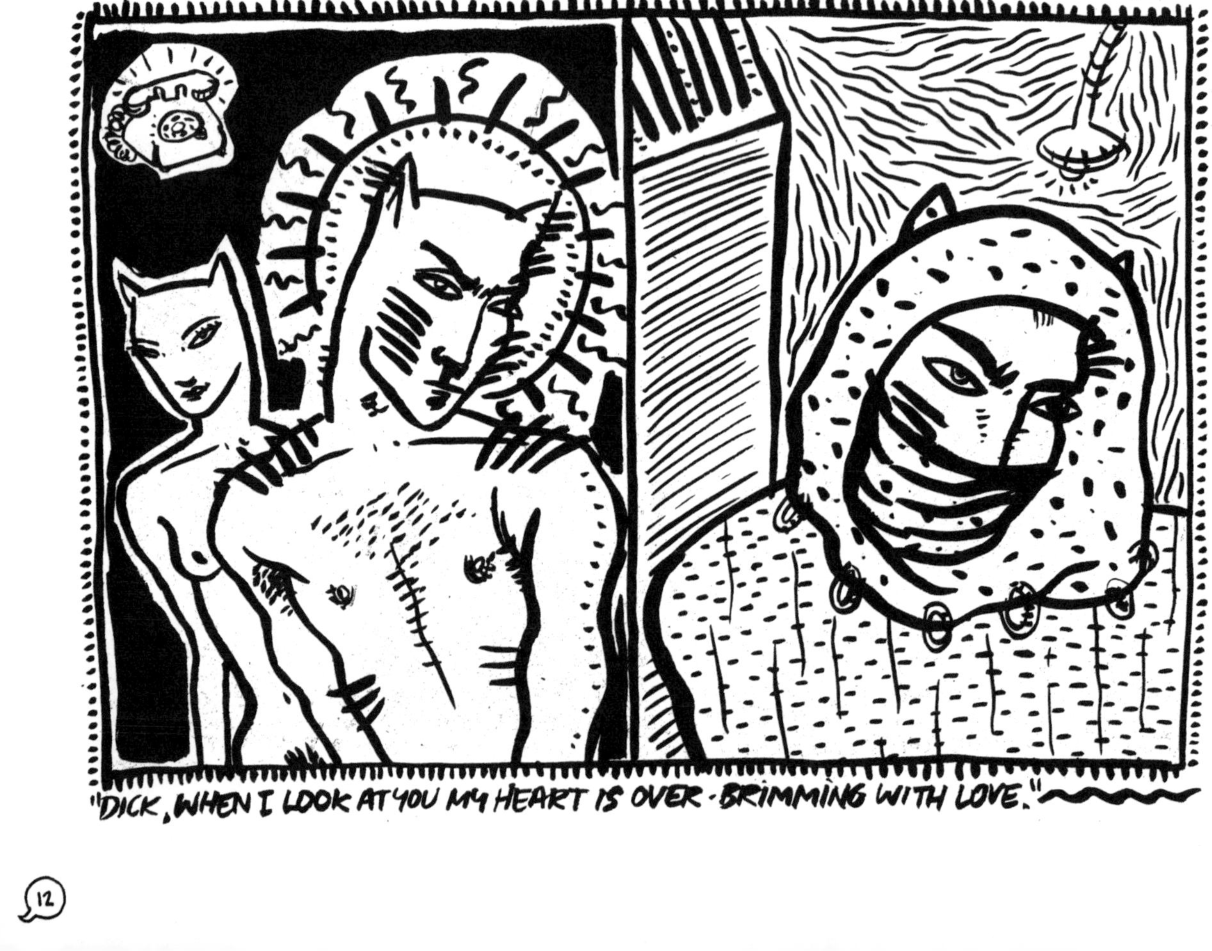

"DICK, WHEN I LOOK AT YOU MY HEART IS OVER-BRIMMING WITH LOVE."

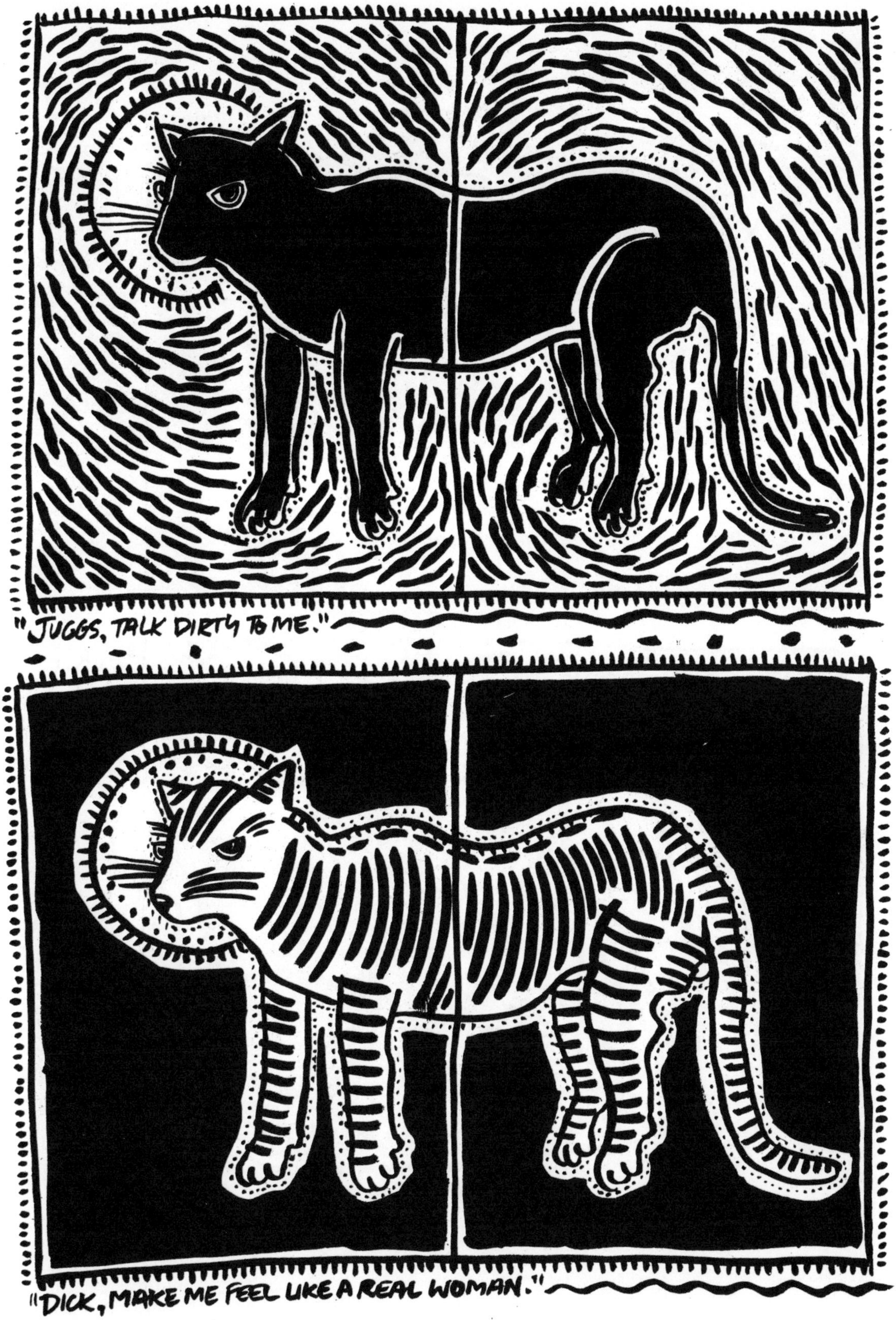
"JUGGS, TALK DIRTY TO ME."
"DICK, MAKE ME FEEL LIKE A REAL WOMAN."

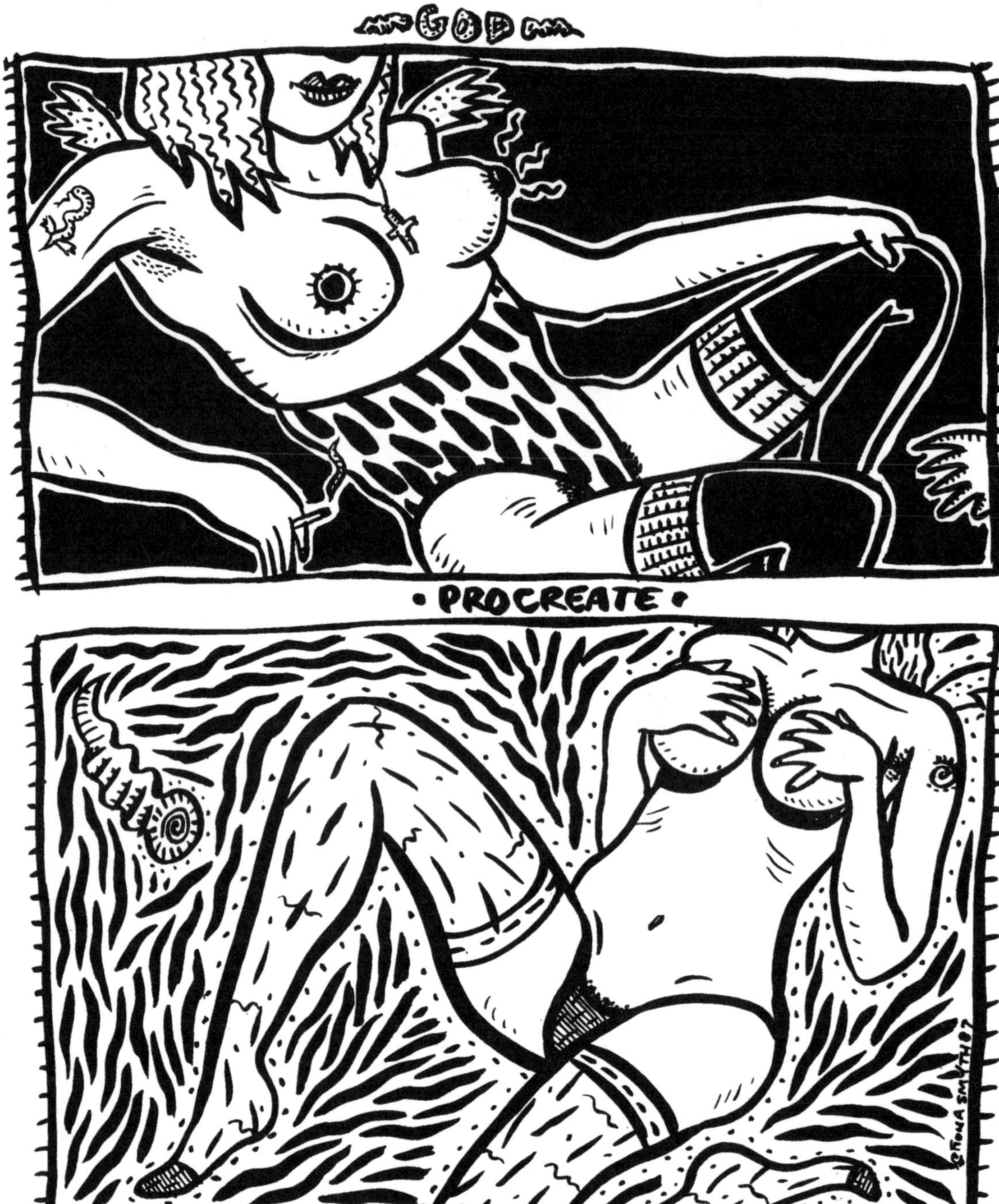
GOD
PROCREATE
DO NOT SIN
©FIONA SMYTH 87

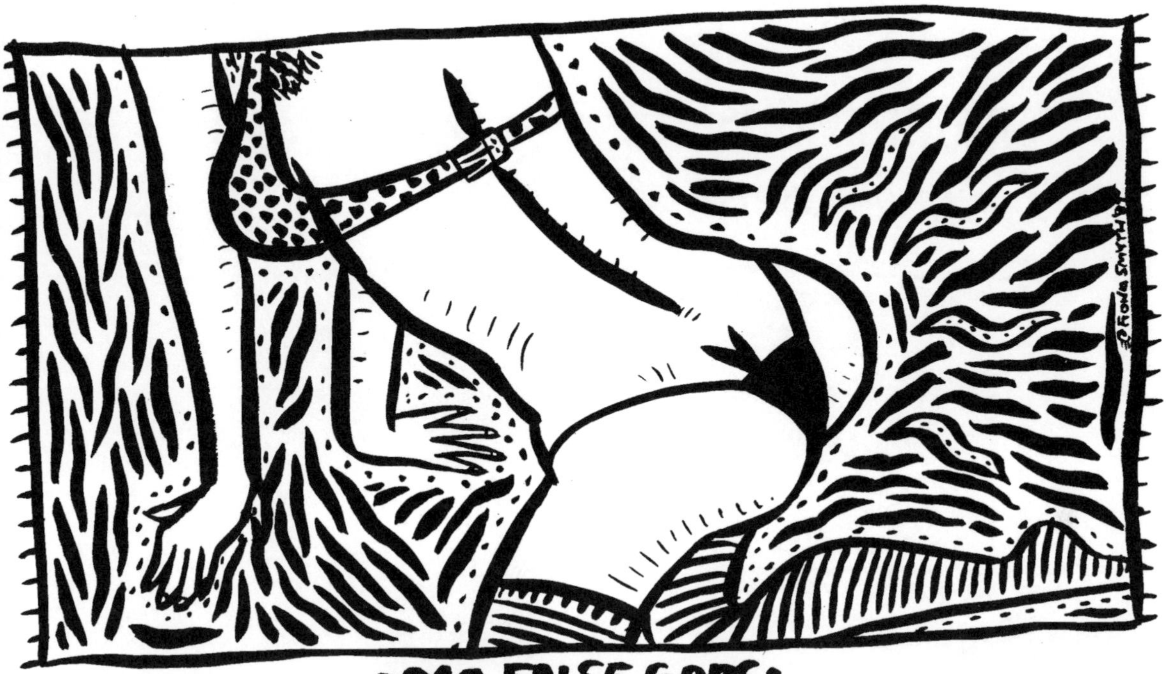
© Fiona Smyth

•NO FALSE GODS•

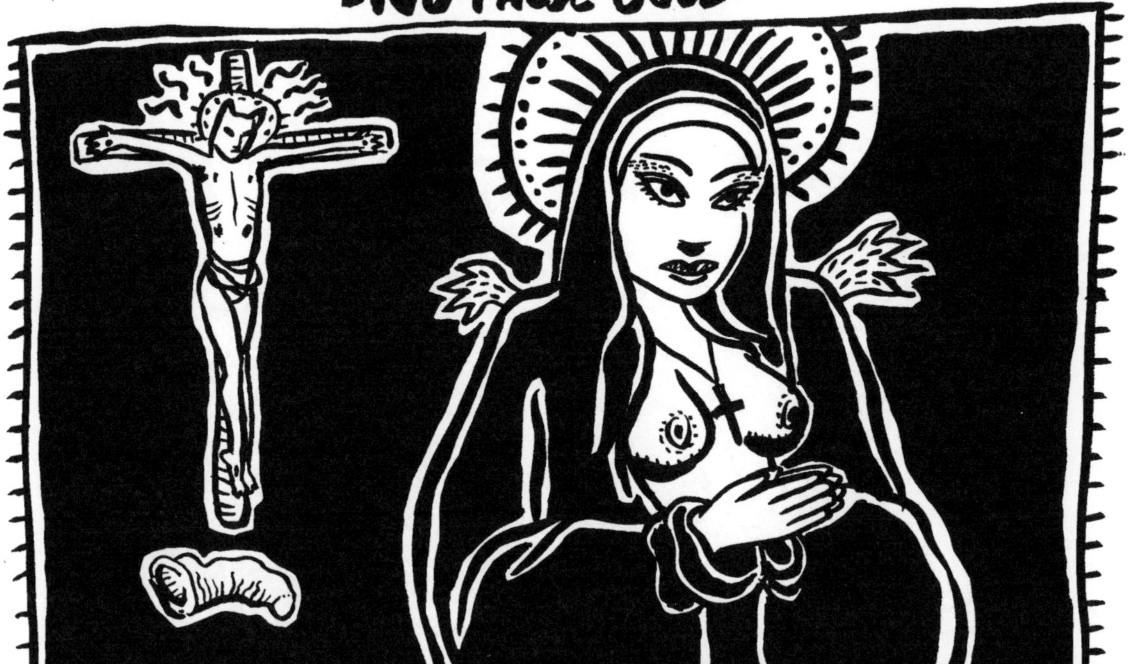

•PRAISE BE TO THE LORD•

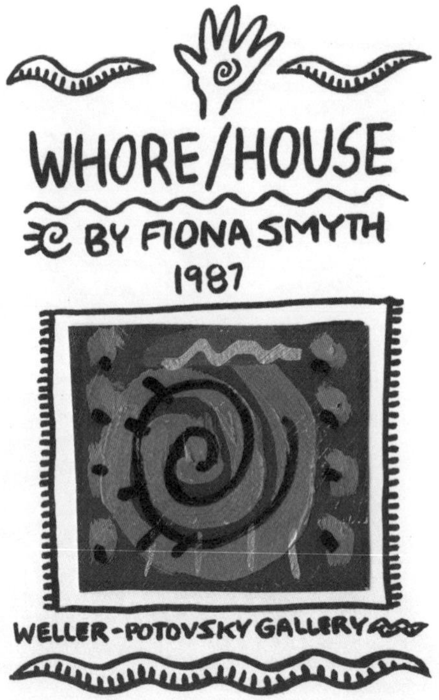
WHORE/HOUSE
BY FIONA SMYTH
1987
WELLER-POTOVSKY GALLERY

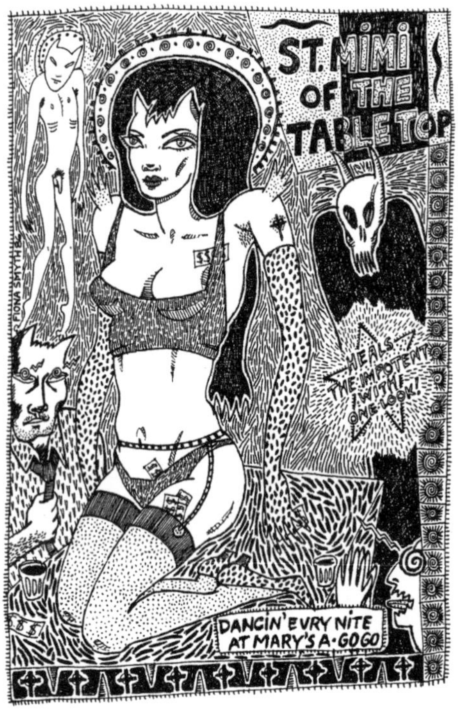
ST. MIMI OF THE TABLE TOP
HEALS THE IMPOTENT WITH ONE LOOK!
DANCIN' EVRY NITE AT MARY'S A-GOGO

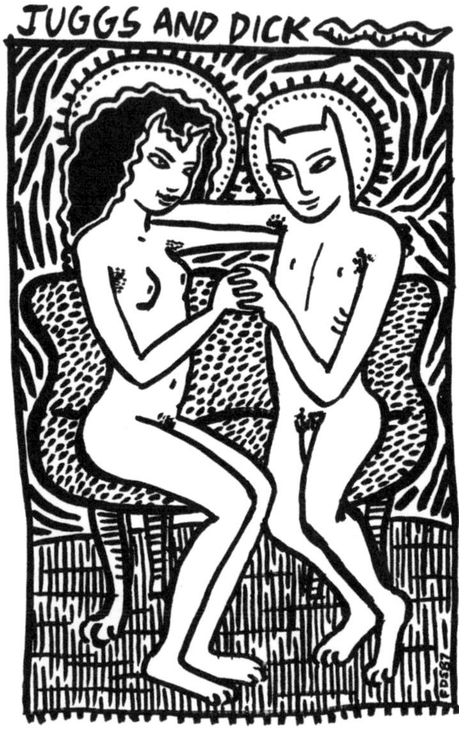
JUGGS AND DICK

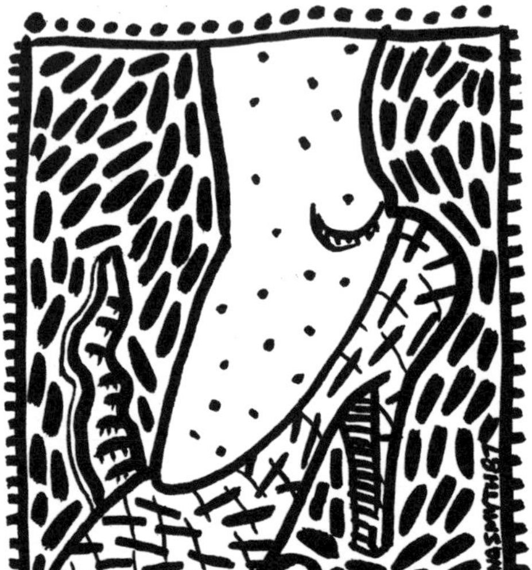
SPERMICIDE

 1987 WHORE/HOUSE - FIRST SOLO SHOW AND ZINE

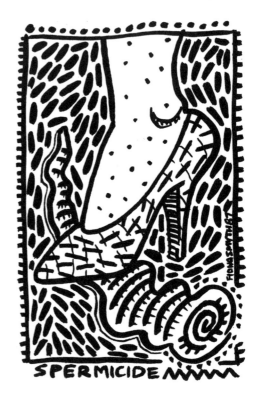

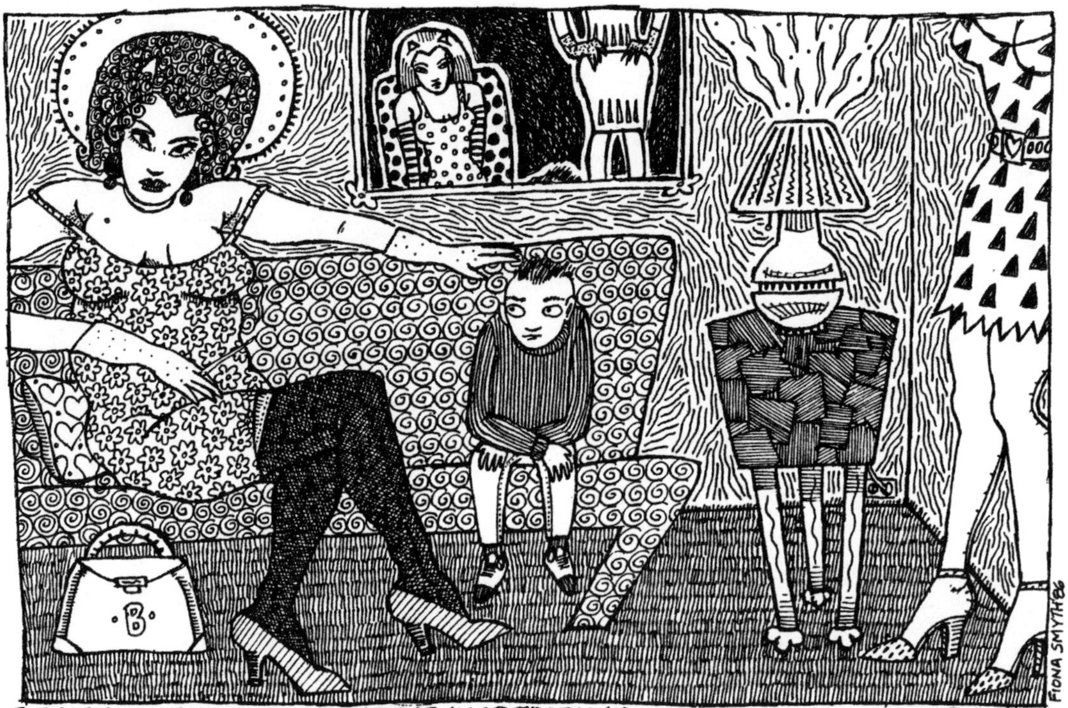
FIONA SMYTH 86

SAM ADMIRES AUNTIE BARB'S INCREDIBLY COMPREHENSIVE VOCABULARY.

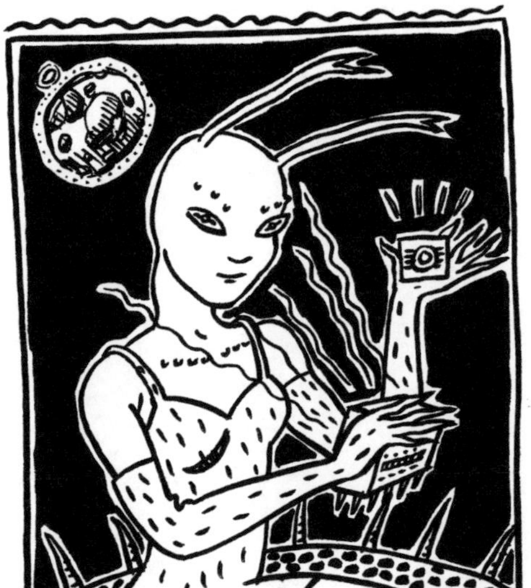

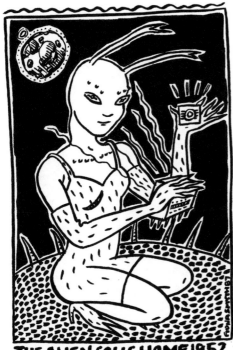

THE ALIEN CALLS HOME. 1952.

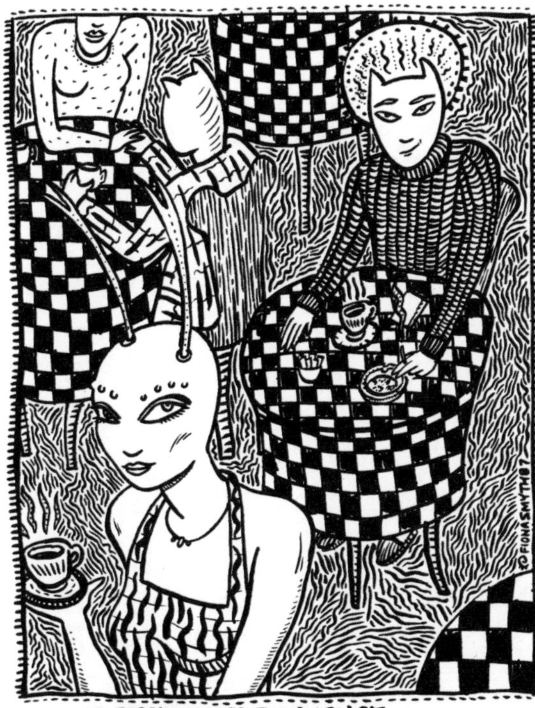
©FIONASMYTH87

FRANK OOGLES THE ALIEN.

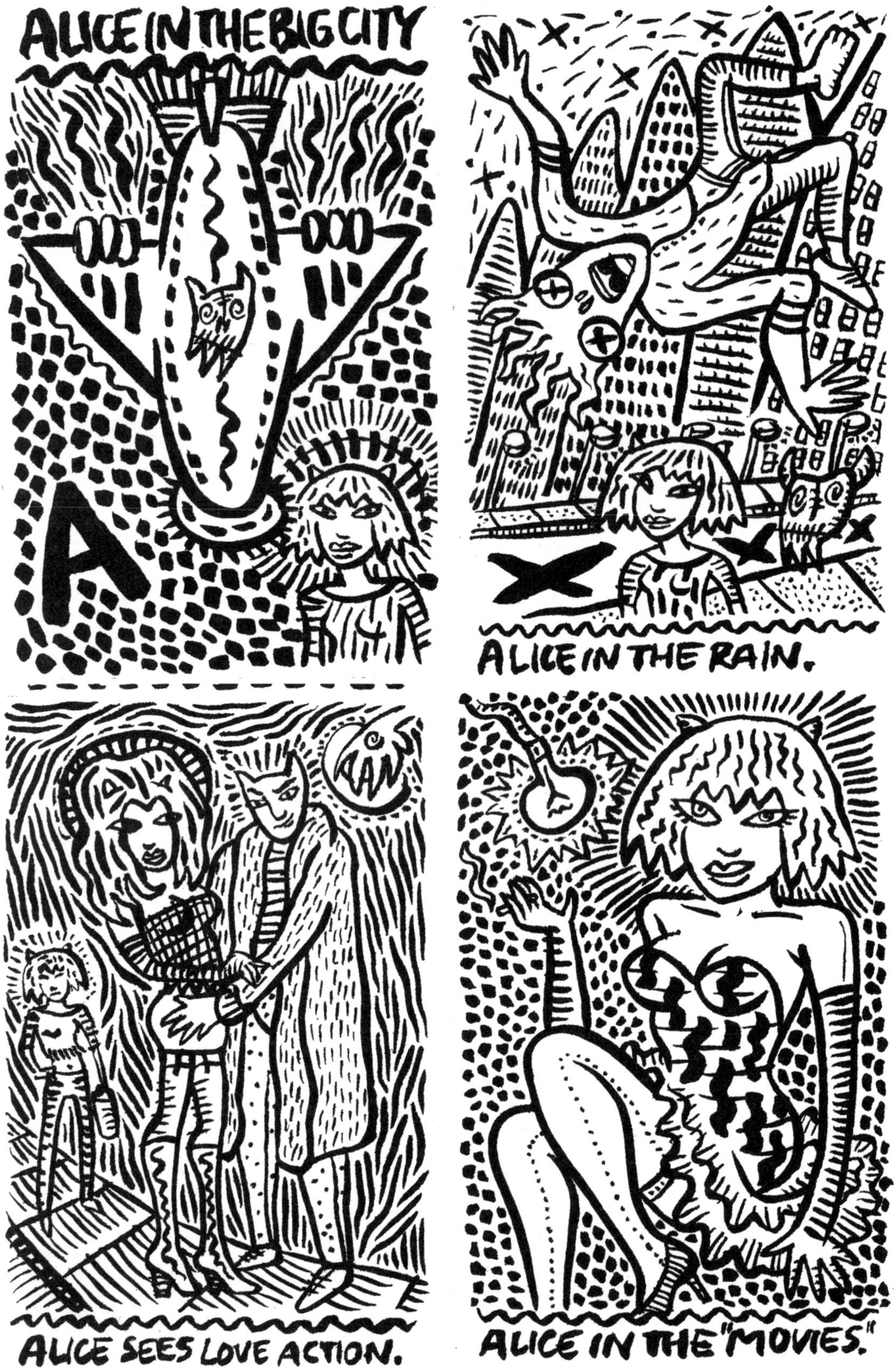
ALICE IN THE BIG CITY
A
ALICE IN THE RAIN.
ALICE SEES LOVE ACTION.
ALICE IN THE "MOVIES."

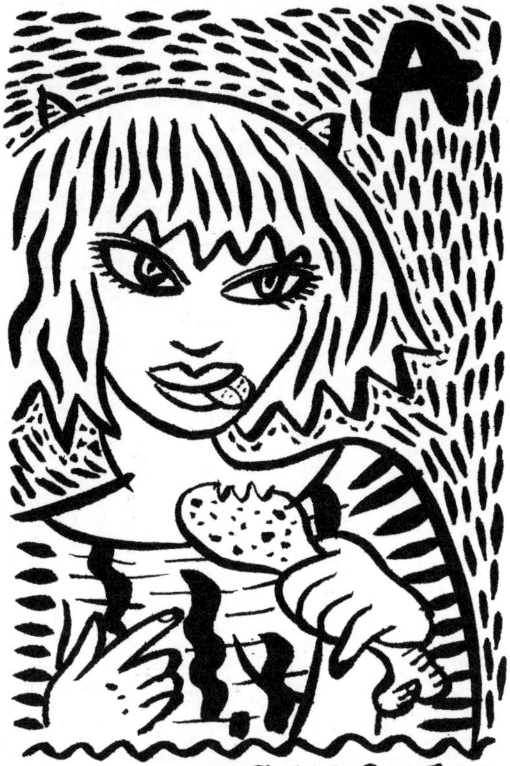
A

ALICE EATS CHICKEN.

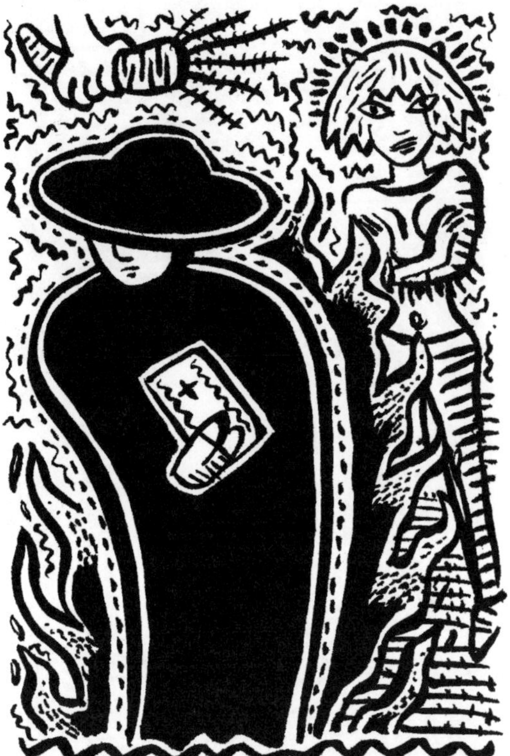

ALICE AND THE PREACHER.

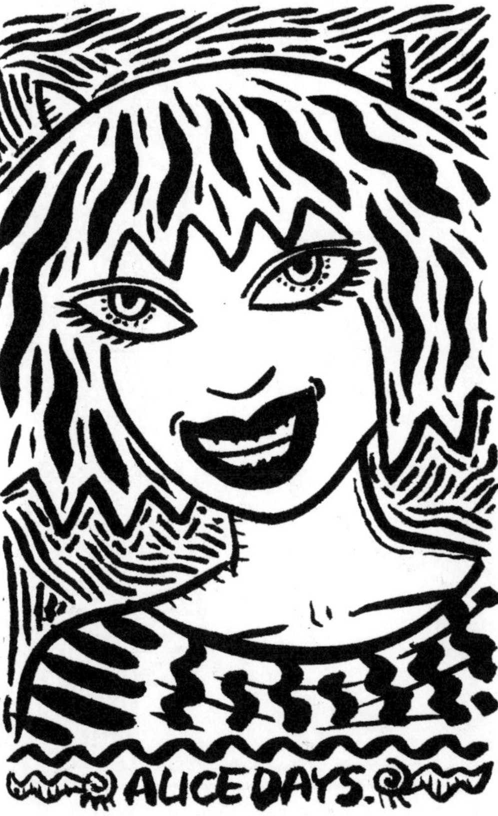

ALICE DAYS.

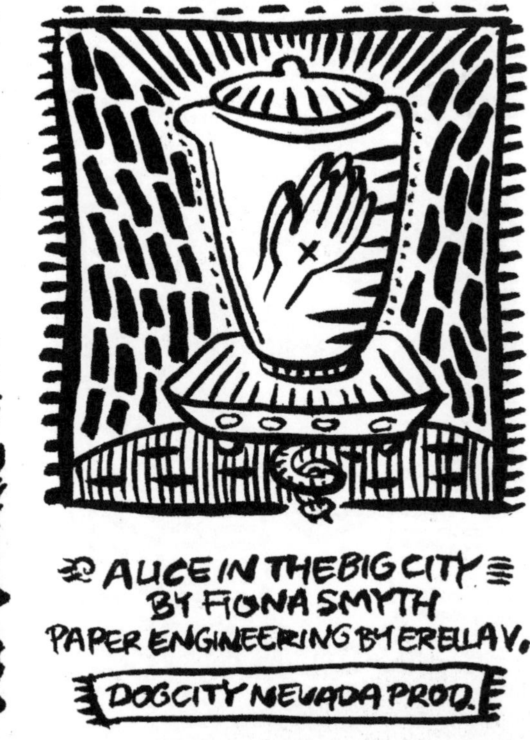

ALICE IN THE BIG CITY
BY FIONA SMYTH
PAPER ENGINEERING BY ERELLA V.

DOGCITY NEVADA PROD.

1988

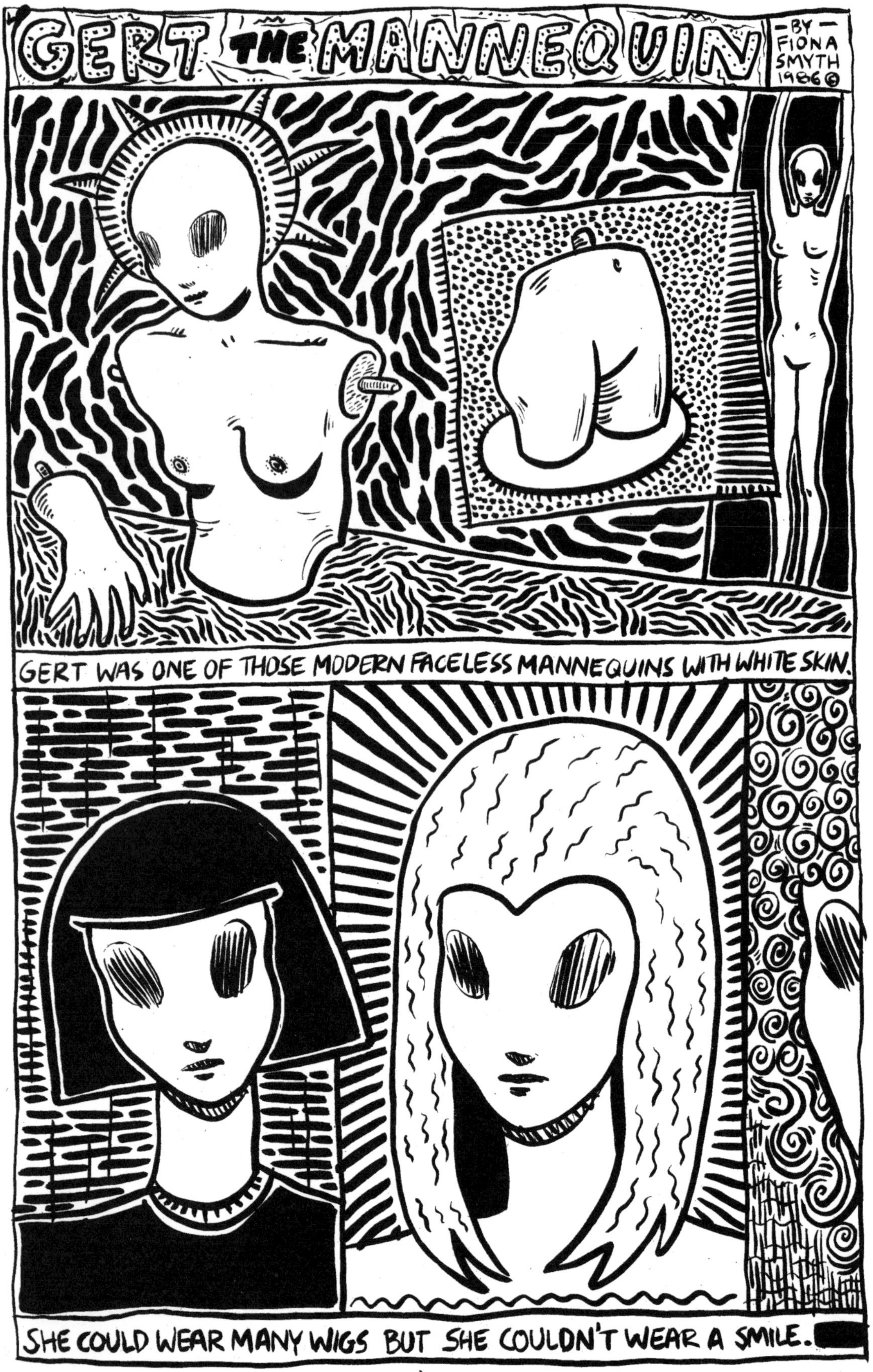
GERT THE MANNEQUIN
-BY- FIONA SMYTH 1986©
GERT WAS ONE OF THOSE MODERN FACELESS MANNEQUINS WITH WHITE SKIN.
SHE COULD WEAR MANY WIGS BUT SHE COULDN'T WEAR A SMILE.

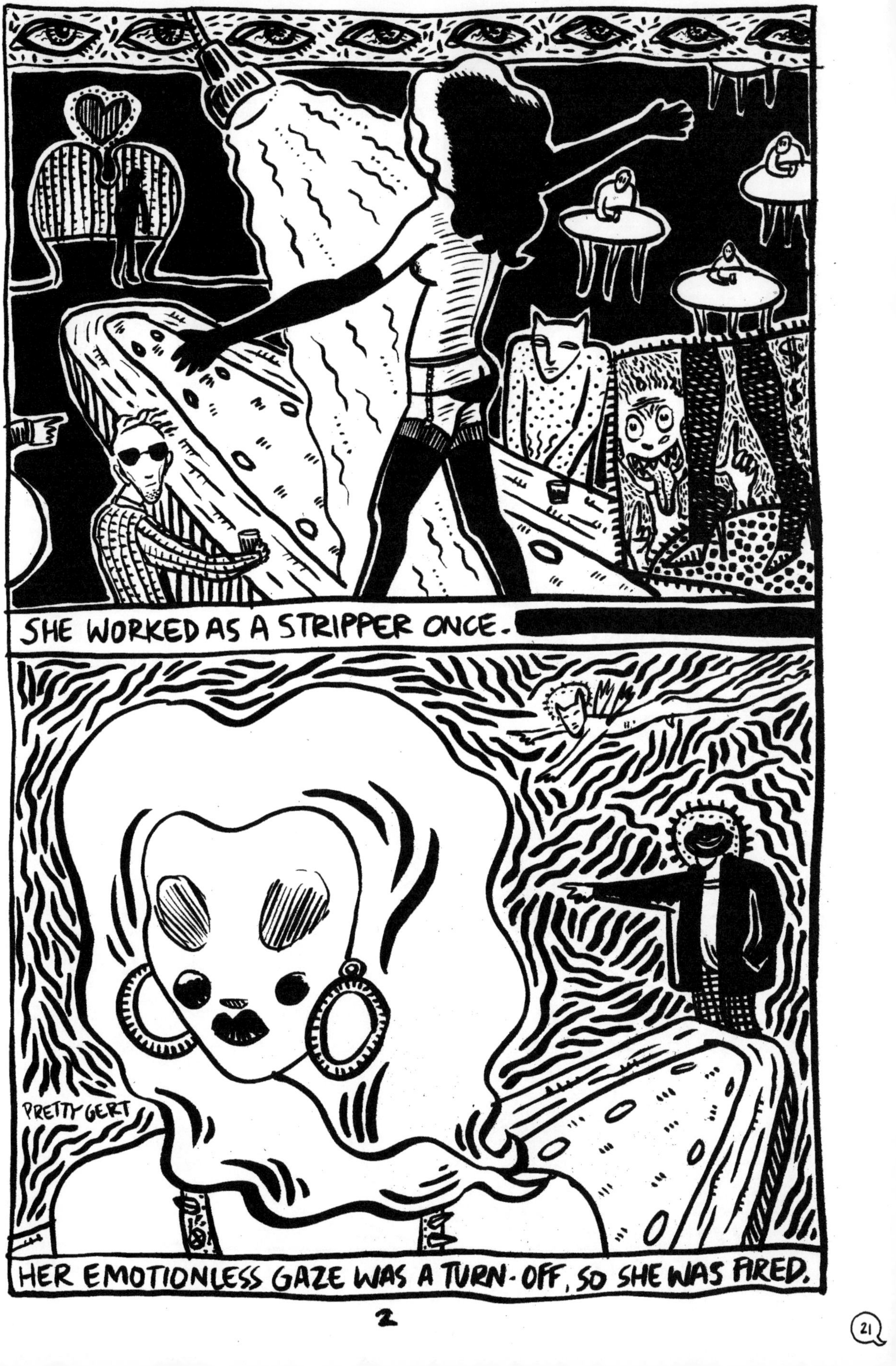
SHE WORKED AS A STRIPPER ONCE.
PRETTY GERT
HER EMOTIONLESS GAZE WAS A TURN-OFF, SO SHE WAS FIRED.

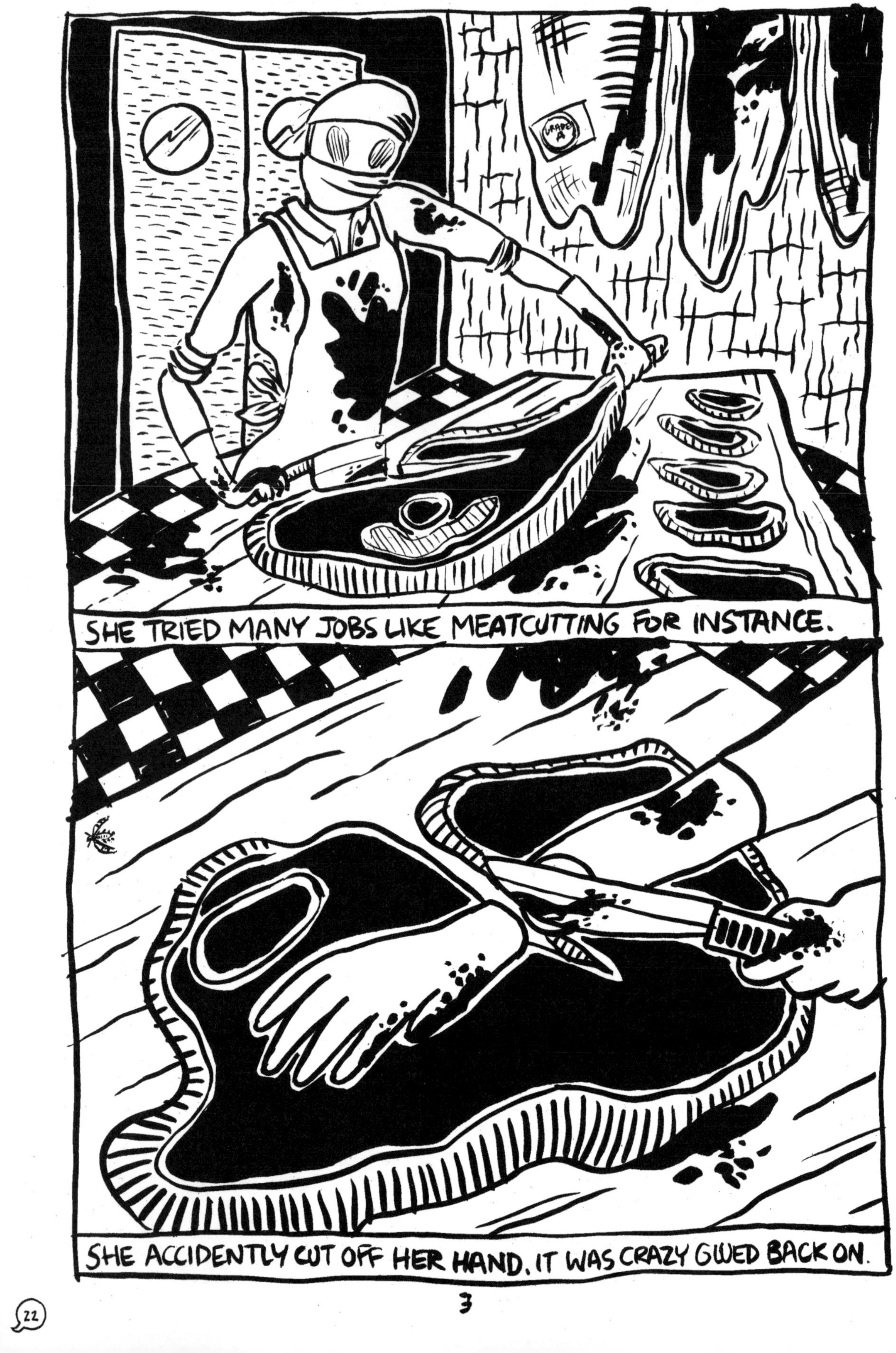
GRADE A
SHE TRIED MANY JOBS LIKE MEATCUTTING FOR INSTANCE.
SHE ACCIDENTLY CUT OFF HER HAND. IT WAS CRAZY GLUED BACK ON.

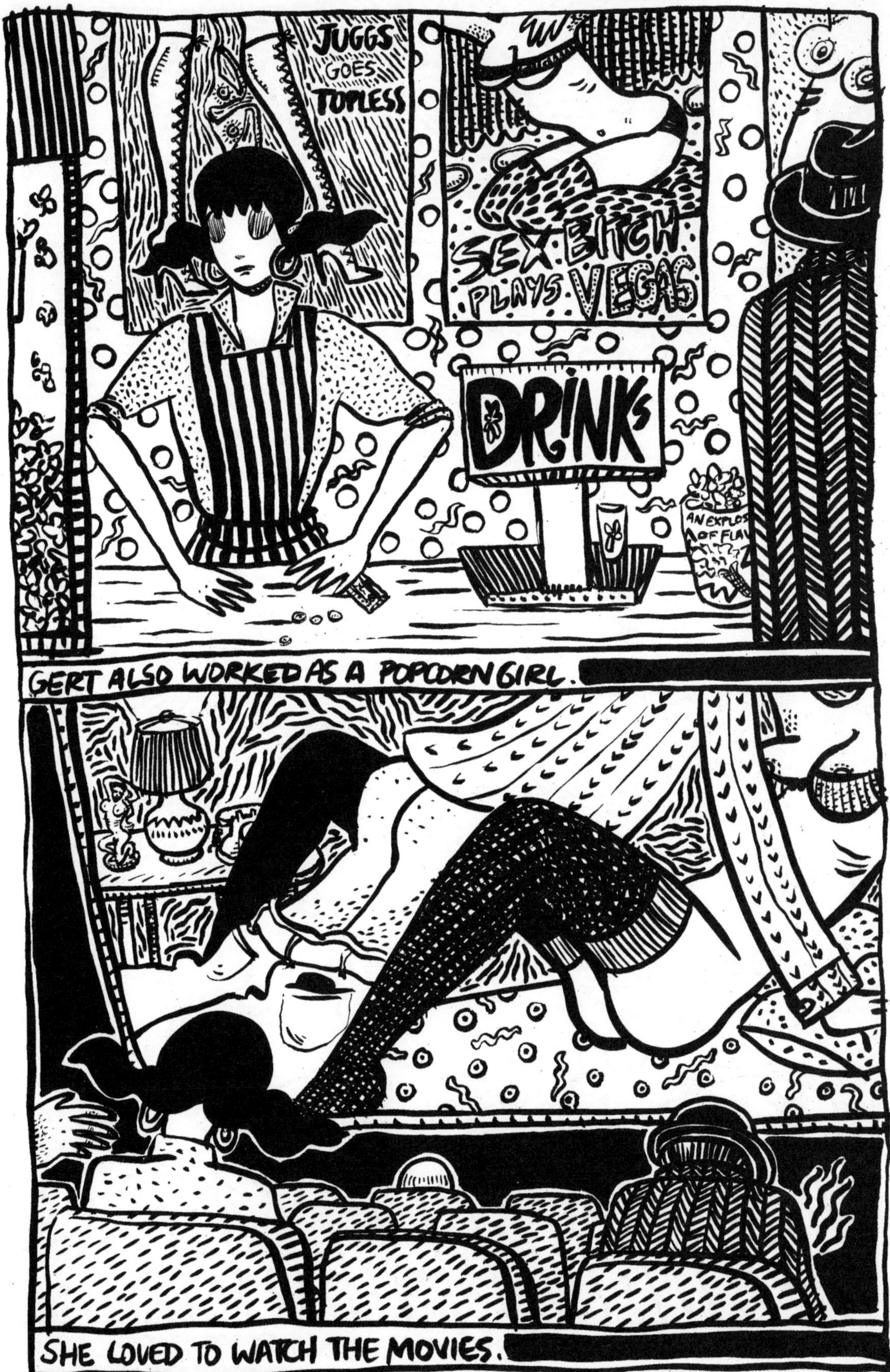
JUGGS GOES TOPLESS
SEX BITCH PLAYS VEGAS
DRINKS
AN EXPLOS OF FLAV
GERT ALSO WORKED AS A POPCORN GIRL.
SHE LOVED TO WATCH THE MOVIES.

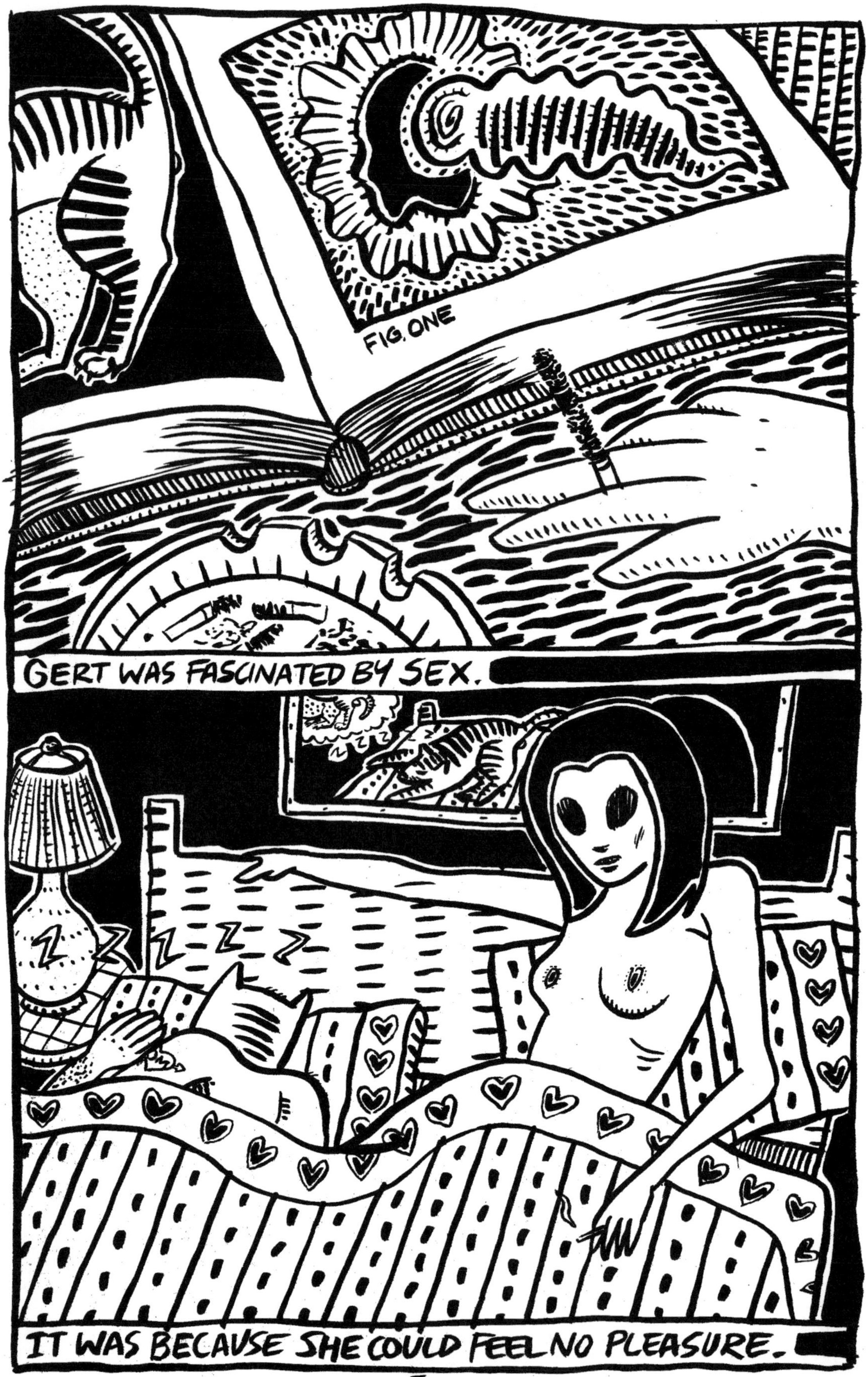
FIG. ONE
GERT WAS FASCINATED BY SEX.
IT WAS BECAUSE SHE COULD FEEL NO PLEASURE.

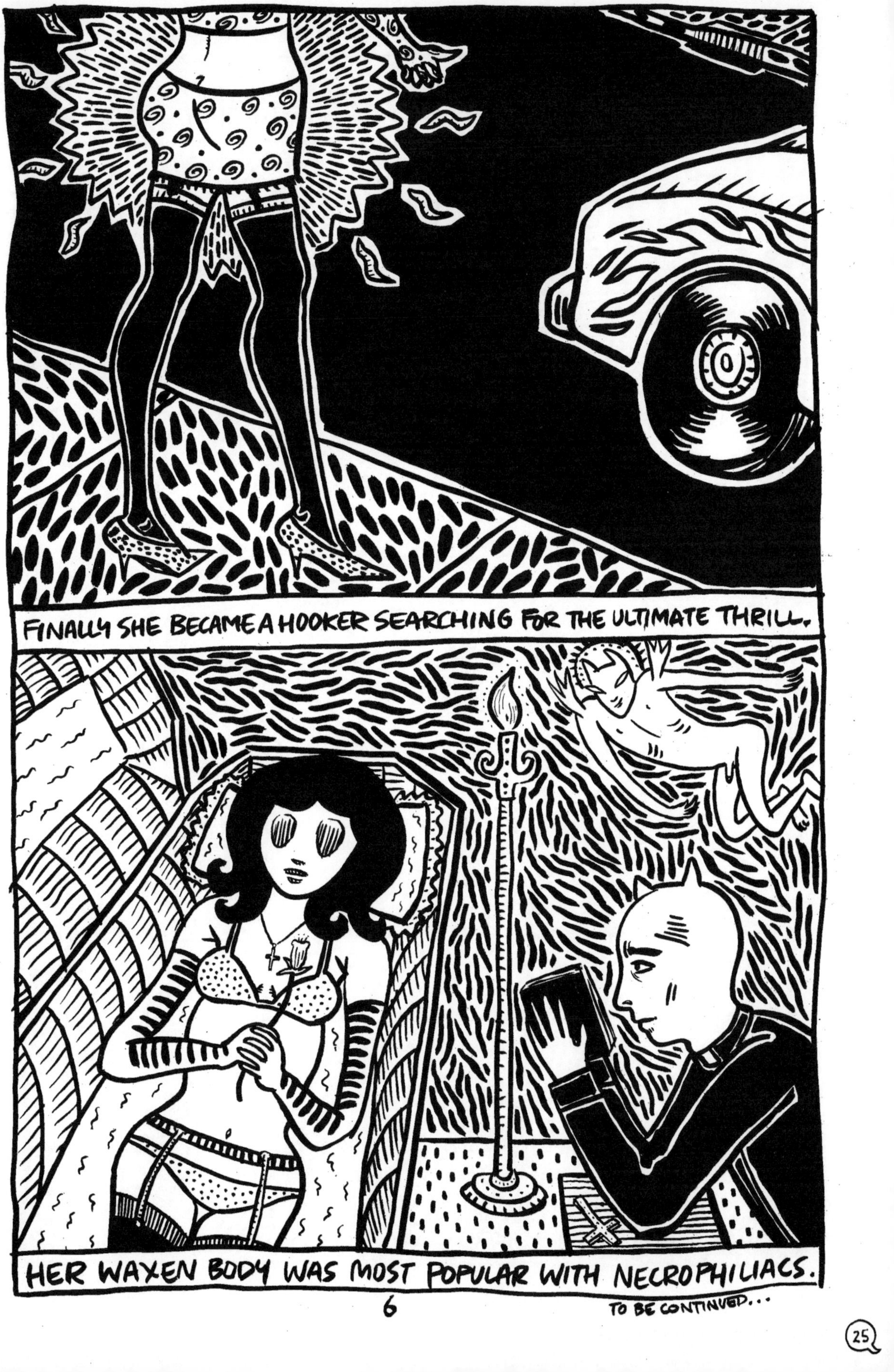
FINALLY SHE BECAME A HOOKER SEARCHING FOR THE ULTIMATE THRILL.
HER WAXEN BODY WAS MOST POPULAR WITH NECROPHILIACS.

6

TO BE CONTINUED...

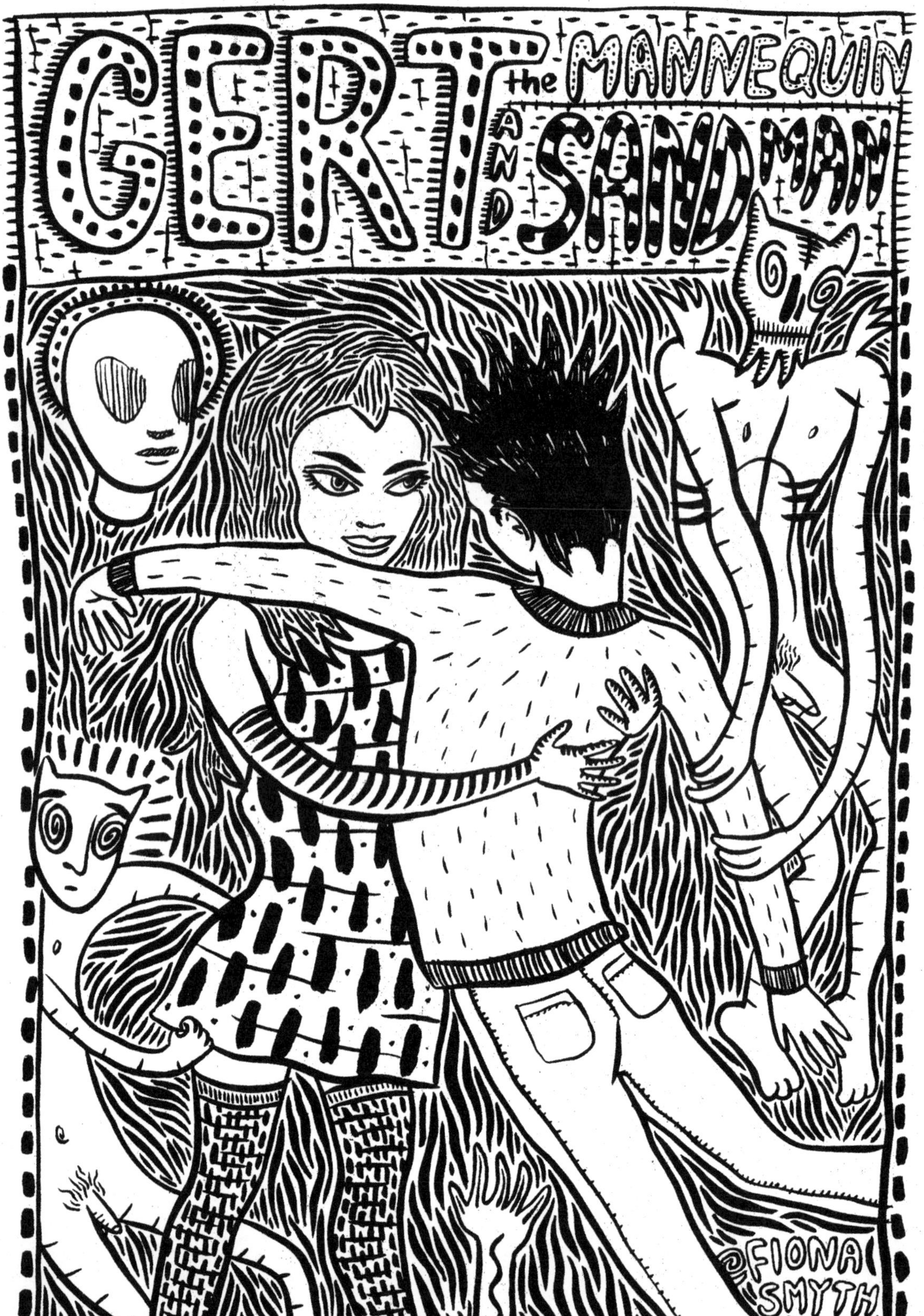
GERT the MANNEQUIN AND SANDMAN
©FIONA SMYTH 1988

© GERT FOUND HERSELF THE PERFECT MAN.

© AND HE TURNED HER INTO THE PERFECT WOMAN.

HER SOUL IS STILL PURE FIBREGLASS.

27

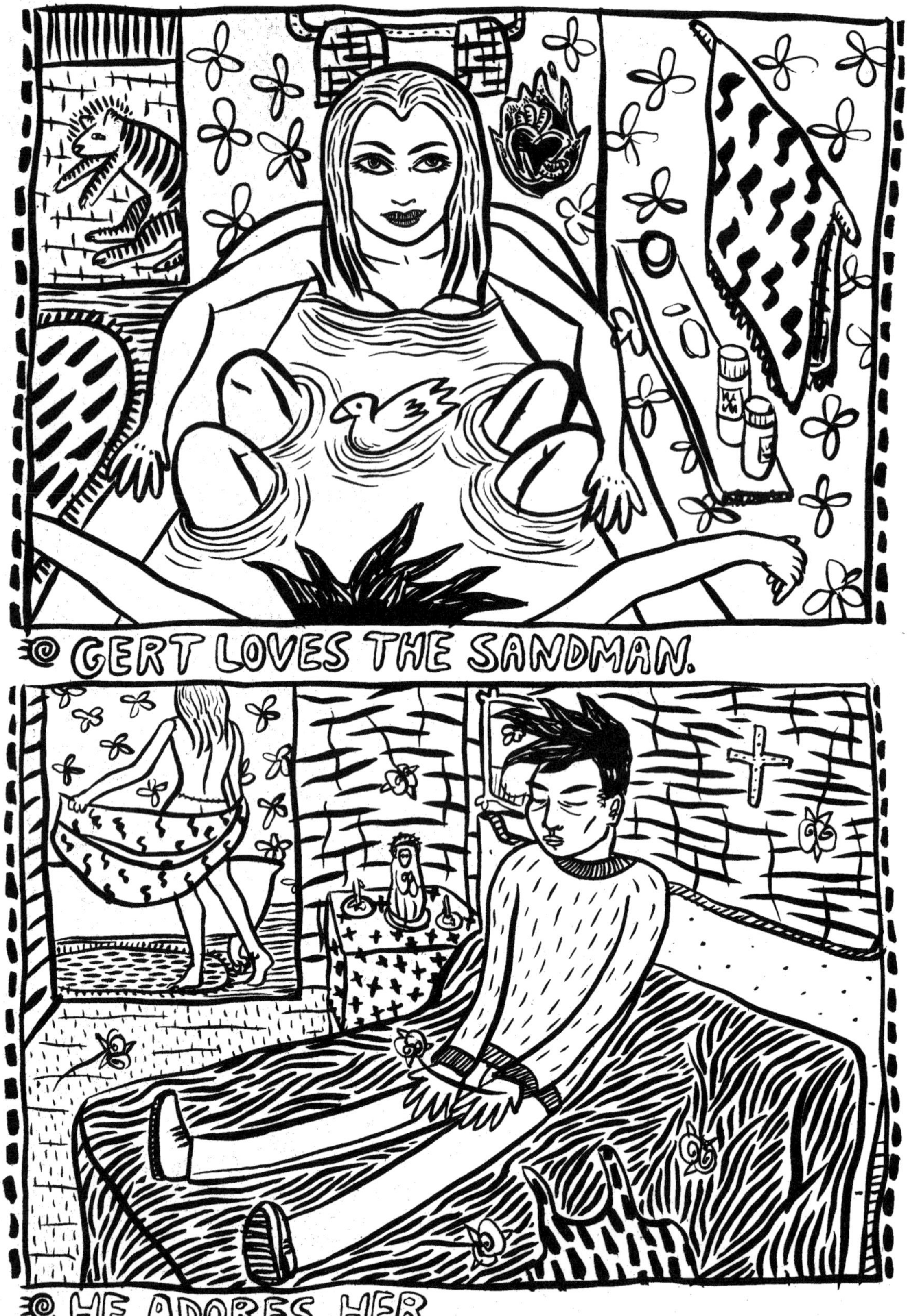
GERT LOVES THE SANDMAN.
HE ADORES HER.

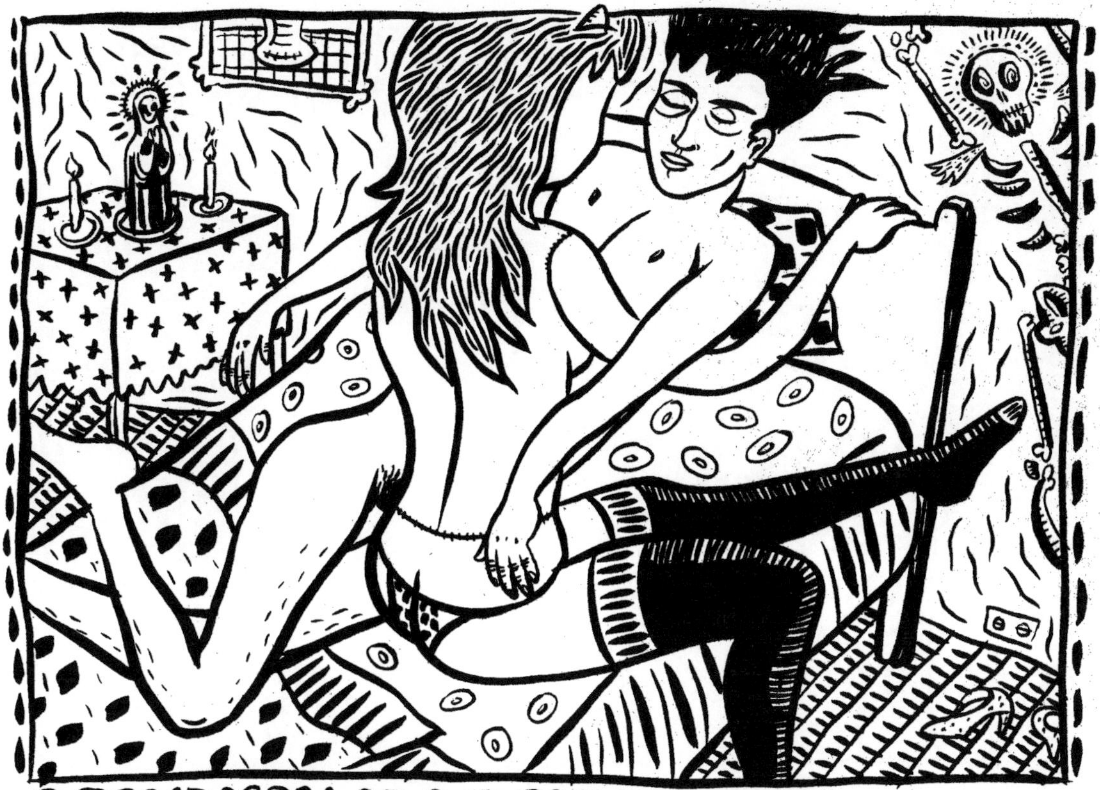

SANDMAN IS A TENDER LOVER.

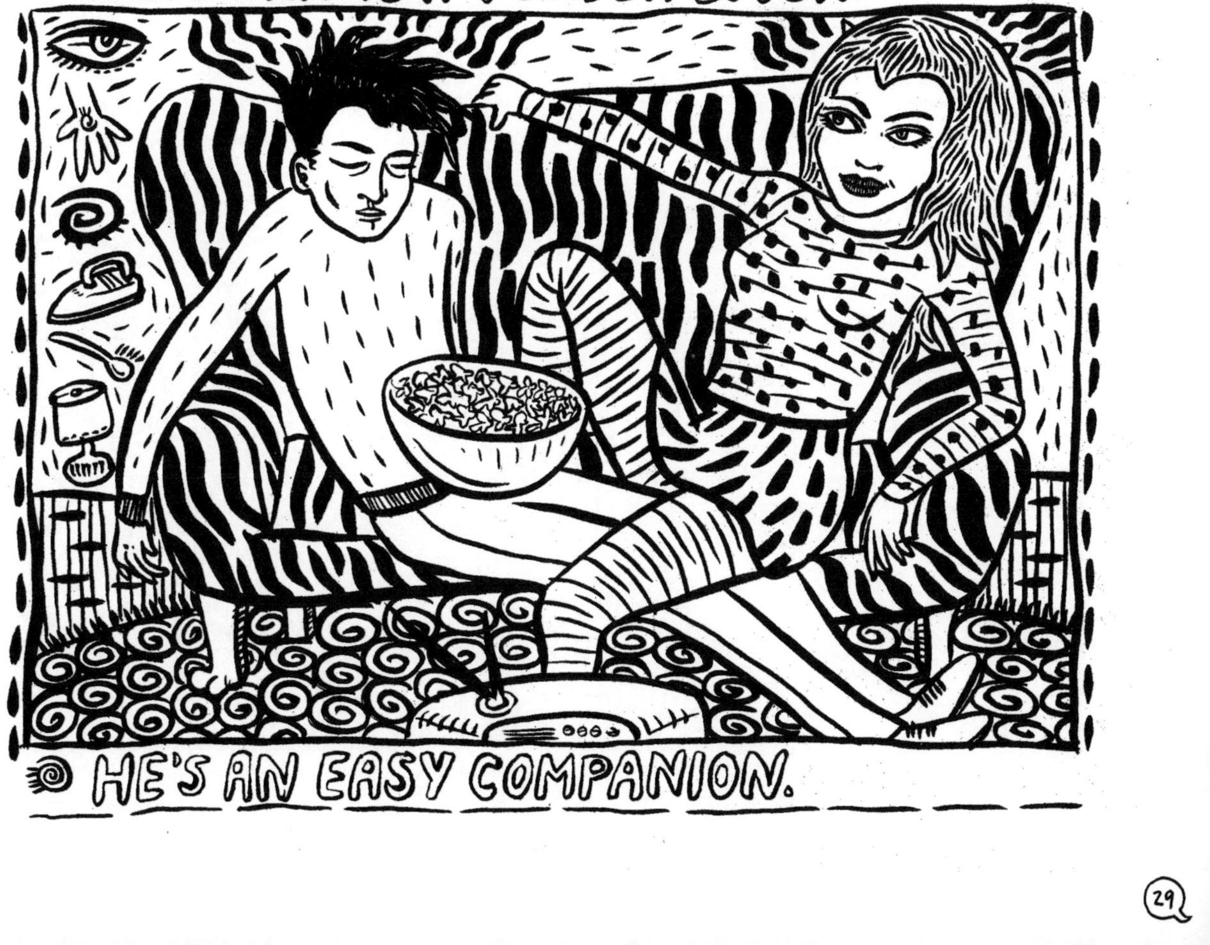

HE'S AN EASY COMPANION.

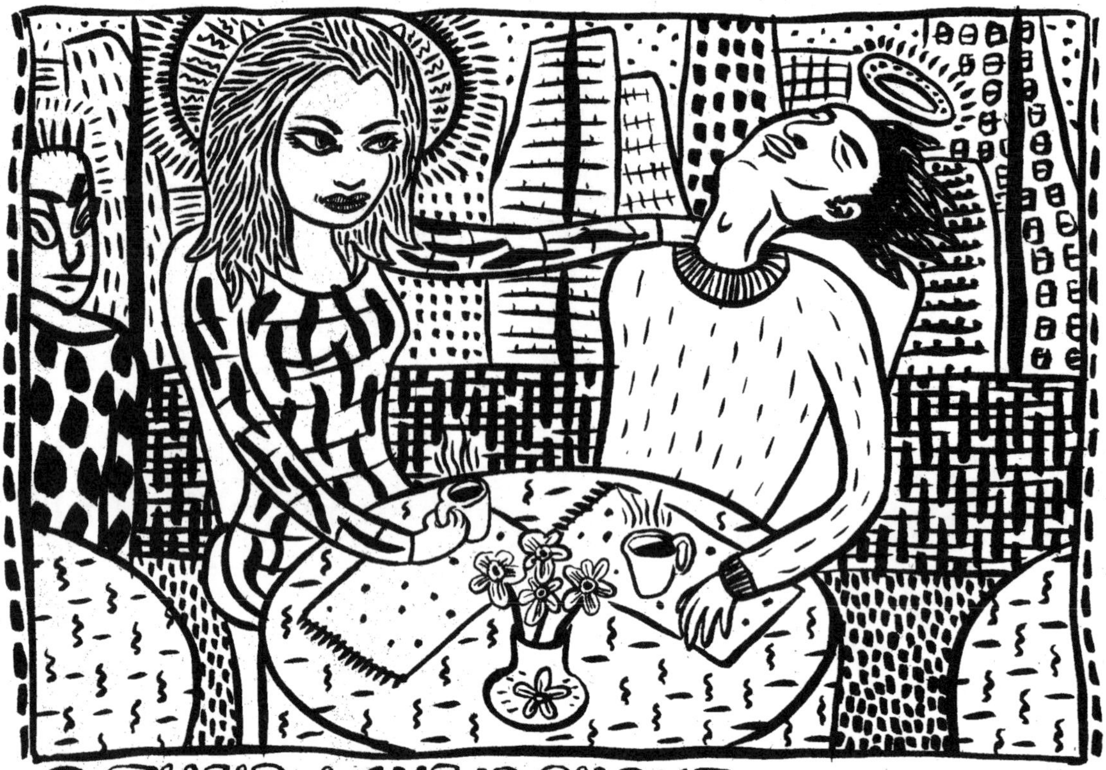

THEIR LOVE IS SILENT.

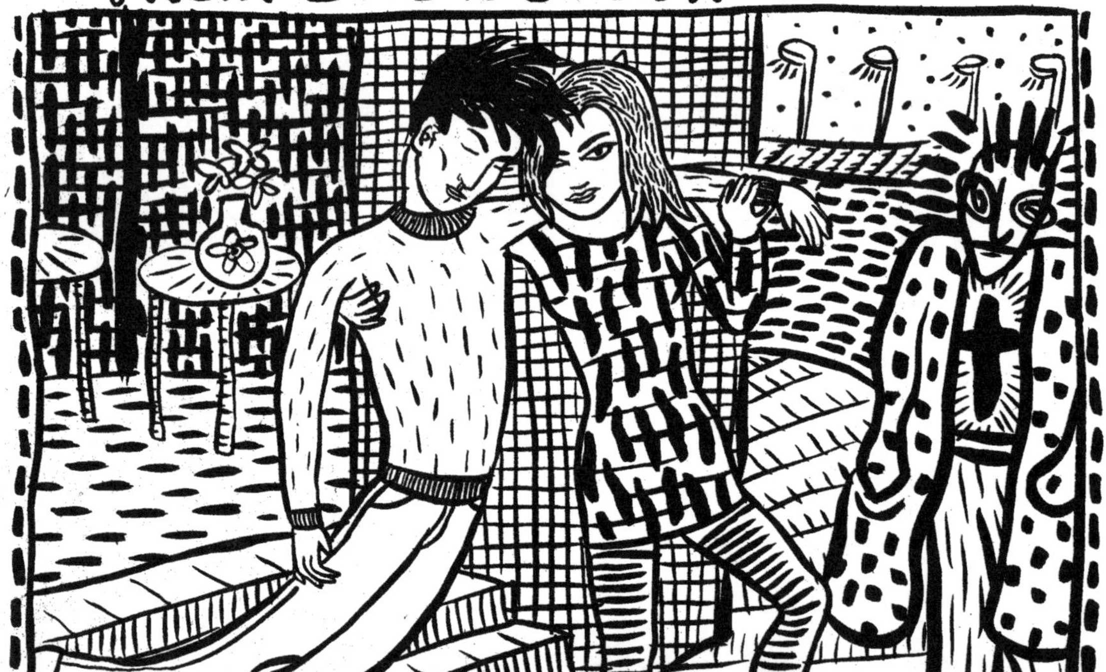

THEIR LOVE RUNS DEEP.

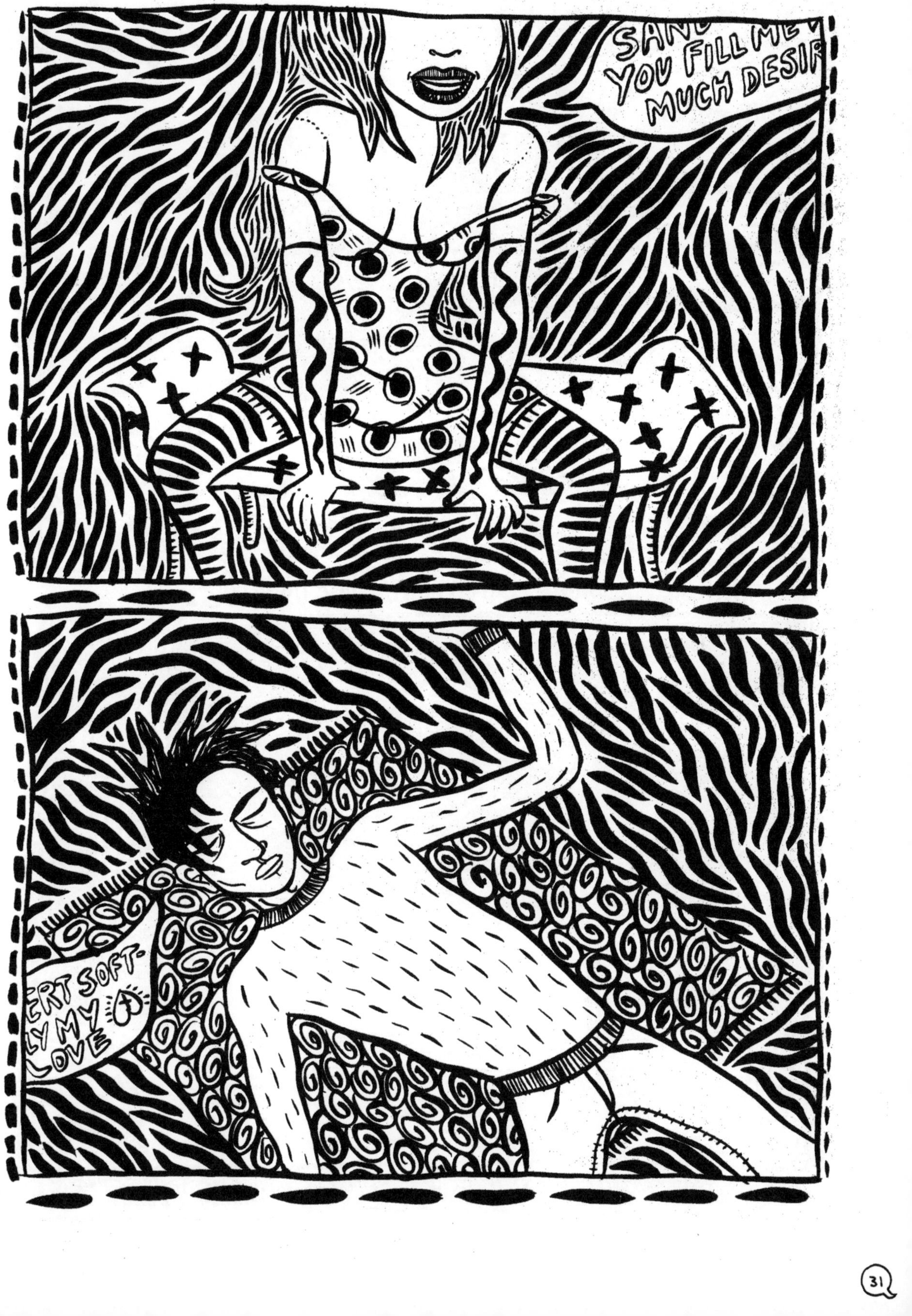
SAN
YOU FILL ME
MUCH DESIR
ERT SOFT-
LY MY
LOVE

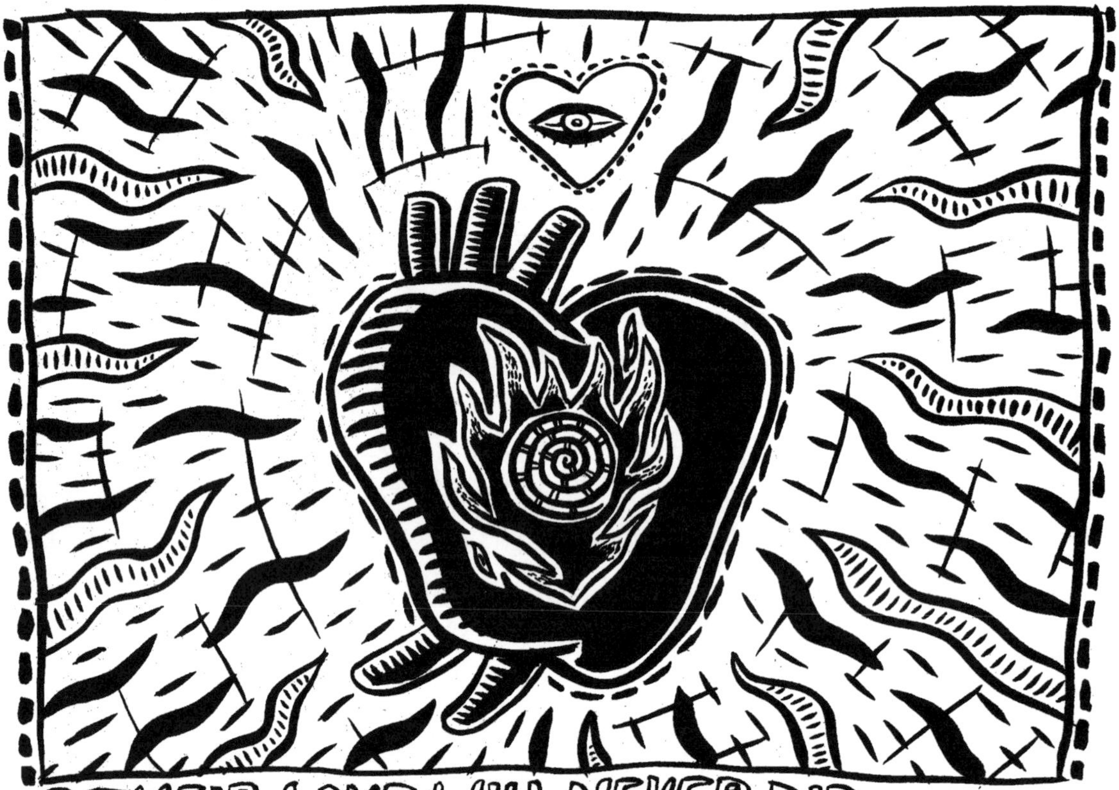

THEIR LOVE WILL NEVER DIE.

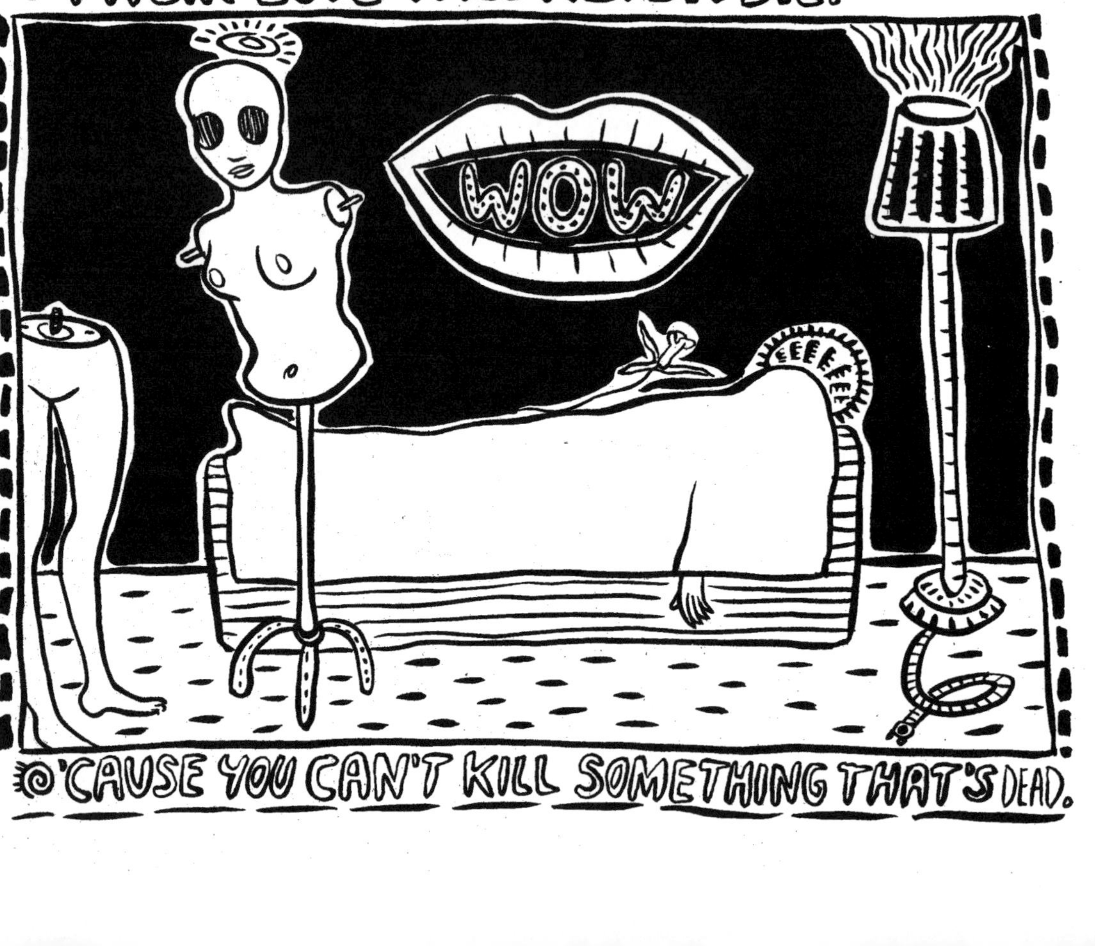
WOW

'CAUSE YOU CAN'T KILL SOMETHING THAT'S DEAD.

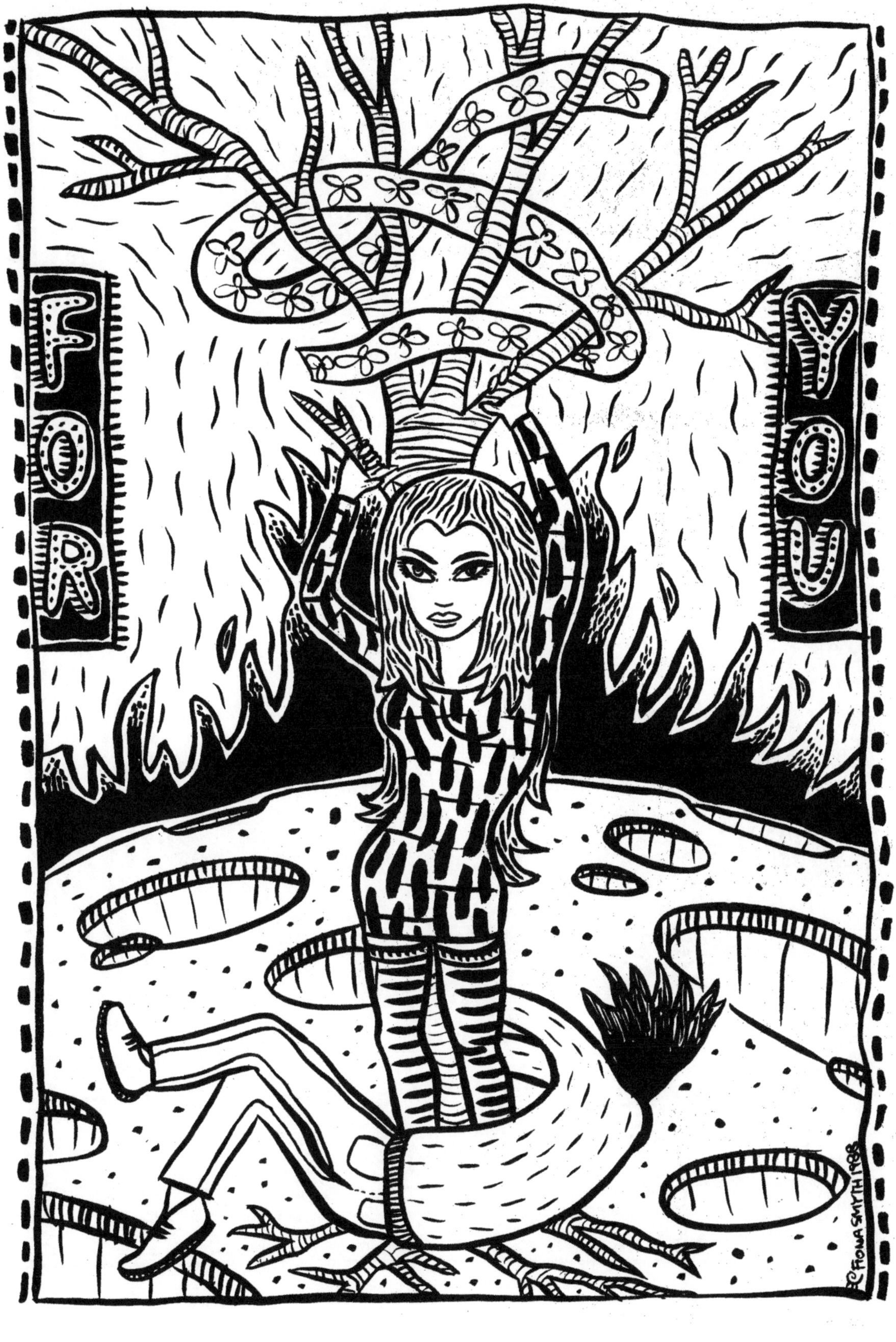
FOR
YOU
©FIONA SMYTH 1988

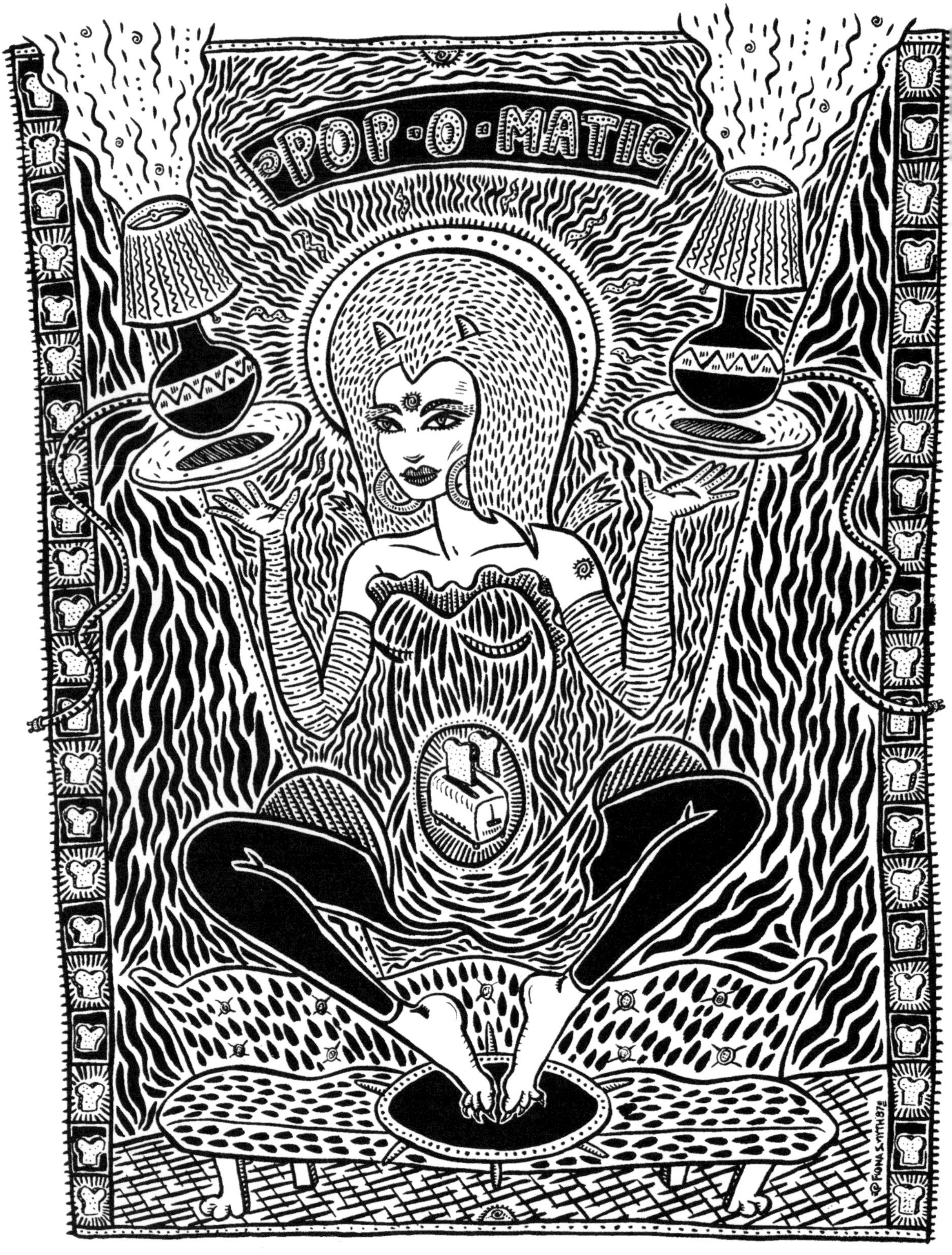
POP-O-MATIC
©FIONA SMYTH 87©

34 1987 REACTOR ART & DESIGN FABULOUS BABES

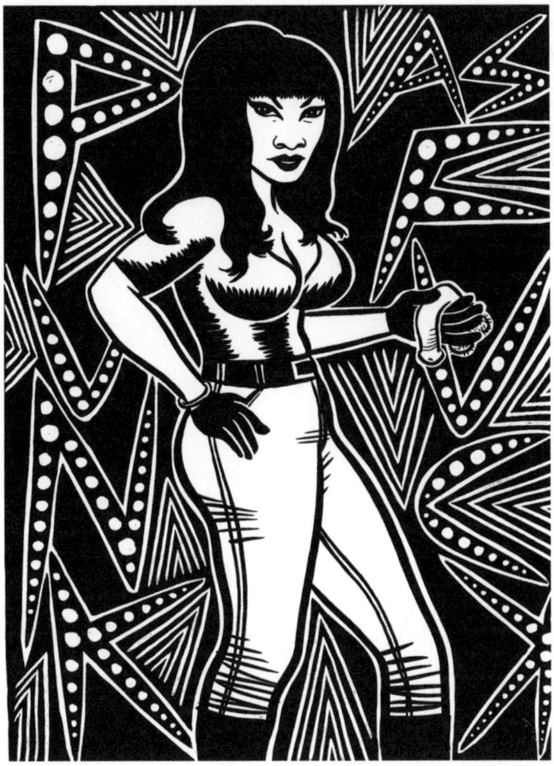

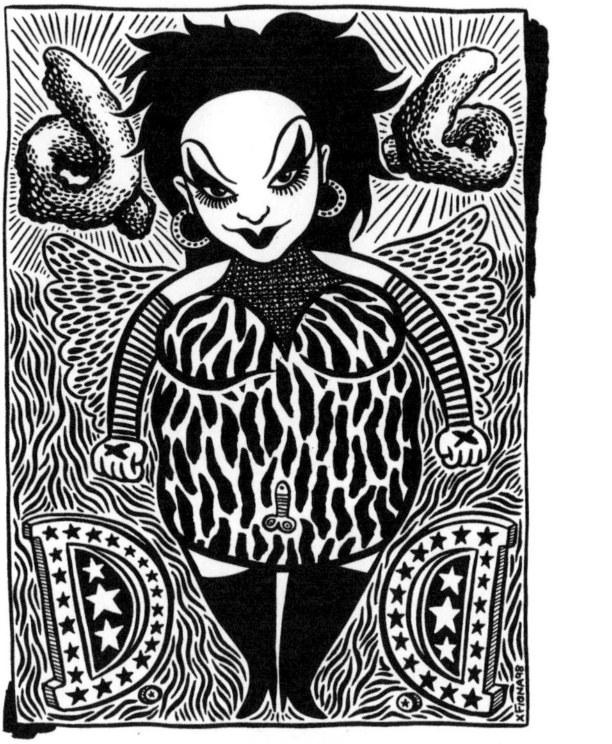

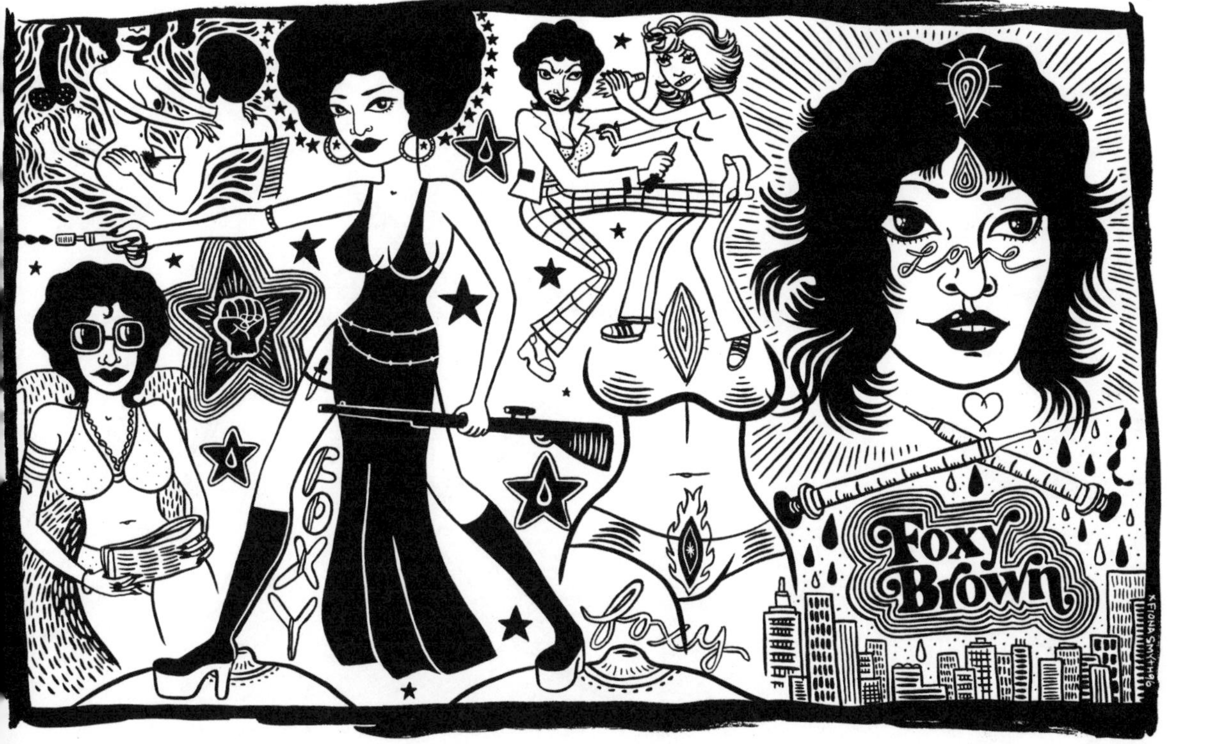
Foxy Brown
love
foxy

1990'S HEROINES: TURA SATANA AND DIVINE IN HEAVY GIRL PRESS ZINE
AND PAM GRIER IN TRASH COMPACTOR ZINE

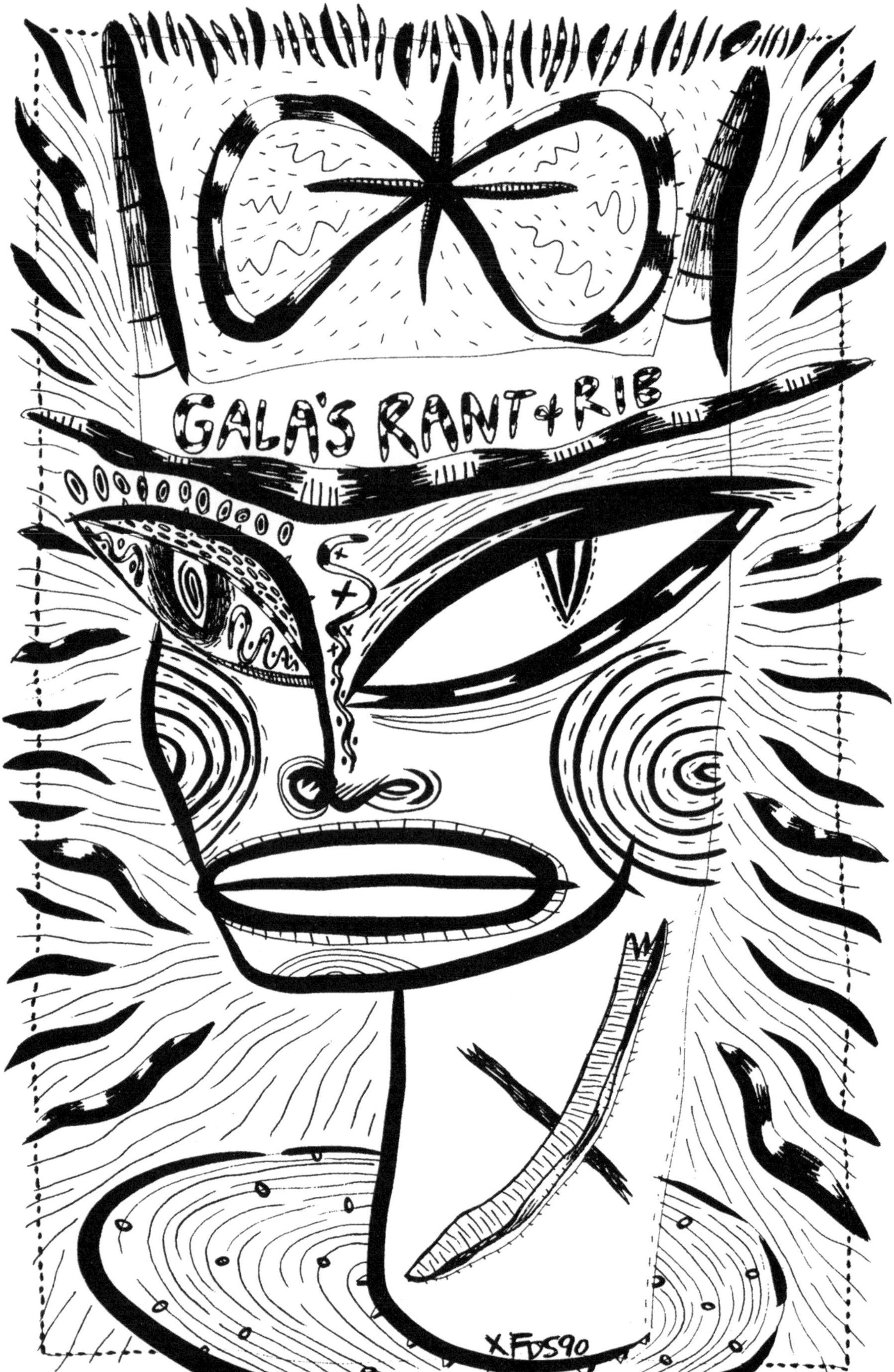
GALA'S RANT + RIB
XFDS90

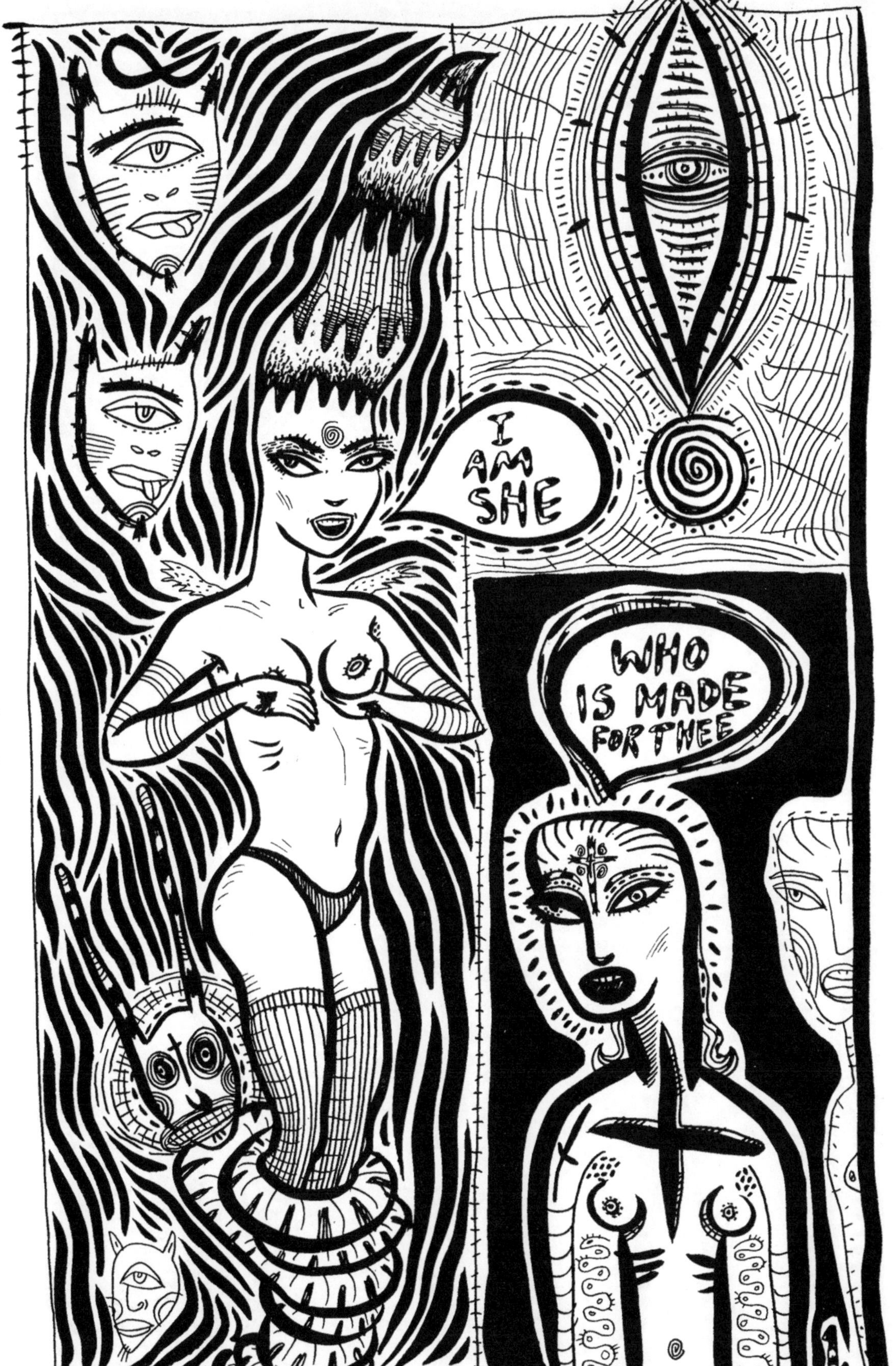
I AM SHE
WHO IS MADE FOR THEE

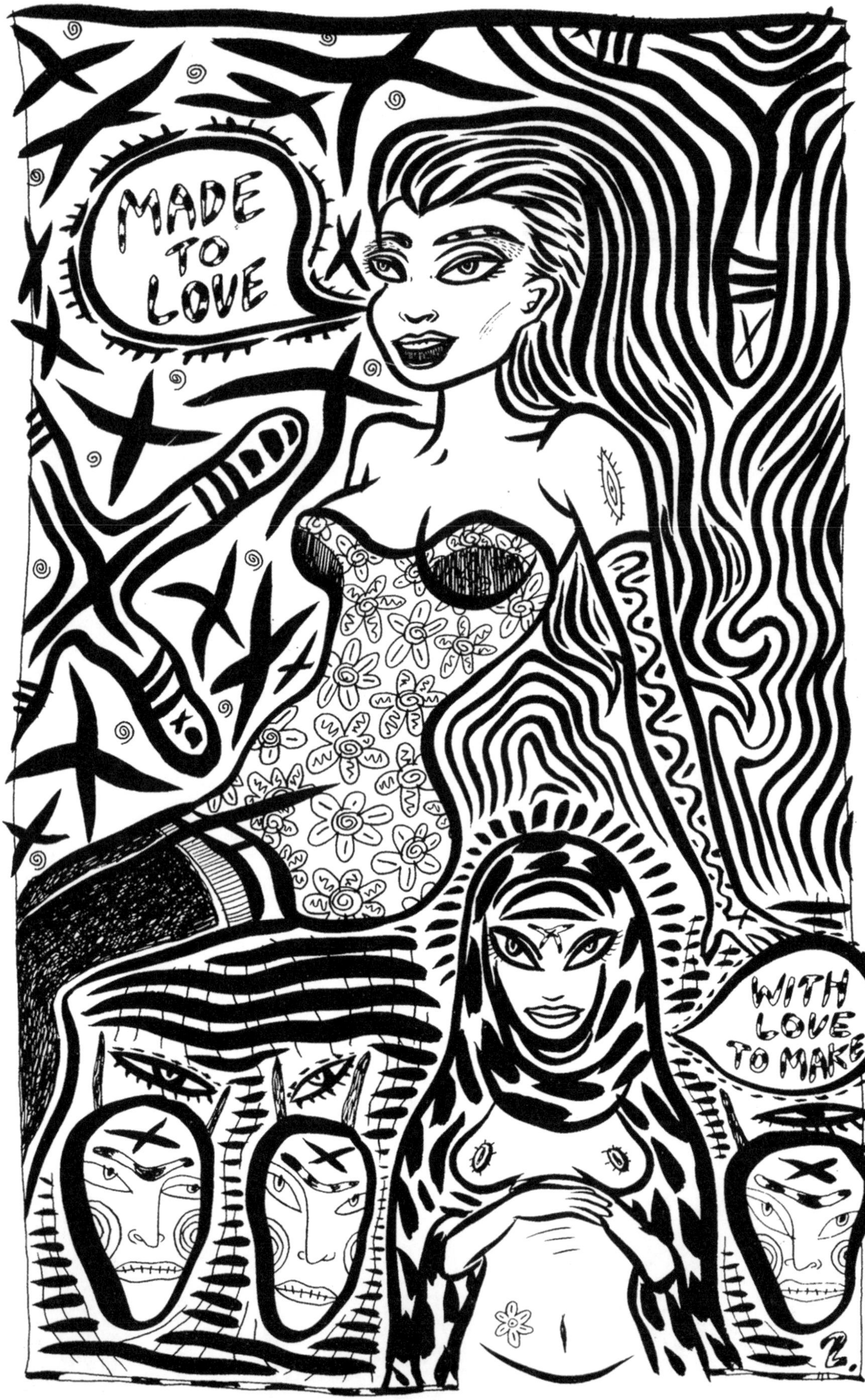
MADE TO LOVE
WITH LOVE TO MAKE

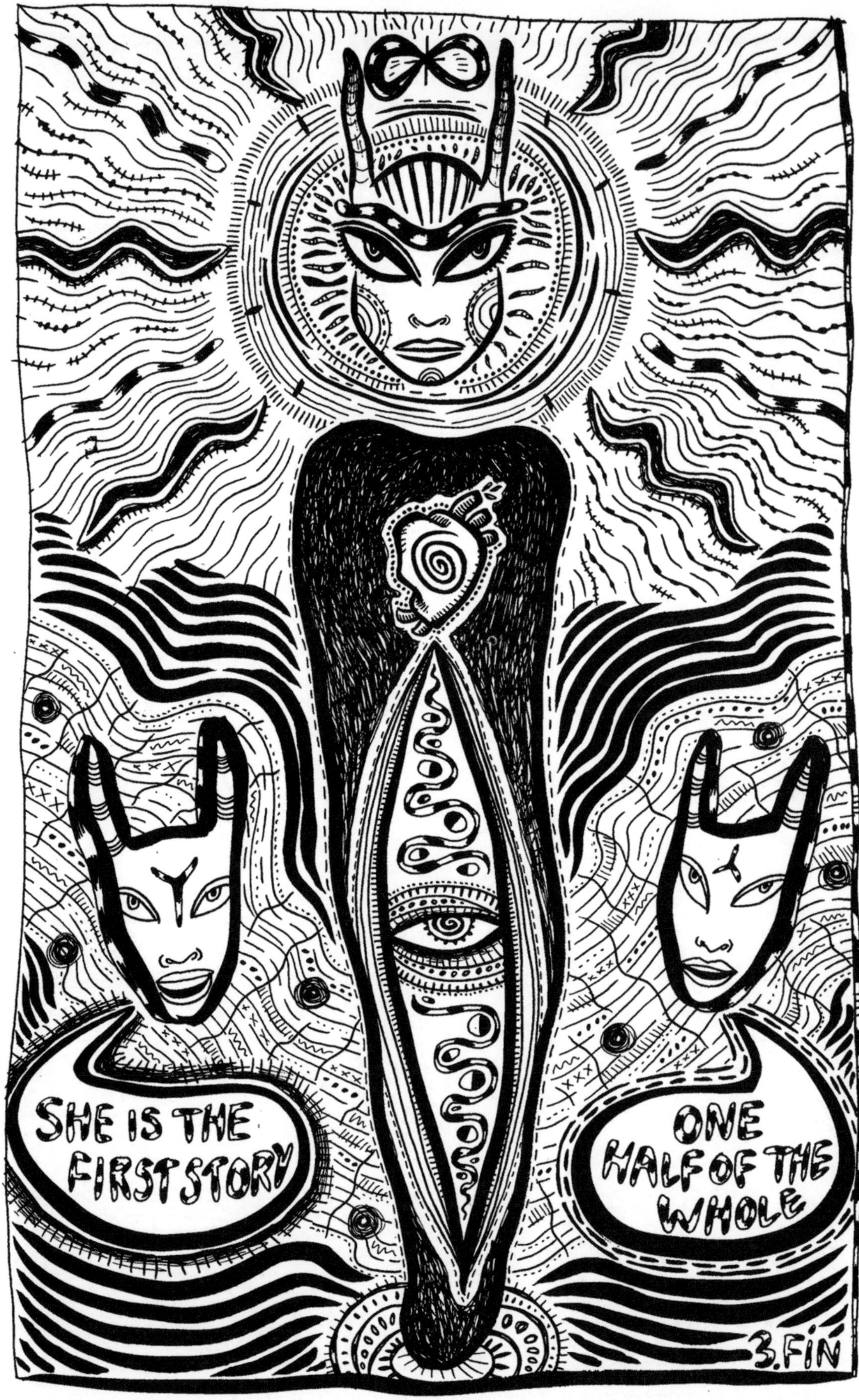
SHE IS THE FIRST STORY
ONE HALF OF THE WHOLE
3.FIN

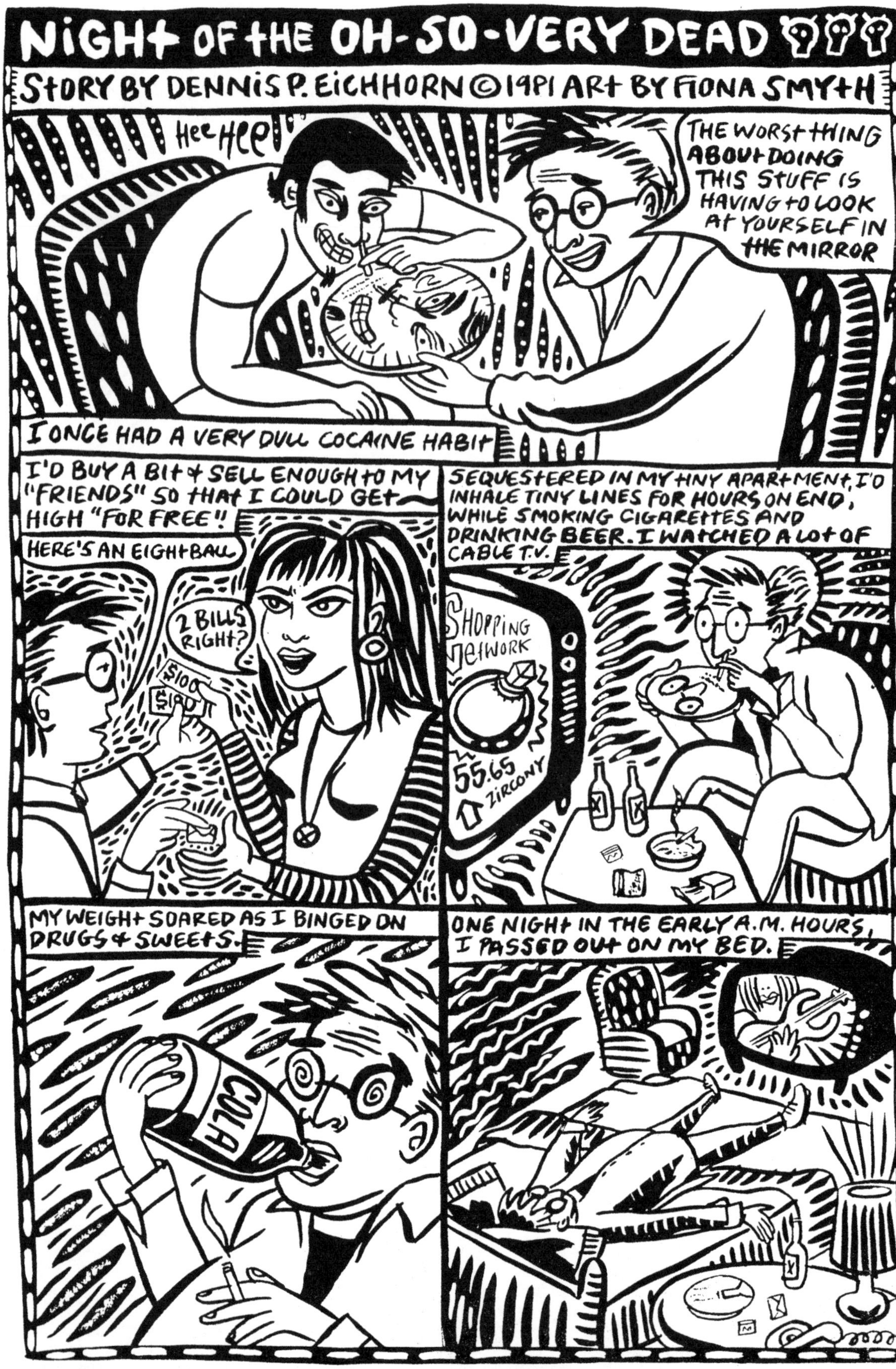
NIGHT OF THE OH-SO-VERY DEAD
STORY BY DENNIS P. EICHHORN © 1991 ART BY FIONA SMYTH
HEE HEE
THE WORST THING ABOUT DOING THIS STUFF IS HAVING TO LOOK AT YOURSELF IN THE MIRROR
I ONCE HAD A VERY DULL COCAINE HABIT
I'D BUY A BIT & SELL ENOUGH TO MY "FRIENDS" SO THAT I COULD GET HIGH "FOR FREE"!
HERE'S AN EIGHTBALL
2 BILLS RIGHT?
$100
$100
SEQUESTERED IN MY TINY APARTMENT, I'D INHALE TINY LINES FOR HOURS ON END, WHILE SMOKING CIGARETTES AND DRINKING BEER. I WATCHED A LOT OF CABLE T.V.
SHOPPING NETWORK
55.65
ZIRCONY
MY WEIGHT SOARED AS I BINGED ON DRUGS & SWEETS.
COLA
ONE NIGHT IN THE EARLY A.M. HOURS, I PASSED OUT ON MY BED.

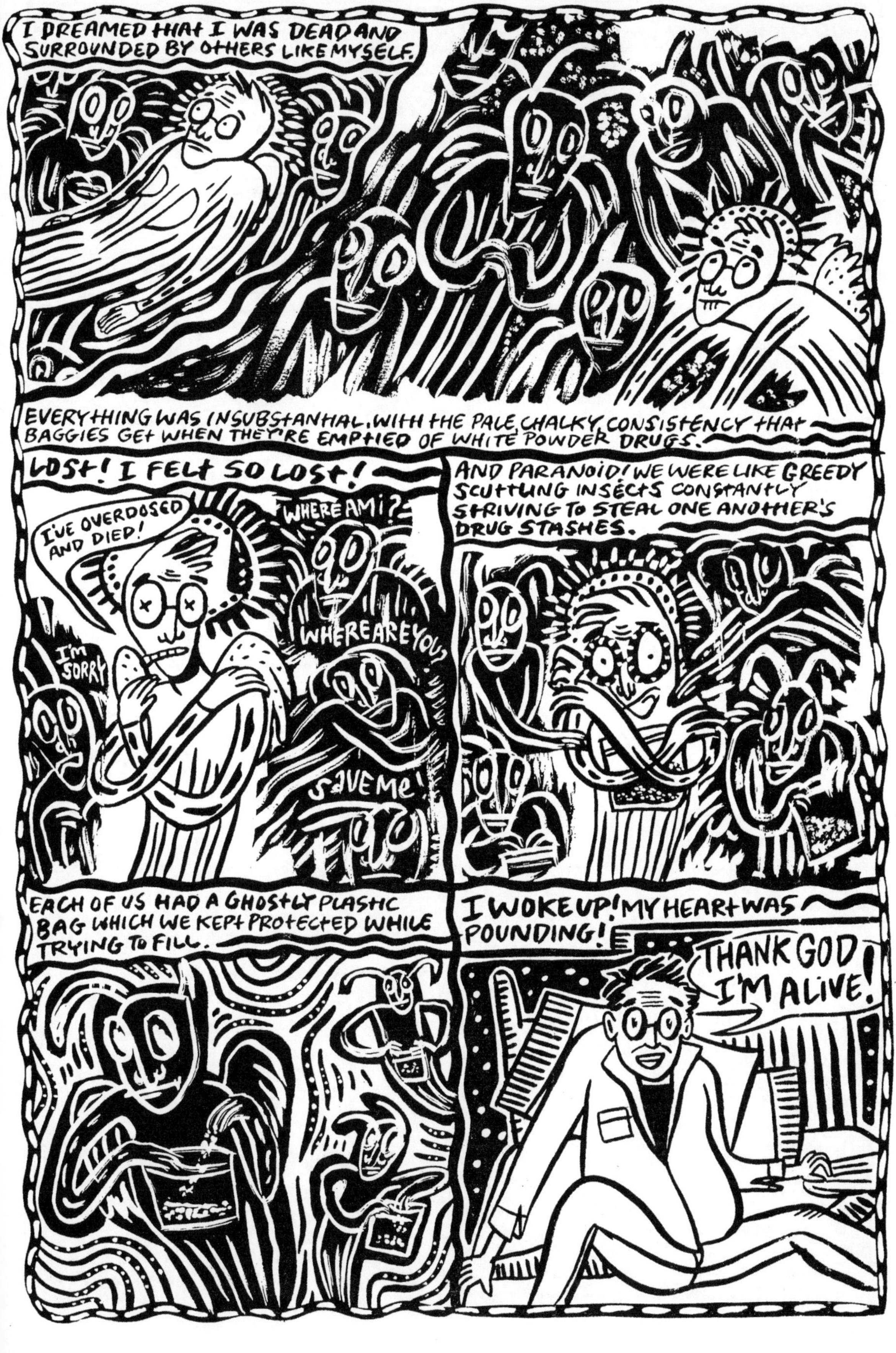

I DREAMED THAT I WAS DEAD AND SURROUNDED BY OTHERS LIKE MYSELF.
EVERYTHING WAS INSUBSTANTIAL, WITH THE PALE, CHALKY, CONSISTENCY THAT BAGGIES GET WHEN THEY'RE EMPTIED OF WHITE POWDER DRUGS.
LOST! I FELT SO LOST!
I'VE OVERDOSED AND DIED!
WHERE AM I?
WHERE ARE YOU?
I'M SORRY
SAVE ME
AND PARANOID! WE WERE LIKE GREEDY SCUTTLING INSECTS CONSTANTLY STRIVING TO STEAL ONE ANOTHER'S DRUG STASHES.
EACH OF US HAD A GHOSTLY PLASTIC BAG WHICH WE KEPT PROTECTED WHILE TRYING TO FILL.
I WOKE UP! MY HEART WAS POUNDING!
THANK GOD I'M ALIVE!

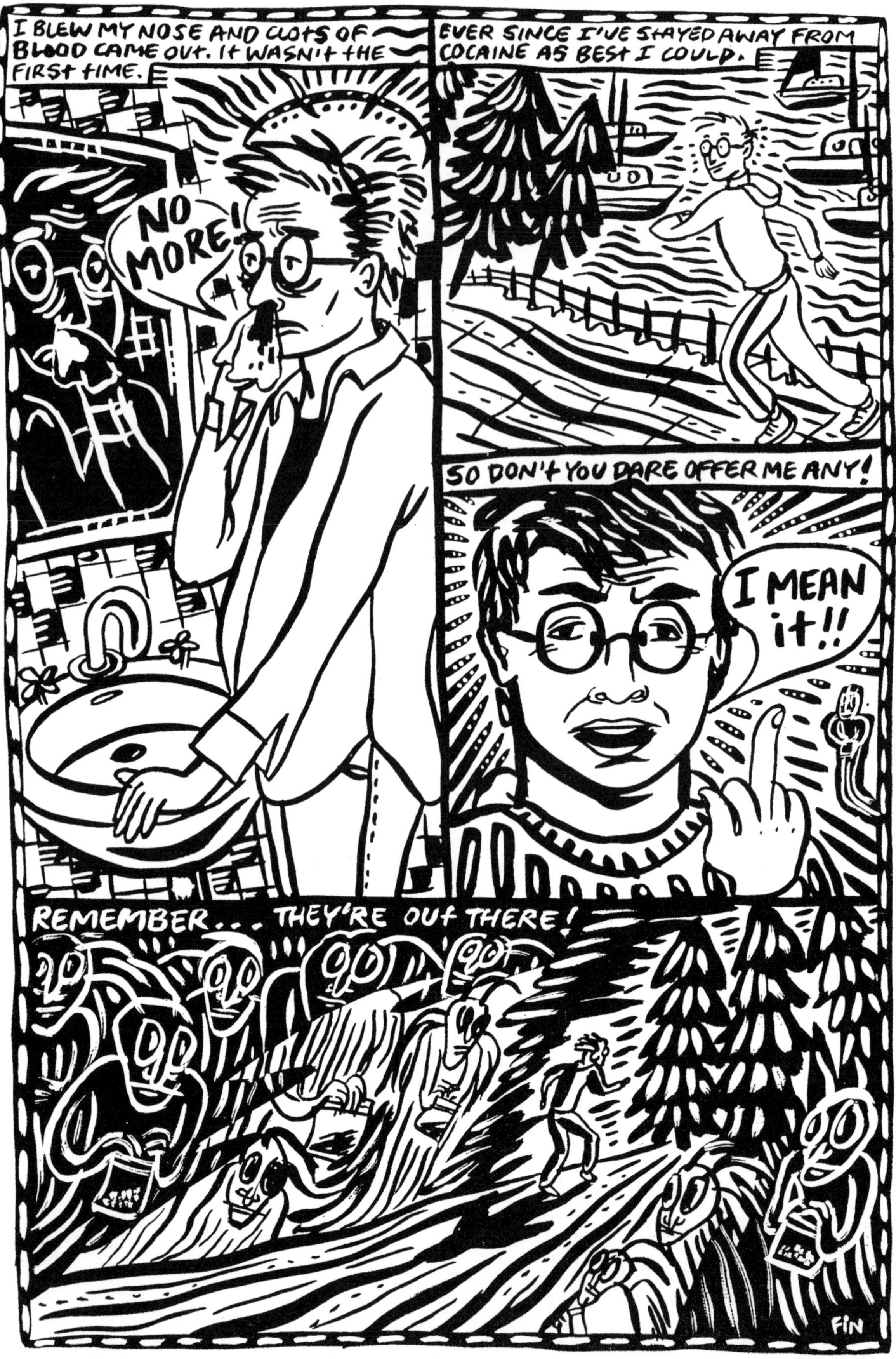
I BLEW MY NOSE AND CLOTS OF BLOOD CAME OUT. IT WASN'T THE FIRST TIME.
NO MORE!
EVER SINCE I'VE STAYED AWAY FROM COCAINE AS BEST I COULD.
SO DON'T YOU DARE OFFER ME ANY!
I MEAN it!!
REMEMBER... THEY'RE OUT THERE!
FIN

I'M O.K.
A. CON-CEIVED
B. IN SIN
C. NOT LOVE
YOU'RE NOT
D. TO LOVE
E. HON-OUR
F. AND OBEY

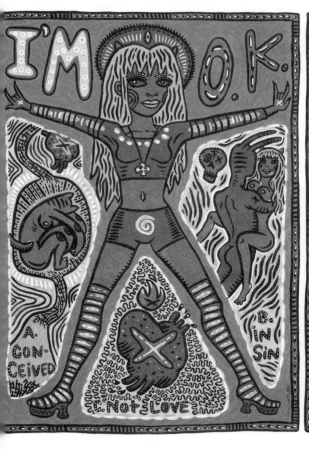

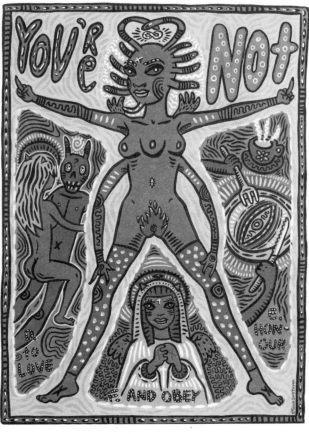

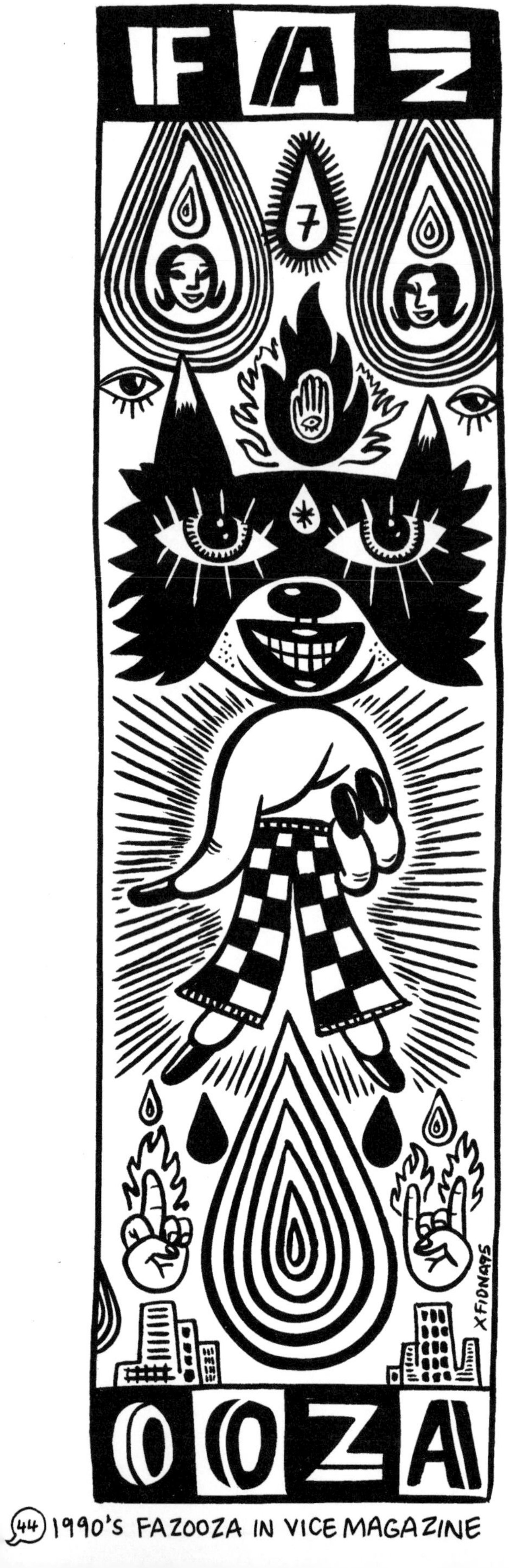
FAZ
7
OOZA
XFIONA95

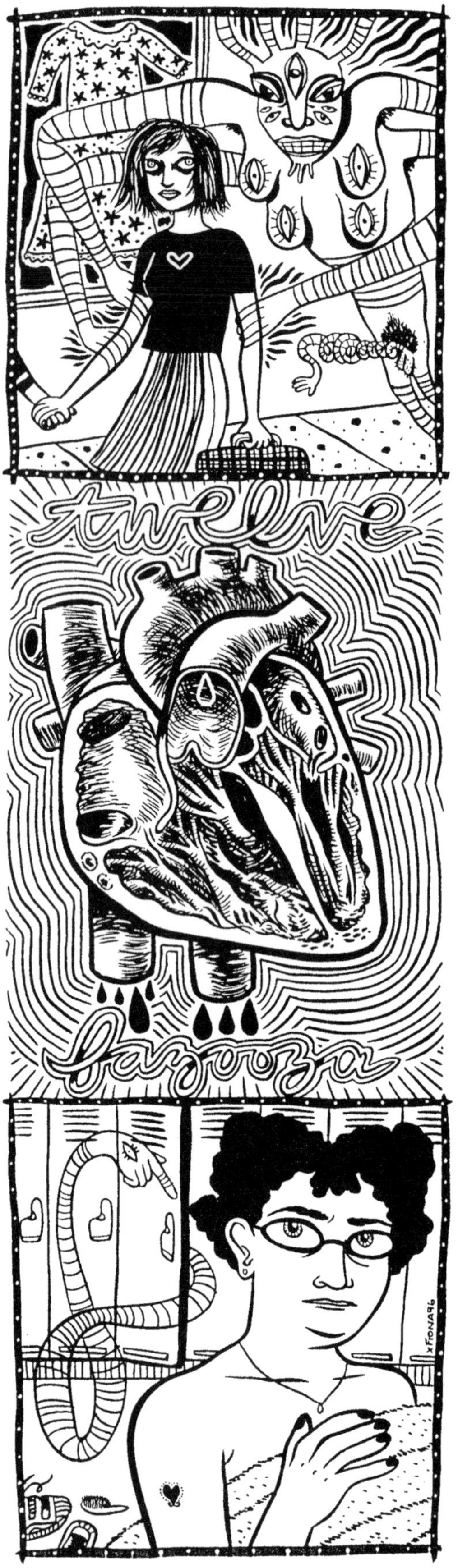
twelve
fazooza
XFIONA96

 1990'S FAZOOZA IN VICE MAGAZINE

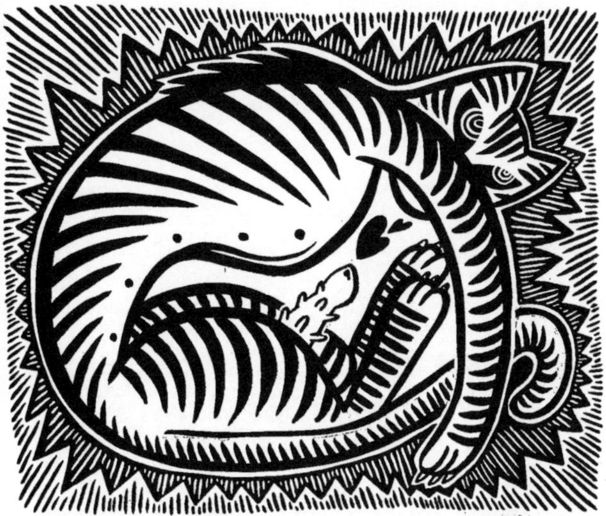

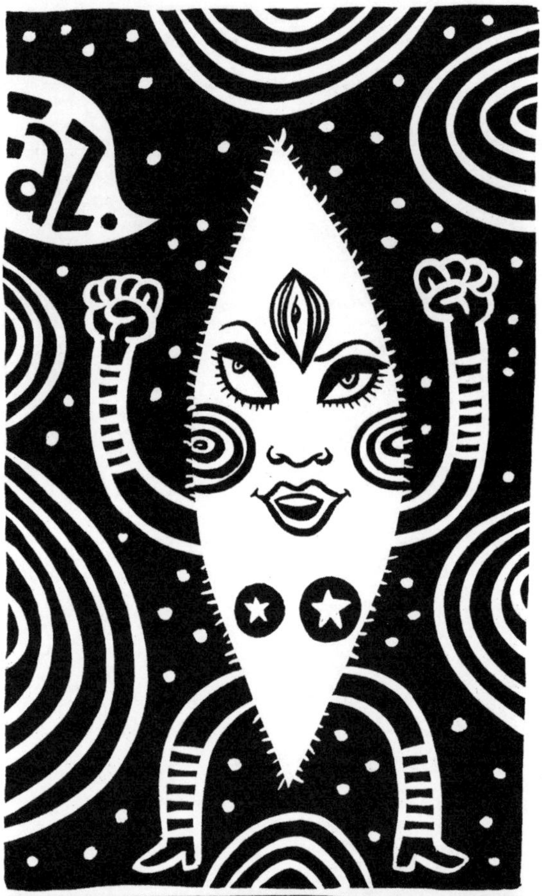
faz.

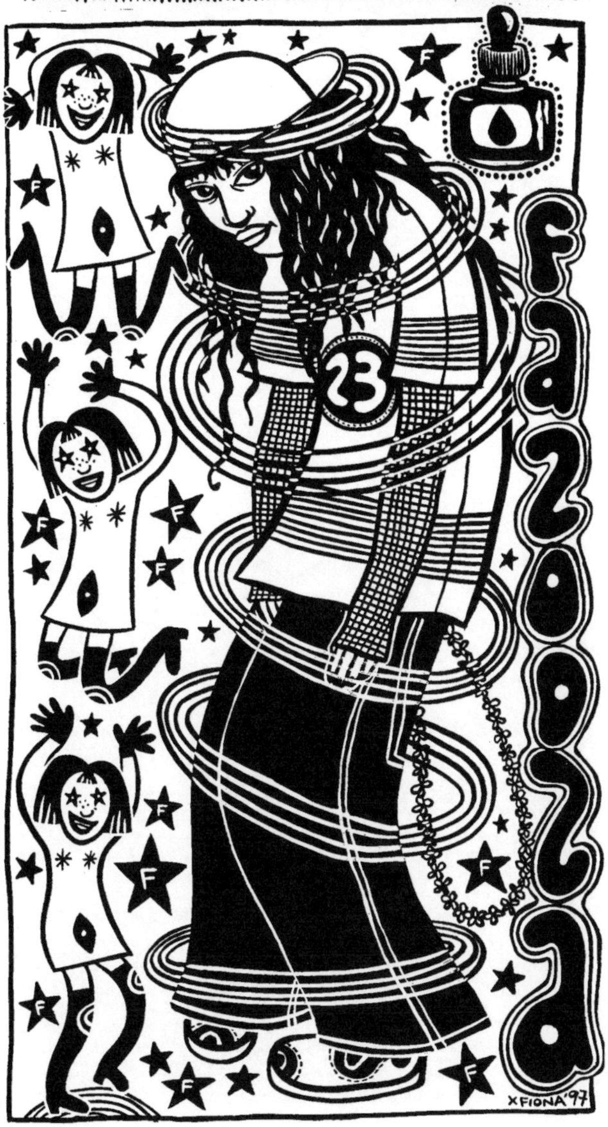
fazooza
23
XFIONA'97

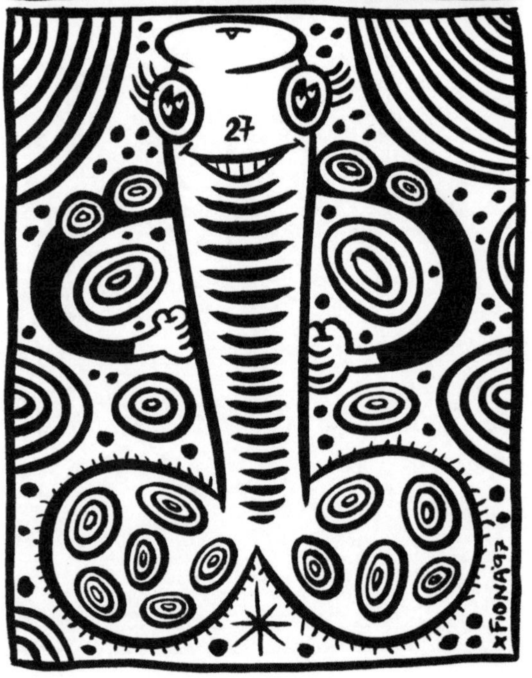
27
XFIONA'97

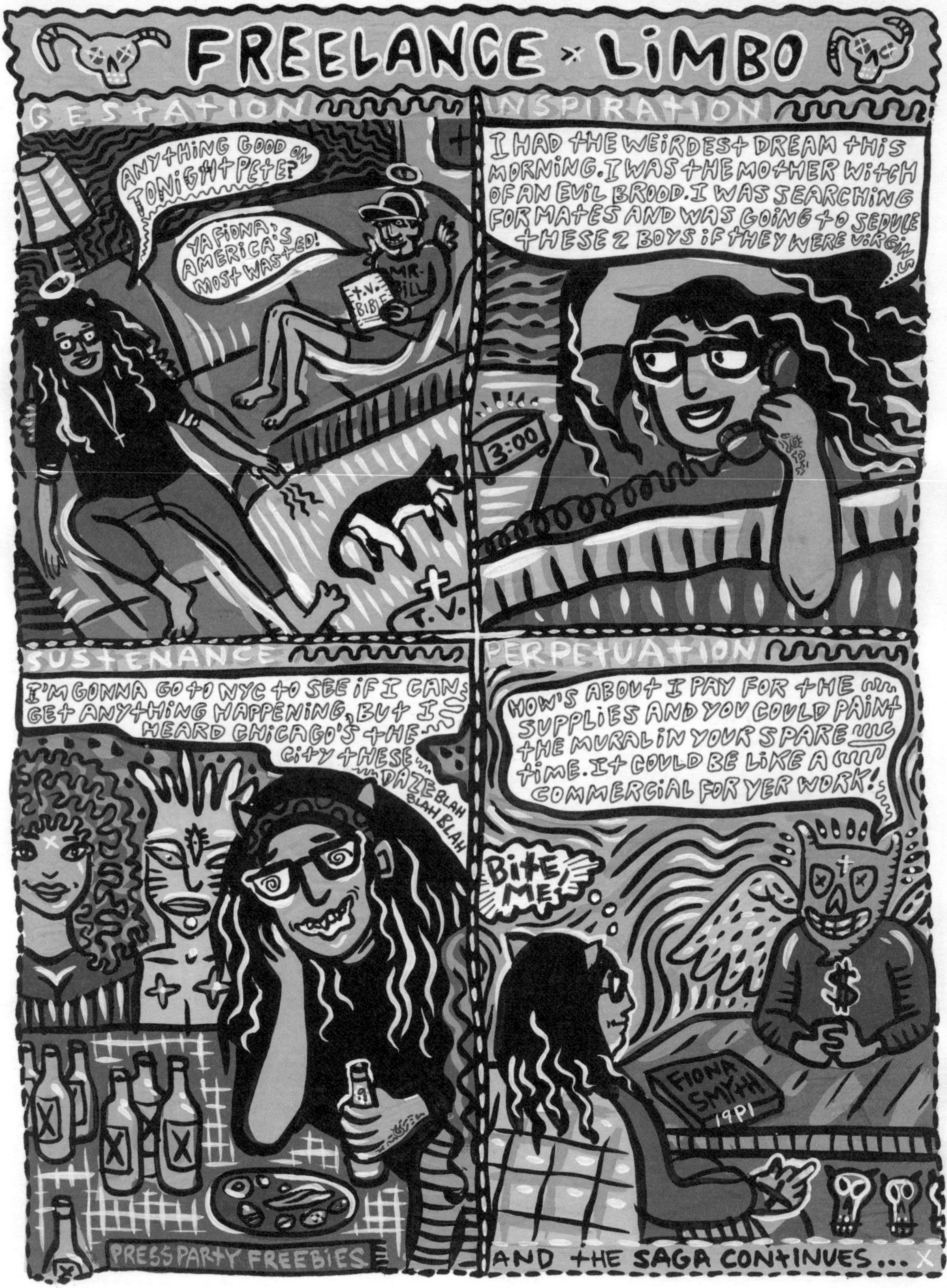
FREELANCE LIMBO
GESTATION
ANYTHING GOOD ON TONIGHT PETE?
YA FIONA: AMERICA'S MOST WASTED!
T.V. BIBLE
MR. BILL
3:00
T.V.
INSPIRATION
I HAD THE WEIRDEST DREAM THIS MORNING. I WAS THE MOTHER WITCH OF AN EVIL BROOD. I WAS SEARCHING FOR MATES AND WAS GOING TO SEDUCE THESE 2 BOYS IF THEY WERE VIRGINS...
SUSTENANCE
I'M GONNA GO TO NYC TO SEE IF I CAN GET ANYTHING HAPPENING, BUT I HEARD CHICAGO'S THE CITY THESE DAZE
BLAH BLAH BLAH
PRESS PARTY FREEBIES
PERPETUATION
HOW'S ABOUT I PAY FOR THE SUPPLIES AND YOU COULD PAINT THE MURAL IN YOUR SPARE TIME. IT COULD BE LIKE A COMMERCIAL FOR YER WORK!
BITE ME!
FIONA SMYTH 1991
AND THE SAGA CONTINUES...

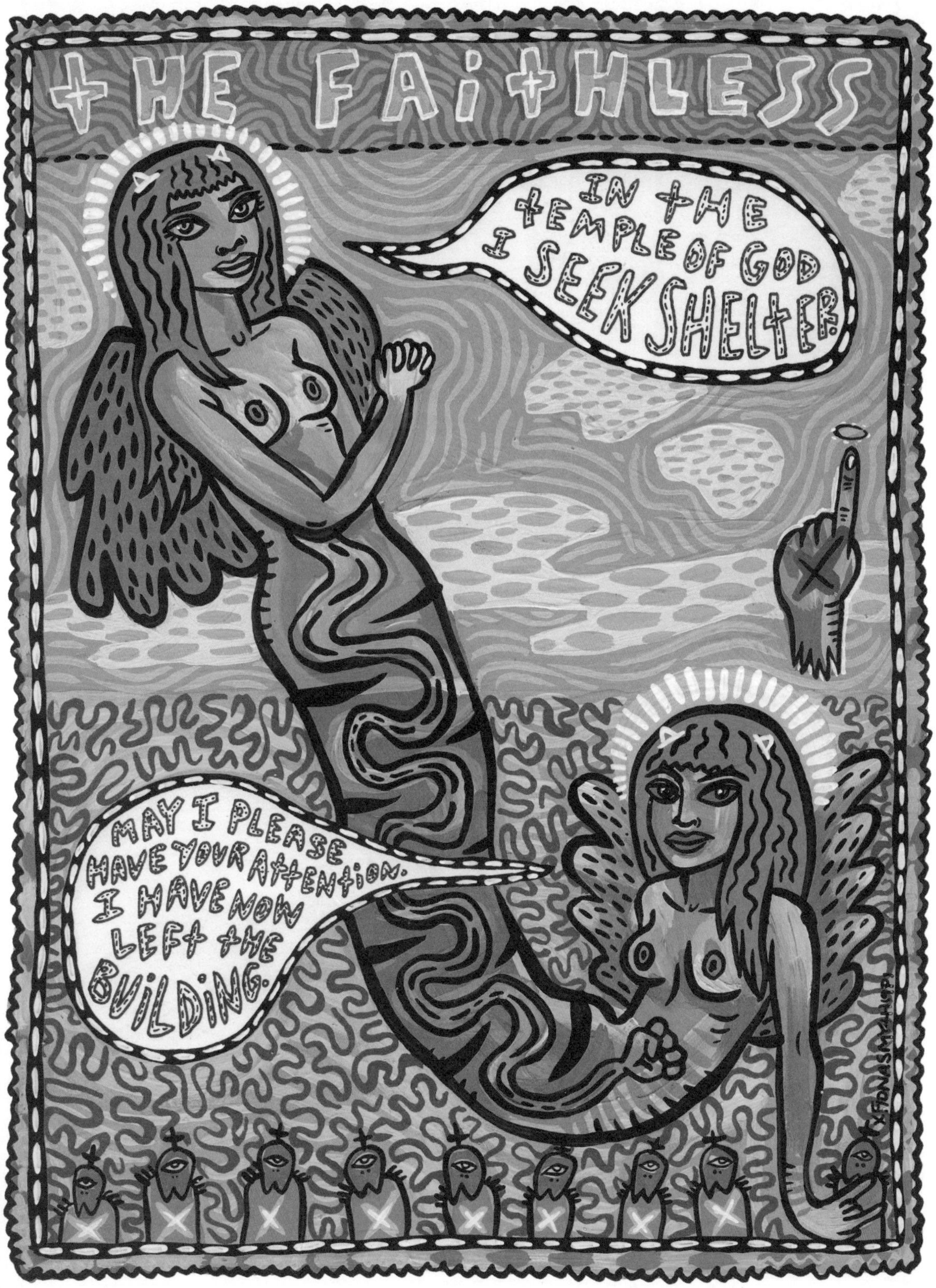
THE FAITHLESS
IN THE TEMPLE OF GOD I SEEK SHELTER.
MAY I PLEASE HAVE YOUR ATTENTION. I HAVE NOW LEFT THE BUILDING.

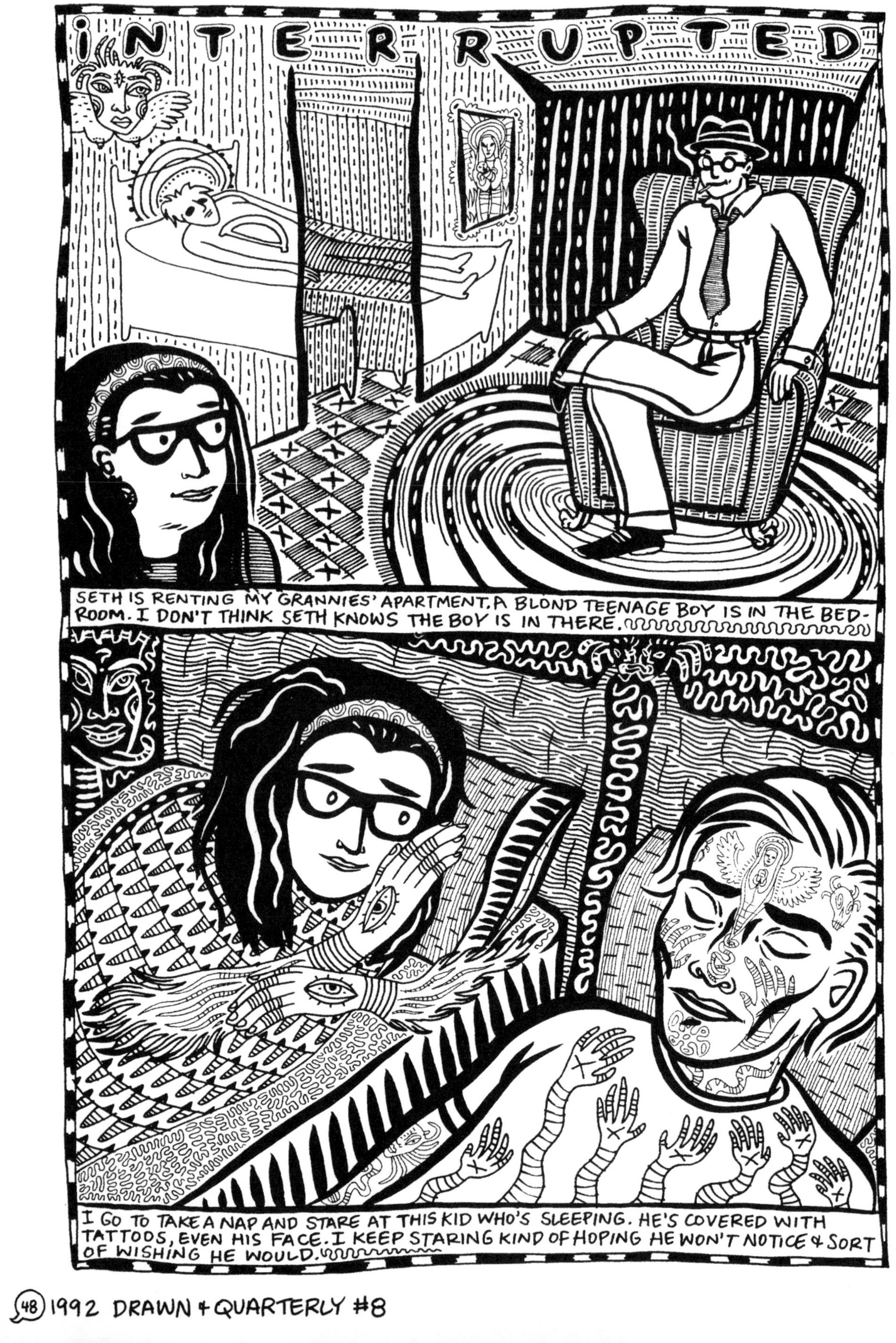
INTERRUPTED
SETH IS RENTING MY GRANNIES' APARTMENT. A BLOND TEENAGE BOY IS IN THE BEDROOM. I DON'T THINK SETH KNOWS THE BOY IS IN THERE.
I GO TO TAKE A NAP AND STARE AT THIS KID WHO'S SLEEPING. HE'S COVERED WITH TATTOOS, EVEN HIS FACE. I KEEP STARING KIND OF HOPING HE WON'T NOTICE & SORT OF WISHING HE WOULD.

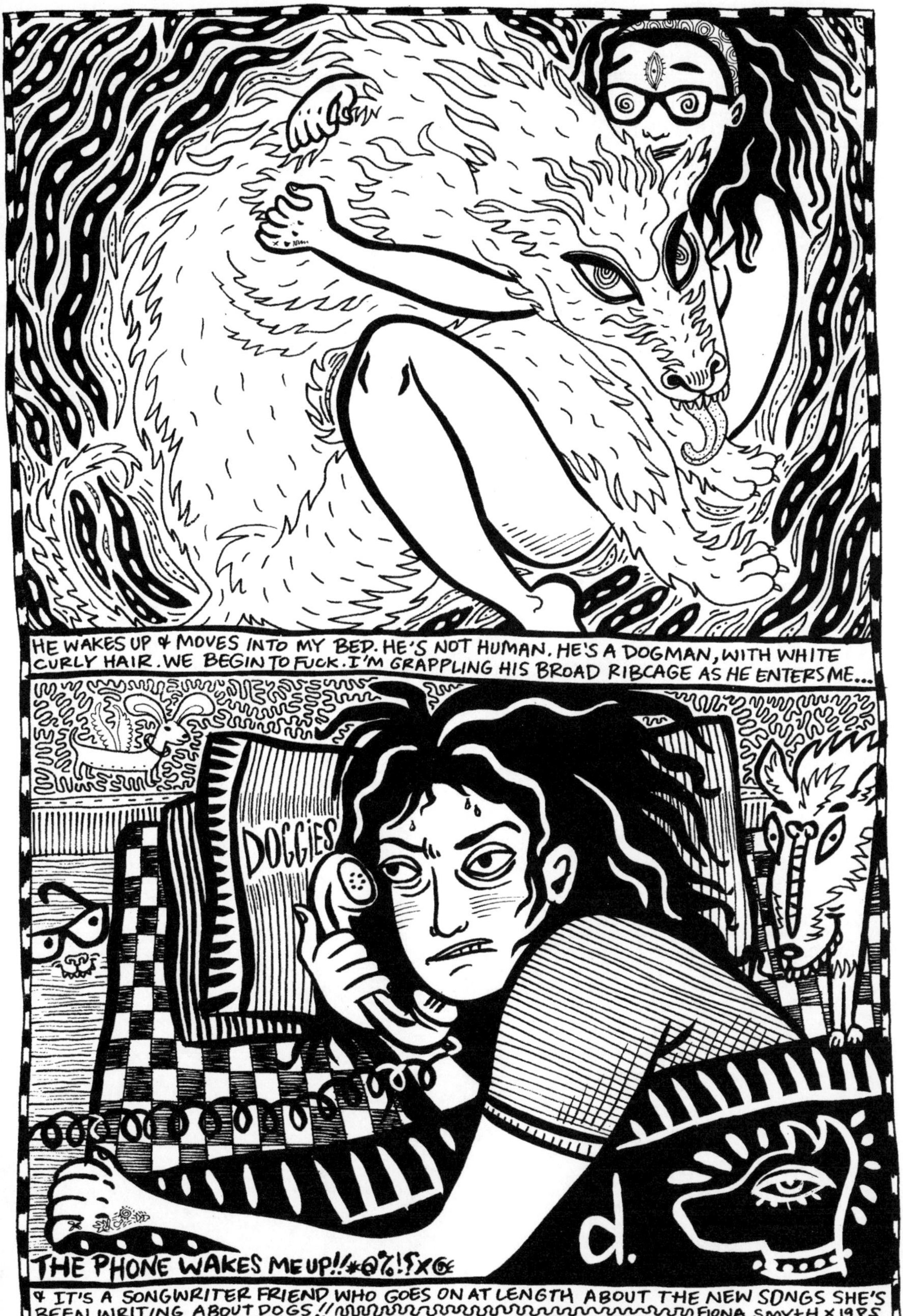
HE WAKES UP & MOVES INTO MY BED. HE'S NOT HUMAN. HE'S A DOGMAN, WITH WHITE CURLY HAIR. WE BEGIN TO FUCK. I'M GRAPPLING HIS BROAD RIBCAGE AS HE ENTERS ME...
DOGGIES
THE PHONE WAKES ME UP!!
d.
& IT'S A SONGWRITER FRIEND WHO GOES ON AT LENGTH ABOUT THE NEW SONGS SHE'S BEEN WRITING ABOUT DOGS!!
FIONA SMYTH

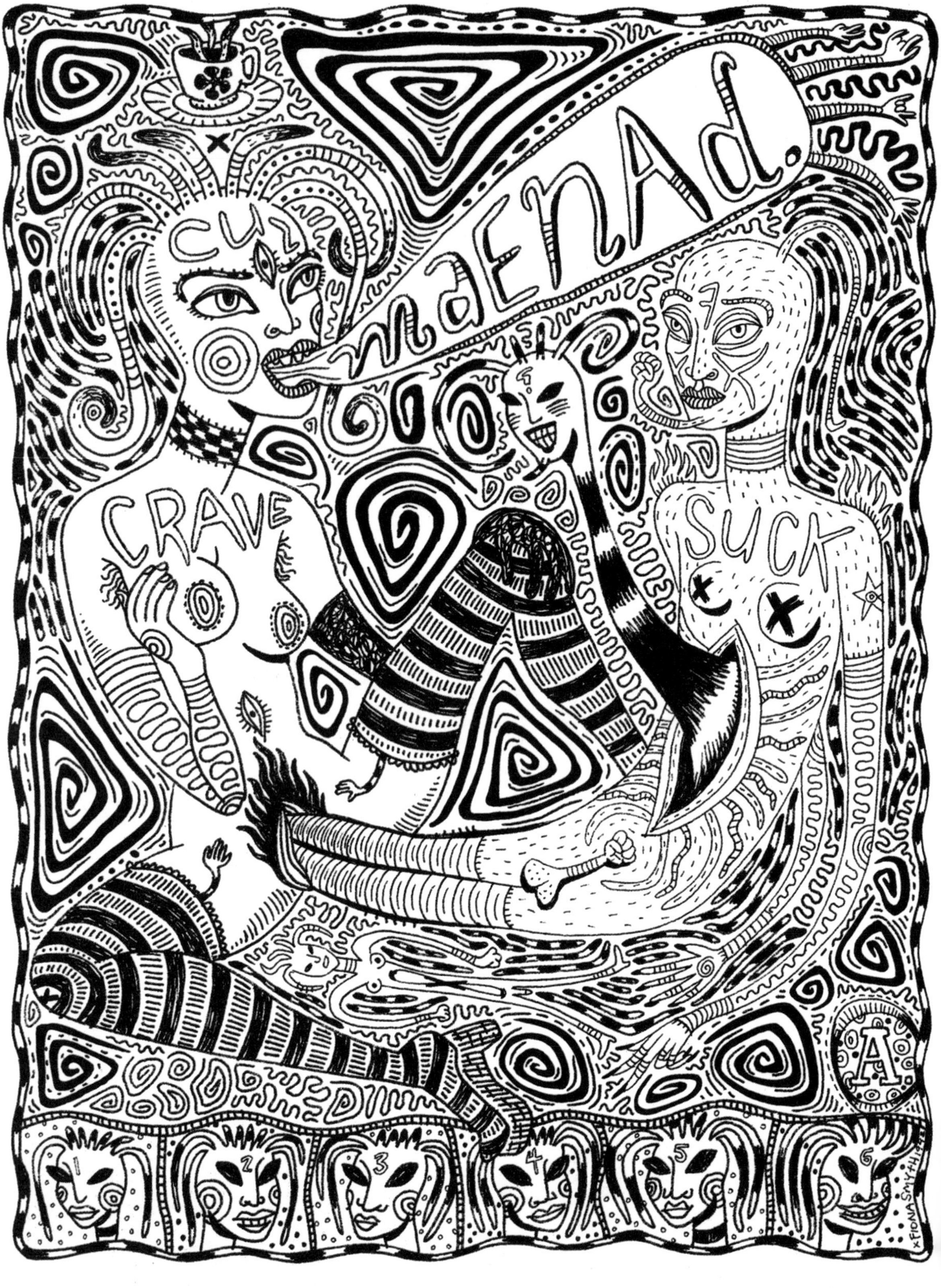
maenad.
CUZ
CRAVE
SUCK
A
1
2
3
4
5
6
x FIONA SMYTH

50 1992 UNTITLED

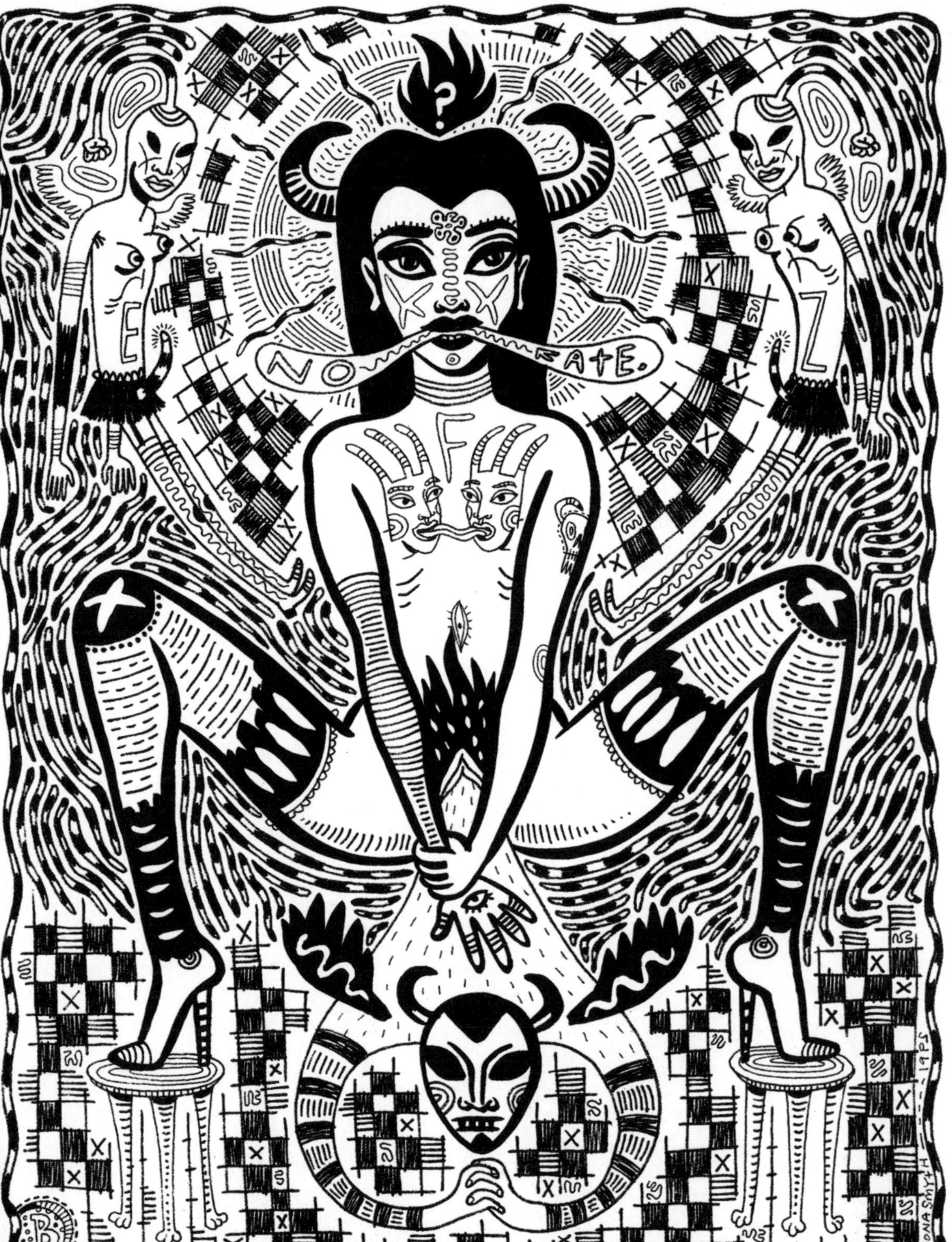
NO FATE.
xFIONA SMYTH 1995

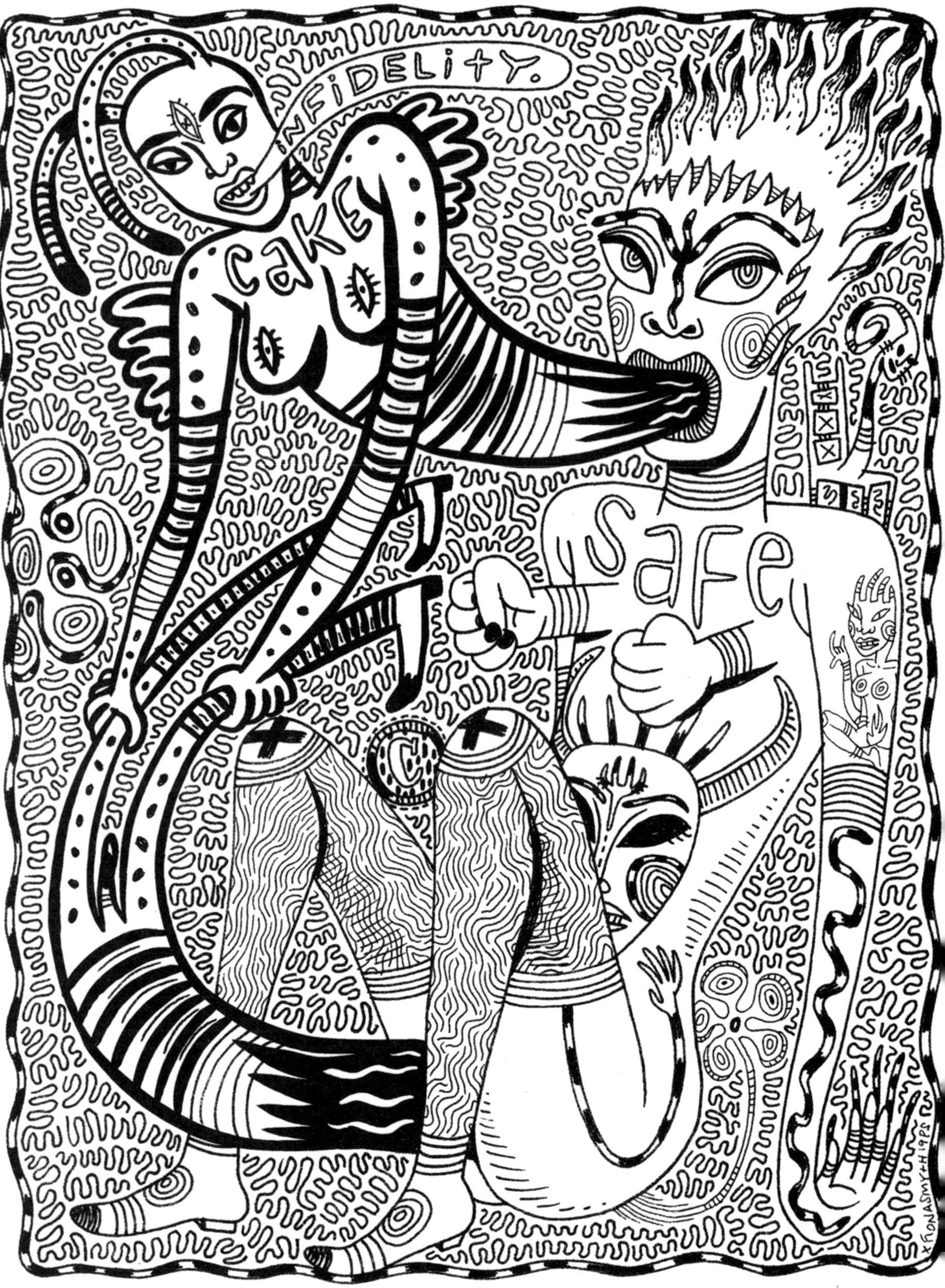
INFIDELITY.
CAKE
SAFE
x FIONASMYTH 1992

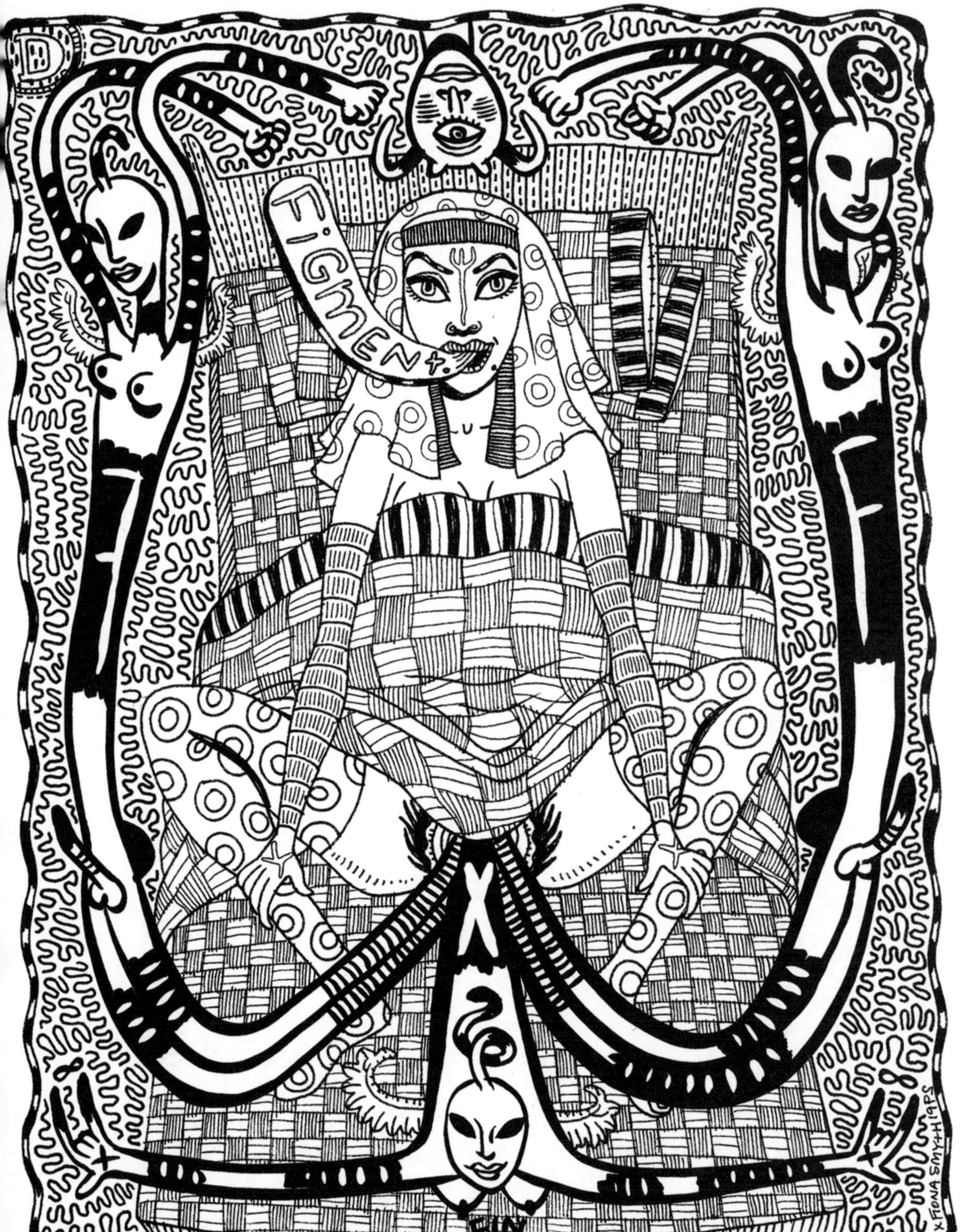

FIGMENT.
FIN
X FIONA SMYTH 1995

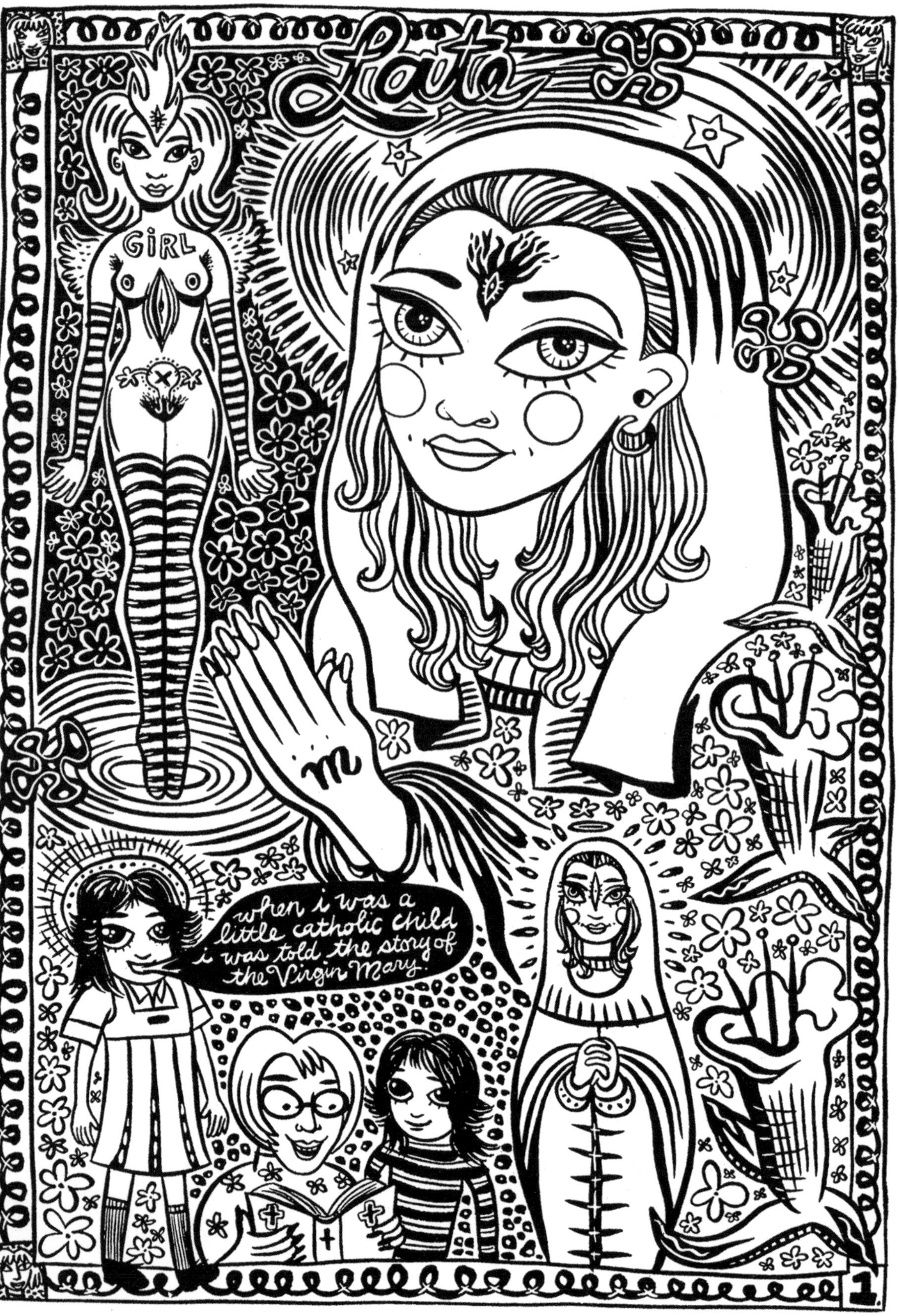
Leith
GIRL
m
when i was a little catholic child i was told the story of the Virgin Mary.
1.

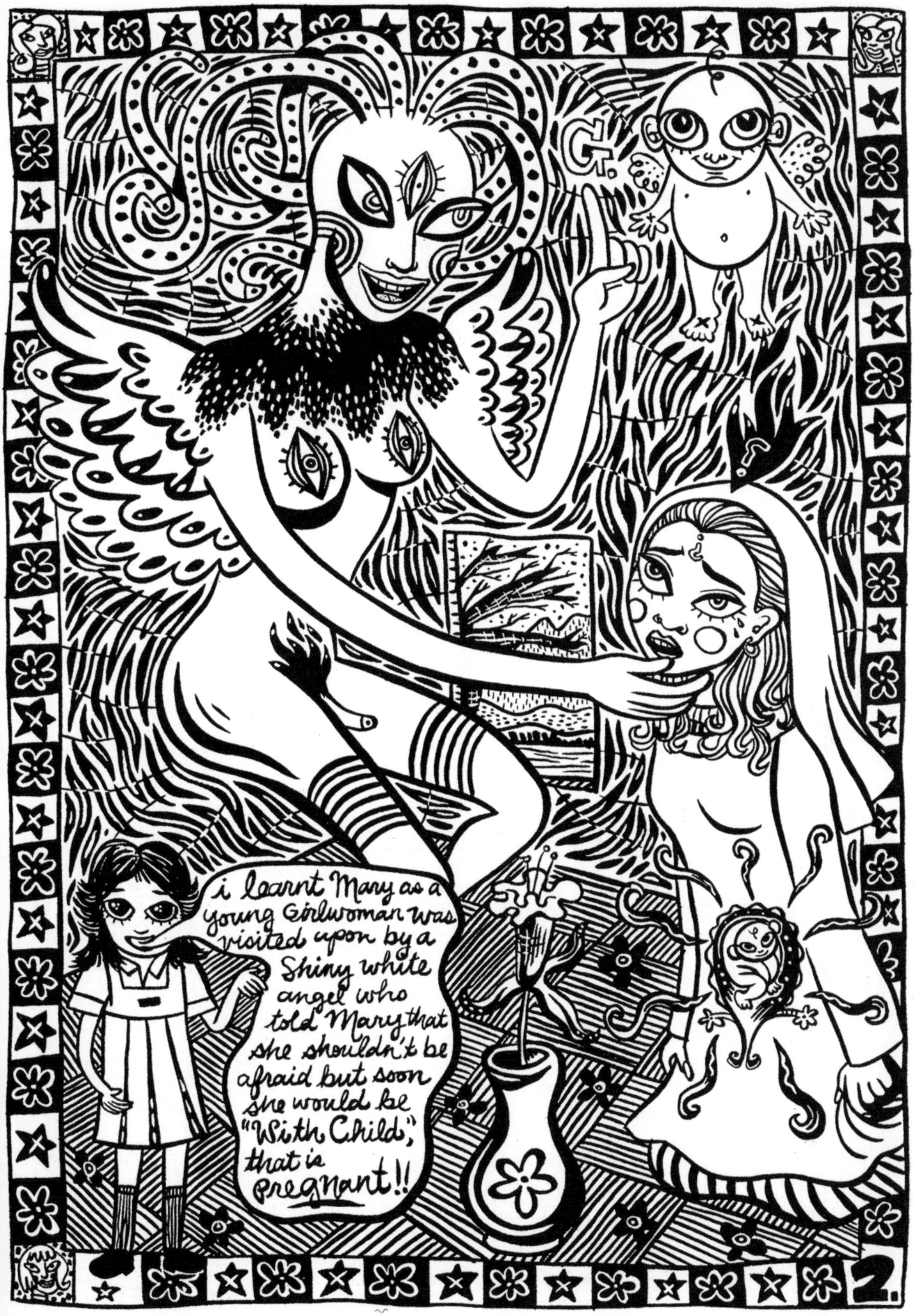
G.
i learnt Mary as a young Girlwoman was visited upon by a Shiny white angel who told Mary that she shouldn't be afraid but soon she would be "With Child", that is pregnant!!
2.

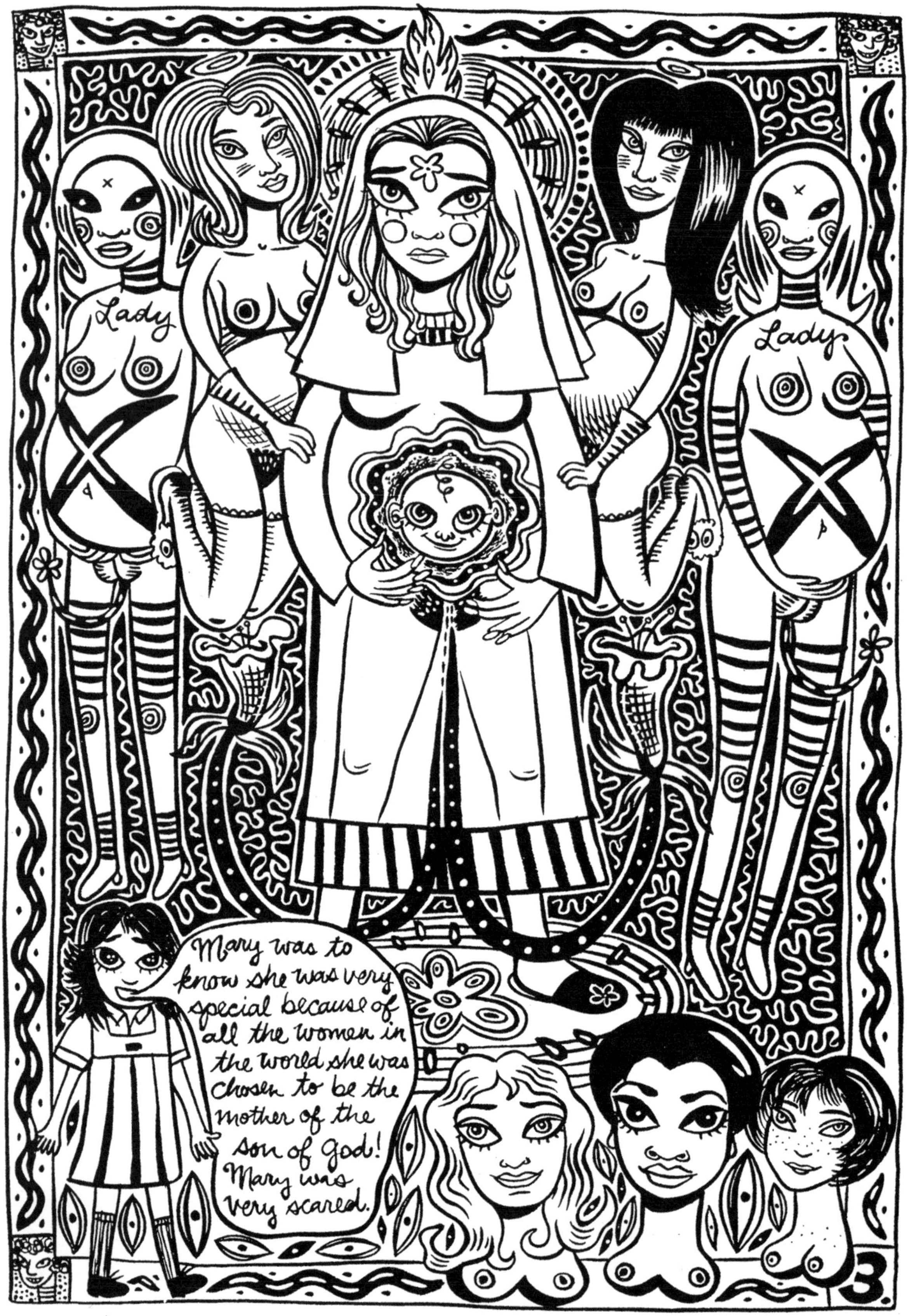
Lady
Lady
Mary was to know she was very special because of all the women in the world she was chosen to be the mother of the son of God! Mary was very scared.
3.

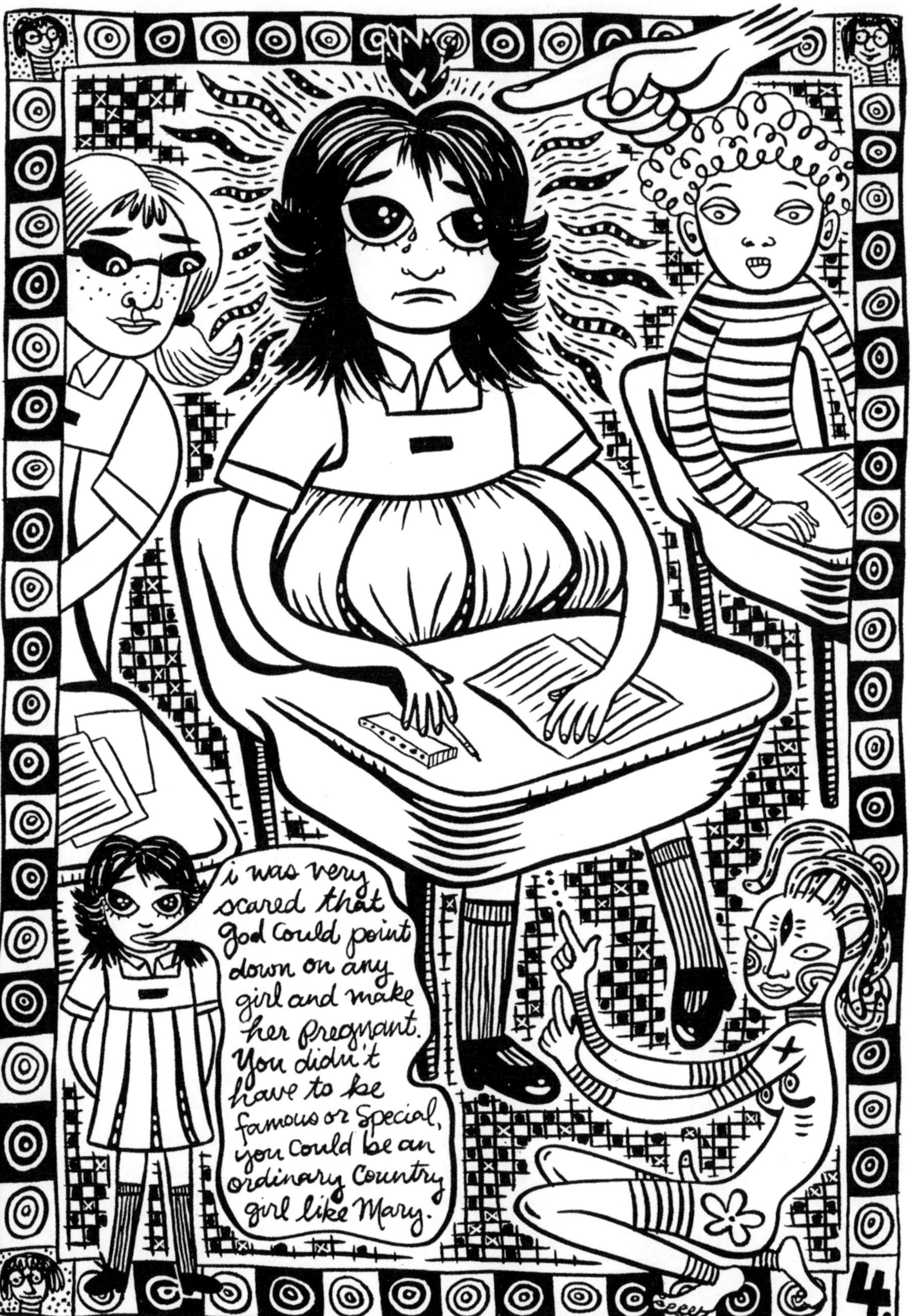
i was very scared that God could point down on any girl and make her pregnant. You didn't have to be famous or Special, you could be an ordinary Country girl like Mary.
4.

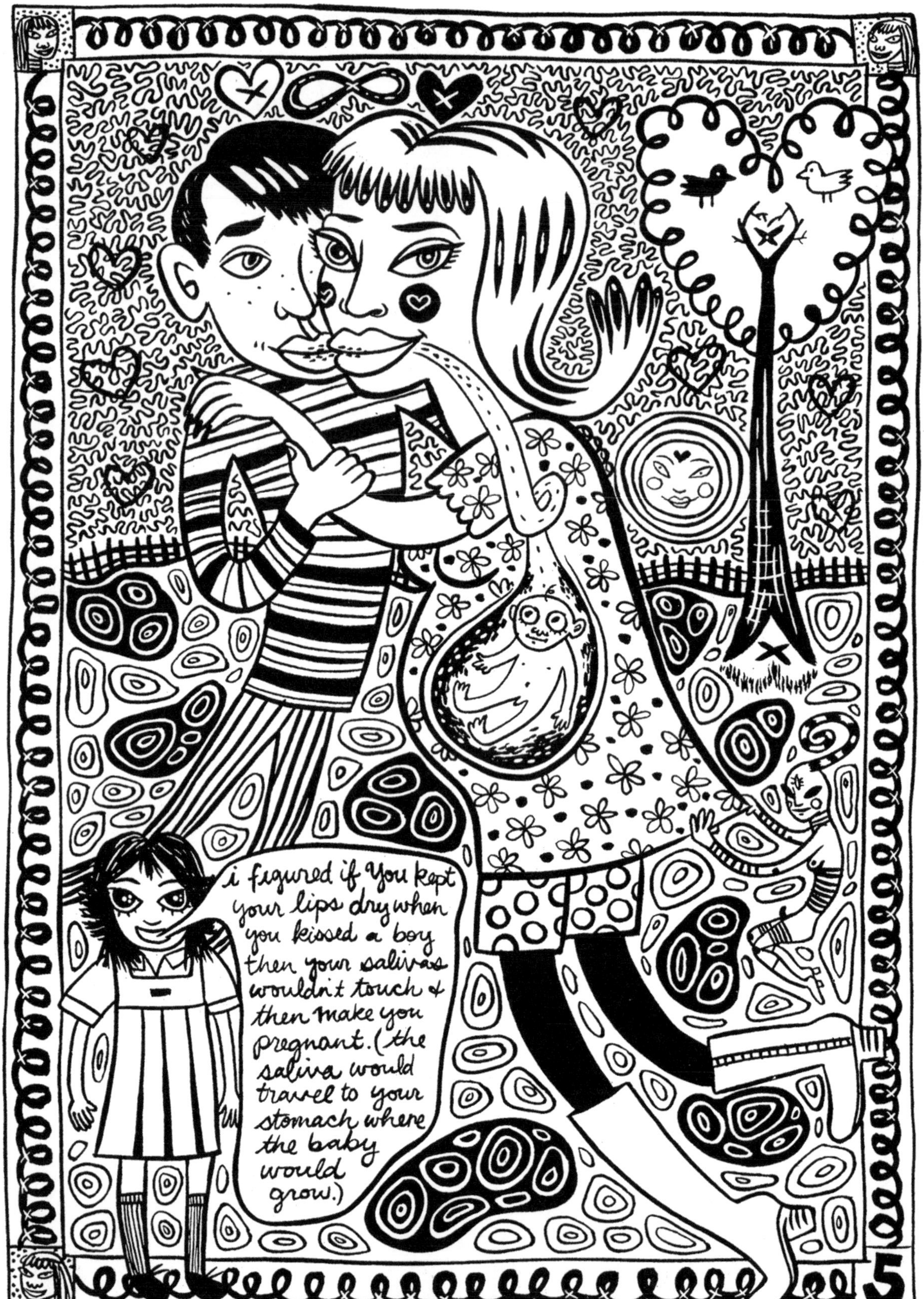
i figured if You kept your lips dry when you kissed a boy then your salivas wouldn't touch & then make you pregnant. (the saliva would travel to your stomach where the baby would grow.)
5.

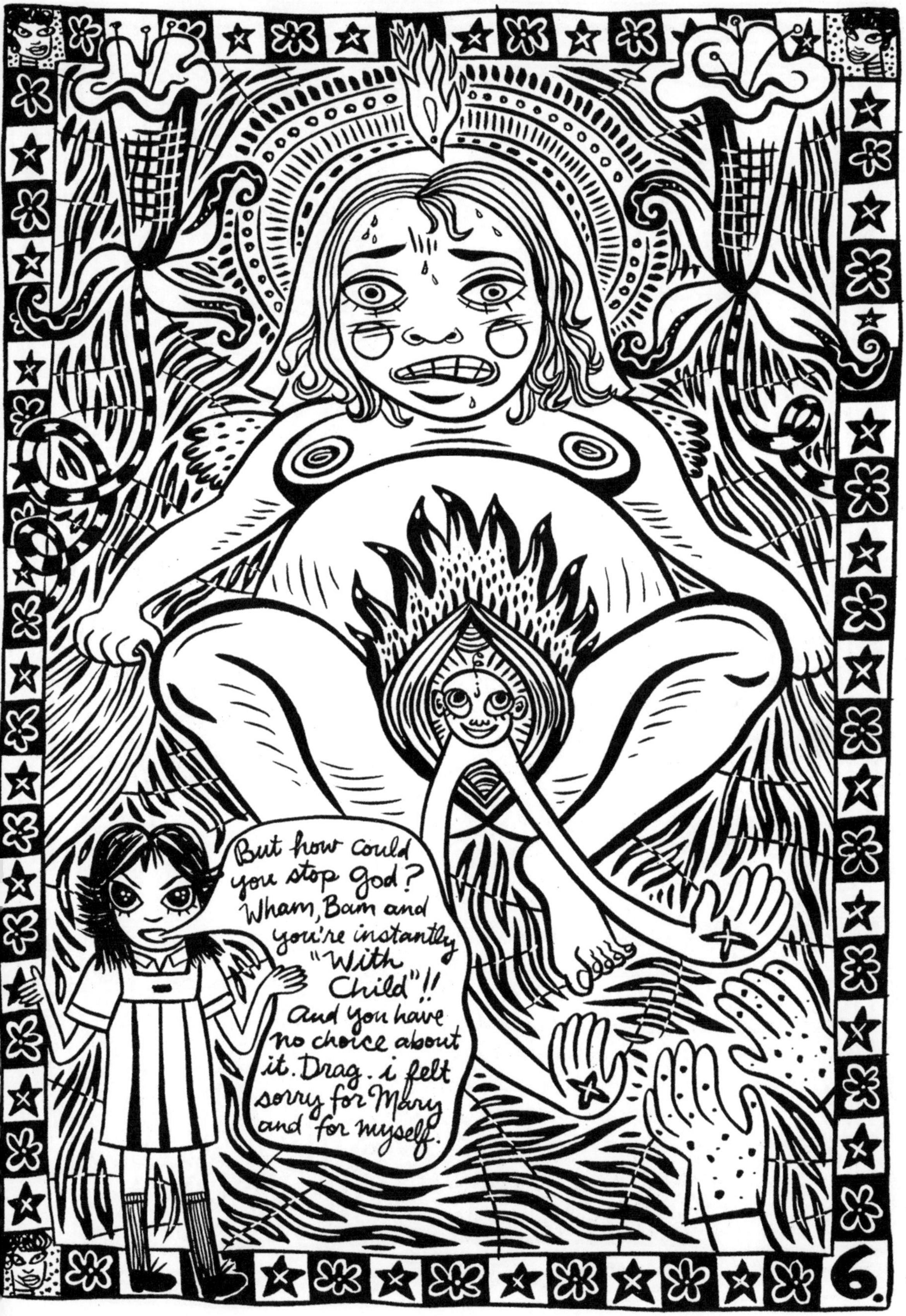
But how could you stop god? Wham, Bam and you're instantly "With Child"!! and you have no choice about it. Drag. i felt sorry for Mary and for myself.
6.

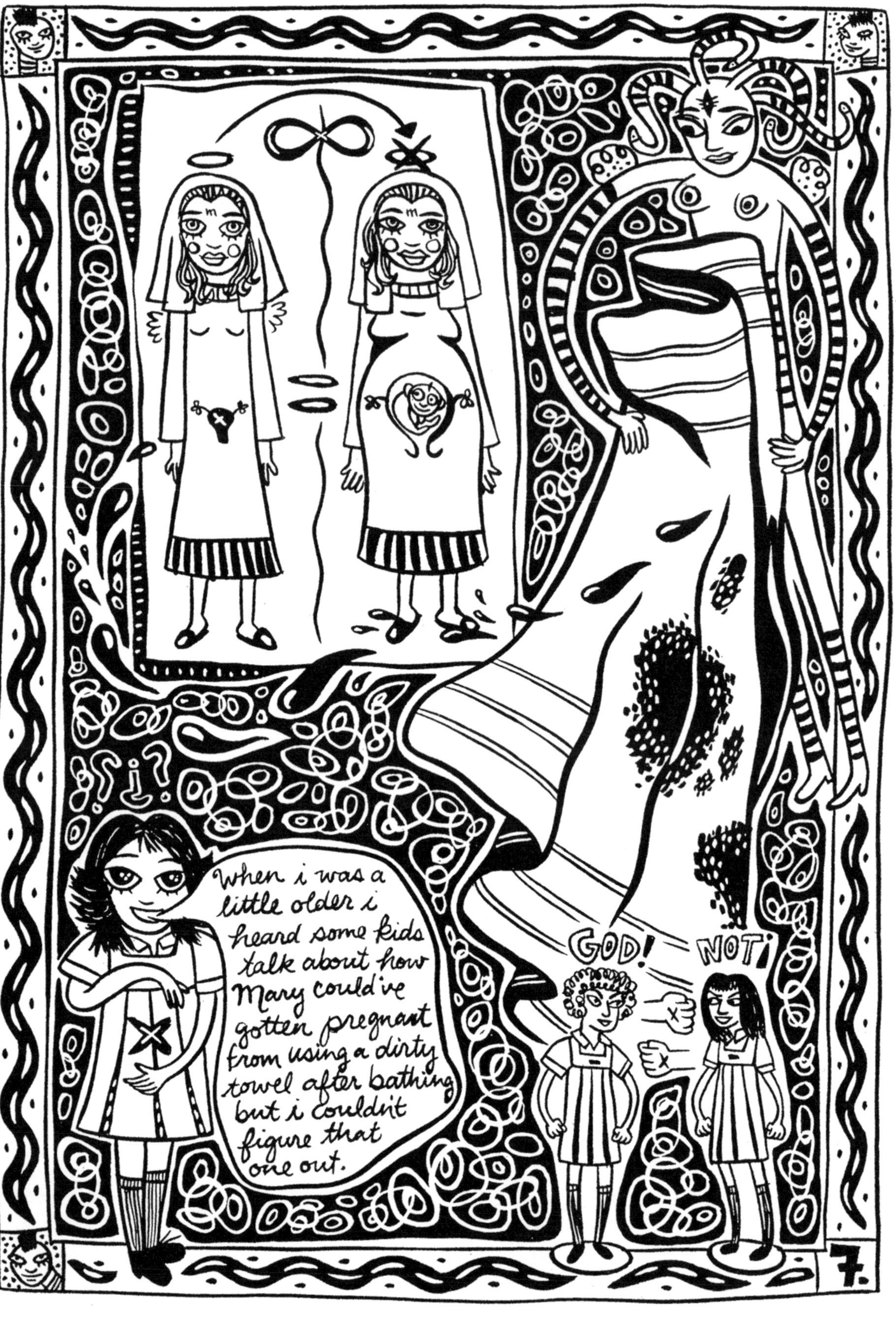
¿i?
When i was a little older i heard some kids talk about how Mary could've gotten pregnant from using a dirty towel after bathing but i couldn't figure that one out.
GOD!
NOT!
7.

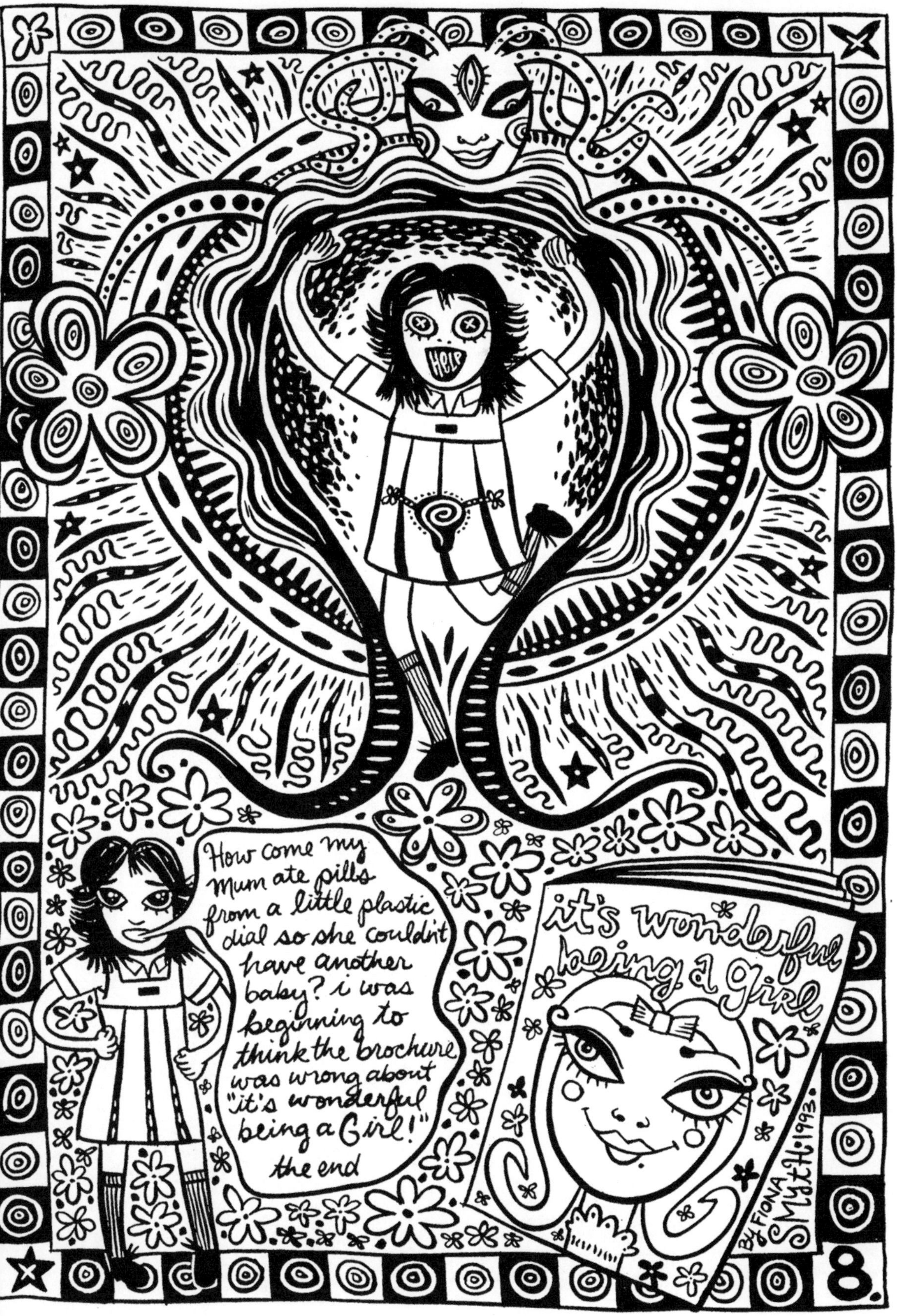
HELP
How come my Mum ate pills from a little plastic dial so she couldn't have another baby? i was beginning to think the brochure was wrong about "it's wonderful being a Girl!"
the end
it's wonderful being a Girl
BY FIONA SMYTH • 1993 •
8.

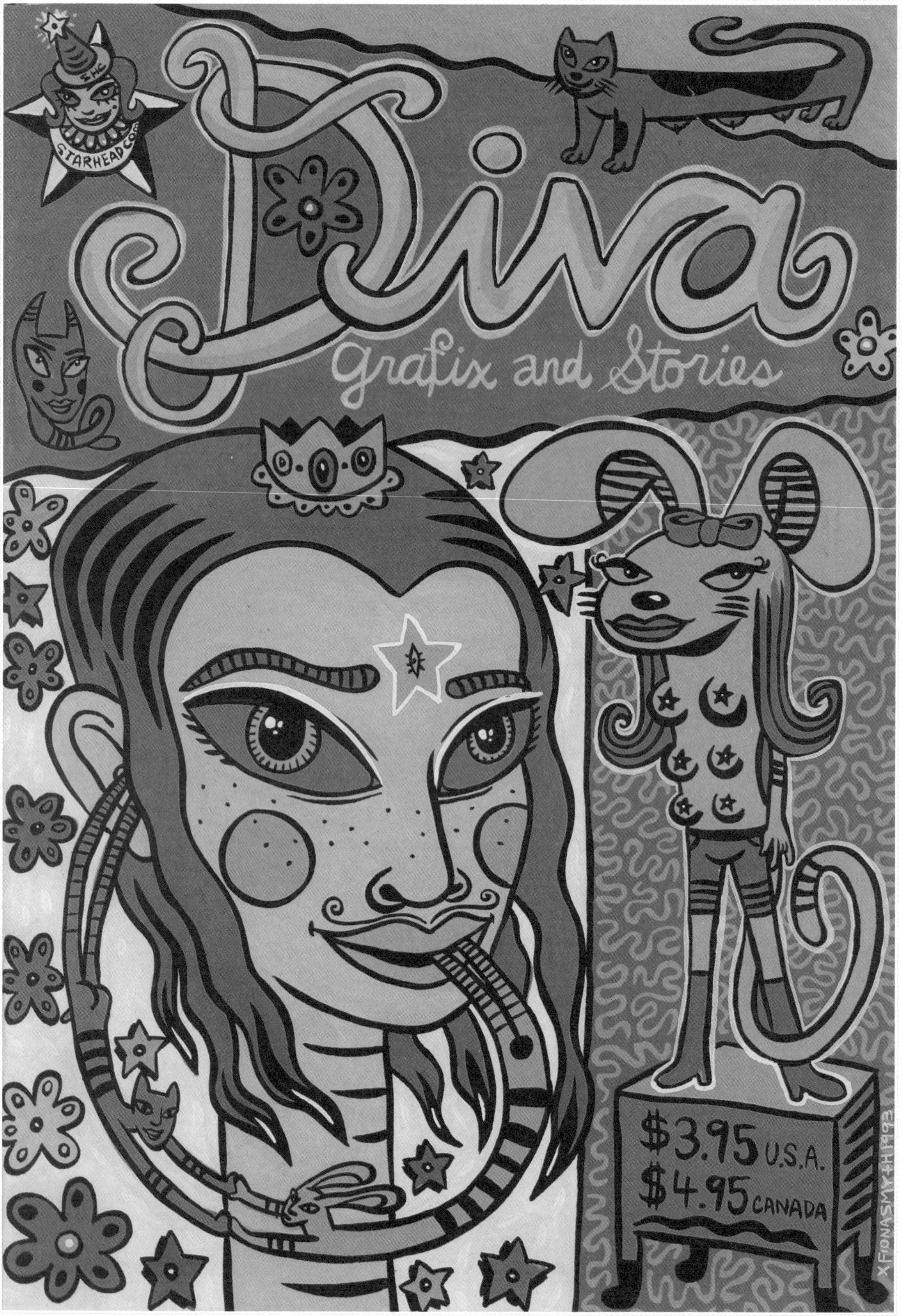
STARHEAD.COM
SHC
Diva
grafix and Stories
$3.95 U.S.A.
$4.95 CANADA
X FIONA SMYTH 1993

 1993 STARHEAD COMIX WITH ELLEN FORNEY AND DAME DARCY

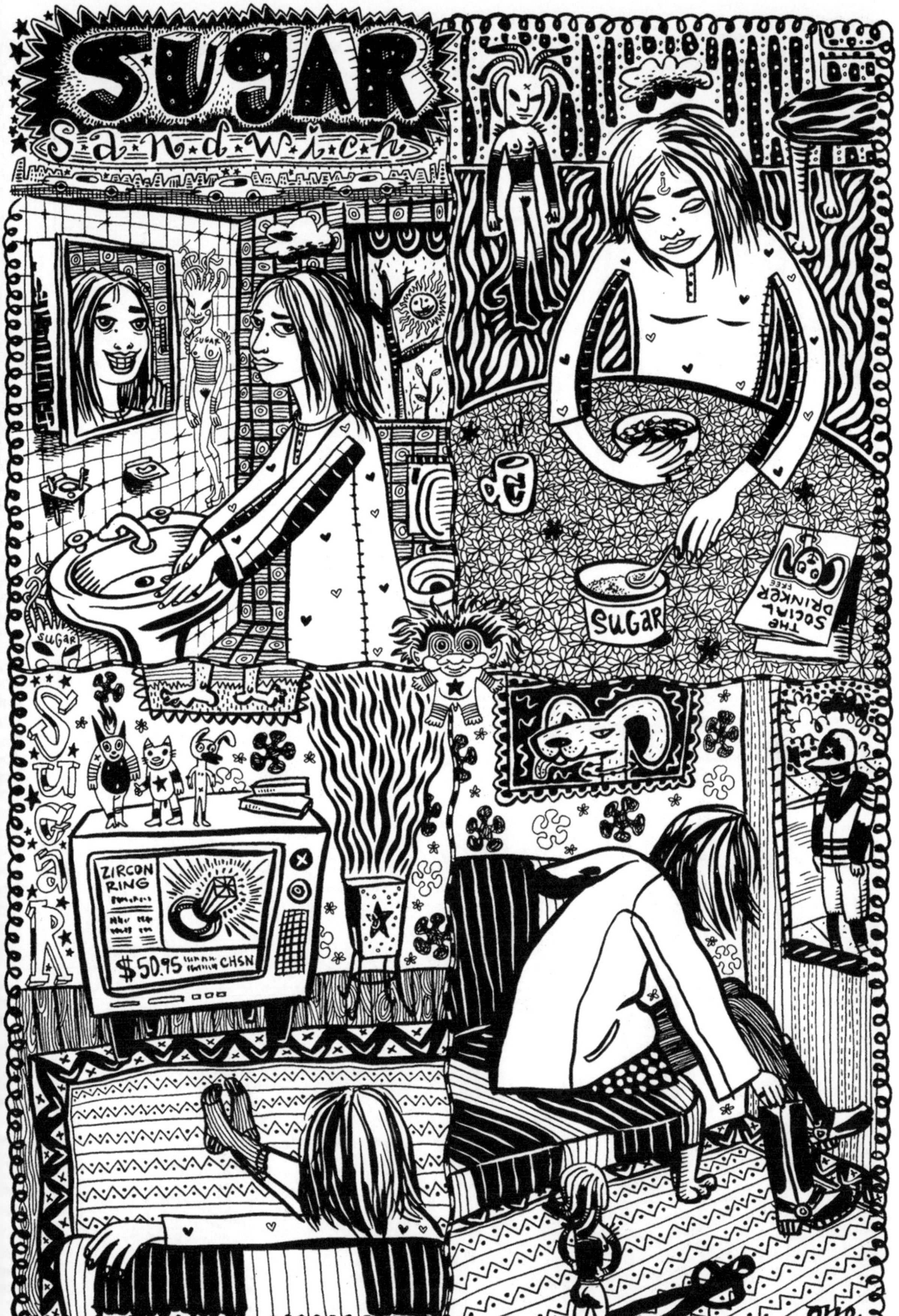
SUGAR
sandwich
SUGAR
SUGAR
SUGAR
THE SOCIAL DRINKER
FREE
SUGAR
ZIRCON RING
$50.95
CHSN
one

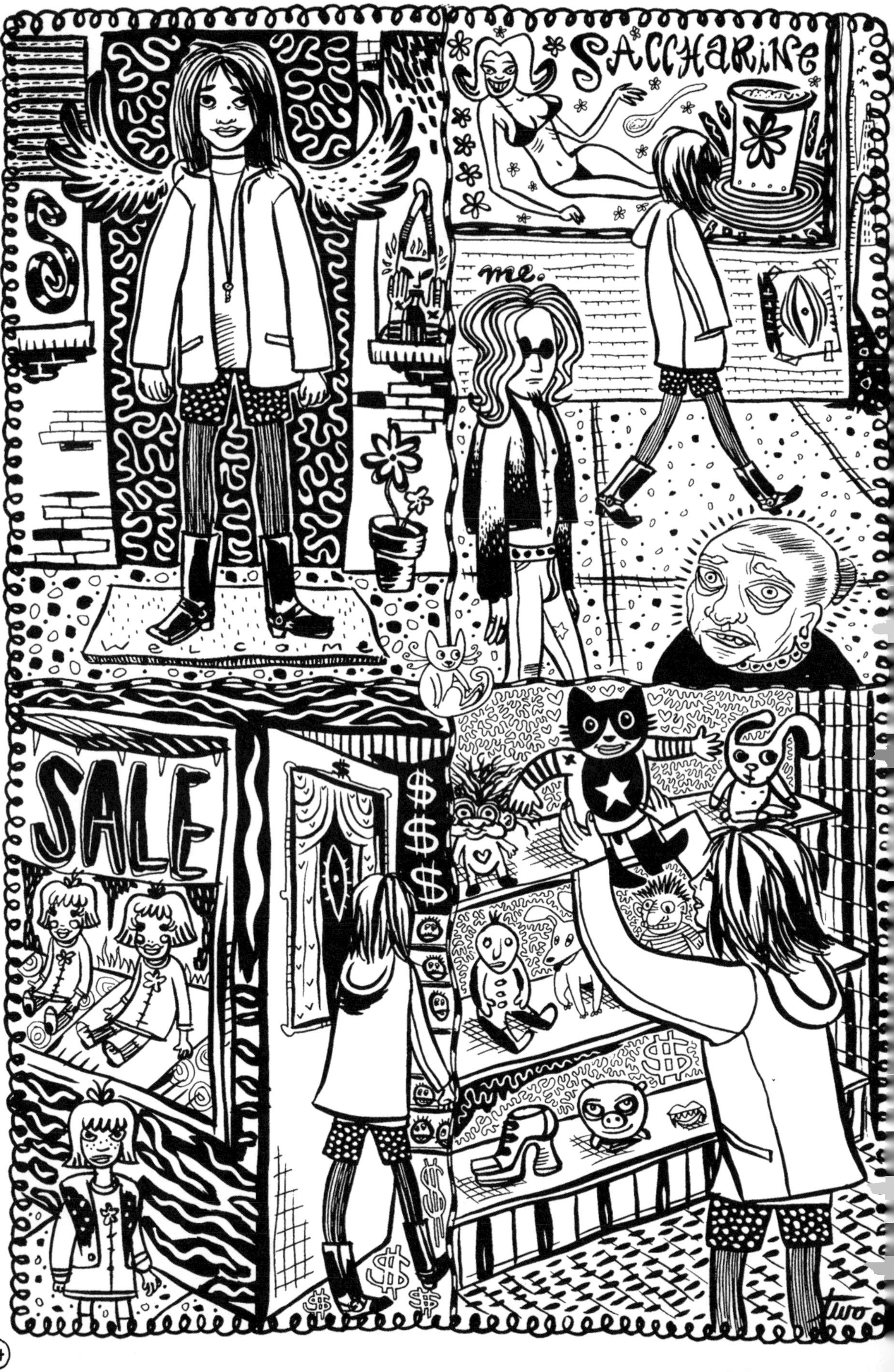
SACCHARINE
me.
welcome
SALE

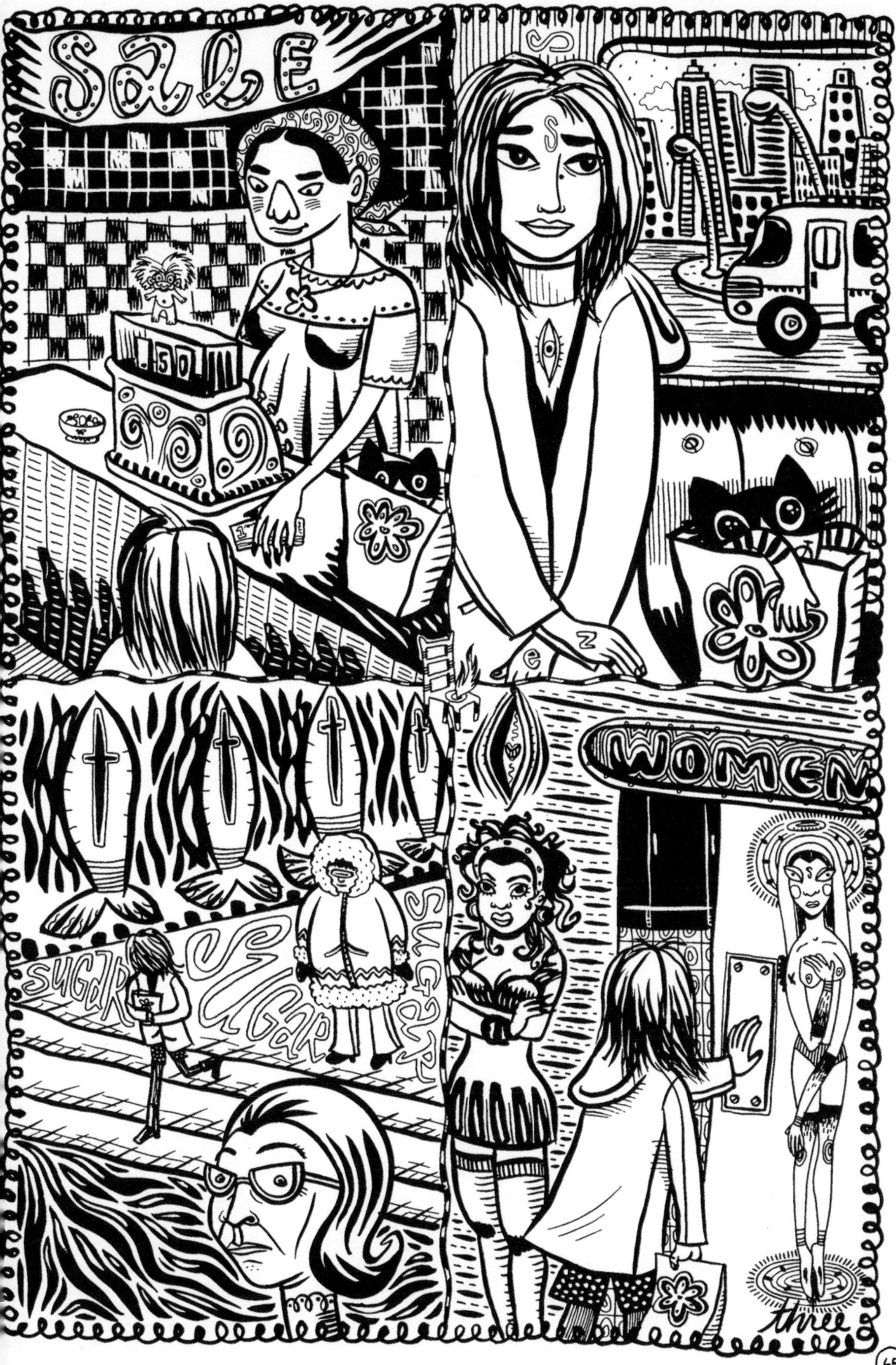
Sale
1.50
WOMEN
SUGAR
SUGAR
SUGAR
three

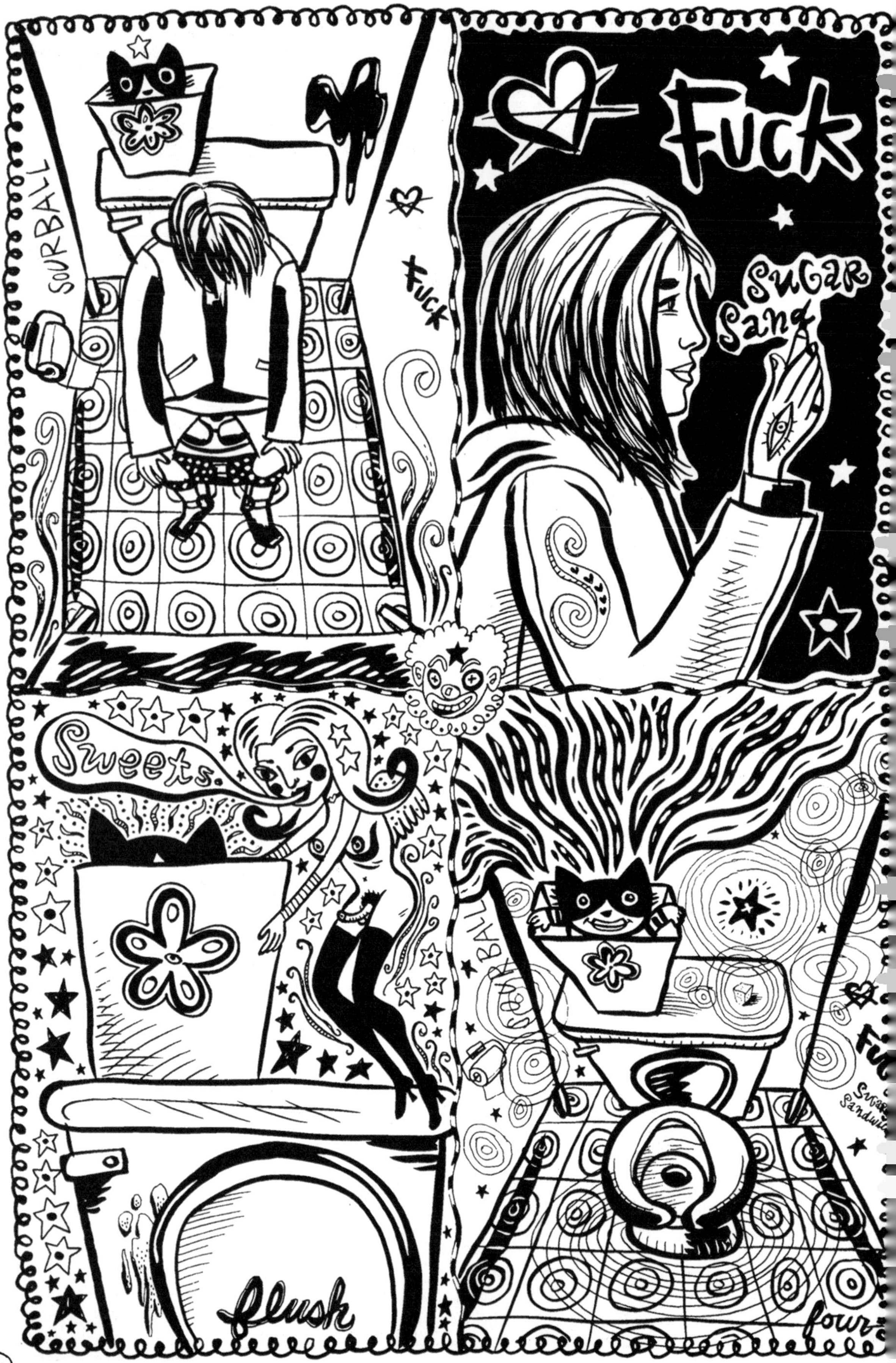
SOURBALL
Fuck
Fuck
Sugar Sang
Sweets.
BALL
flush
four

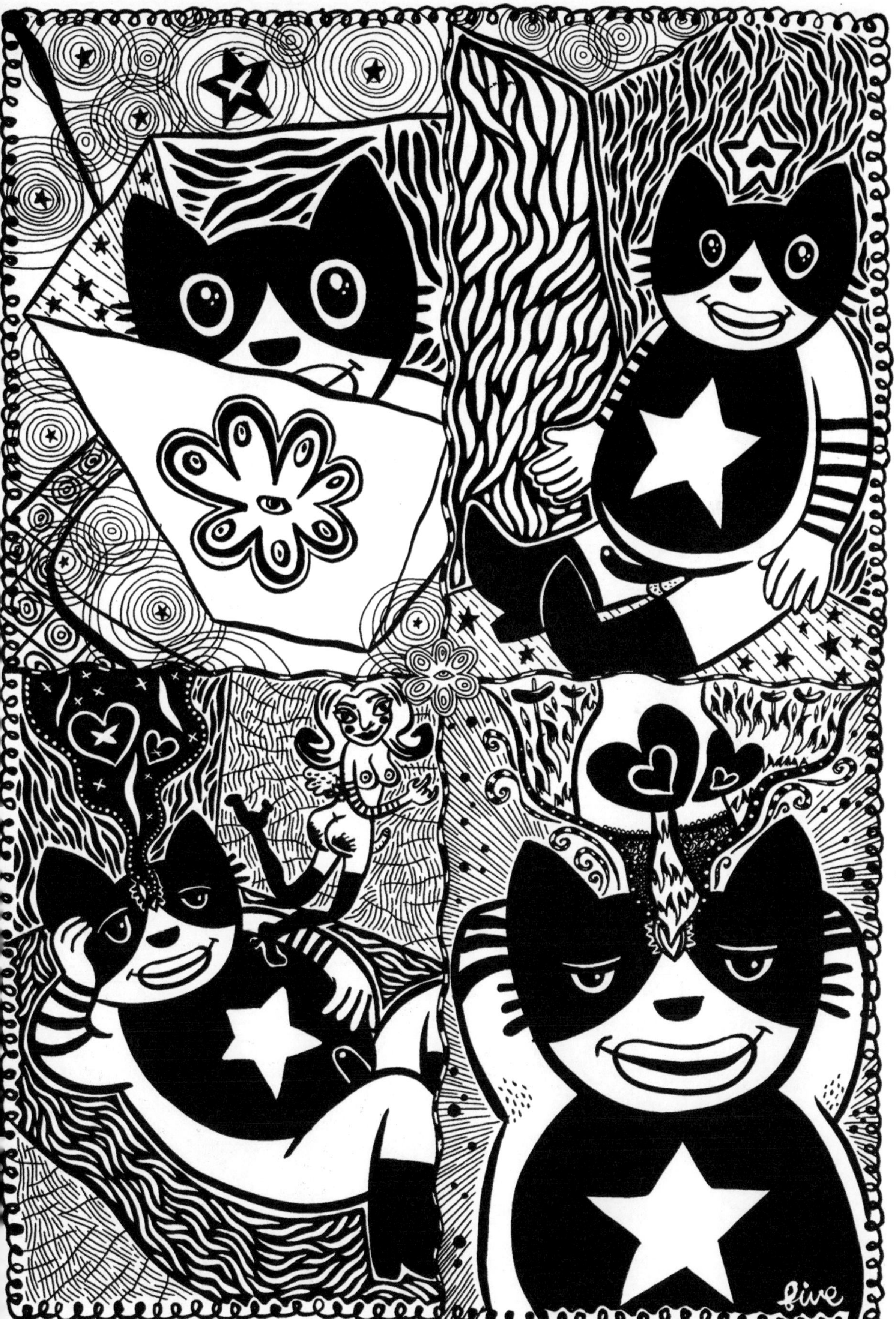
five

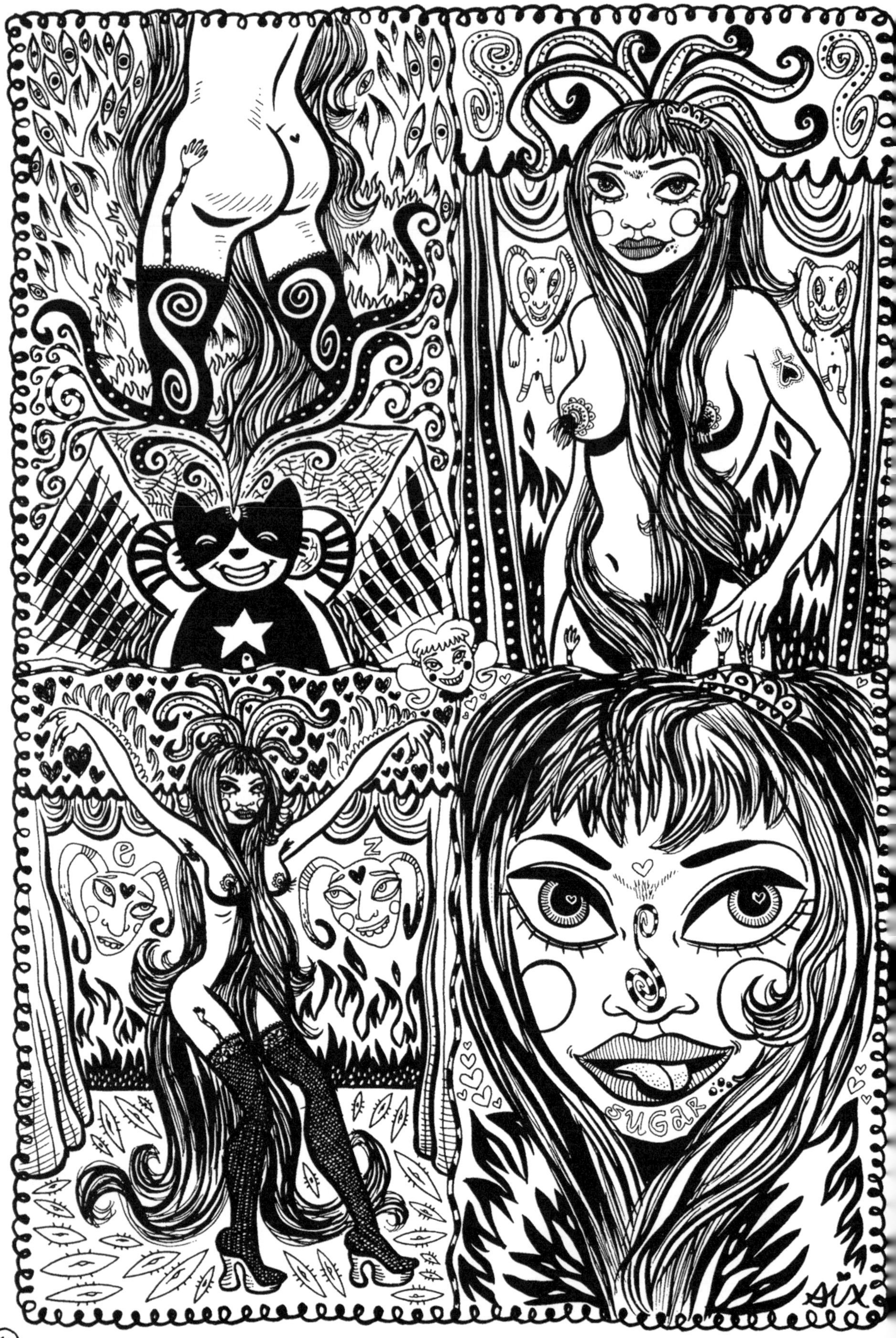
e
z
sugar
aix

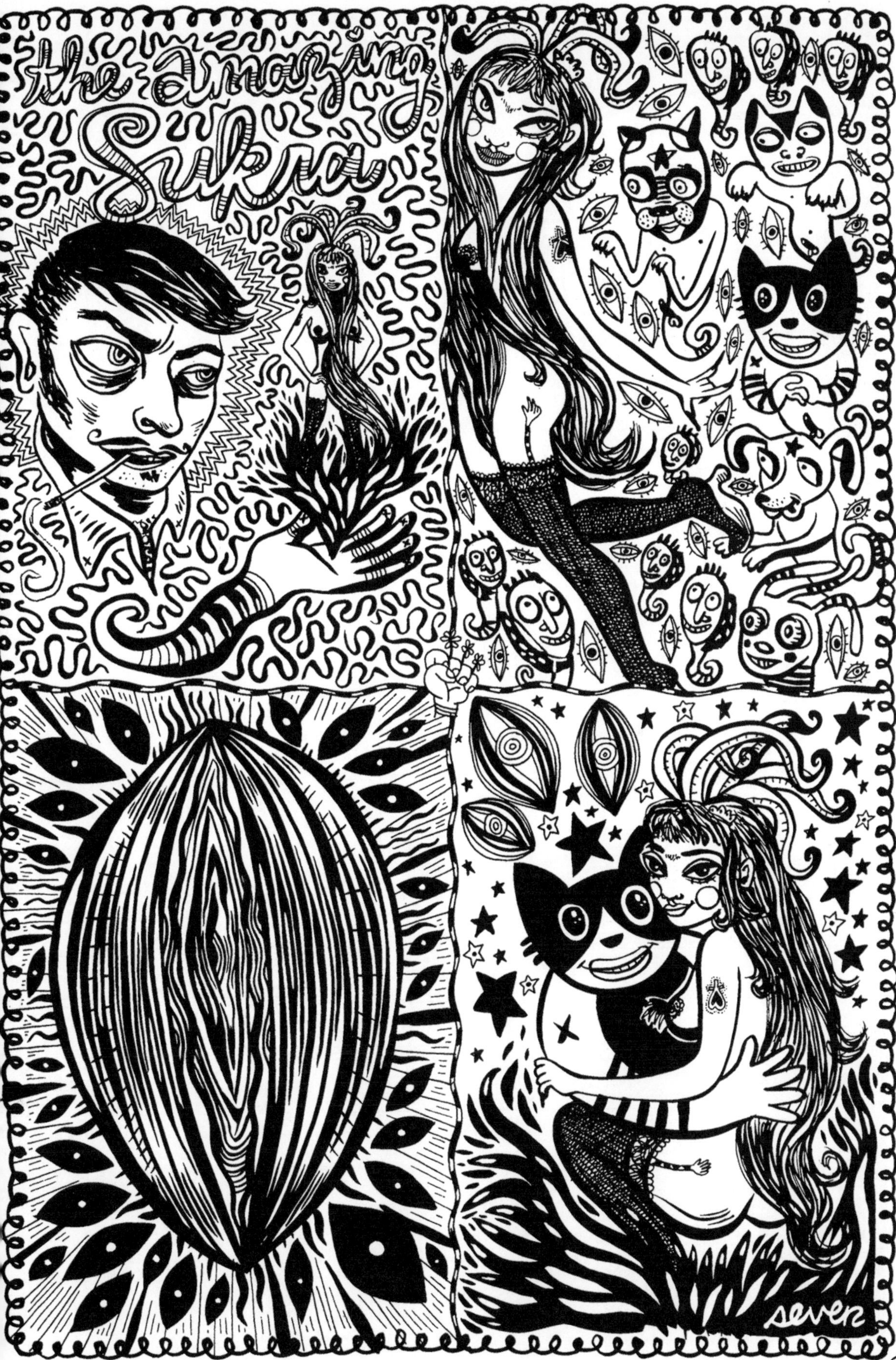
the amazing Sukra
sever

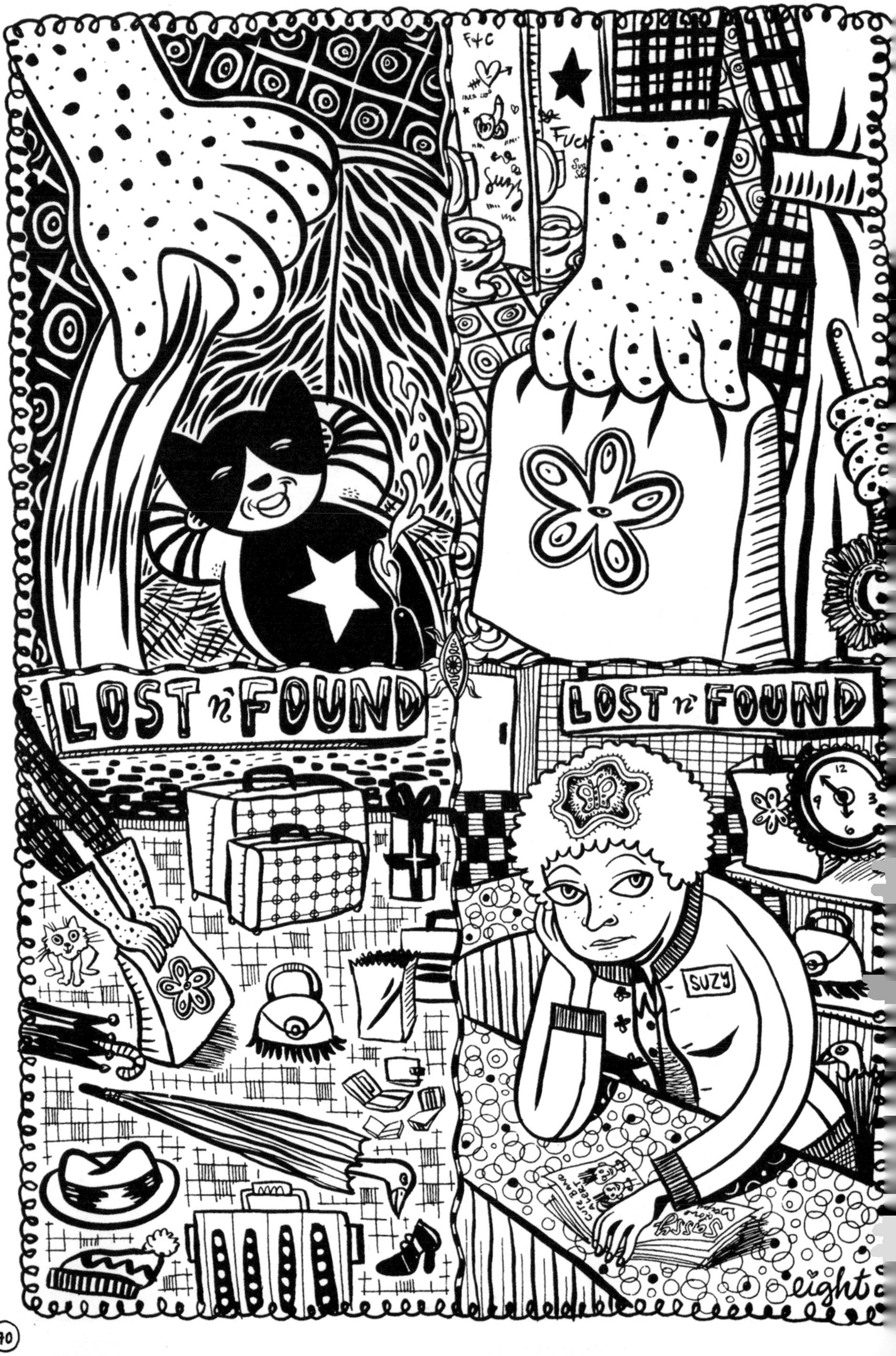
F+C
Fuck
Suzy
LOST n' FOUND
LOST n' FOUND
SUZY
CUTE BAND ALERT
Sassy
eight

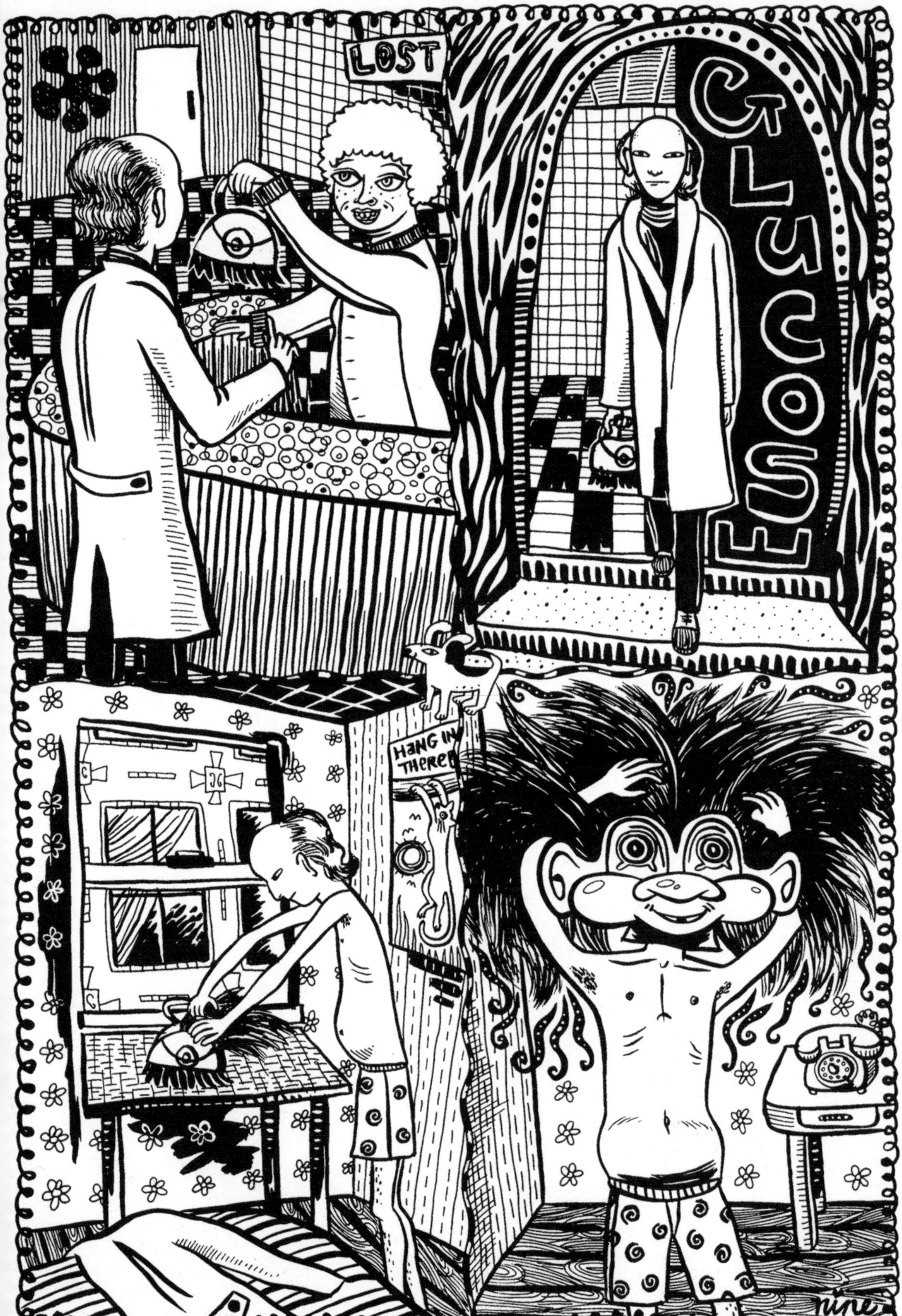
LOST
GLUCOSE
HANG IN THERE
nine

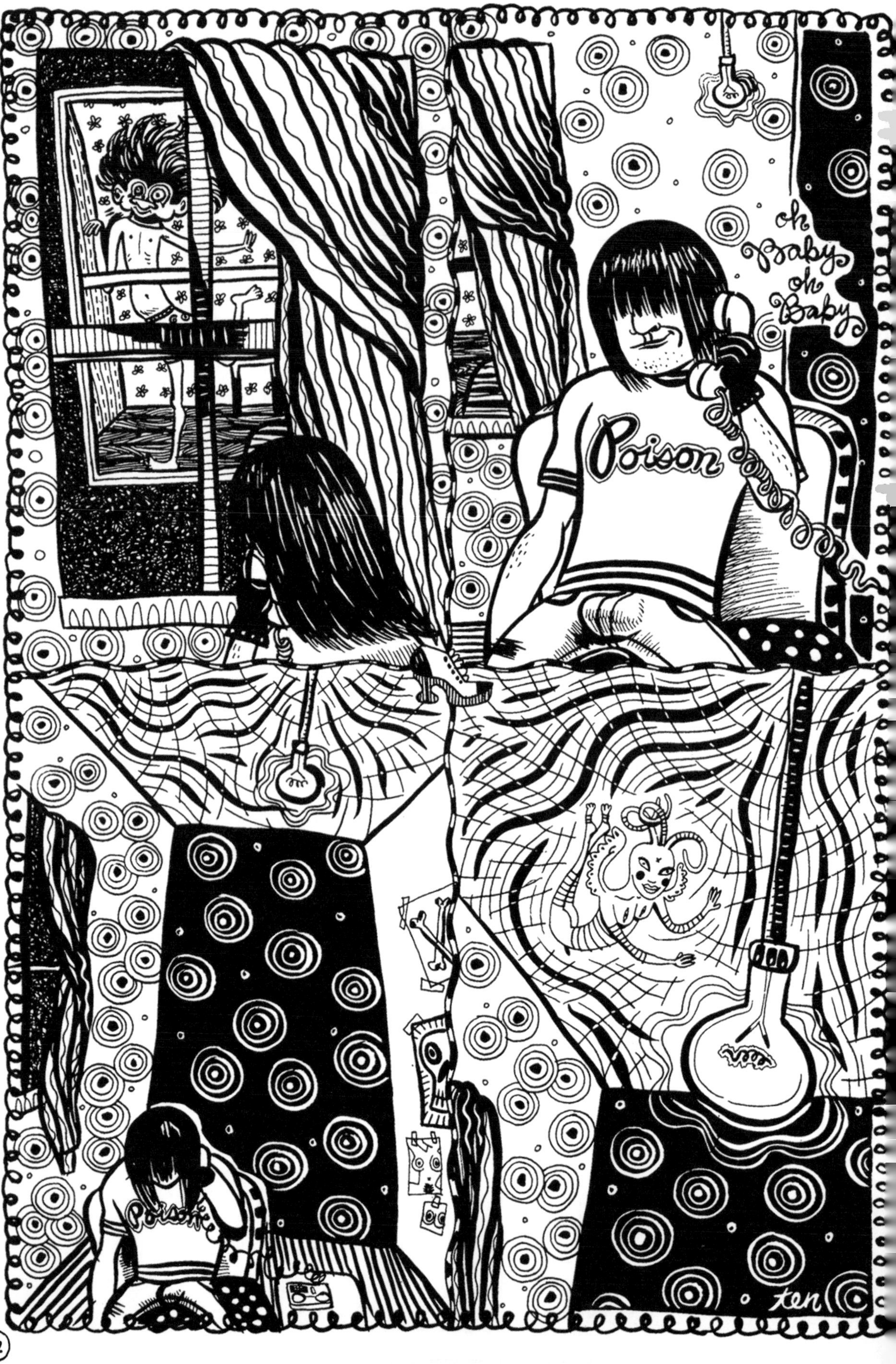

oh Baby oh Baby
Poison
Poison
ten

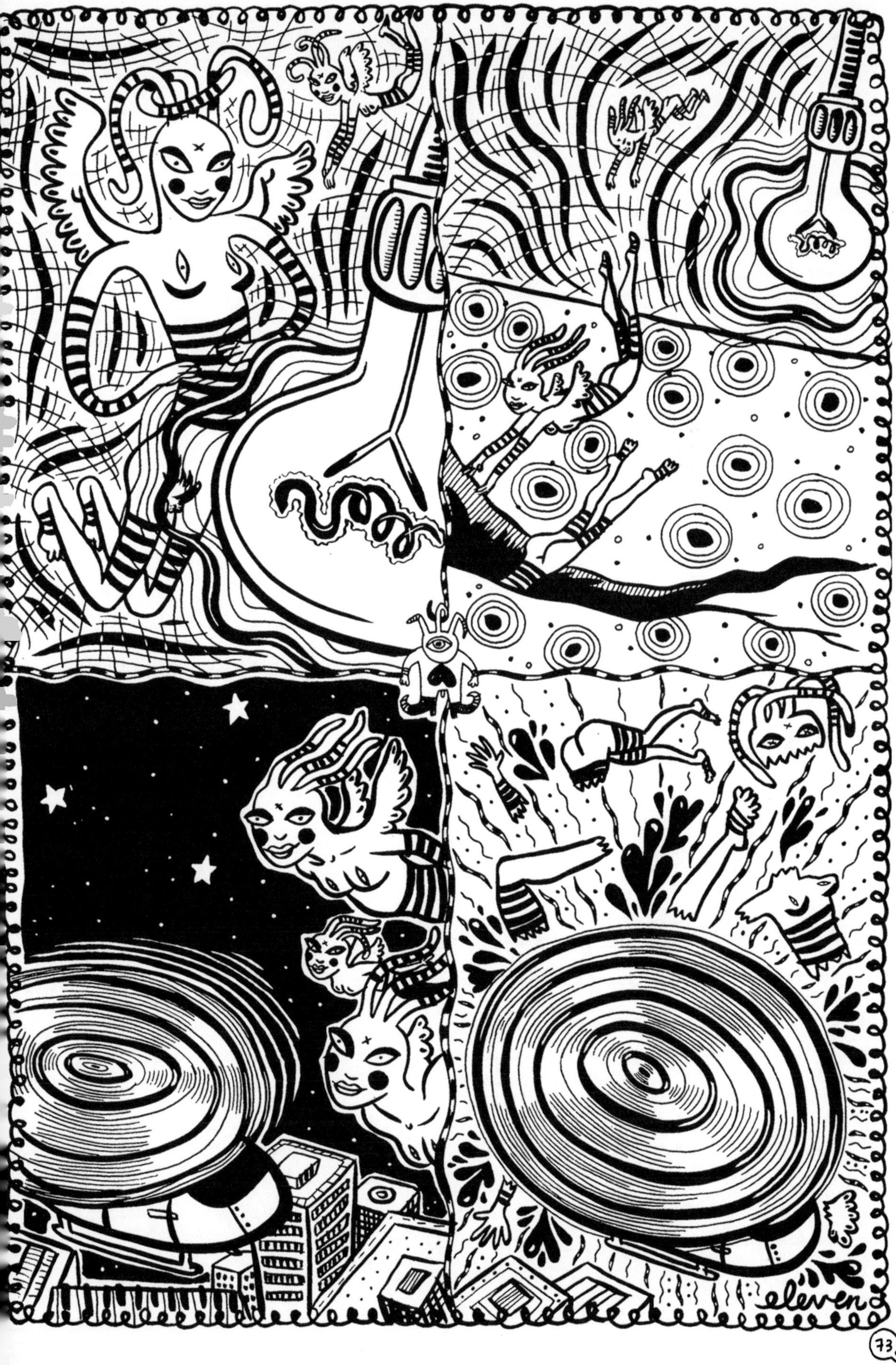
eleven

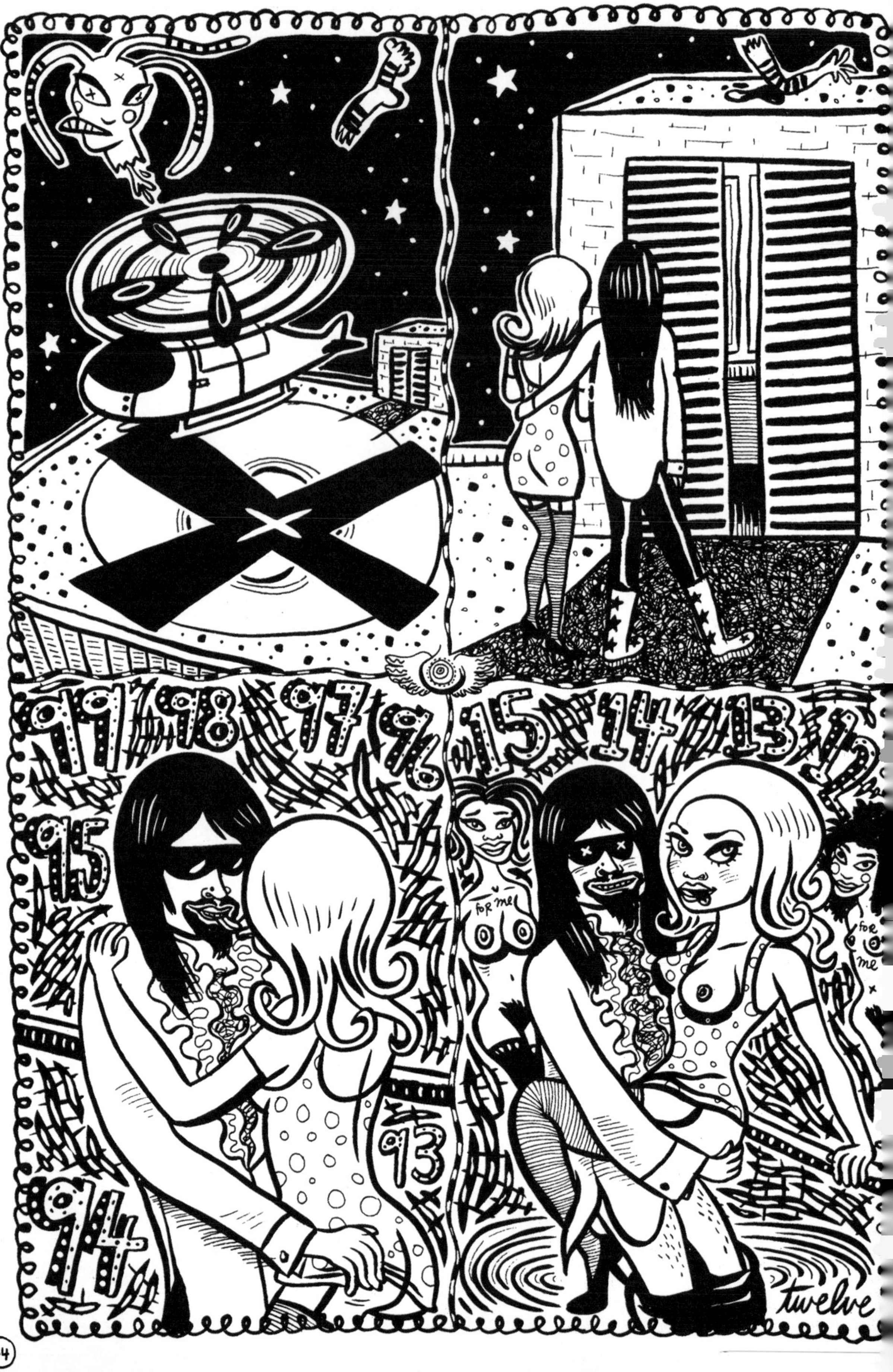
99 98 97 96
15 14 13 12
95
94
93
for me
for me
twelve

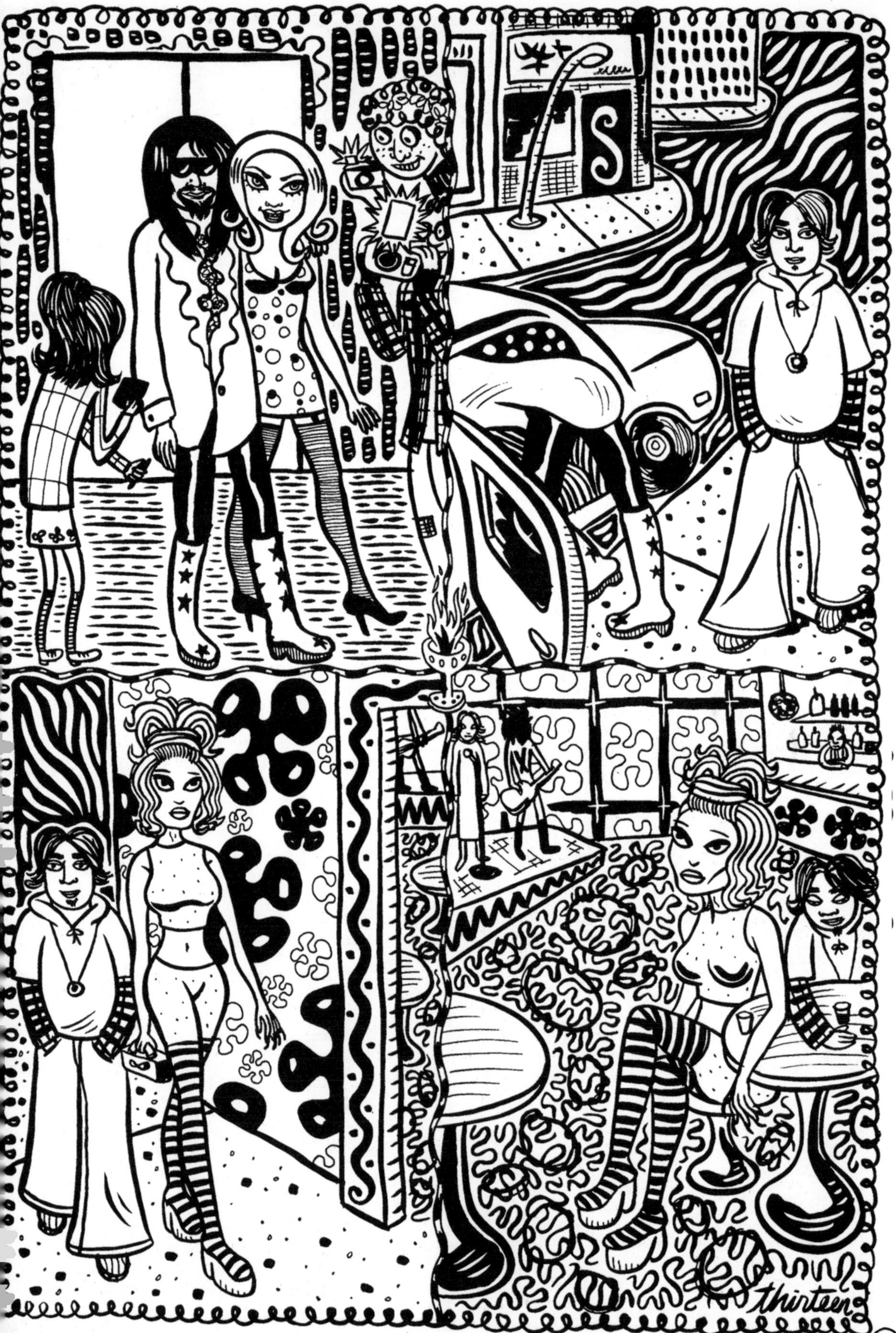
S
thirteen

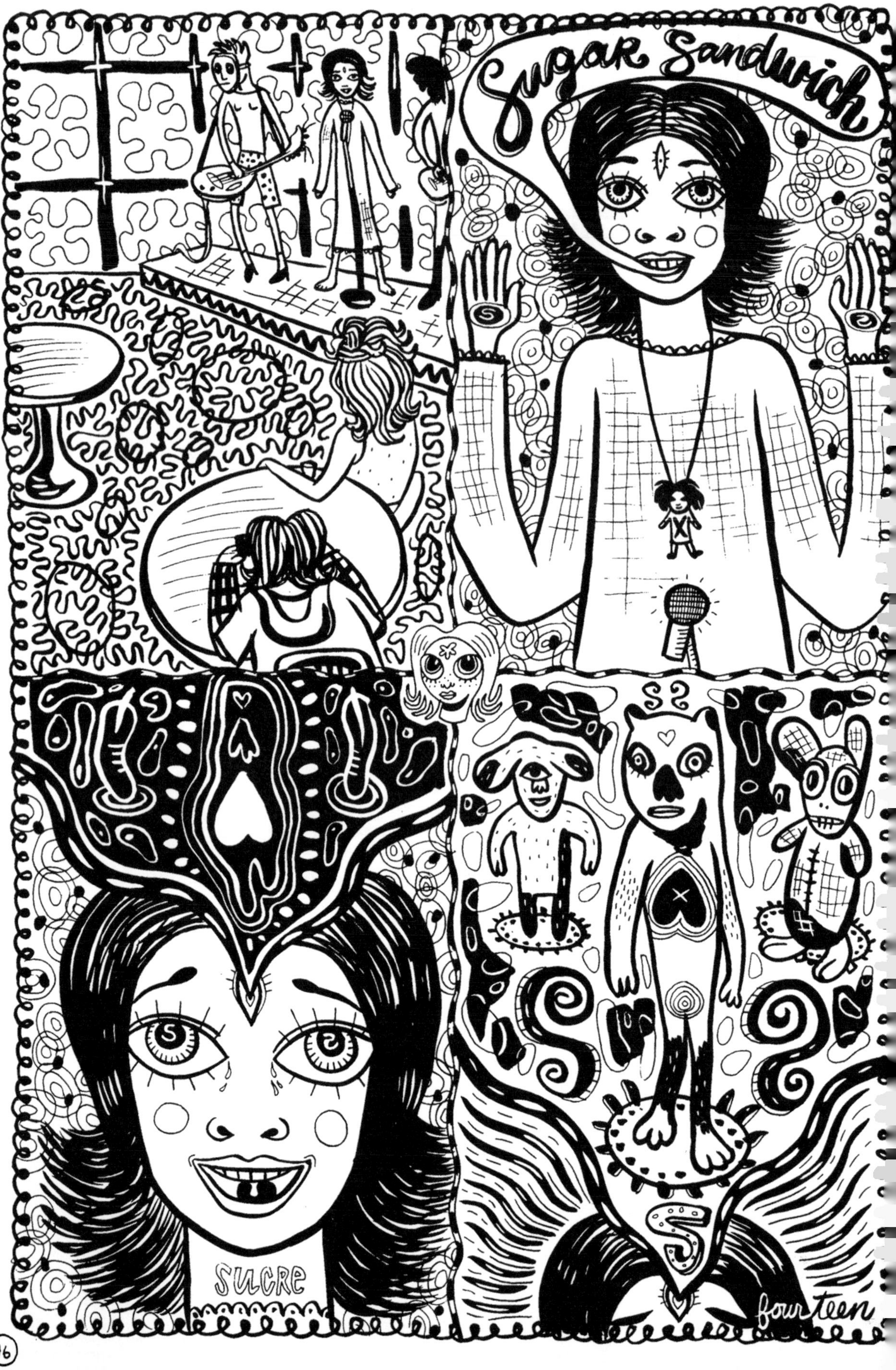

Sugar Sandwich
SUCRE
fourteen

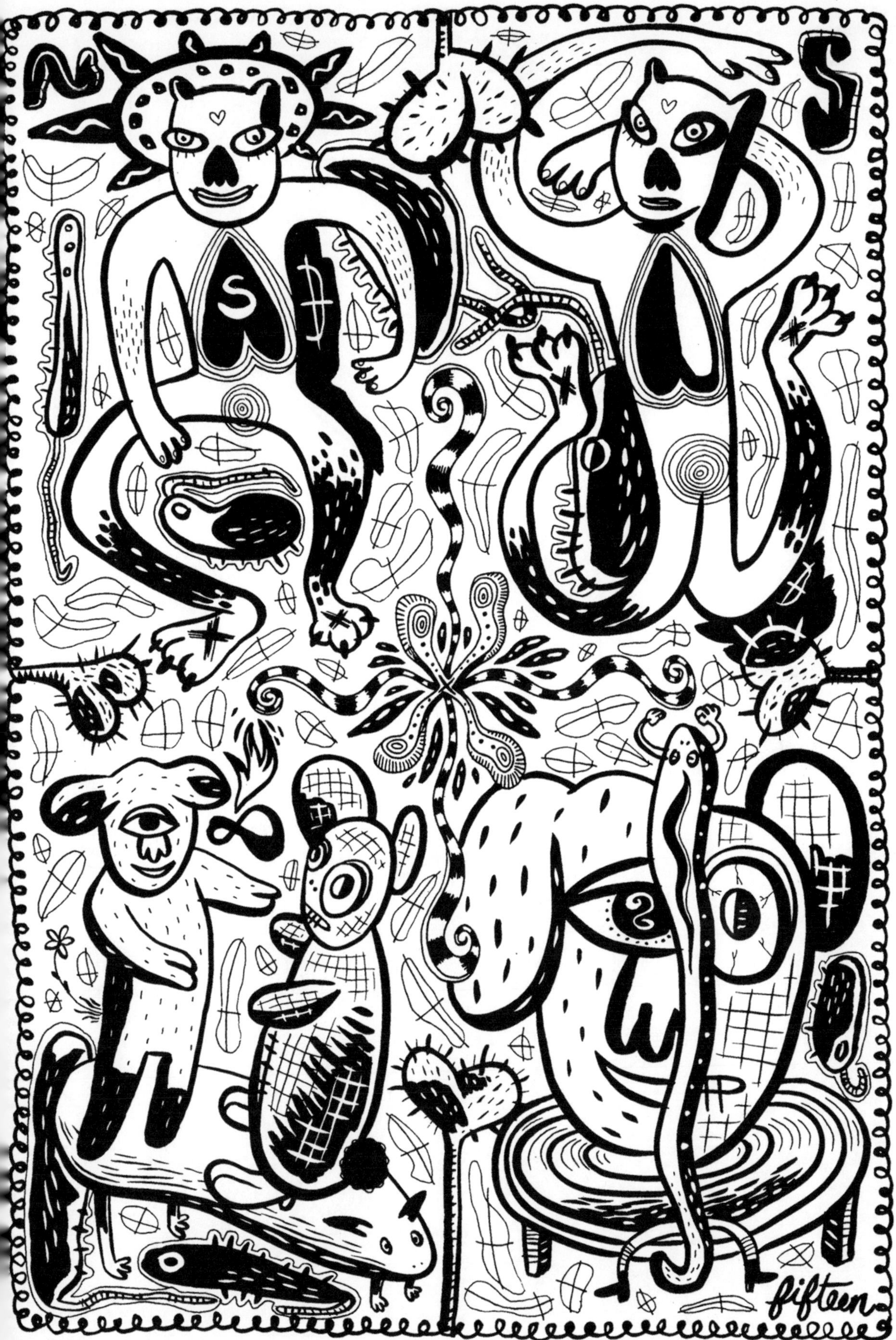
fifteen

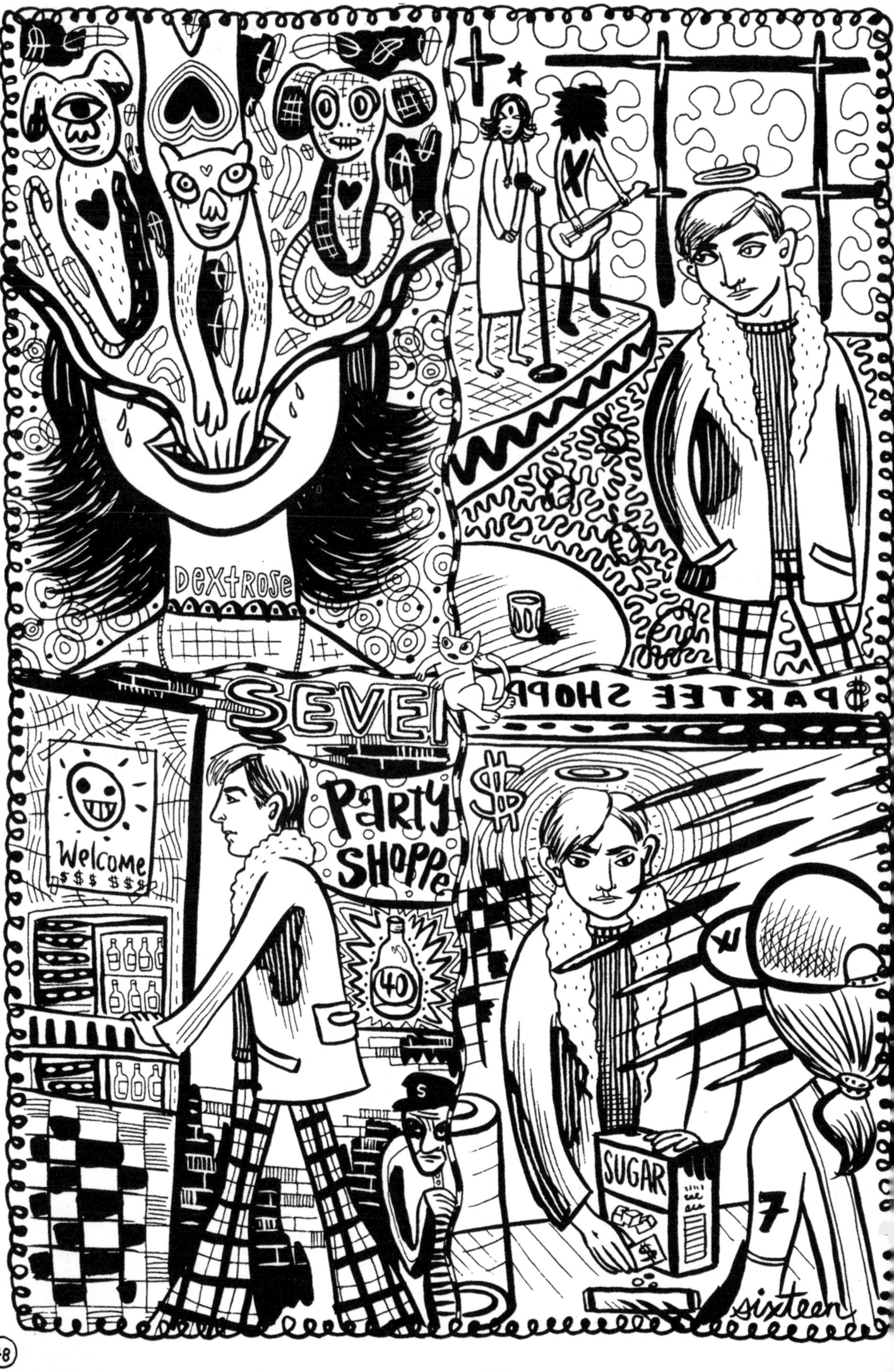
dextrose
SEVEN
PARTEE SHOPP
Party SHOPPe
Welcome
$$$ $$$
40
SUGAR
7
sixteen

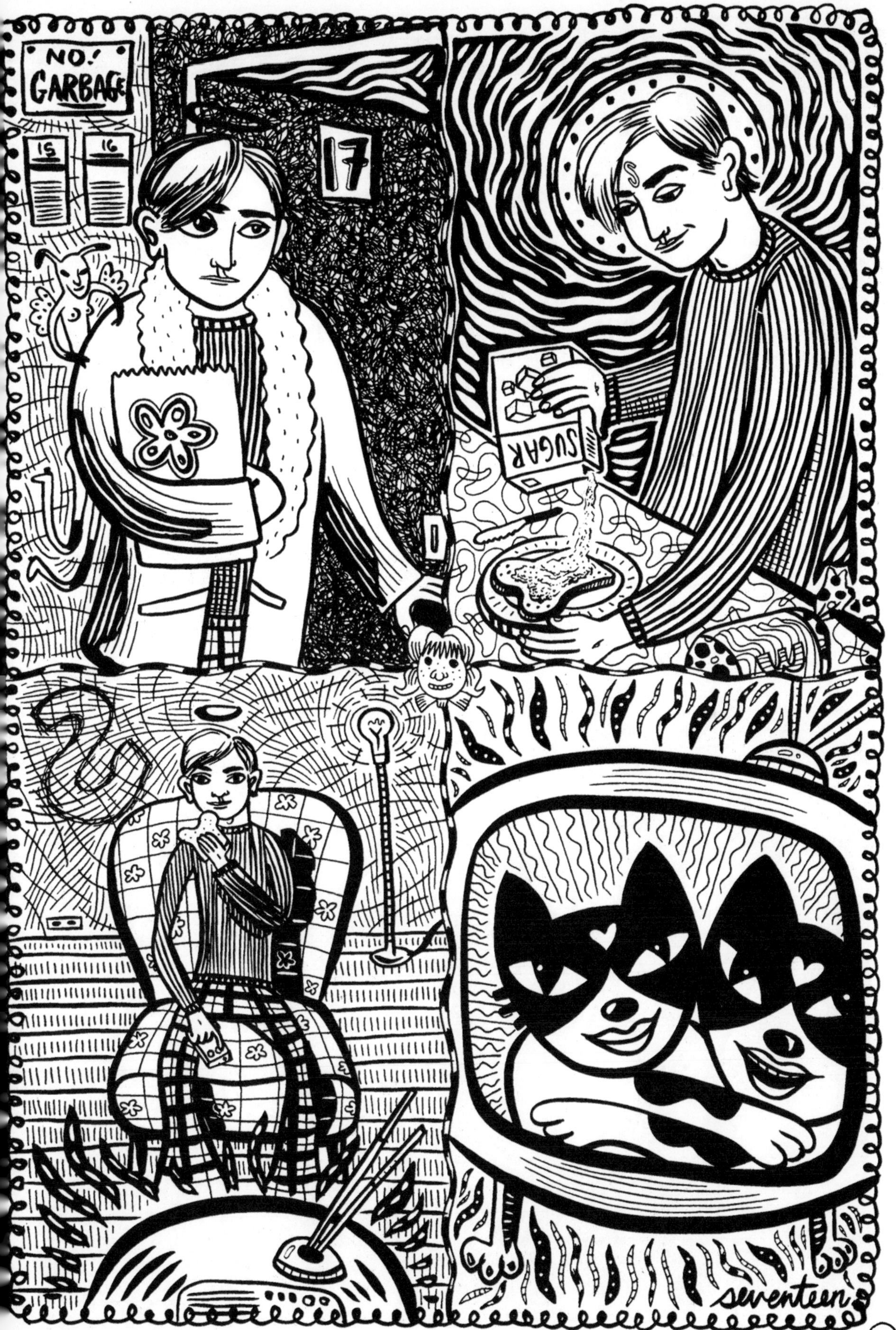
NO!
GARBAGE
15
16
17
SUGAR
seventeen

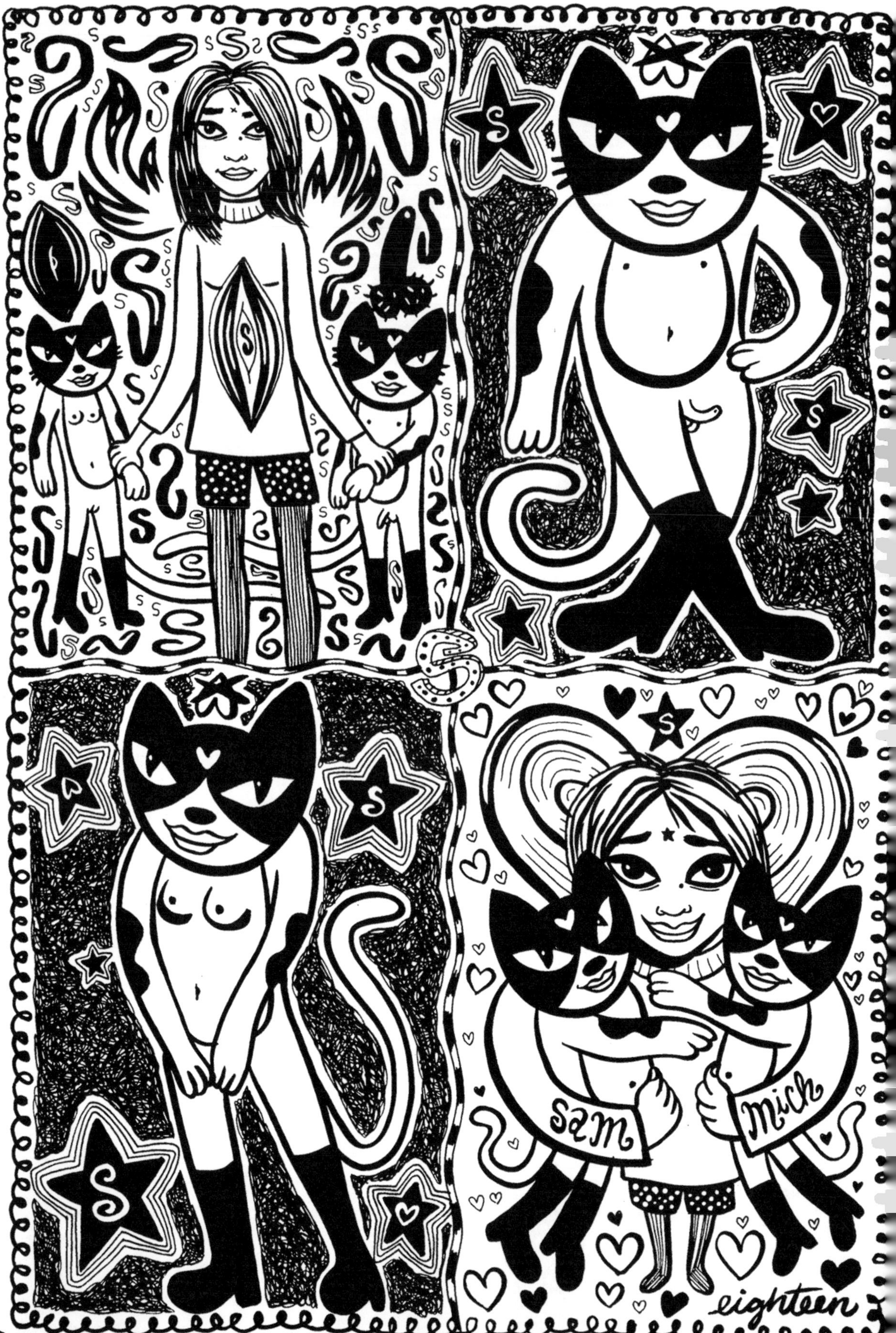
sam
mich
eighteen

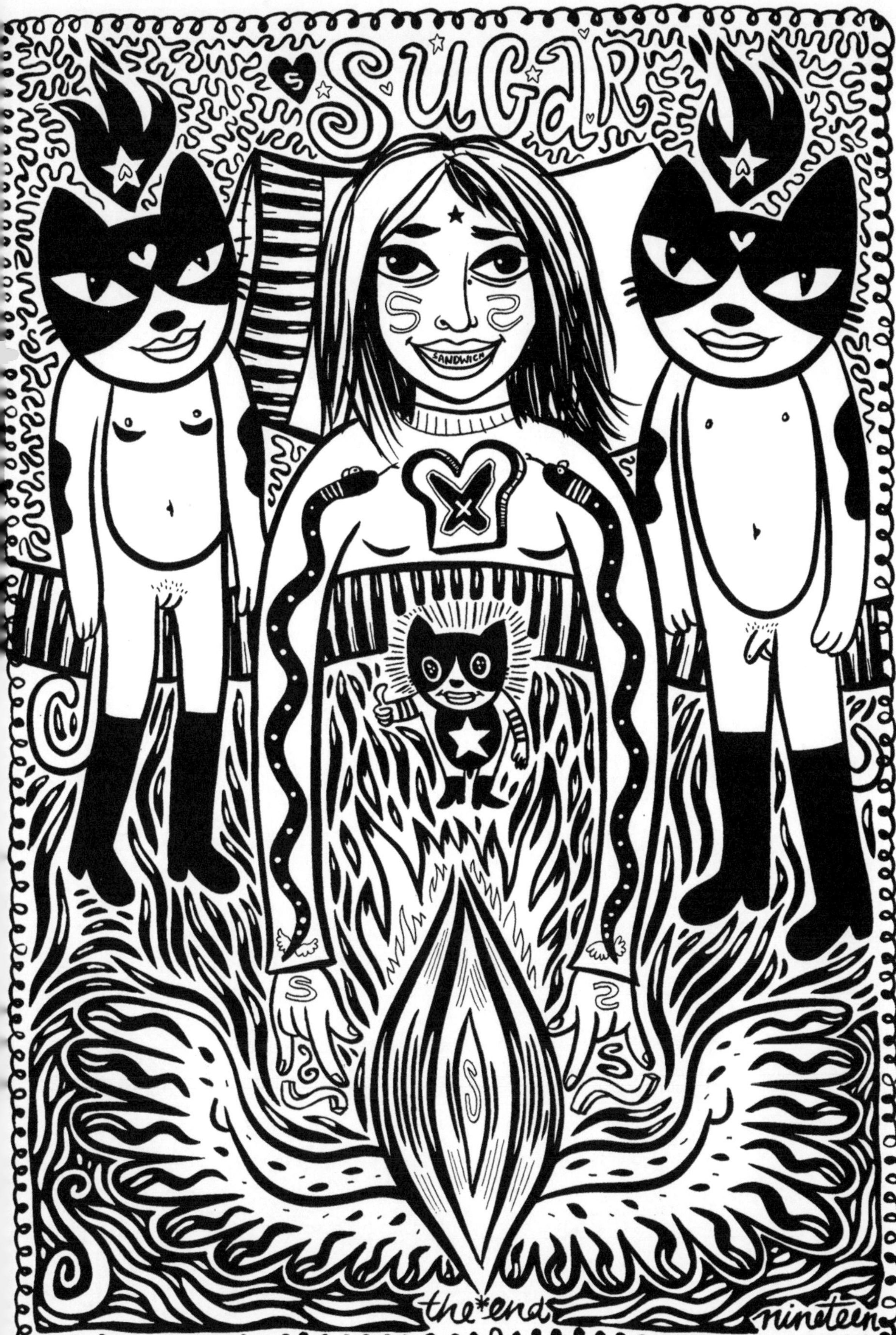
SUGAR
SANDWICH
the*end
nineteen

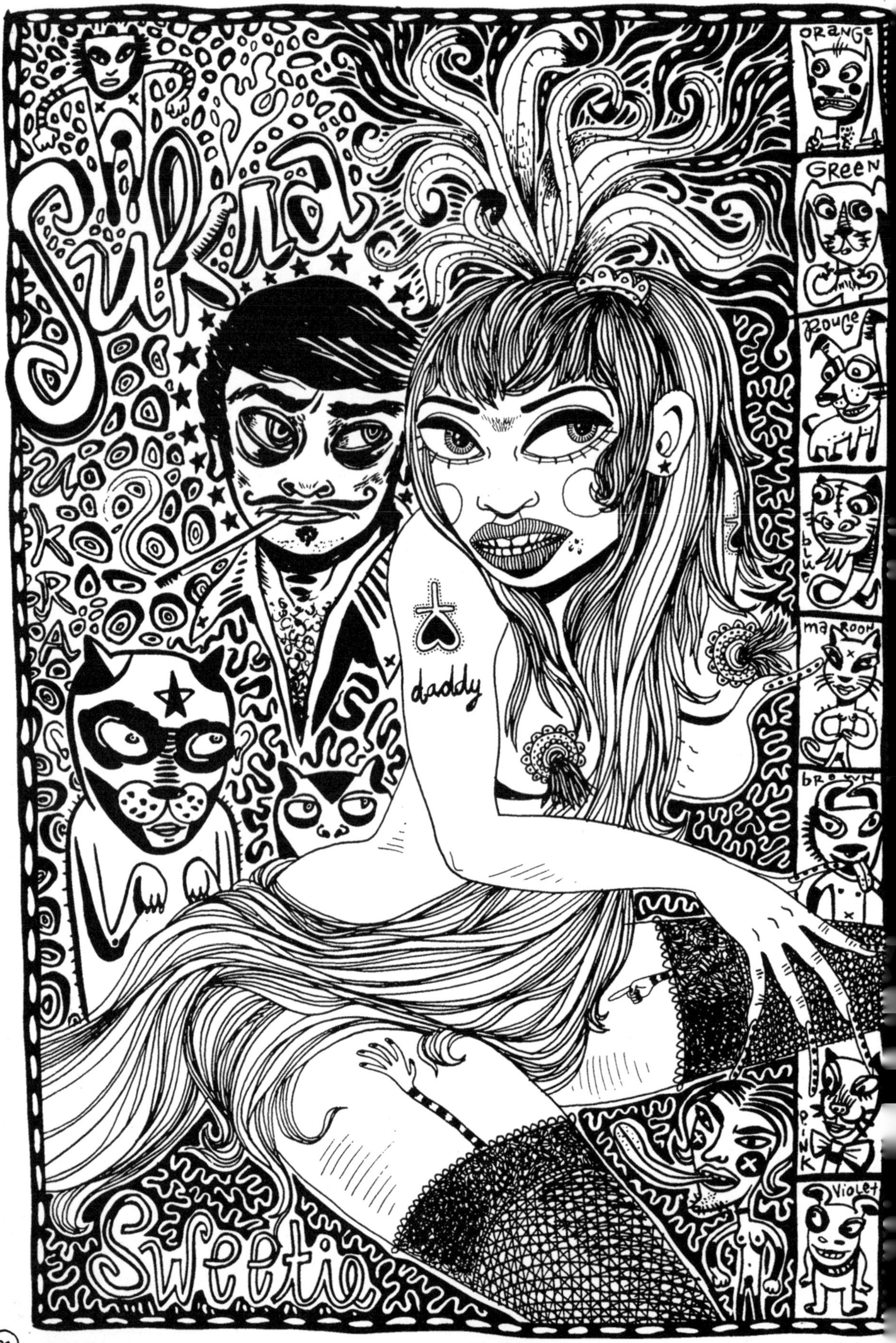
orange
GReeN
Rouge
blue
maROON
brown
PINK
Violet
daddy
Sweetie

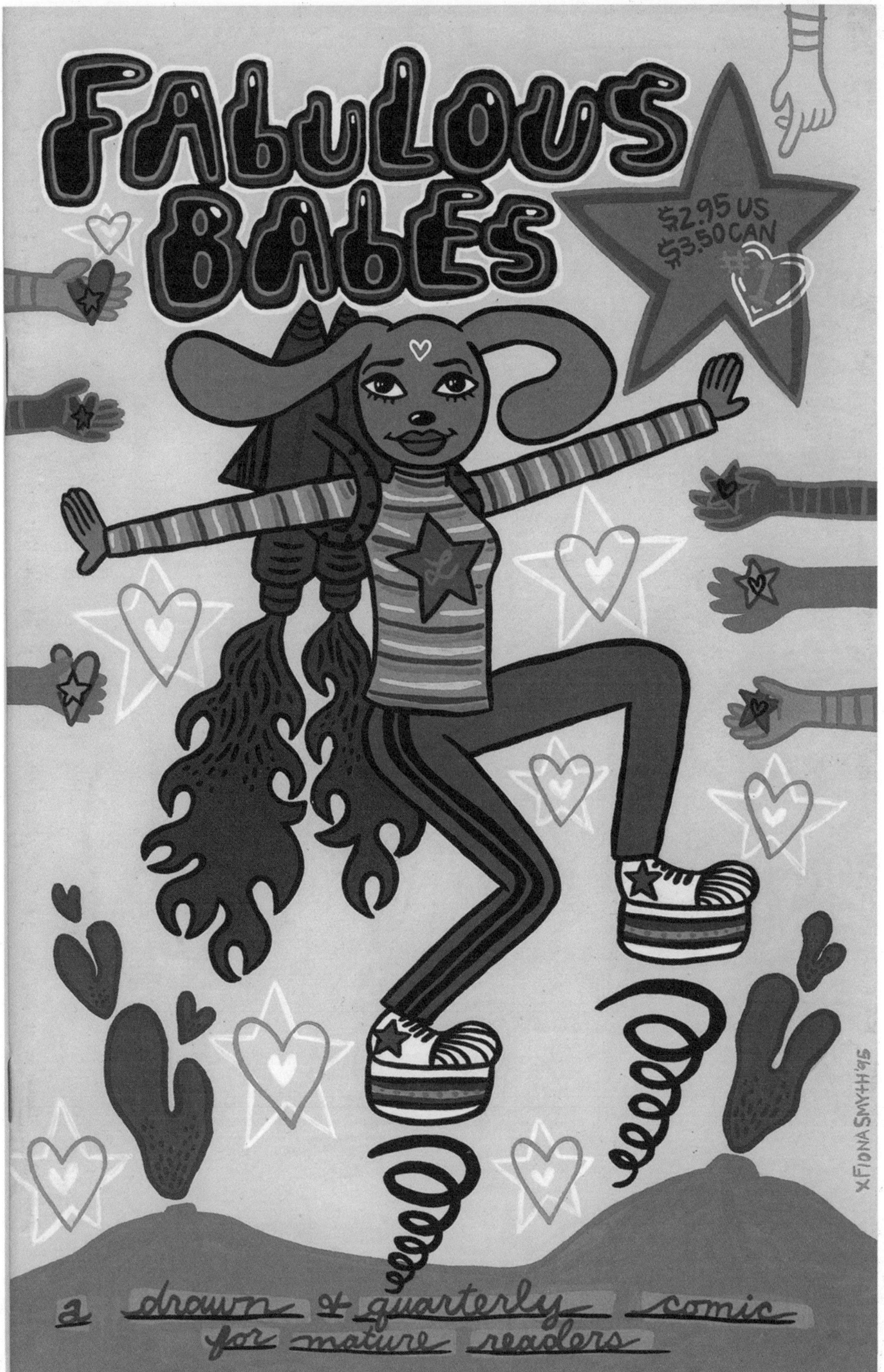
FABULOUS BABES
$2.95 US
$3.50 CAN
#1
XFIONA SMYTH '95
a drawn & quarterly comic for mature readers

1995 DRAWN & QUARTERLY WITH MAURICE VELLEKOOP AND ROXANNA BIKADOROFF

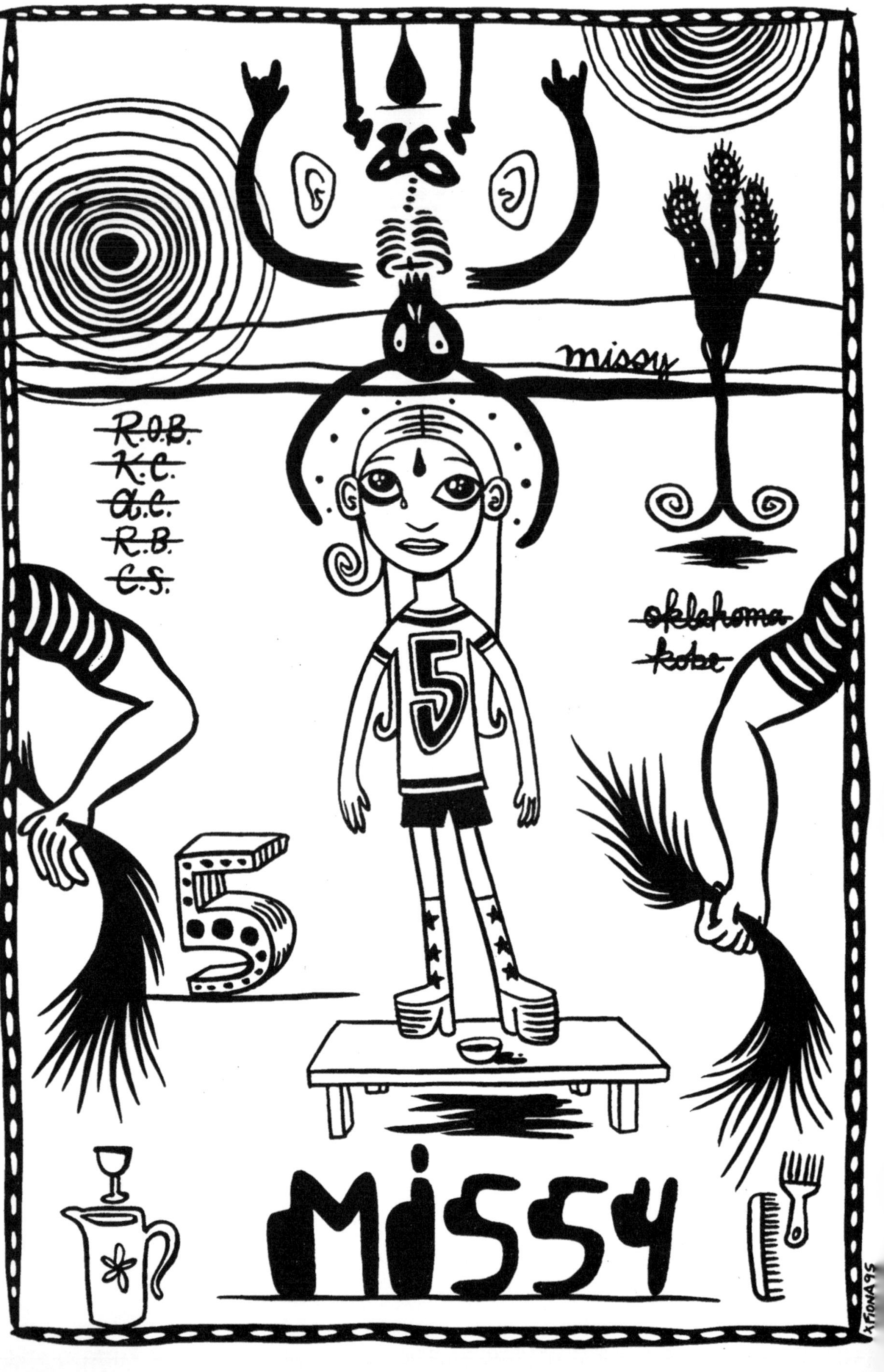
missy
R.O.B.
K.C.
A.C.
R.B.
C.S.
oklahoma
kobe
5
5
MISSY
xFIONA95

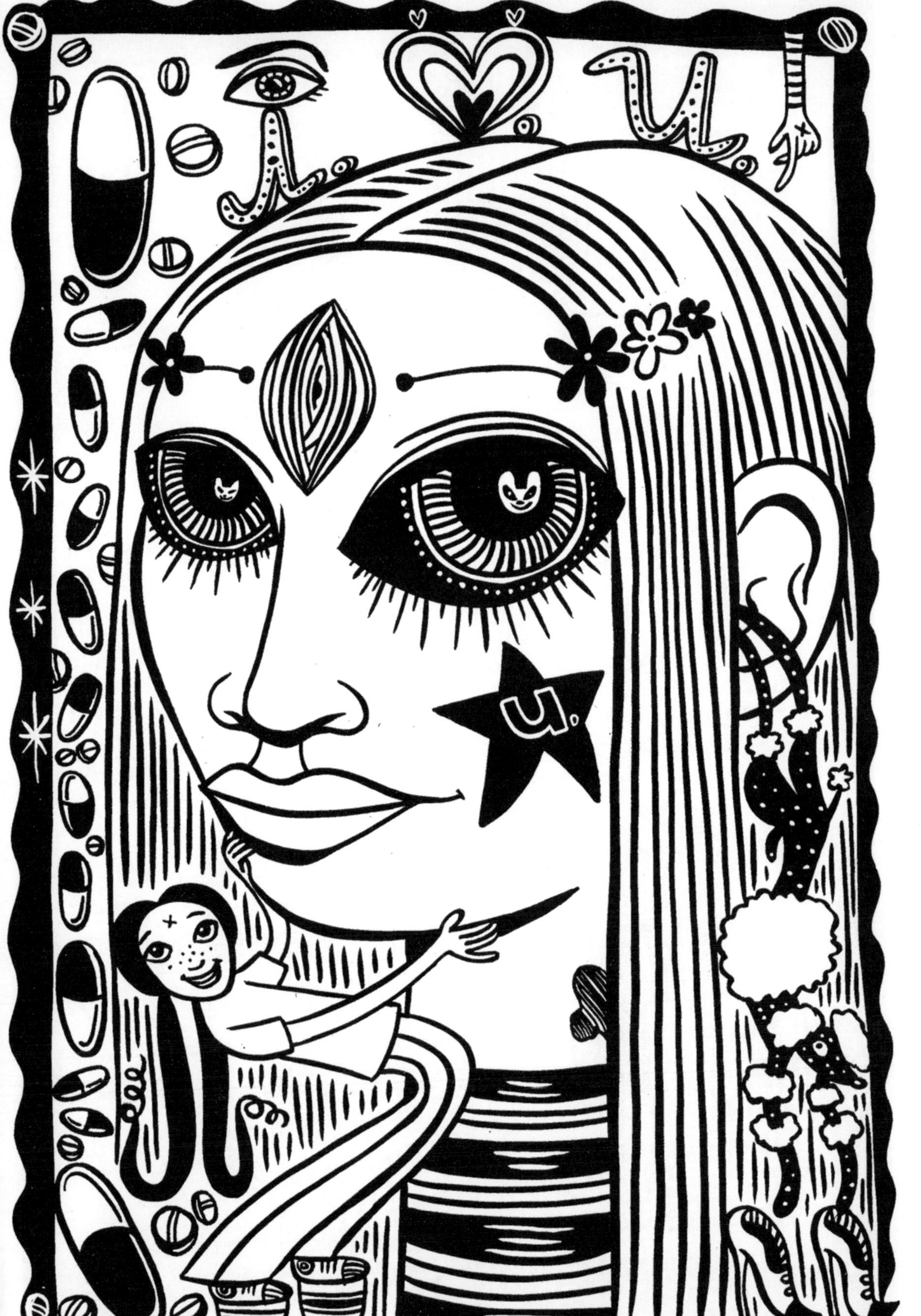
U!
U.
×FIONA95

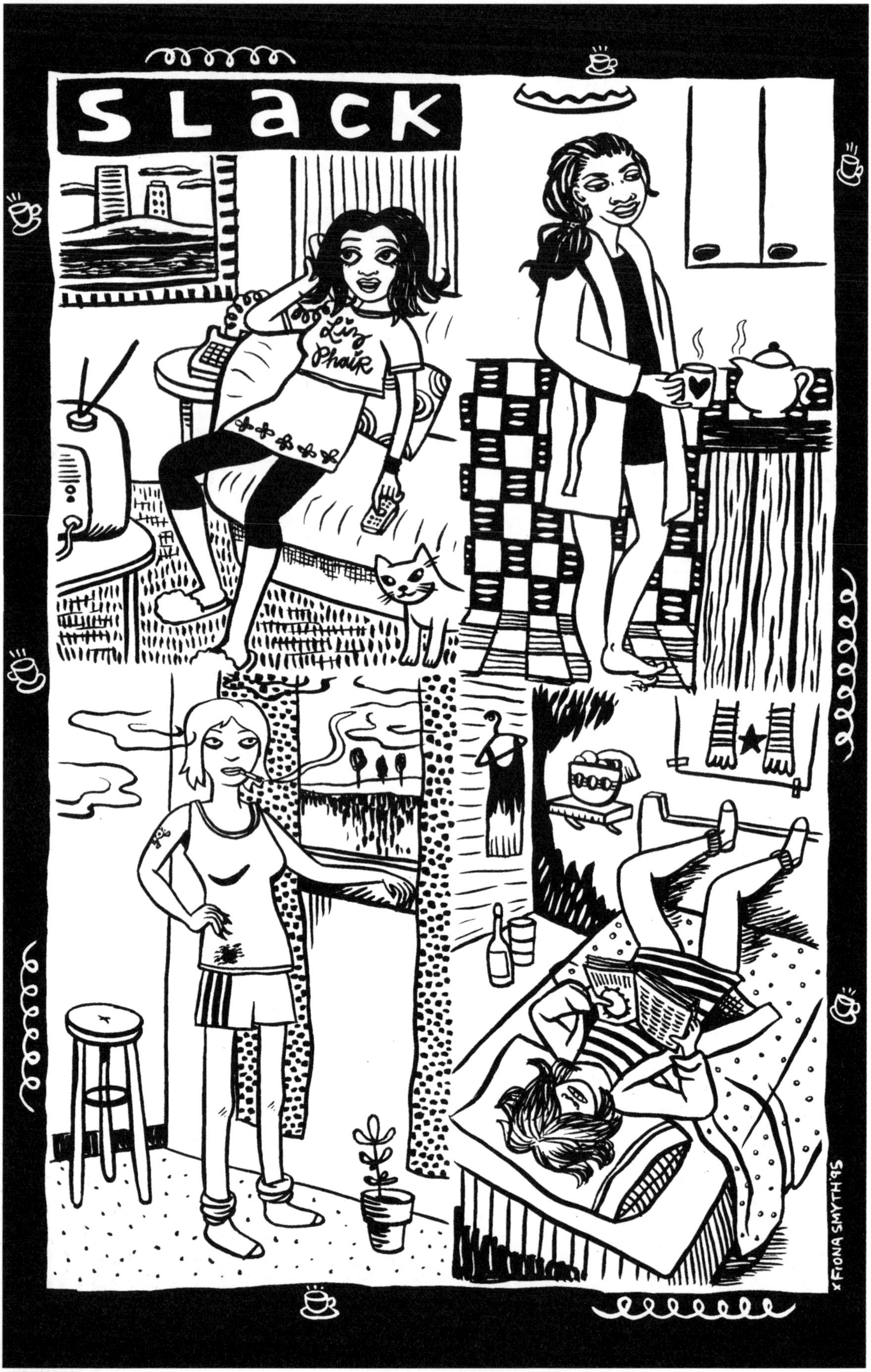
SLACK
Liz Phair
xFIONA SMYTH '95

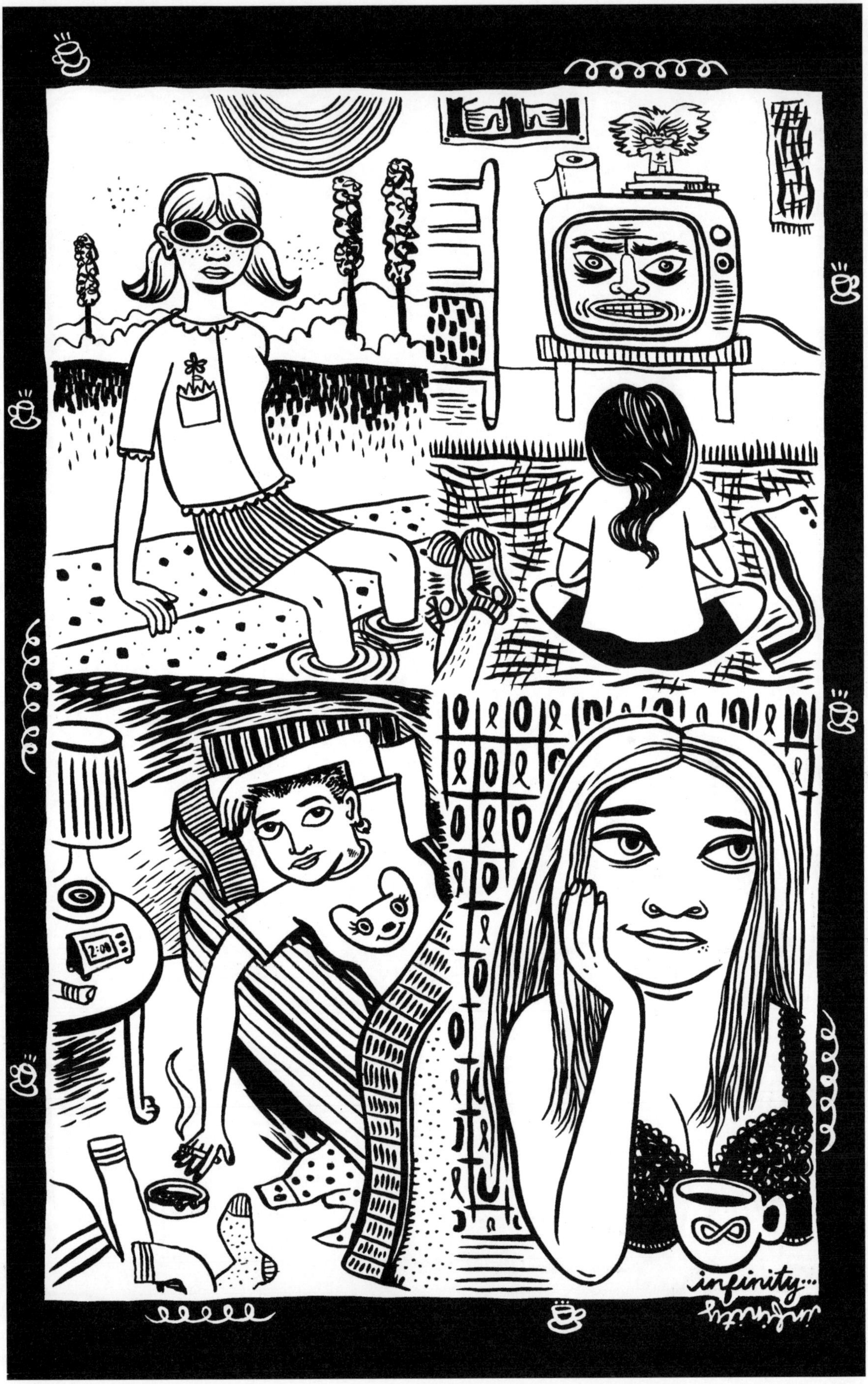
2:00
infinity...

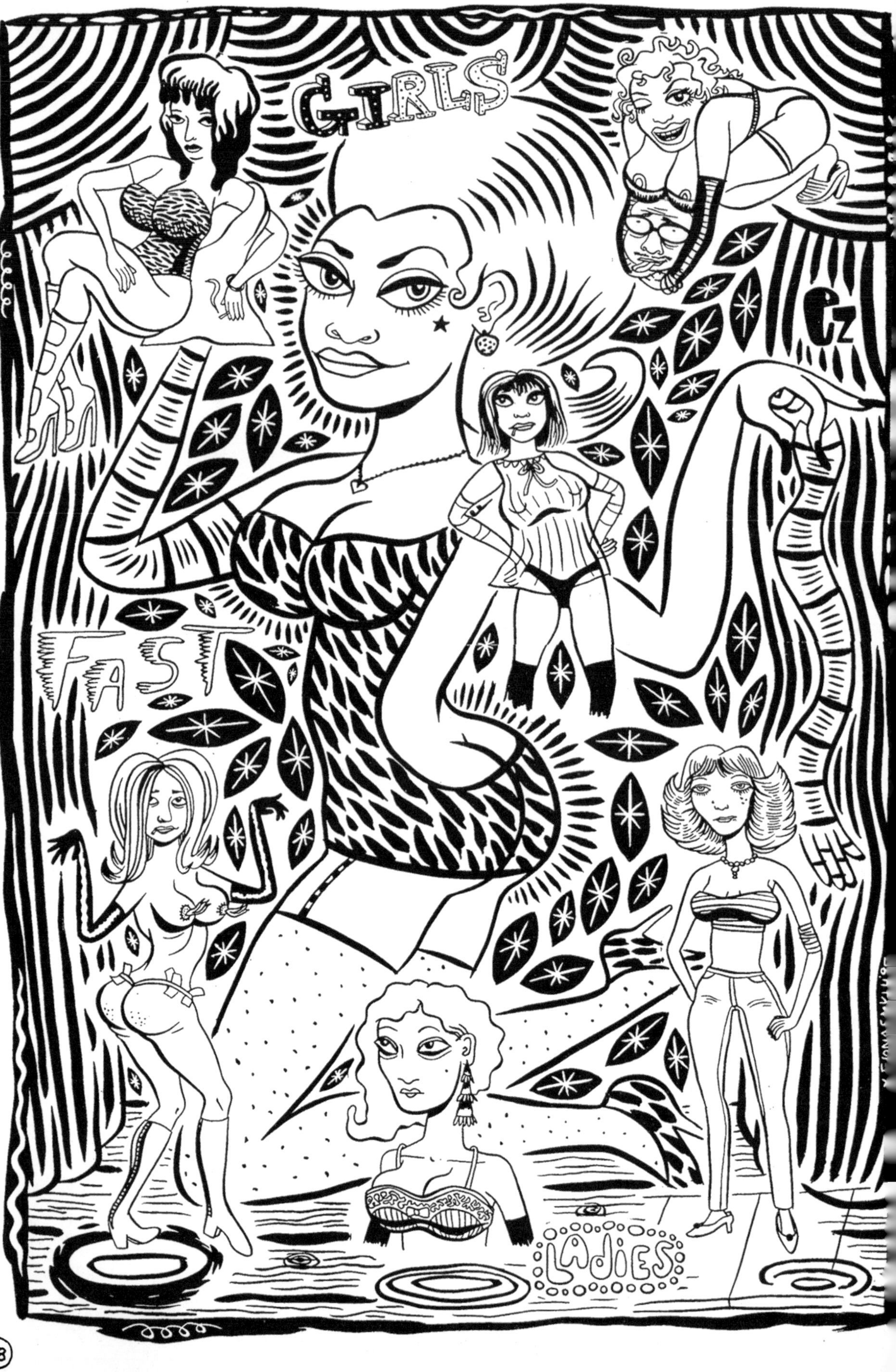
GIRLS
FAST
LADIES

VIVA LA FRIDA

NOCTURNAL
EMISSIONS
#1
$2.50
$3.00
CANADA
ADULTS ONLY
VORTEX COMICS
FIONA SMYTH

1991 VORTEX COMICS

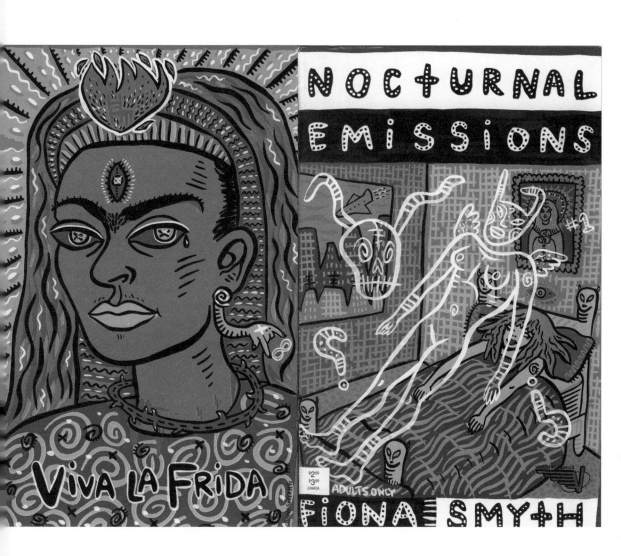

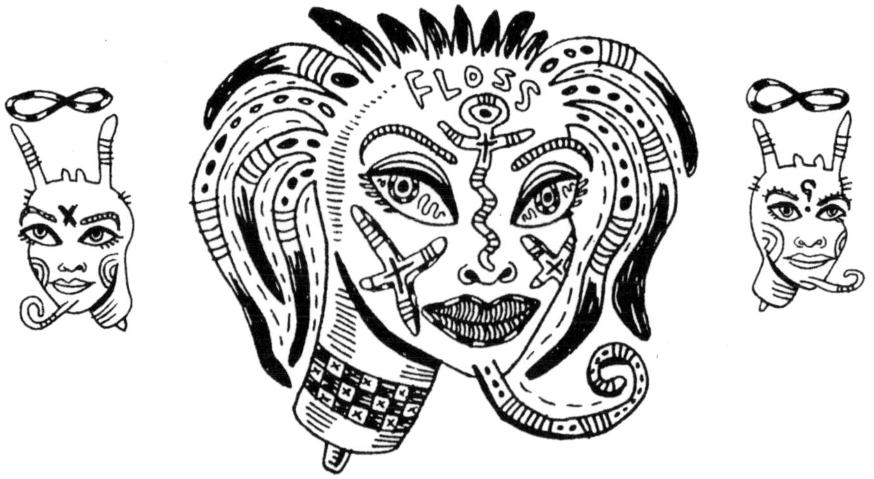
FLOSS

"THAT'S WHY THE LADY IS A TRAMP"

WHO IS FIONA SMYTH? GOOD QUESTION. LOOKING AT HER WORK YOU'D PROBABLY GET THE IDEA THAT SHE'S SOME SORT OF WIGGED-OUT, OVER-SEXED WHORE/GODDESS... AND TO BE PERFECTLY HONEST -- YOU WOULDN'T BE TOO FAR WRONG.

WHEN I FIRST MET FIONA SHE WAS MY GIRLFRIEND'S BEST FRIEND'S SISTER (GOT THAT?). THAT WAS BACK IN THE BIG HAIR DAYS. WE GOT TO KNOW EACH OTHER BETTER WHEN WE BOTH CAME DOWN IN HEIGHT & VOLUME (HAIR-WISE THAT IS) AND I ALSO CAME TO RESPECT & APPRECIATE HER WORK. FIONA'S COME A LONG WAY SINCE THOSE DAYS. BACK THEN SHE WAS A CANDY GIRL... NOW SHE'S A KANDY KOLORED, TANGERINE FLAKE, STREAMLINE BABY. LET'S FACE IT, SHE OWNS THIS TOWN. IT'S HARD TO FIND A SQUARE INCH OF DOWNTOWN TORONTO THAT SHE HASN'T COVERED WITH ONE OF HER MURALS.

FIONA'S A POP-CULTURE BLACK HOLE -- ANYTHING PASSING BY GETS SUCKED IN. SHE'S A GRAB-BAG, REACH IN AND YOU'LL PULL OUT A HANDFULL OF BLASPHEMY, BABES, CAMP AND CASTRATION. SHE'S THE GREASY-SPOON WHERE MR. HIGH-BROW HAS BREAKFAST WITH MISS LOW-BROW. SHE'S A 24 HOUR GIN-JOINT, SNOOTY ART GALLERY BY DAY, SLEAZY STRIP PALACE BY NIGHT. LOOK OUT... SHE'S A HOOCHIE KOOCHIE GIRL.

YOU'RE A LUCKY BUNCH, THOSE OF YOU WHO ARE SEEING FIONA'S WORK FOR THE FIRST TIME - IT'S A FULLY REALIZED WORLD. CHARACTERS POPPING UP OUT OF NOWHERE OFTEN HAVE A COMPLICATED HISTORY THAT RUNS BACK THRU YEARS OF PAINTINGS & MINI COMICS. FIONA'S WORLD REVEALS ITSELF SLOWLY. SO BE PATIENT. BUT GO ON, DIVE INTO THAT OBSESSIVE, PSYCHEDELIC, CUM-STICKY WORLD... AND REMEMBER AS FIONA SAYS, "THAT'S GOOD CHICKEN."

SETH
PALOOKA-VILLE
19PS

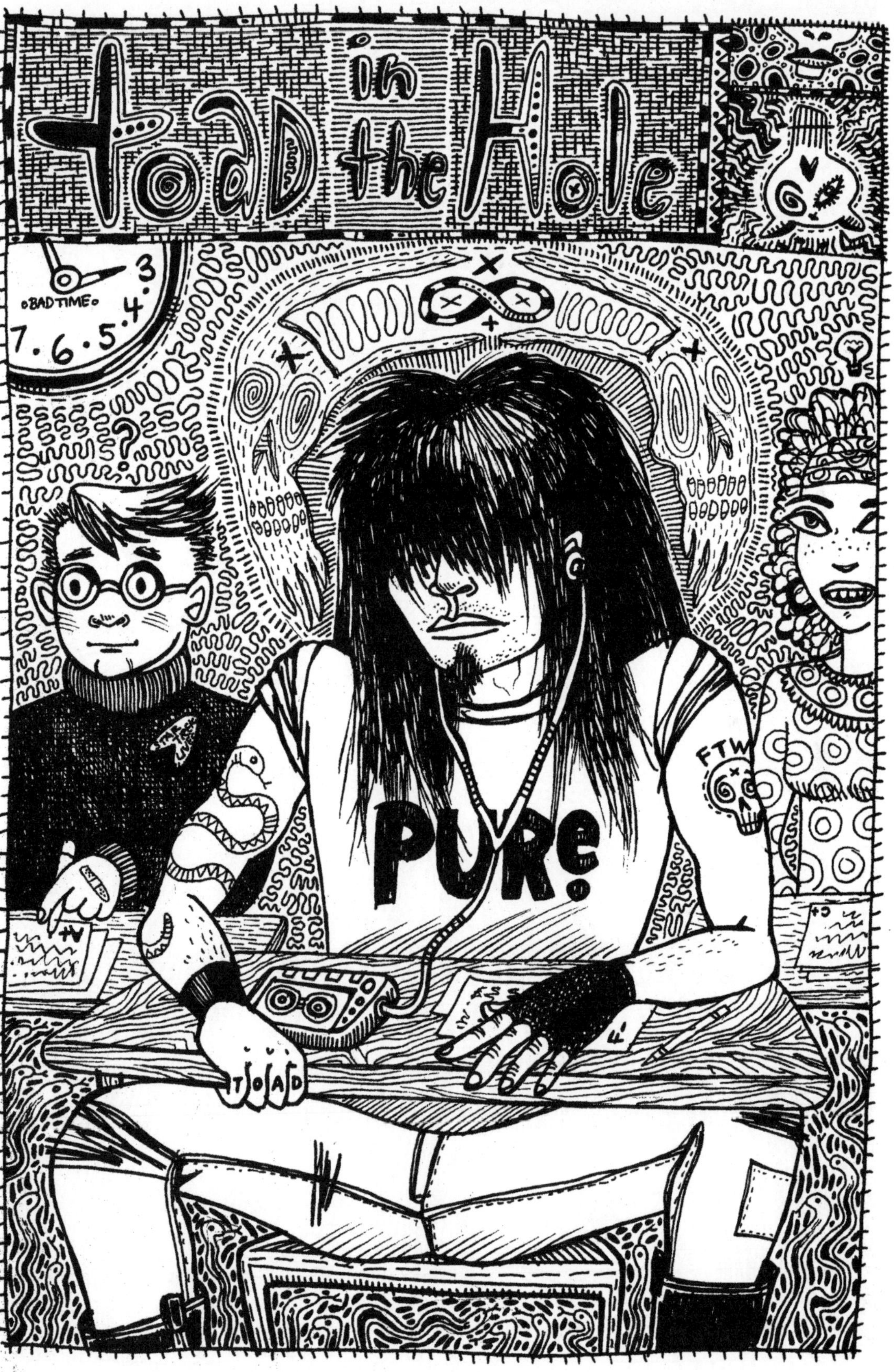
Toad in the Hole
BAD TIME
3
4
5
6
7
PURE
FTW
TOAD

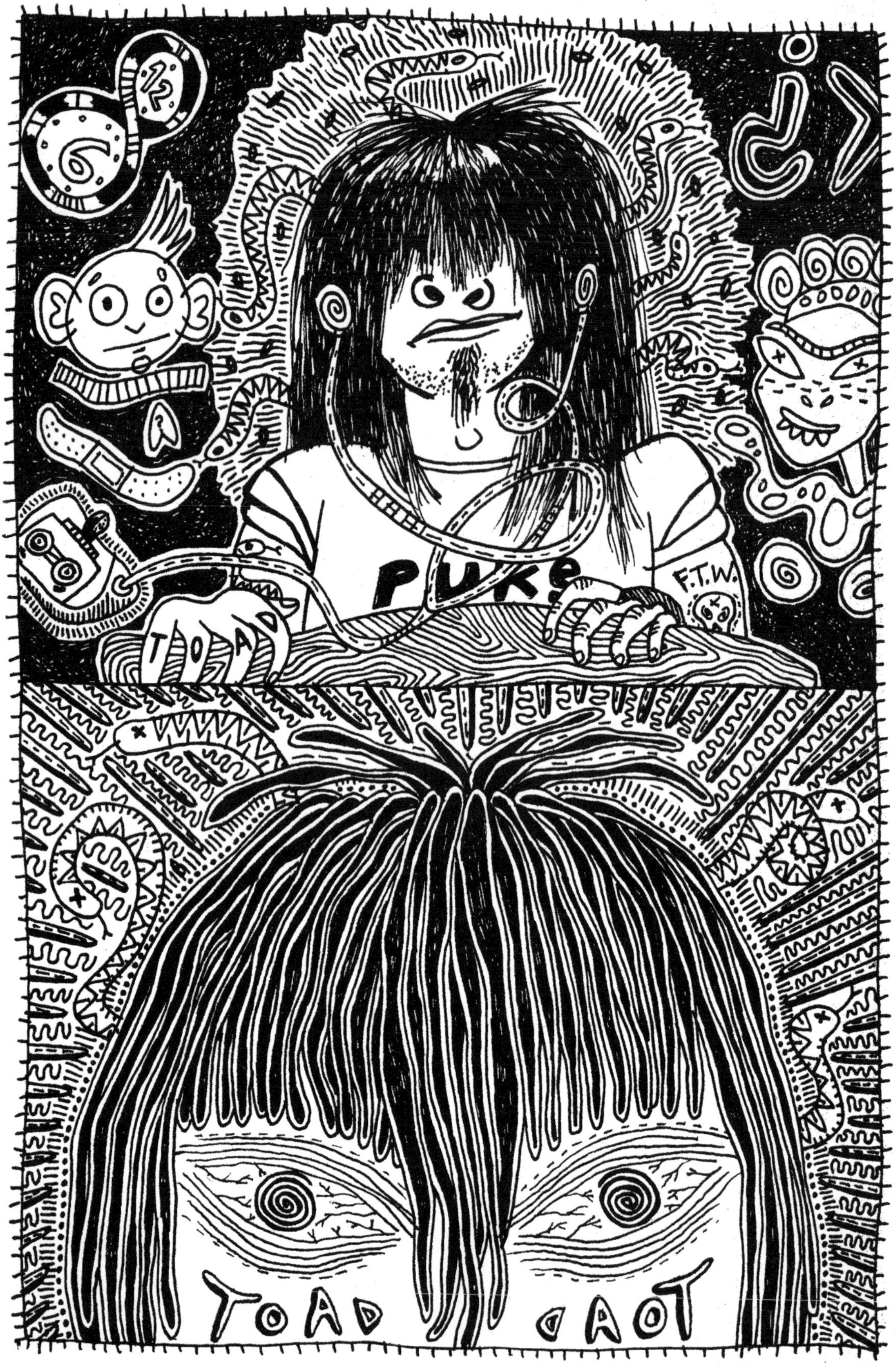
12
6
PUKE
F.T.W.
TOAD
TOAD

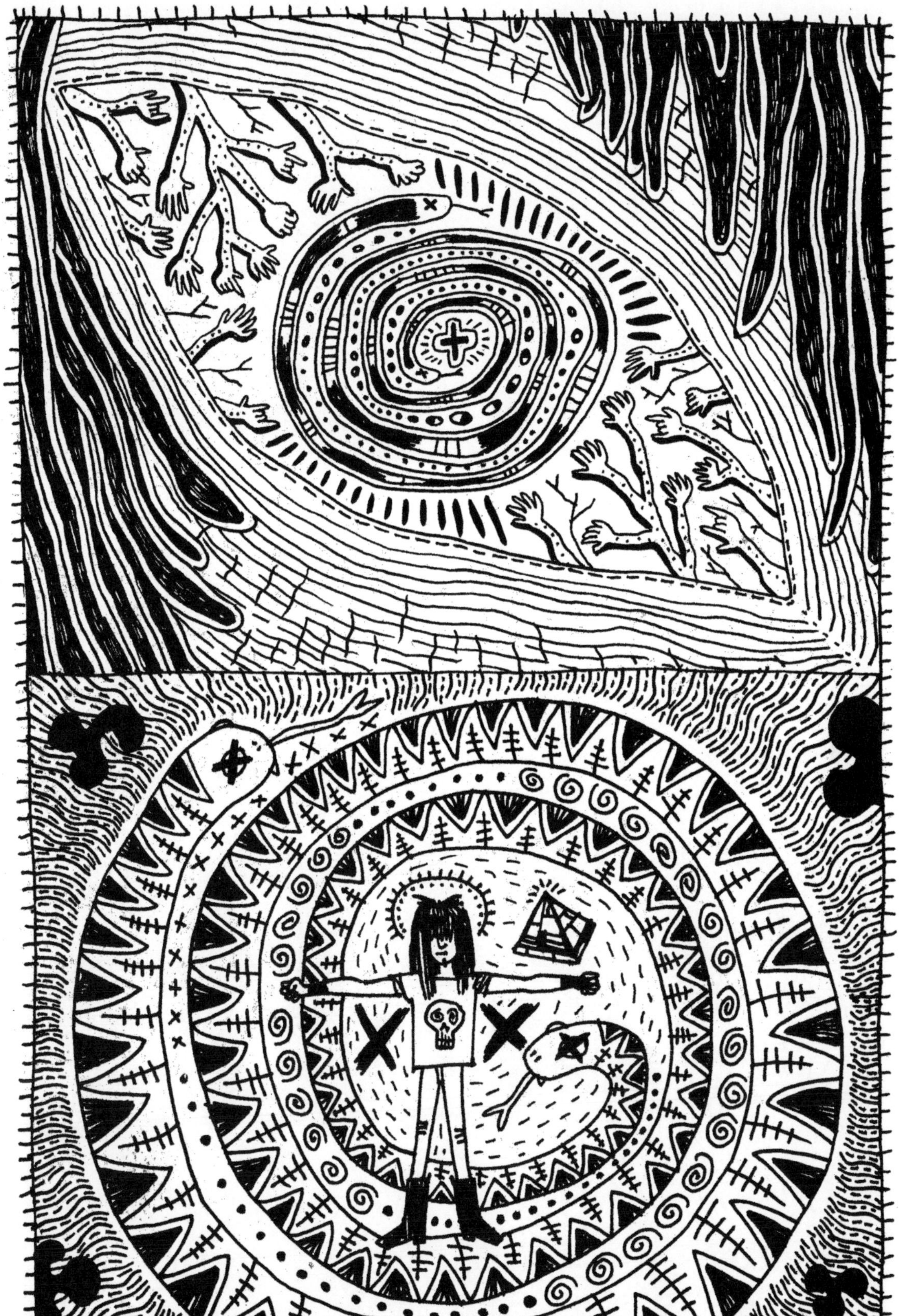

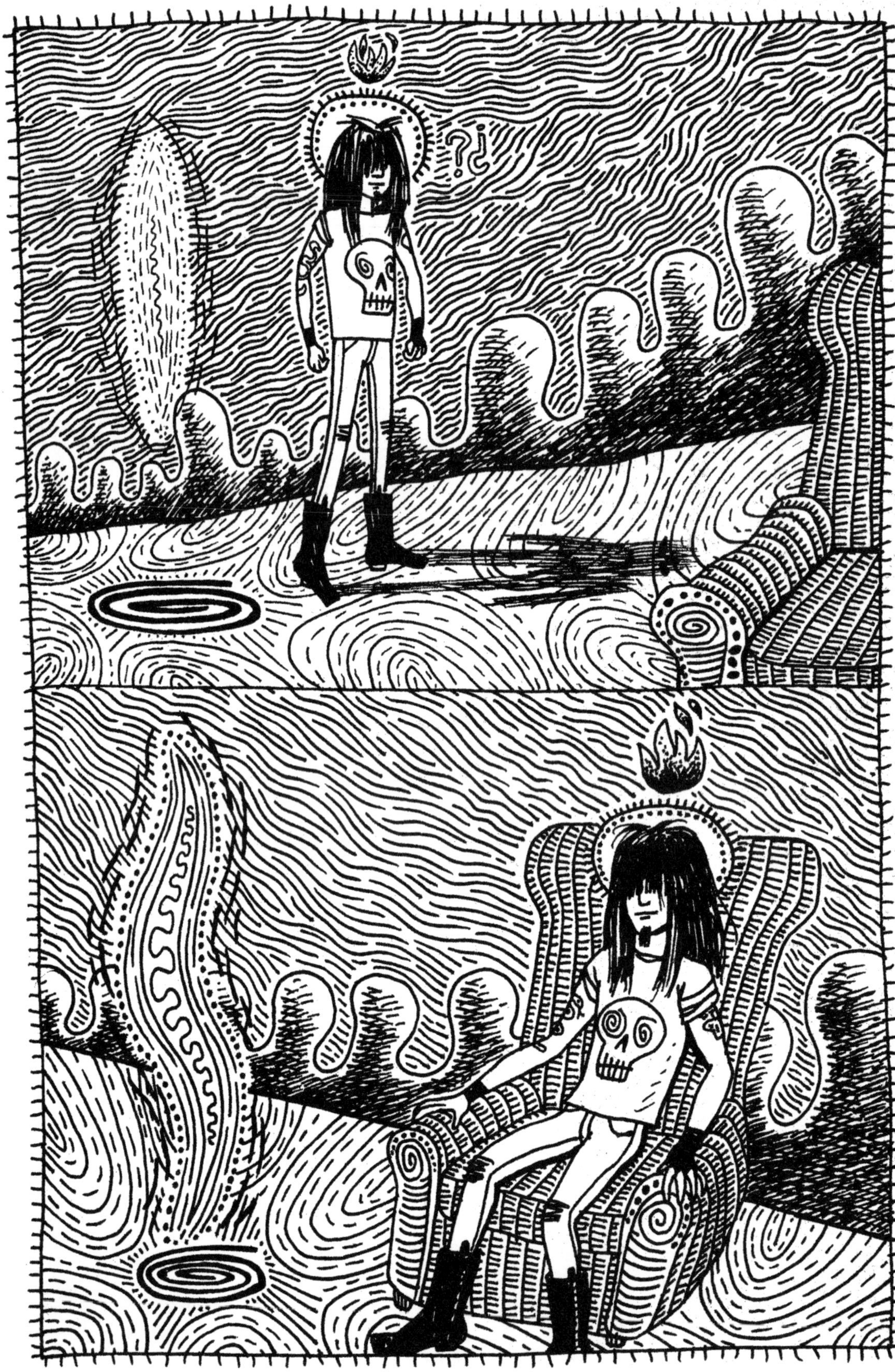
?¿

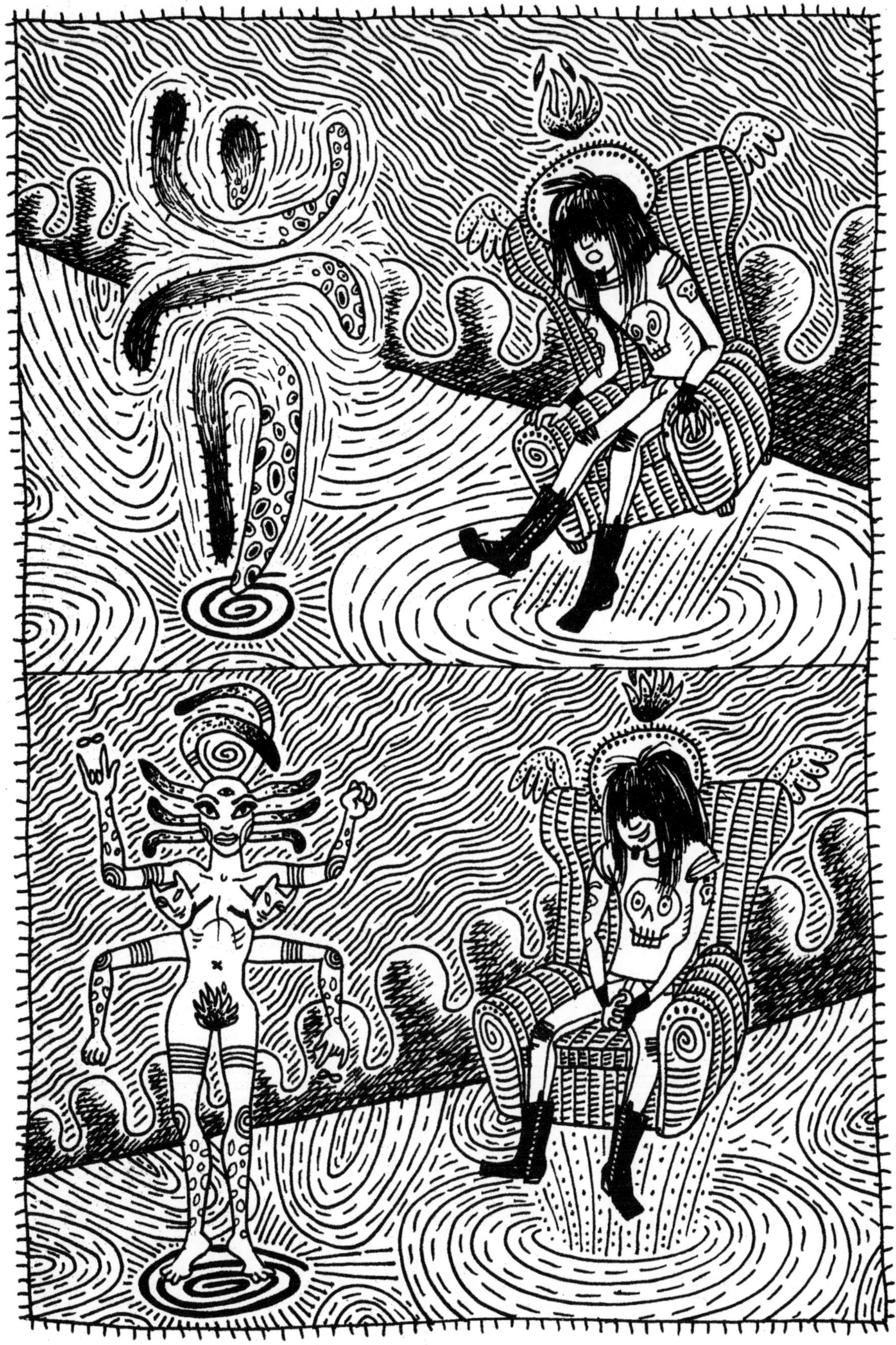

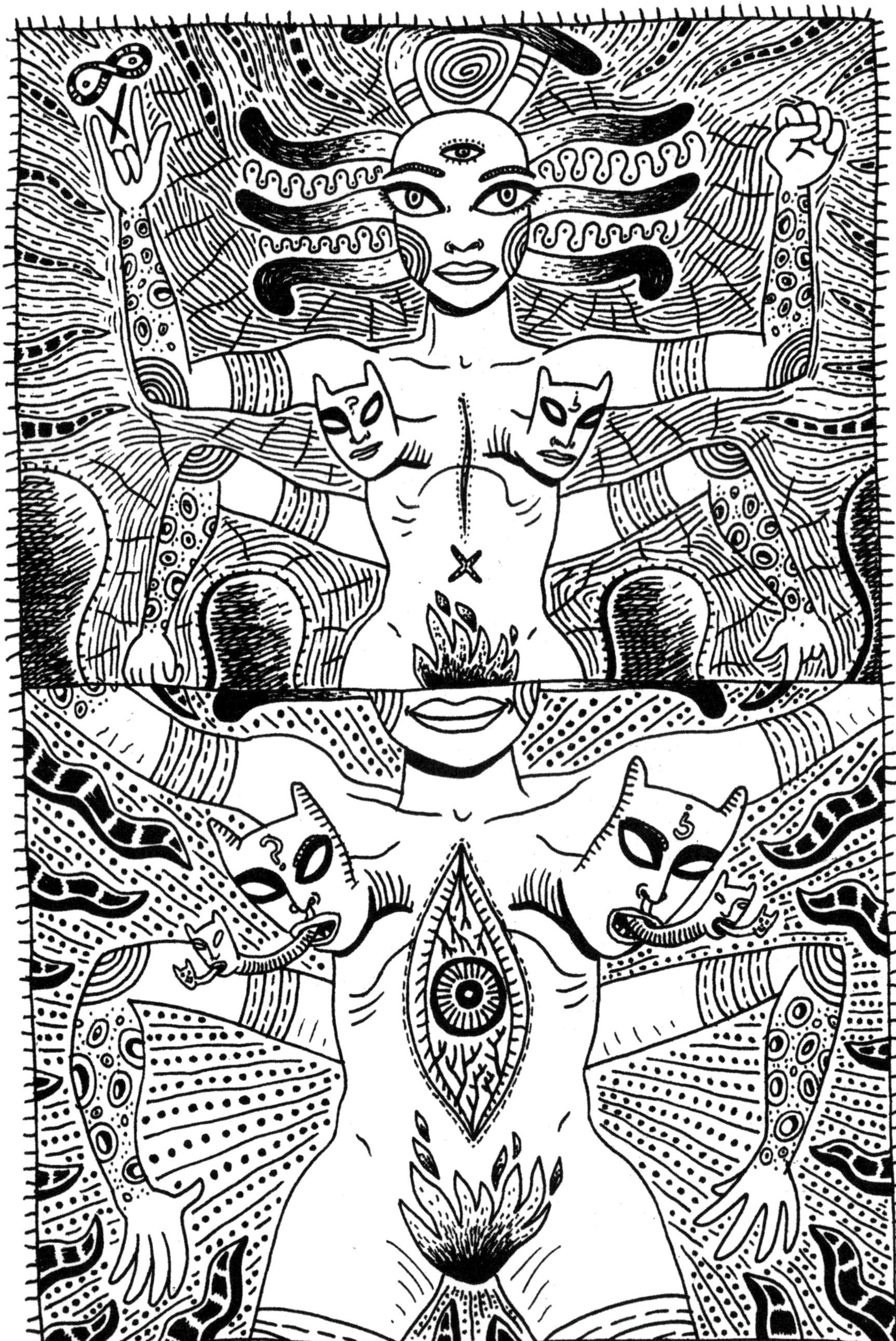

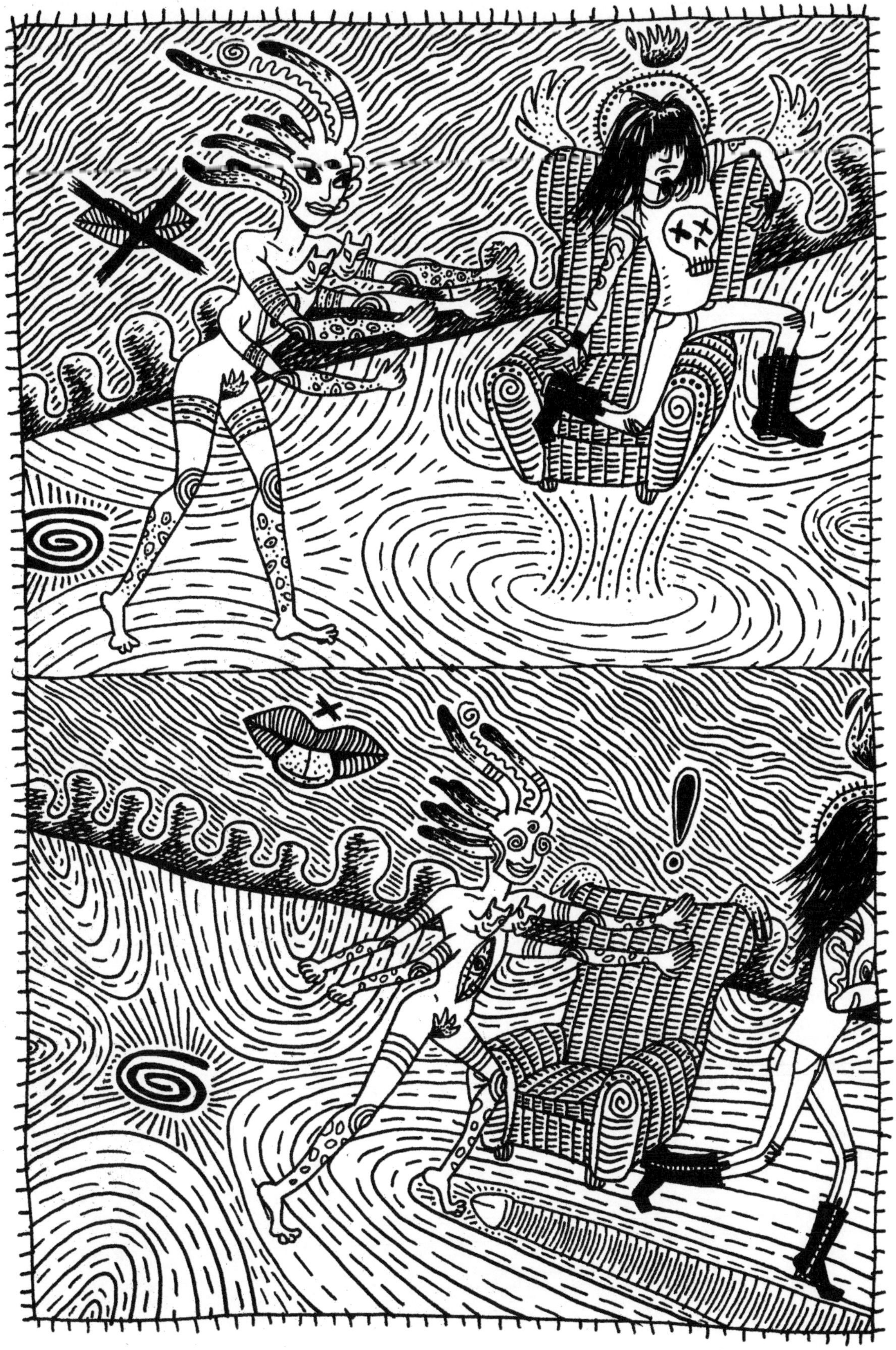
!

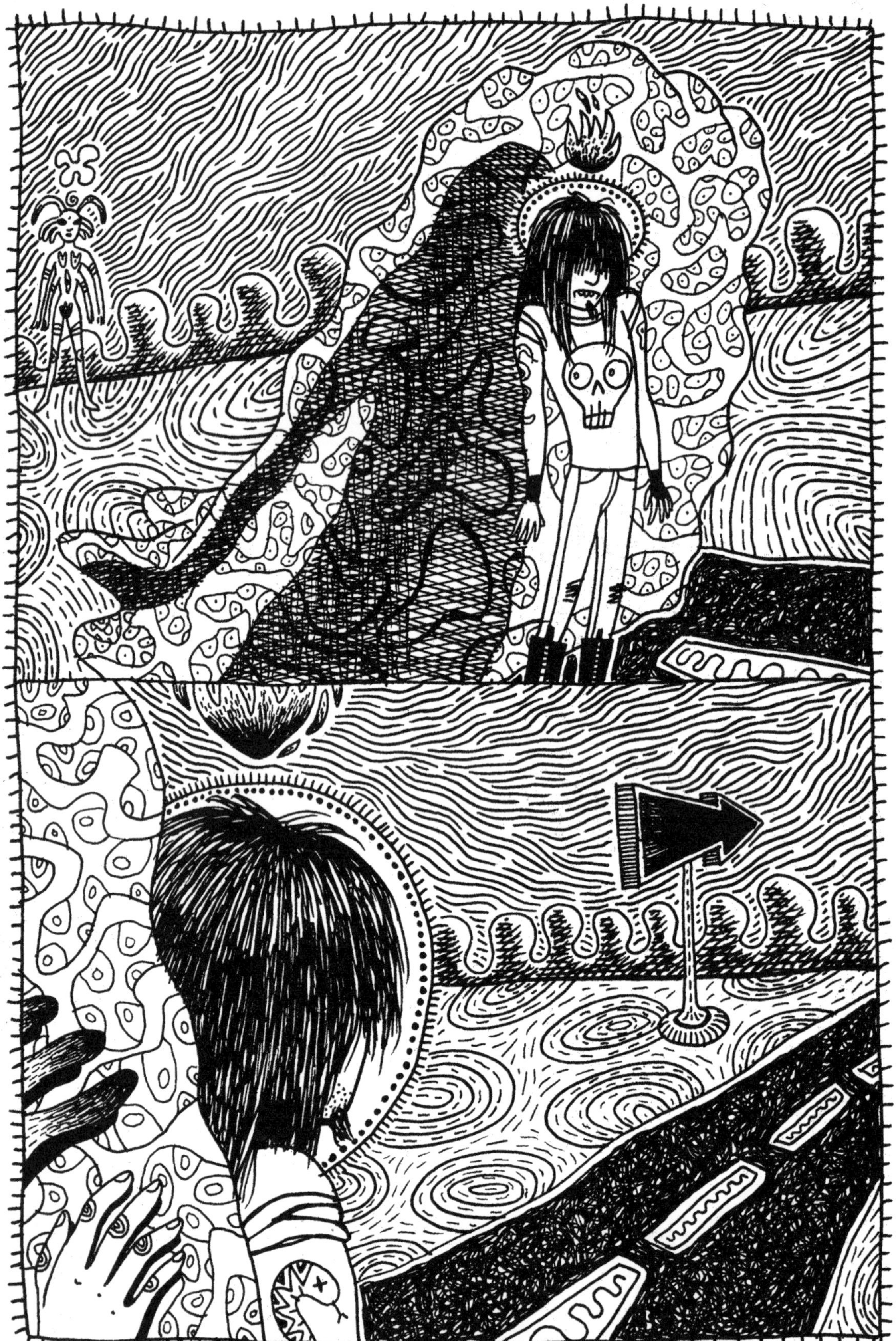

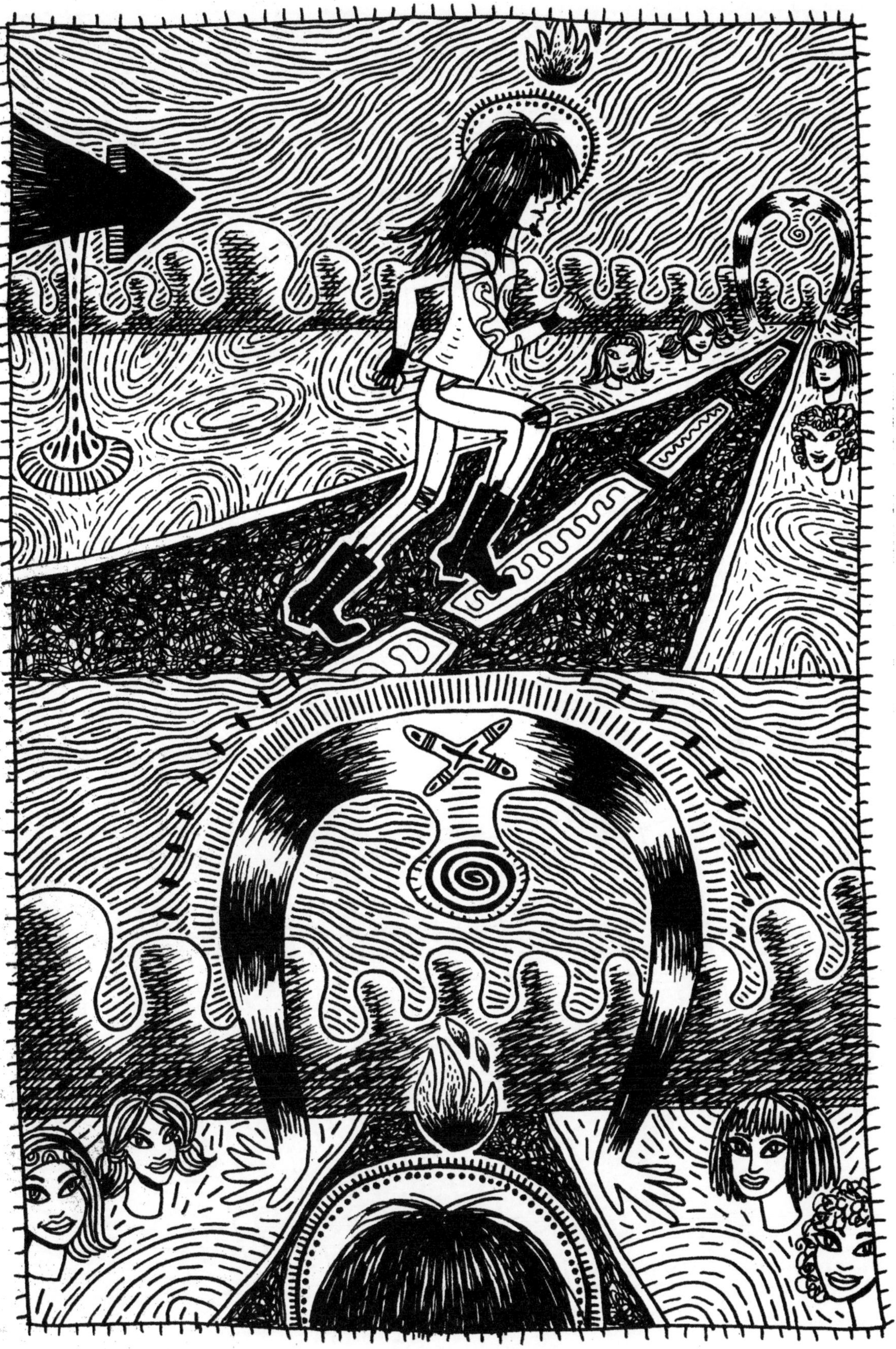

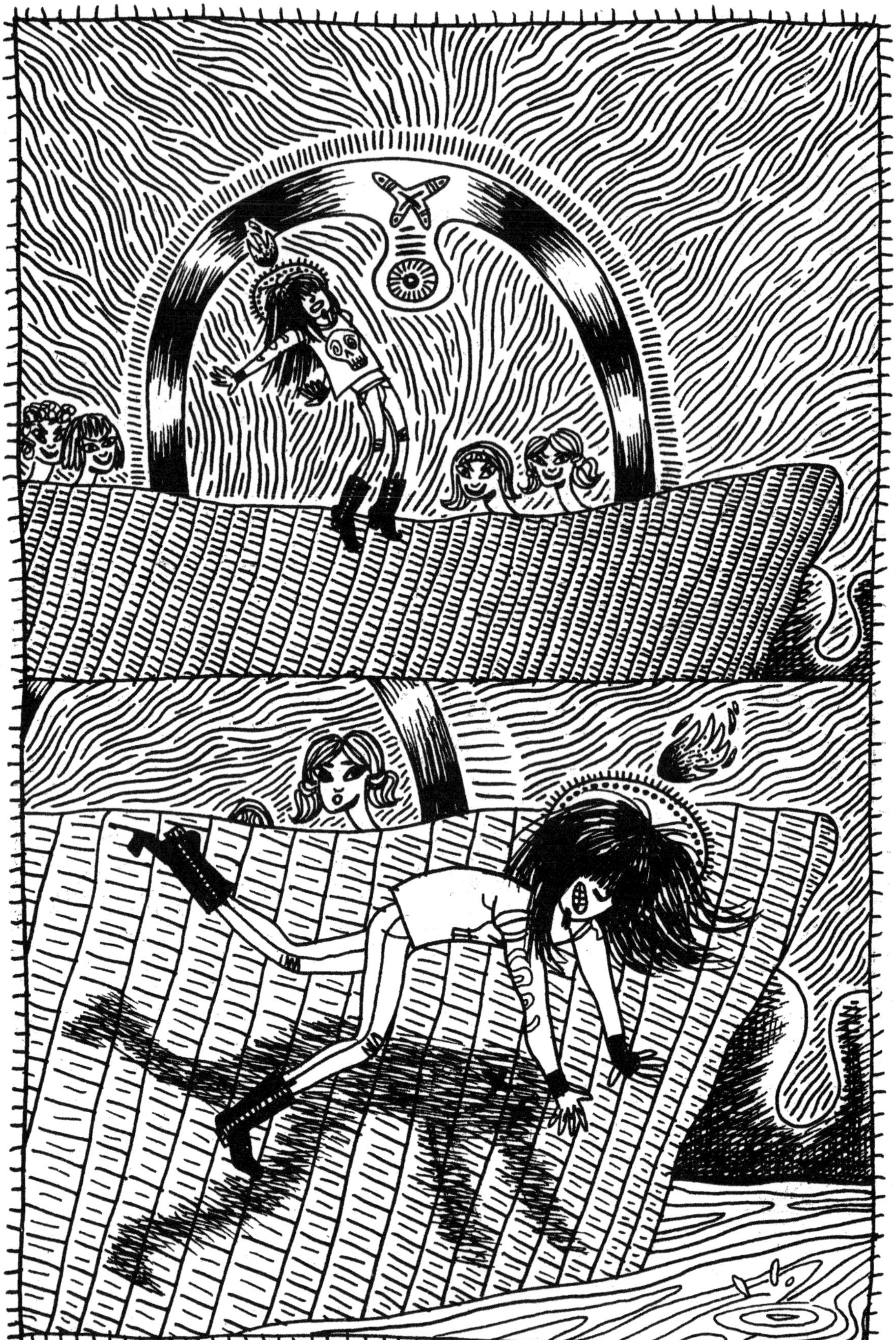

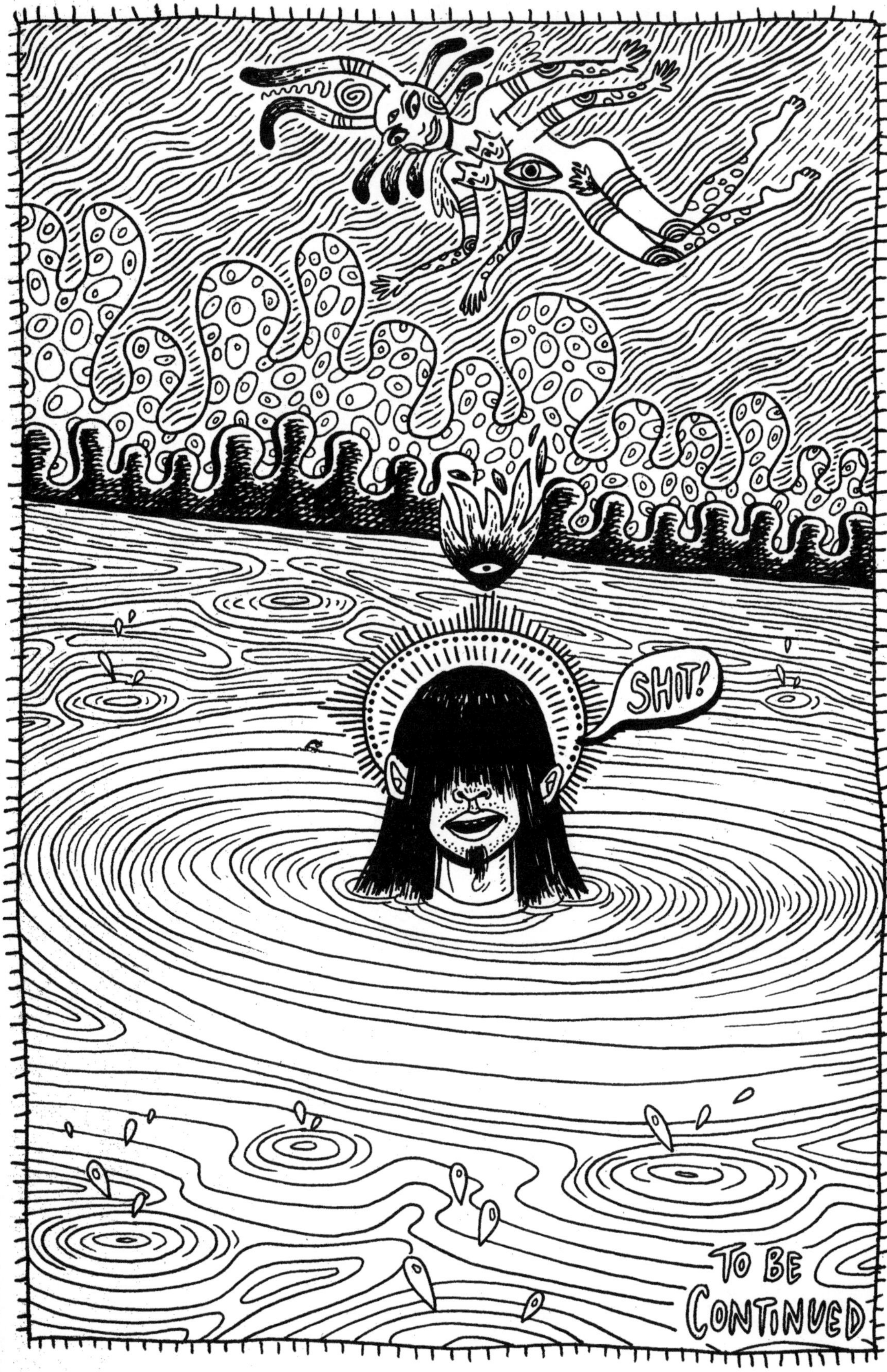
SHIT!
TO BE CONTINUED

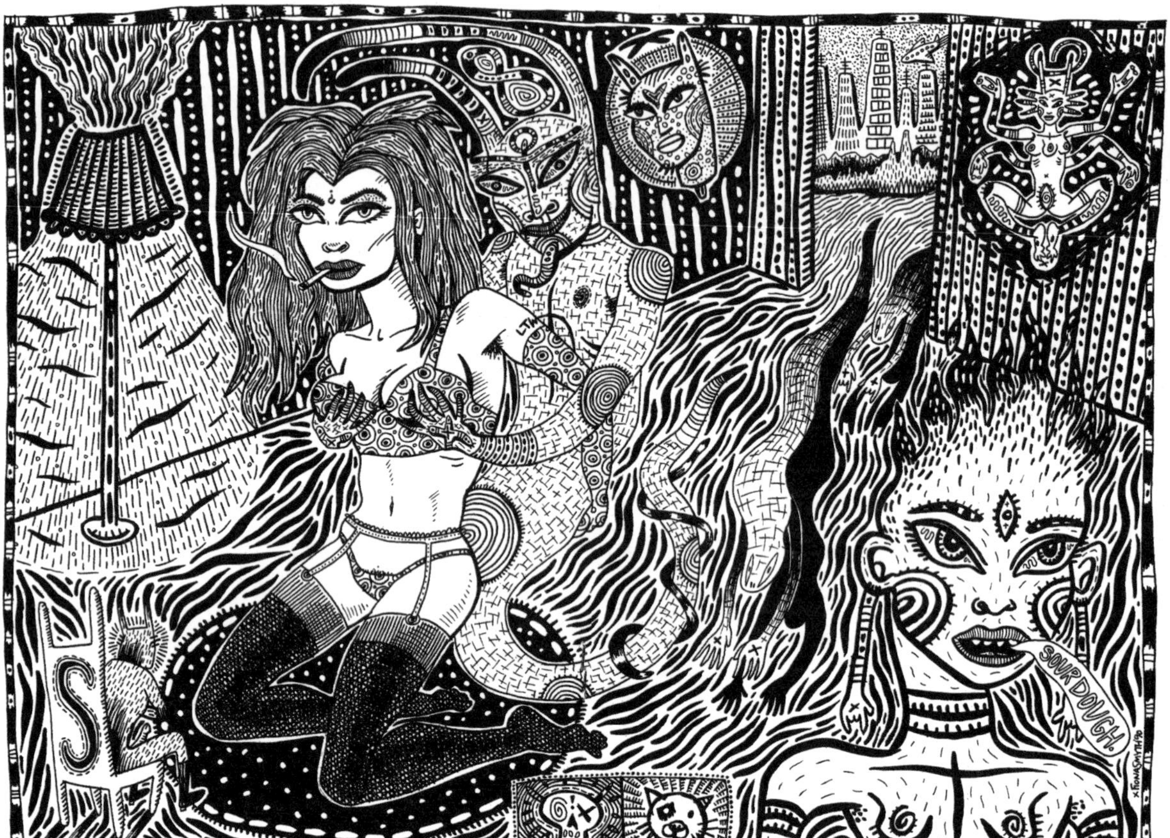
SOURDOUGH.
x FIONA SMYTH 90

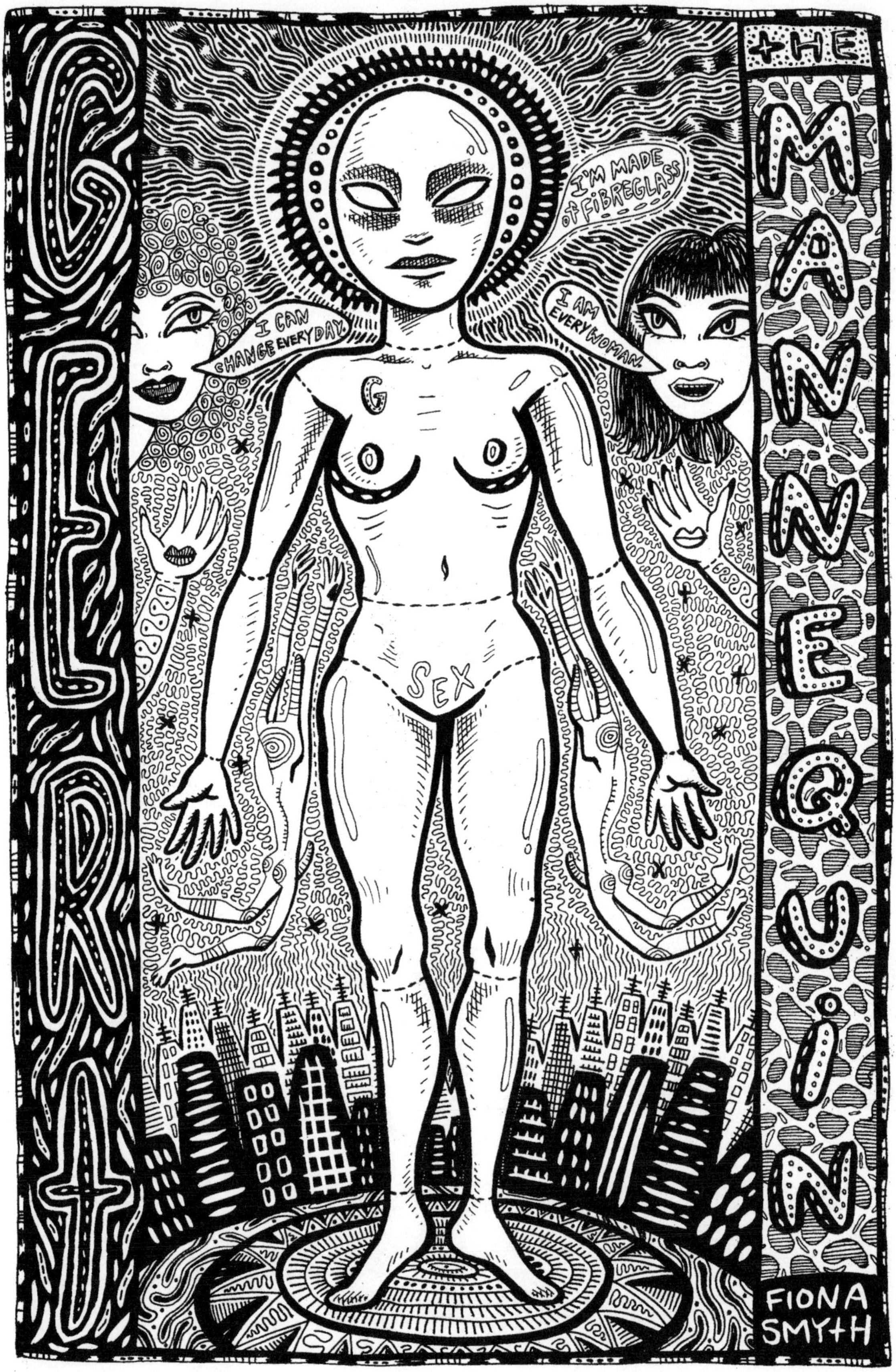
GIRL
THE MANNEQUIN
I'M MADE of FIBREGLASS
I CAN CHANGE EVERY DAY.
I AM EVERY WOMAN.
G
O O
SEX
FIONA SMYTH

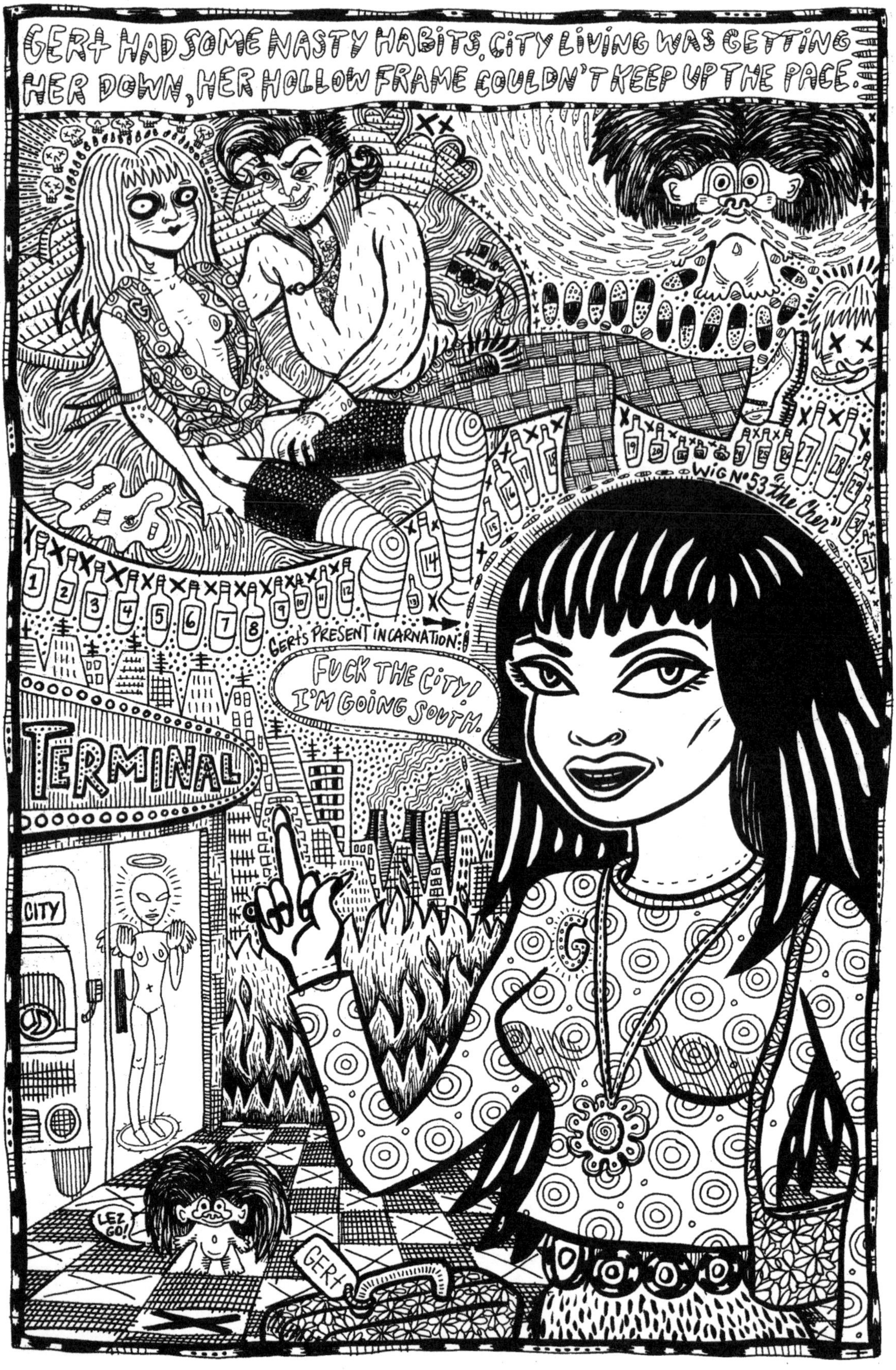
GERT HAD SOME NASTY HABITS, CITY LIVING WAS GETTING HER DOWN, HER HOLLOW FRAME COULDN'T KEEP UP THE PACE.
WIG No 53 "the Cher"
GERT'S PRESENT INCARNATION:
FUCK THE CITY! I'M GOING SOUTH.
TERMINAL
CITY
LEZ GO!
GERT

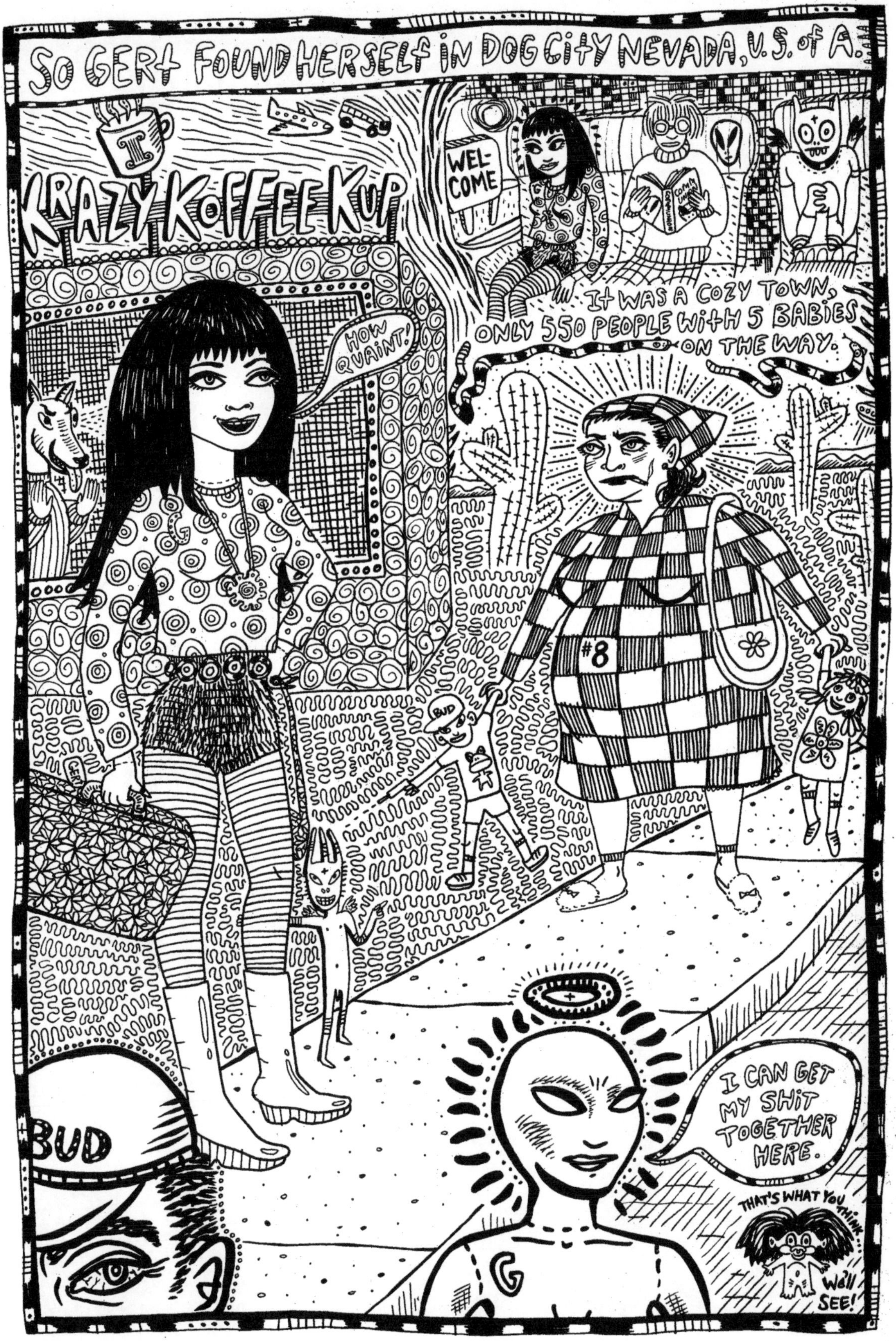

SO GERT FOUND HERSELF IN DOG CITY NEVADA, U.S. of A.
KRAZY KOFFEE KUP
WEL-COME
IT WAS A COZY TOWN, ONLY 550 PEOPLE WITH 5 BABIES ON THE WAY.
HOW QUAINT!
#8
BUD
I CAN GET MY SHIT TOGETHER HERE.
THAT'S WHAT YOU THINK...
WE'LL SEE!
BUD

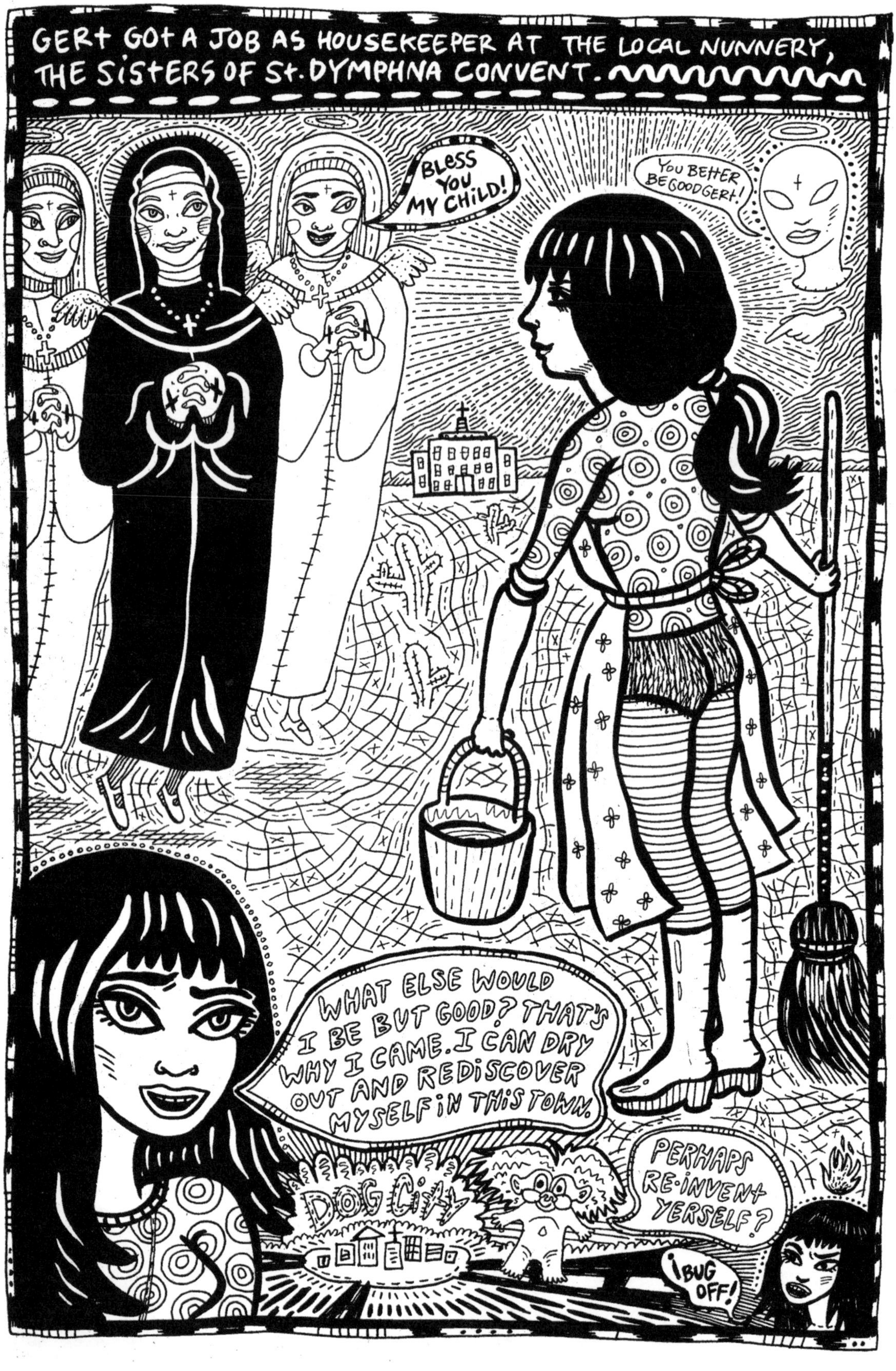

GERT GOT A JOB AS HOUSEKEEPER AT THE LOCAL NUNNERY, THE SISTERS OF ST. DYMPHNA CONVENT.
BLESS YOU MY CHILD!
YOU BETTER BE GOOD GERT!
WHAT ELSE WOULD I BE BUT GOOD? THAT'S WHY I CAME. I CAN DRY OUT AND REDISCOVER MYSELF IN THIS TOWN.
DOG CITY
PERHAPS RE-INVENT YERSELF?
¡BUG OFF!

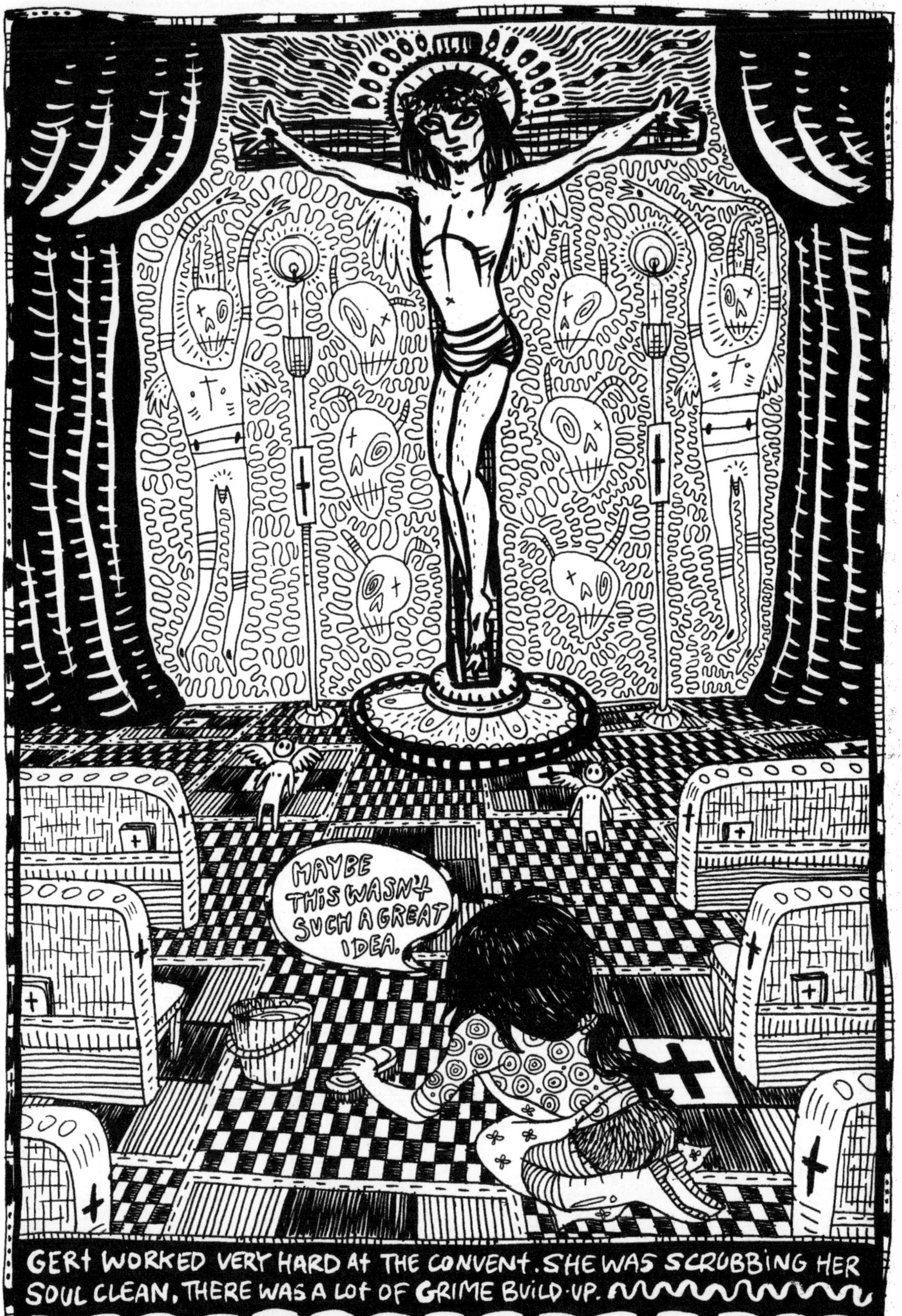
MAYBE THIS WASN'T SUCH A GREAT IDEA.
GERT WORKED VERY HARD AT THE CONVENT. SHE WAS SCRUBBING HER SOUL CLEAN. THERE WAS A LOT OF GRIME BUILD-UP.

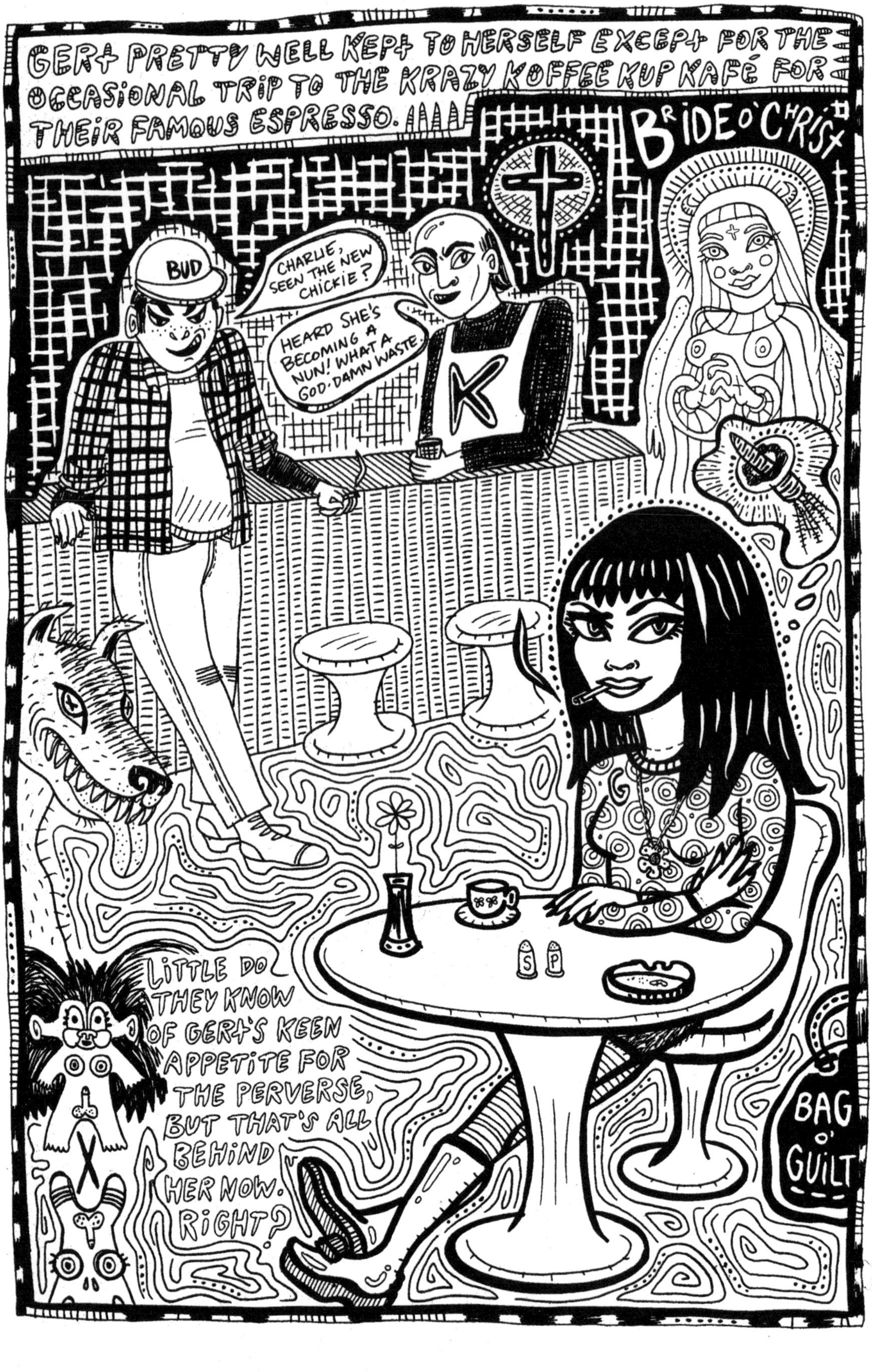
GERT PRETTY WELL KEPT TO HERSELF EXCEPT FOR THE OCCASIONAL TRIP TO THE KRAZY KOFFEE KUP KAFÉ FOR THEIR FAMOUS ESPRESSO.
BRIDE O' CHRIST
BUD
CHARLIE, SEEN THE NEW CHICKIE?
HEARD SHE'S BECOMING A NUN! WHAT A GOD-DAMN WASTE.
K
S
P
LITTLE DO THEY KNOW OF GERT'S KEEN APPETITE FOR THE PERVERSE, BUT THAT'S ALL BEHIND HER NOW. RIGHT?
BAG O' GUILT

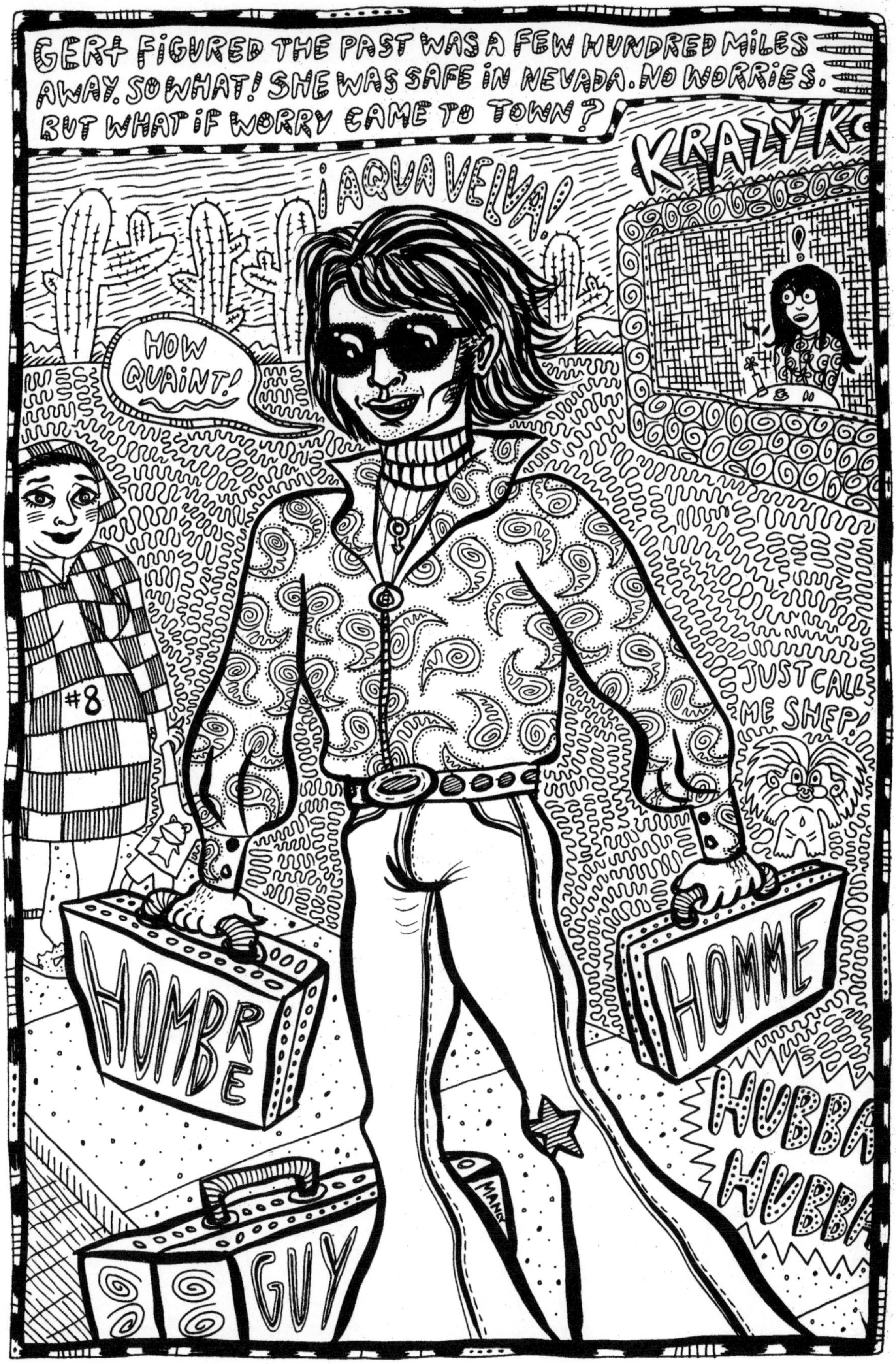

GERT FIGURED THE PAST WAS A FEW HUNDRED MILES AWAY. SO WHAT! SHE WAS SAFE IN NEVADA. NO WORRIES. BUT WHAT IF WORRY CAME TO TOWN?
¡AQUA VELVA!
KRAZY KO
HOW QUAINT!
#8
JUST CALL ME SHEP!
HOMBRE
HOMME
HUBBA HUBBA
GUY
MANLY

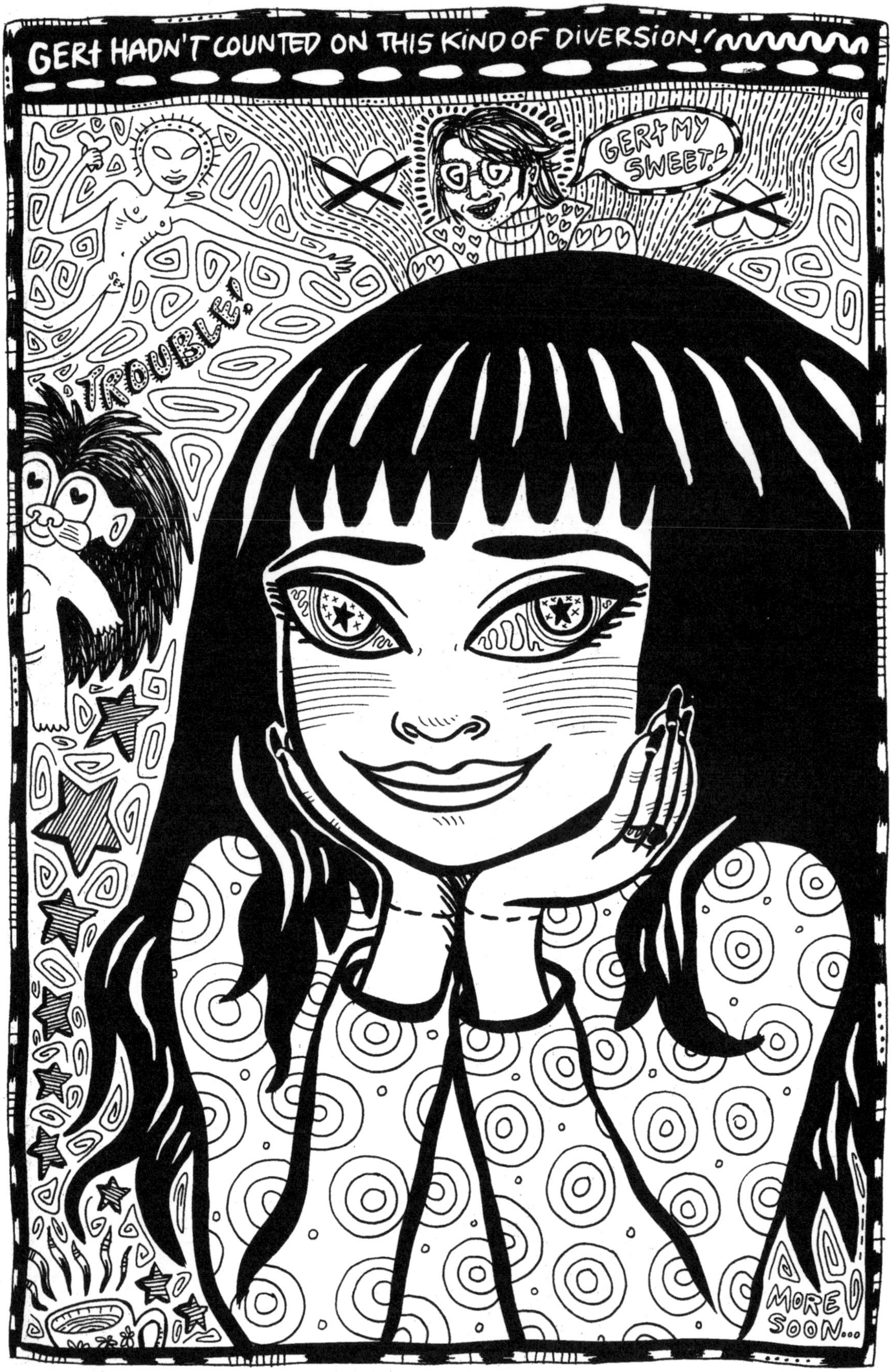
GERT HADN'T COUNTED ON THIS KIND OF DIVERSION!
GERT MY SWEET!
SEX
TROUBLE!
MORE SOON...

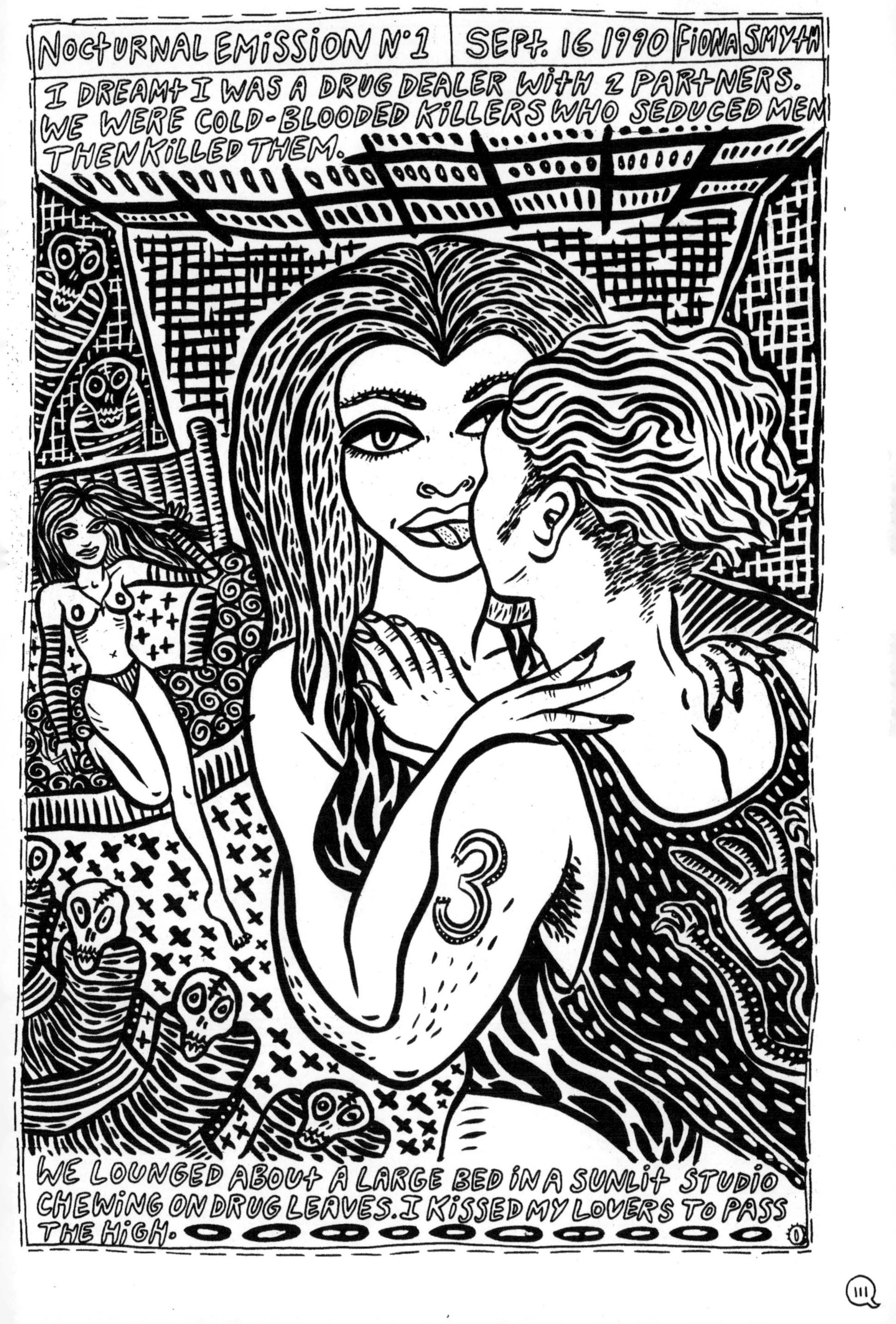
NOCTURNAL EMISSION N°1
SEPT. 16 1990
FIONA SMYTH
I DREAMT I WAS A DRUG DEALER WITH 2 PARTNERS. WE WERE COLD-BLOODED KILLERS WHO SEDUCED MEN THEN KILLED THEM.
3
WE LOUNGED ABOUT A LARGE BED IN A SUNLIT STUDIO CHEWING ON DRUG LEAVES. I KISSED MY LOVERS TO PASS THE HIGH.

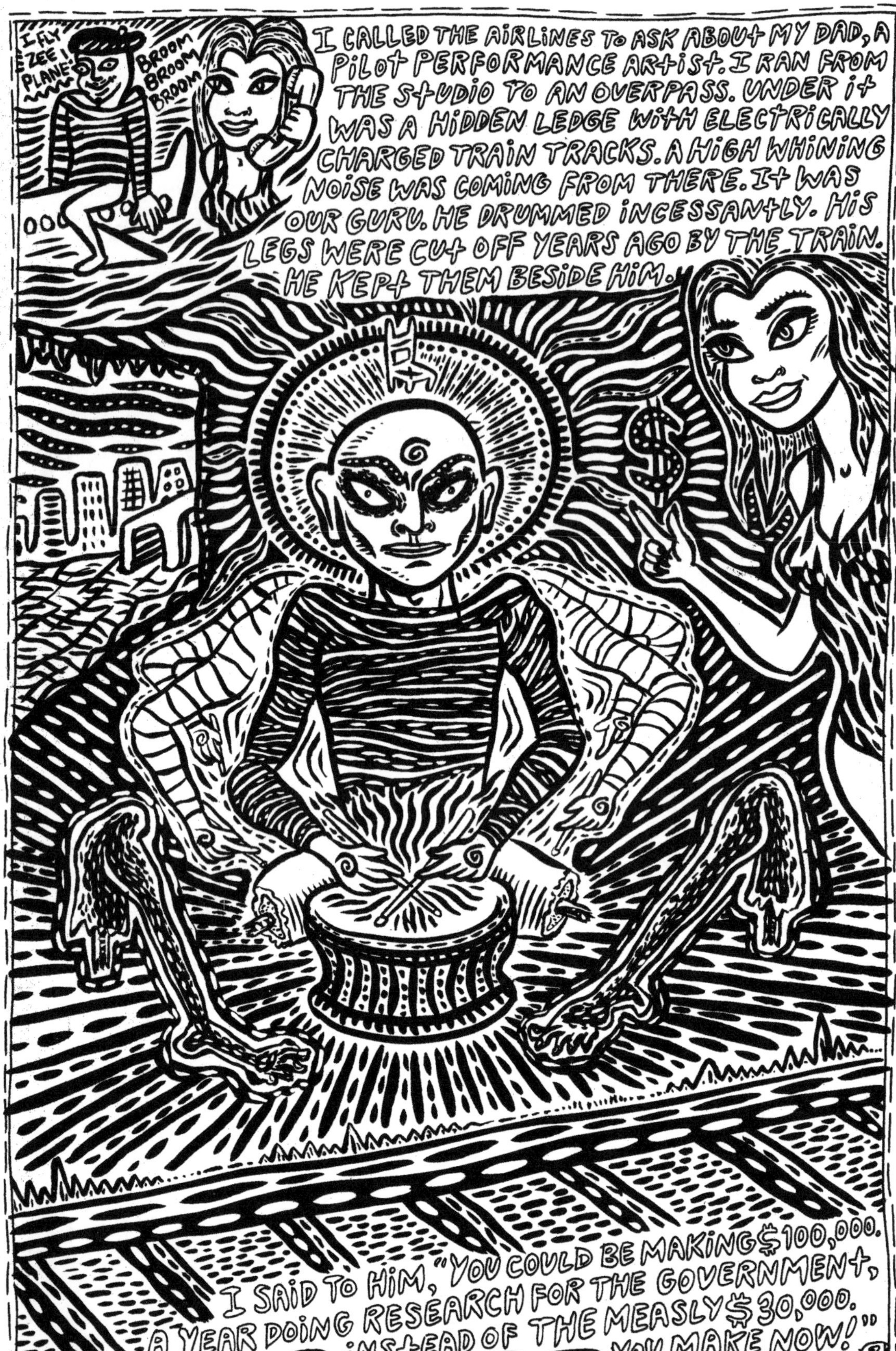
I FLY ZEE! PLANE!
BROOM BROOM BROOM
I CALLED THE AIRLINES TO ASK ABOUT MY DAD, A PILOT PERFORMANCE ARTIST. I RAN FROM THE STUDIO TO AN OVERPASS. UNDER IT WAS A HIDDEN LEDGE WITH ELECTRICALLY CHARGED TRAIN TRACKS. A HIGH WHINING NOISE WAS COMING FROM THERE. IT WAS OUR GURU. HE DRUMMED INCESSANTLY. HIS LEGS WERE CUT OFF YEARS AGO BY THE TRAIN. HE KEPT THEM BESIDE HIM.
$
I SAID TO HIM, "YOU COULD BE MAKING $100,000. A YEAR DOING RESEARCH FOR THE GOVERNMENT, INSTEAD OF THE MEASLY $30,000. YOU MAKE NOW!"

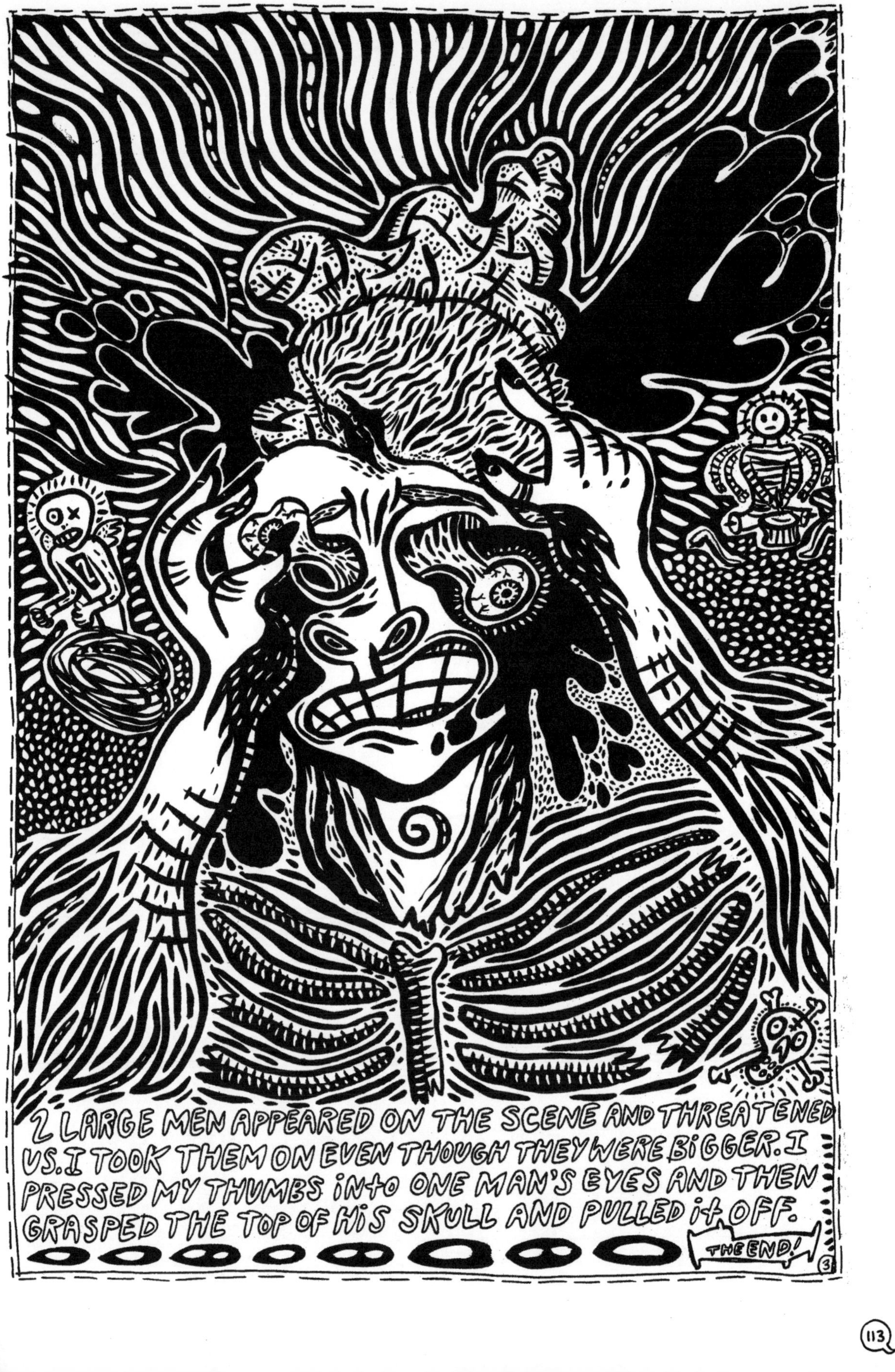
2 LARGE MEN APPEARED ON THE SCENE AND THREATENED US. I TOOK THEM ON EVEN THOUGH THEY WERE BIGGER. I PRESSED MY THUMBS INTO ONE MAN'S EYES AND THEN GRASPED THE TOP OF HIS SKULL AND PULLED IT OFF.
THE END!
3

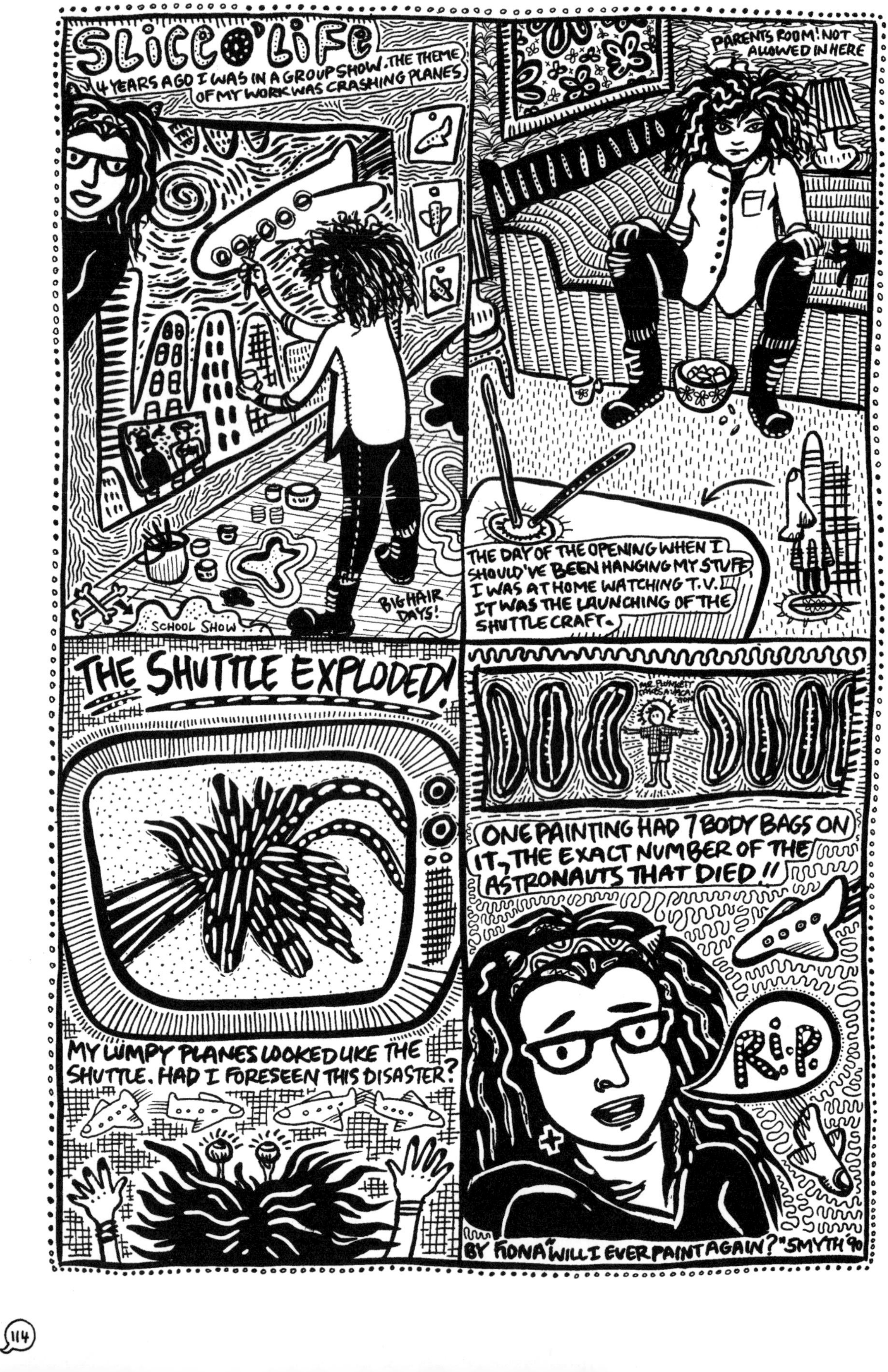
SLICE O' LIFE
4 YEARS AGO I WAS IN A GROUP SHOW. THE THEME OF MY WORK WAS CRASHING PLANES
SCHOOL SHOW
BIG HAIR DAYS!
PARENTS ROOM! NOT ALLOWED IN HERE
THE DAY OF THE OPENING WHEN I SHOULD'VE BEEN HANGING MY STUFF, I WAS AT HOME WATCHING T.V. IT WAS THE LAUNCHING OF THE SHUTTLE CRAFT.
THE SHUTTLE EXPLODED!
MY LUMPY PLANES LOOKED LIKE THE SHUTTLE. HAD I FORESEEN THIS DISASTER?
MR. PLUNKETT TAKES A VACATION
ONE PAINTING HAD 7 BODY BAGS ON IT, THE EXACT NUMBER OF THE ASTRONAUTS THAT DIED!!
R.I.P.
BY FIONA "WILL I EVER PAINT AGAIN?" SMYTH '90

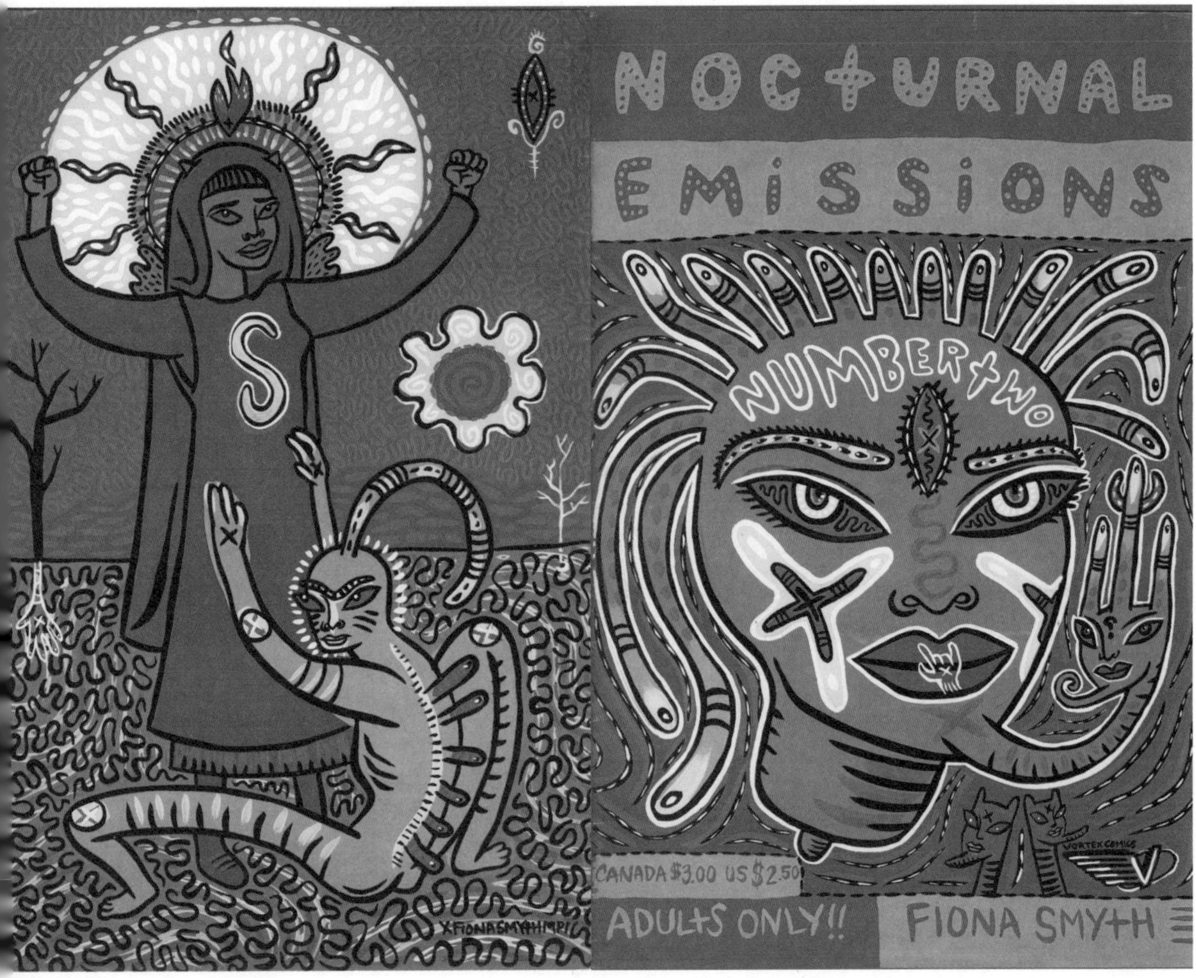
NOCTURNAL
EMISSIONS
NUMBER TWO
CANADA $3.00 US $2.50
VORTEX COMICS
ADULTS ONLY!!
FIONA SMYTH

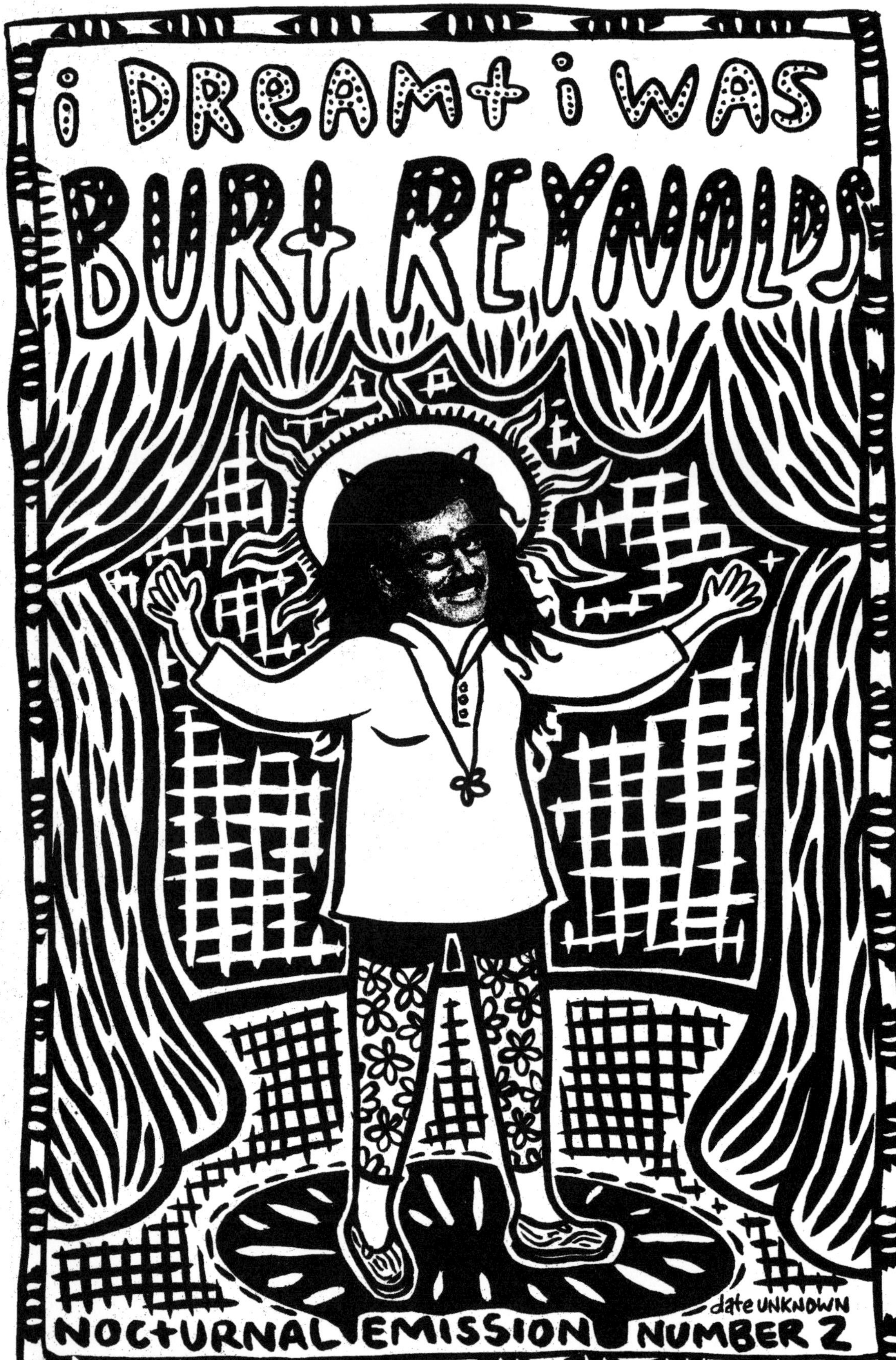

i DREAM+ i WAS
BURt REYNOLDS
date UNKNOWN
NOCtURNAL EMISSION NUMBER 2

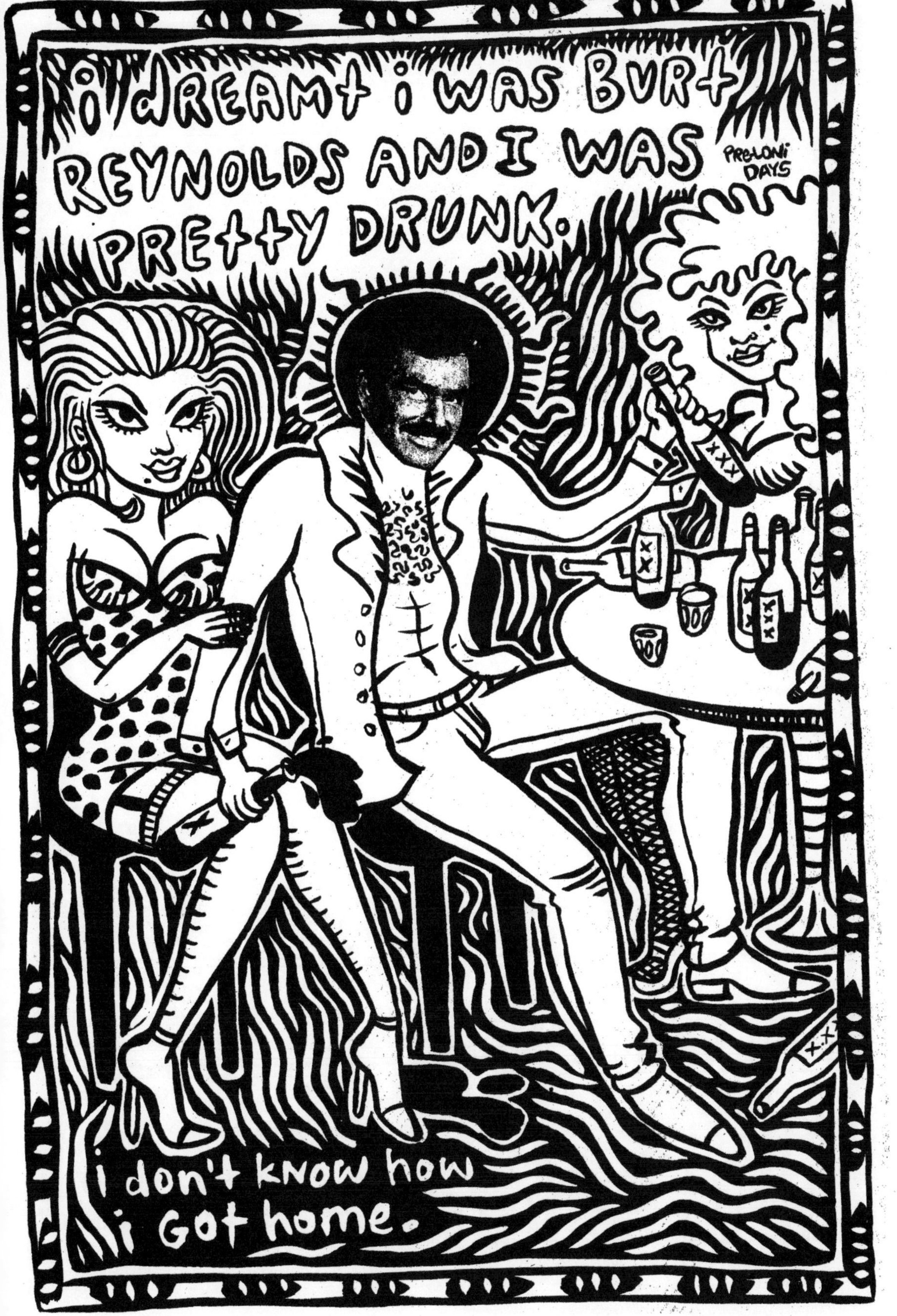
i dreamt i was Burt Reynolds and I was pretty drunk.
PRE-LONi DAYS
XXX
i don't know how i Got home.

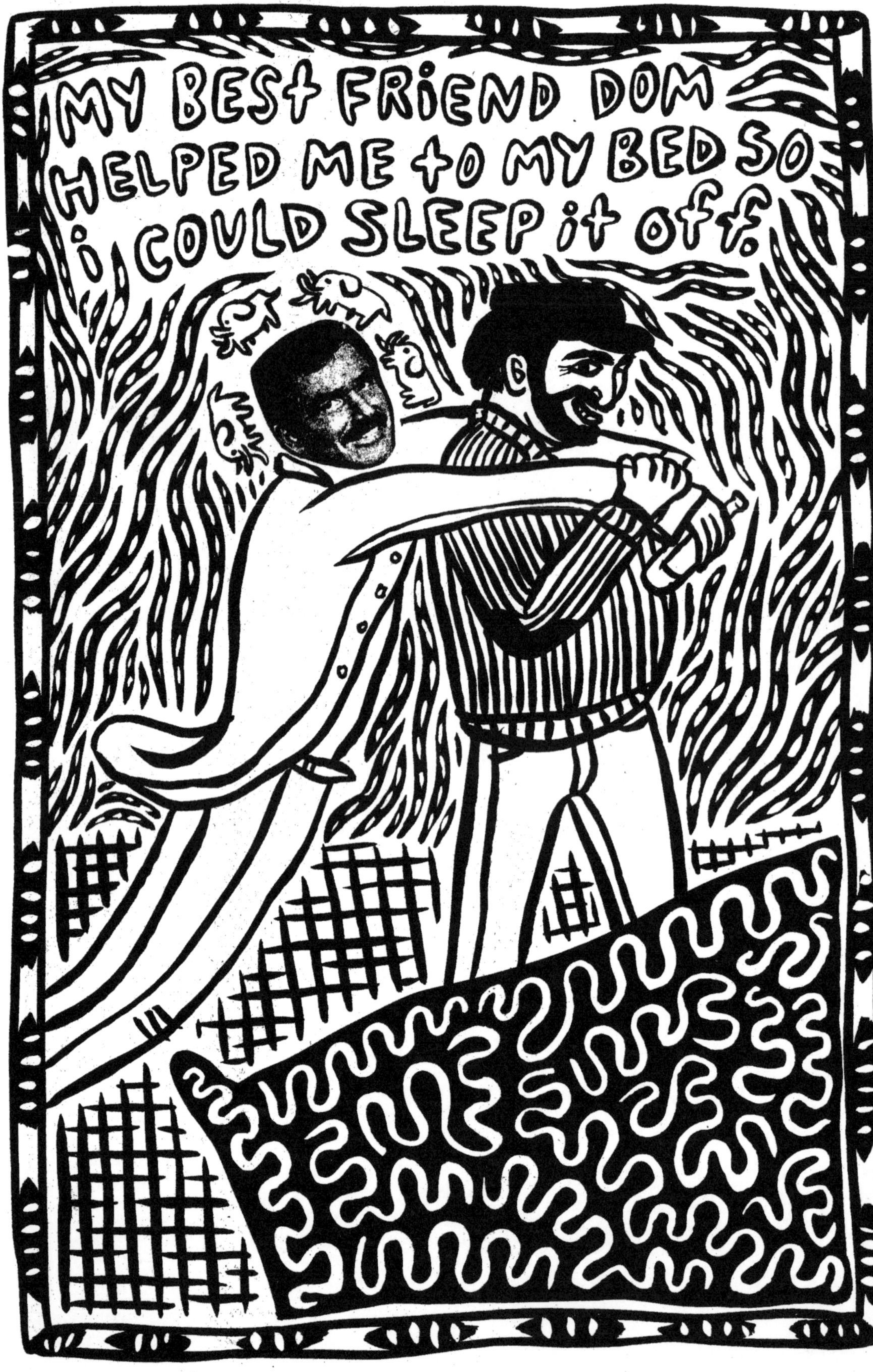
MY BEST FRIEND DOM HELPED ME TO MY BED SO i COULD SLEEP it off.

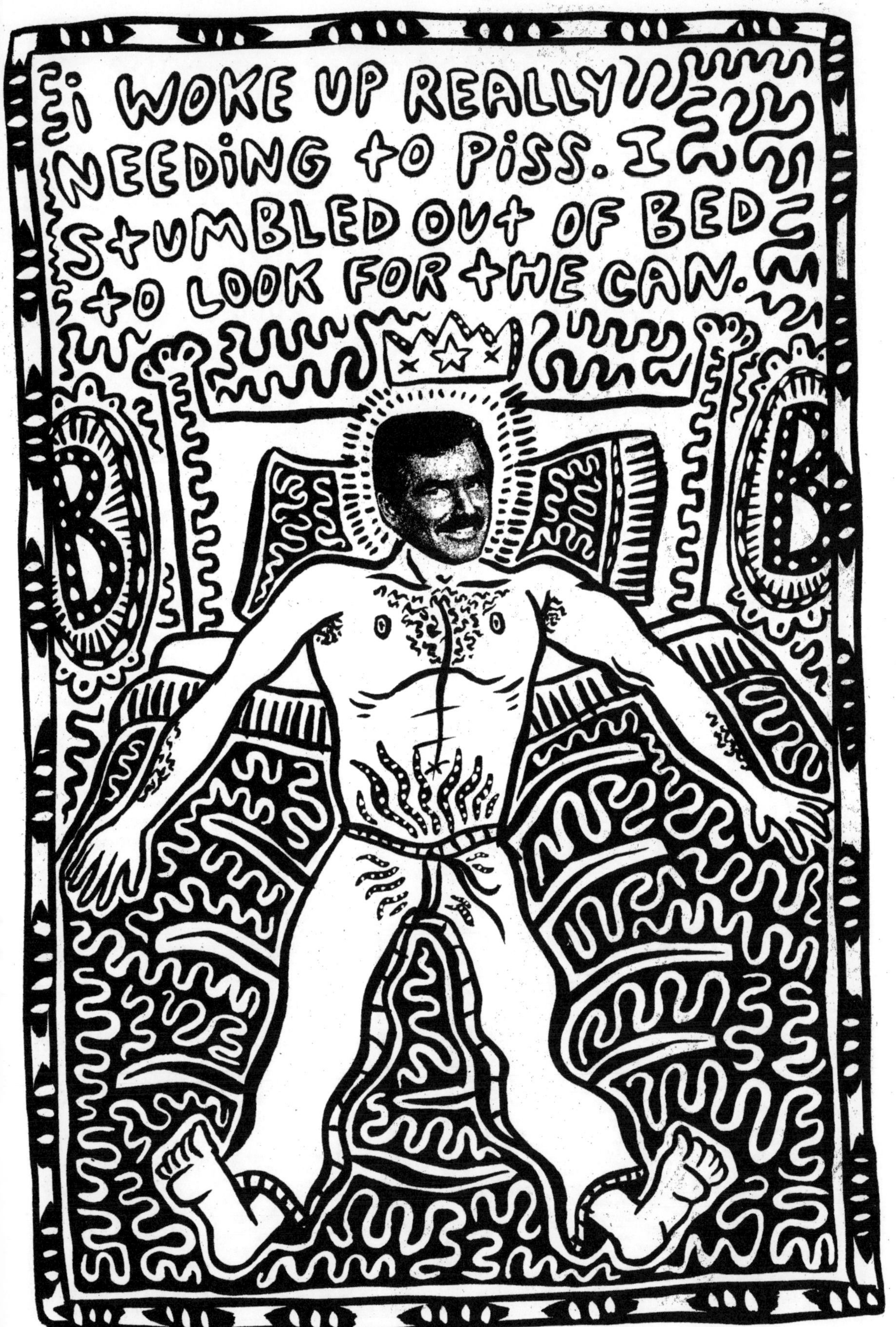
i WOKE UP REALLY NEEDING TO PISS. I STUMBLED OUT OF BED TO LOOK FOR THE CAN.
B
B

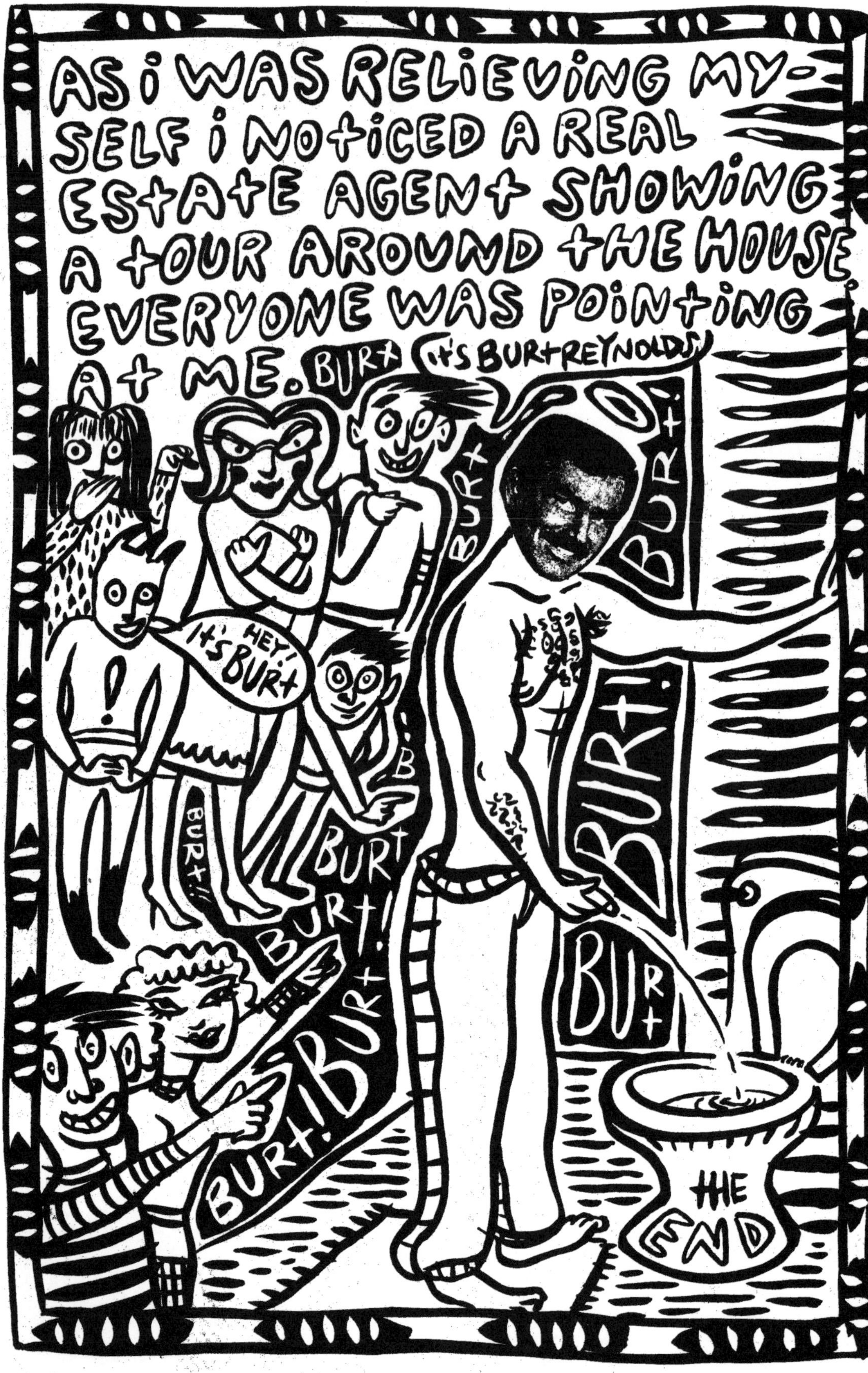
AS I WAS RELIEVING MYSELF I NOTICED A REAL ESTATE AGENT SHOWING A TOUR AROUND THE HOUSE. EVERYONE WAS POINTING AT ME.
BURT
IT'S BURT REYNOLDS
HEY! IT'S BURT
BURT
BURT
BURT
BURT!
BURT!
BURT
BURT!
BURT.
BURT
BURT
THE END

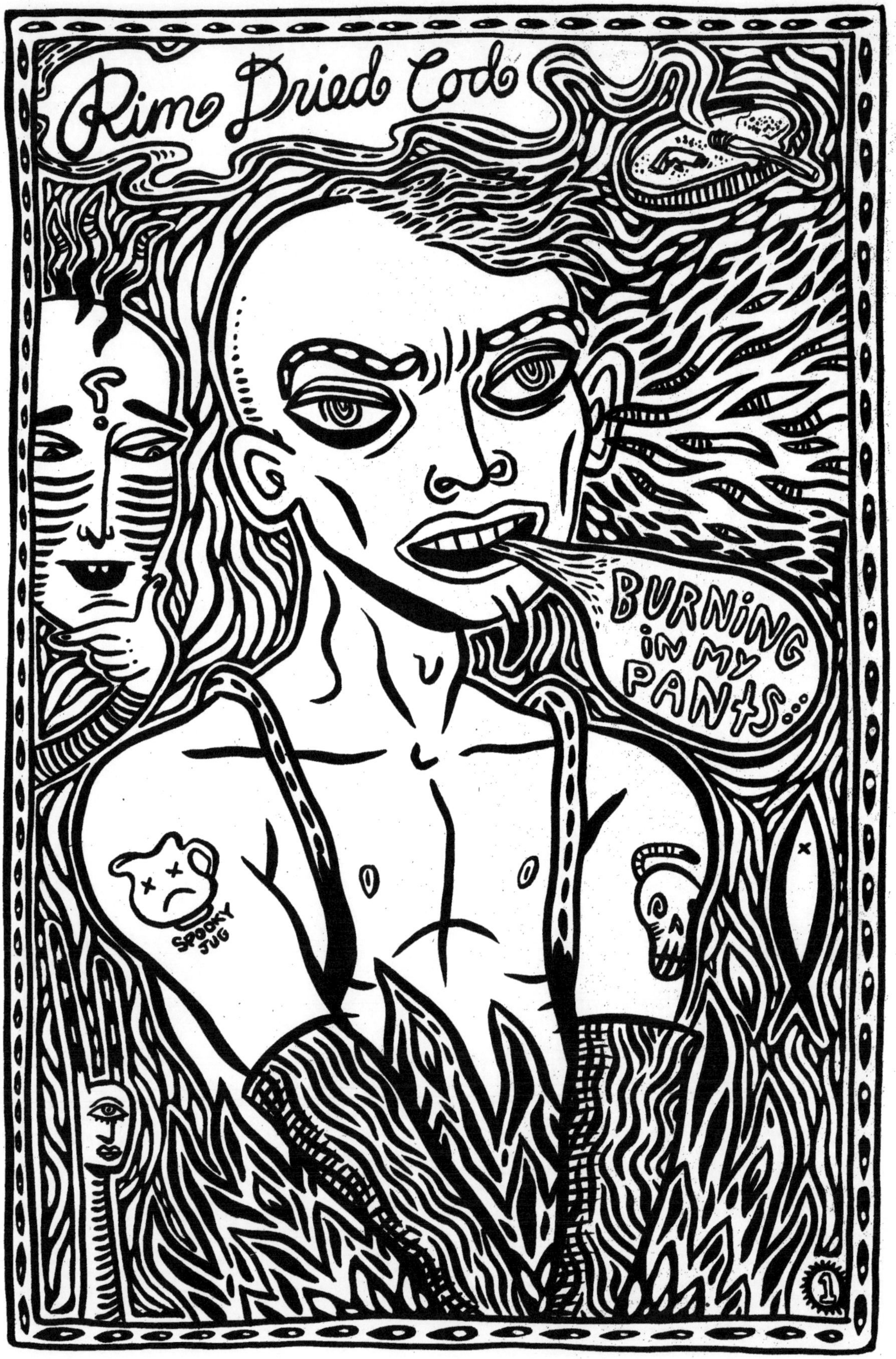

Rime Dried Cod
BURNING IN MY PANTS...
SPOOKY JUG
1

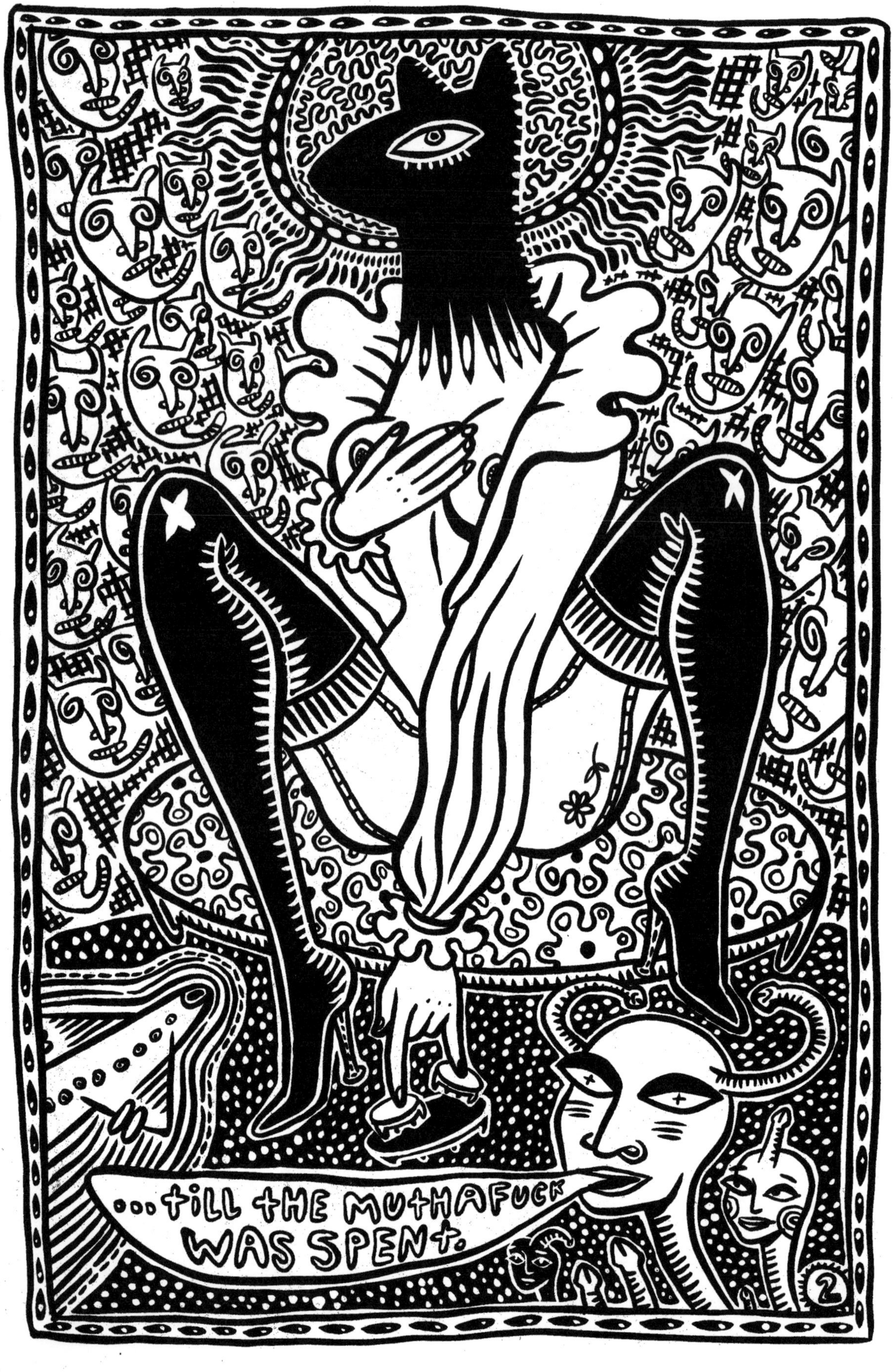
...till the muthafuck
WAS SPENT.
2

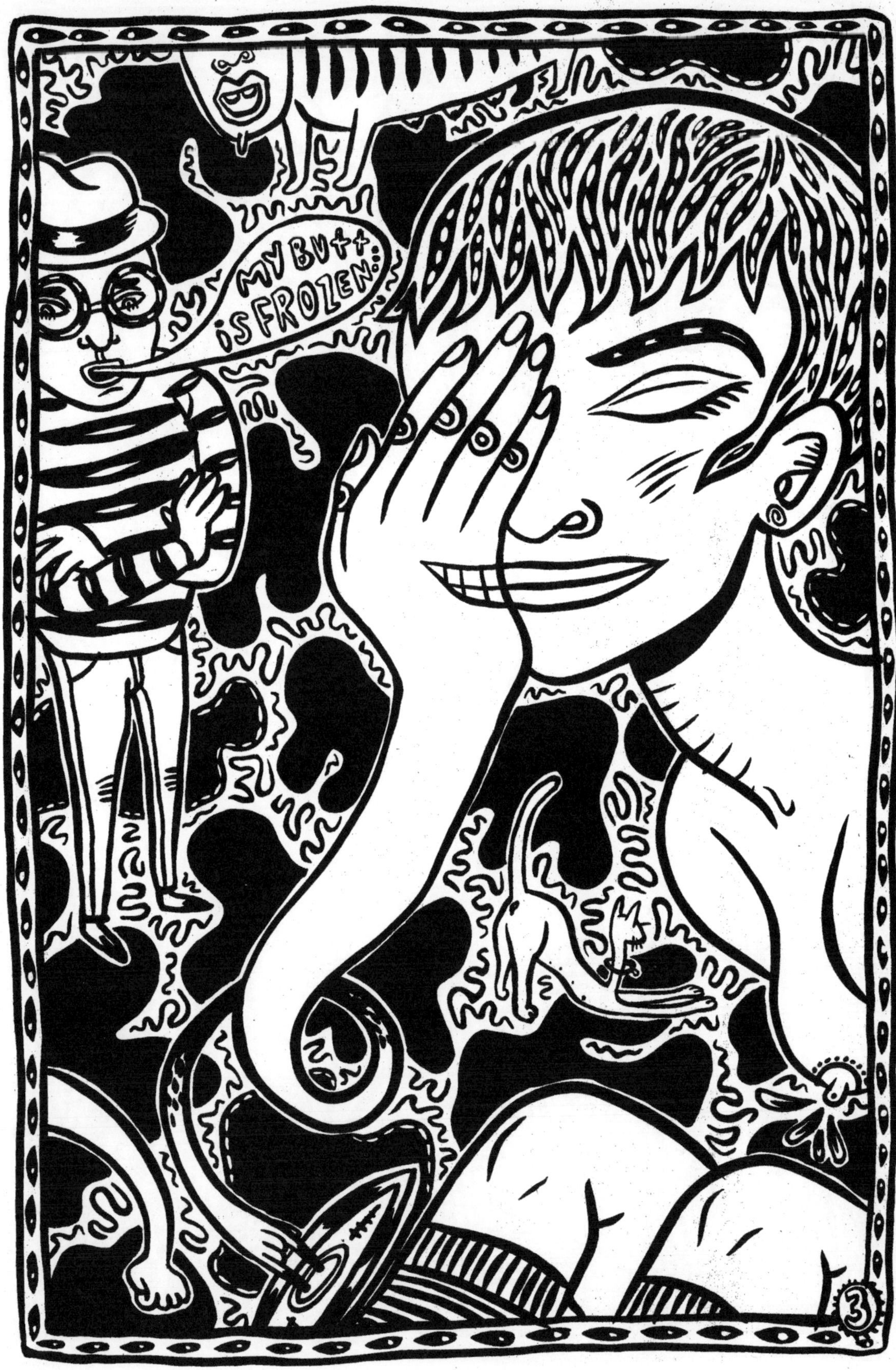
MY BUTT IS FROZEN...
3

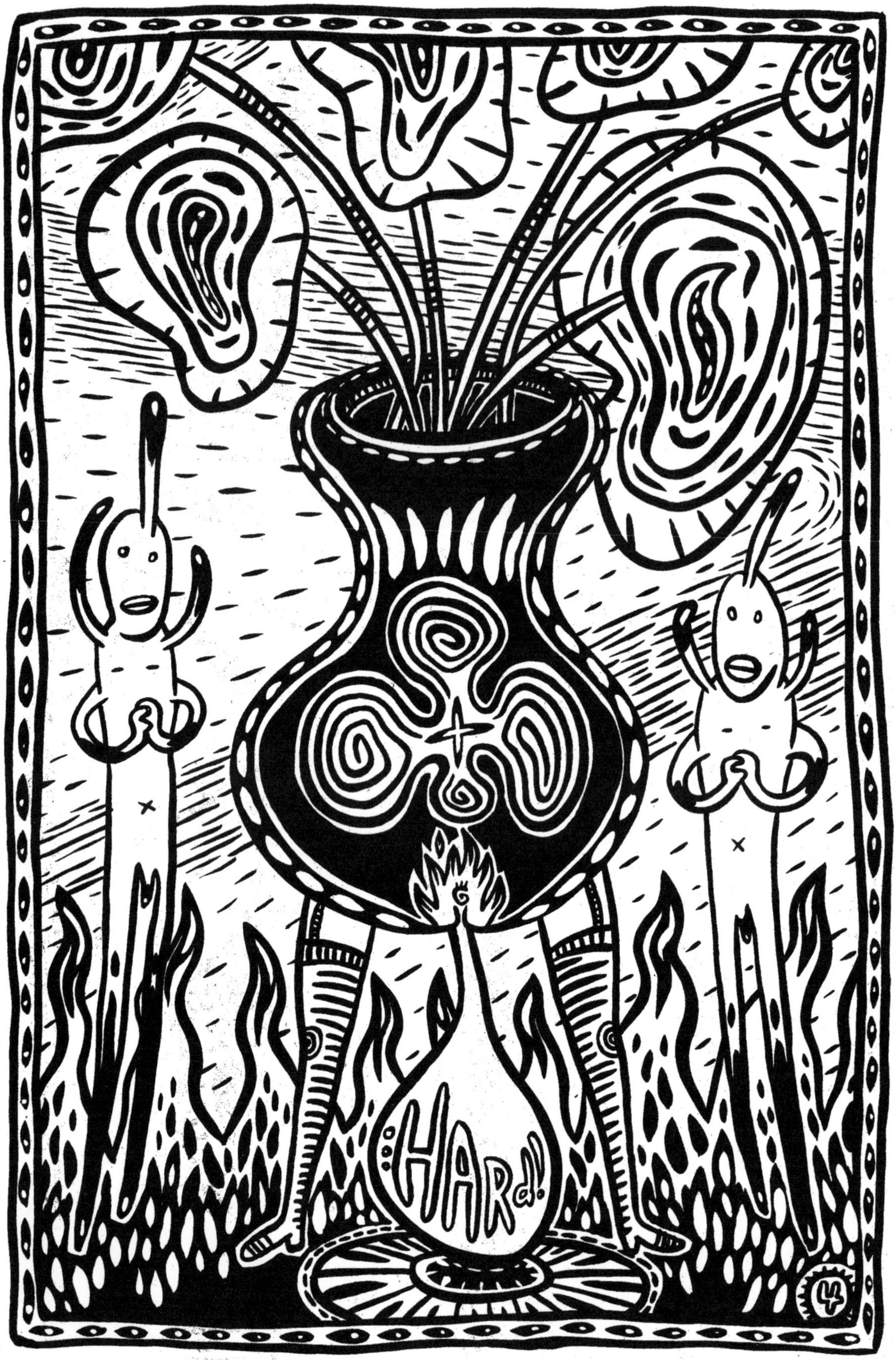
HARd!

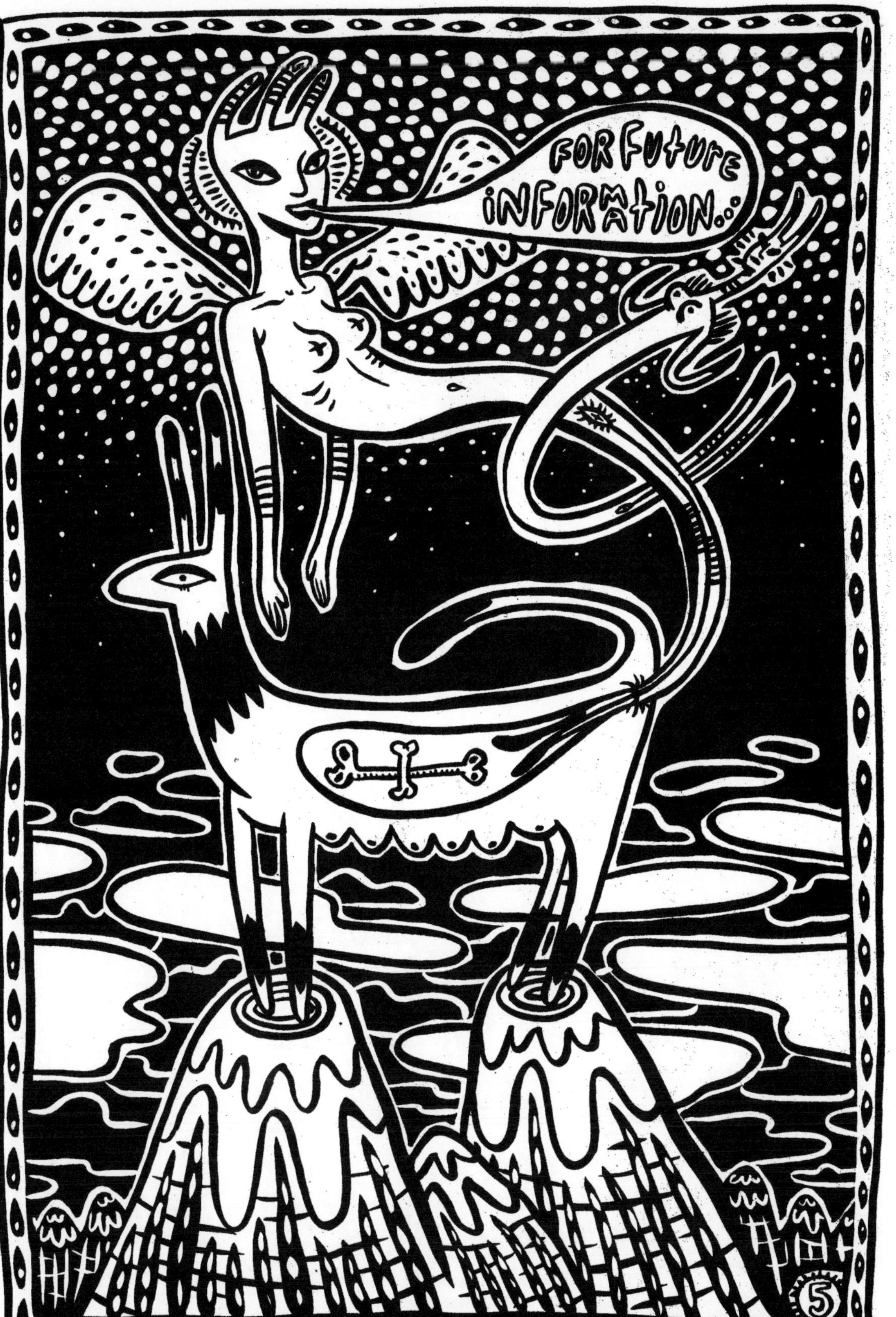
FOR FUTURE INFORMATION...
5

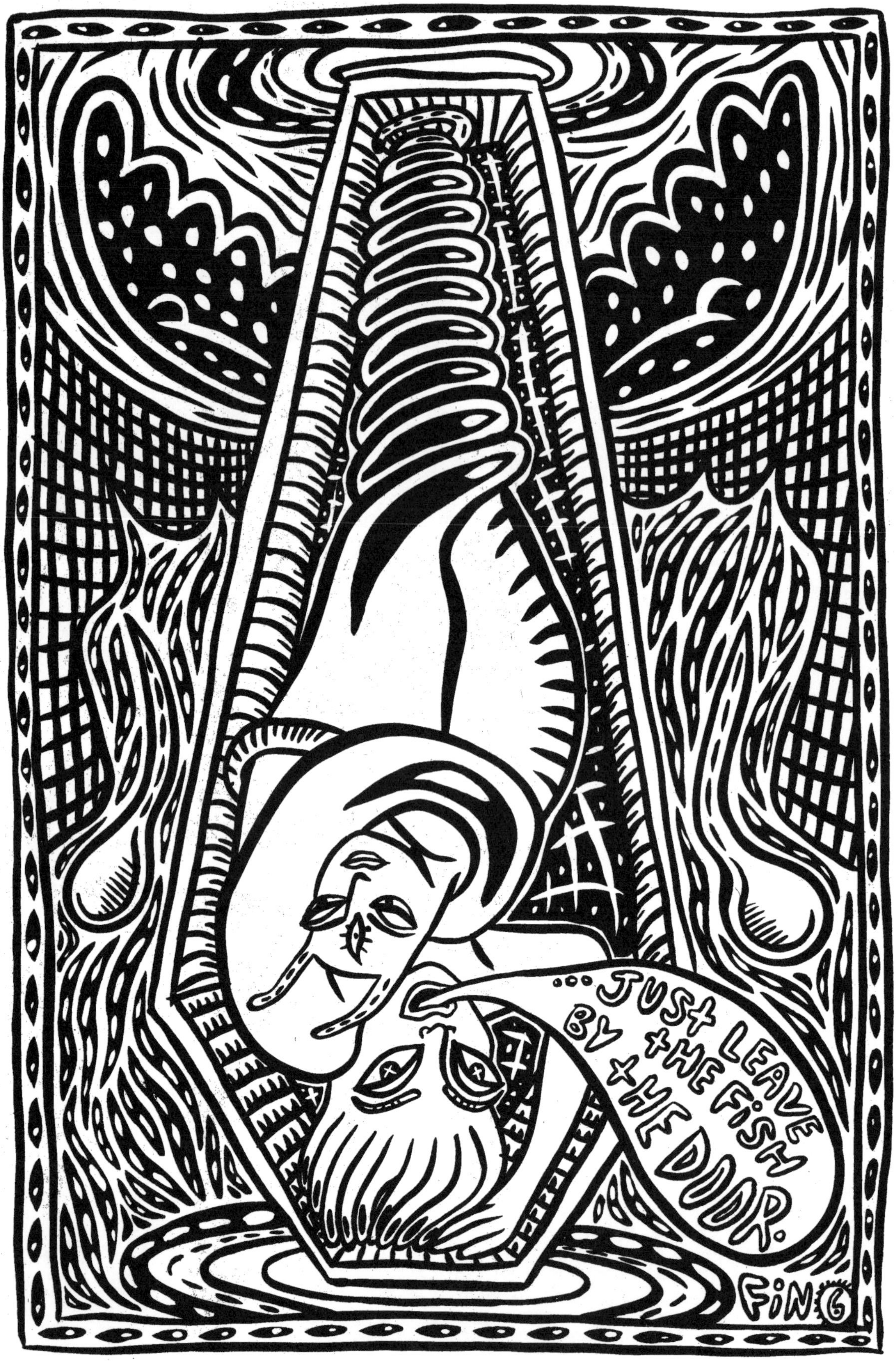
...JUST LEAVE BY THE FISH THE DOOR.
FiNG

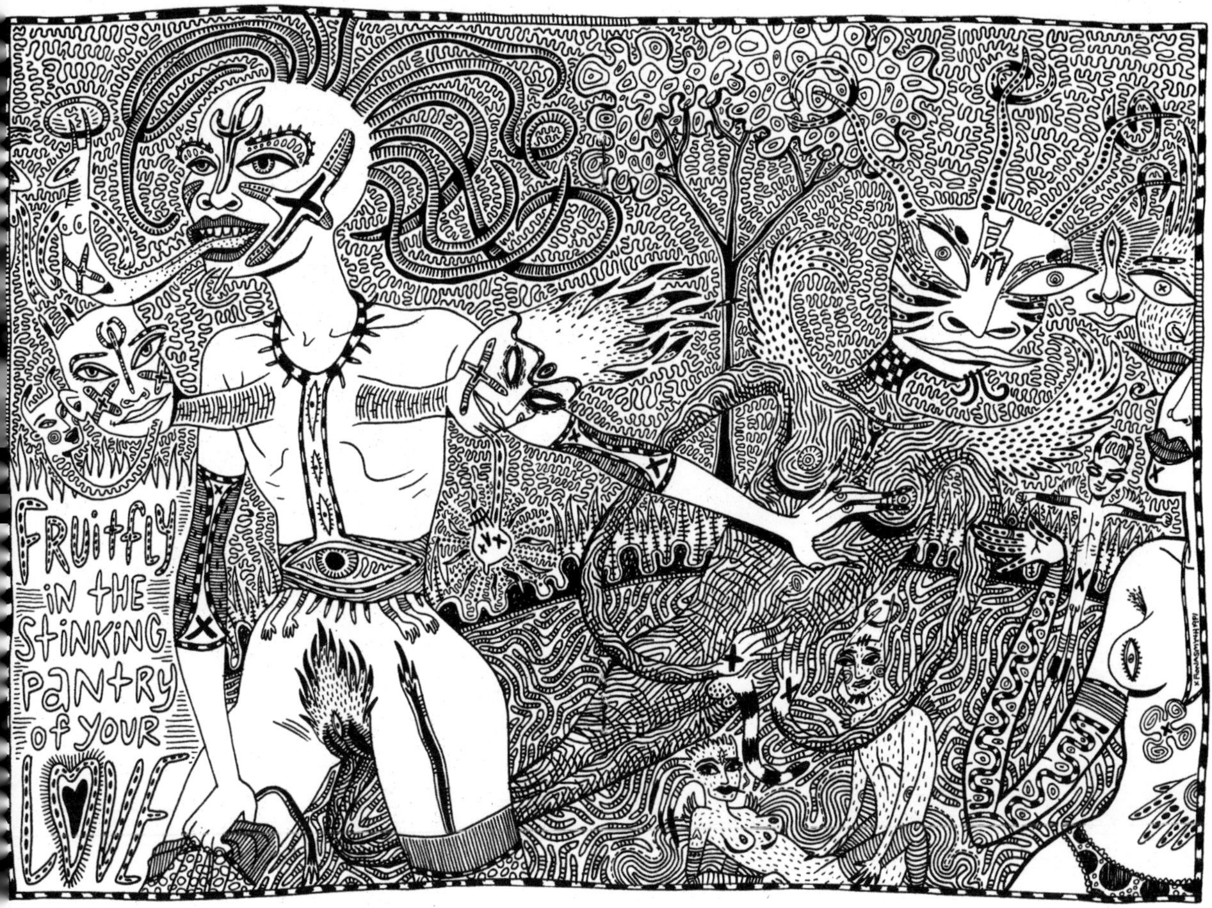
Fruitfly
in the
stinking
pantry
of your
LOVE

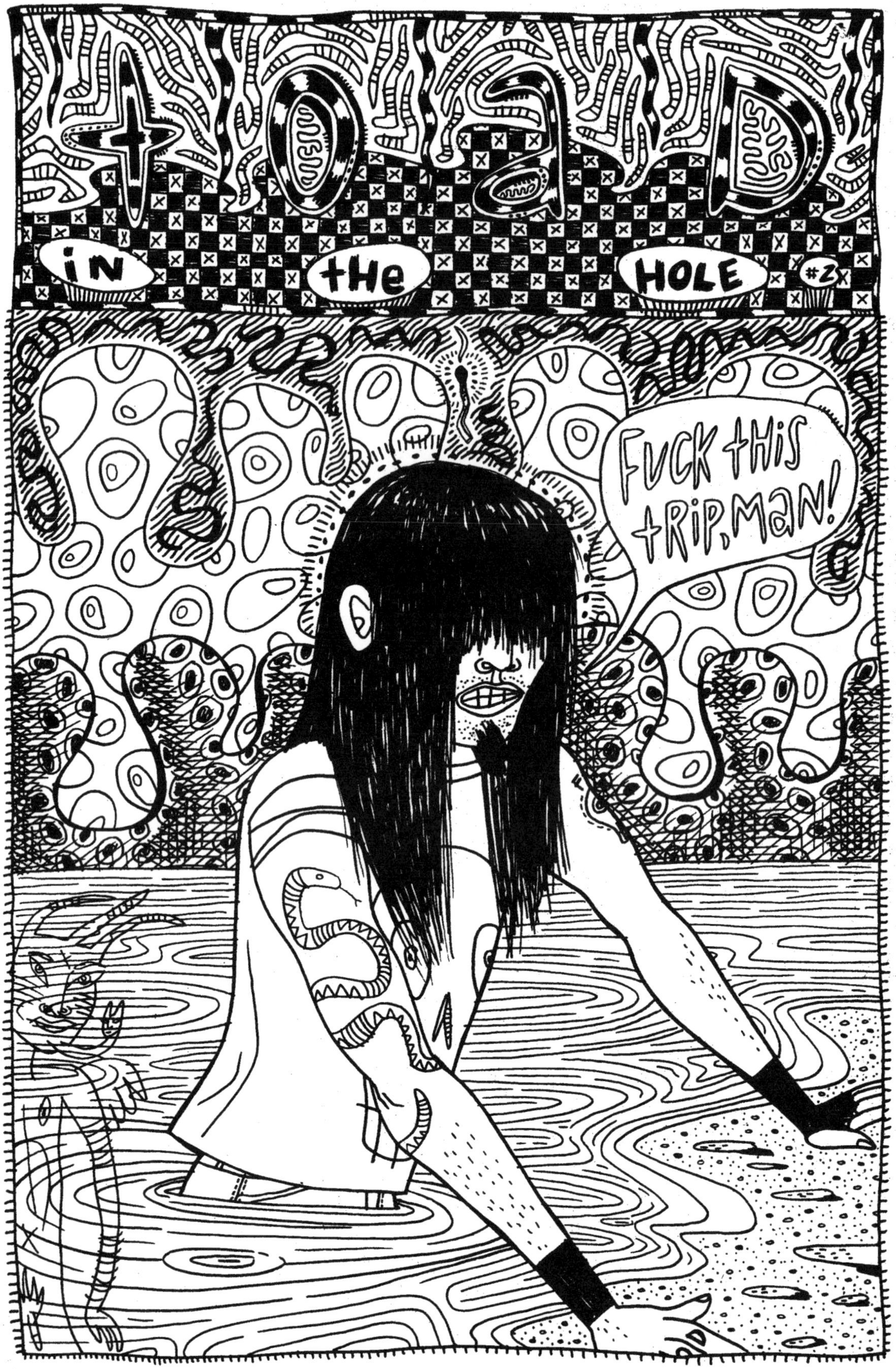
toaD
in tHe HOLE #2
FUCK tHiS tRip, MAN!

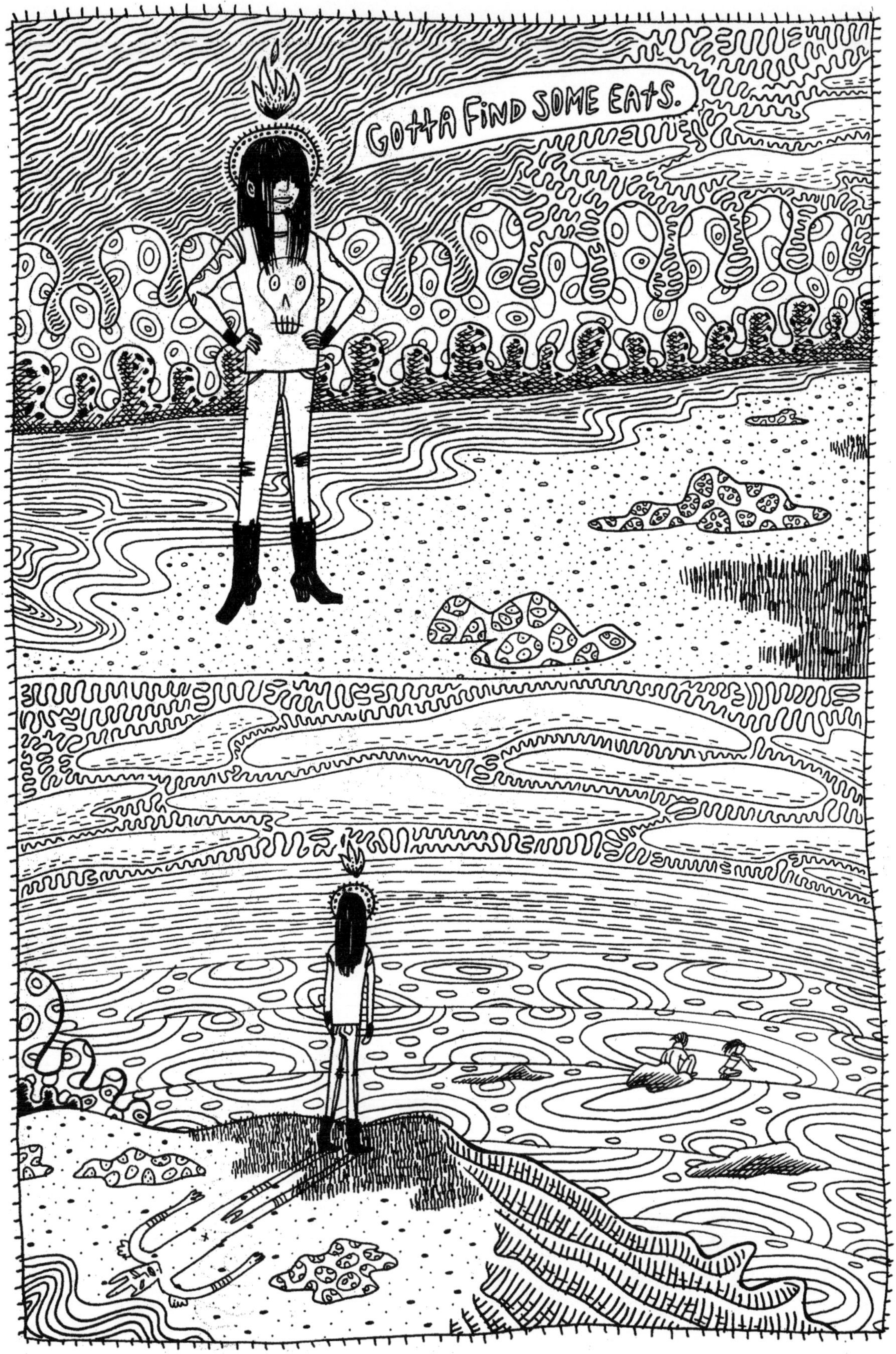

GOTTA FIND SOME EATS.

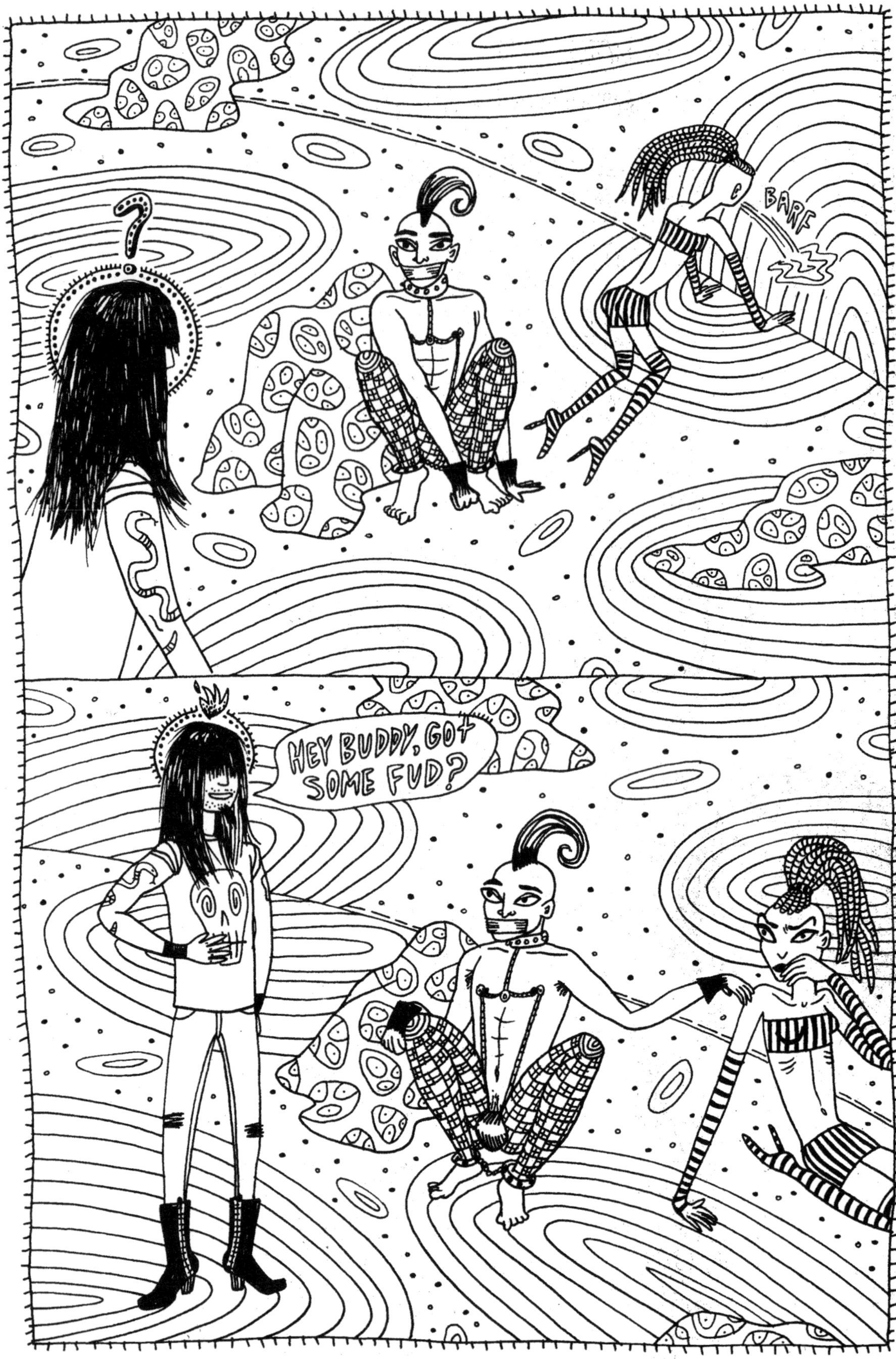
?
BARF
HEY BUDDY, GOT SOME FUD?

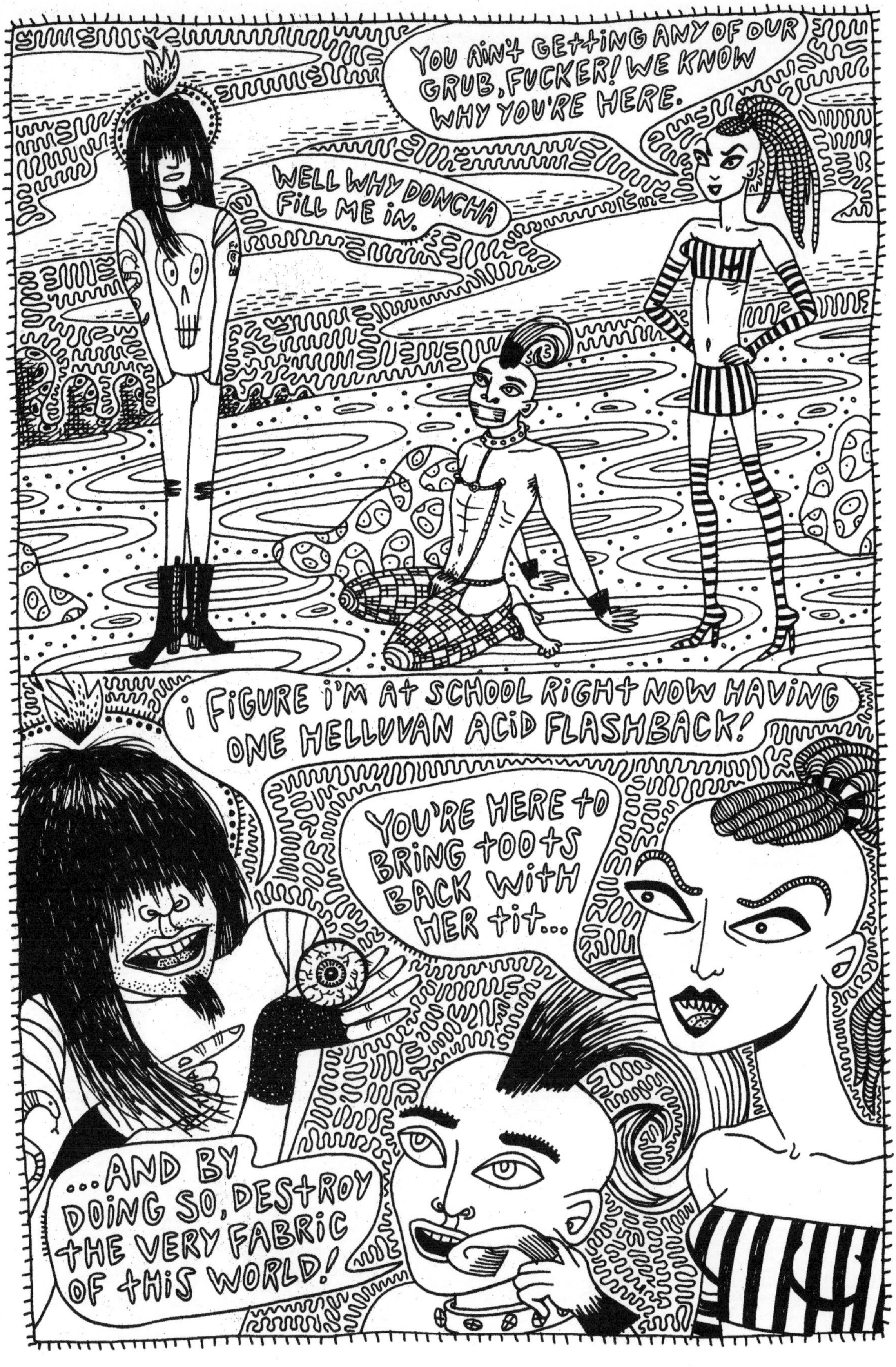
YOU AIN'T GETTING ANY OF OUR GRUB, FUCKER! WE KNOW WHY YOU'RE HERE.
WELL WHY DONCHA FILL ME IN.
I FIGURE I'M AT SCHOOL RIGHT NOW HAVING ONE HELLUVAN ACID FLASHBACK!
YOU'RE HERE TO BRING TOOTS BACK WITH HER TIT...
...AND BY DOING SO, DESTROY THE VERY FABRIC OF THIS WORLD!

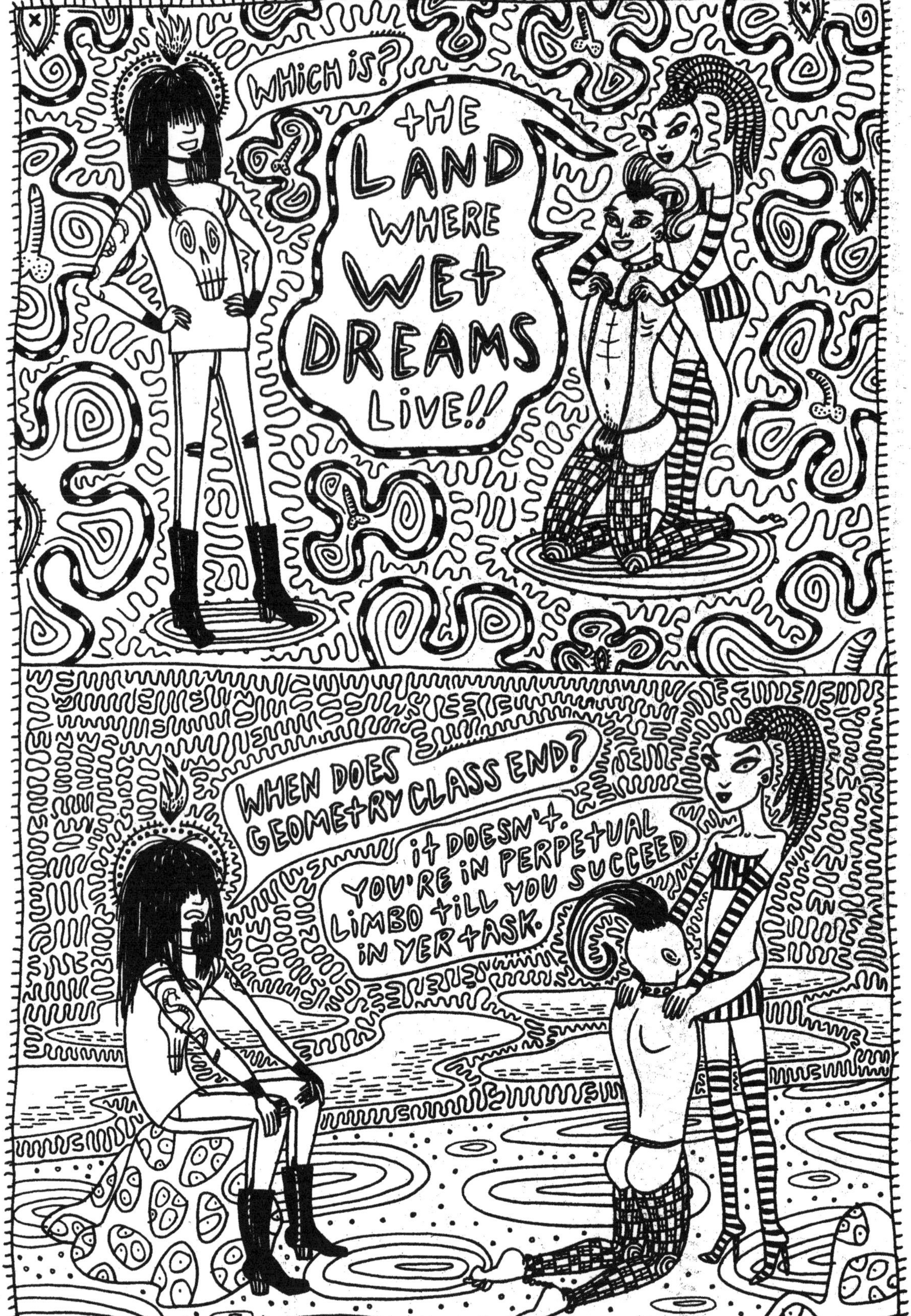
WHICH IS?
THE LAND WHERE WET DREAMS LIVE!!
WHEN DOES GEOMETRY CLASS END?
IT DOESN'T. YOU'RE IN PERPETUAL LIMBO TILL YOU SUCCEED IN YER TASK.

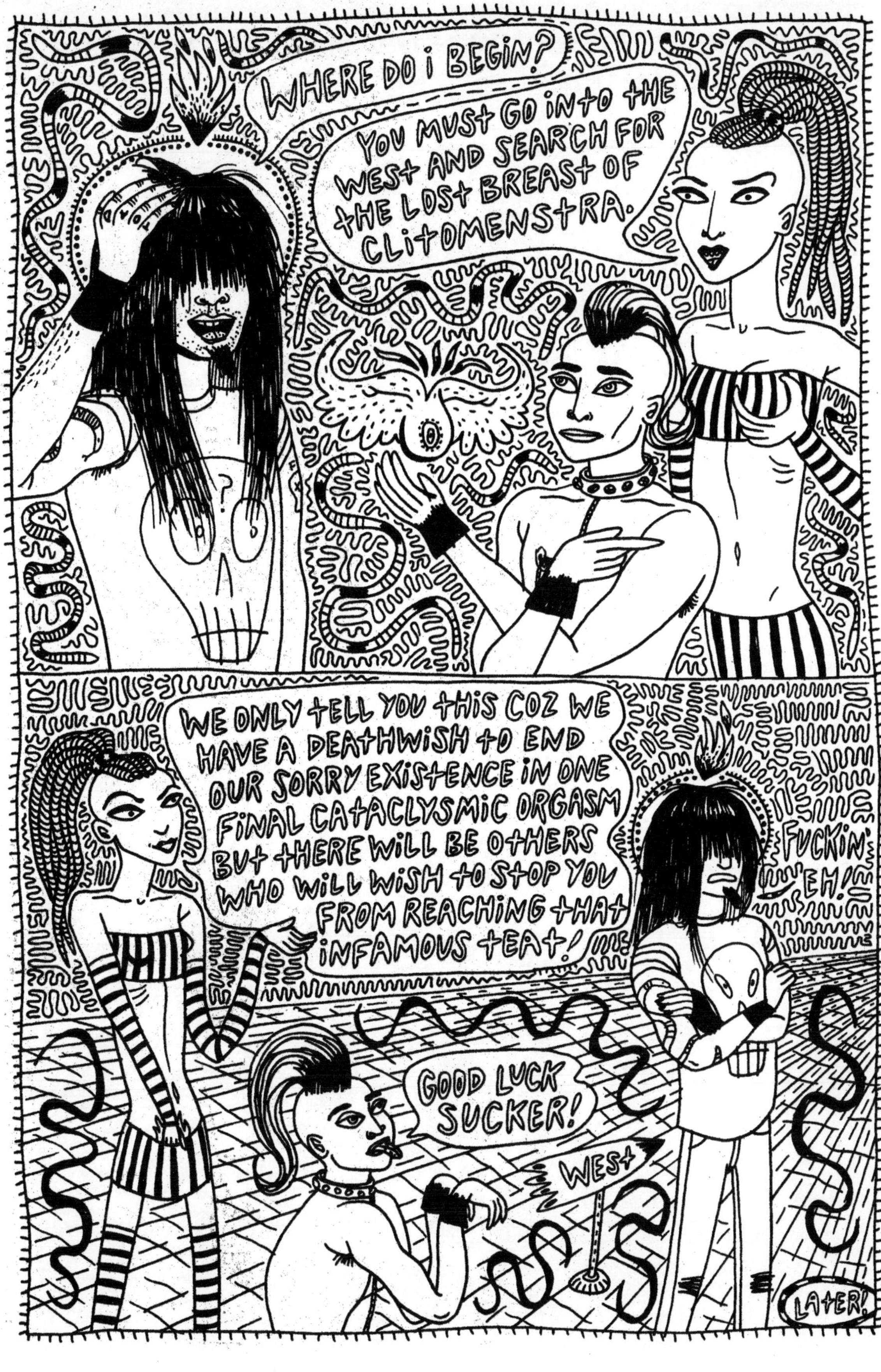

WHERE DO i BEGIN?
YOU MUST GO iNTO THE WEST AND SEARCH FOR THE LOST BREAST OF CLITOMENSTRA.
WE ONLY TELL YOU THIS COZ WE HAVE A DEATHWISH TO END OUR SORRY EXISTENCE IN ONE FINAL CATACLYSMIC ORGASM BUT THERE WILL BE OTHERS WHO WILL WISH TO STOP YOU FROM REACHING THAT INFAMOUS TEAT!
FUCKIN' EH!
GOOD LUCK SUCKER!
WEST
LATER!

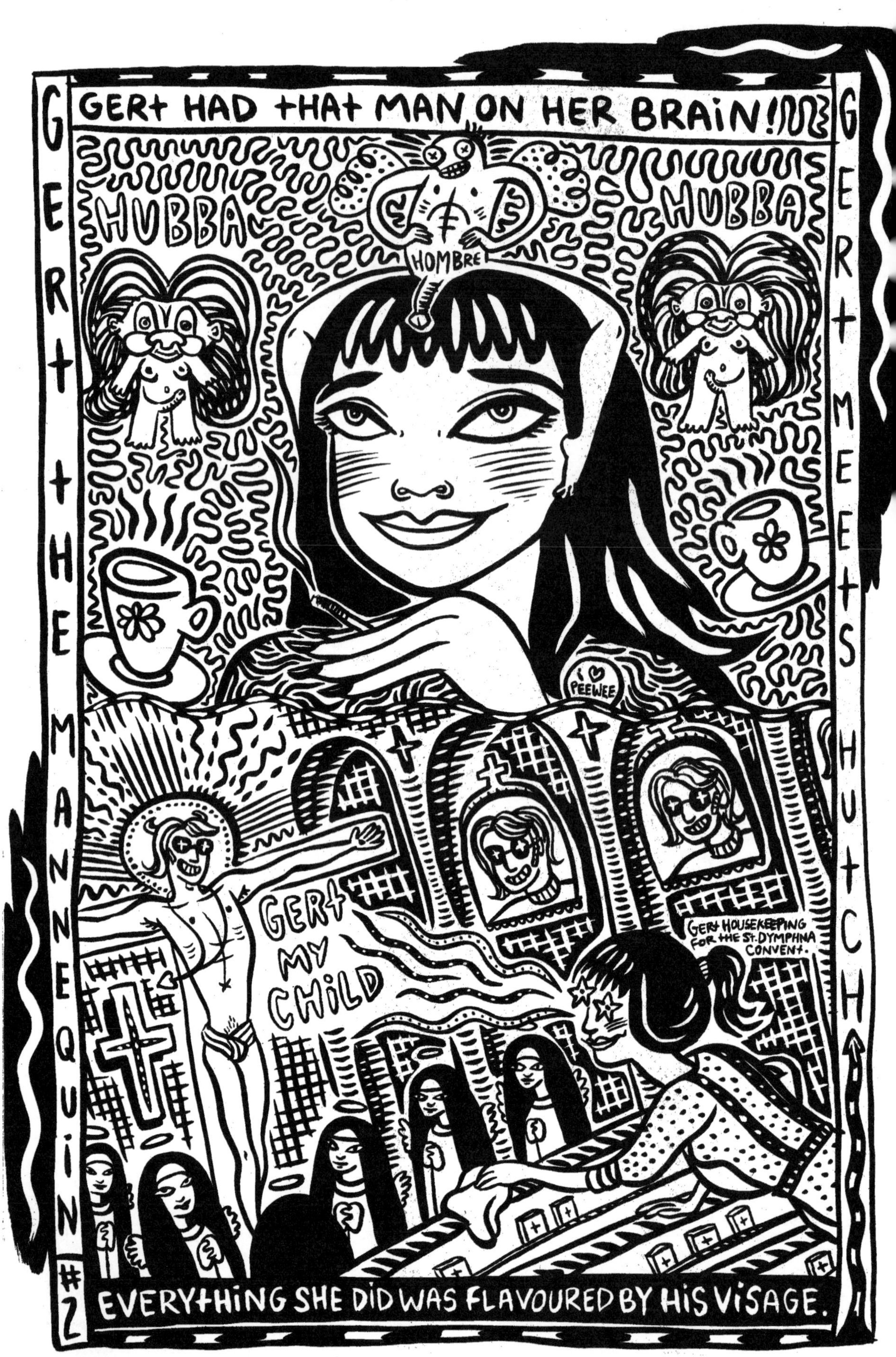
GERT HAD THAT MAN ON HER BRAIN!
GERT THE MANNEQUIN #2
GERT MEETS HUTCH
HUBBA
HUBBA
HOMBRE
I ♥ PEEWEE
GERT MY CHILD
GERT HOUSEKEEPING FOR THE ST. DYMPHNA CONVENT.
EVERYTHING SHE DID WAS FLAVOURED BY HIS VISAGE.

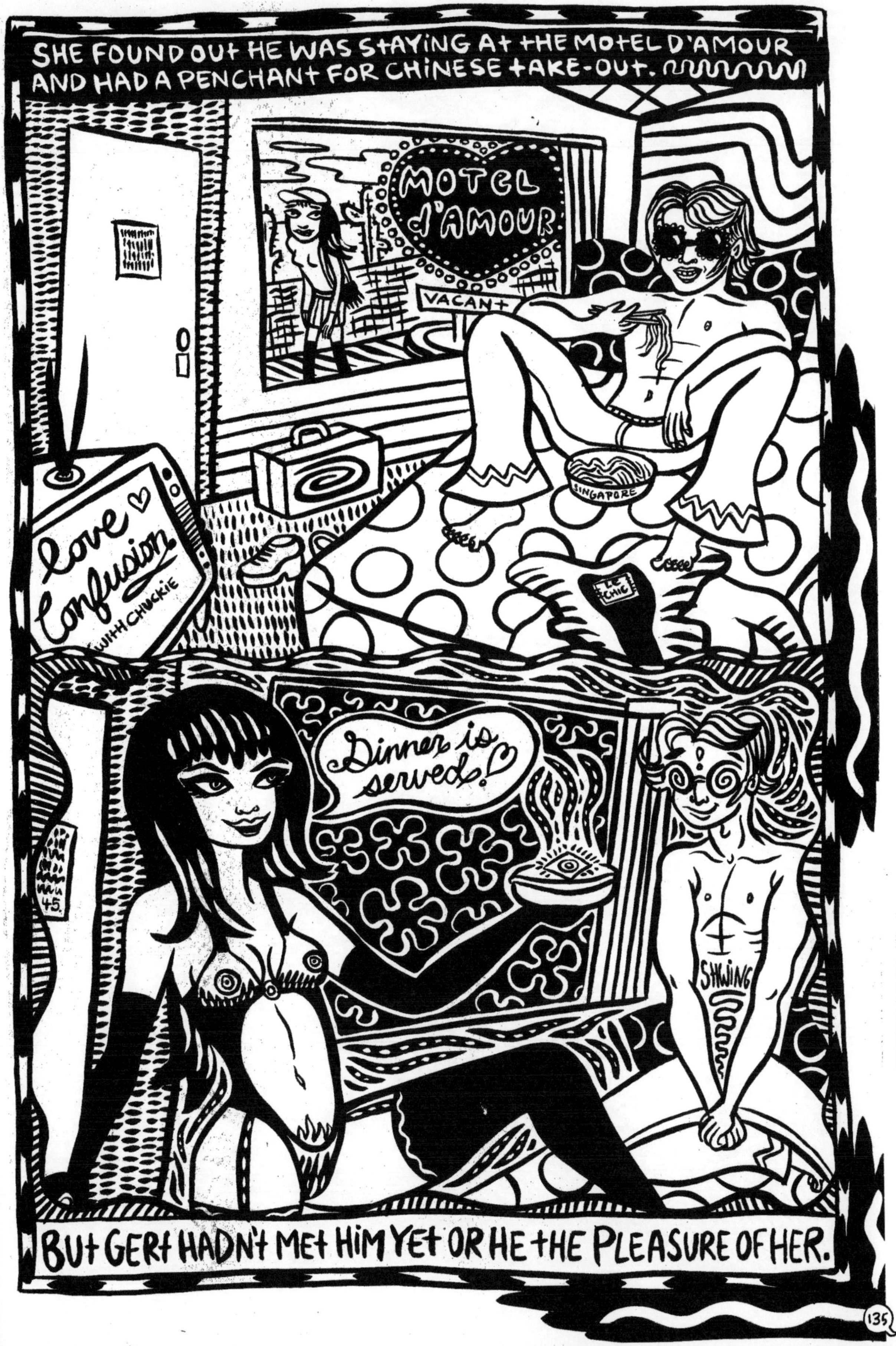
SHE FOUND OUT HE WAS STAYING AT THE MOTEL D'AMOUR AND HAD A PENCHANT FOR CHINESE TAKE-OUT.
MOTEL d'AMOUR
VACANT
SINGAPORE
LE CHIC
love Confusion
WITH CHUCKIE
Dinner is served!
45.
SHWING
BUT GERT HADN'T MET HIM YET OR HE THE PLEASURE OF HER.

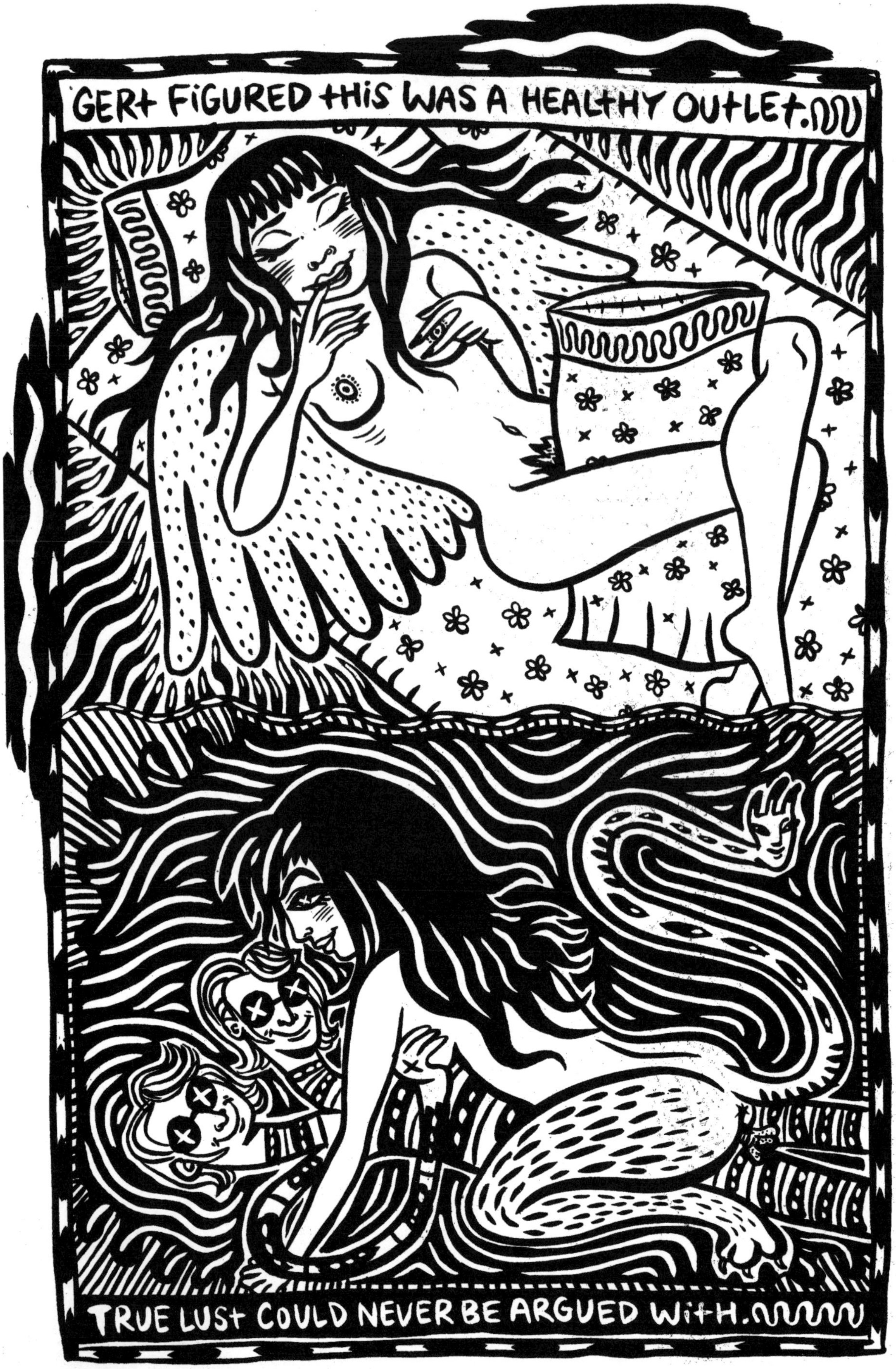
GERT FIGURED THIS WAS A HEALTHY OUTLET.
TRUE LUST COULD NEVER BE ARGUED WITH.

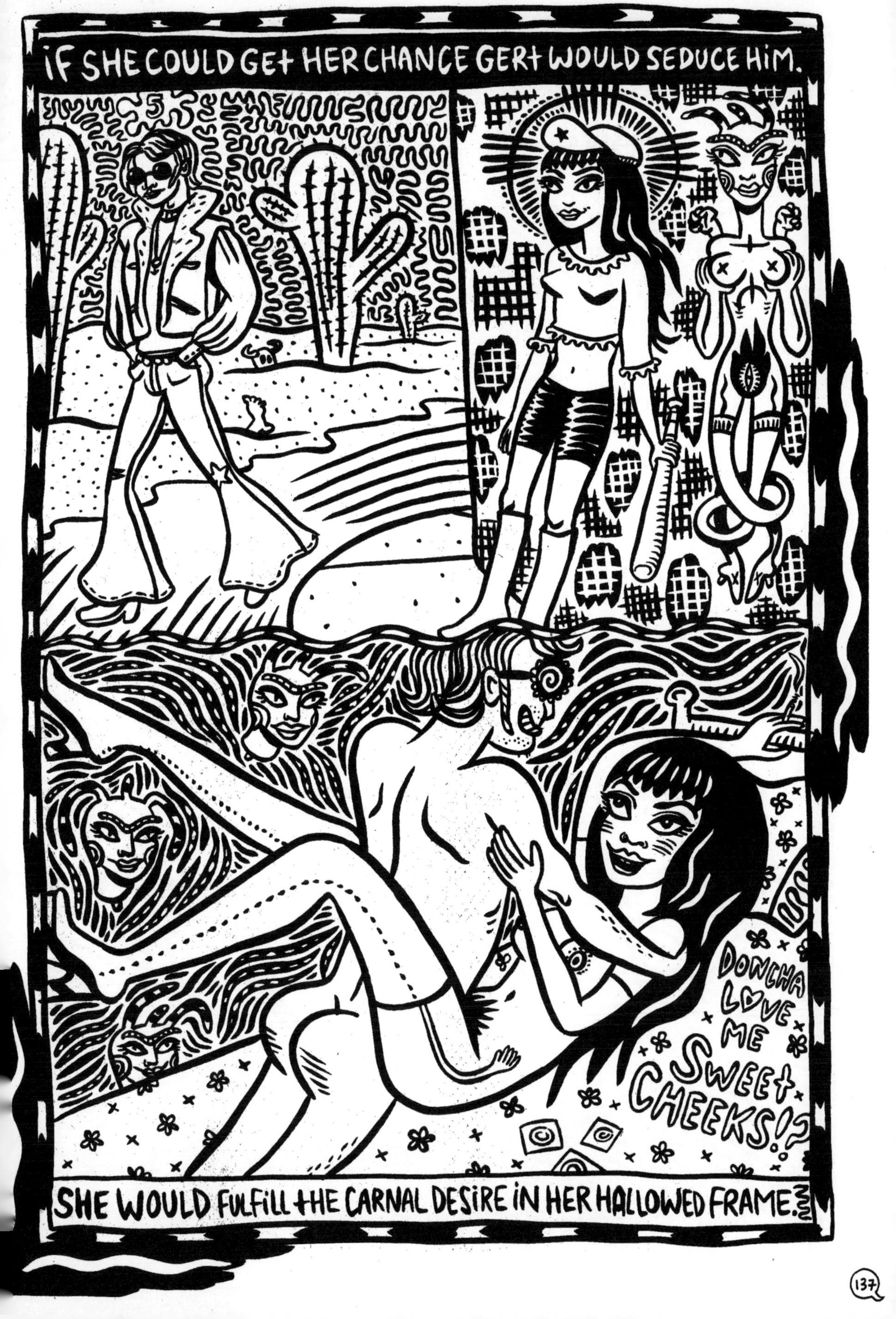
IF SHE COULD GET HER CHANCE GERT WOULD SEDUCE HIM.
DONCHA LOVE ME SWEET CHEEKS!?
SHE WOULD FULFILL THE CARNAL DESIRE IN HER HALLOWED FRAME.

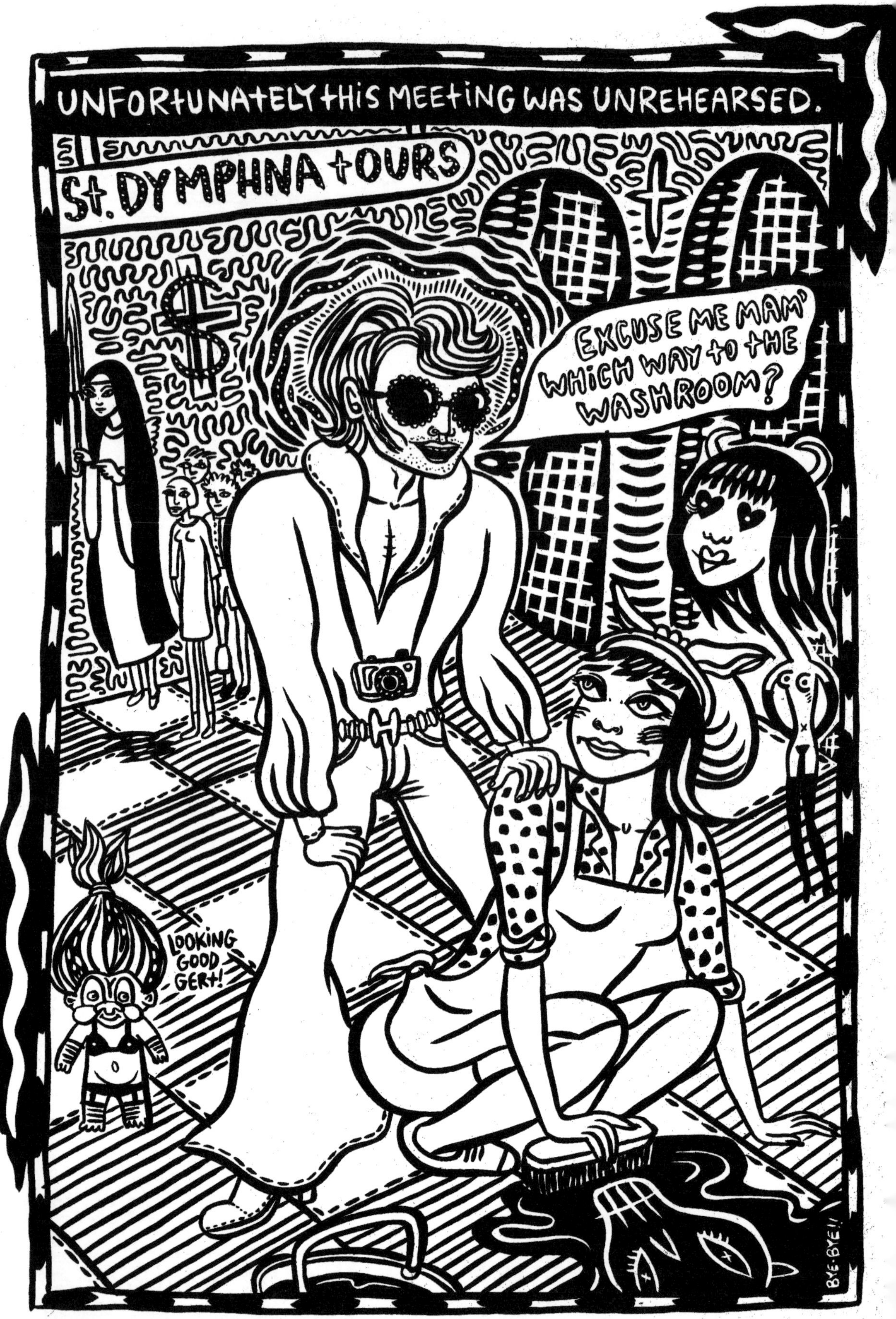
UNFORTUNATELY THIS MEETING WAS UNREHEARSED.
St. DYMPHNA TOURS
EXCUSE ME MAM' WHICH WAY TO THE WASHROOM?
LOOKING GOOD GERT!
BYE-BYE!!

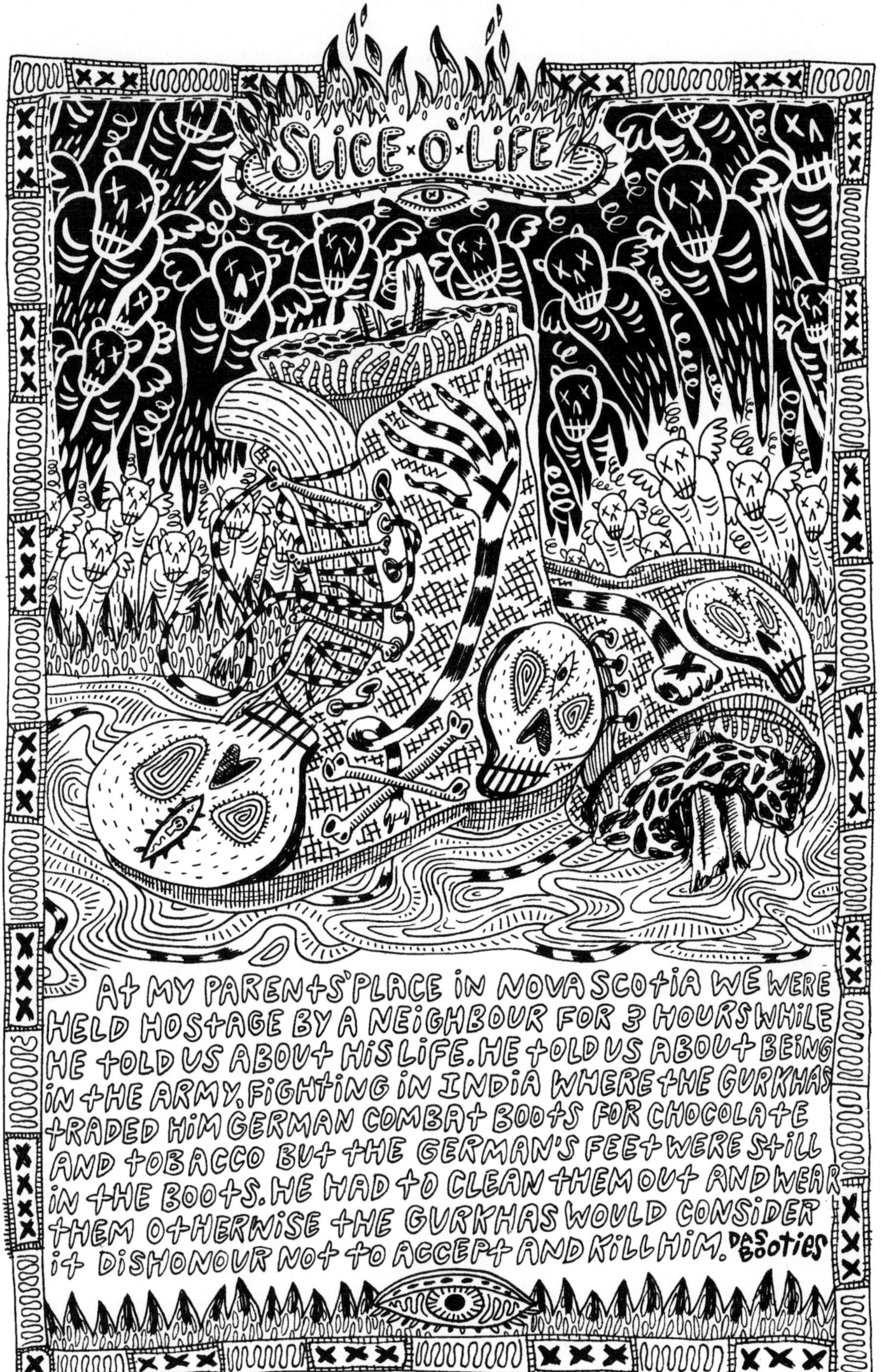
SLICE O LIFE
AT MY PARENTS' PLACE IN NOVA SCOTIA WE WERE HELD HOSTAGE BY A NEIGHBOUR FOR 3 HOURS WHILE HE TOLD US ABOUT HIS LIFE. HE TOLD US ABOUT BEING IN THE ARMY, FIGHTING IN INDIA WHERE THE GURKHAS TRADED HIM GERMAN COMBAT BOOTS FOR CHOCOLATE AND TOBACCO BUT THE GERMAN'S FEET WERE STILL IN THE BOOTS. HE HAD TO CLEAN THEM OUT AND WEAR THEM OTHERWISE THE GURKHAS WOULD CONSIDER IT DISHONOUR NOT TO ACCEPT AND KILL HIM.
DAS BOOTIES

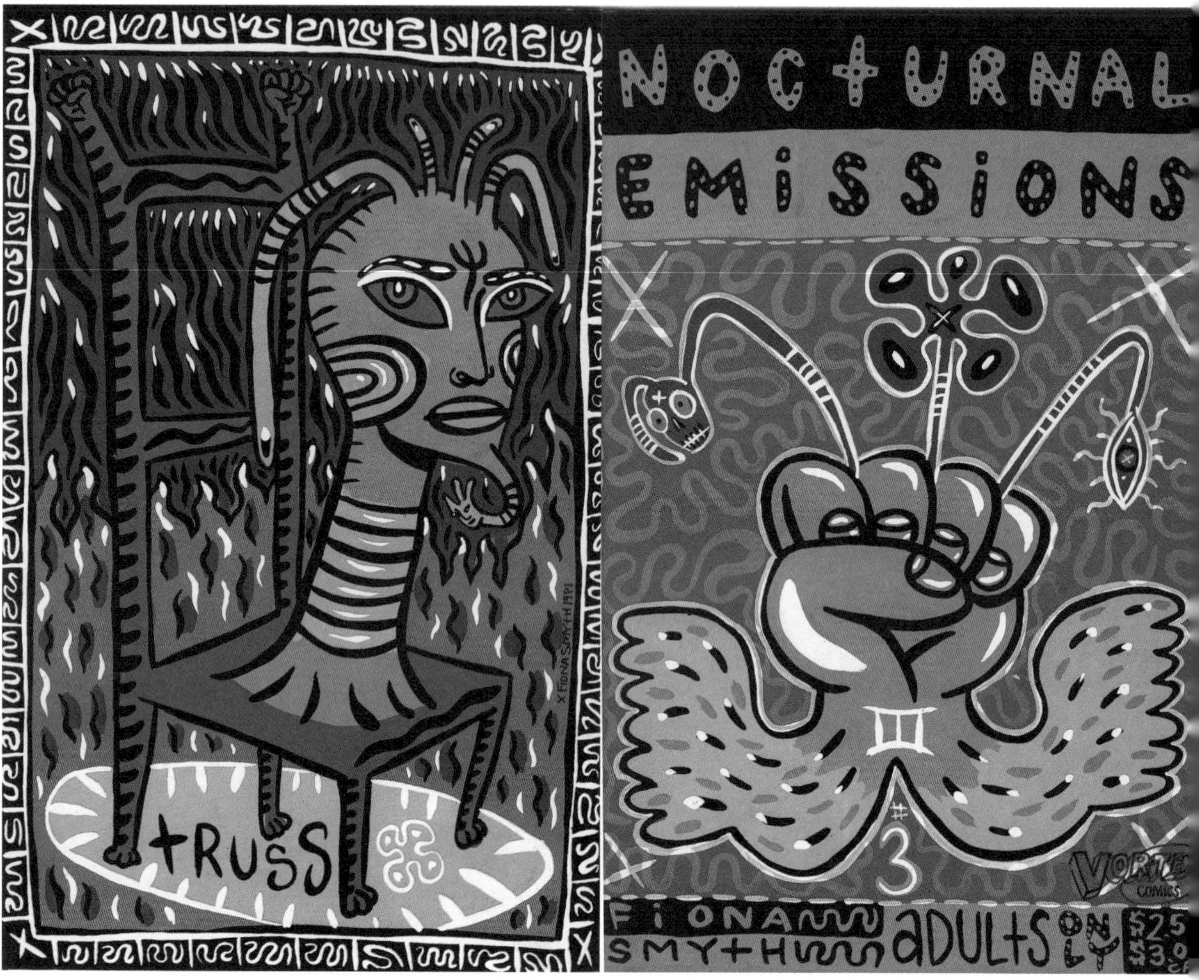
TRUSS
NOCTURNAL
EMISSIONS
#3
VORTEX COMICS
FIONA
SMYTH
ADULTS ONLY

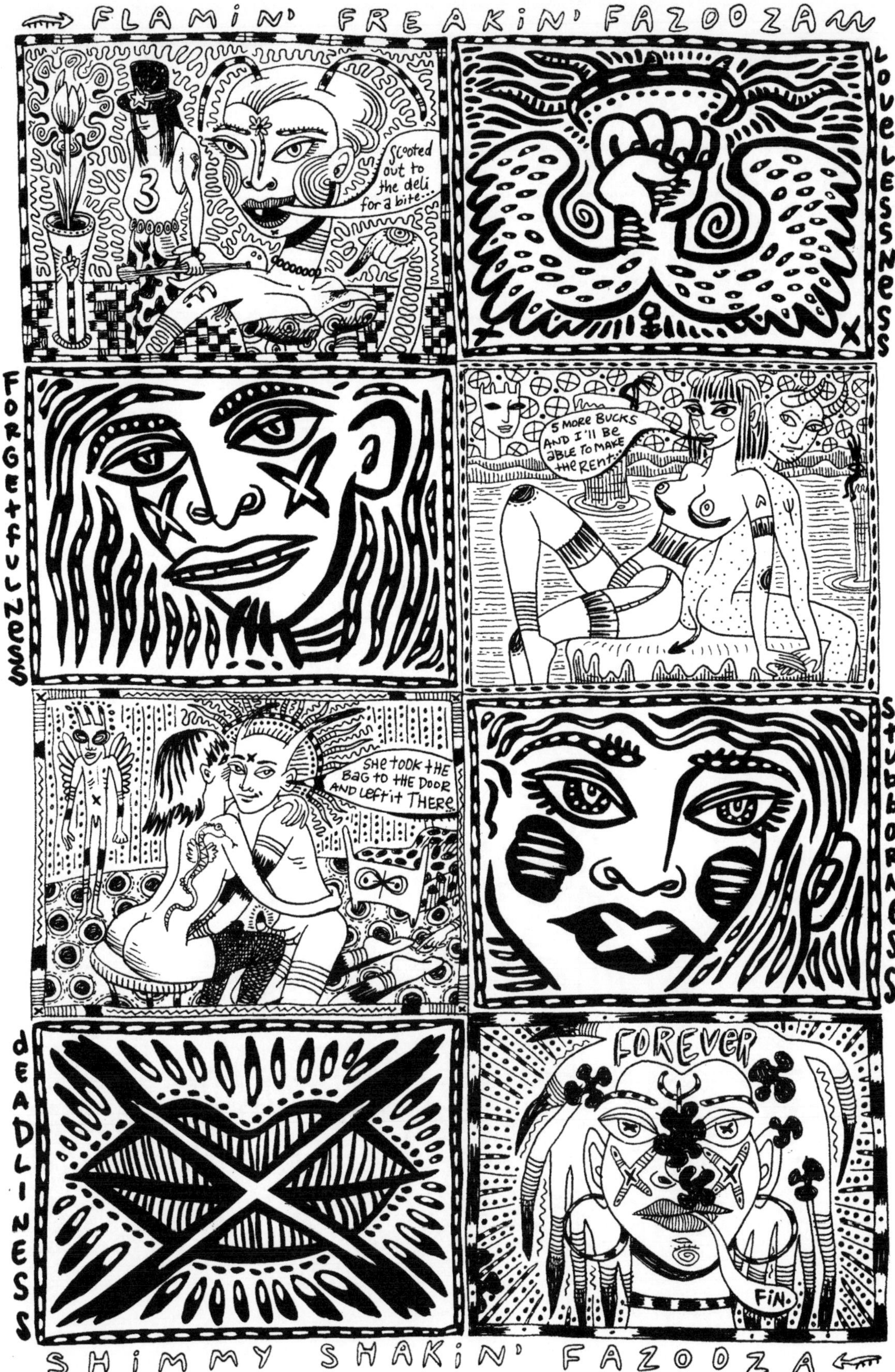
FLAMIN' FREAKIN' FAZOOZA
Scooted out to the deli for a bite
LOVELESSNESS
FORGETFULNESS
5 MORE BUCKS AND I'LL BE ABLE TO MAKE THE RENT
SHE TOOK THE BAG TO THE DOOR AND LEFT IT THERE
STUBBORNESS
DEADLINESS
FOREVER
FIN
SHIMMY SHAKIN' FAZOOZA

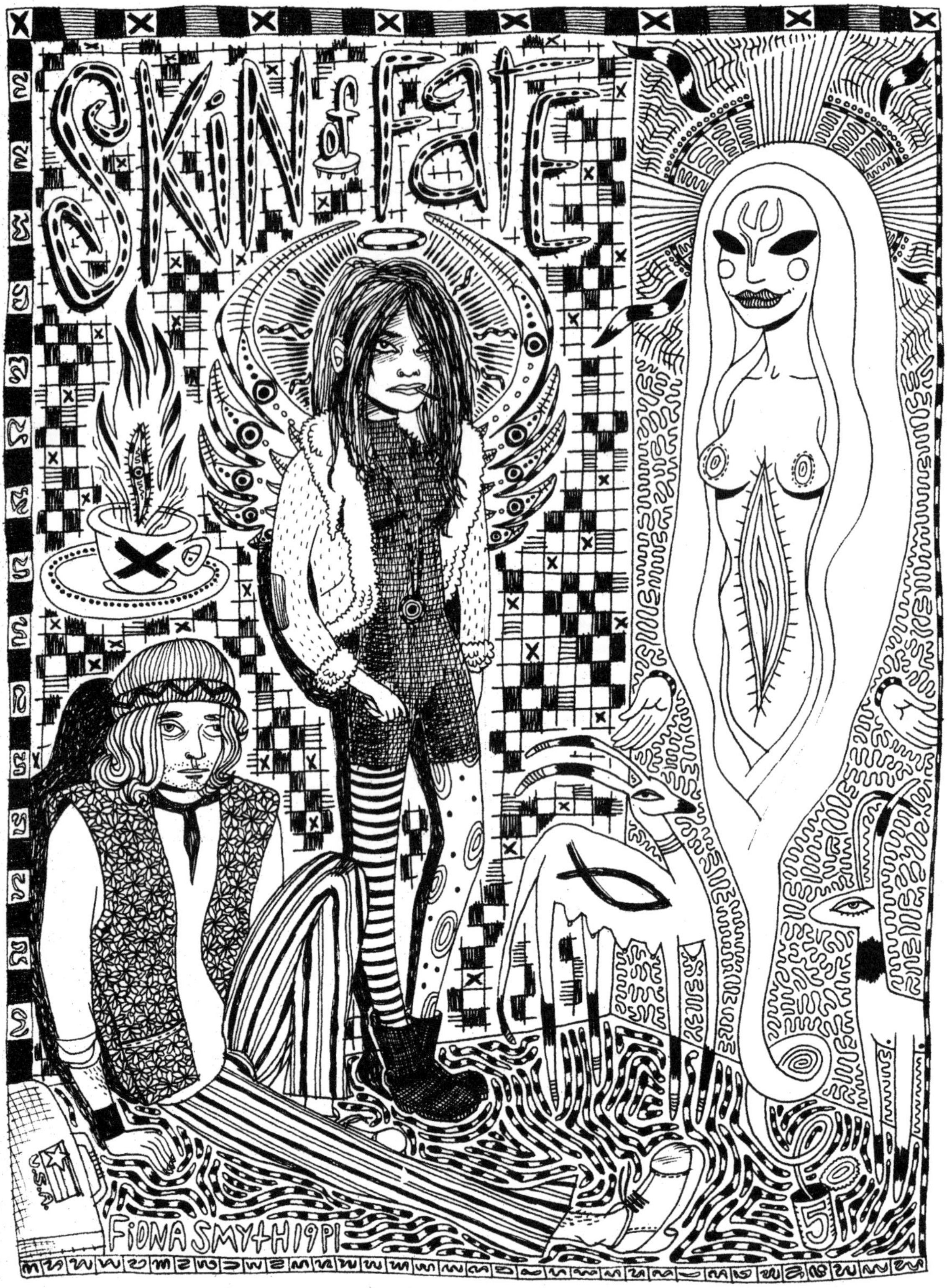
SKIN of FATE
U.S.A.
FIONA SMYTH 1991
5

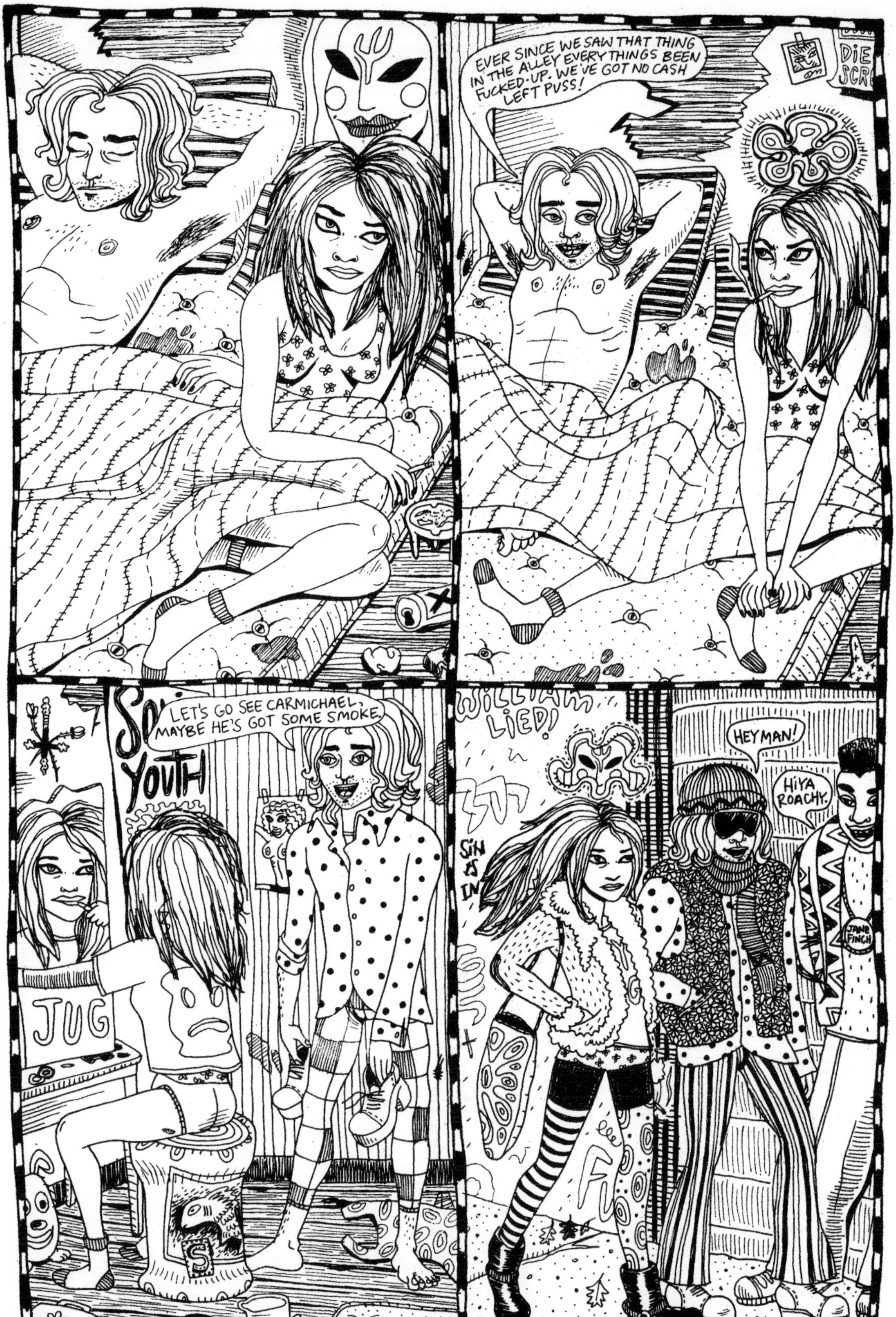
EVER SINCE WE SAW THAT THING IN THE ALLEY EVERYTHINGS BEEN FUCKED-UP. WE'VE GOT NO CASH LEFT PUSS!
DIE
LET'S GO SEE CARMICHAEL, MAYBE HE'S GOT SOME SMOKE.
YOUTH
JUG
WILLIAM LIED!
SIN IS IN
HEYMAN!
HIYA ROACHY.
JANE FINCH

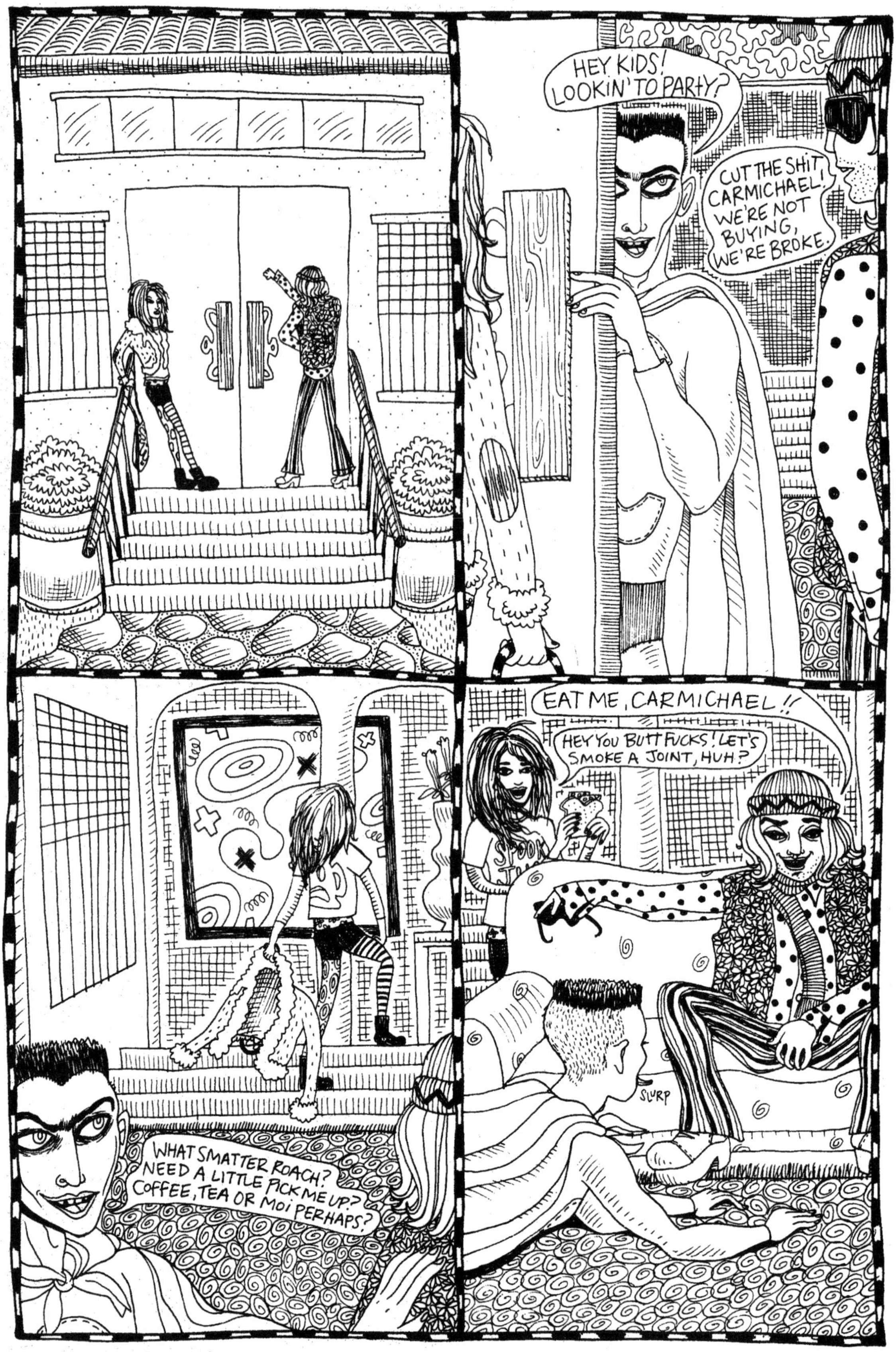
HEY KIDS! LOOKIN' TO PARTY?
CUT THE SHIT CARMICHAEL! WE'RE NOT BUYING, WE'RE BROKE.
WHATSMATTER ROACH? NEED A LITTLE PICK ME UP? COFFEE, TEA OR MOI PERHAPS?
EAT ME, CARMICHAEL!!
HEY YOU BUTT FUCKS! LET'S SMOKE A JOINT, HUH?
SLURP

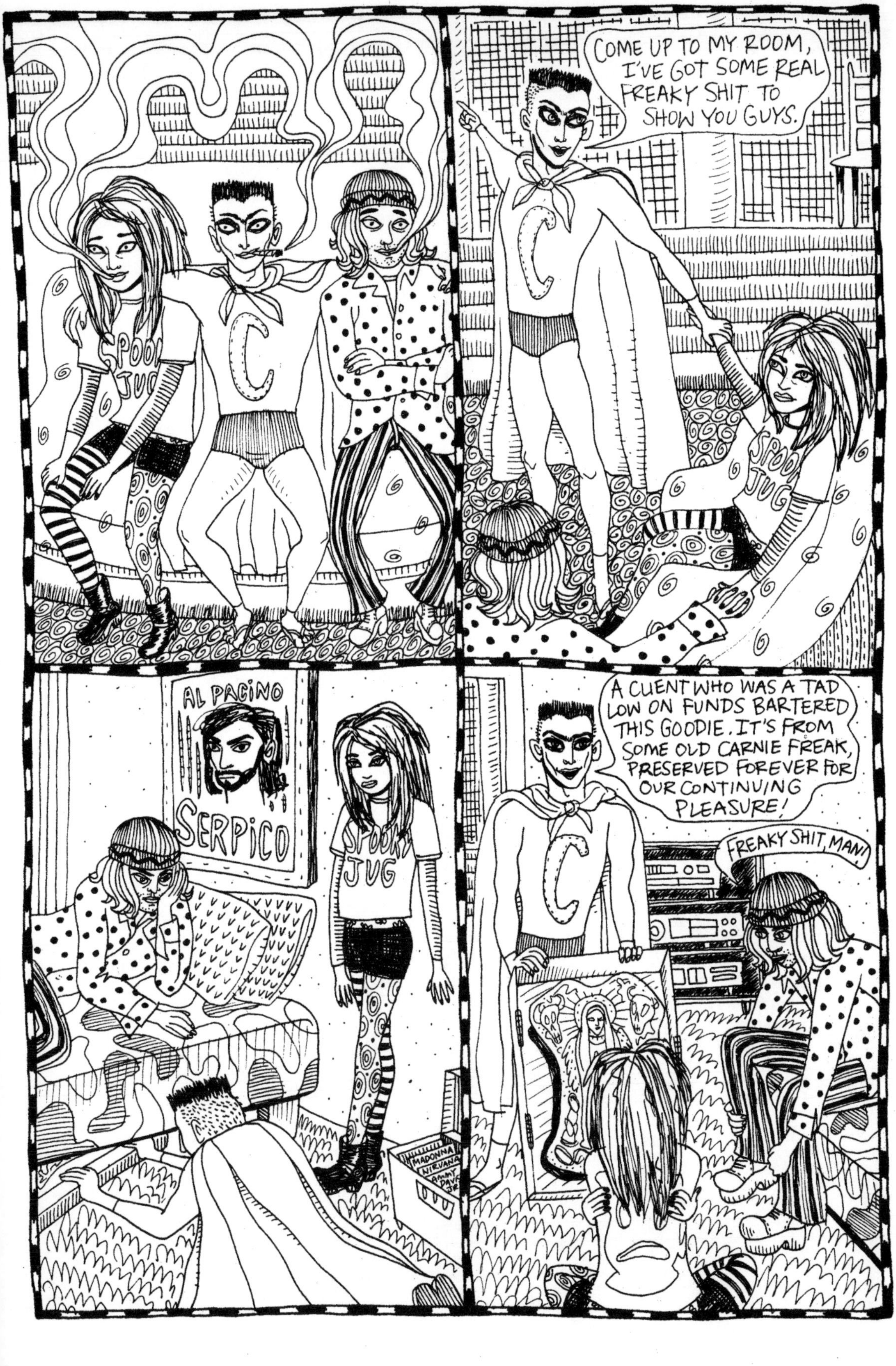
SPOOKY JUG
COME UP TO MY ROOM, I'VE GOT SOME REAL FREAKY SHIT TO SHOW YOU GUYS.
SPOOKY JUG
AL PACINO
SERPICO
SPOOKY JUG
MADONNA
NIRVANA
SAMMY DAVIS JR
A CLIENT WHO WAS A TAD LOW ON FUNDS BARTERED THIS GOODIE. IT'S FROM SOME OLD CARNIE FREAK, PRESERVED FOREVER FOR OUR CONTINUING PLEASURE!
FREAKY SHIT, MAN!

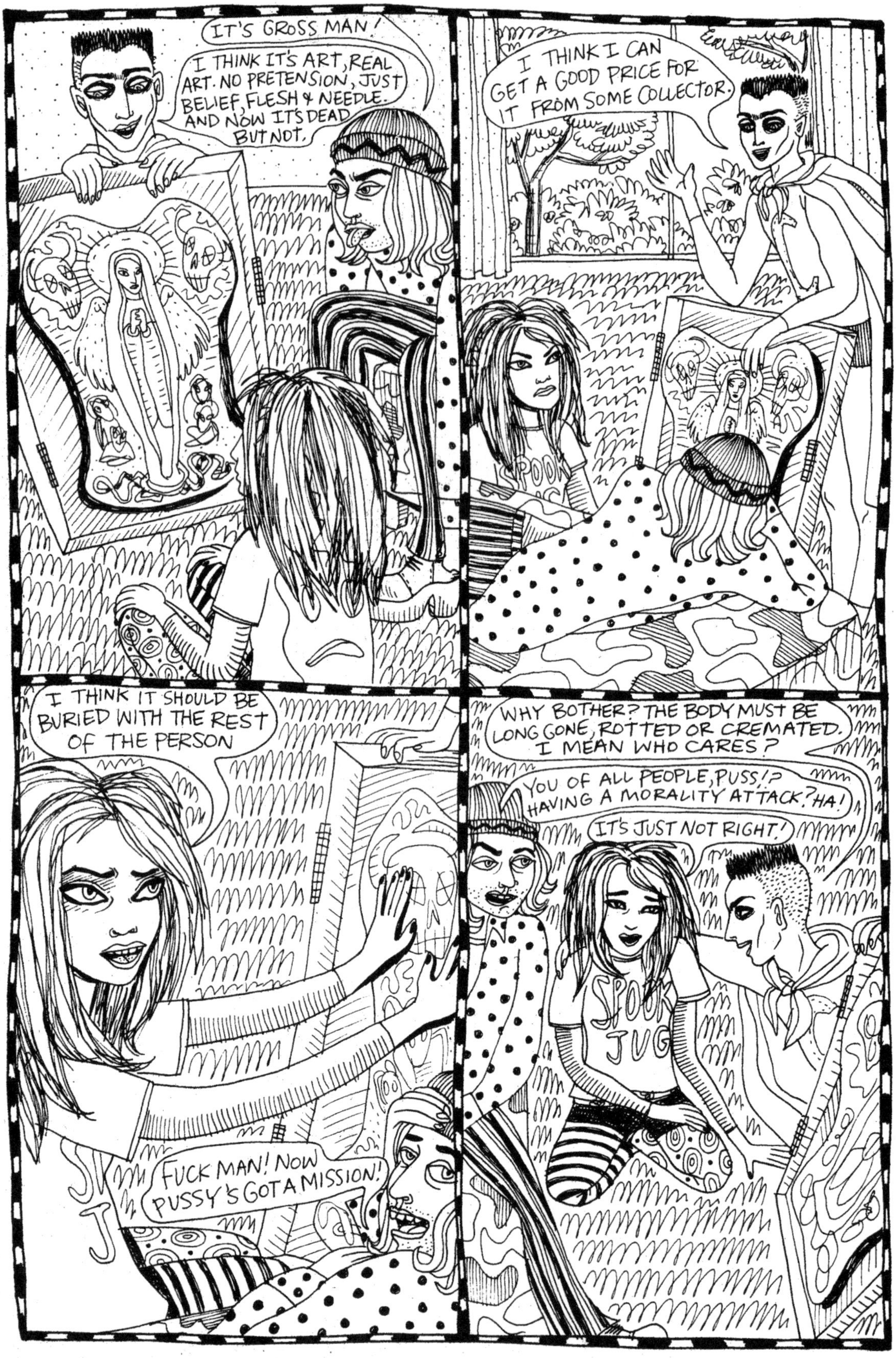
IT'S GROSS MAN!
I THINK IT'S ART, REAL ART. NO PRETENSION, JUST BELIEF, FLESH & NEEDLE. AND NOW IT'S DEAD BUT NOT.
I THINK I CAN GET A GOOD PRICE FOR IT FROM SOME COLLECTOR.
I THINK IT SHOULD BE BURIED WITH THE REST OF THE PERSON
FUCK MAN! NOW PUSSY'S GOT A MISSION!
WHY BOTHER? THE BODY MUST BE LONG GONE, ROTTED OR CREMATED. I MEAN WHO CARES?
YOU OF ALL PEOPLE, PUSS!? HAVING A MORALITY ATTACK? HA!
IT'S JUST NOT RIGHT!
SPOOK JUG

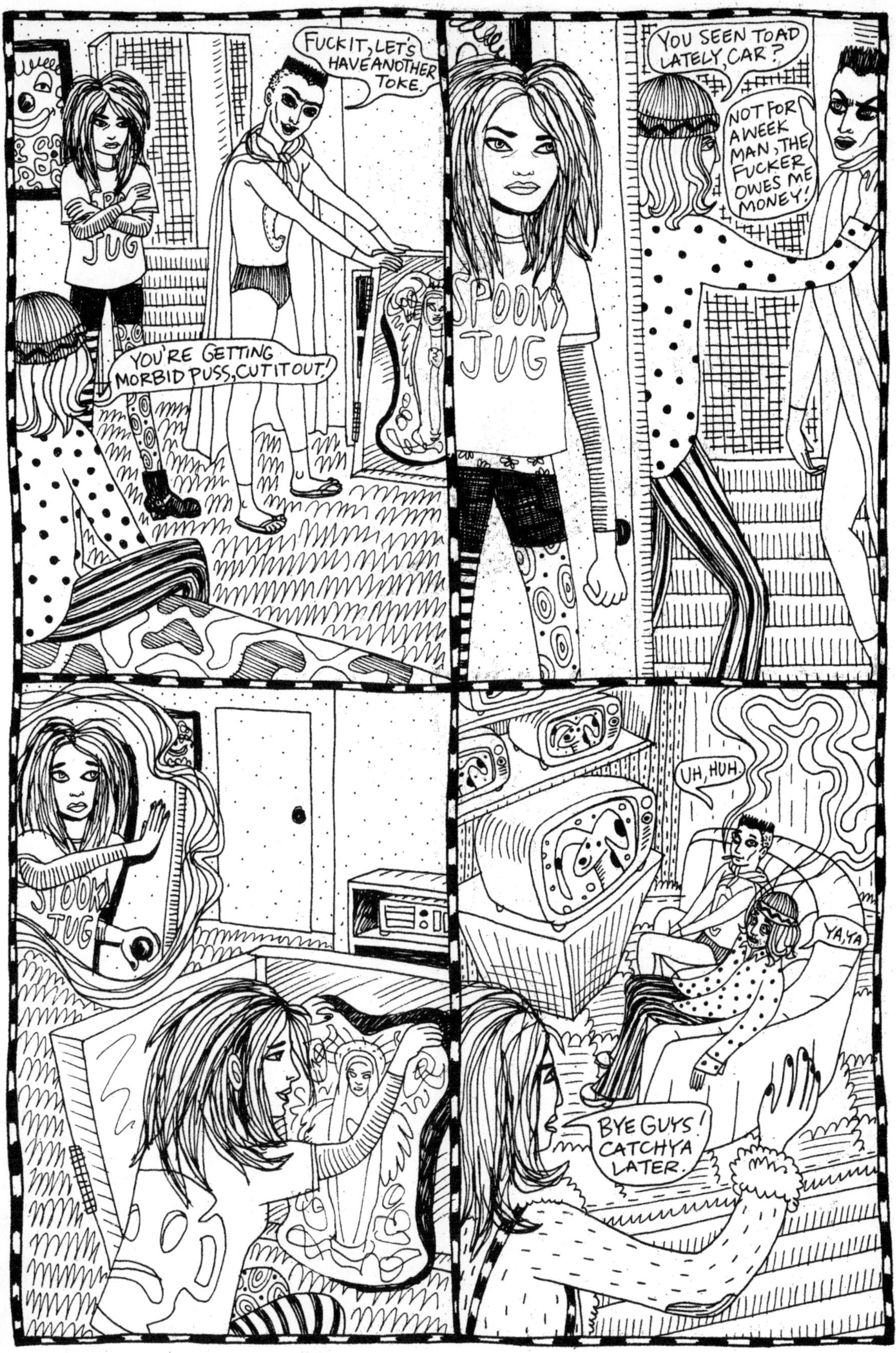
FUCKIT, LET'S HAVE ANOTHER TOKE.
YOU'RE GETTING MORBID PUSS, CUT IT OUT!
SPOOKY JUG
YOU SEEN TOAD LATELY, CAR?
NOT FOR A WEEK MAN, THE FUCKER OWES ME MONEY!
BYE GUYS! CATCHYA LATER.
UH, HUH.
YA, YA

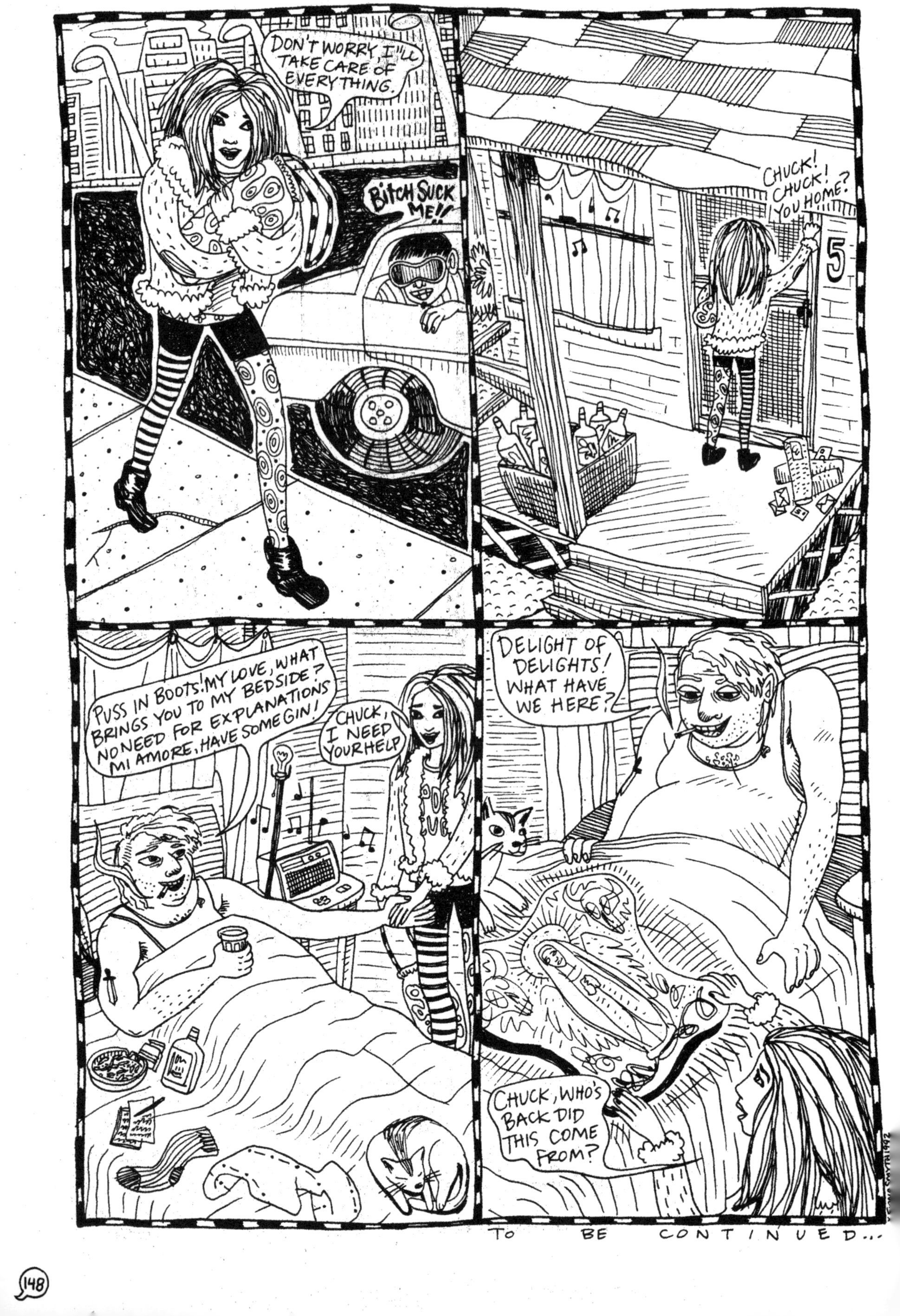
DON'T WORRY, I'LL TAKE CARE OF EVERYTHING.
BITCH SUCK ME!!
CHUCK! CHUCK! YOU HOME?
5
PUSS IN BOOTS! MY LOVE, WHAT BRINGS YOU TO MY BEDSIDE? NO NEED FOR EXPLANATIONS MI AMORE, HAVE SOME GIN!
CHUCK, I NEED YOUR HELP
DELIGHT OF DELIGHTS! WHAT HAVE WE HERE?
CHUCK, WHO'S BACK DID THIS COME FROM?

TO BE CONTINUED...

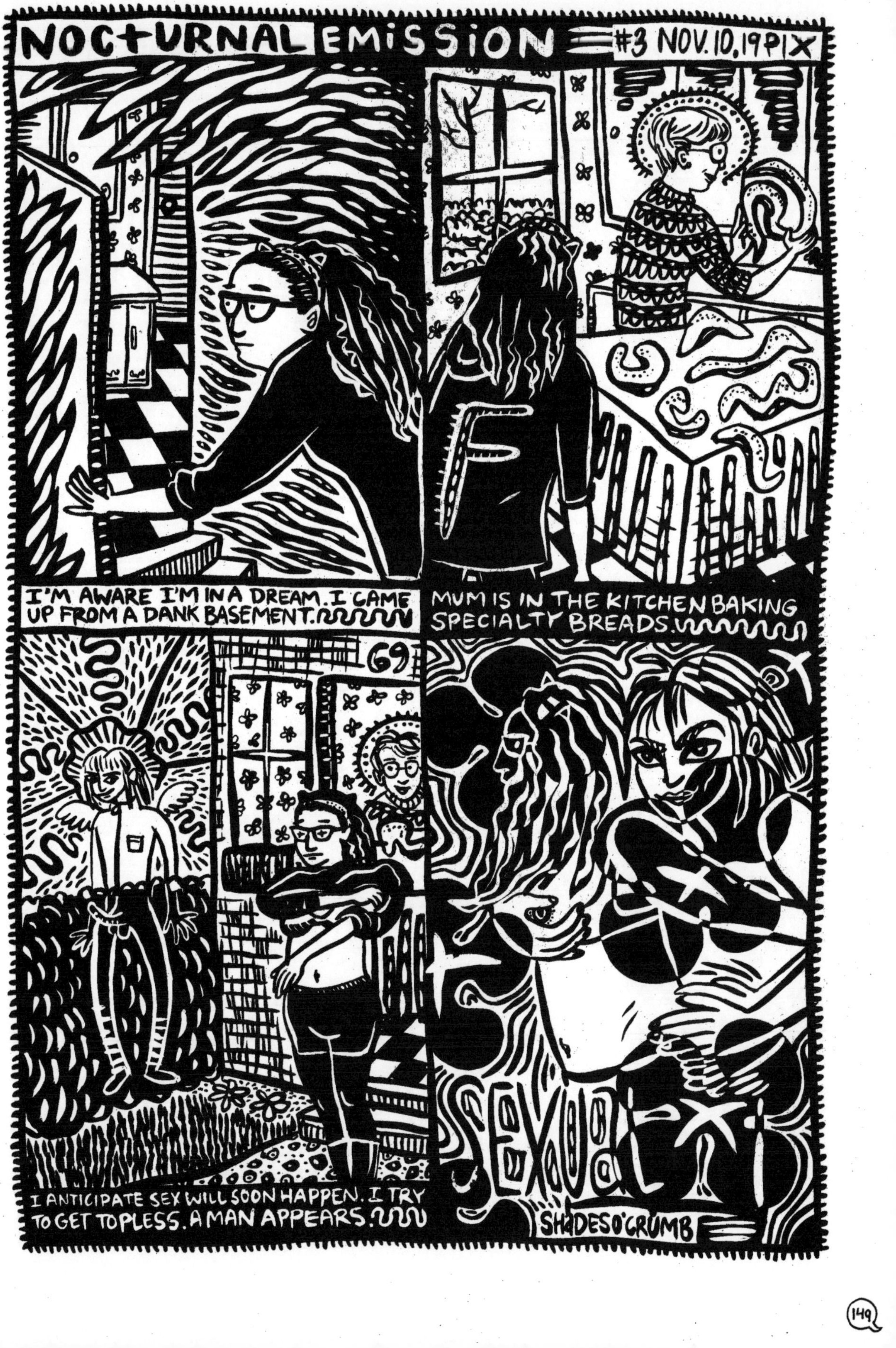
NOCTURNAL EMISSION
#3 NOV.10,19PIX
I'M AWARE I'M IN A DREAM. I CAME UP FROM A DANK BASEMENT.
MUM IS IN THE KITCHEN BAKING SPECIALTY BREADS.
69
I ANTICIPATE SEX WILL SOON HAPPEN. I TRY TO GET TOPLESS. A MAN APPEARS.
SEXUALiXi
SHADES O' CRUMB

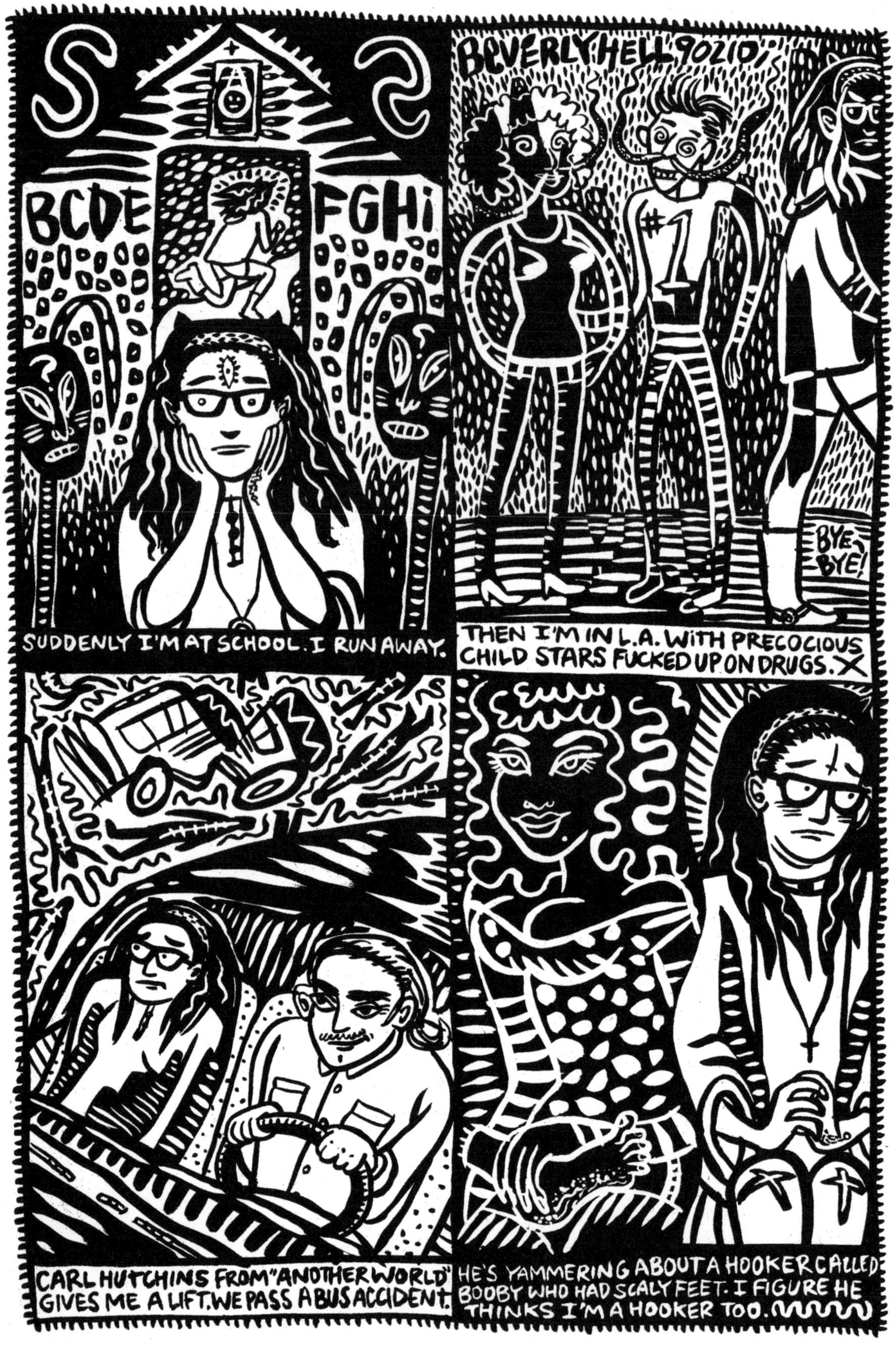

BCDE
FGHi
SUDDENLY I'M AT SCHOOL. I RUN AWAY.
BEVERLY HELL 90210!
#1
BYE-BYE!
THEN I'M IN L.A. WITH PRECOCIOUS CHILD STARS FUCKED UP ON DRUGS.
CARL HUTCHINS FROM "ANOTHER WORLD" GIVES ME A LIFT. WE PASS A BUS ACCIDENT.
HE'S YAMMERING ABOUT A HOOKER CALLED BOOBY WHO HAD SCALY FEET. I FIGURE HE THINKS I'M A HOOKER TOO.

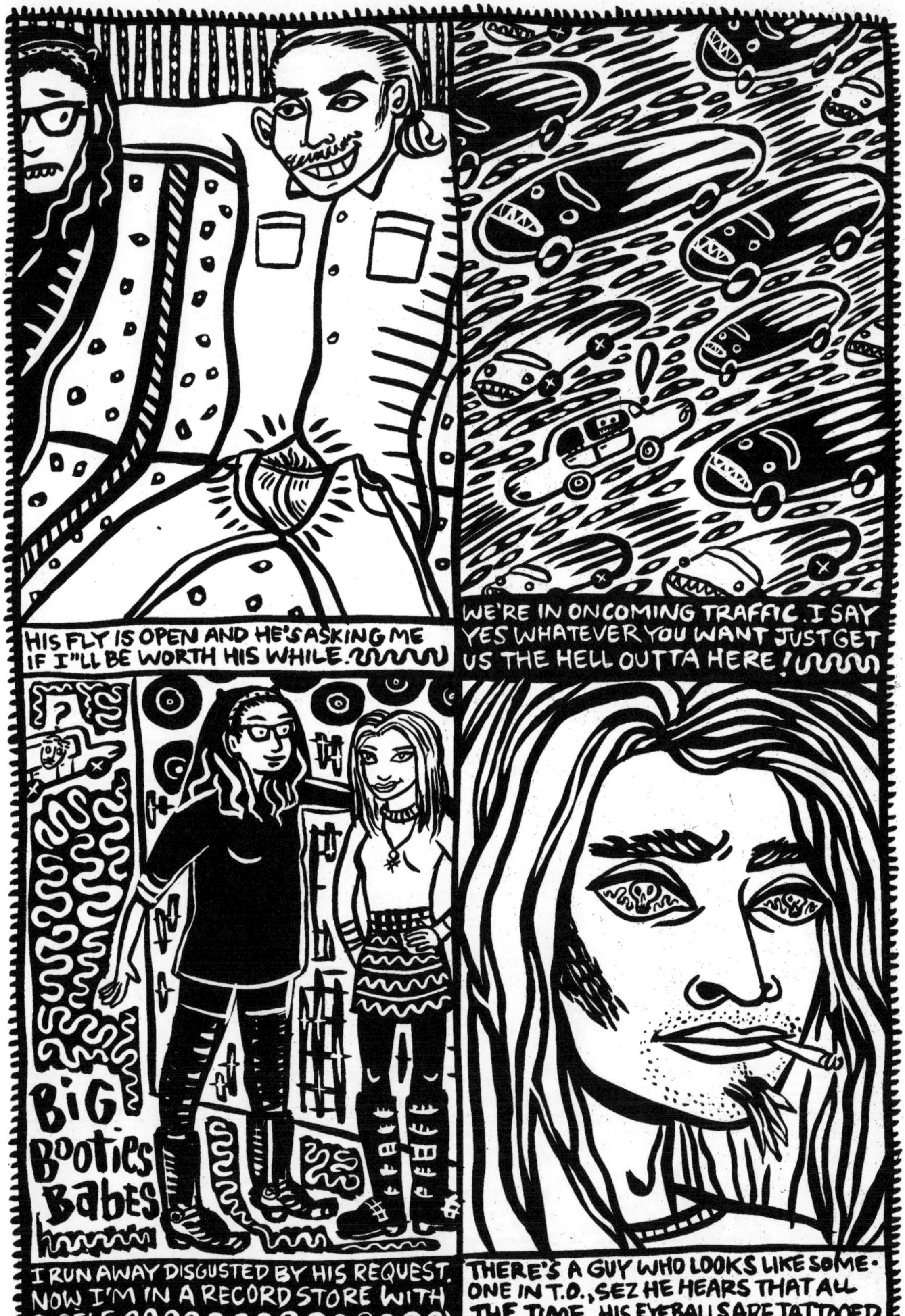
HIS FLY IS OPEN AND HE'S ASKING ME IF I'LL BE WORTH HIS WHILE.
WE'RE IN ONCOMING TRAFFIC. I SAY YES WHATEVER YOU WANT JUST GET US THE HELL OUTTA HERE!
BIG BOOTIES BABES
I RUN AWAY DISGUSTED BY HIS REQUEST. NOW I'M IN A RECORD STORE WITH GISELE.
THERE'S A GUY WHO LOOKS LIKE SOMEONE IN T.O., SEZ HE HEARS THAT ALL THE TIME. HIS EYEBALLS ARE TATTOOED.

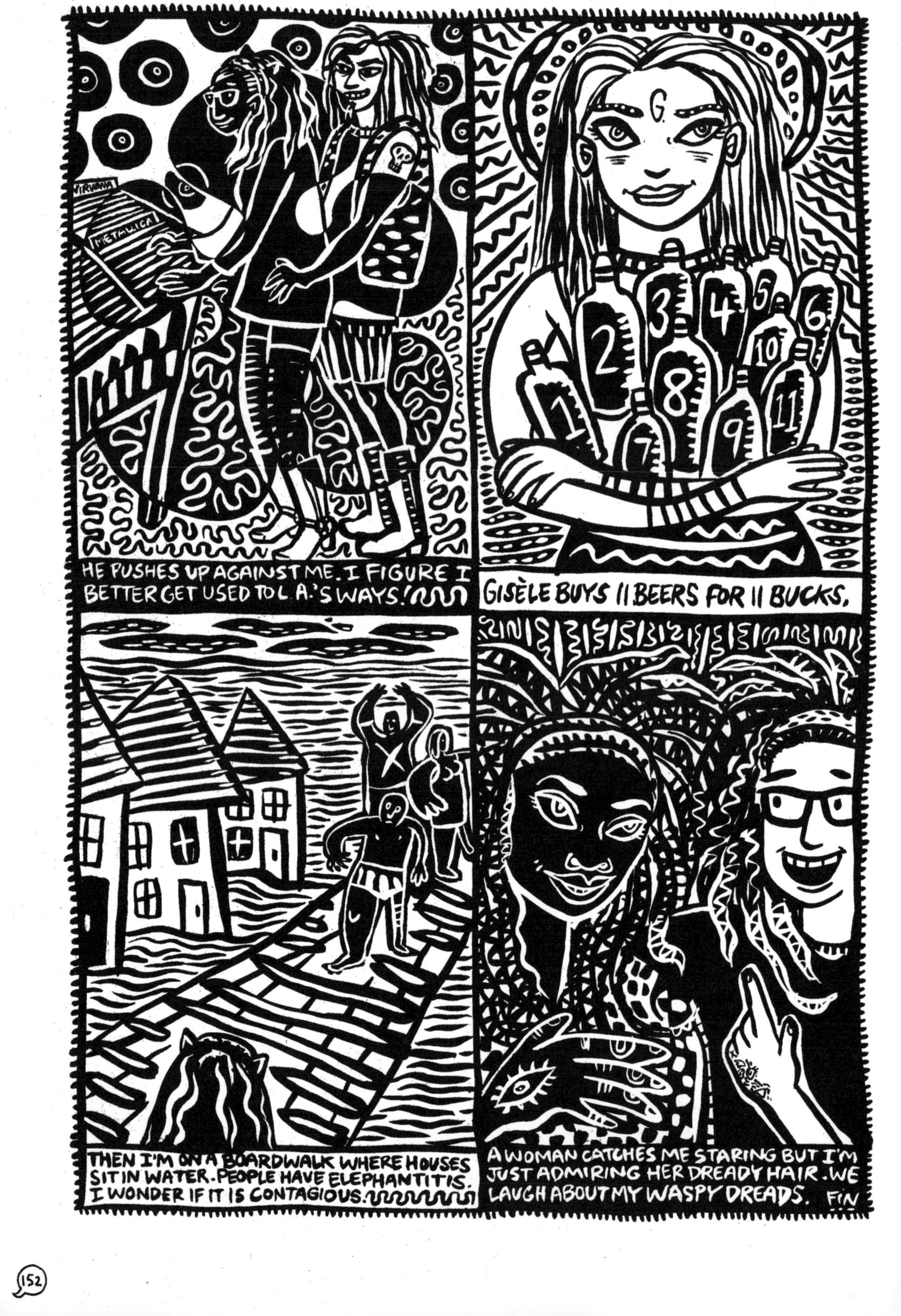
NIRVANA
METALLICA
HE PUSHES UP AGAINST ME. I FIGURE I BETTER GET USED TO L.A.'S WAYS!
GISÈLE BUYS 11 BEERS FOR 11 BUCKS.
THEN I'M ON A BOARDWALK WHERE HOUSES SIT IN WATER. PEOPLE HAVE ELEPHANTITIS. I WONDER IF IT IS CONTAGIOUS.
A WOMAN CATCHES ME STARING BUT I'M JUST ADMIRING HER DREADY HAIR. WE LAUGH ABOUT MY WASPY DREADS.
FIN

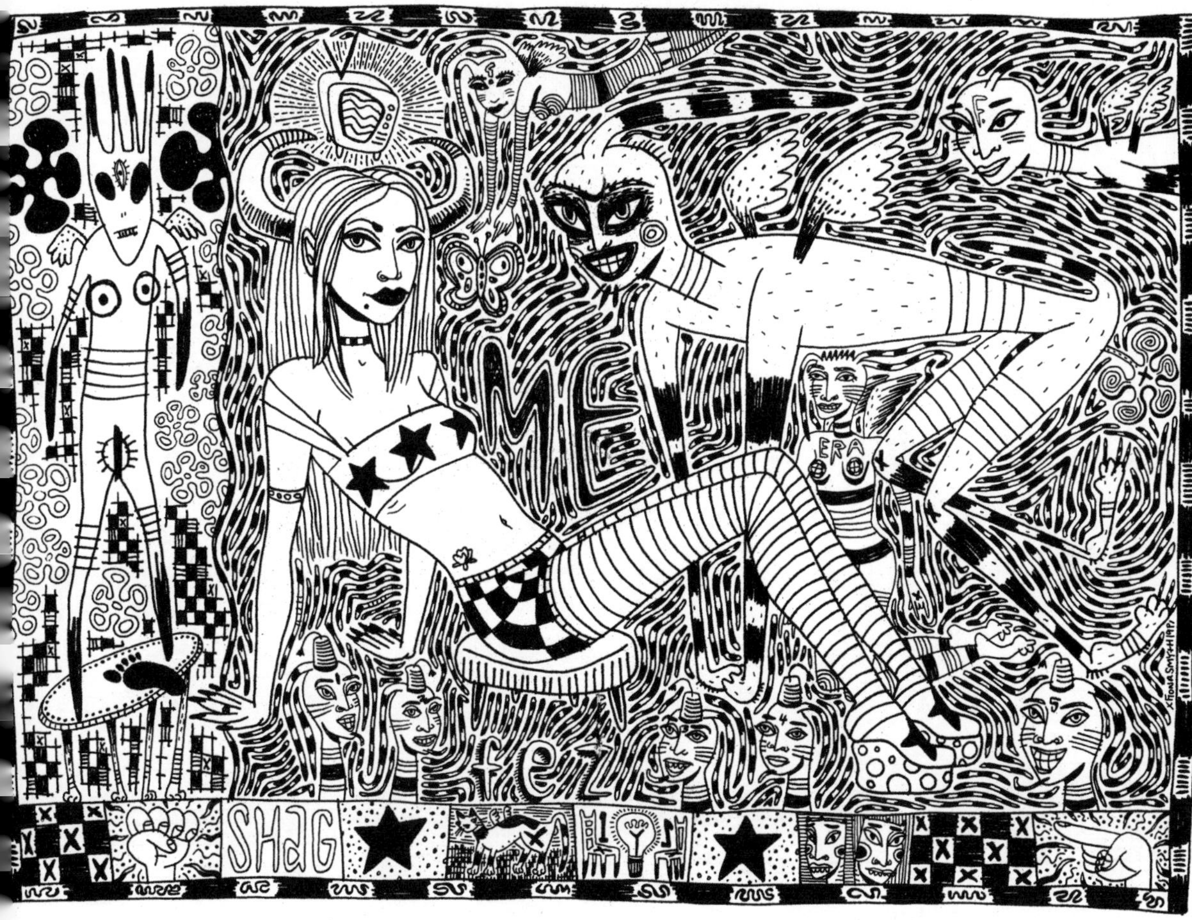
ME
ERA
fez
SHAG

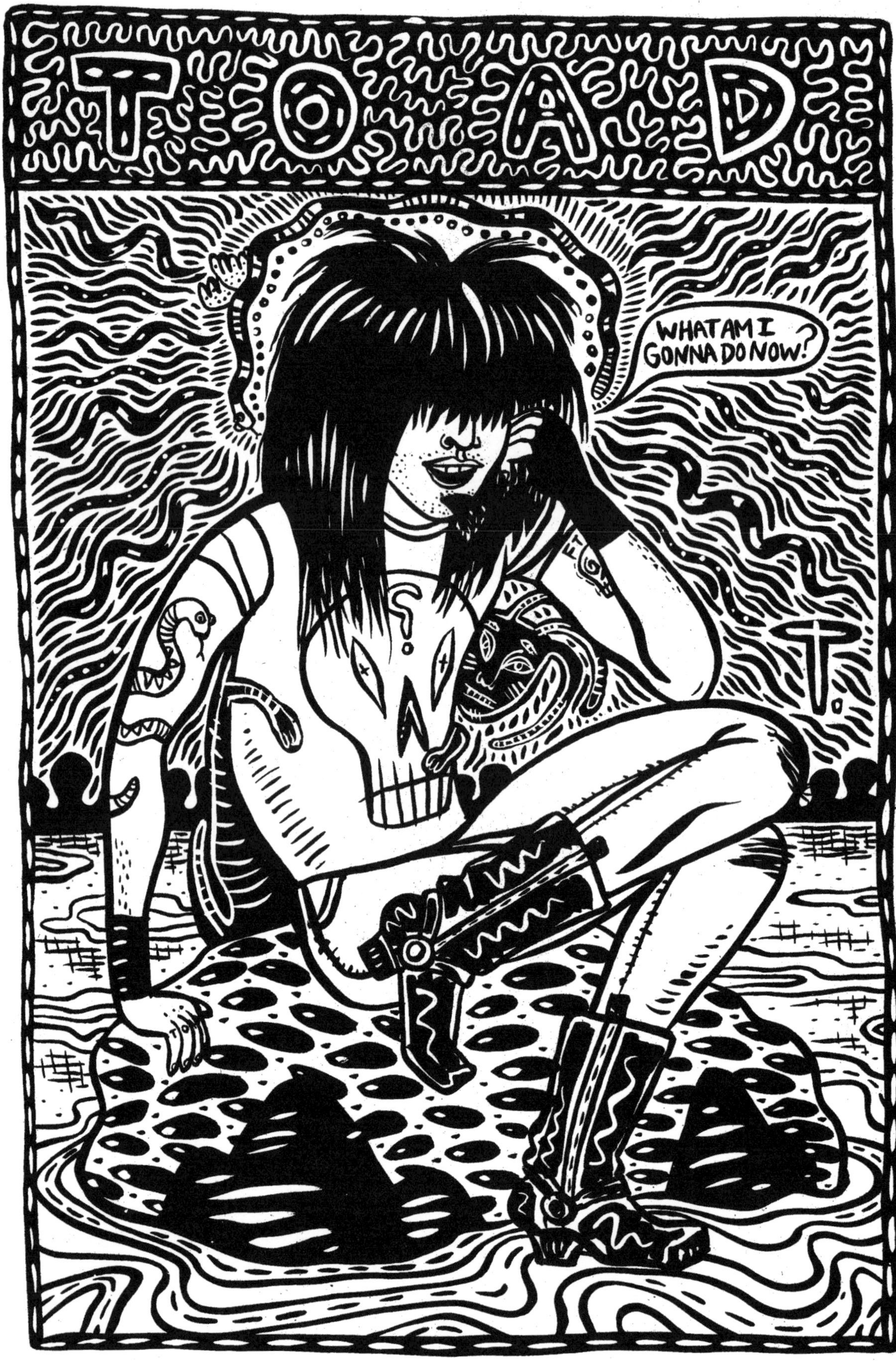
TOAD
WHAT AM I GONNA DO NOW?

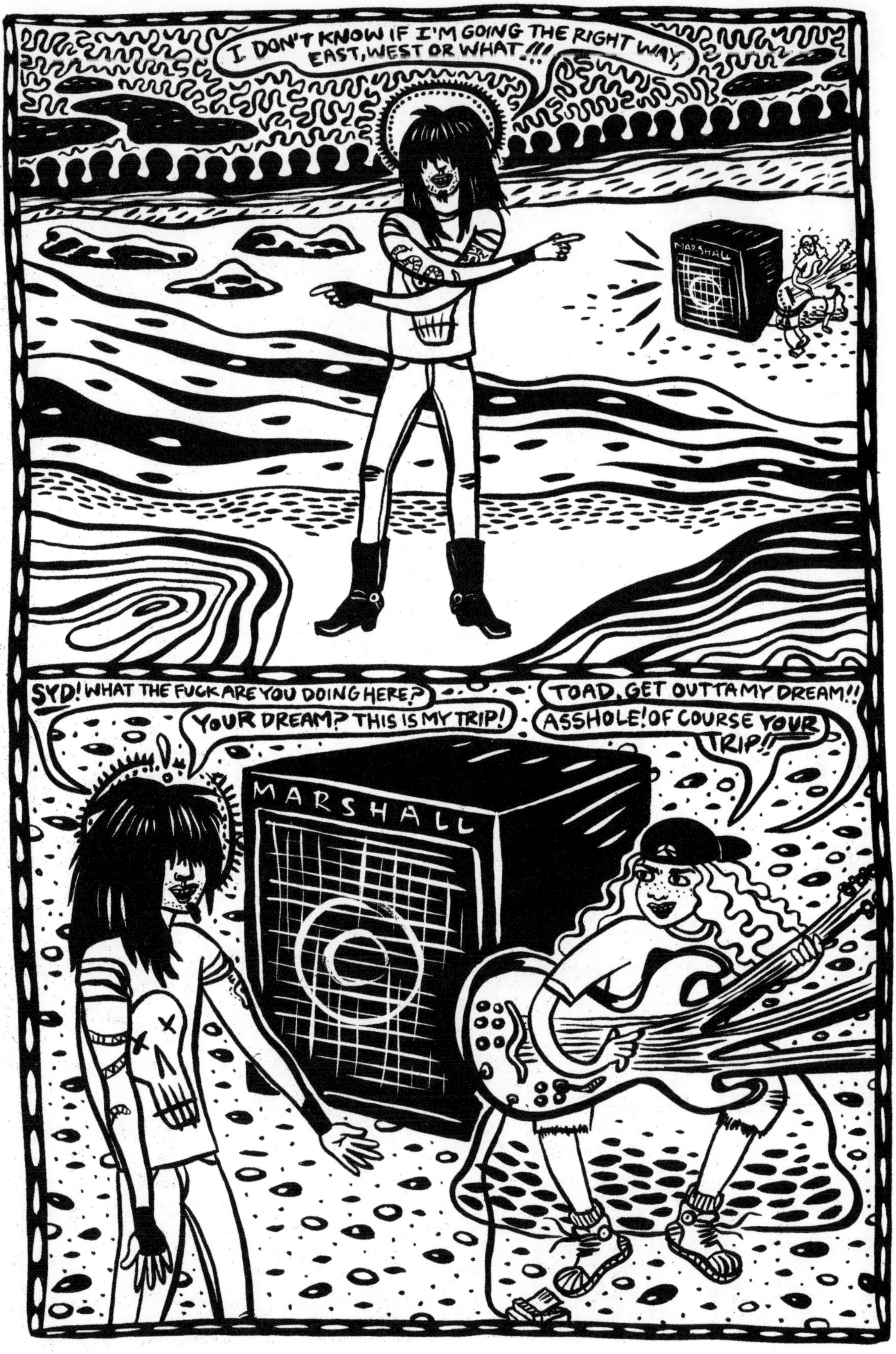
I DON'T KNOW IF I'M GOING THE RIGHT WAY, EAST, WEST OR WHAT!!!
MARSHALL
SYD! WHAT THE FUCK ARE YOU DOING HERE?
TOAD, GET OUTTA MY DREAM!!
YOUR DREAM? THIS IS MY TRIP!
ASSHOLE! OF COURSE YOUR TRIP!!
MARSHALL

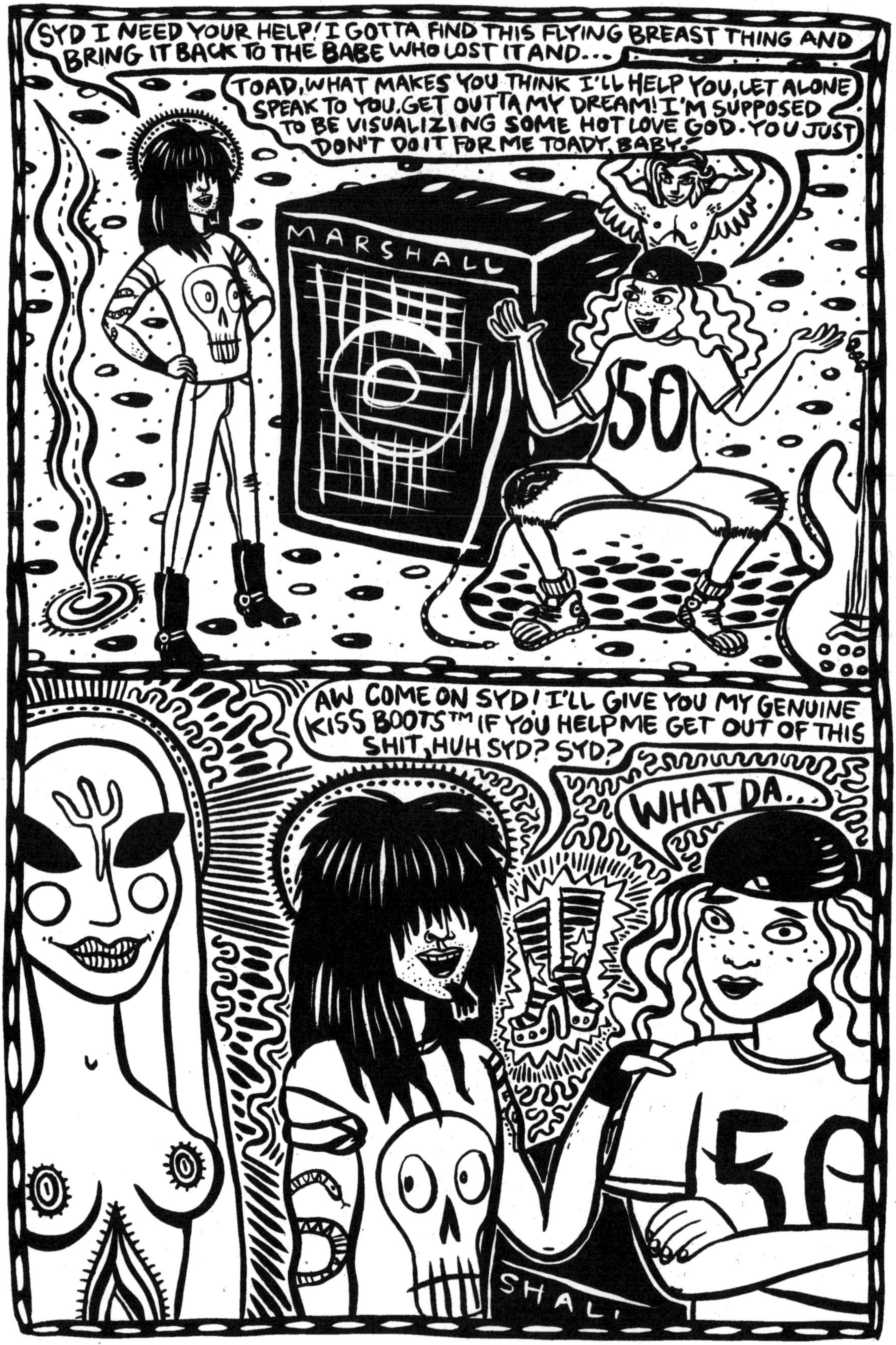
SYD I NEED YOUR HELP! I GOTTA FIND THIS FLYING BREAST THING AND BRING IT BACK TO THE BABE WHO LOST IT AND...
TOAD, WHAT MAKES YOU THINK I'LL HELP YOU, LET ALONE SPEAK TO YOU. GET OUTTA MY DREAM! I'M SUPPOSED TO BE VISUALIZING SOME HOT LOVE GOD. YOU JUST DON'T DO IT FOR ME TOADY, BABY!
MARSHALL
50
AW COME ON SYD! I'LL GIVE YOU MY GENUINE KISS BOOTS™ IF YOU HELP ME GET OUT OF THIS SHIT, HUH SYD? SYD?
WHAT DA...
50
SHALI

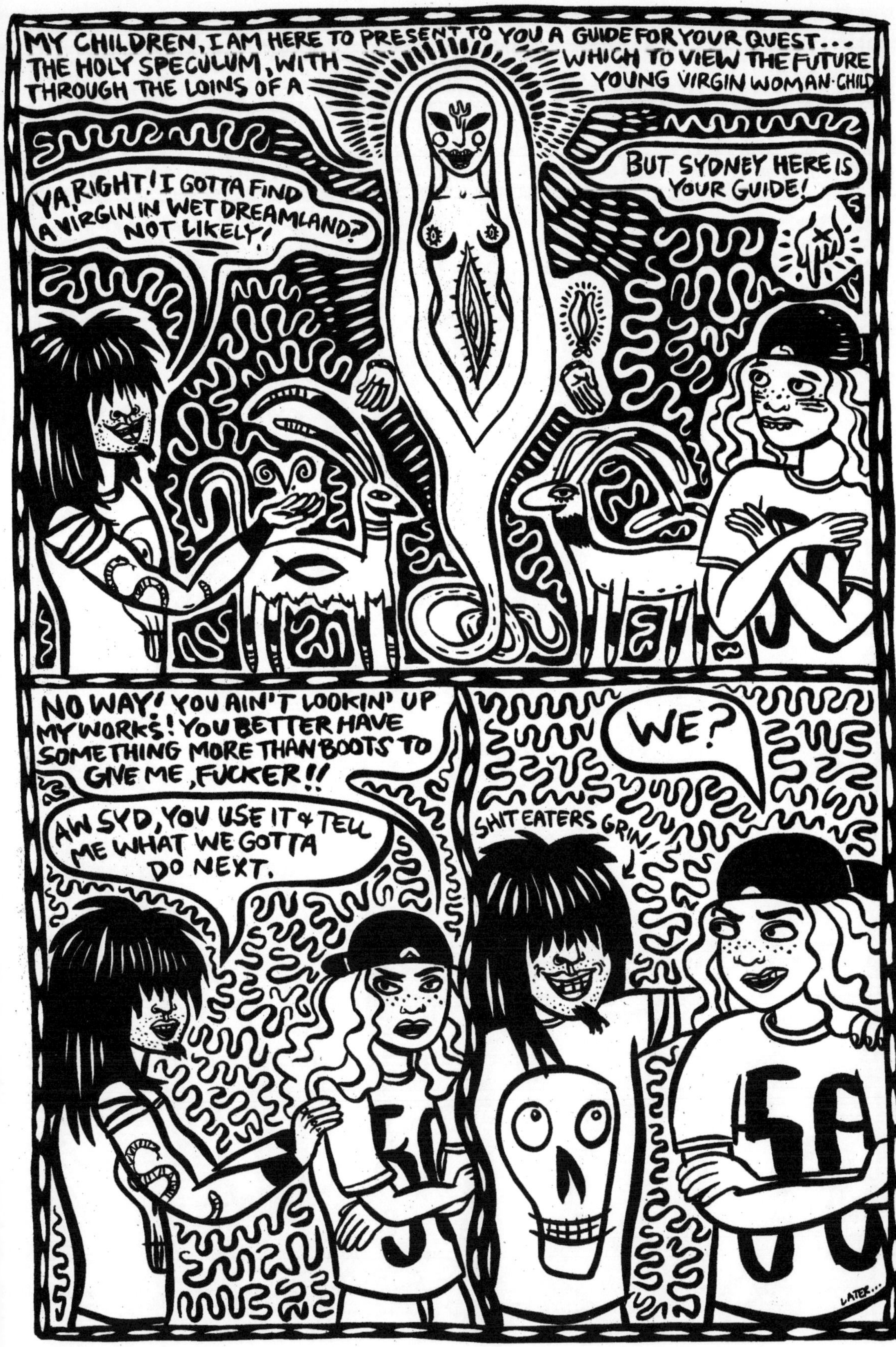
MY CHILDREN, I AM HERE TO PRESENT TO YOU A GUIDE FOR YOUR QUEST... THE HOLY SPECULUM, WITH WHICH TO VIEW THE FUTURE THROUGH THE LOINS OF A YOUNG VIRGIN WOMAN·CHILD
YA, RIGHT! I GOTTA FIND A VIRGIN IN WET DREAMLAND? NOT LIKELY!
BUT SYDNEY HERE IS YOUR GUIDE!
NO WAY! YOU AIN'T LOOKIN' UP MY WORKS! YOU BETTER HAVE SOMETHING MORE THAN BOOTS TO GIVE ME, FUCKER!!
AW SYD, YOU USE IT & TELL ME WHAT WE GOTTA DO NEXT.
WE?
SHIT EATERS GRIN!
LATER...

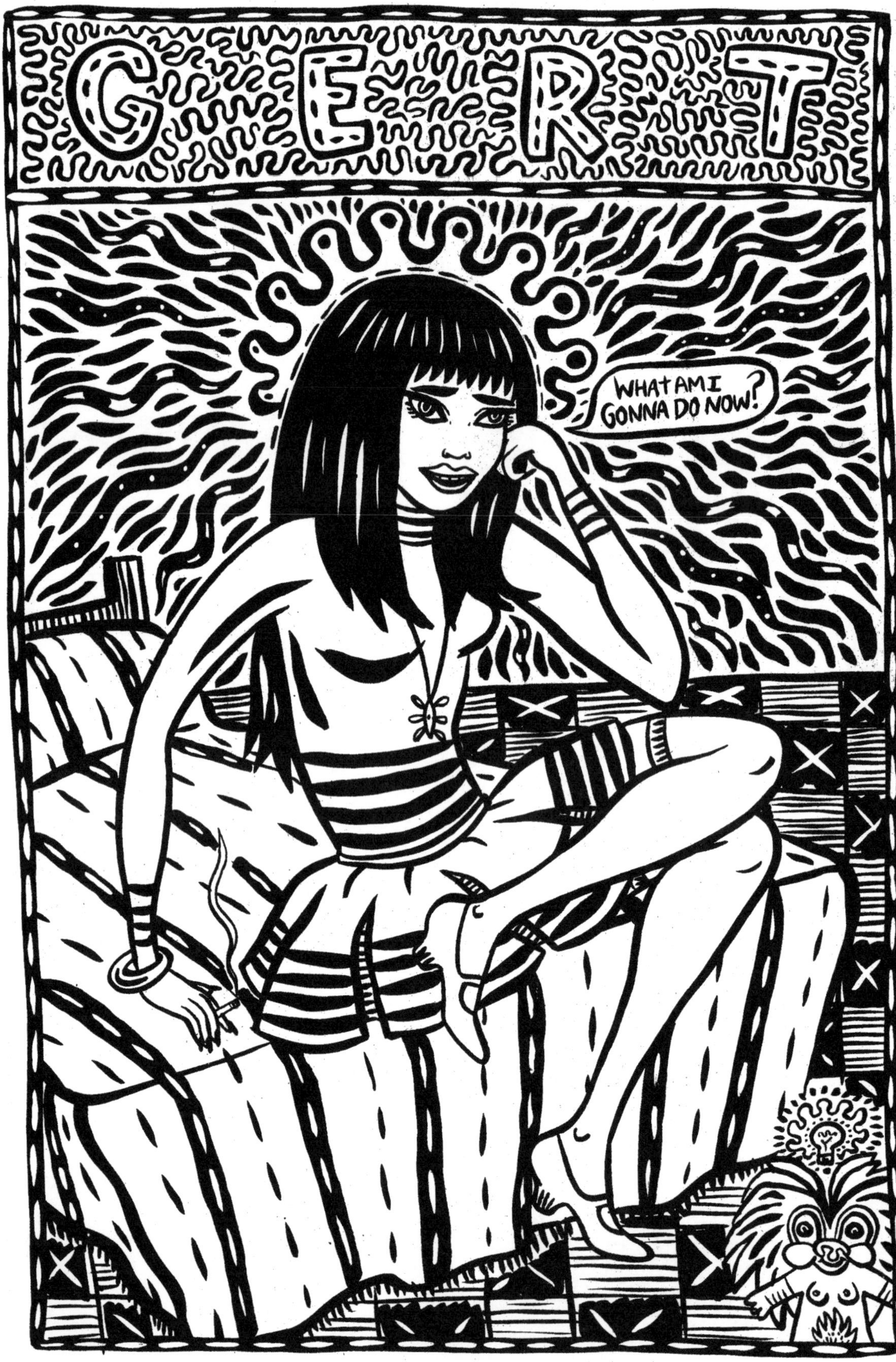
GERT
WHAT AM I GONNA DO NOW?

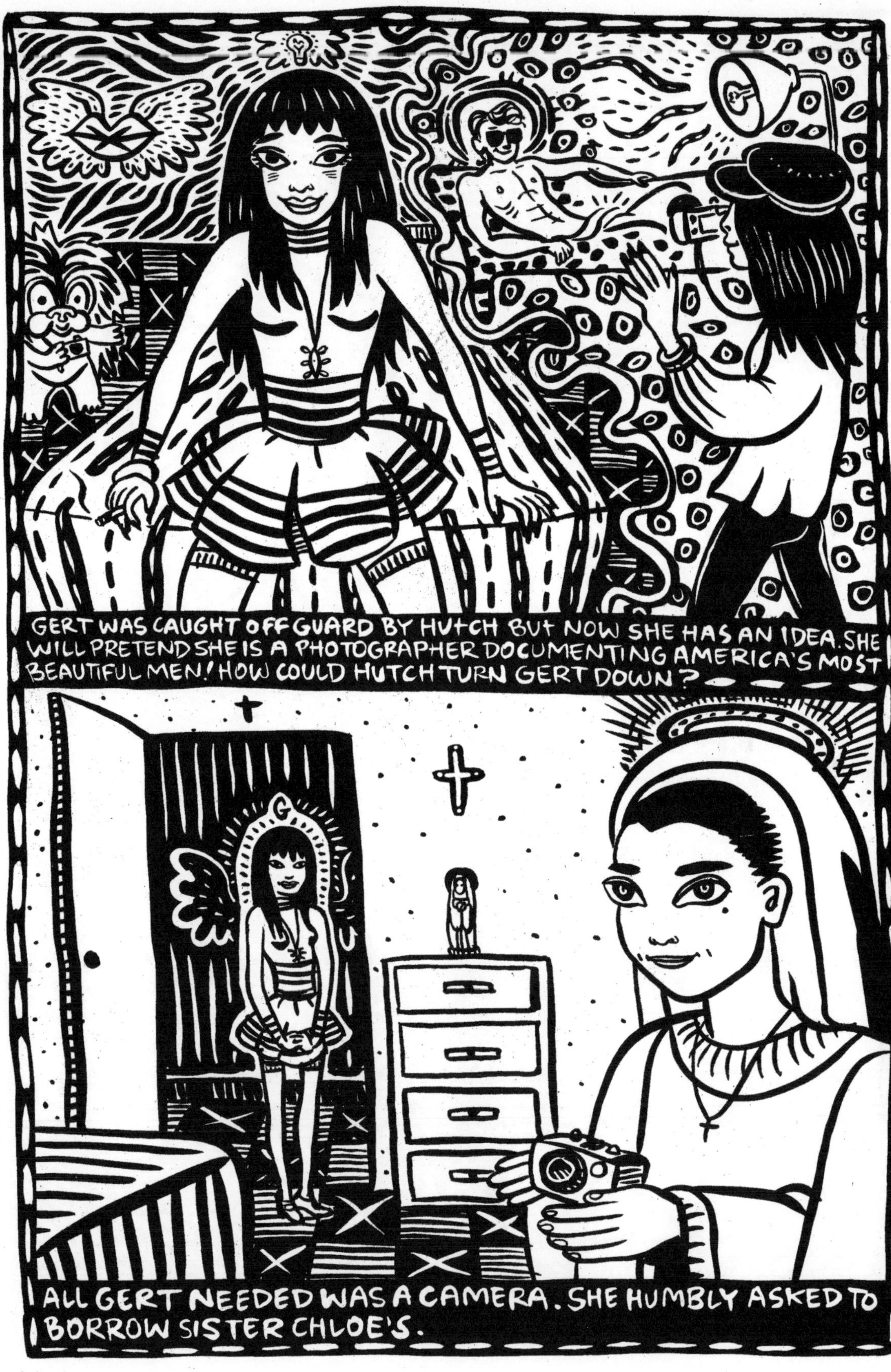
GERT WAS CAUGHT OFF GUARD BY HUTCH BUT NOW SHE HAS AN IDEA. SHE WILL PRETEND SHE IS A PHOTOGRAPHER DOCUMENTING AMERICA'S MOST BEAUTIFUL MEN! HOW COULD HUTCH TURN GERT DOWN?
ALL GERT NEEDED WAS A CAMERA. SHE HUMBLY ASKED TO BORROW SISTER CHLOE'S.

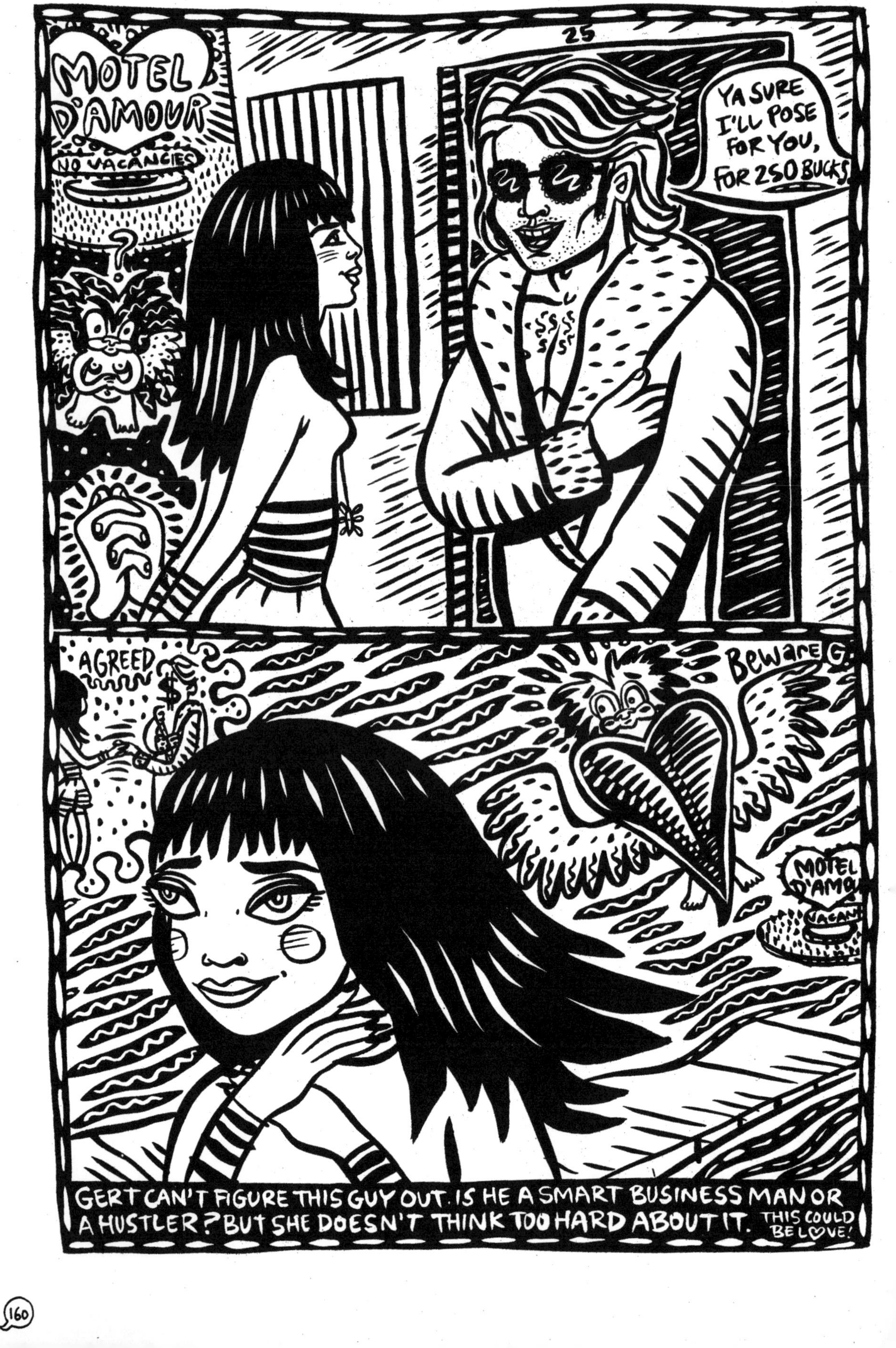
MOTEL D'AMOUR
NO VACANCIES
25
YA SURE I'LL POSE FOR YOU, FOR 250 BUCKS.
AGREED
Beware
GERT CAN'T FIGURE THIS GUY OUT. IS HE A SMART BUSINESS MAN OR A HUSTLER? BUT SHE DOESN'T THINK TOO HARD ABOUT IT.
THIS COULD BE LOVE!

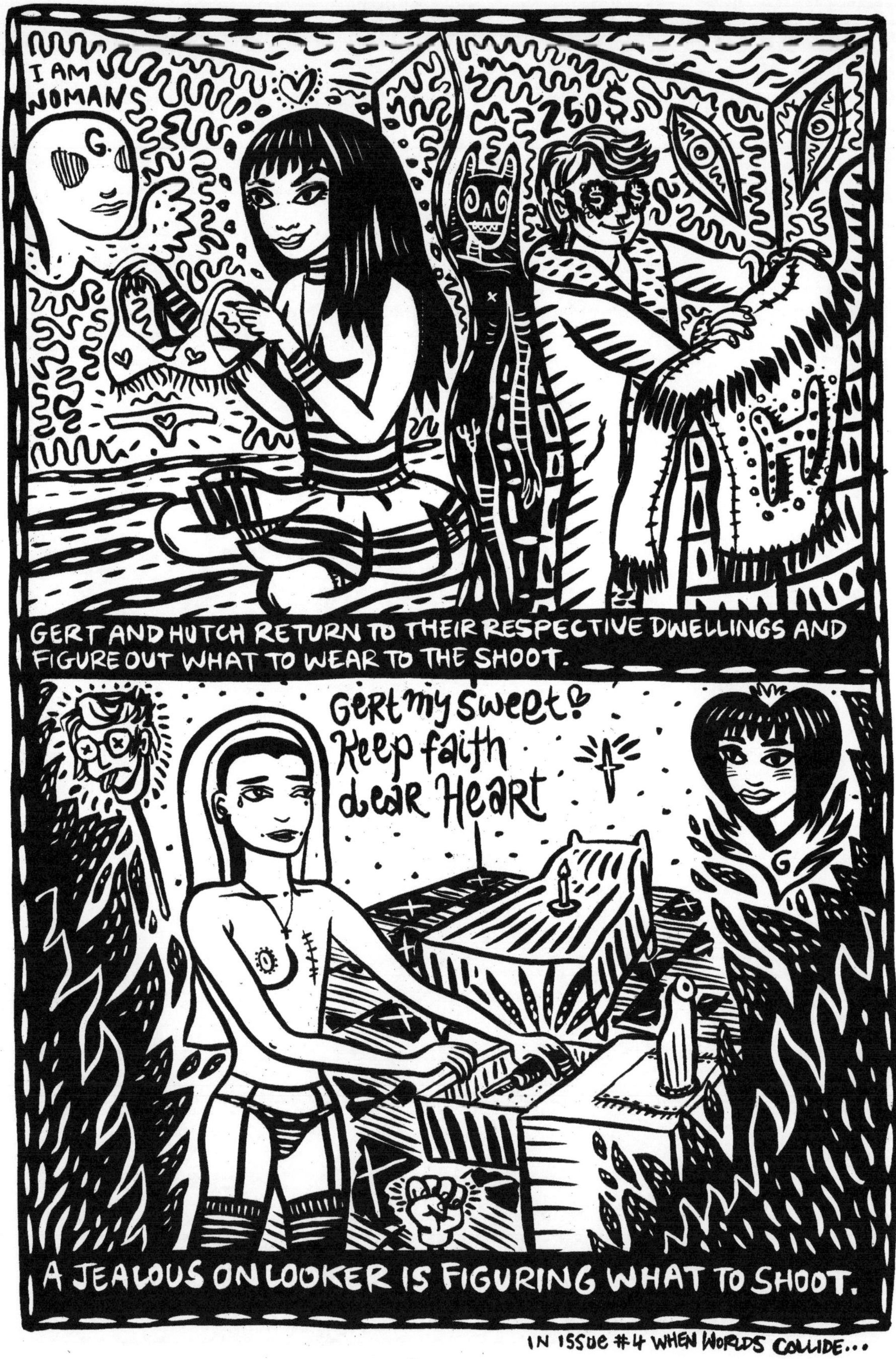
I AM WOMANS
250$
GERT AND HUTCH RETURN TO THEIR RESPECTIVE DWELLINGS AND FIGURE OUT WHAT TO WEAR TO THE SHOOT.
Gert my sweet!
Keep faith dear Heart
A JEALOUS ONLOOKER IS FIGURING WHAT TO SHOOT.

IN ISSUE #4 WHEN WORLDS COLLIDE...

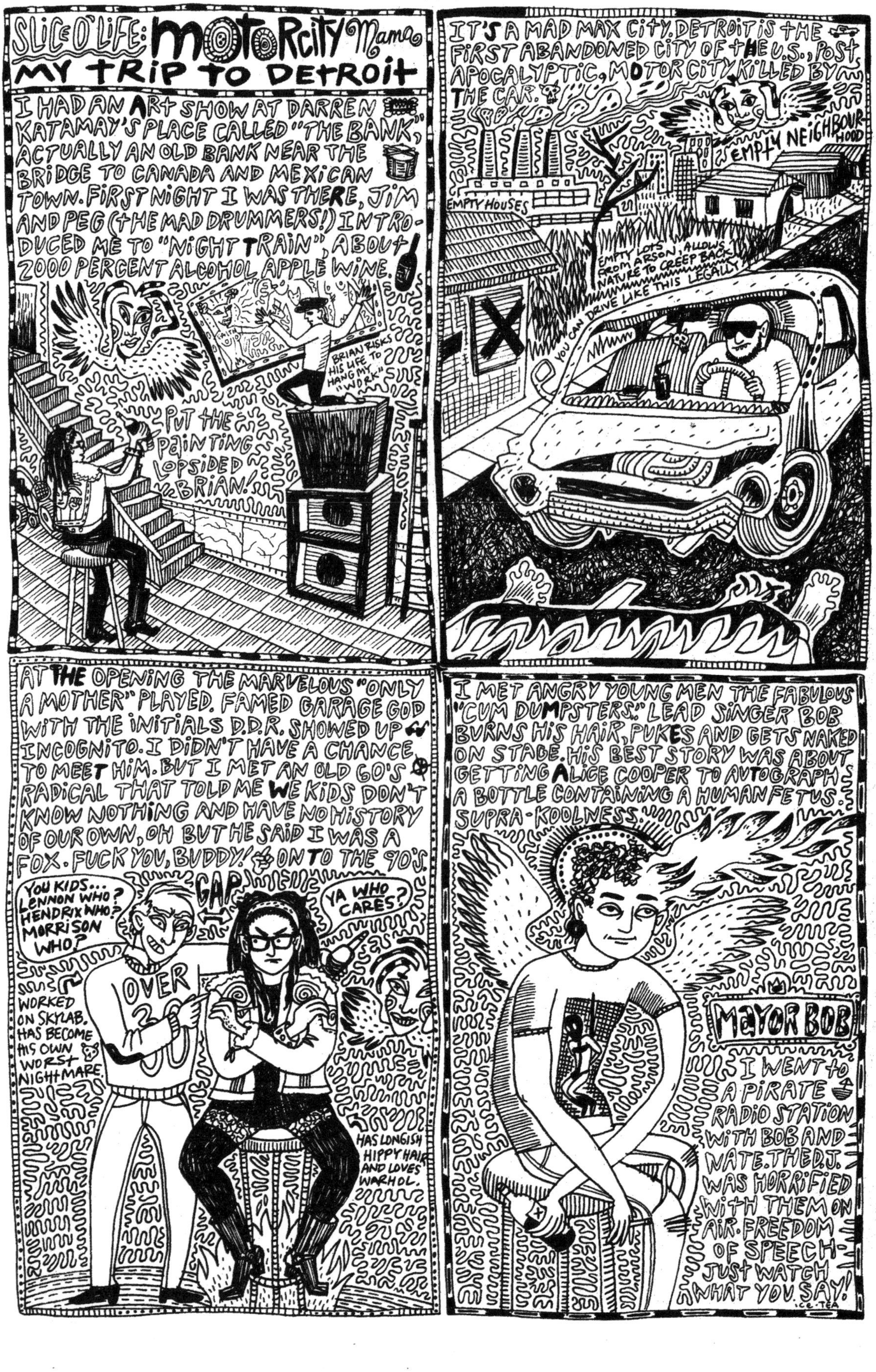
SLICE O' LIFE: MOTORCITY Mama
MY TRIP TO DETROIT
I HAD AN ART SHOW AT DARREN KATAMAY'S PLACE CALLED "THE BANK", ACTUALLY AN OLD BANK NEAR THE BRIDGE TO CANADA AND MEXICAN TOWN. FIRST NIGHT I WAS THERE, JIM AND PEG (THE MAD DRUMMERS!) INTRODUCED ME TO "NIGHT TRAIN", ABOUT 2000 PERCENT ALCOHOL APPLE WINE.
BRIAN RISKS HIS LIFE TO HANG MY "WORK"
PUT THE PAINTING LOPSIDED BRIAN!
IT'S A MAD MAX CITY. DETROIT IS THE FIRST ABANDONED CITY OF THE U.S., POST APOCALYPTIC, MOTOR CITY KILLED BY THE CAR.
EMPTY NEIGHBOURHOOD
EMPTY HOUSES
EMPTY LOTS FROM ARSON, ALLOWS NATURE TO CREEP BACK
YOU CAN DRIVE LIKE THIS LEGALLY
AT THE OPENING THE MARVELOUS "ONLY A MOTHER" PLAYED. FAMED GARAGE GOD WITH THE INITIALS D.D.R. SHOWED UP INCOGNITO. I DIDN'T HAVE A CHANCE TO MEET HIM. BUT I MET AN OLD 60'S RADICAL THAT TOLD ME WE KIDS DON'T KNOW NOTHING AND HAVE NO HISTORY OF OUR OWN, OH BUT HE SAID I WAS A FOX. FUCK YOU, BUDDY! ONTO THE 90'S.
YOU KIDS... LENNON WHO? HENDRIX WHO? MORRISON WHO?
GAP
YA WHO CARES?
OVER 30
WORKED ON SKYLAB. HAS BECOME HIS OWN WORST NIGHTMARE.
HAS LONGISH HIPPY HAIR AND LOVES WARHOL.
I MET ANGRY YOUNG MEN THE FABULOUS "CUM DUMPSTERS." LEAD SINGER BOB BURNS HIS HAIR, PUKES AND GETS NAKED ON STAGE. HIS BEST STORY WAS ABOUT GETTING ALICE COOPER TO AUTOGRAPH A BOTTLE CONTAINING A HUMAN FETUS. SUPRA-KOOLNESS.
MAYOR BOB
I WENT TO A PIRATE RADIO STATION WITH BOB AND NATE. THE D.J. WAS HORRIFIED WITH THEM ON AIR. FREEDOM OF SPEECH - JUST WATCH WHAT YOU SAY!

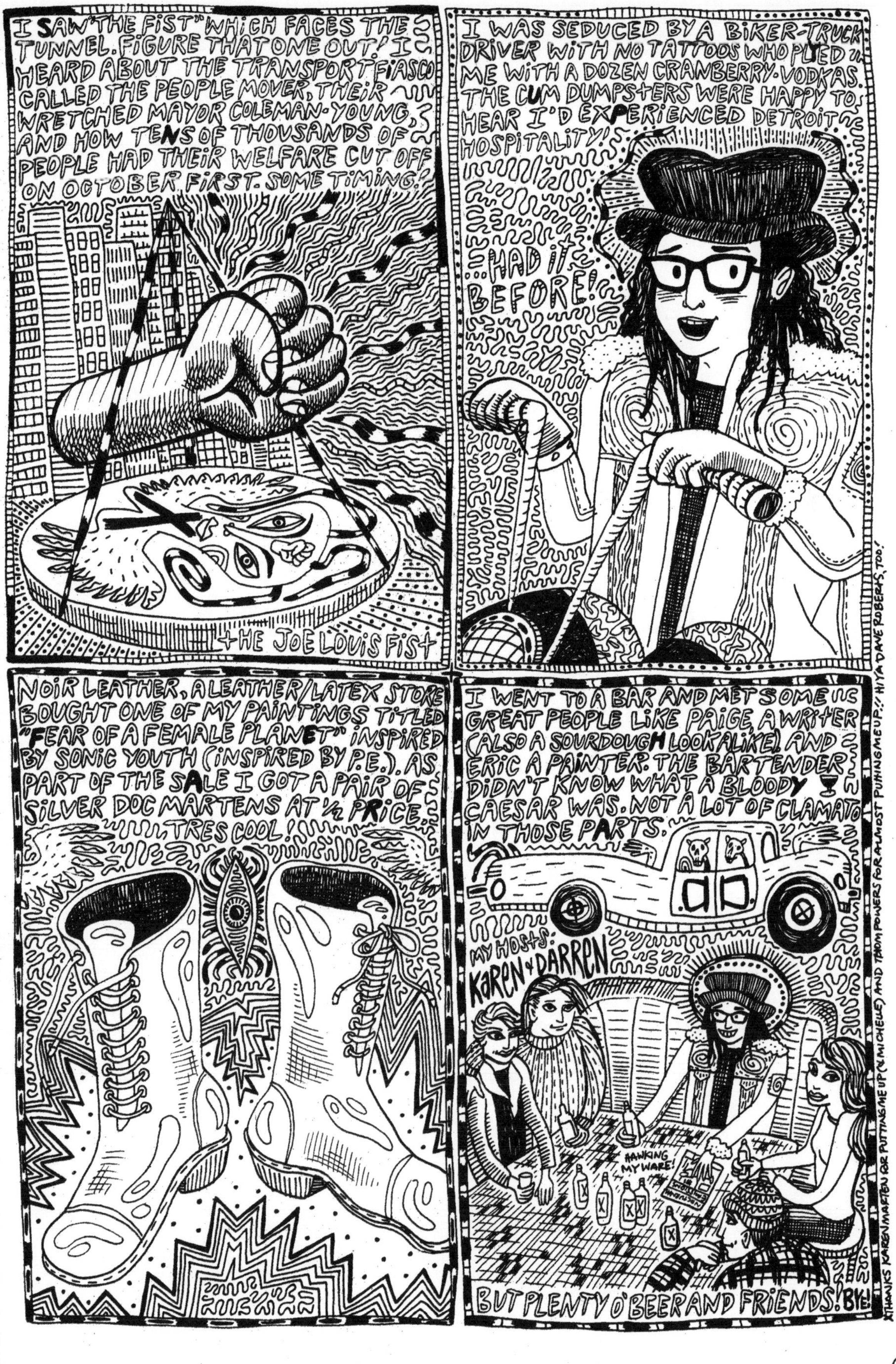
I SAW "THE FIST" WHICH FACES THE TUNNEL. FIGURE THAT ONE OUT! I HEARD ABOUT THE TRANSPORT FIASCO CALLED THE PEOPLE MOVER, THEIR WRETCHED MAYOR COLEMAN-YOUNG, AND HOW TENS OF THOUSANDS OF PEOPLE HAD THEIR WELFARE CUT OFF ON OCTOBER FIRST. SOME TIMING!
THE JOE LOUIS FIST
I WAS SEDUCED BY A BIKER-TRUCK DRIVER WITH NO TATTOOS WHO PLIED ME WITH A DOZEN CRANBERRY-VODKAS. THE CUM DUMPSTERS WERE HAPPY TO HEAR I'D EXPERIENCED DETROIT HOSPITALITY!
...HAD IT BEFORE!
NOIR LEATHER, A LEATHER/LATEX STORE BOUGHT ONE OF MY PAINTINGS TITLED "FEAR OF A FEMALE PLANET" INSPIRED BY SONIC YOUTH (INSPIRED BY P.E.). AS PART OF THE SALE I GOT A PAIR OF SILVER DOC MARTENS AT ½ PRICE. TRES COOL!
I WENT TO A BAR AND MET SOME GREAT PEOPLE LIKE PAIGE, A WRITER (ALSO A SOURDOUGH LOOKALIKE) AND ERIC A PAINTER. THE BARTENDER DIDN'T KNOW WHAT A BLOODY CAESAR WAS. NOT A LOT OF CLAMATO IN THOSE PARTS.
MY HOSTS: KAREN & DARREN
HAWKING MY WARE!
BUT PLENTY O' BEER AND FRIENDS! BYE!
THANKS KAREN MARTEN FOR PUTTING ME UP (& MICHELLE) AND THOM POWERS FOR ALMOST PUTTING ME UP!! HIYA DAVE ROBERTS, TOO!

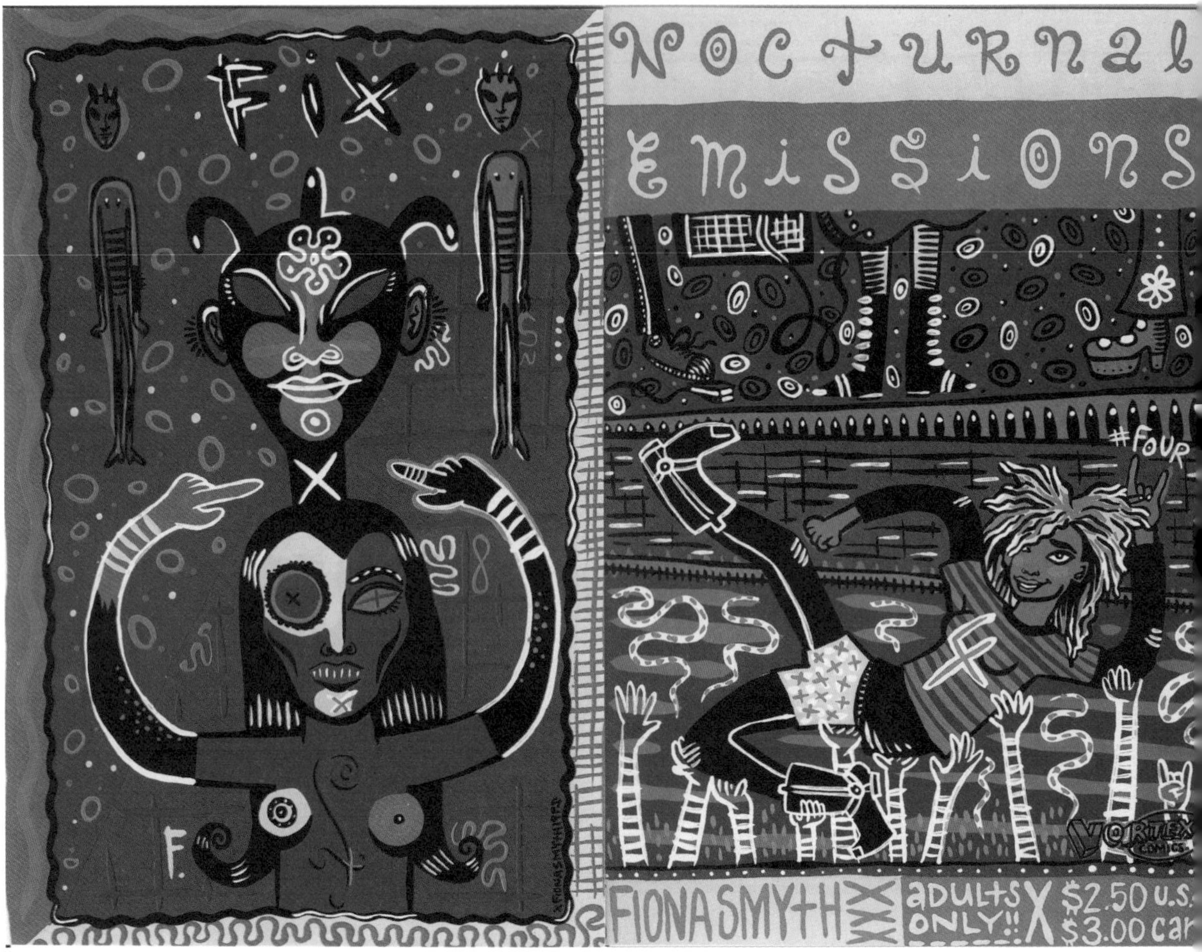
FIX
F.
NOCTURNAL
EMISSIONS
#FOUR
VORTEX COMICS
FIONA SMYTH
XXX
adults ONLY!! X
$2.50 U.S.
$3.00 can

 1992 VORTEX COMICS

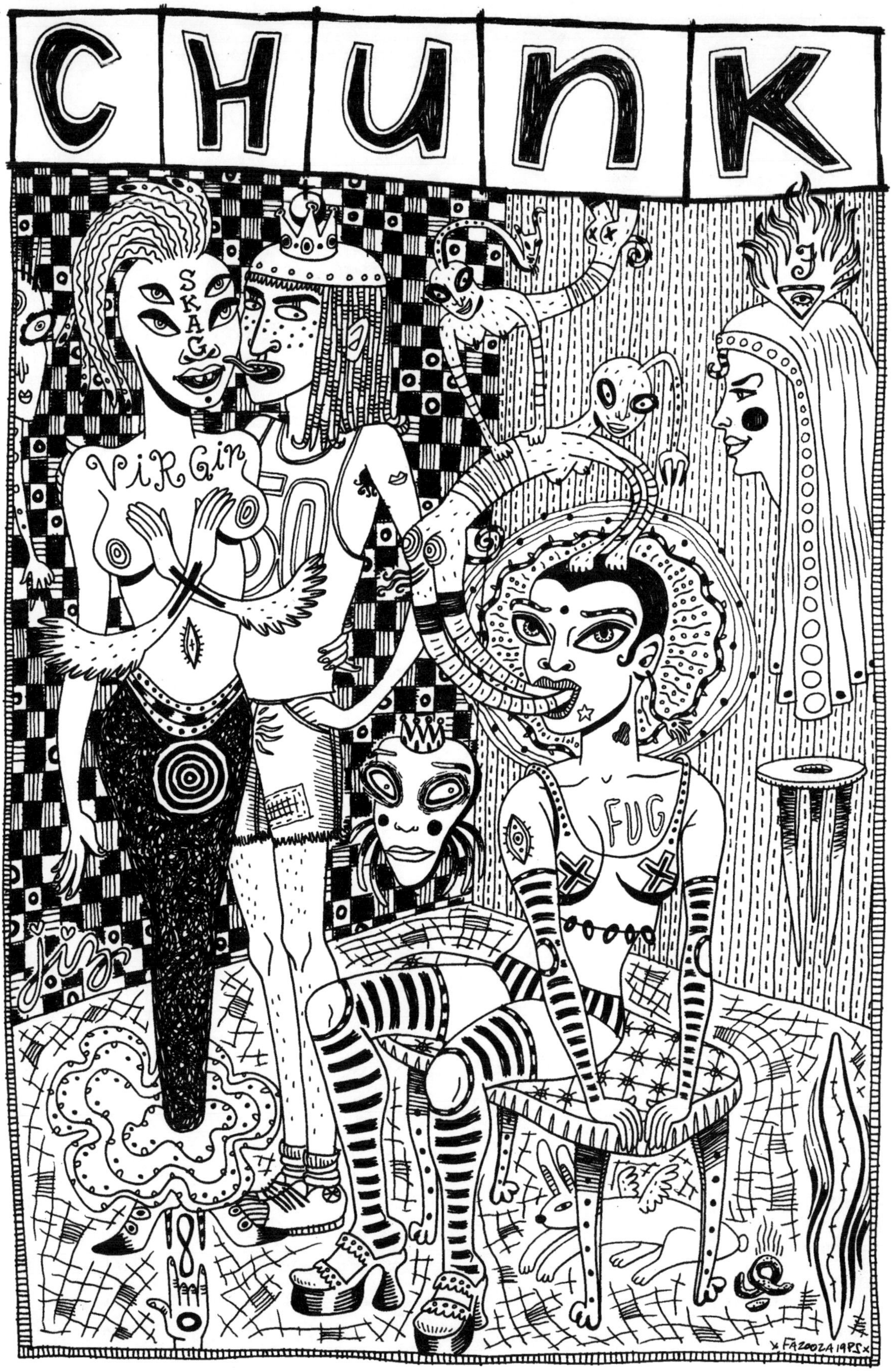
CHUNK
SKAG
VIRGIN
FUG
FAZOOZA 1995

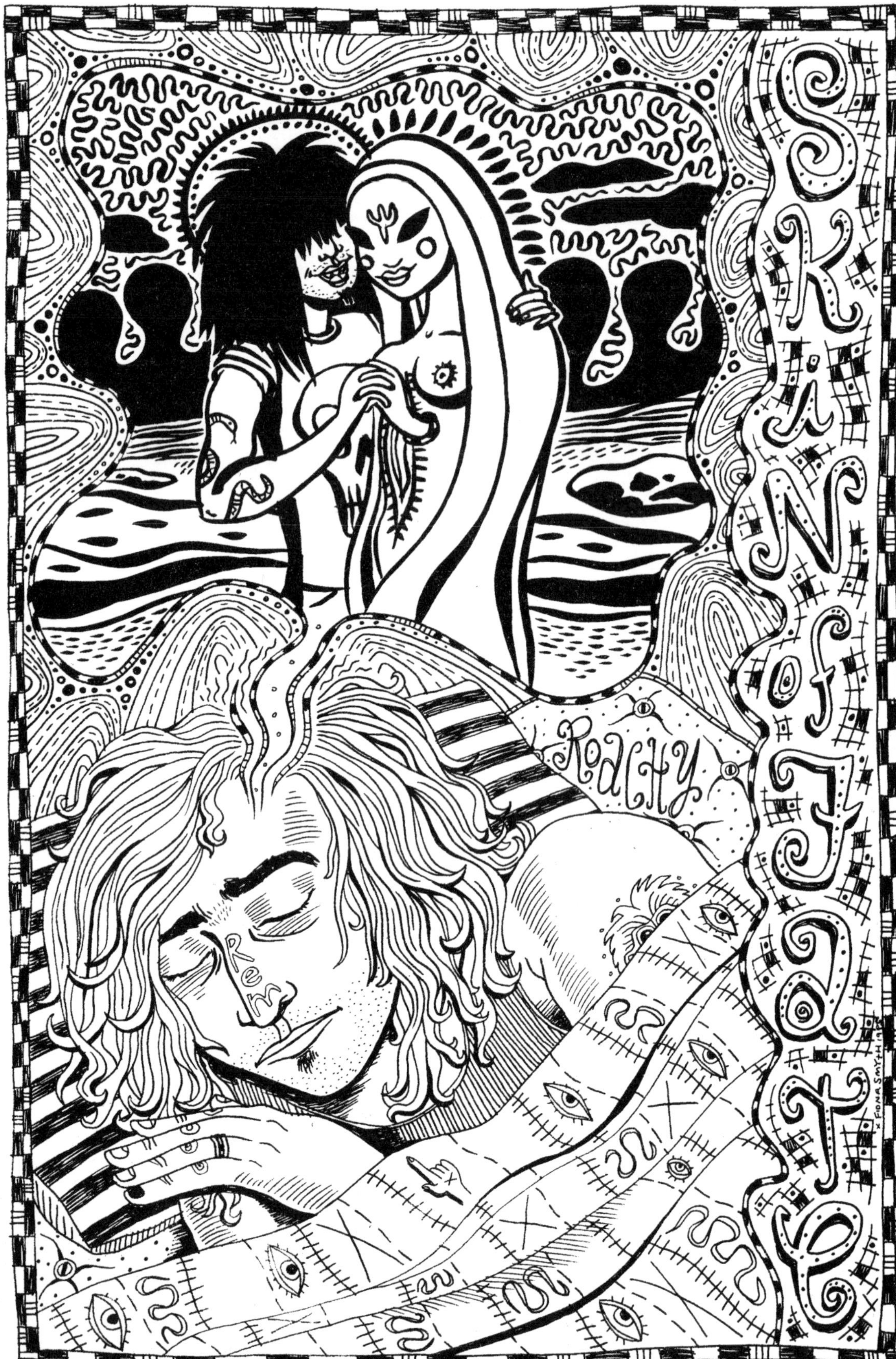
Skin of Jate
Roachy
Rem
FIONA SMYTH

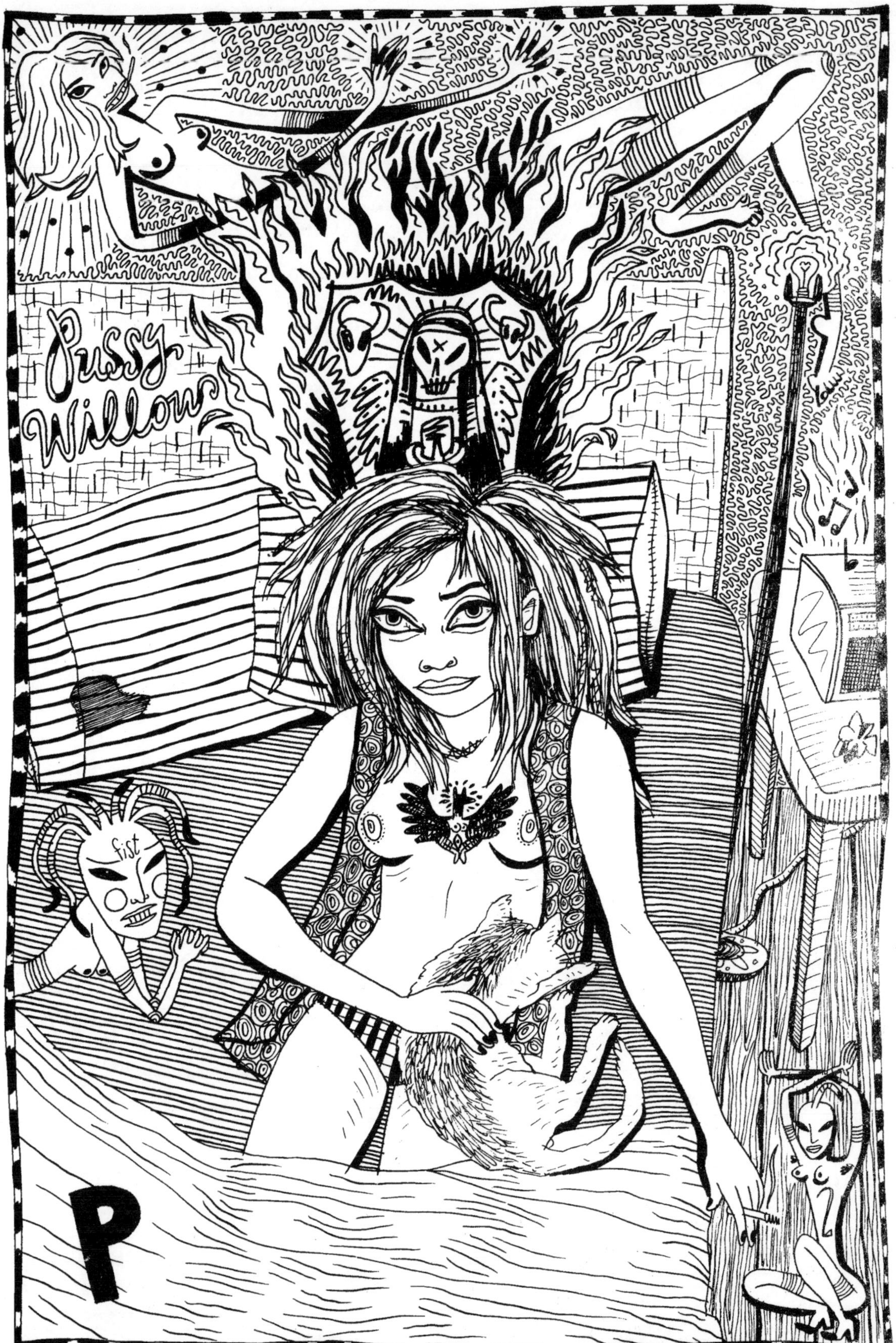

Pussy Willows
fist
P

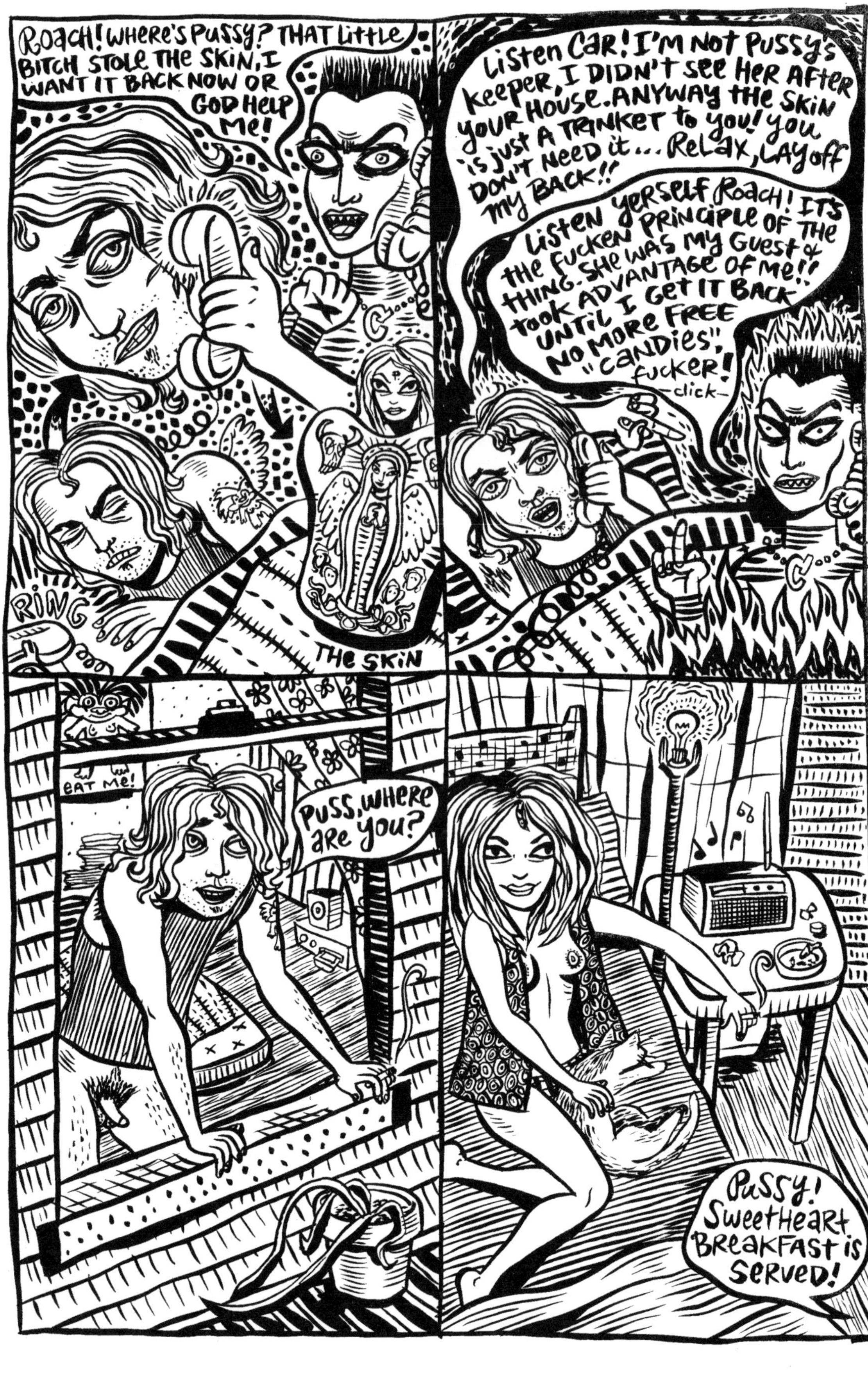
ROACH! WHERE'S PUSSY? THAT LITTLE BITCH STOLE THE SKIN, I WANT IT BACK NOW OR GOD HELP ME!
RING
THE SKIN
LISTEN CAR! I'M NOT PUSSY'S KEEPER, I DIDN'T SEE HER AFTER YOUR HOUSE. ANYWAY THE SKIN IS JUST A TRINKET TO YOU! YOU DON'T NEED IT... RELAX, LAY OFF MY BACK!!
LISTEN YERSELF ROACH! IT'S THE FUCKEN PRINCIPLE OF THE THING. SHE WAS MY GUEST & TOOK ADVANTAGE OF ME!! UNTIL I GET IT BACK NO MORE FREE "CANDIES", FUCKER!
—click—
EAT ME!
PUSS, WHERE ARE YOU?
PUSSY! SWEETHEART BREAKFAST IS SERVED!

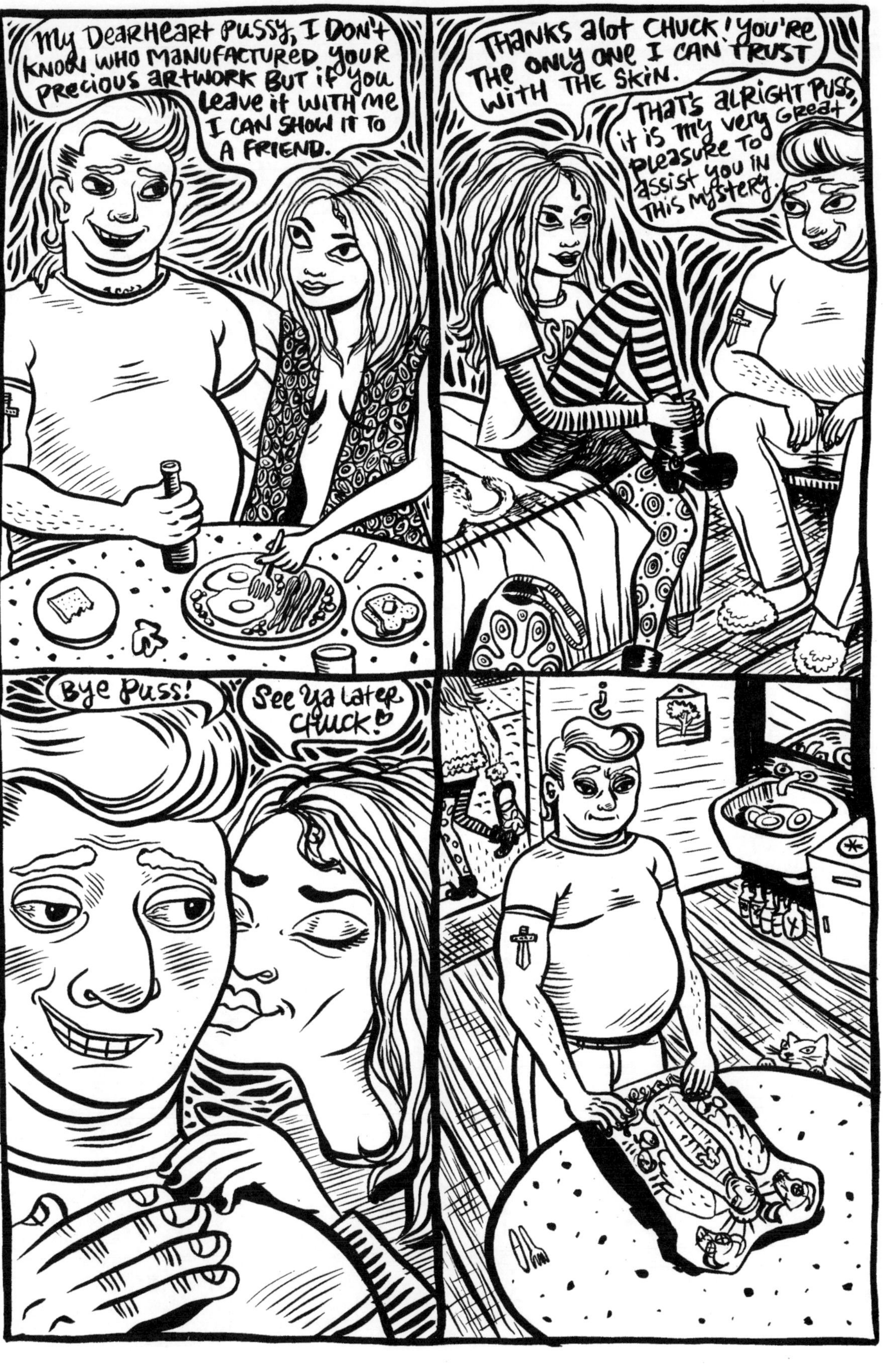
My DearHeart Pussy, I Don't know who manufactured your precious artwork but if you leave it with me I can show it to a friend.
Thanks alot Chuck! You're the only one I can trust with the skin.
That's alright Puss, it is my very great pleasure to assist you in this mystery.
Bye Puss!
See ya later Chuck!
¿

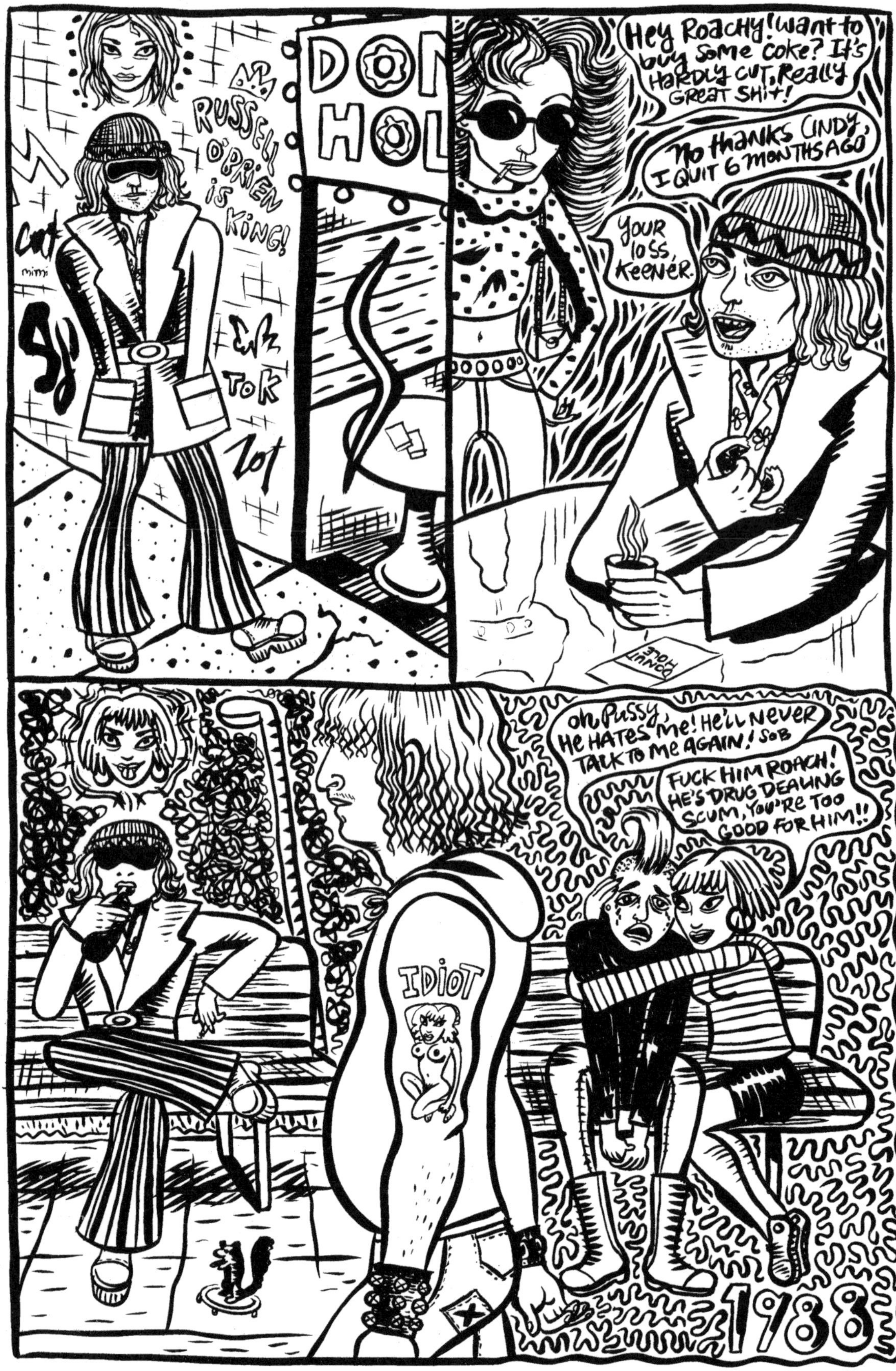
RUSSELL O'BRIEN IS KING!
TOK
DO
HOL
Hey Roachy! want to buy some coke? It's HARDLY CUT, Really GREAT SHIT!
No thanks CINDY, I QUIT 6 MONTHS AGO
YOUR loss, Keener.
DONUT HOLE
oh Pussy, He HATES me! He'll NEVER TALK TO me AGAIN! SOB
FUCK HIM ROACH! HE'S DRUG DEALING SCUM, YOU'RE TOO GOOD FOR HIM!!
IDIOT
1988

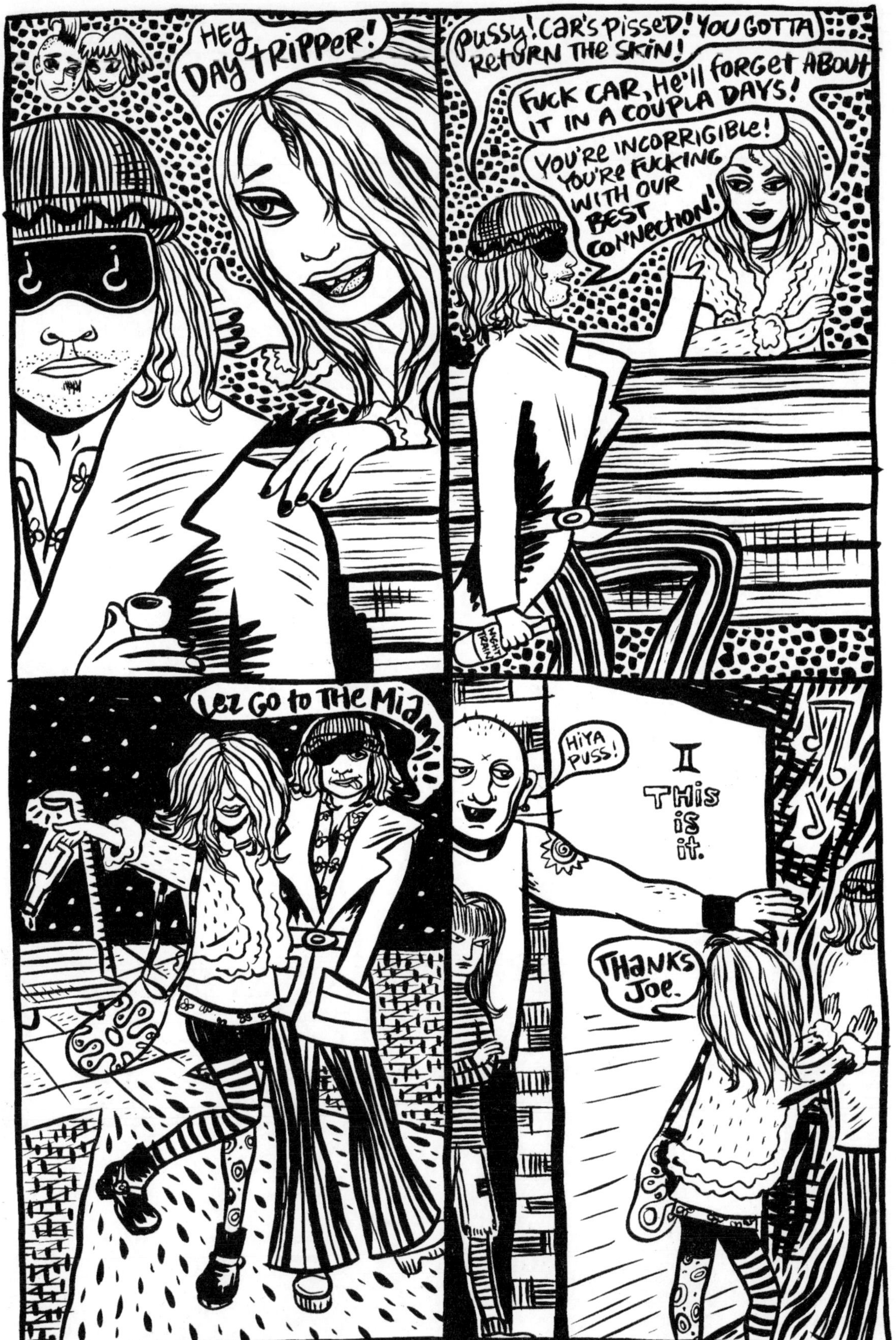

HEY DAY TRIPPER!
PUSSY! CAR'S PISSED! YOU GOTTA RETURN THE SKIN!
FUCK CAR, HE'LL FORGET ABOUT IT IN A COUPLA DAYS!
YOU'RE INCORRIGIBLE! YOU'RE FUCKING WITH OUR BEST CONNECTION!
NIGHT TRAIN
LEZ GO TO THE MIAMI!!!
HIYA PUSS!
THIS is it.
THANKS JOE.

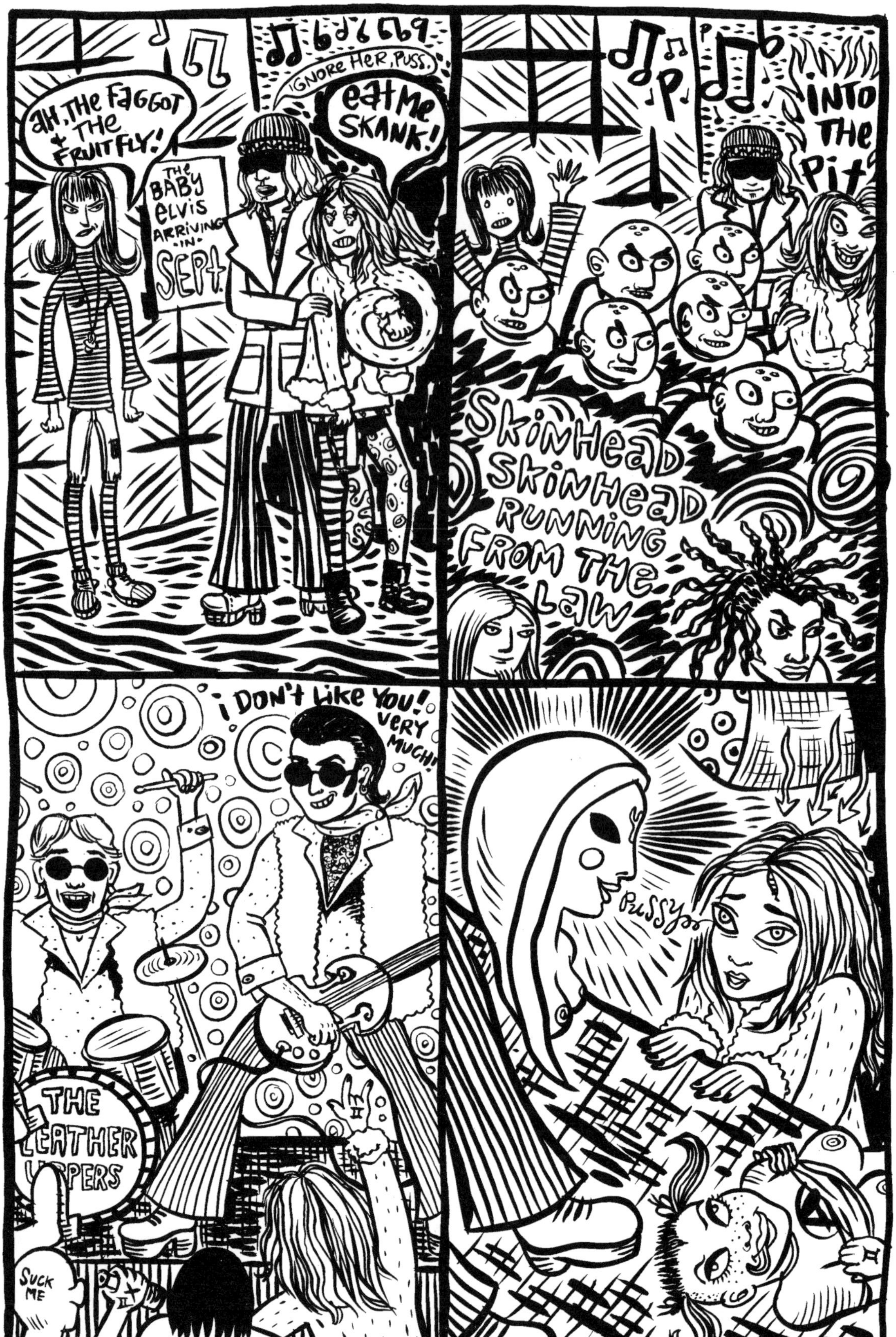

AH, THE FAGGOT & THE FRUITFLY!
IGNORE HER, PUSS.
EAT ME SKANK!
THE BABY ELVIS ARRIVING -IN- SEPT.
INTO THE PIT
SKINHEAD SKINHEAD RUNNING FROM THE LAW
I DON'T LIKE YOU! VERY MUCH!
THE LEATHER UPPERS
SUCK ME
PUSSY...

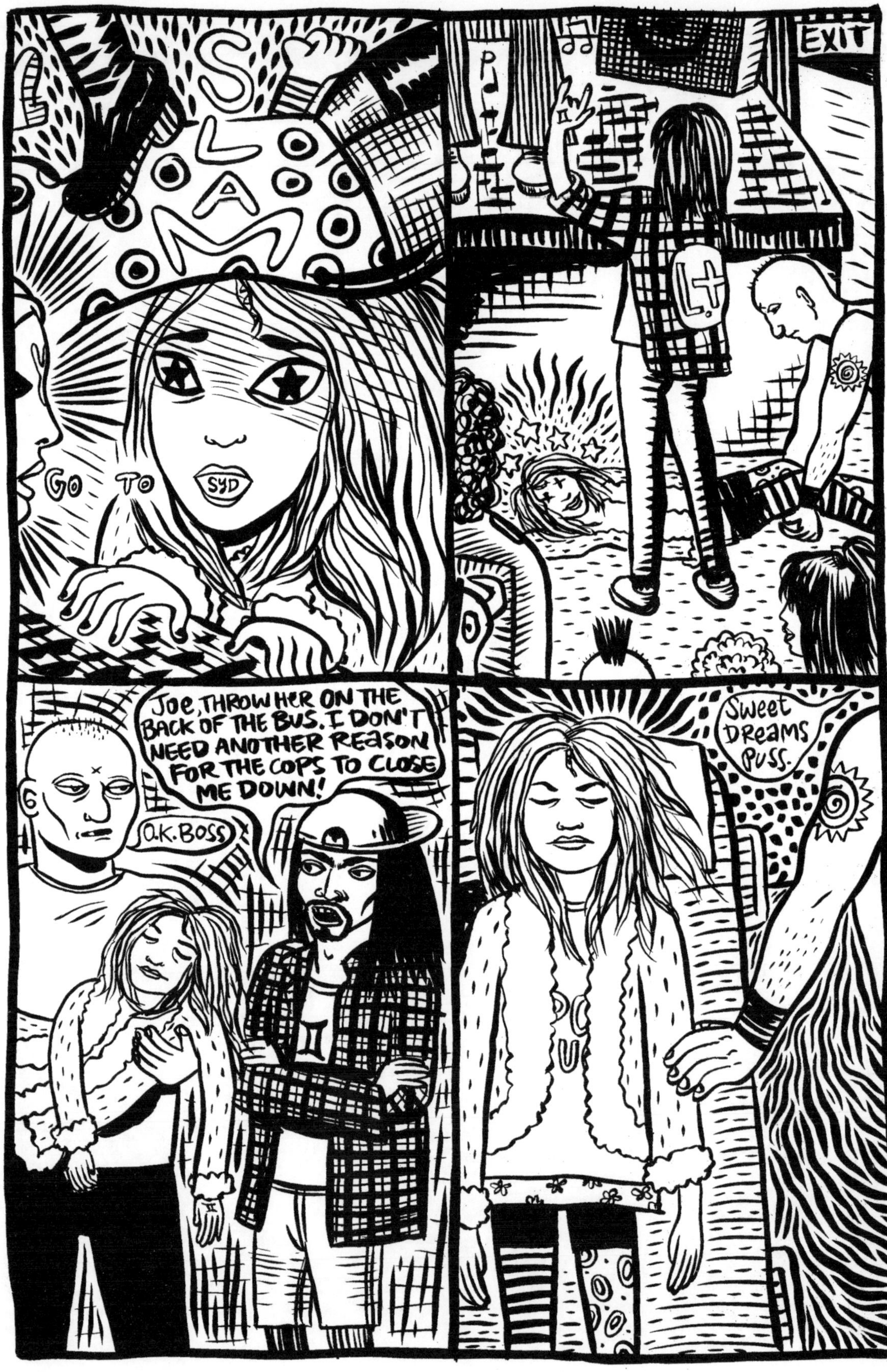
EXIT
GO TO SYD
JOE, THROW HER ON THE BACK OF THE BUS. I DON'T NEED ANOTHER REASON FOR THE COPS TO CLOSE ME DOWN!
O.K. BOSS
SWEET DREAMS PUSS.

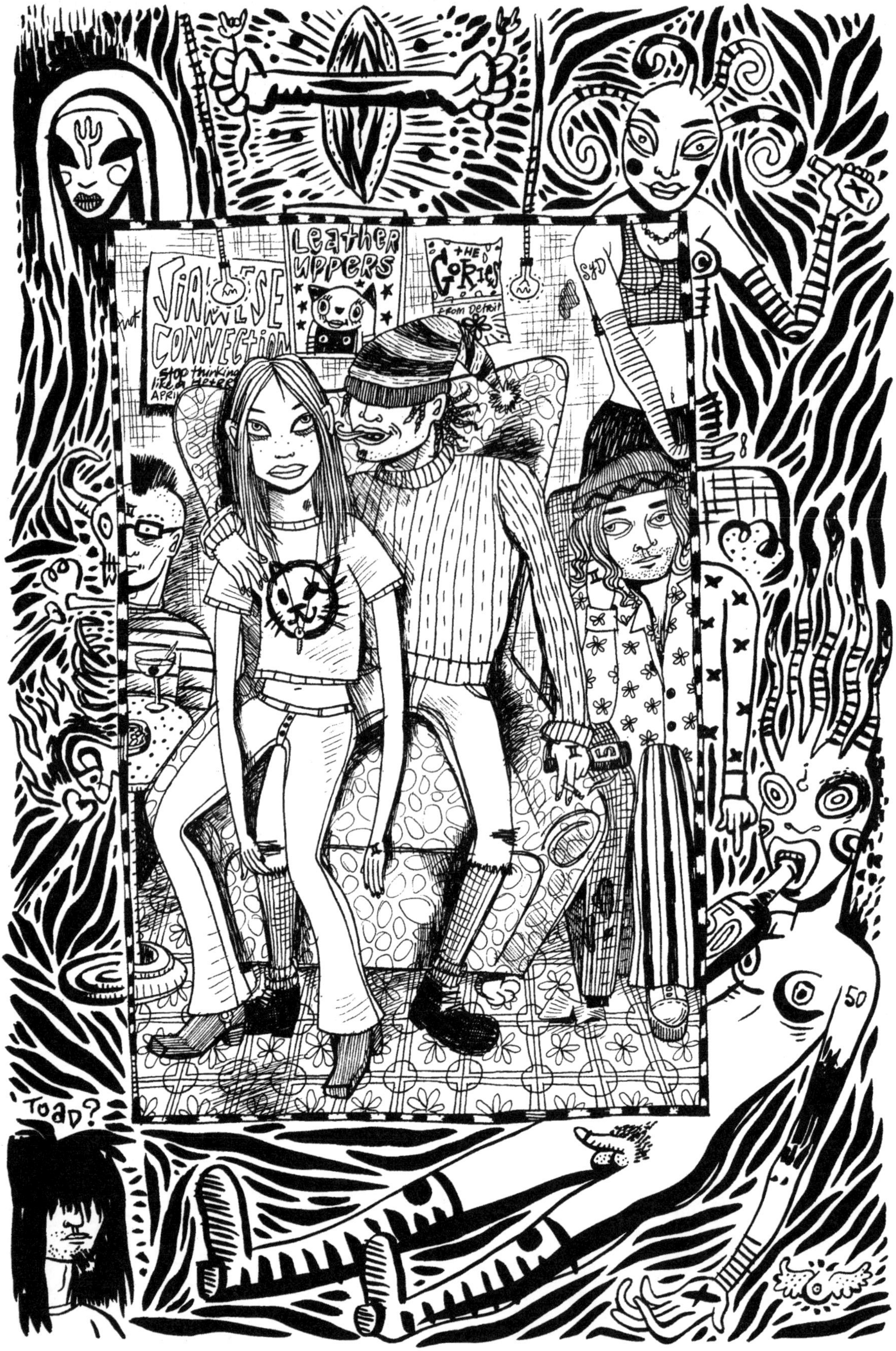
CONNECTION
stop thinking
Leather Uppers
THE GORIES
FROM DETROIT
TOAD?
50

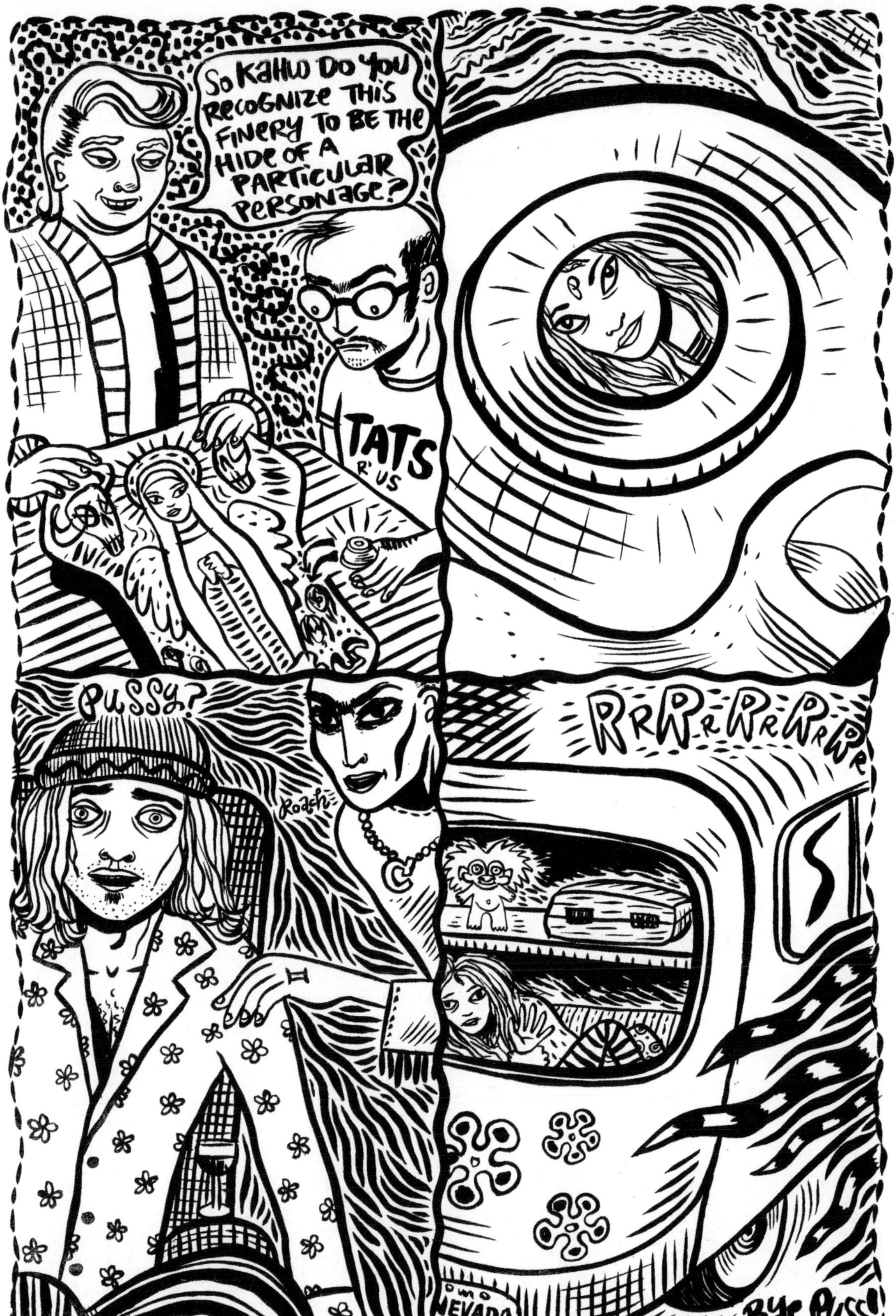
So Kahlo Do You Recognize This Finery To Be The Hide Of A Particular Personage?
TATS R'US
Pussy?
Roach
RRRRRRRRRRRRRR
NEVADA
Bye Puss!

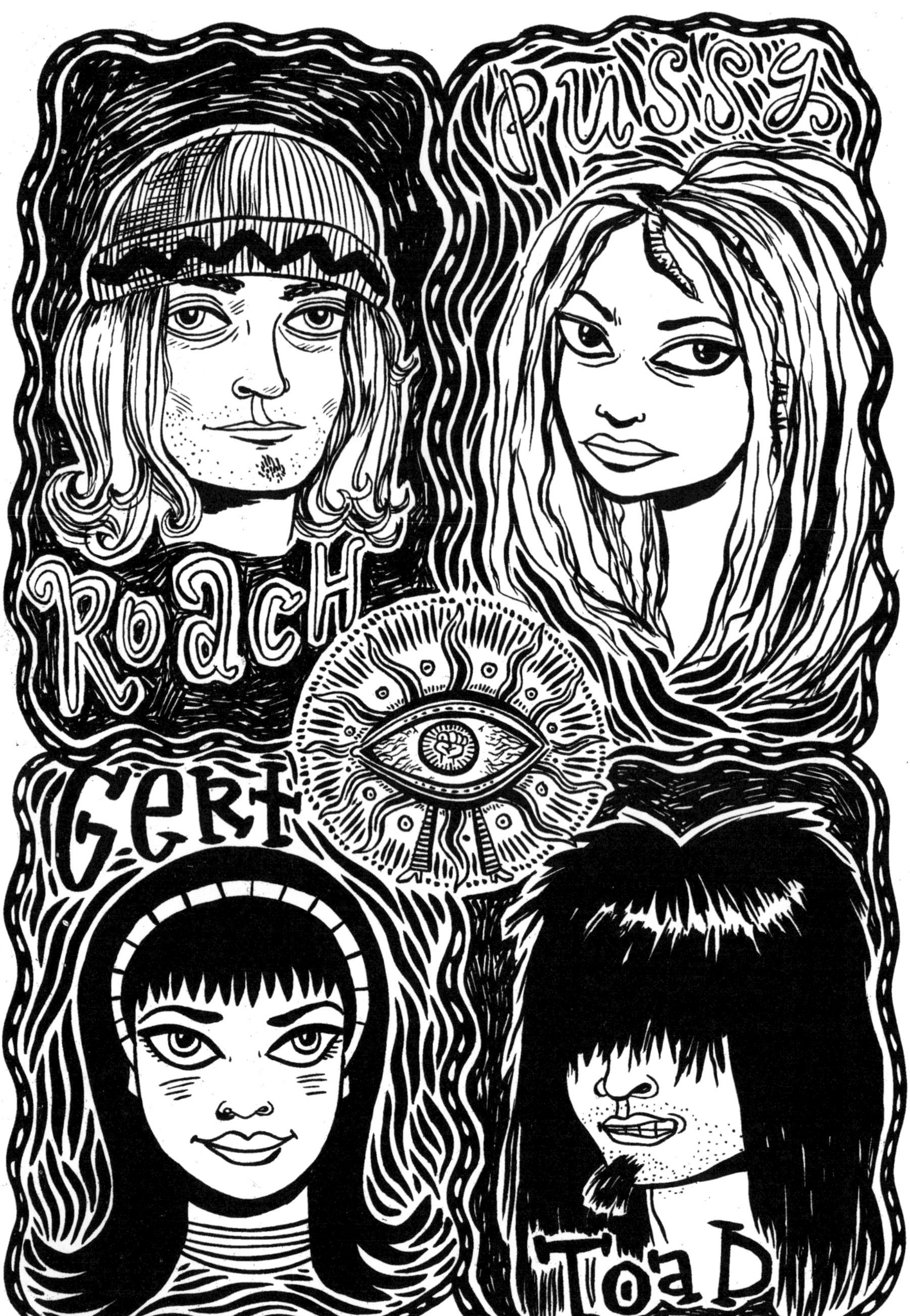
Pussy
Roach
Gert
Toad

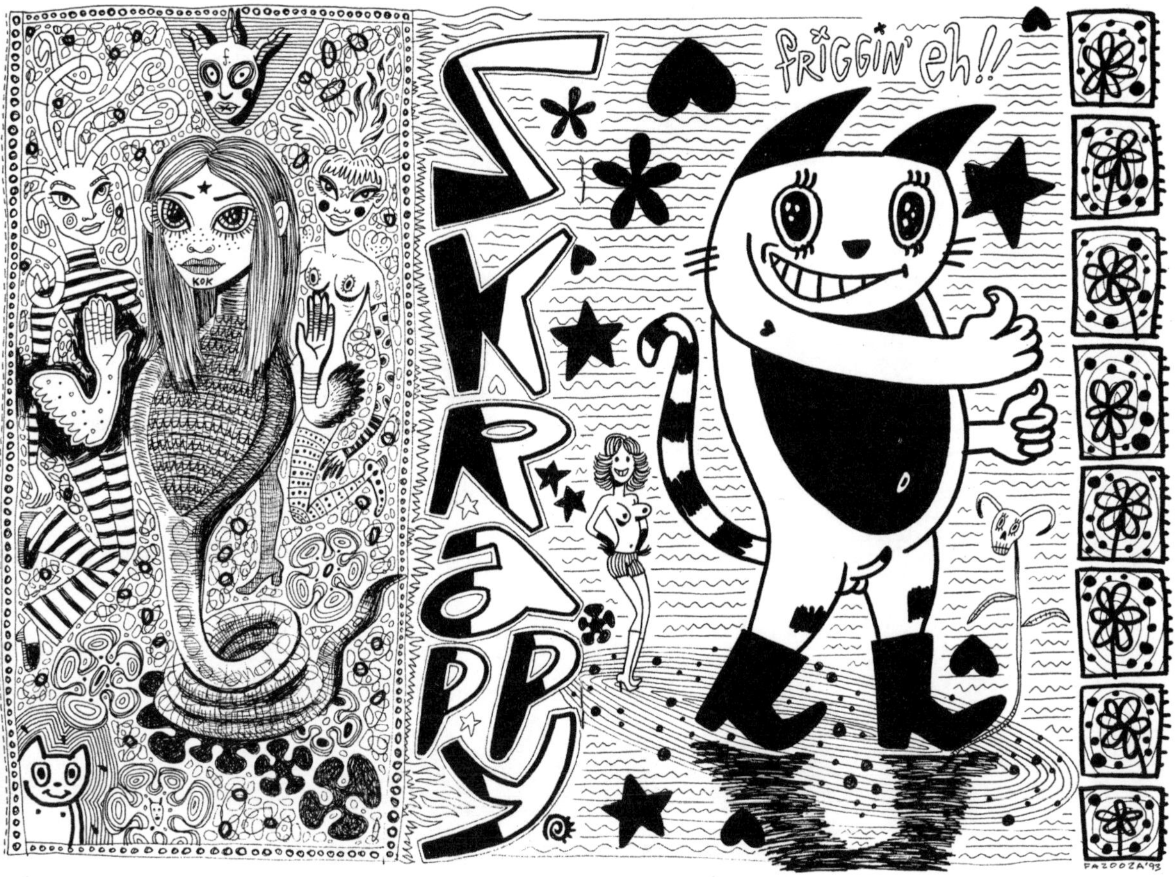
SKRAPPY
friggin' eh!!
KOK
FAZOOZA'93

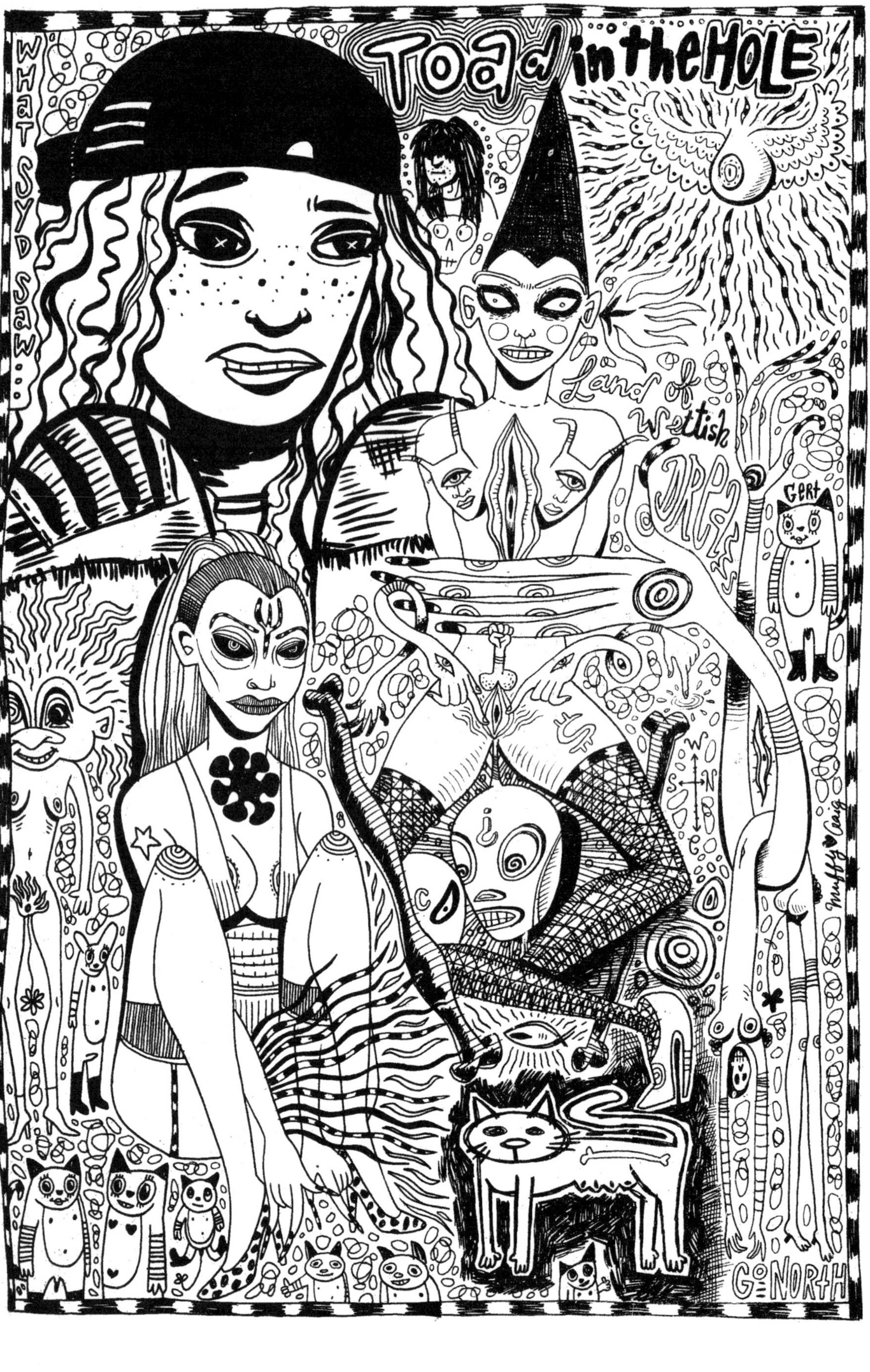
WHAT SYD SAW...
Toad in the HOLE
Land of Wettish DREAMS
Gert
W N S E
muffy ♥ craig
Go NORTH

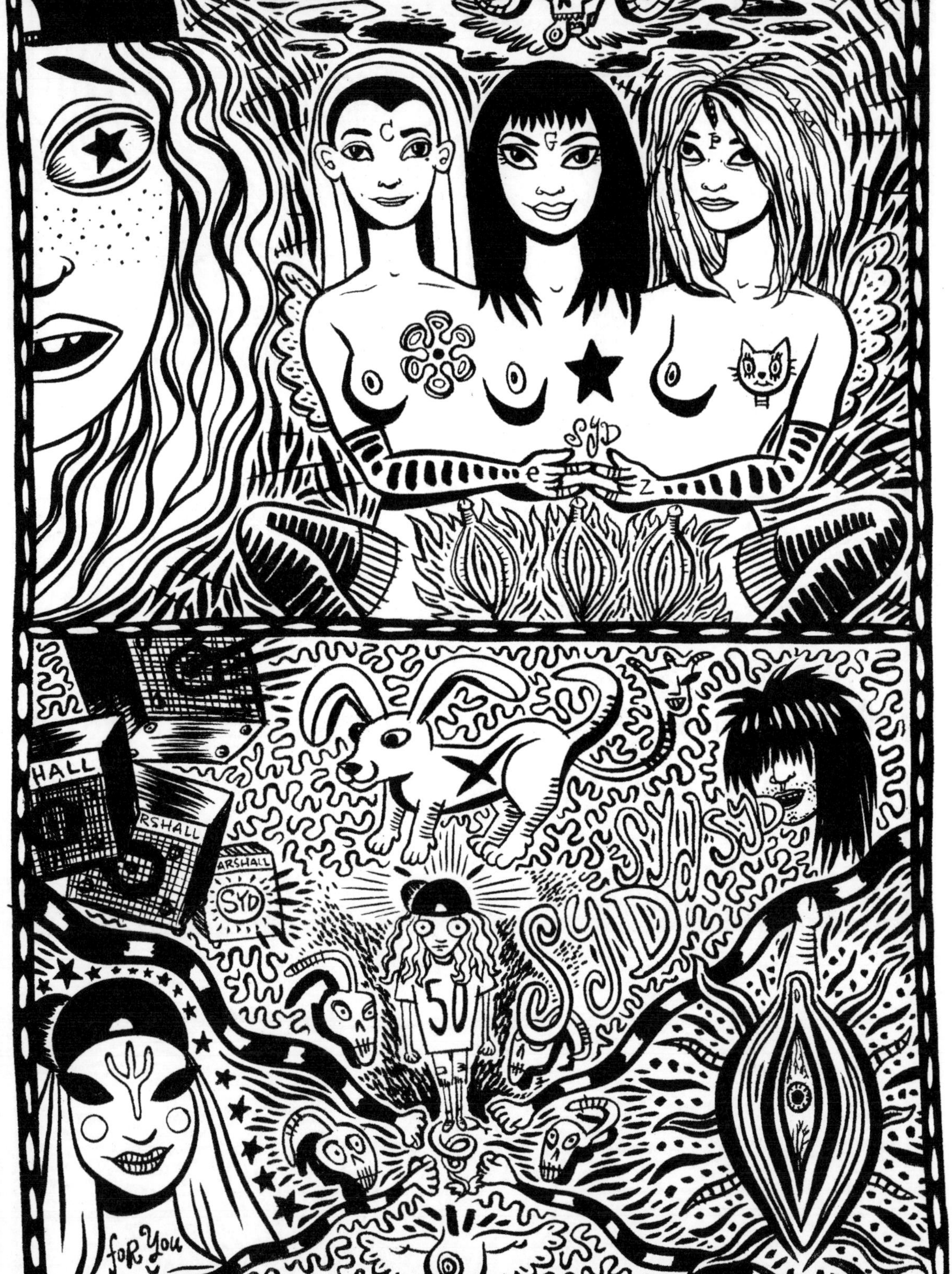

SYD
HALL
RSHALL
ARSHALL
SYD
SYD
SYD
SYD
50
for You

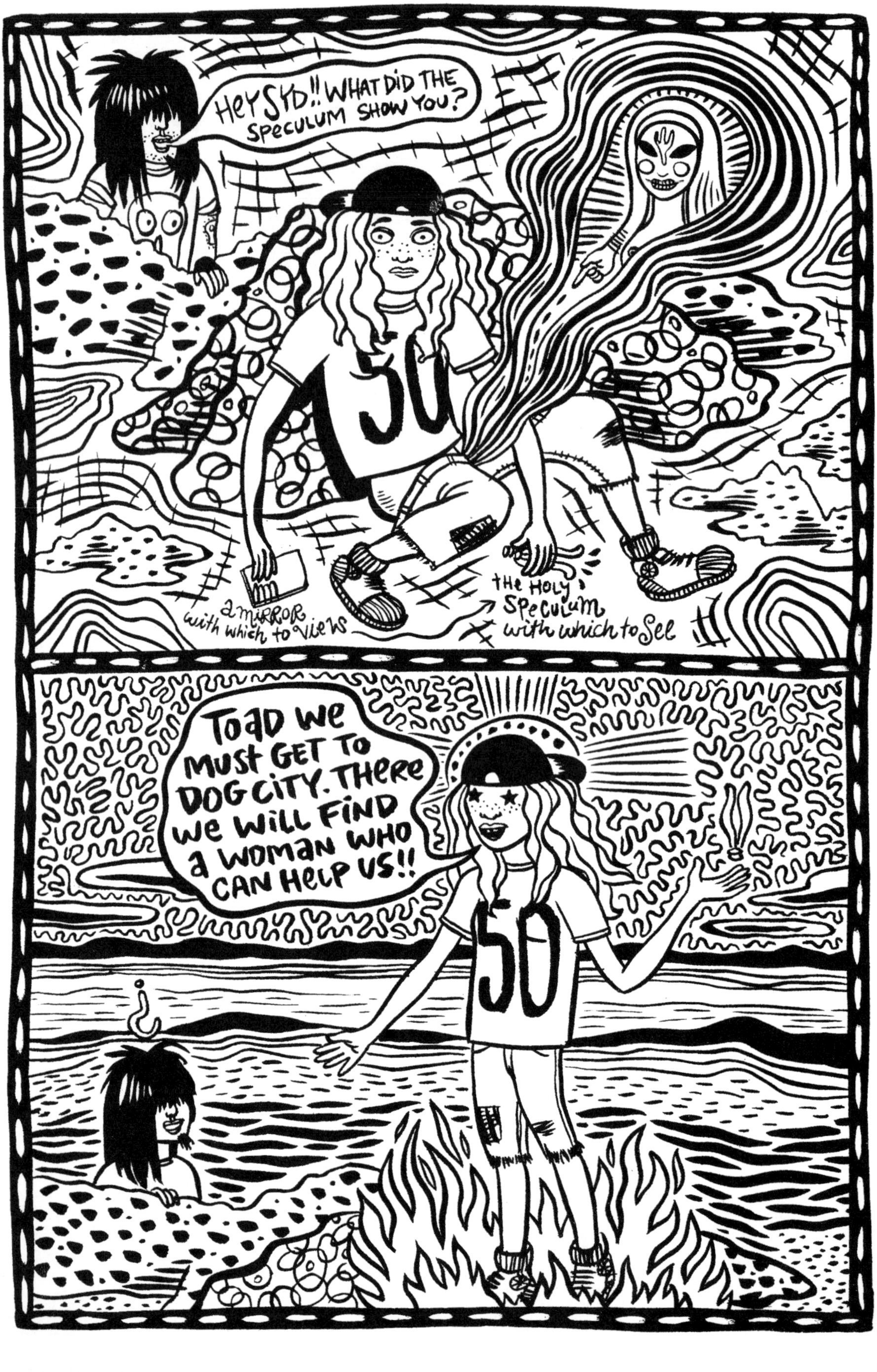
HEY SYD!! WHAT DID THE SPECULUM SHOW YOU?
a MIRROR with which to view
THE HOLY SPECULUM with which to see
TOAD WE MUST GET TO DOG CITY. THERE WE WILL FIND A WOMAN WHO CAN HELP US!!

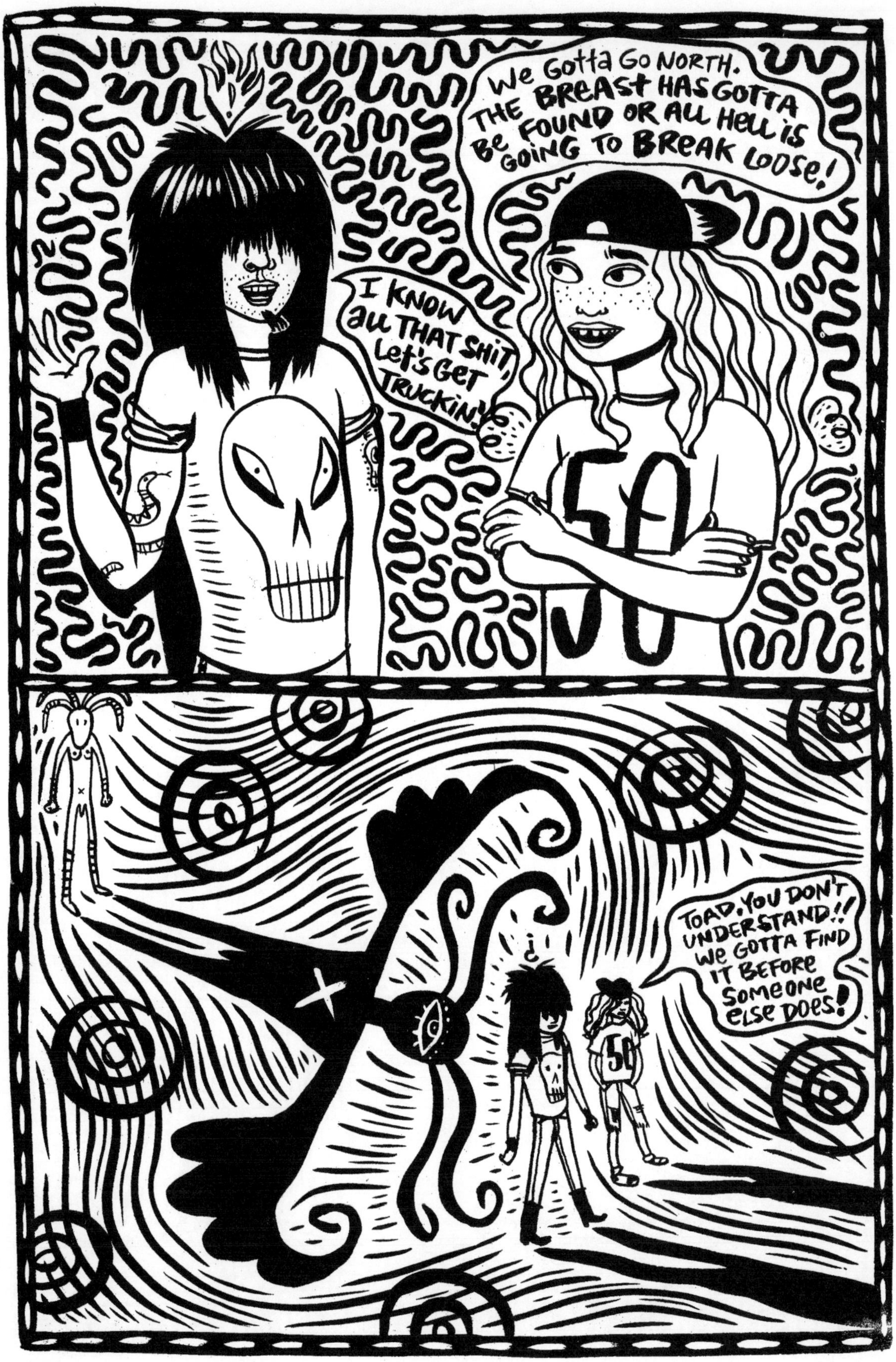
We Gotta Go NORTH. THE BREAST HAS GOTTA Be FOUND OR ALL HELL IS GOING TO BREAK LOOSE!
I KNOW ALL THAT SHIT, Let's GET TRUCKIN'!
TOAD, YOU DON'T UNDERSTAND!! We GOTTA FIND IT BEFORE SOMEONE ELSE DOES!
50

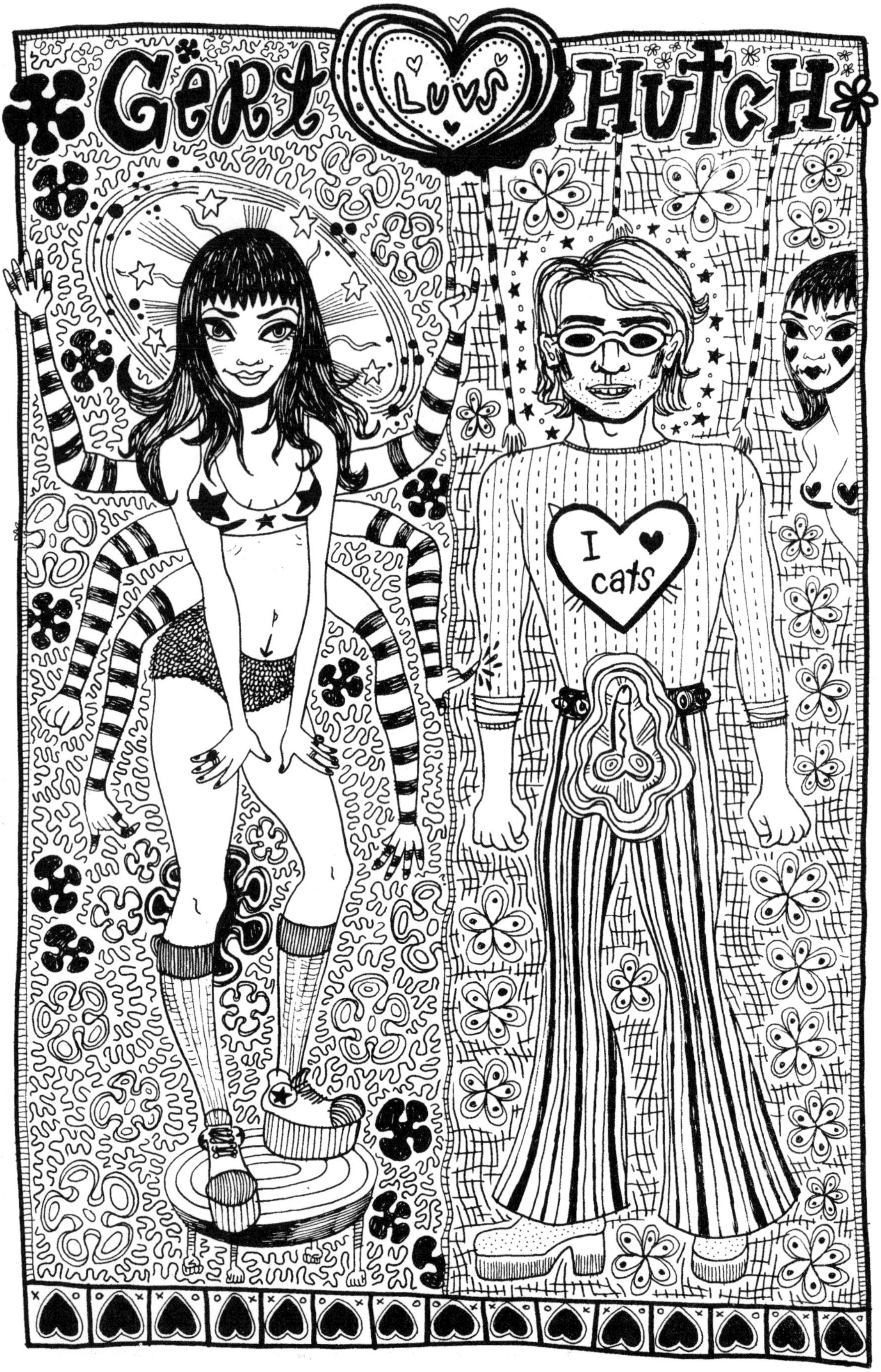

Gert
Luvs
Hutch
I ♥ cats

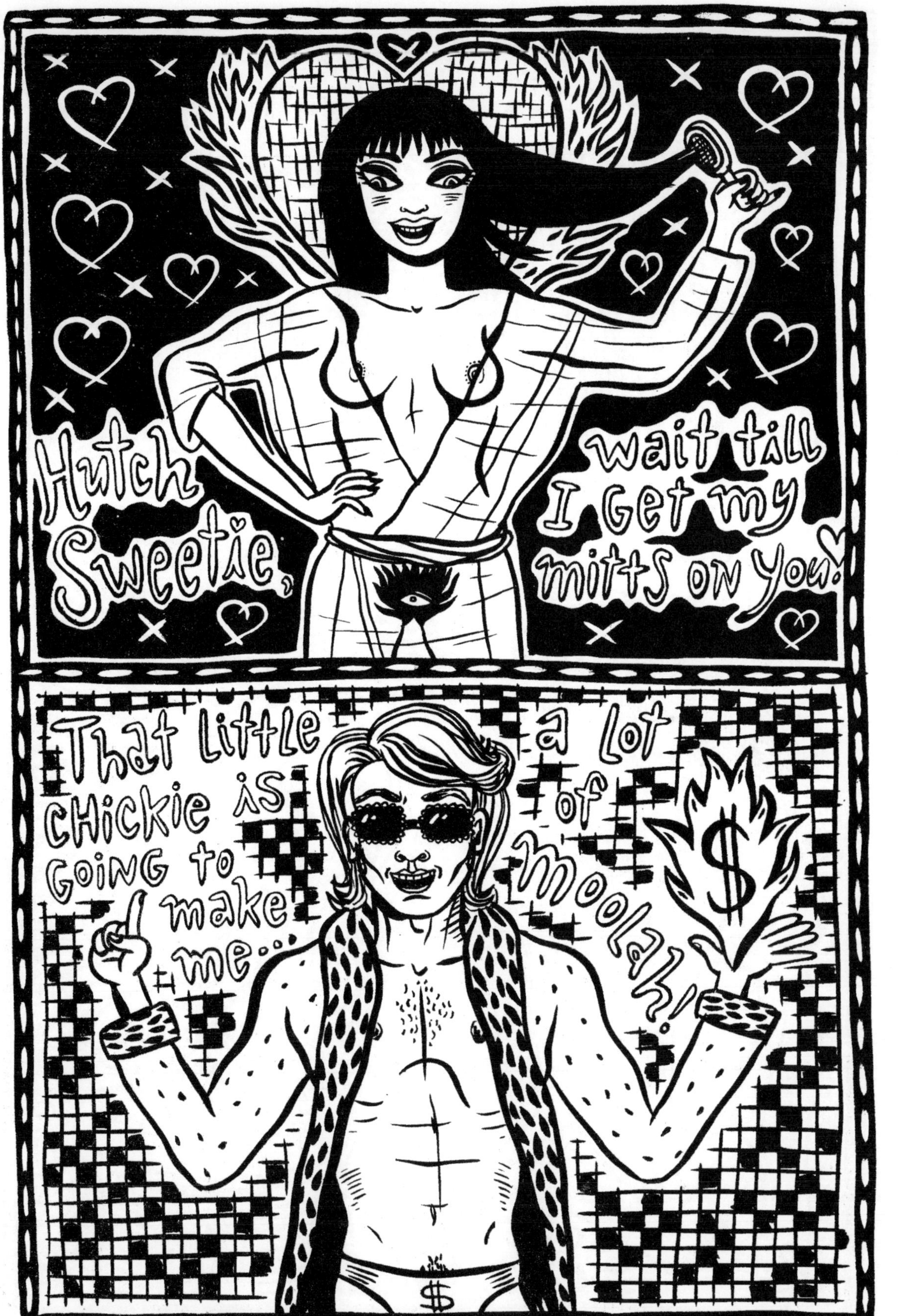
Hutch Sweetie,
wait till I get my mitts on you!
That little chickie is going to make me...
a lot of moolah?!
$
$

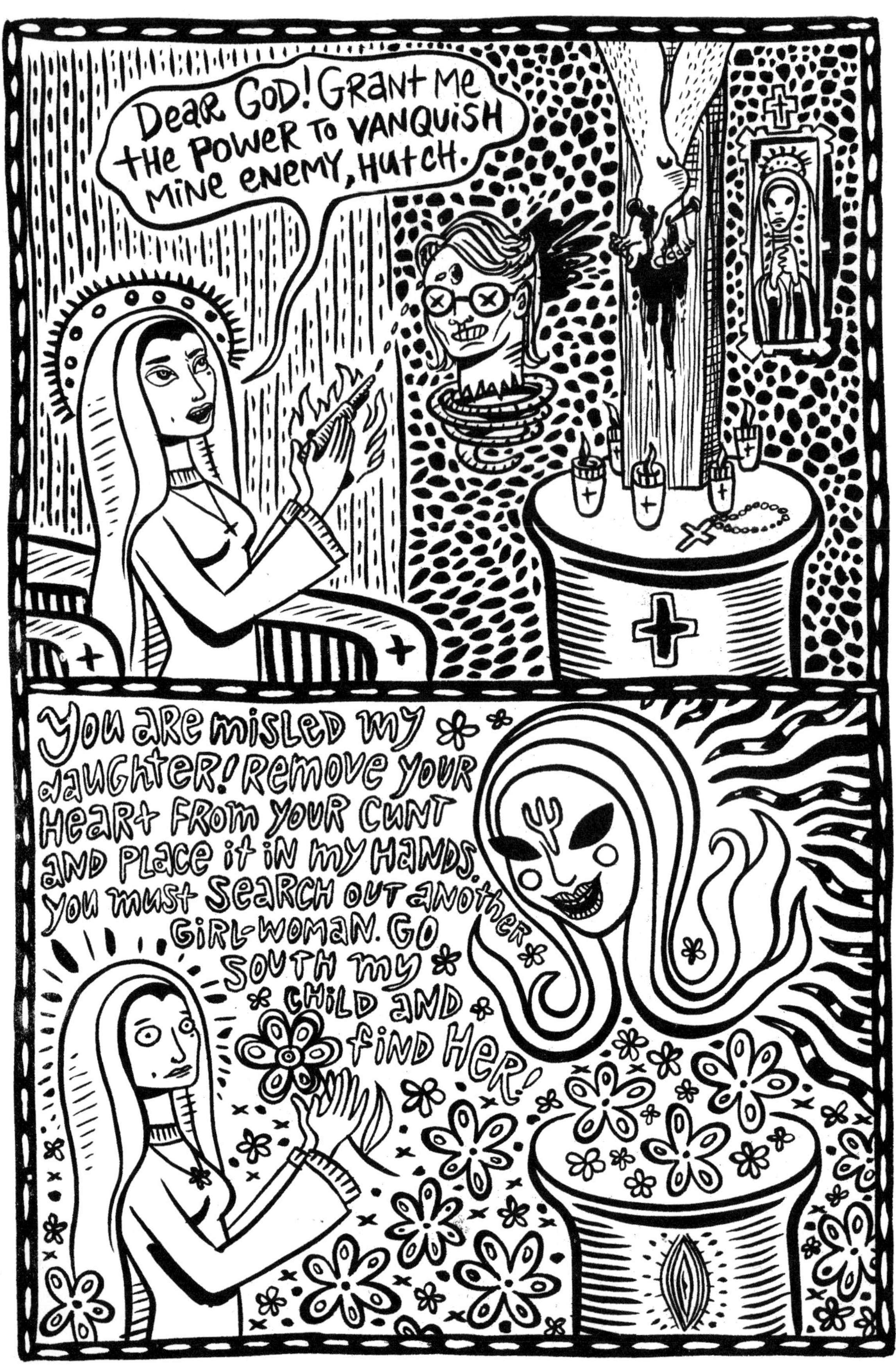
DEAR GOD! GRANT ME THE POWER TO VANQUISH MINE ENEMY, HUTCH.
YOU ARE MISLED MY DAUGHTER! REMOVE YOUR HEART FROM YOUR CUNT AND PLACE IT IN MY HANDS. YOU MUST SEARCH OUT ANOTHER GIRL-WOMAN. GO SOUTH MY CHILD AND FIND HER!

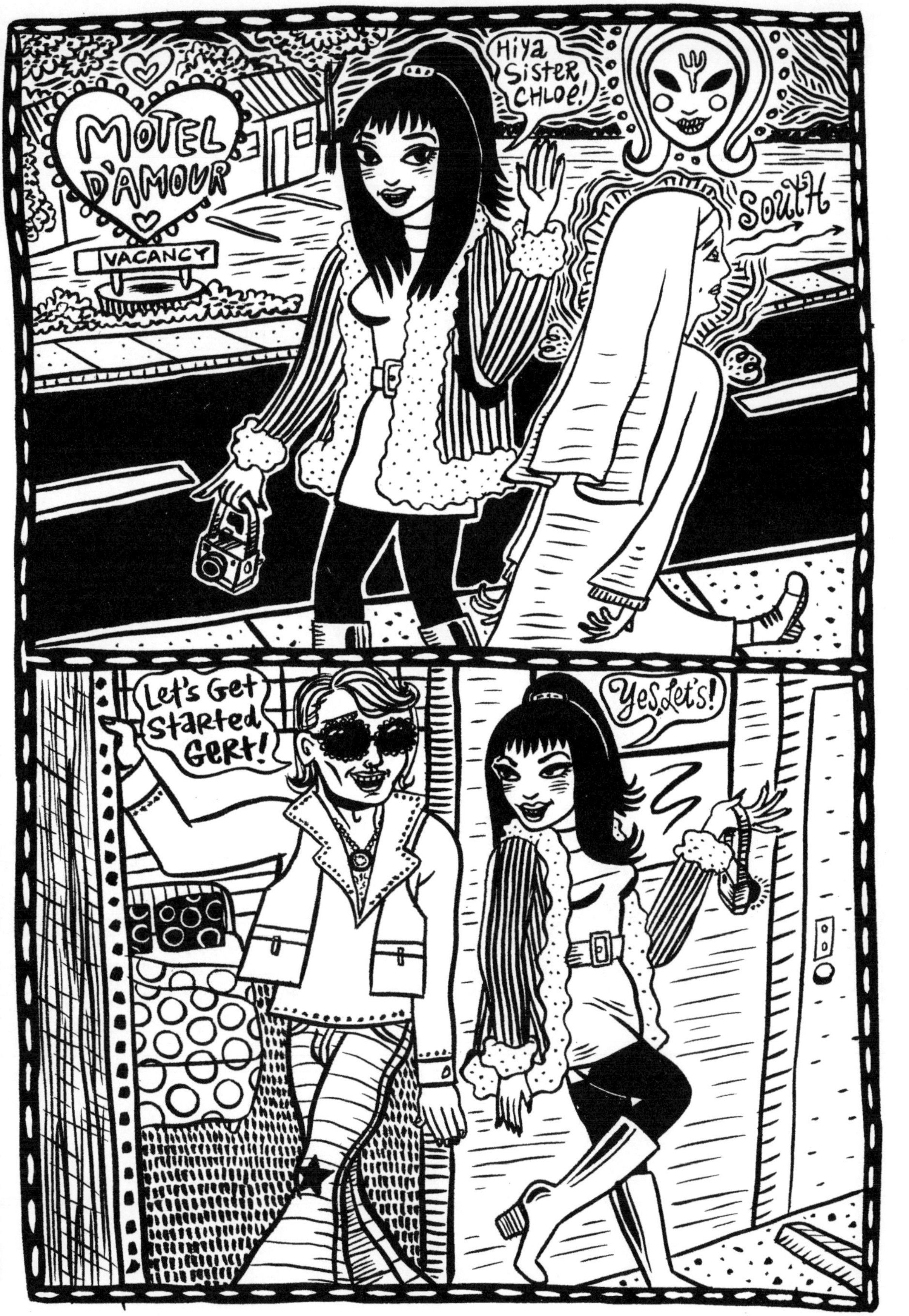
MOTEL D'AMOUR
VACANCY
Hiya Sister CHLOE!
SOUTH
Let's Get started Gert!
Yes, Let's!

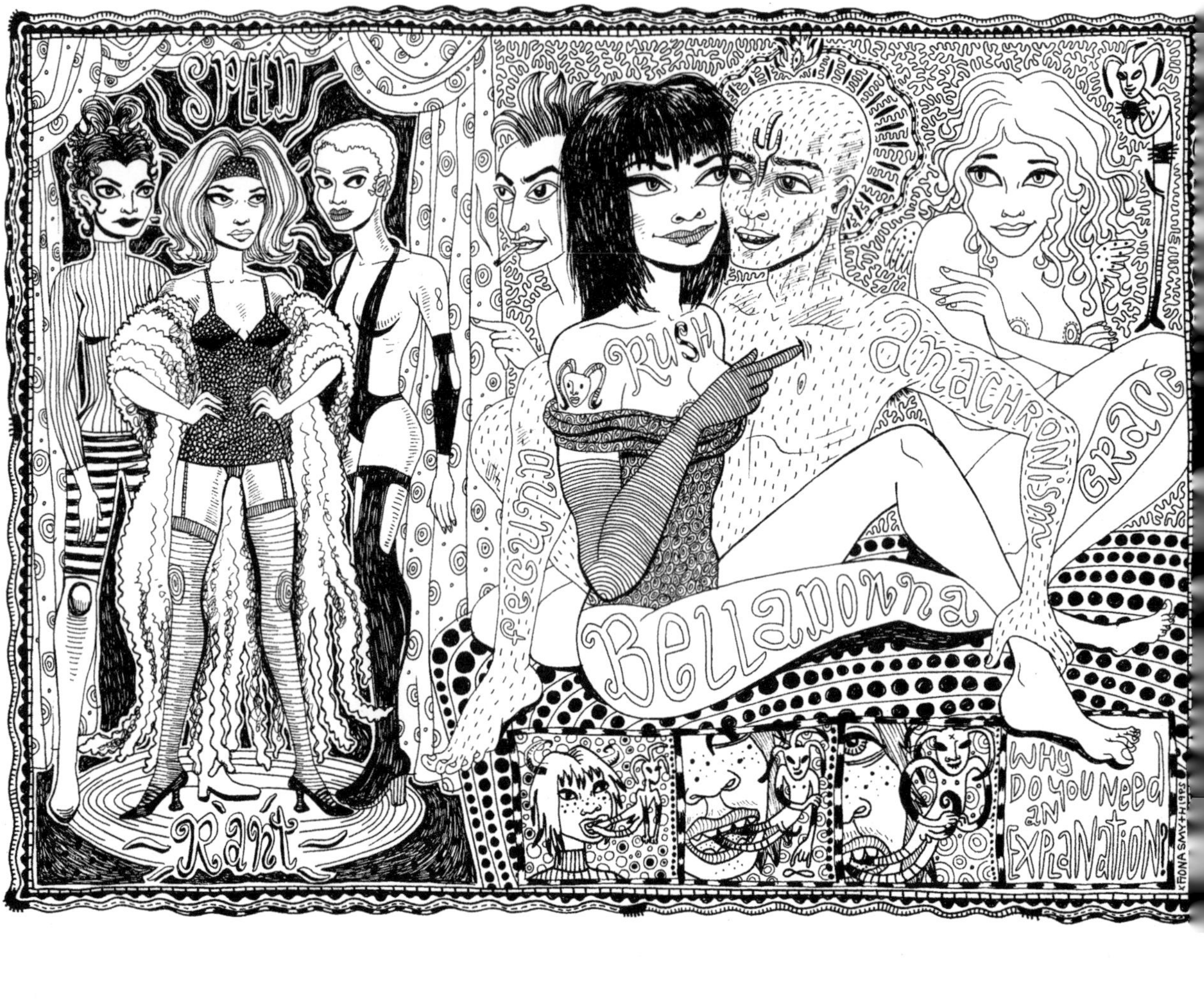
SPEED
Rant
RUSH
fecunda
Anachronism
Grace
Belladonna
WHY DO YOU NEED AN EXPLANATION?
FIONA SMYTH 1995

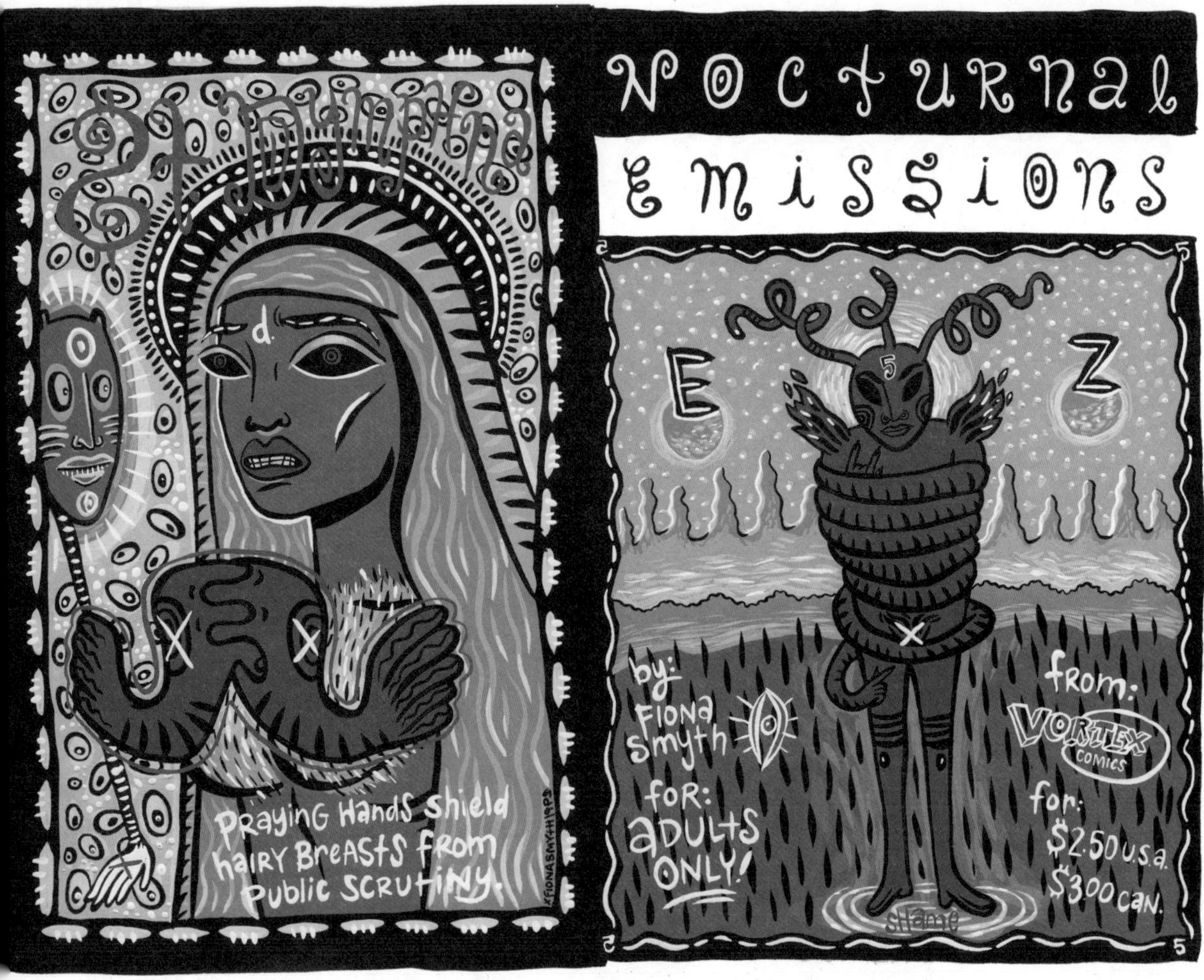
St. Dymphna
d
Praying Hands Shield hairy Breasts from Public SCRUtiny.
Nocturnal Emissions
E
Z
5
by: Fiona Smyth
for: adults only!
from: Vortex Comics
for: $2.50 u.s.a. $3.00 can.
shame
5

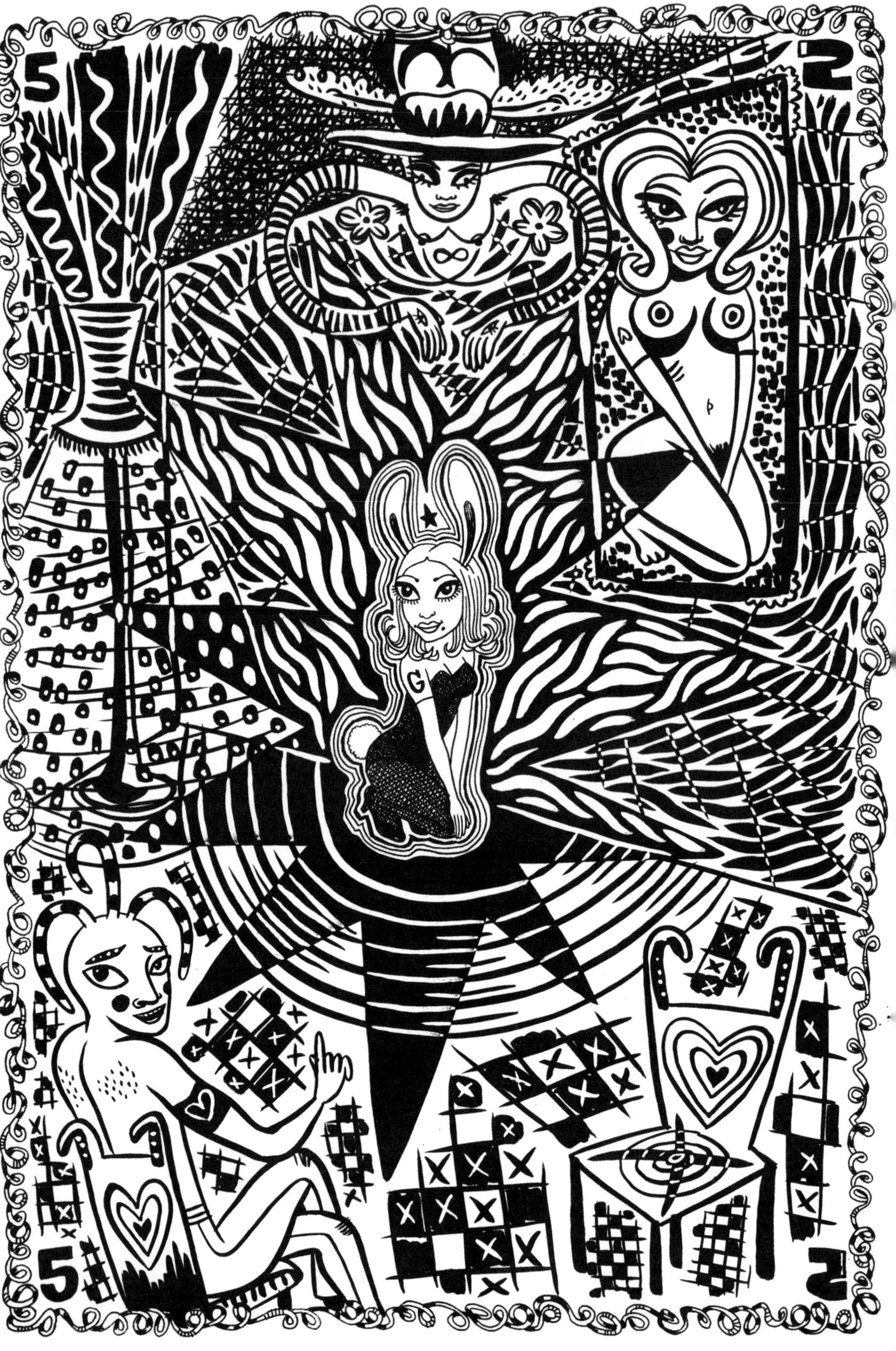
5
2
G
5
2

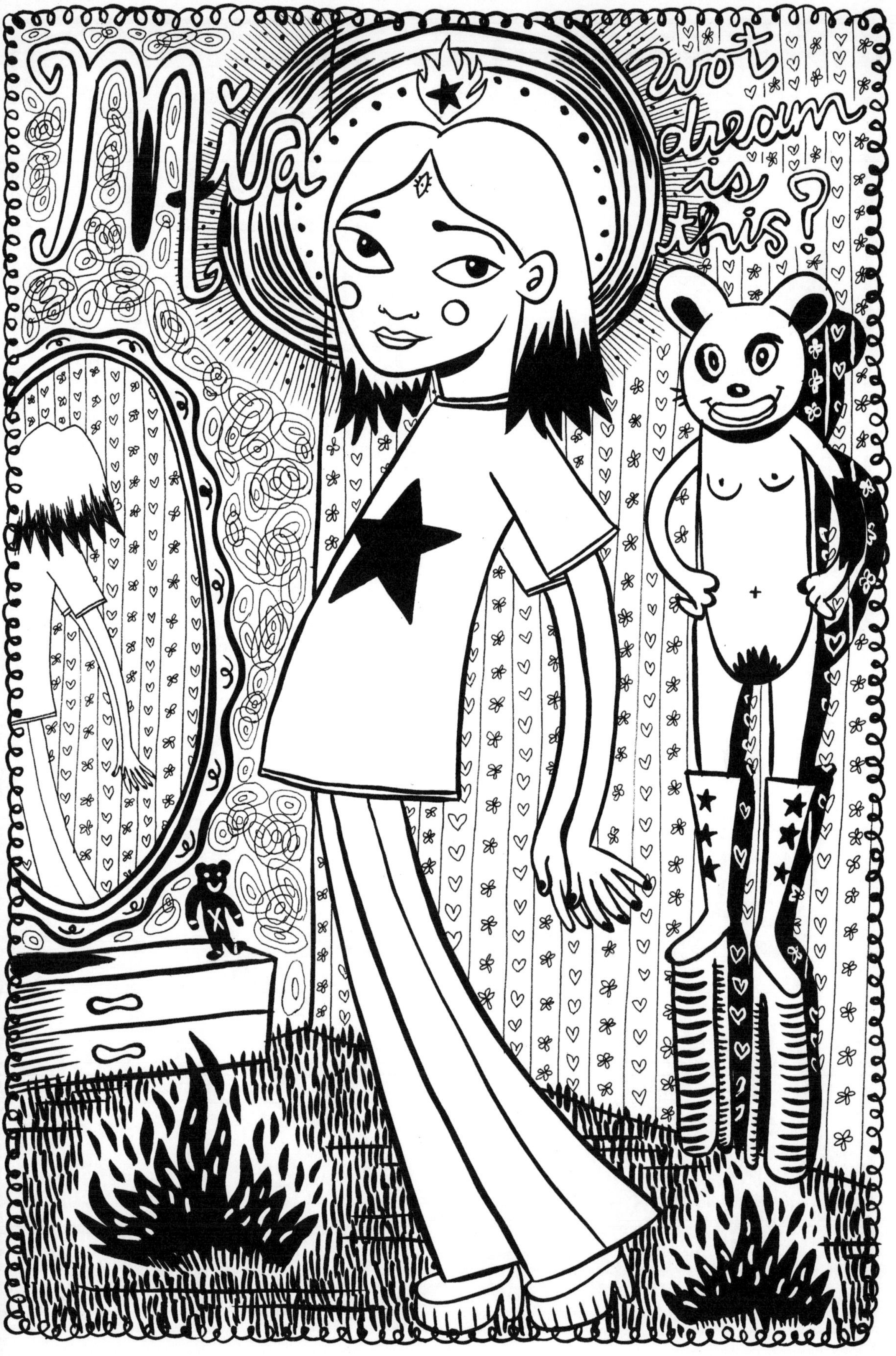
Mia
wot dream is this?

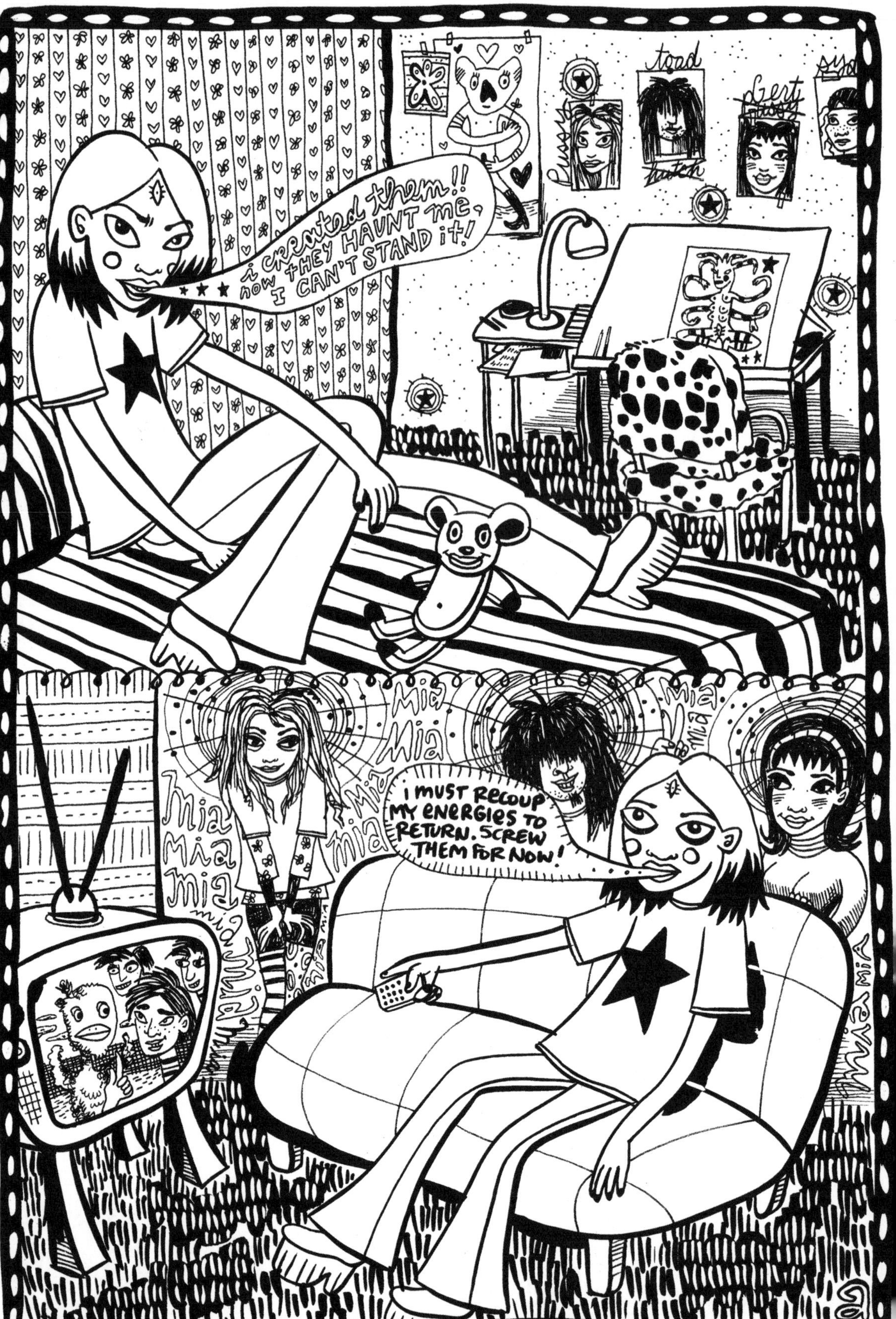
i created them!! now THEY HAUNT me, I CAN'T STAND it!
toad
Gert
I MUST RECOUP MY ENERGIES TO RETURN. SCREW THEM FOR NOW!
mia mia mia mia mia mia mia mia mia

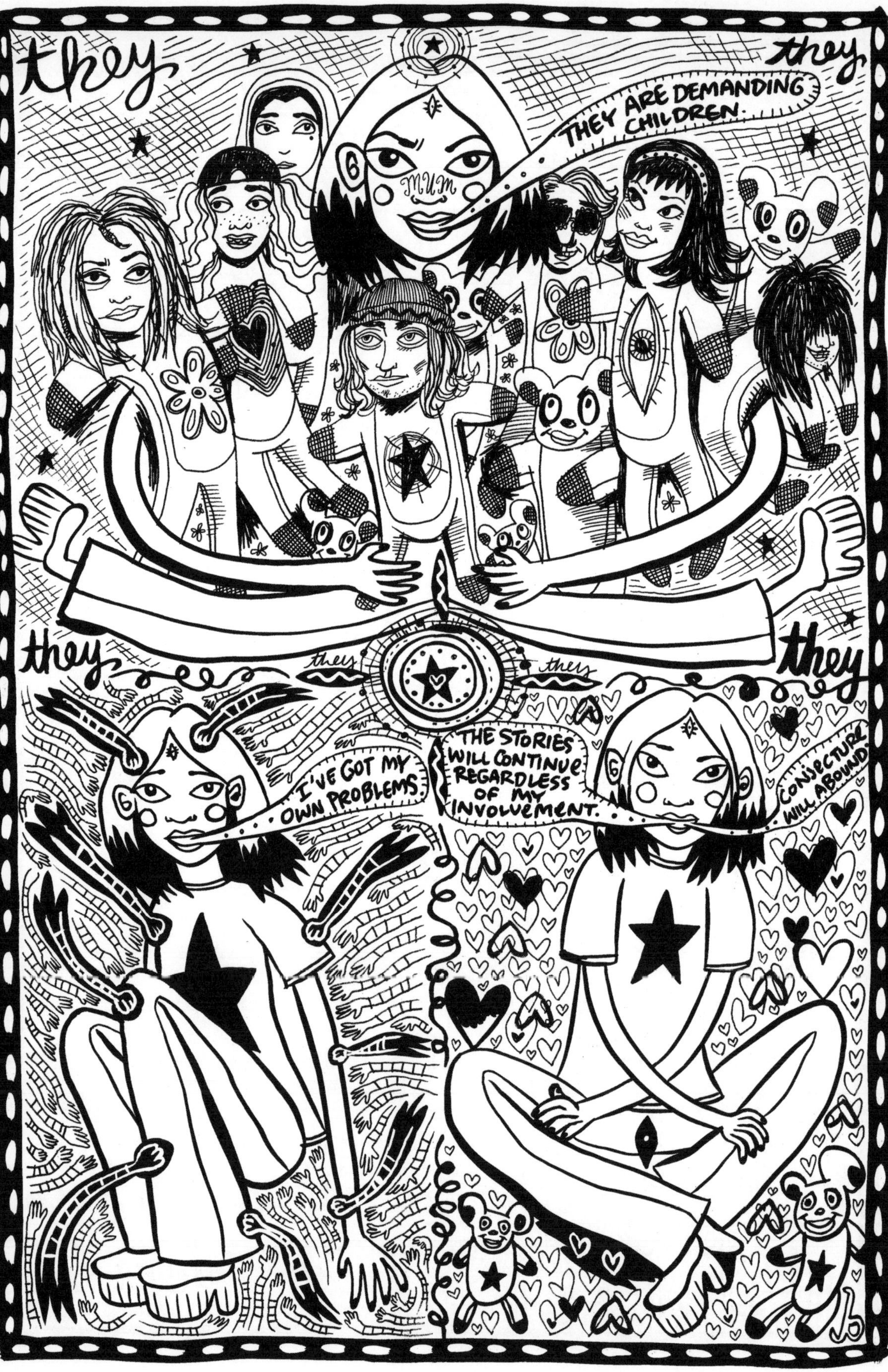
they
they
THEY ARE DEMANDING CHILDREN.
MUM
they
they
they
they
they
they
I'VE GOT MY OWN PROBLEMS.
THE STORIES WILL CONTINUE REGARDLESS OF MY INVOLVEMENT.
CONJECTURE WILL ABOUND.

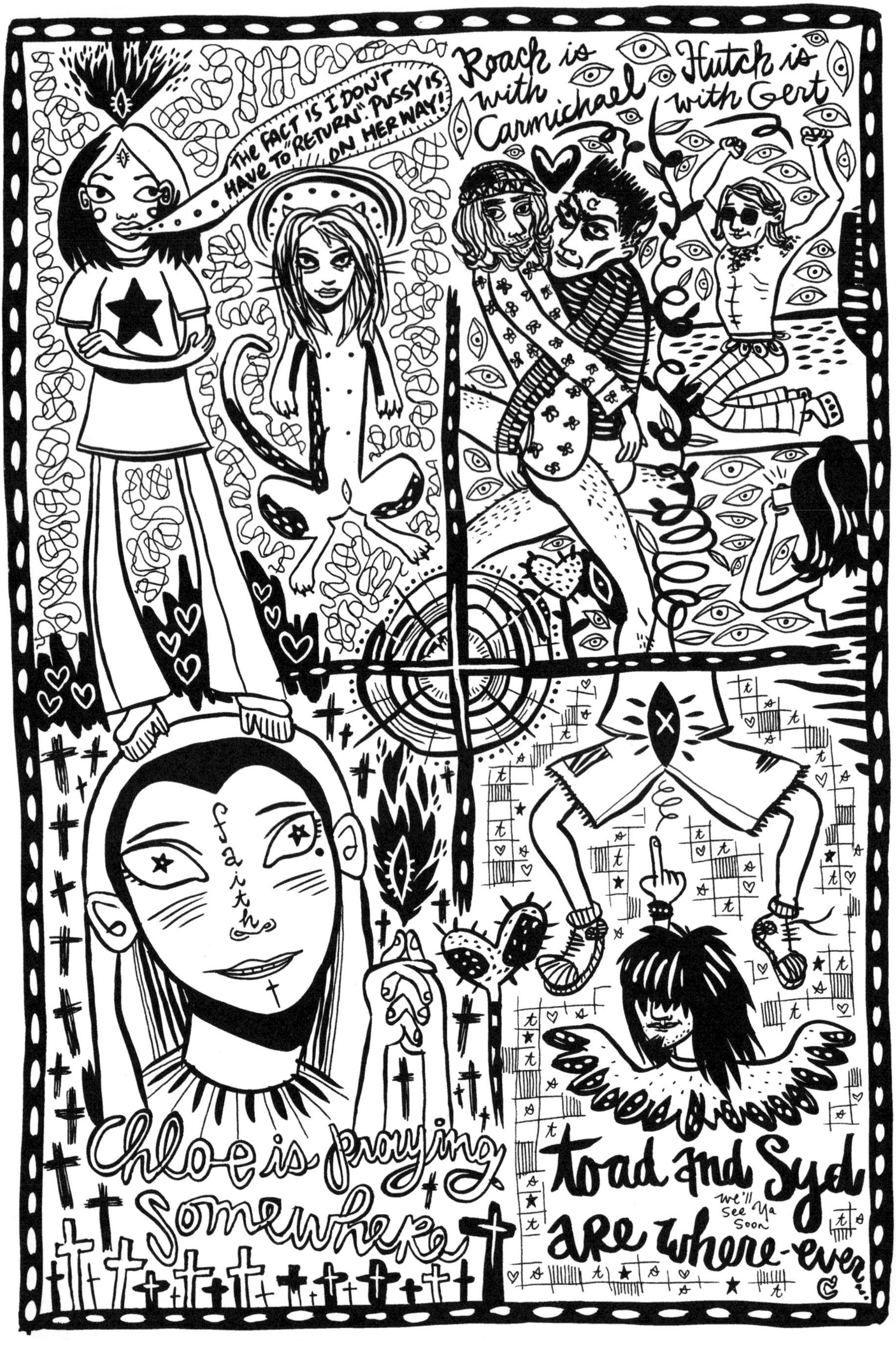
THE FACT IS I DON'T HAVE TO "RETURN". PUSSY IS ON HER WAY!
Roach is with Carmichael
Hutch is with Gert
faith
Chloe is praying somewhere
toad and Syd are where-ever...
we'll see ya soon

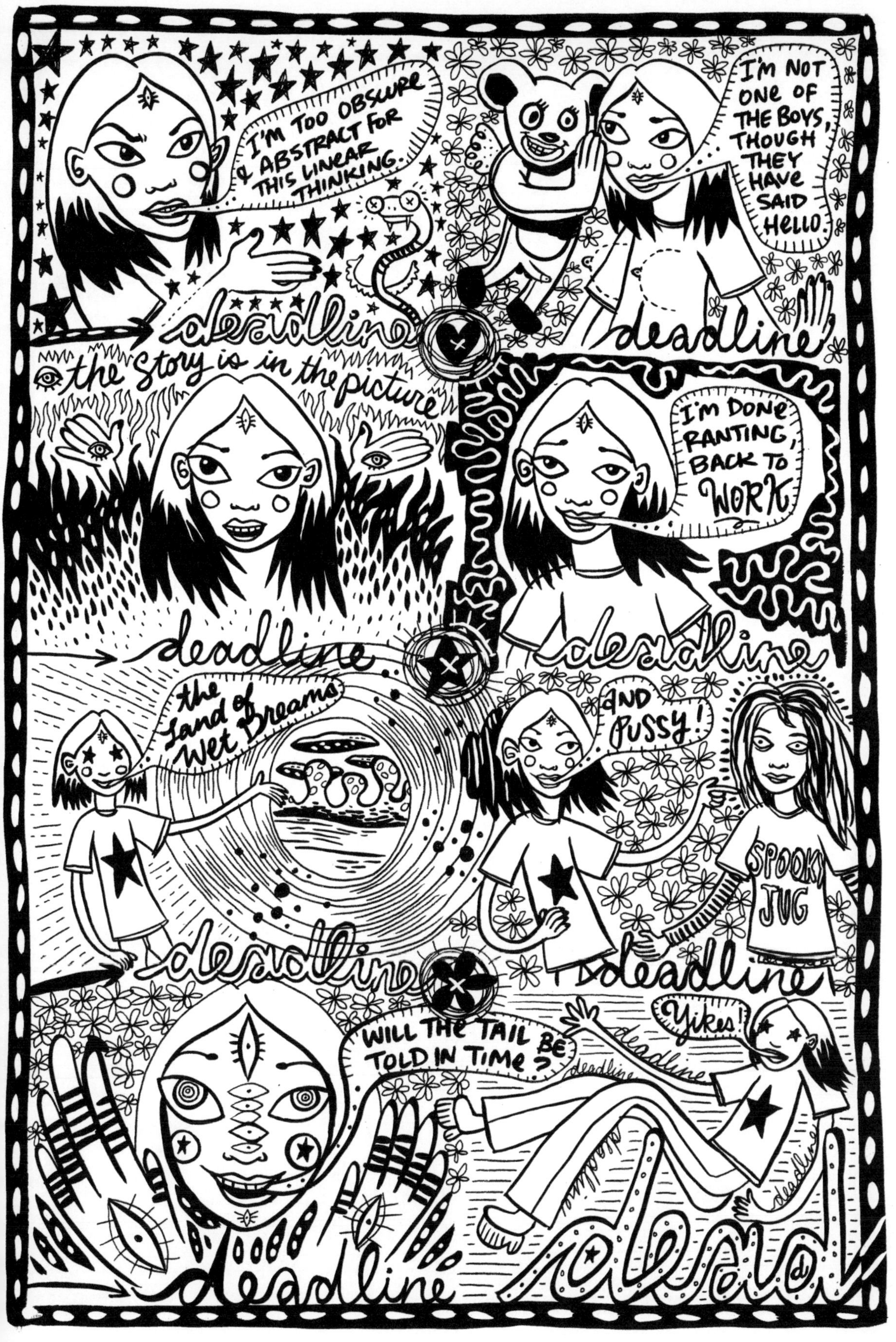
I'M TOO OBSCURE & ABSTRACT FOR THIS LINEAR THINKING.
I'M NOT ONE OF THE BOYS, THOUGH THEY HAVE SAID HELLO.
deadline
deadline
the story is in the picture
I'M DONE RANTING, BACK TO WORK
deadline
deadline
the Land of Wet Dreams
AND PUSSY!
SPOOKY JUG
deadline
deadline
WILL THE TAIL BE TOLD IN TIME?
Yikes!
deadline
dead

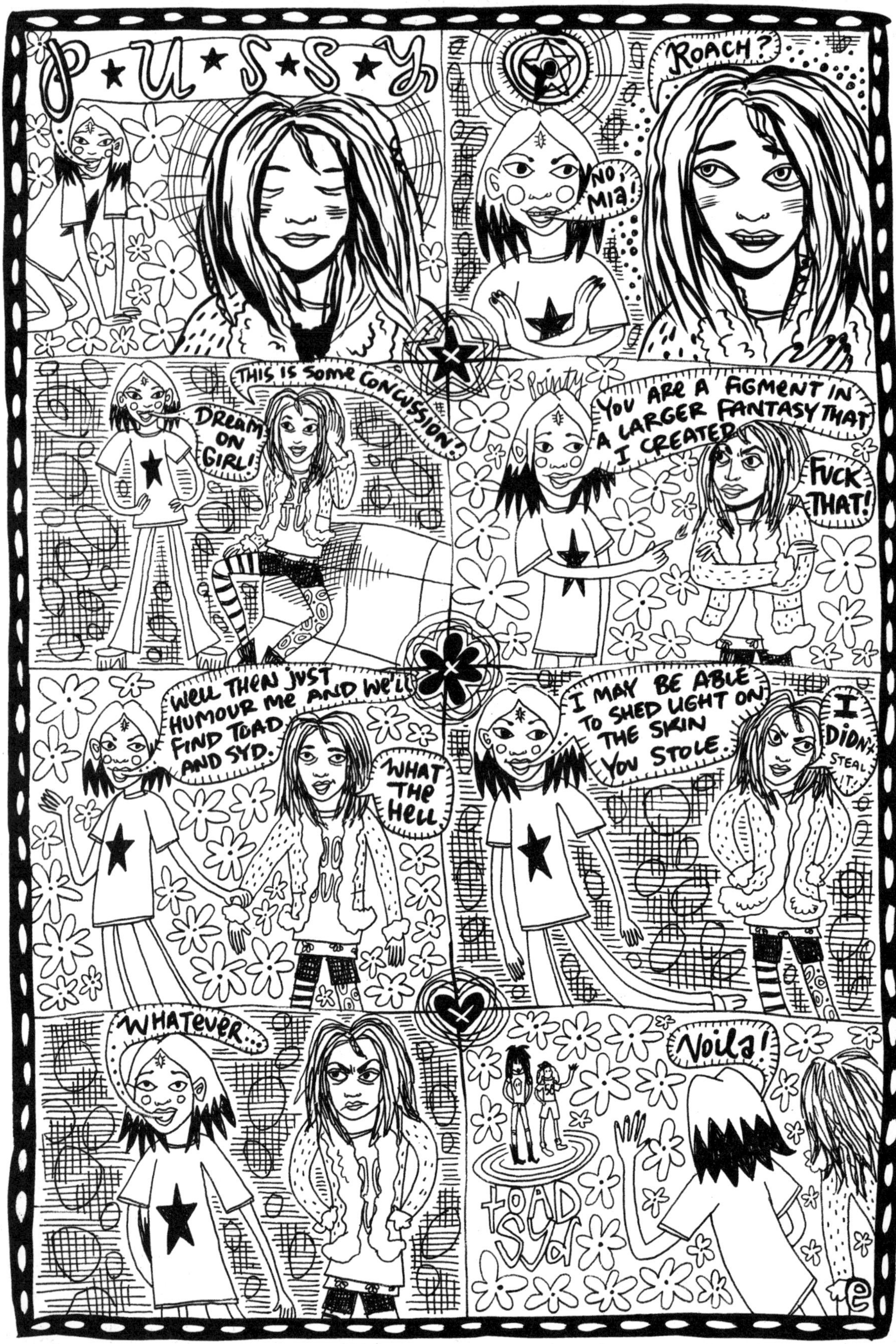

PUSSY
ROACH?
NO, MIA!
THIS IS SOME CONCUSSION!
DREAM ON GIRL!
Pointy
YOU ARE A FIGMENT IN A LARGER FANTASY THAT I CREATED
FUCK THAT!
WELL THEN JUST HUMOUR ME AND WE'LL FIND TOAD AND SYD.
WHAT THE HELL
I MAY BE ABLE TO SHED LIGHT ON THE SKIN YOU STOLE.
I DIDN'T STEAL IT.
WHATEVER...
Voila!
TOAD
SYD

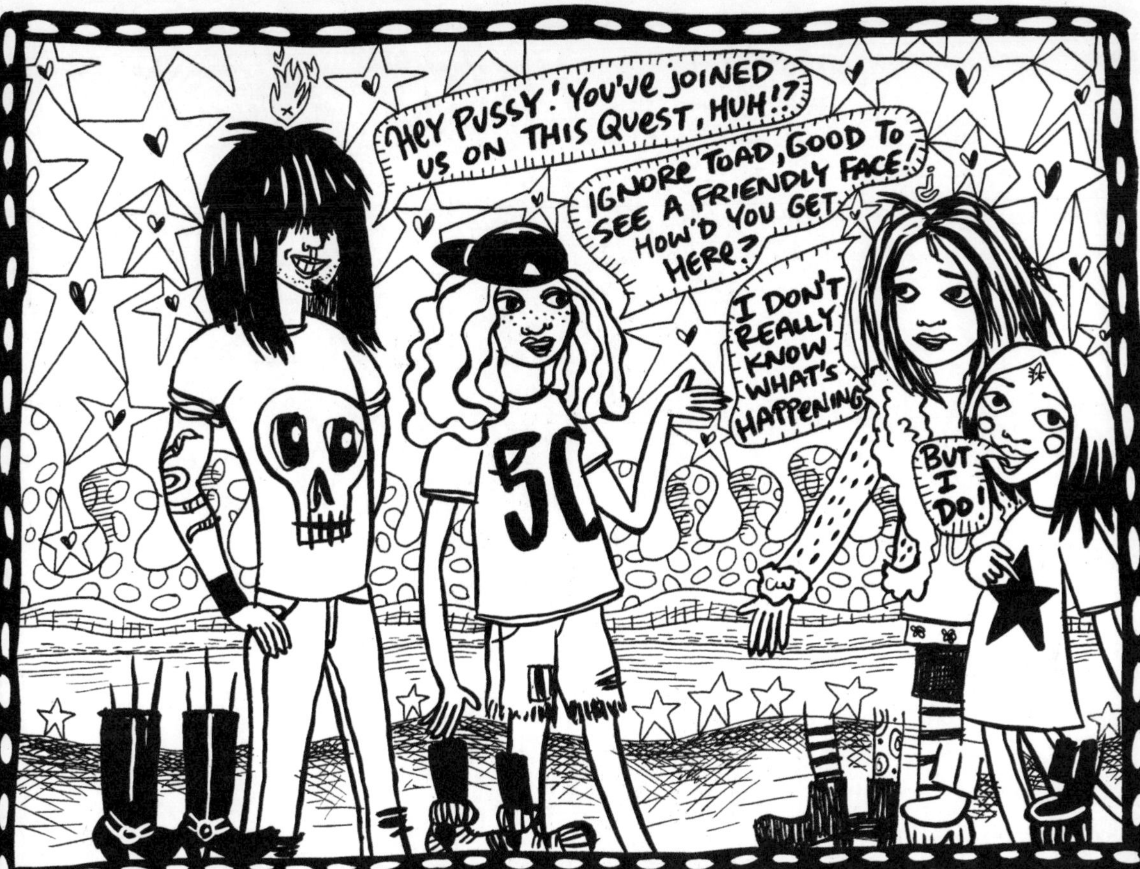
HEY PUSSY! YOU'VE JOINED US ON THIS QUEST, HUH!?
IGNORE TOAD, GOOD TO SEE A FRIENDLY FACE! HOW'D YOU GET HERE?
I DON'T REALLY KNOW WHAT'S HAPPENING
BUT I DO!

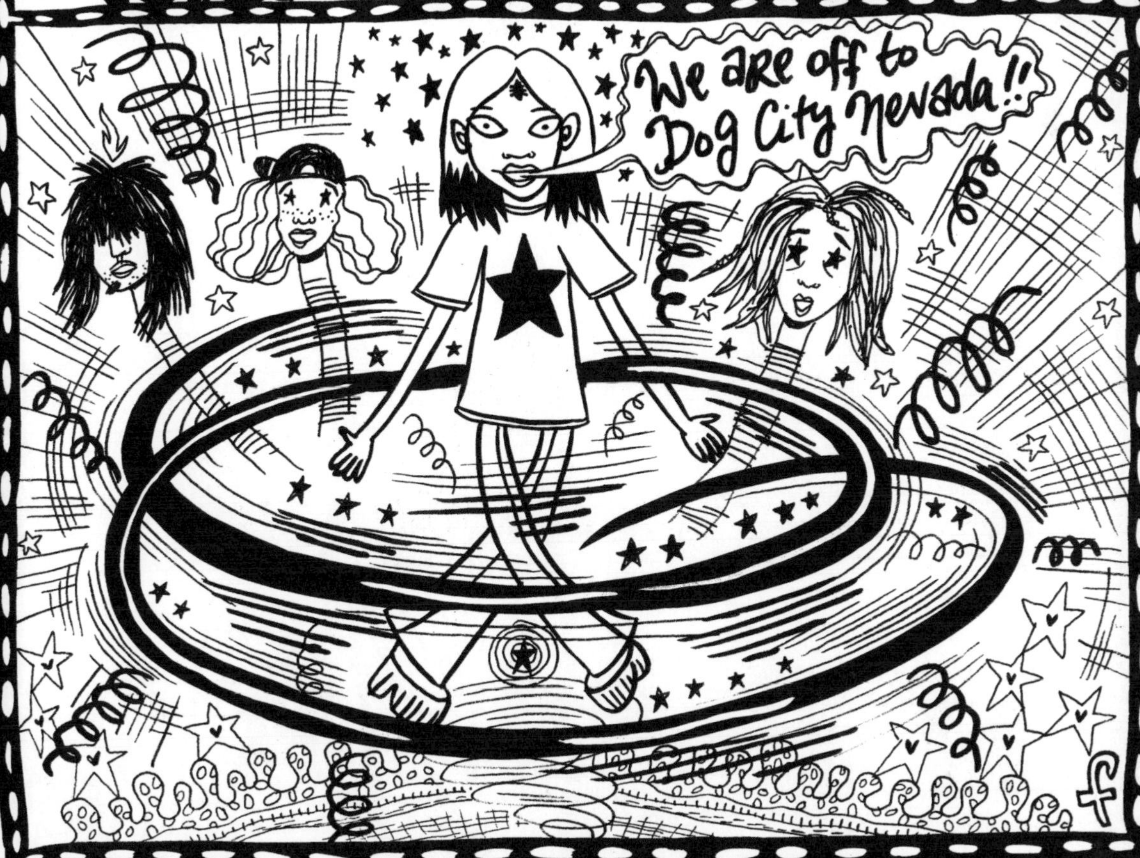
We are off to Dog City Nevada!!

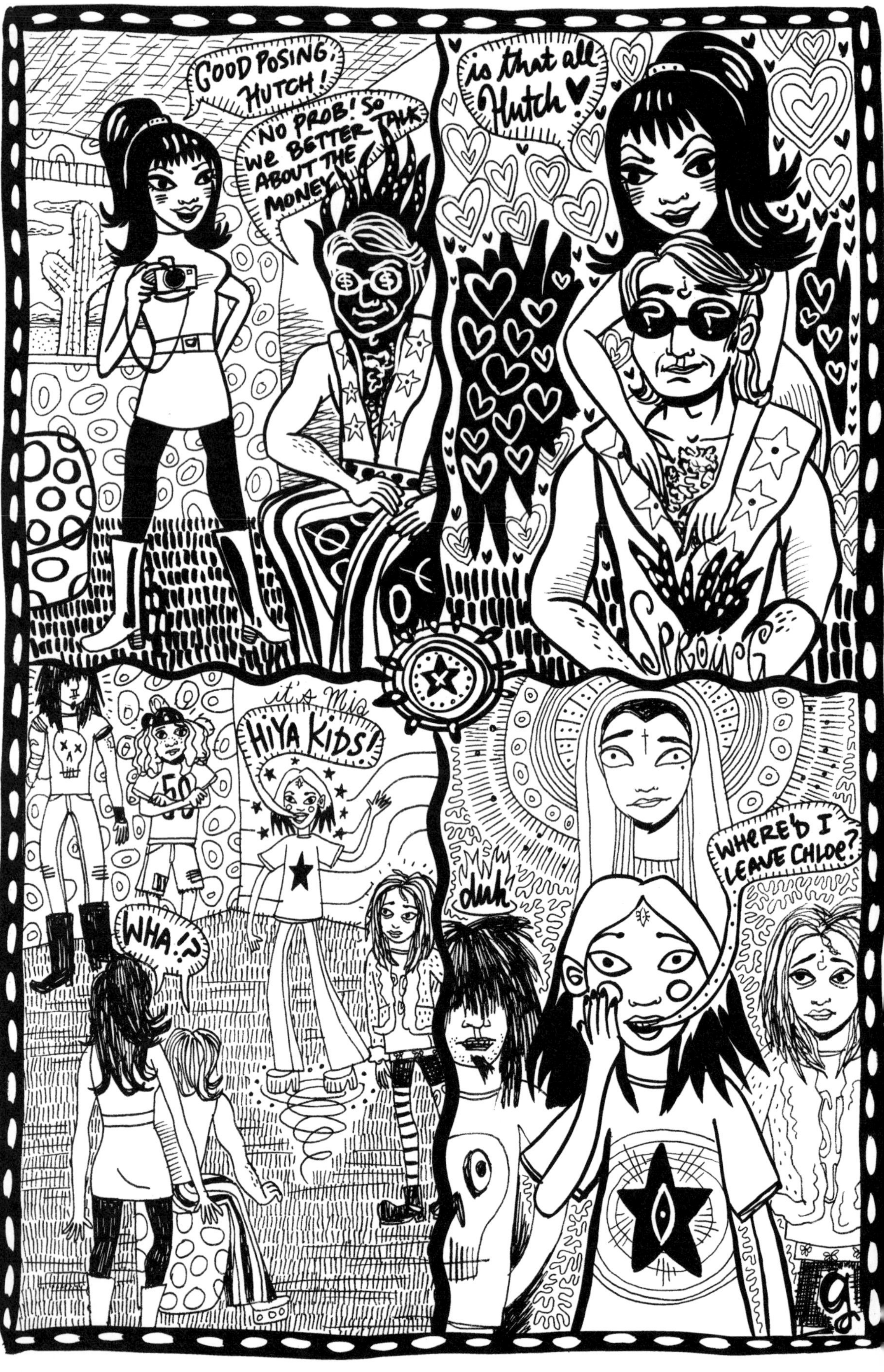
GOOD POSING, HUTCH!
NO PROB! SO WE BETTER TALK ABOUT THE MONEY
is that all Hutch ♥
SPROING
it's Mia
HiYA KIDS!
WHA!?
duh
WHERE'D I LEAVE CHLOE?

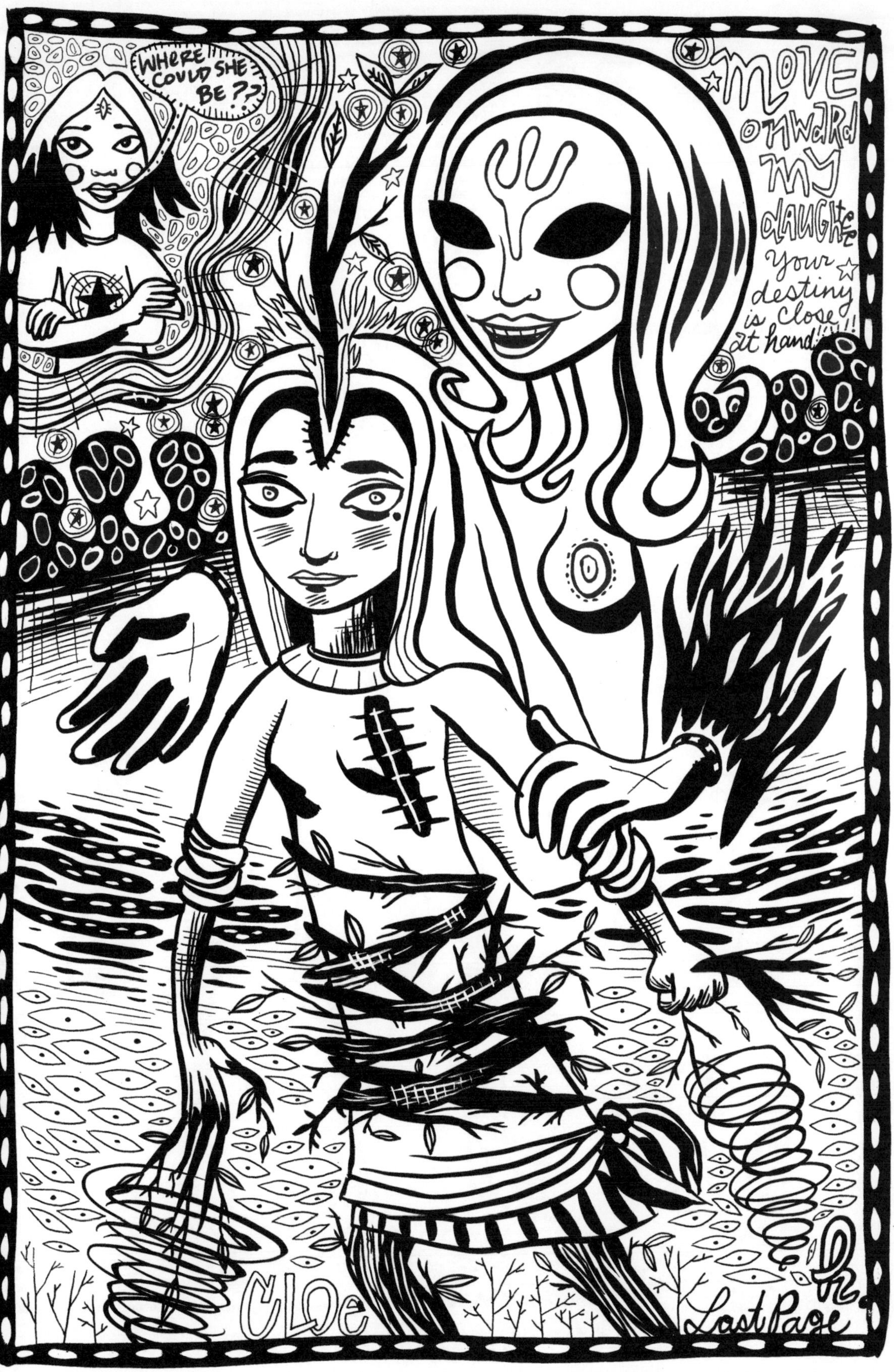
WHERE COULD SHE BE??
MOVE ONWARD MY DAUGHTER
your destiny is close at hand!!!!
CLOe
Last Page

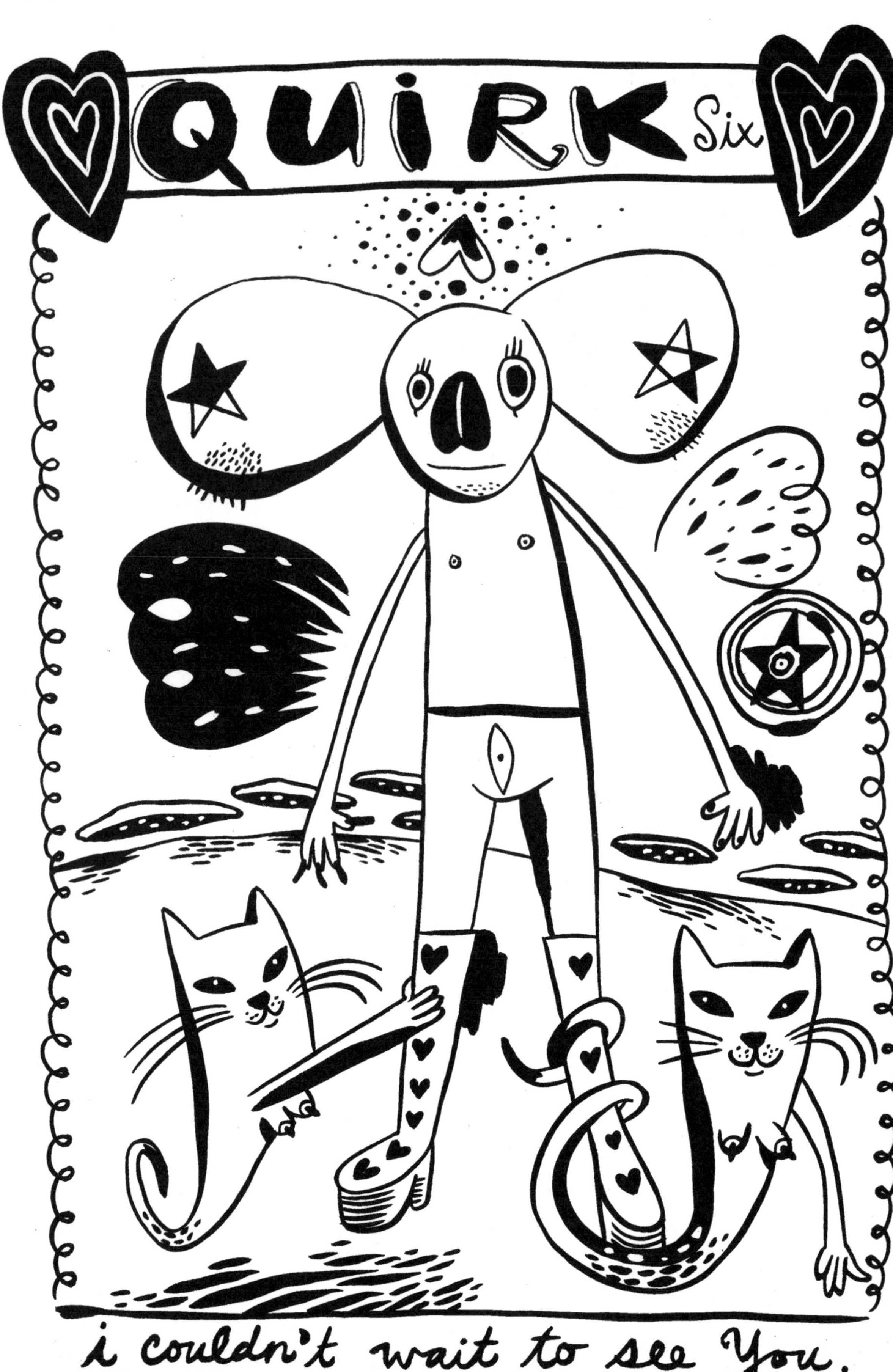
QUIRK Six

i couldn't wait to see You.

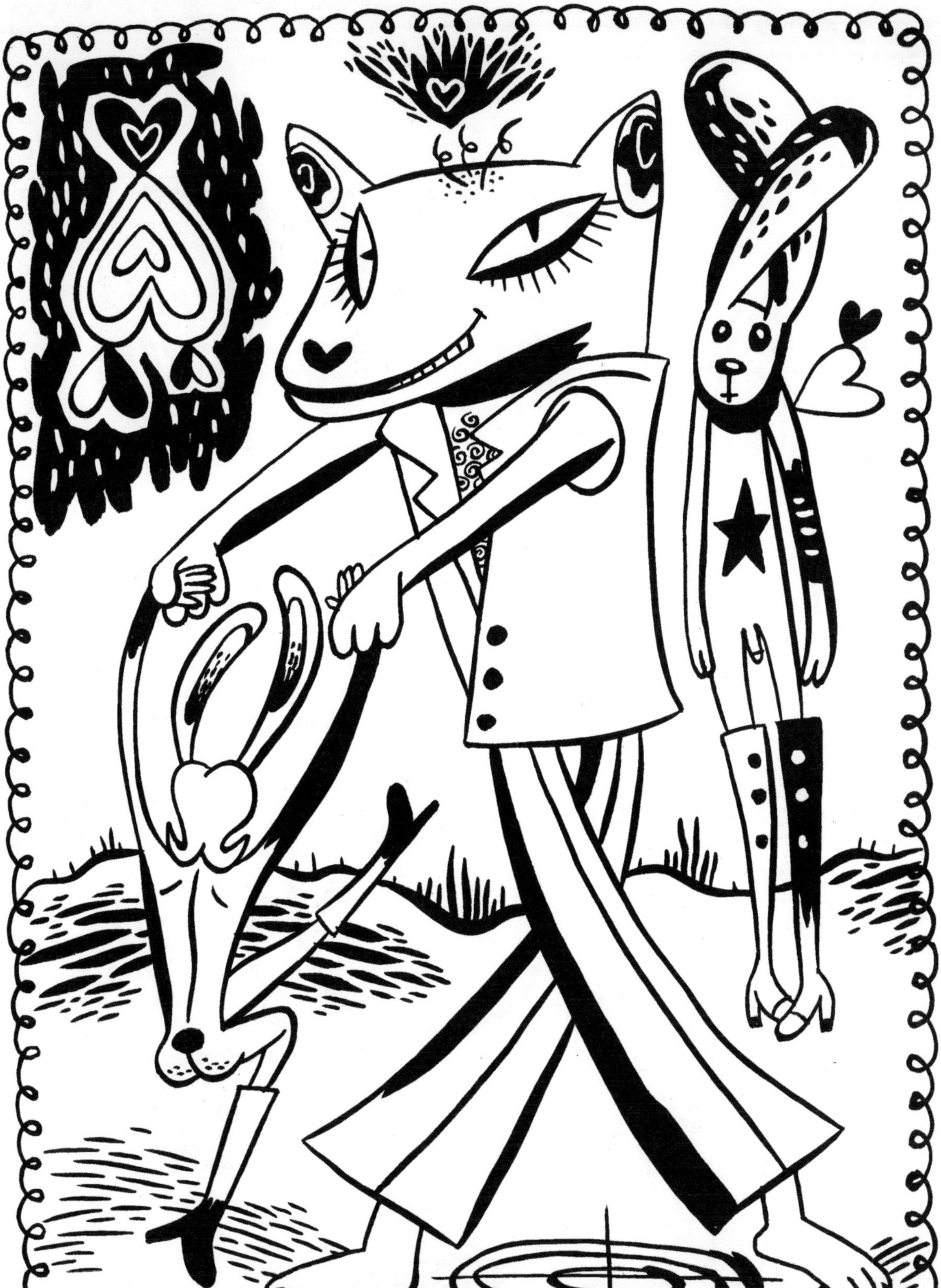

and to feel Your hair against me.

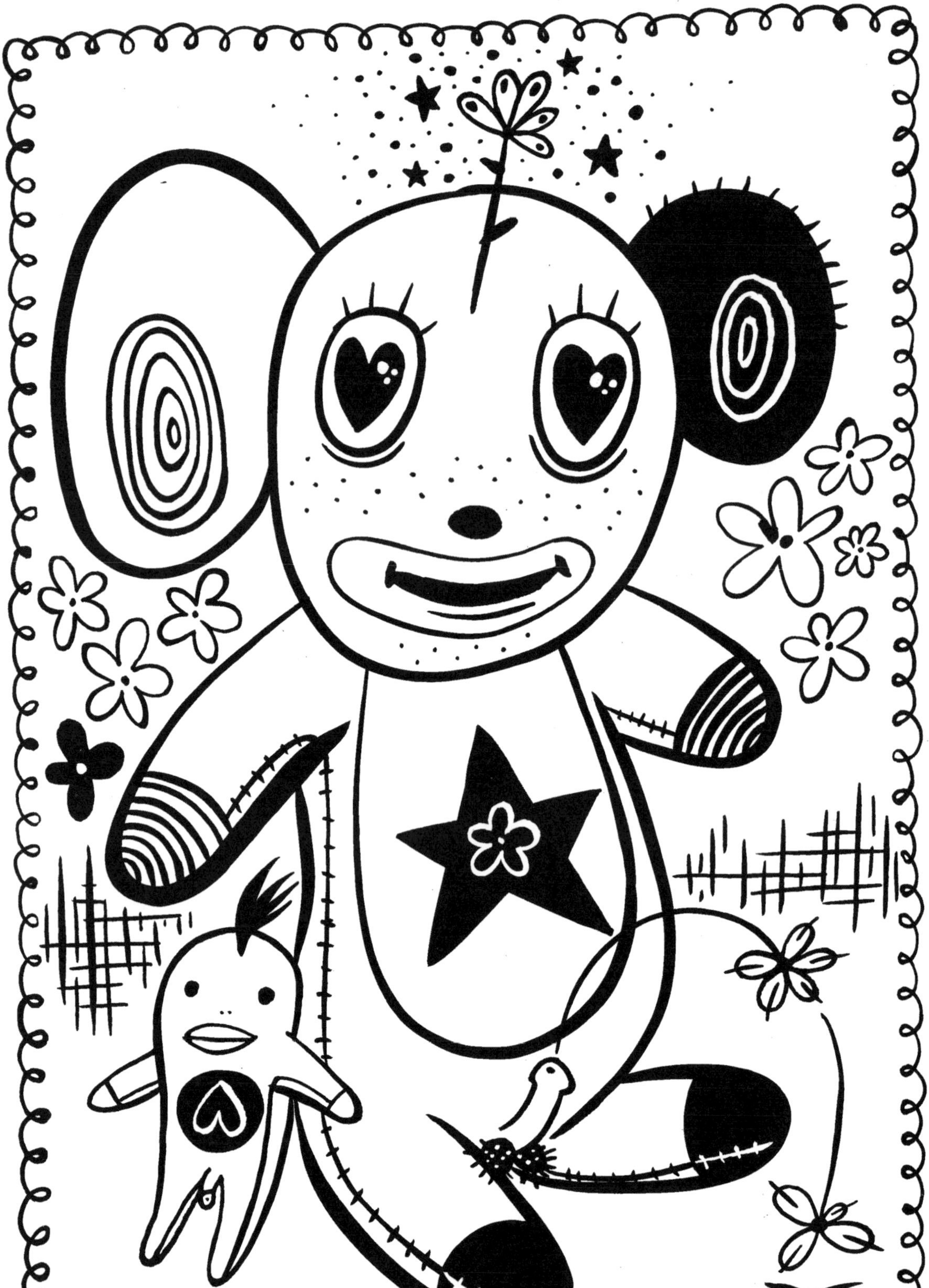

i want to hear what you have to say.

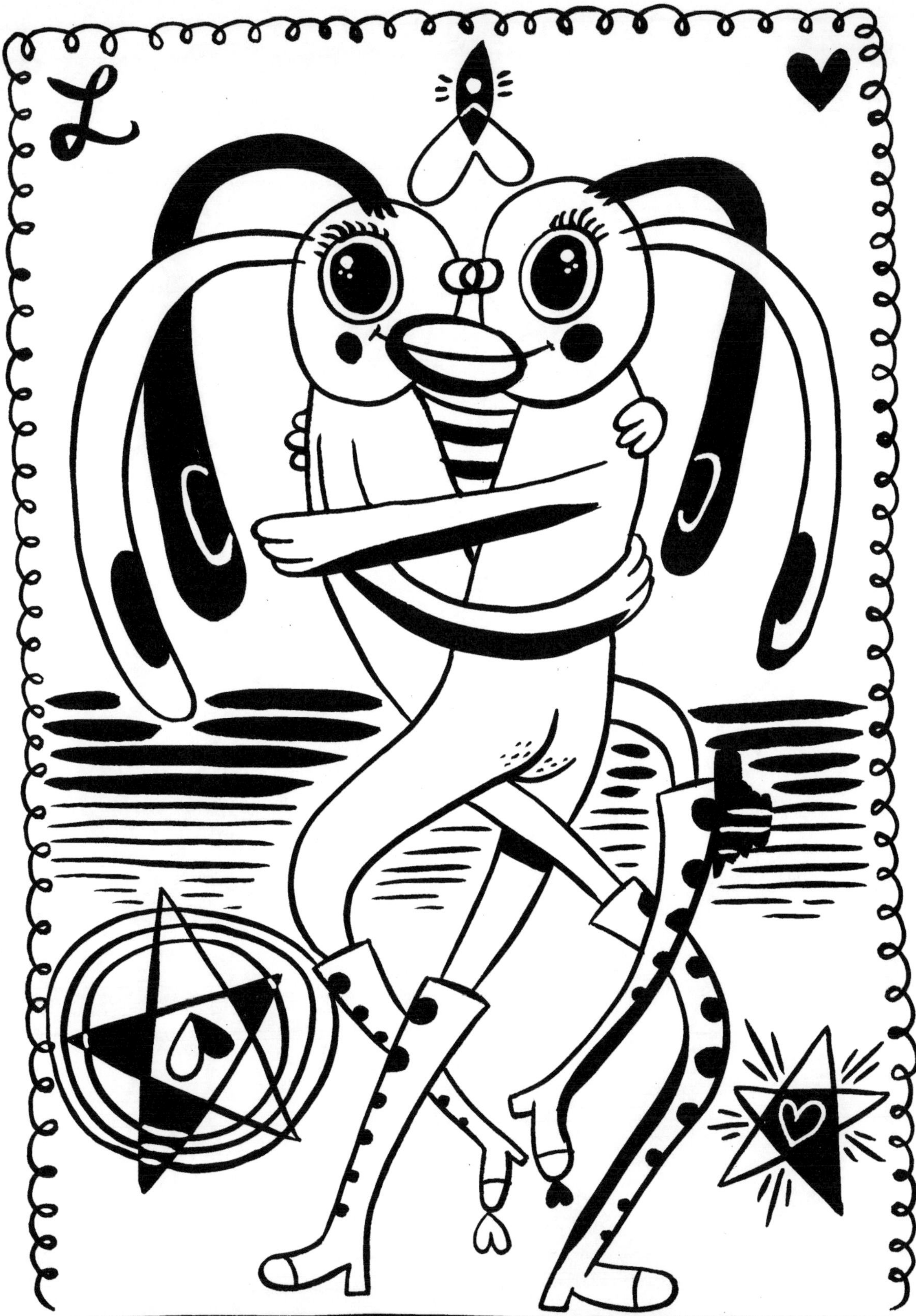
L
so whisper in my ear, make me giddy.

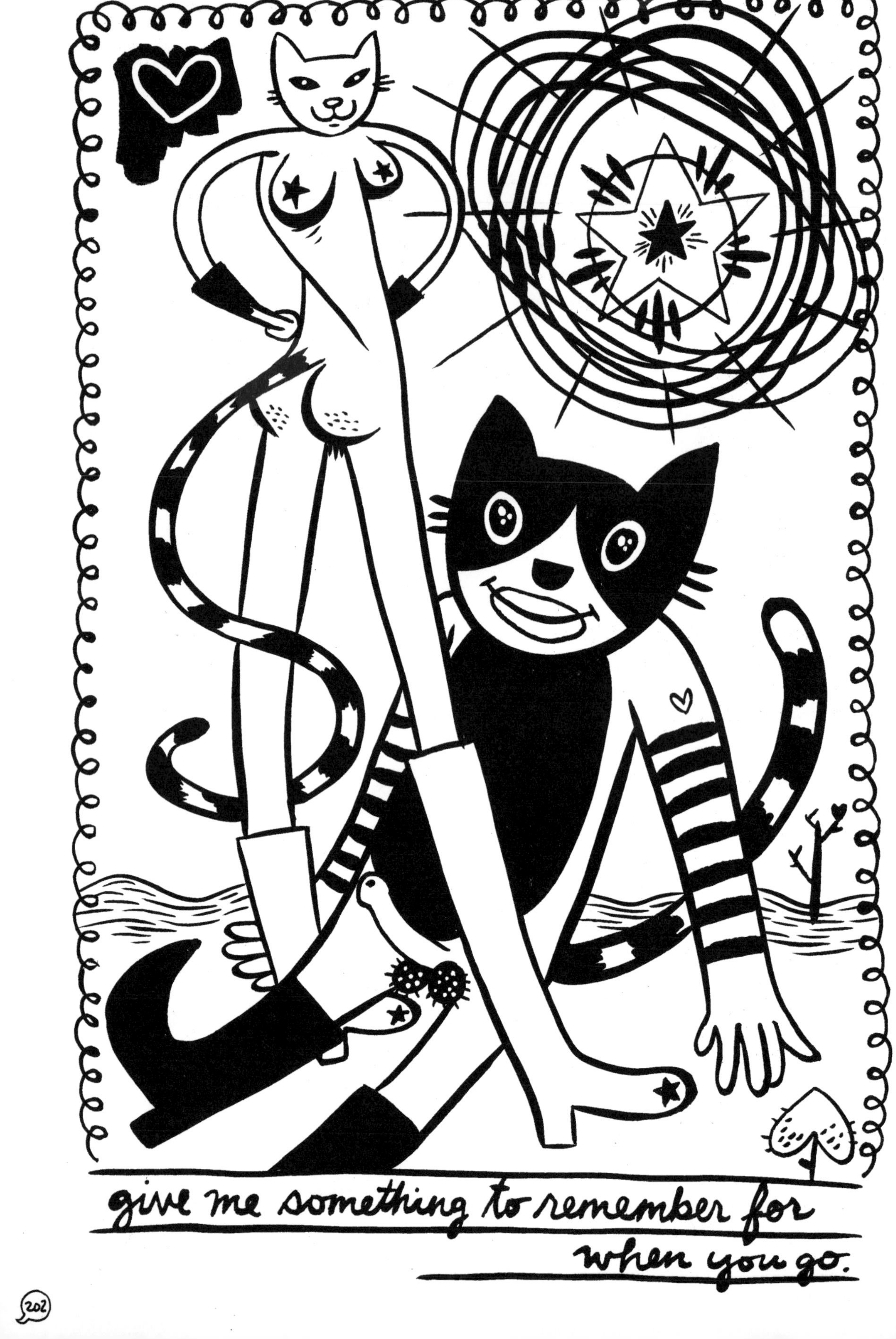

give me something to remember for
when you go.

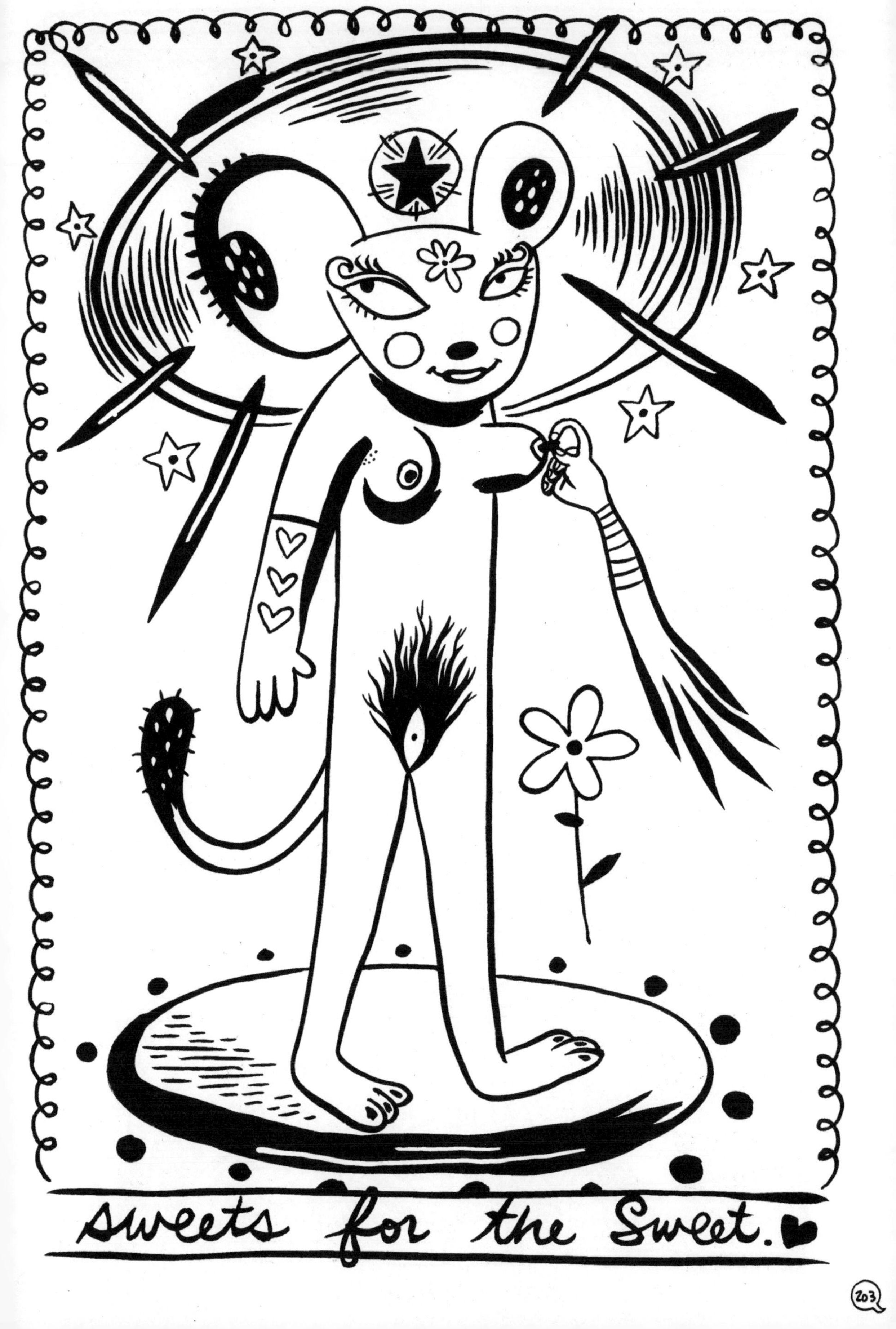

sweets for the Sweet. ♥

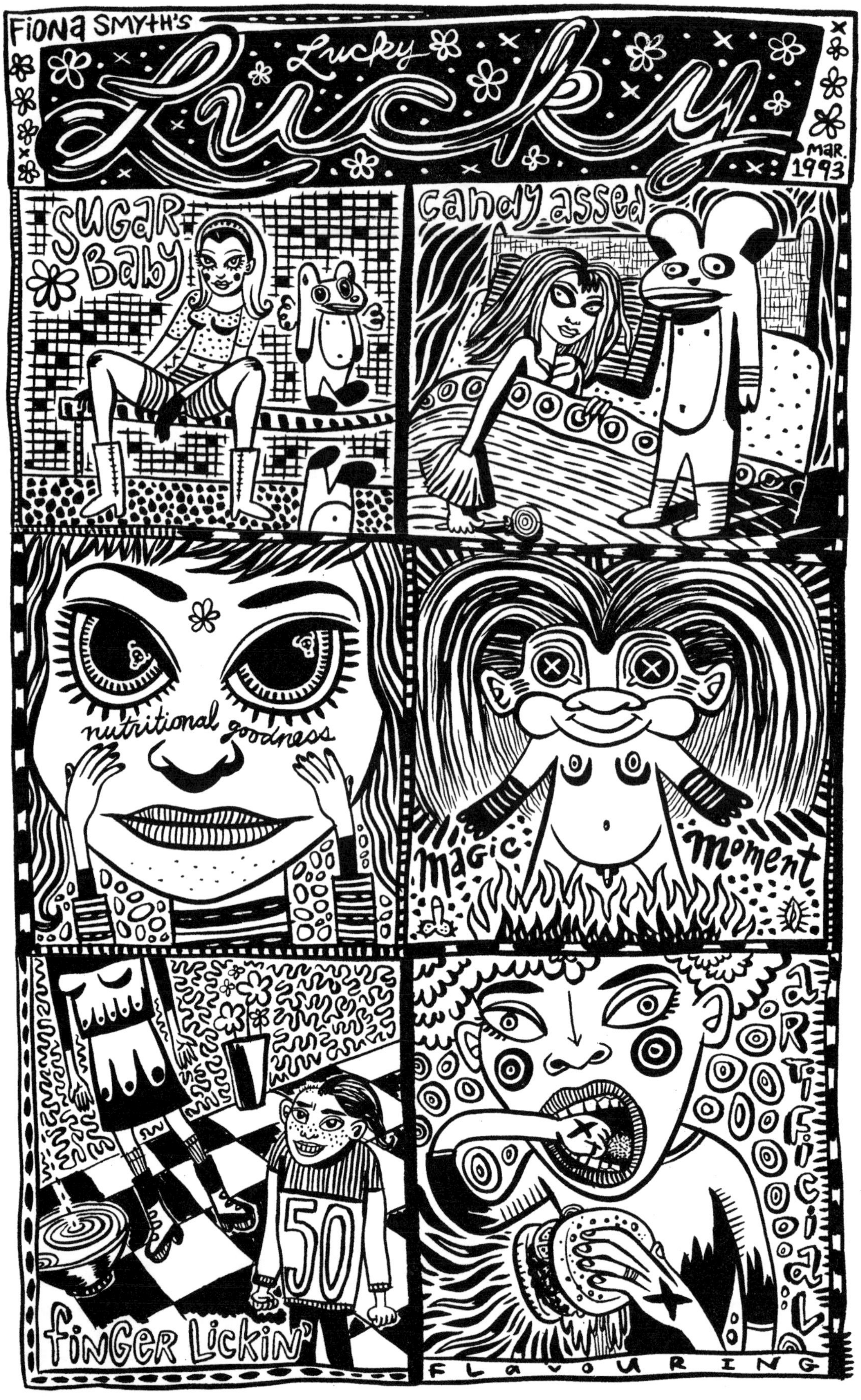
FIONA SMYTH'S
Lucky
Lucky
MAR. 1993
SUGAR Baby
candy assed
nutritional goodness
magic moment
finGER LicKin'
aRTificiaL
FLAVOURING

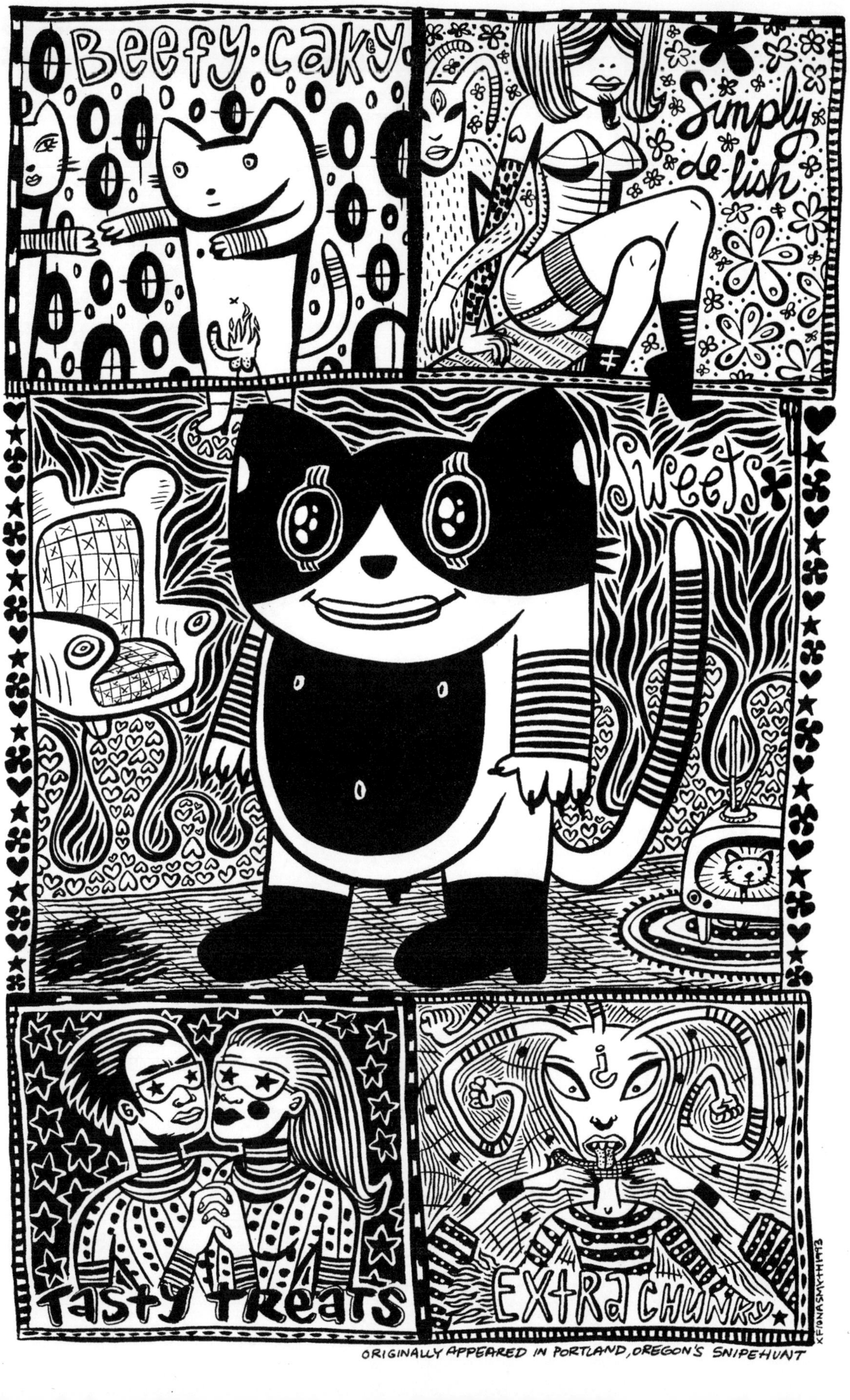
Beefy·caky
Simply de-lish
Sweets
Tasty Treats
Extra Chunky
FIONA SMYTH 1993

ORIGINALLY APPEARED IN PORTLAND, OREGON'S SNIPEHUNT

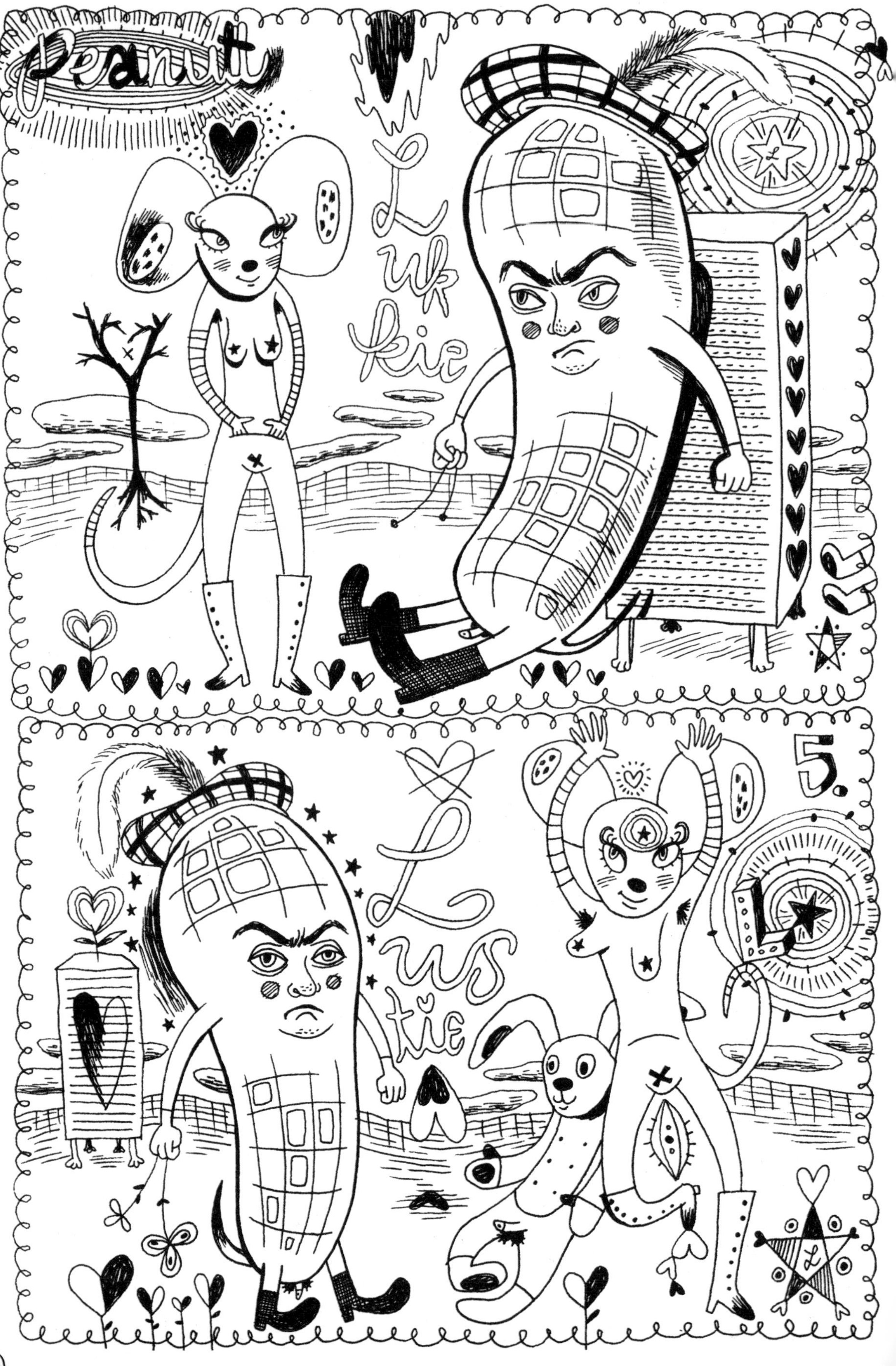
Peanut
5.

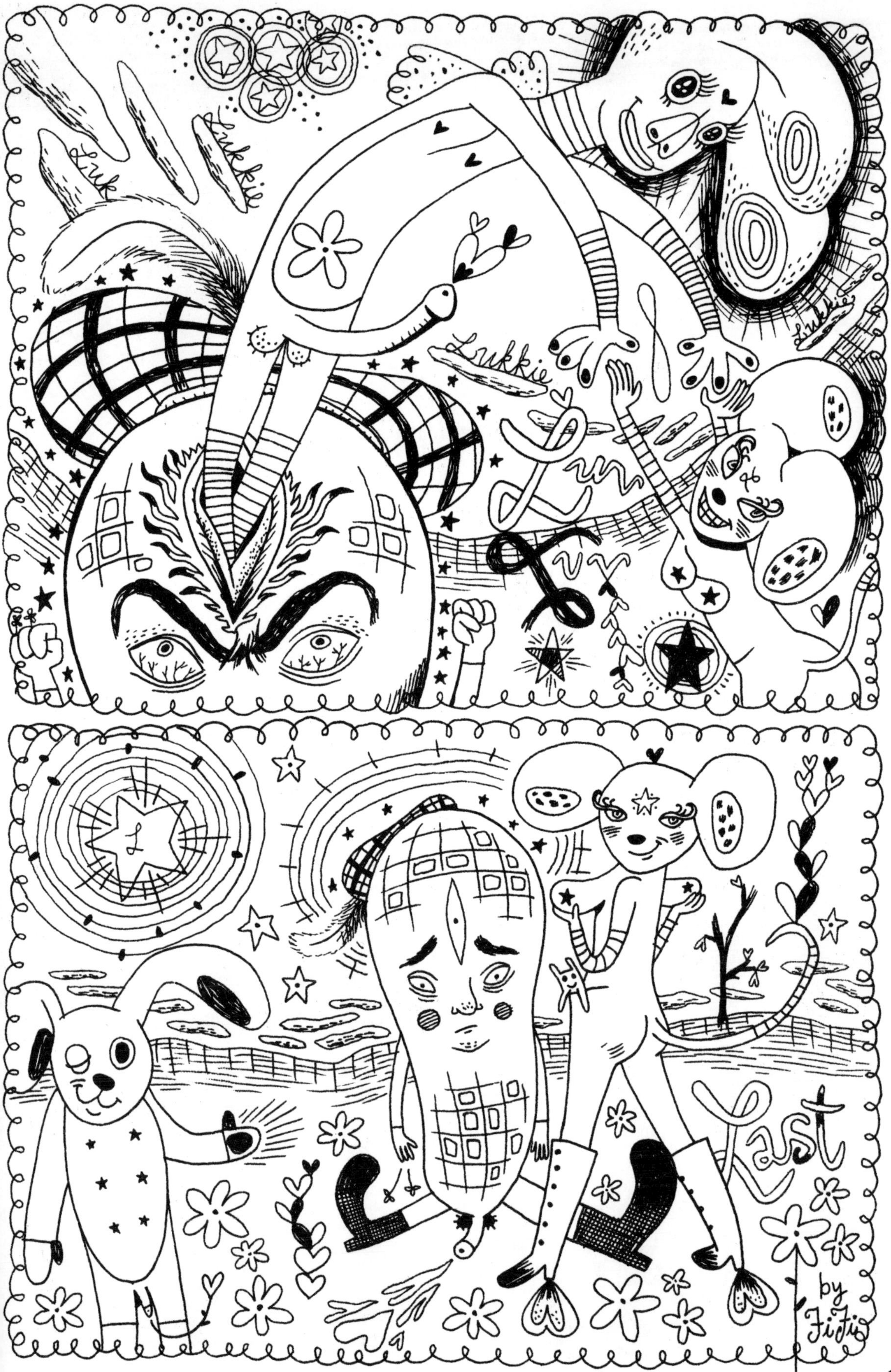
Lukkie
Lukkie
Lukkie
Last
by FiFi

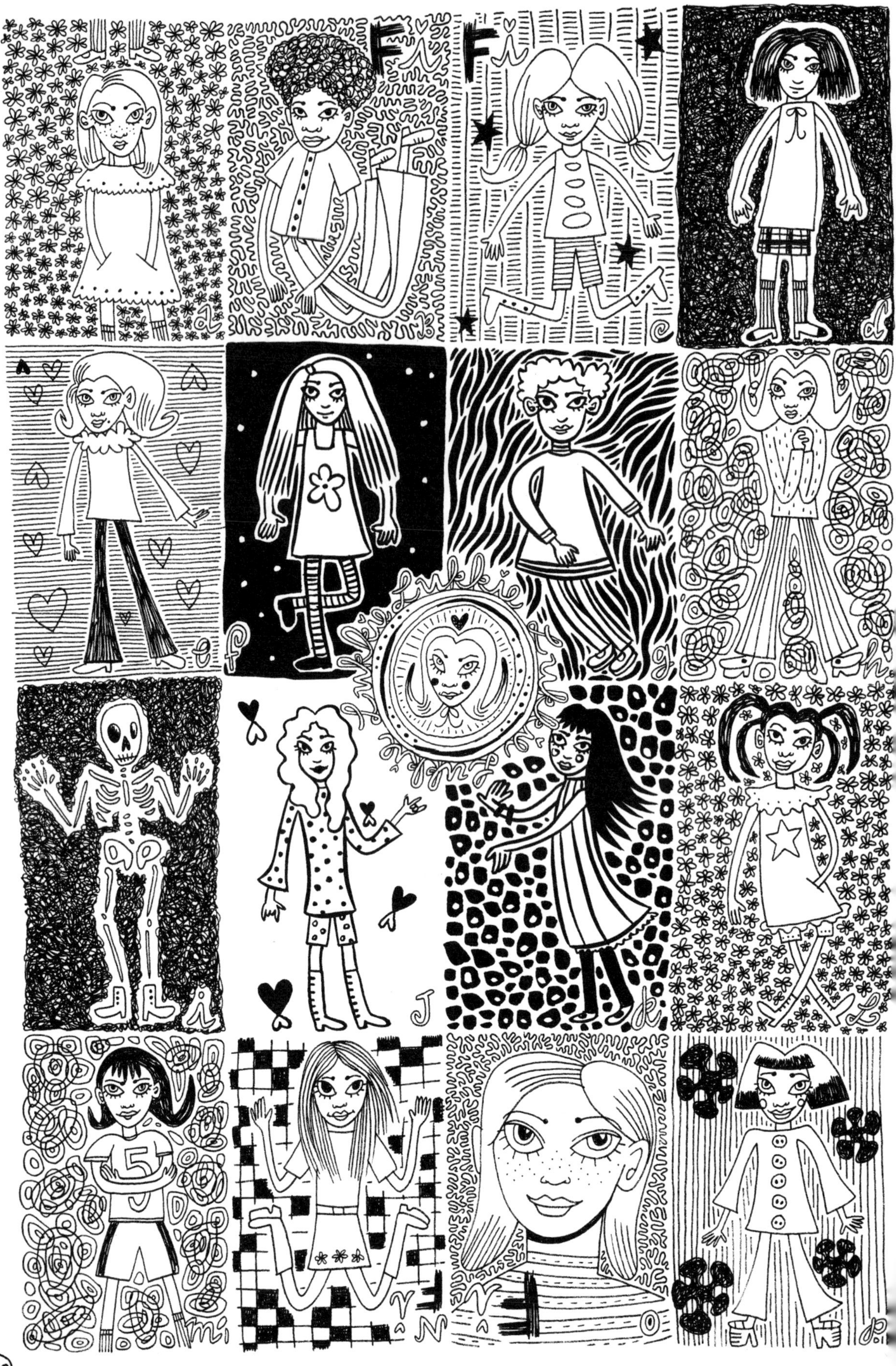

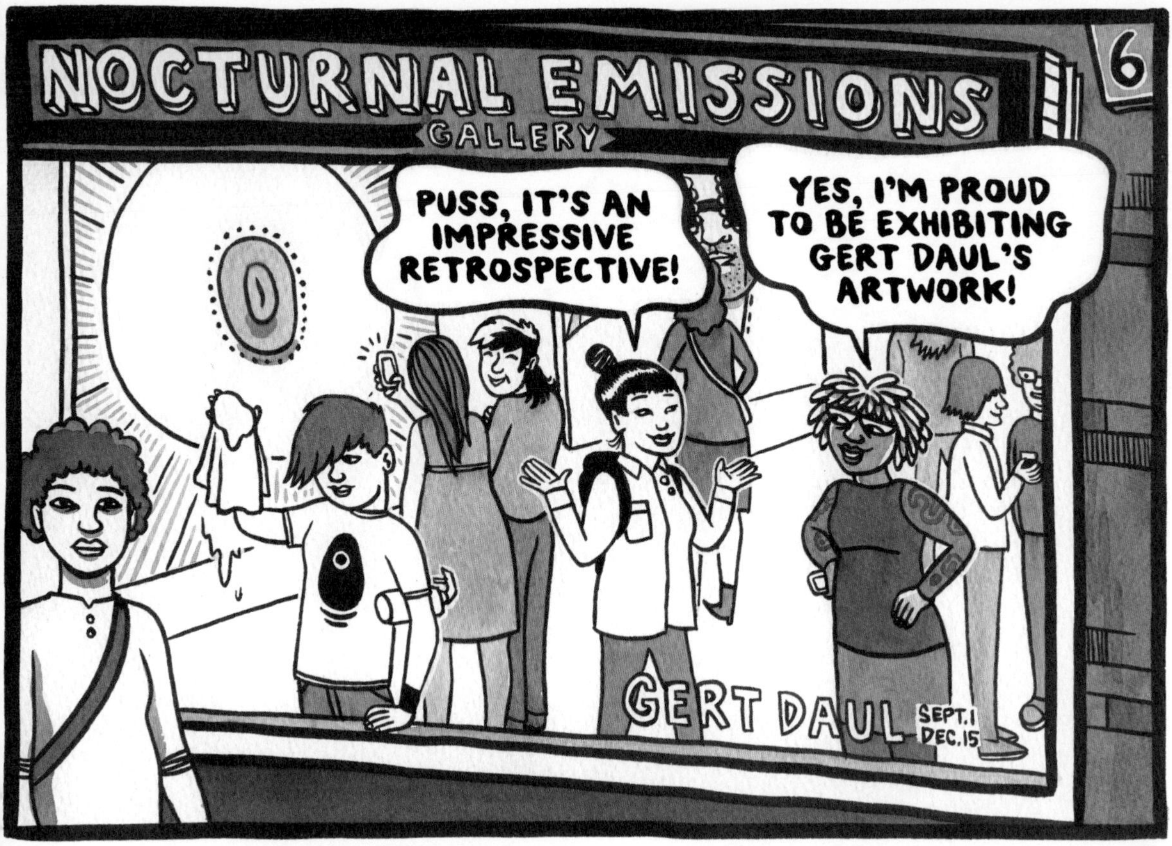
NOCTURNAL EMISSIONS
GALLERY
6
PUSS, IT'S AN IMPRESSIVE RETROSPECTIVE!
YES, I'M PROUD TO BE EXHIBITING GERT DAUL'S ARTWORK!
GERT DAUL
SEPT.1
DEC.15

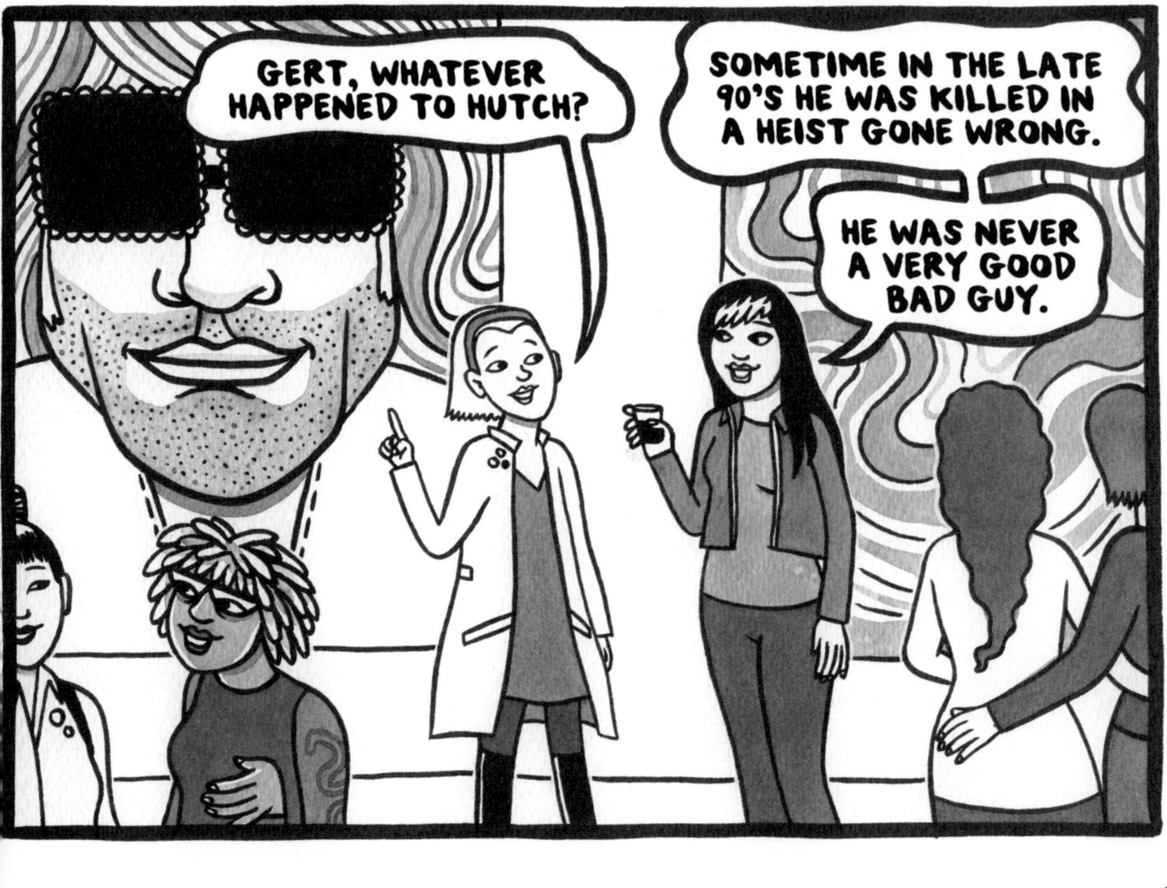
GERT, WHATEVER HAPPENED TO HUTCH?
SOMETIME IN THE LATE 90'S HE WAS KILLED IN A HEIST GONE WRONG.
HE WAS NEVER A VERY GOOD BAD GUY.

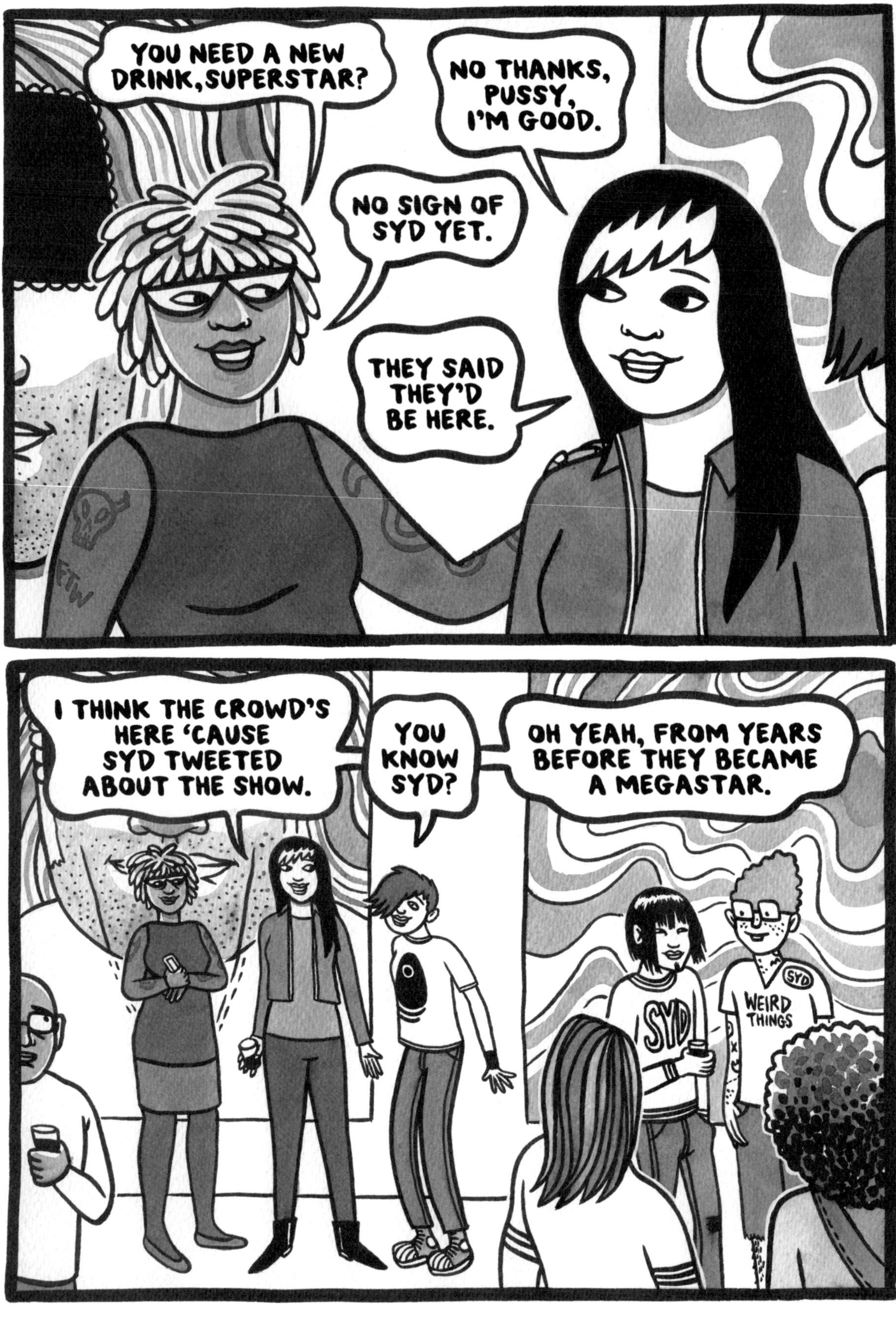
YOU NEED A NEW DRINK, SUPERSTAR?
NO THANKS, PUSSY, I'M GOOD.
NO SIGN OF SYD YET.
THEY SAID THEY'D BE HERE.
I THINK THE CROWD'S HERE 'CAUSE SYD TWEETED ABOUT THE SHOW.
YOU KNOW SYD?
OH YEAH, FROM YEARS BEFORE THEY BECAME A MEGASTAR.
SYD
SYD
WEIRD THINGS

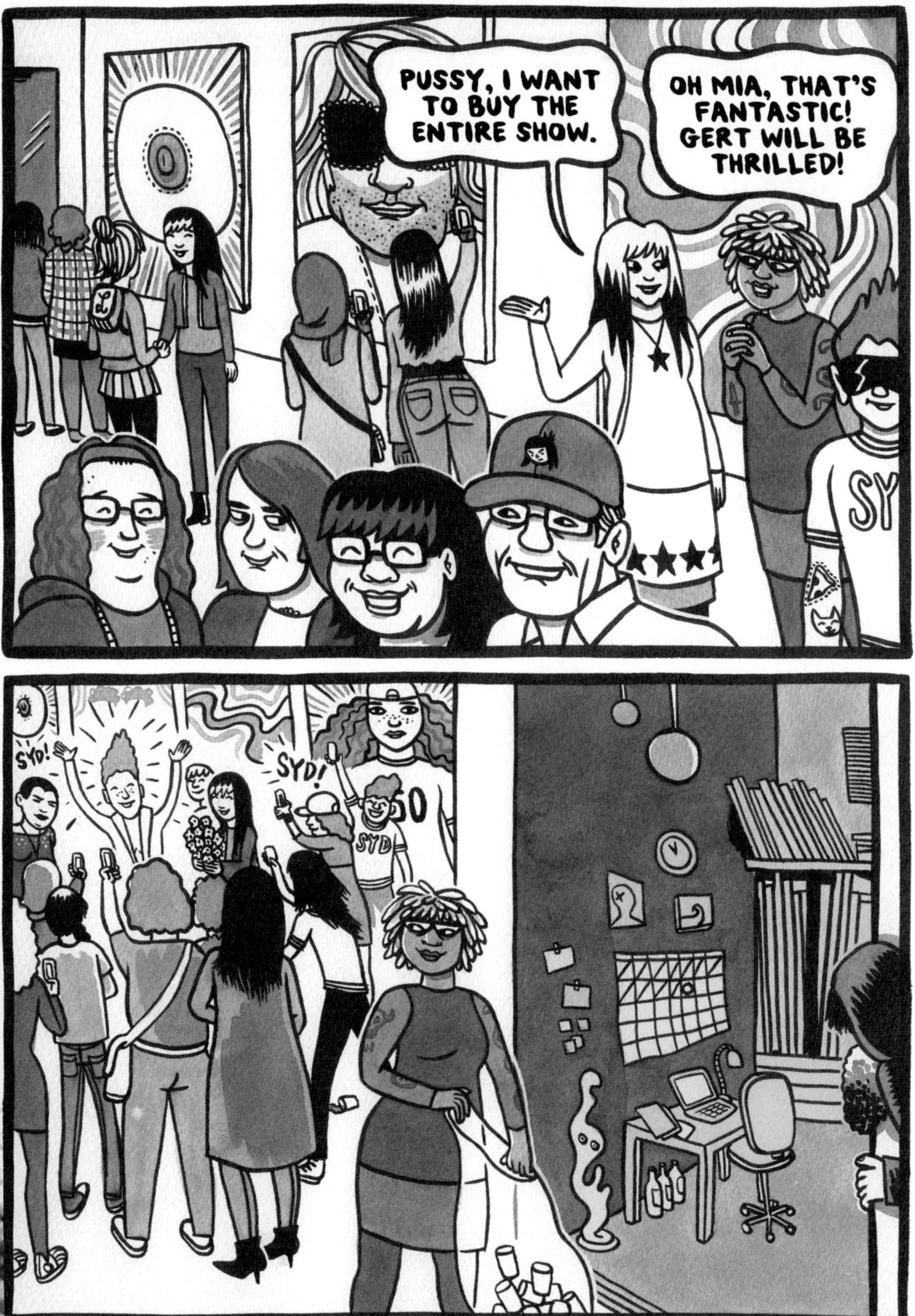
PUSSY, I WANT TO BUY THE ENTIRE SHOW.
OH MIA, THAT'S FANTASTIC! GERT WILL BE THRILLED!
SY
SYD!
SYD!
SYD
60

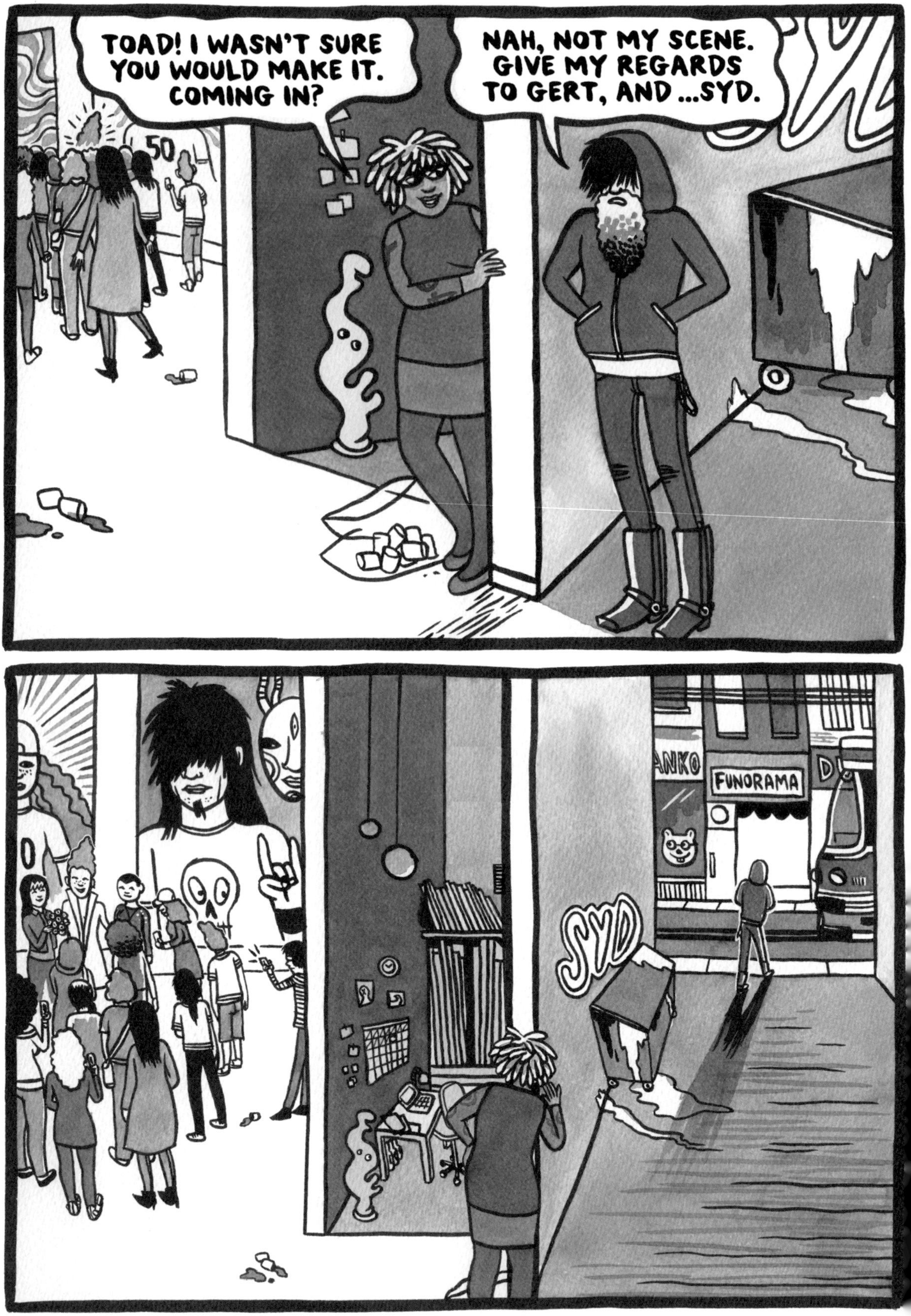
TOAD! I WASN'T SURE YOU WOULD MAKE IT. COMING IN?
NAH, NOT MY SCENE. GIVE MY REGARDS TO GERT, AND ...SYD.
50
ANKO
FUNORAMA
SYD

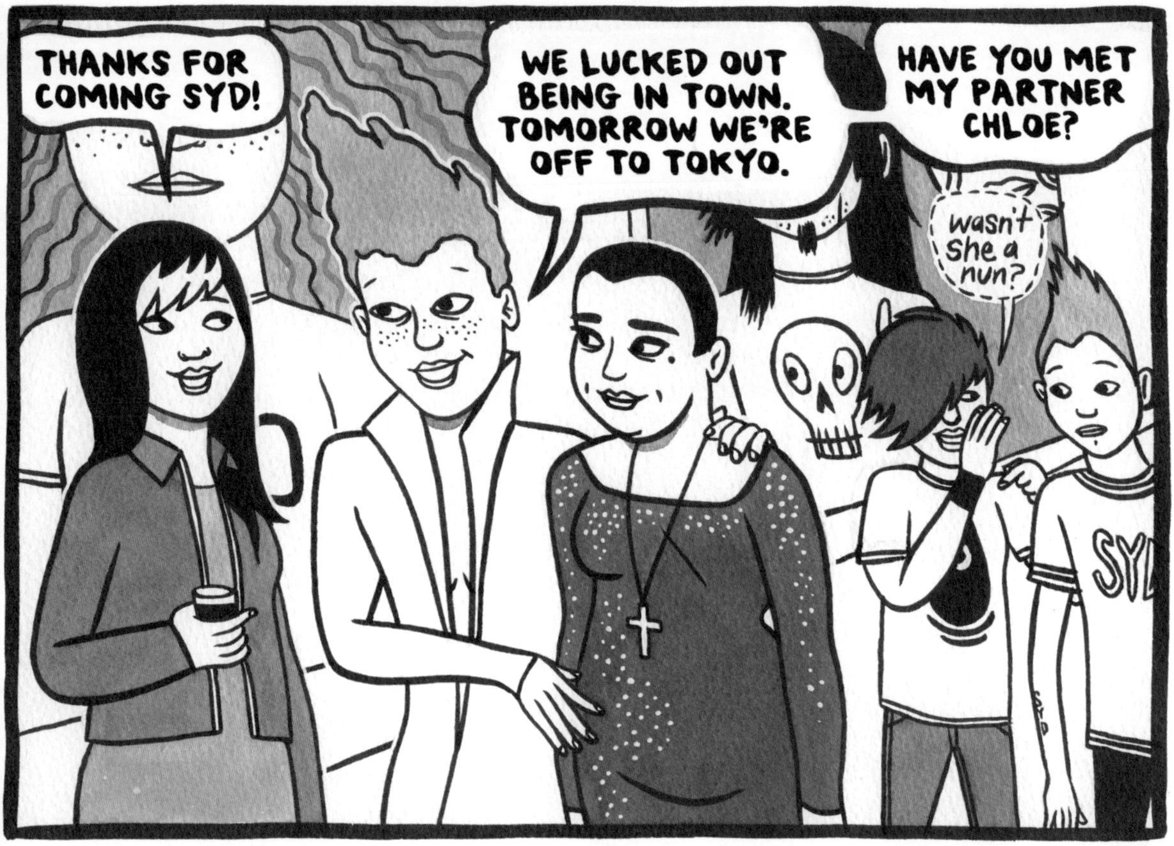
THANKS FOR COMING SYD!
WE LUCKED OUT BEING IN TOWN. TOMORROW WE'RE OFF TO TOKYO.
HAVE YOU MET MY PARTNER CHLOE?
wasn't she a nun?
SYD
SYD

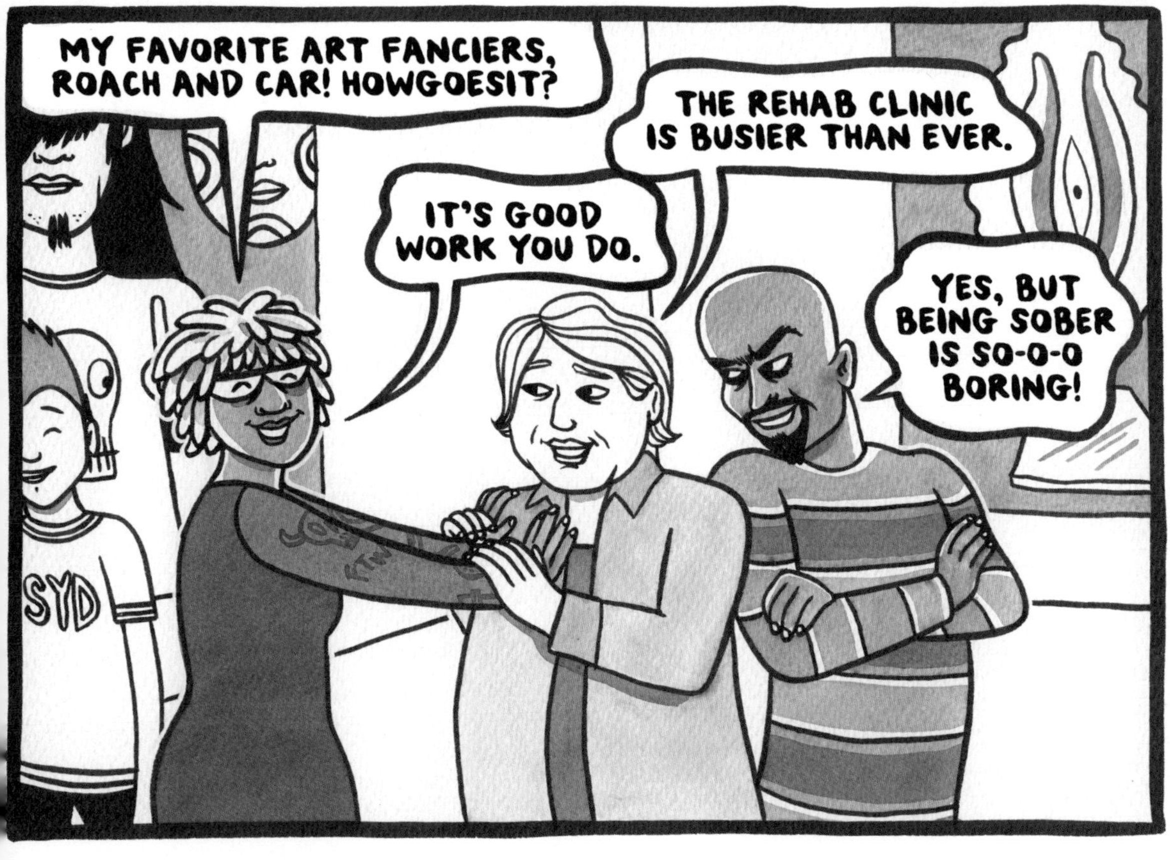
MY FAVORITE ART FANCIERS, ROACH AND CAR! HOWGOESIT?
THE REHAB CLINIC IS BUSIER THAN EVER.
IT'S GOOD WORK YOU DO.
YES, BUT BEING SOBER IS SO-O-O BORING!
SYD

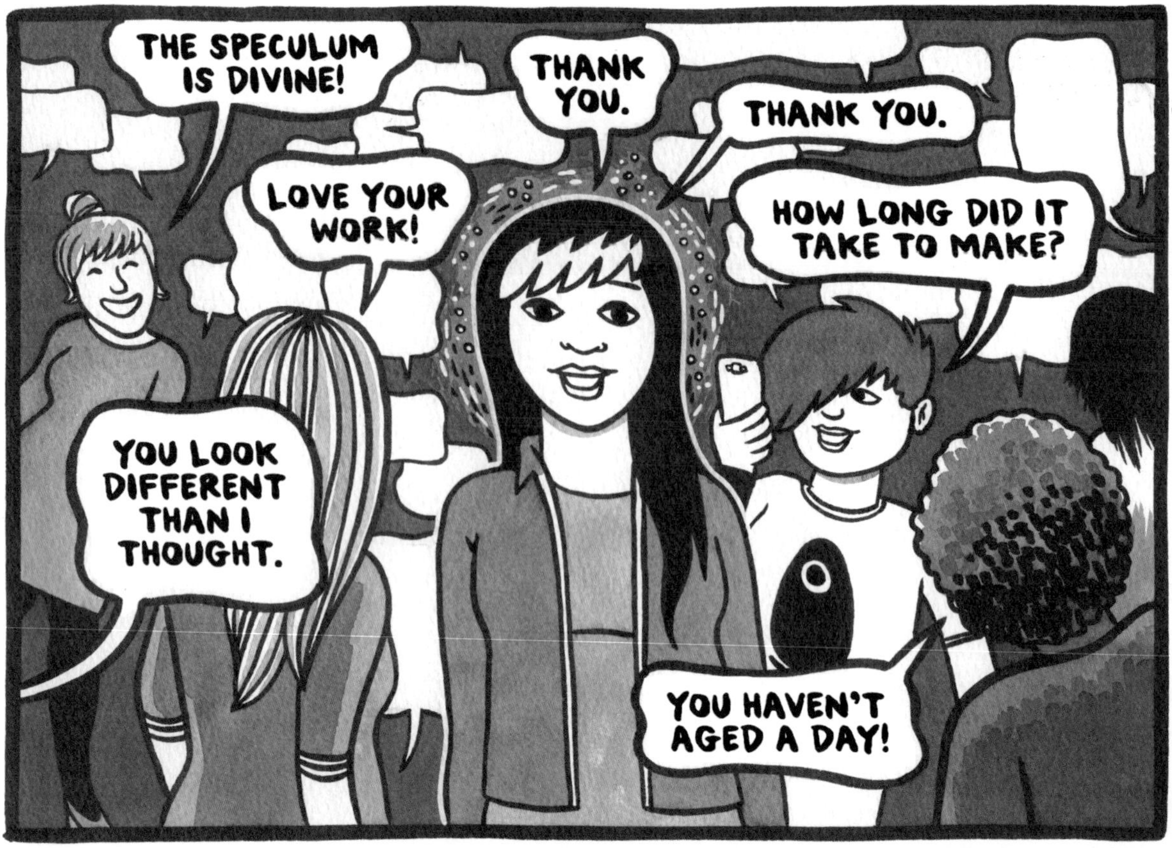
THE SPECULUM IS DIVINE!
THANK YOU.
THANK YOU.
LOVE YOUR WORK!
HOW LONG DID IT TAKE TO MAKE?
YOU LOOK DIFFERENT THAN I THOUGHT.
YOU HAVEN'T AGED A DAY!

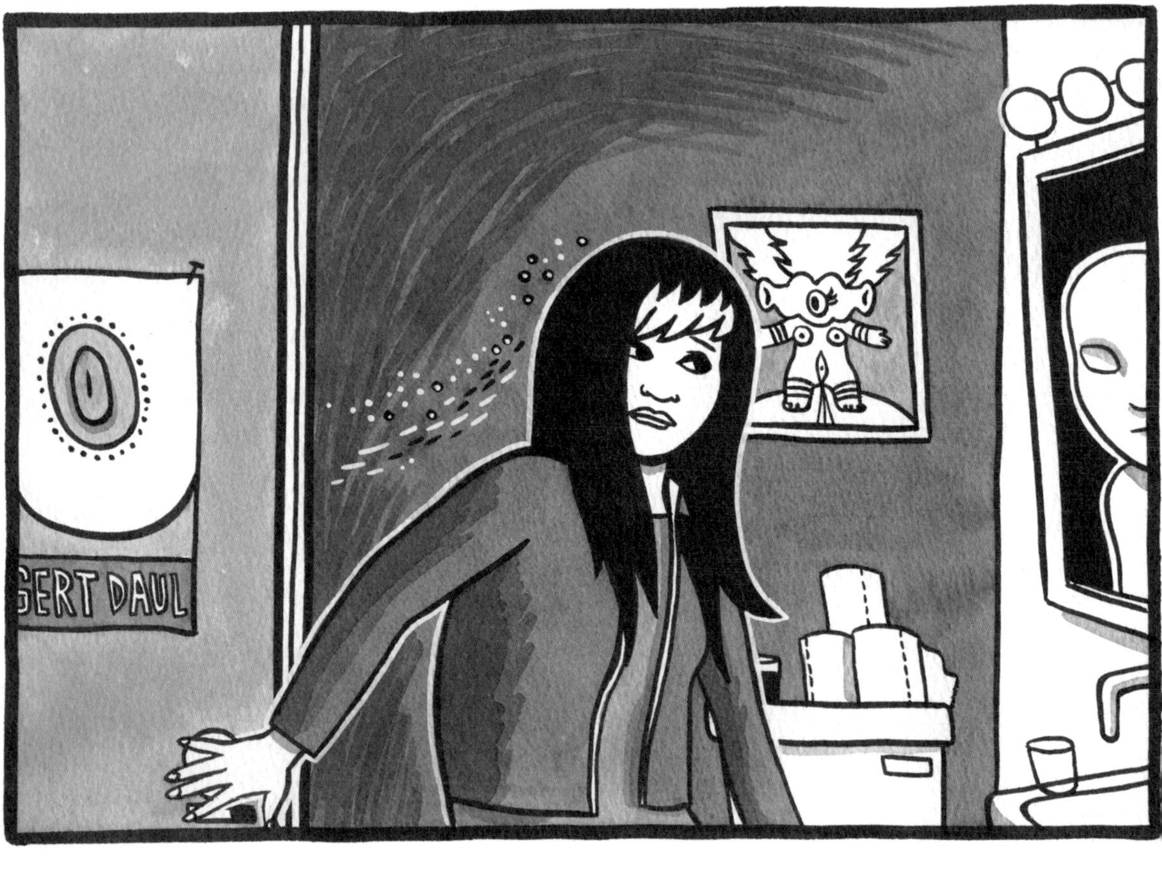
GERT DAUL

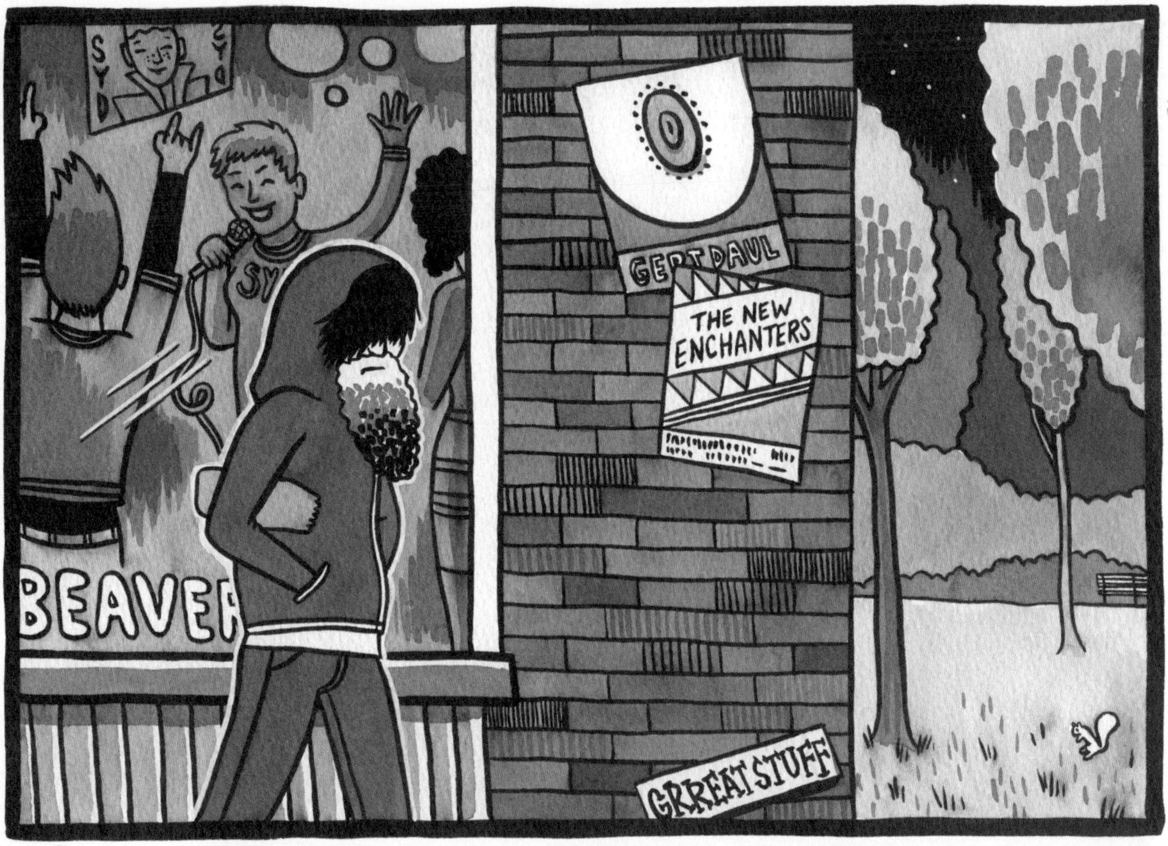
SYD
SYD
BEAVER
THE NEW ENCHANTERS
GRREAT STUFF

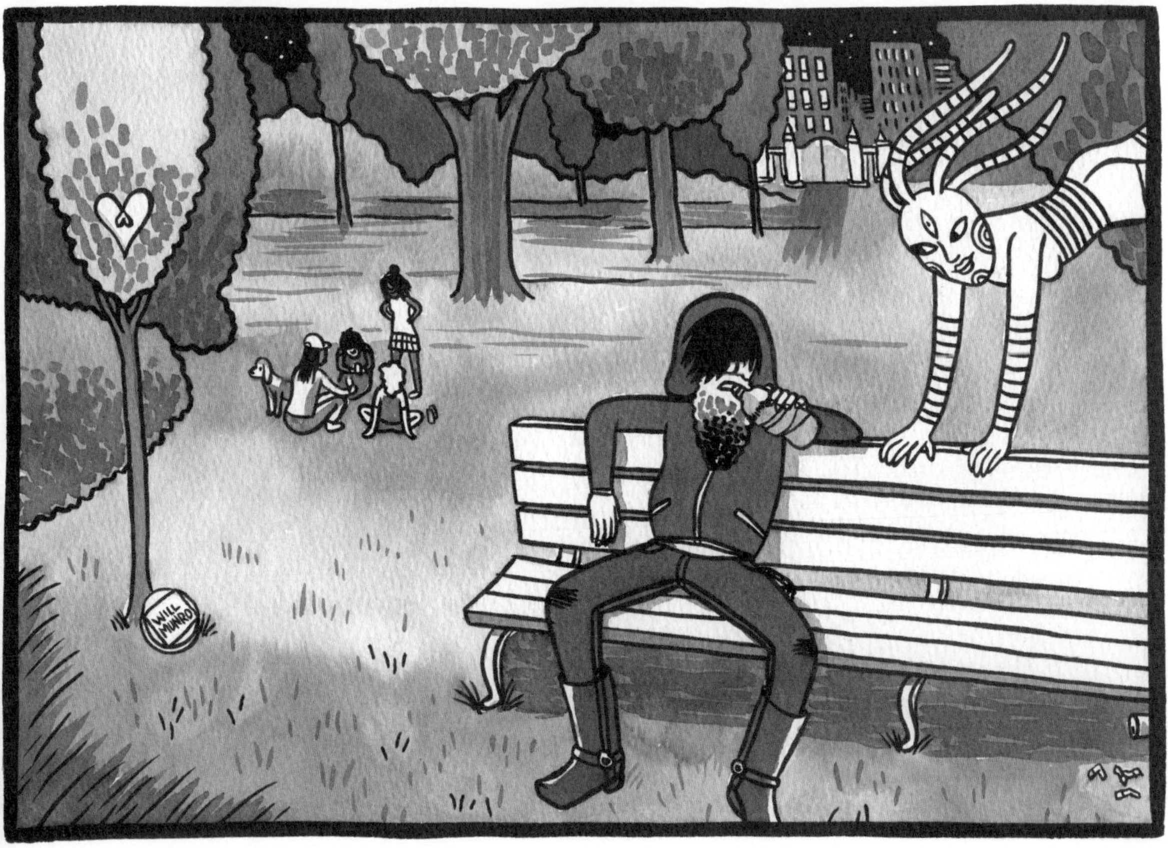
WILL MUNRO

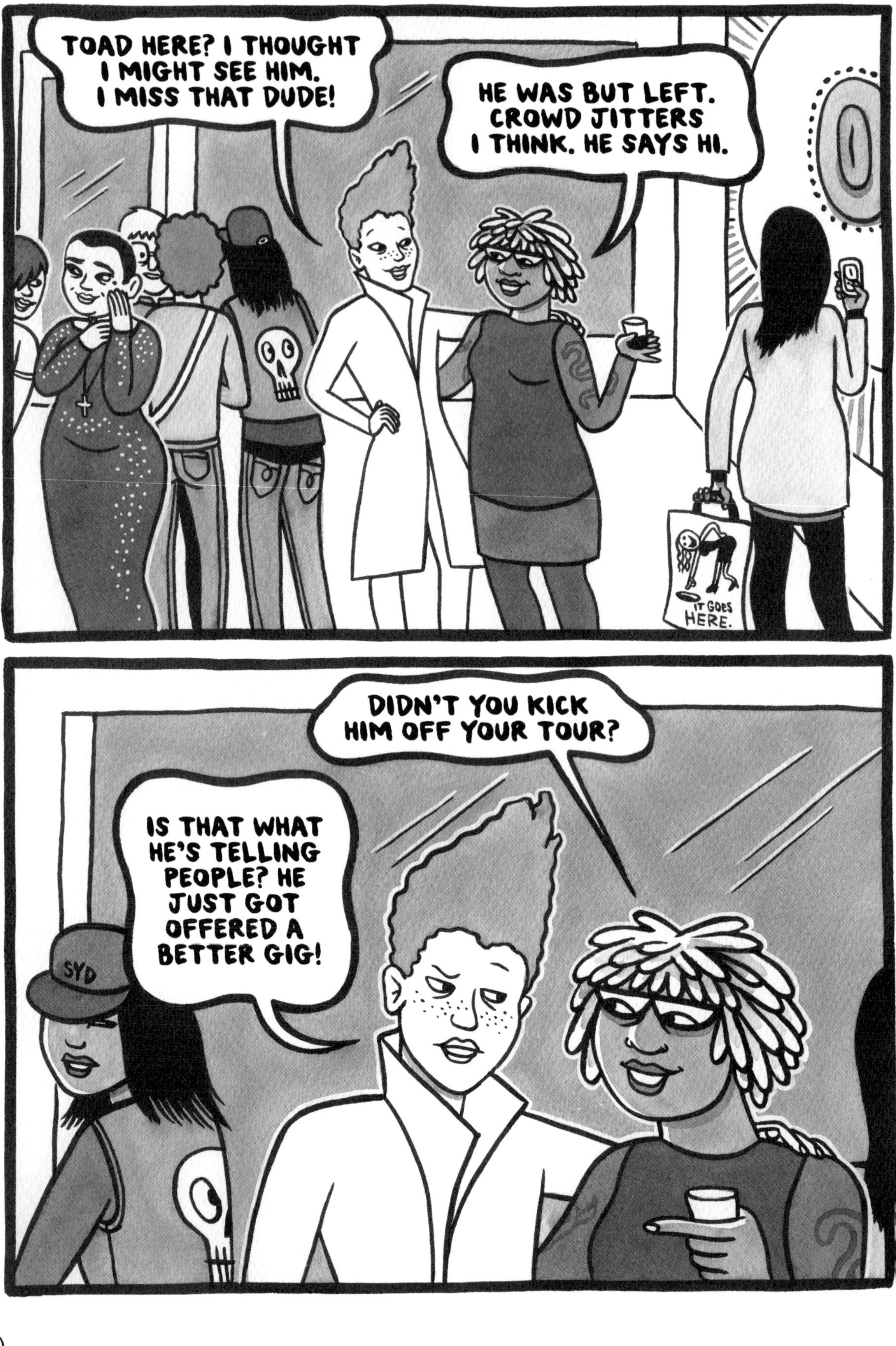
TOAD HERE? I THOUGHT I MIGHT SEE HIM. I MISS THAT DUDE!
HE WAS BUT LEFT. CROWD JITTERS I THINK. HE SAYS HI.
IT GOES HERE.
DIDN'T YOU KICK HIM OFF YOUR TOUR?
IS THAT WHAT HE'S TELLING PEOPLE? HE JUST GOT OFFERED A BETTER GIG!
SYD

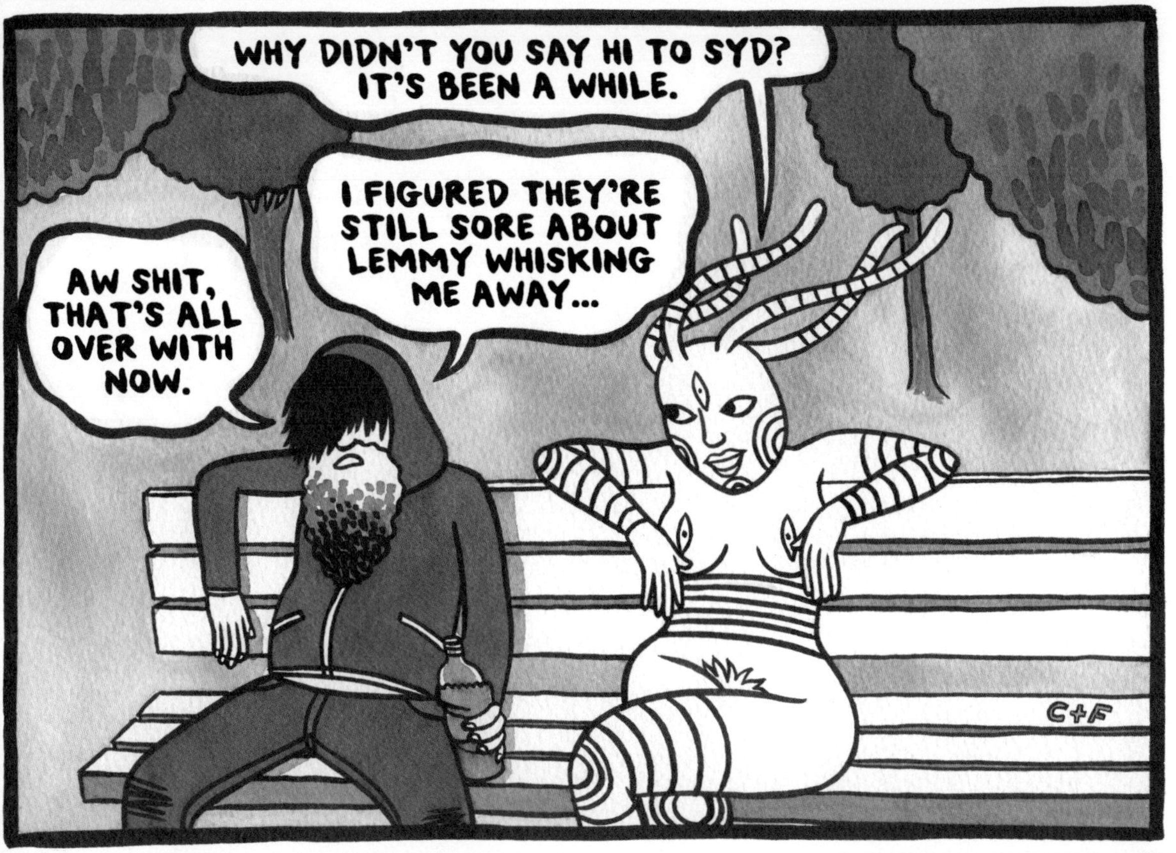
WHY DIDN'T YOU SAY HI TO SYD? IT'S BEEN A WHILE.
I FIGURED THEY'RE STILL SORE ABOUT LEMMY WHISKING ME AWAY...
AW SHIT, THAT'S ALL OVER WITH NOW.
C+F

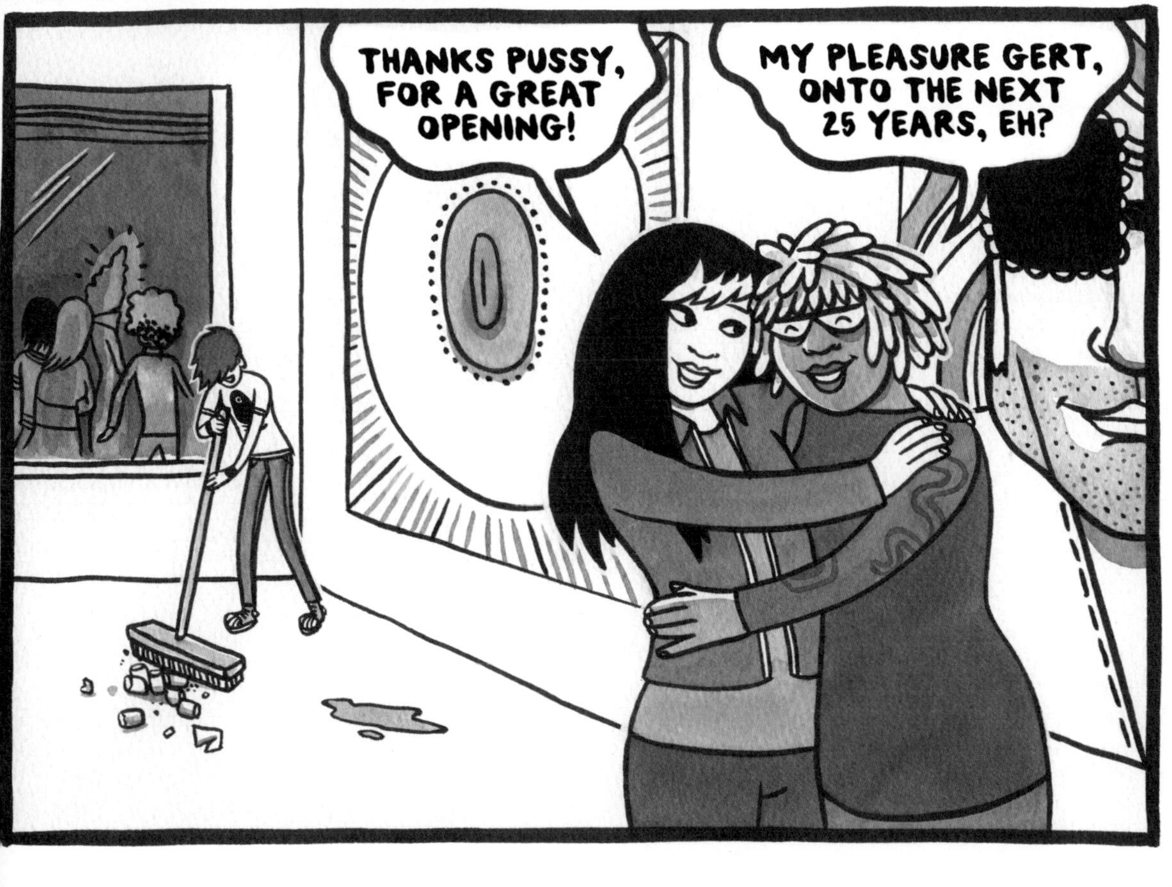
THANKS PUSSY, FOR A GREAT OPENING!
MY PLEASURE GERT, ONTO THE NEXT 25 YEARS, EH?

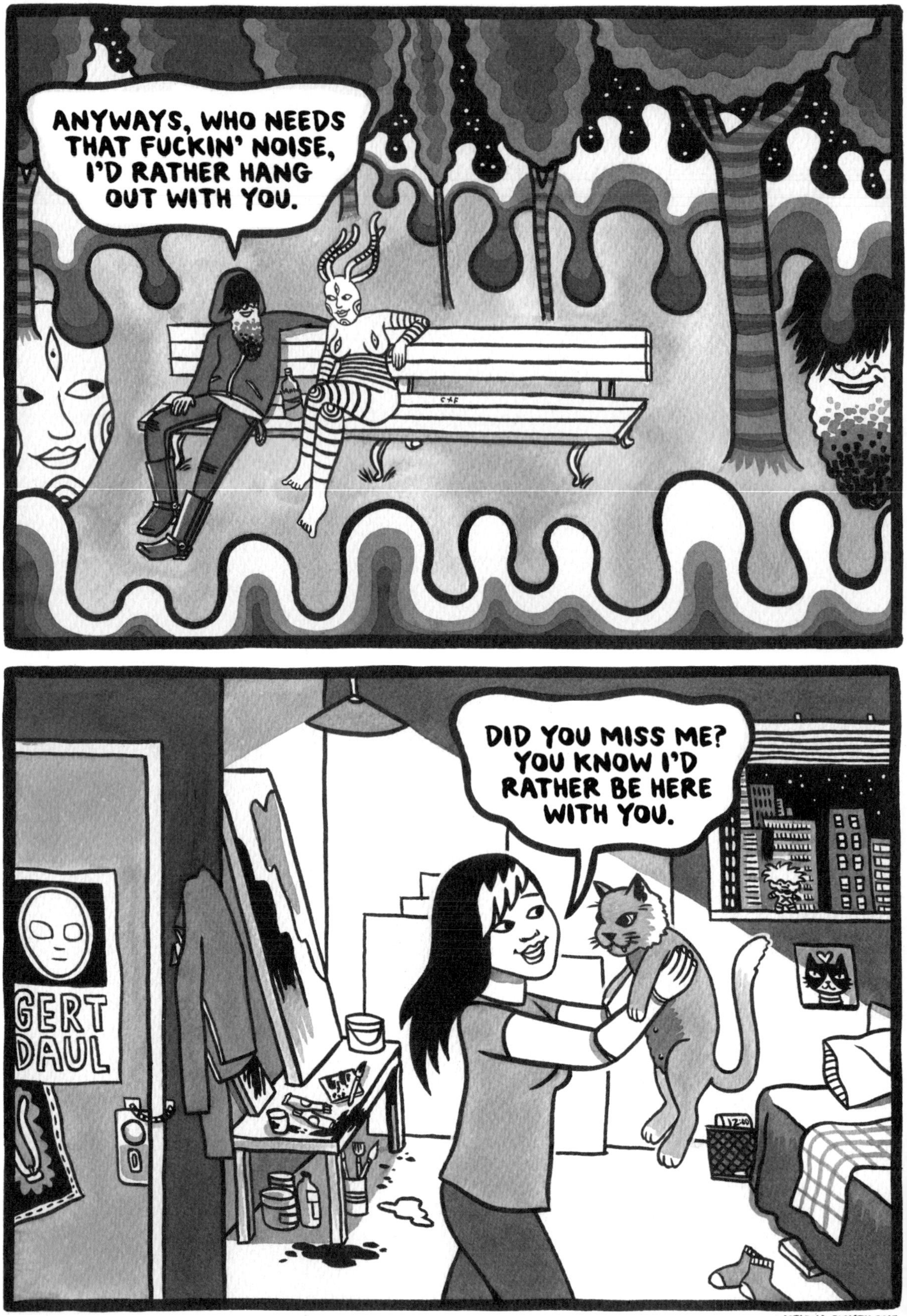
ANYWAYS, WHO NEEDS THAT FUCKIN' NOISE, I'D RATHER HANG OUT WITH YOU.
GERT DAUL
DID YOU MISS ME? YOU KNOW I'D RATHER BE HERE WITH YOU.

XFIONA SMYTH 2017

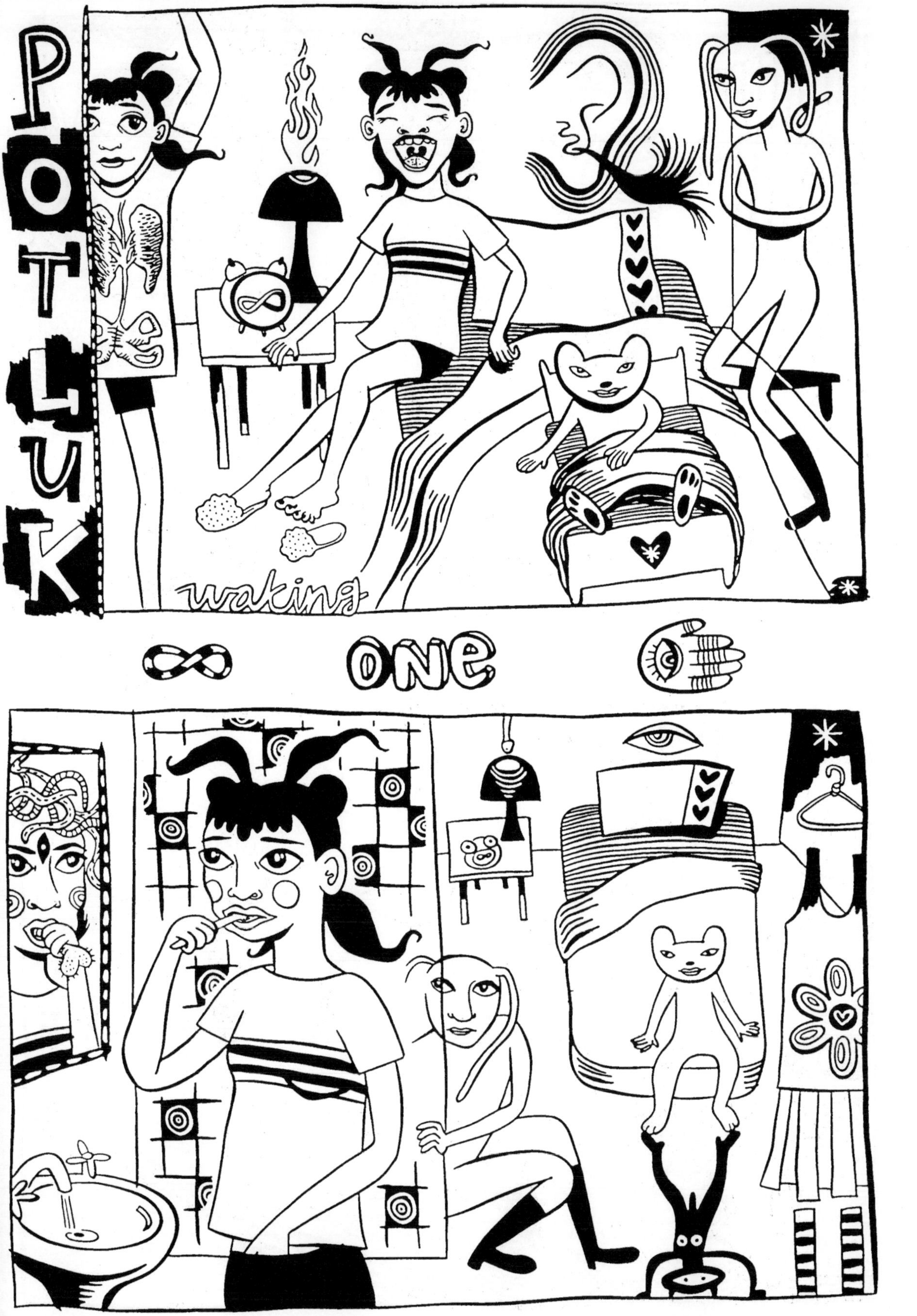
POTLUK
waking
ONE

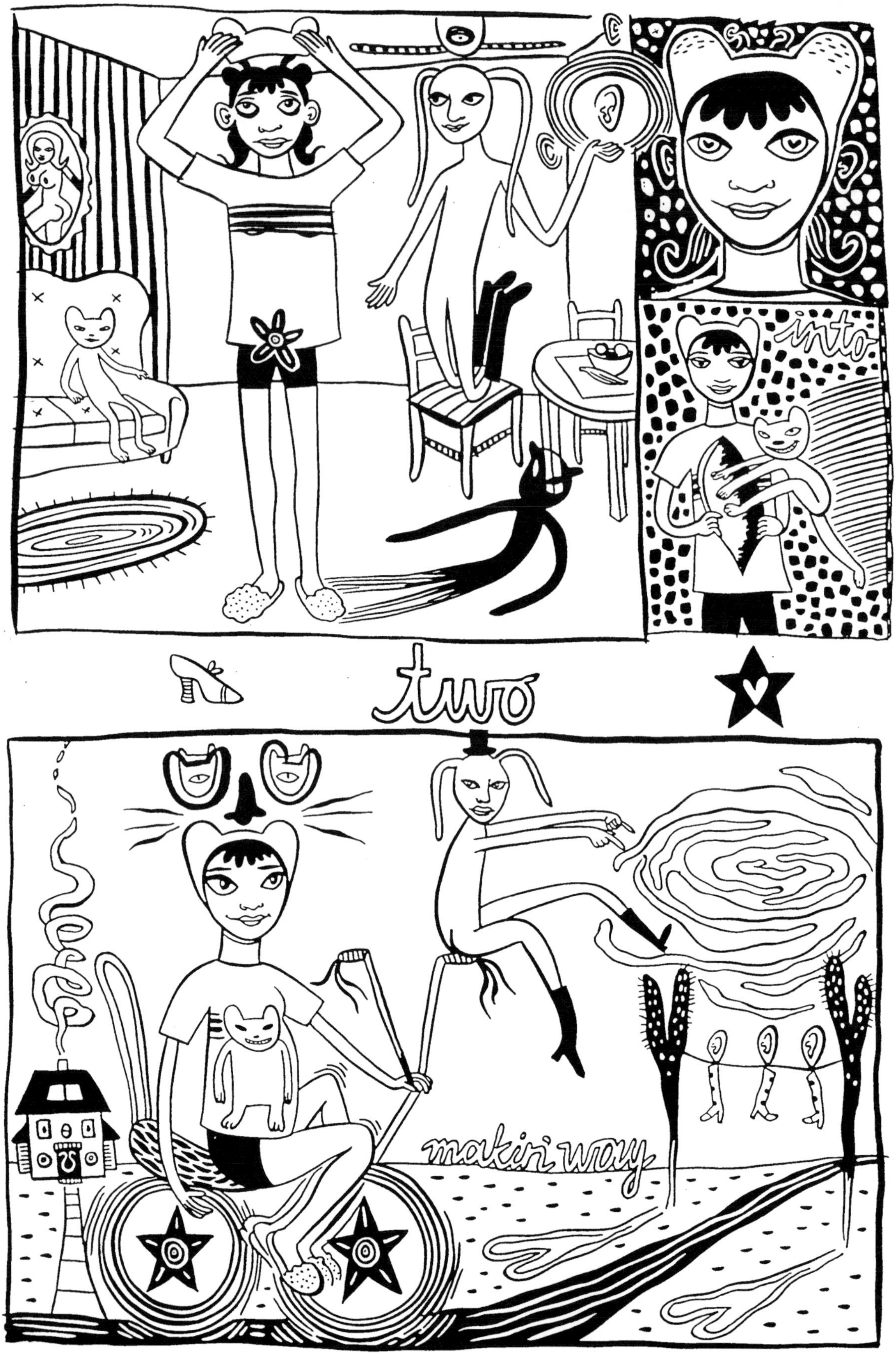
into
two
makin' way

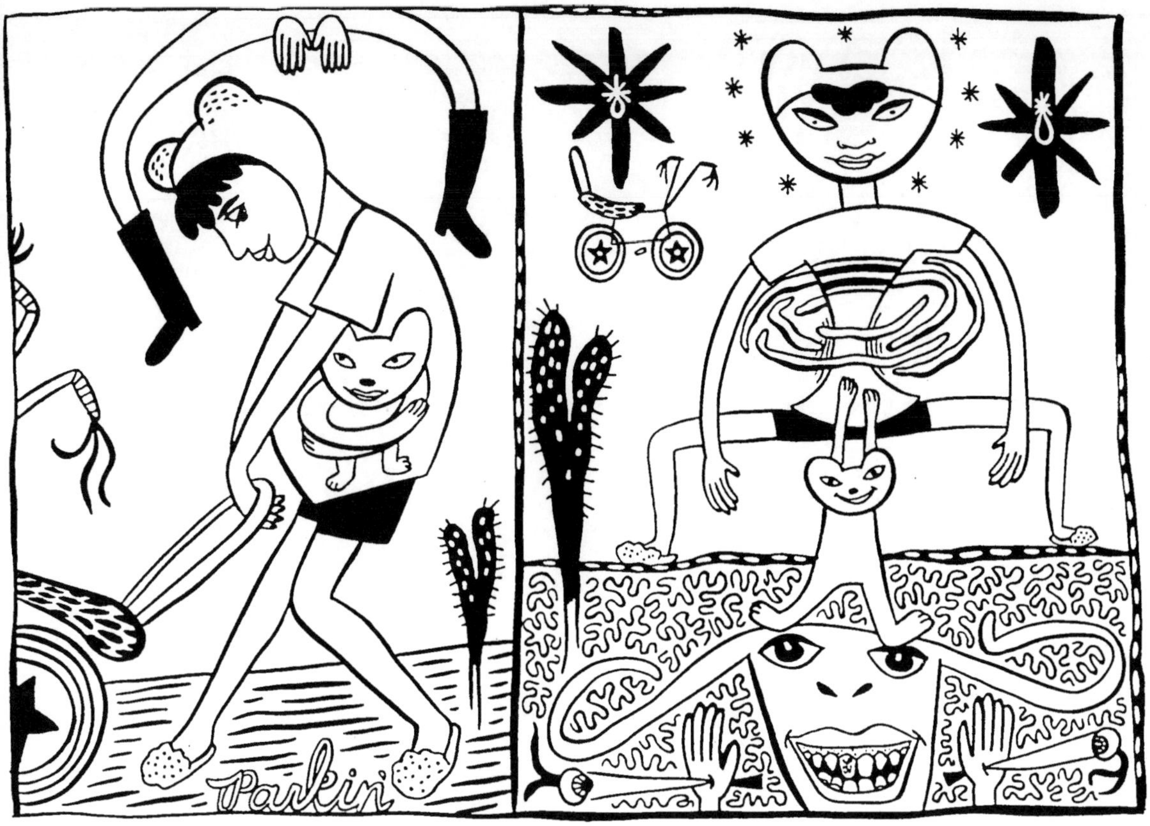
Parkin'

THREE

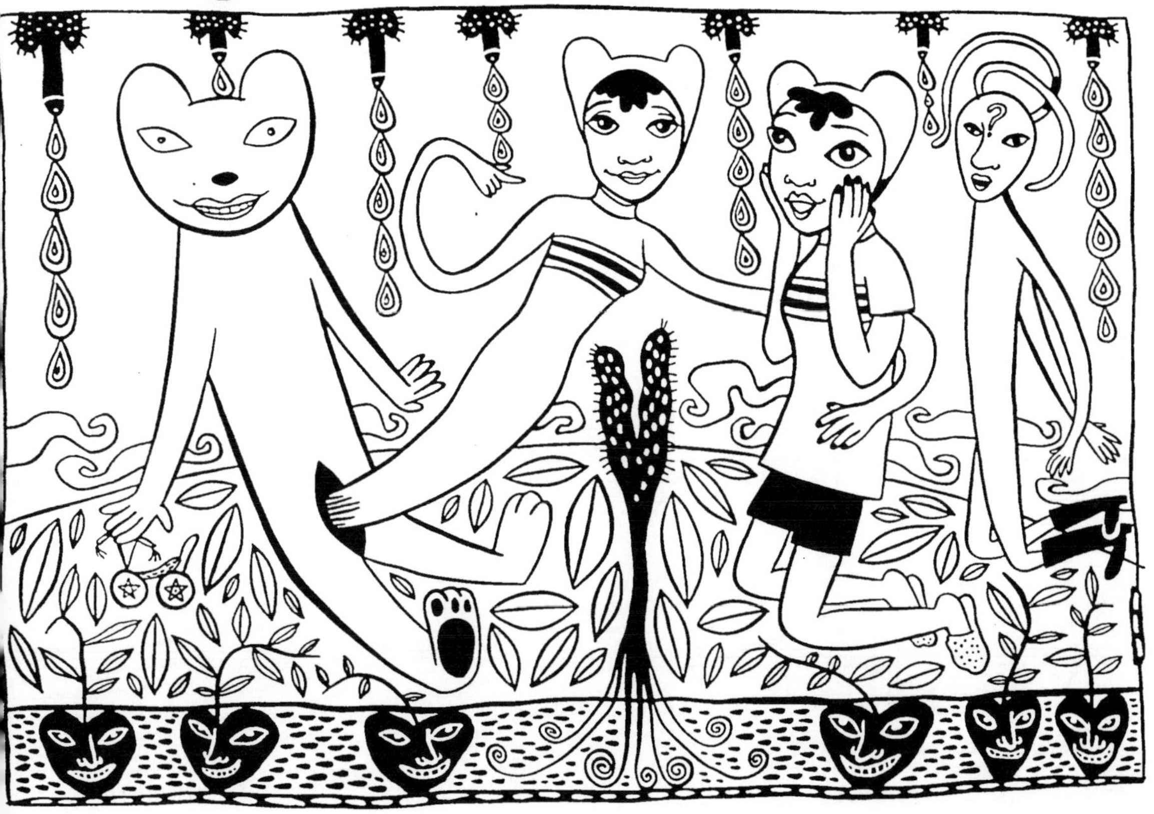

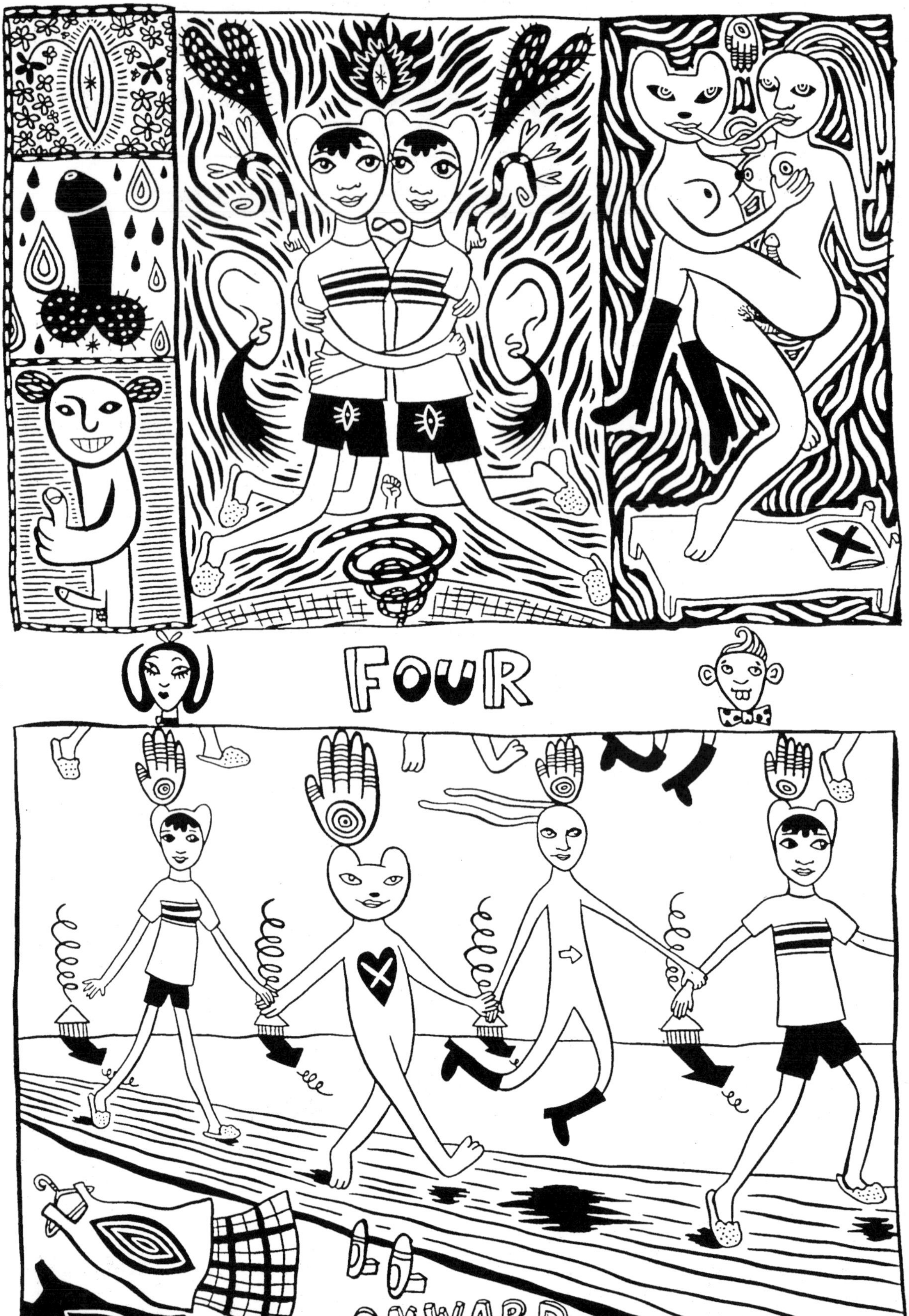
FOUR
ONWARD

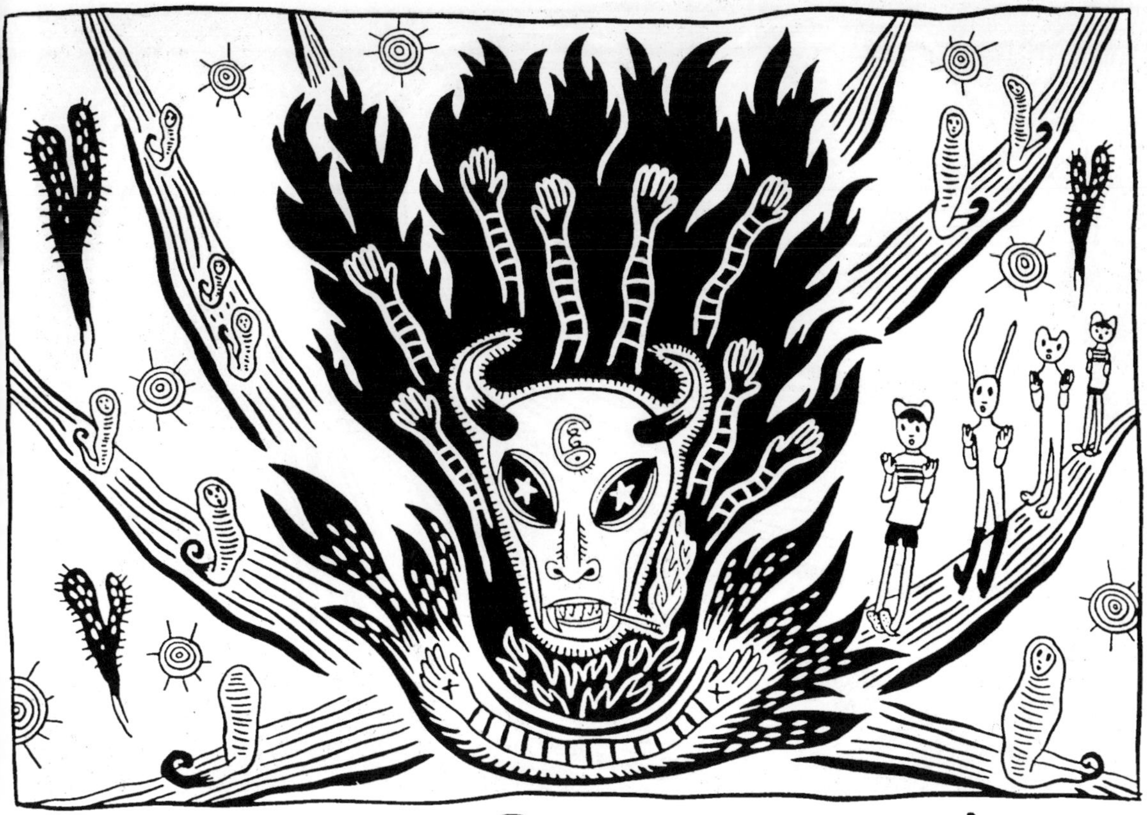

Five

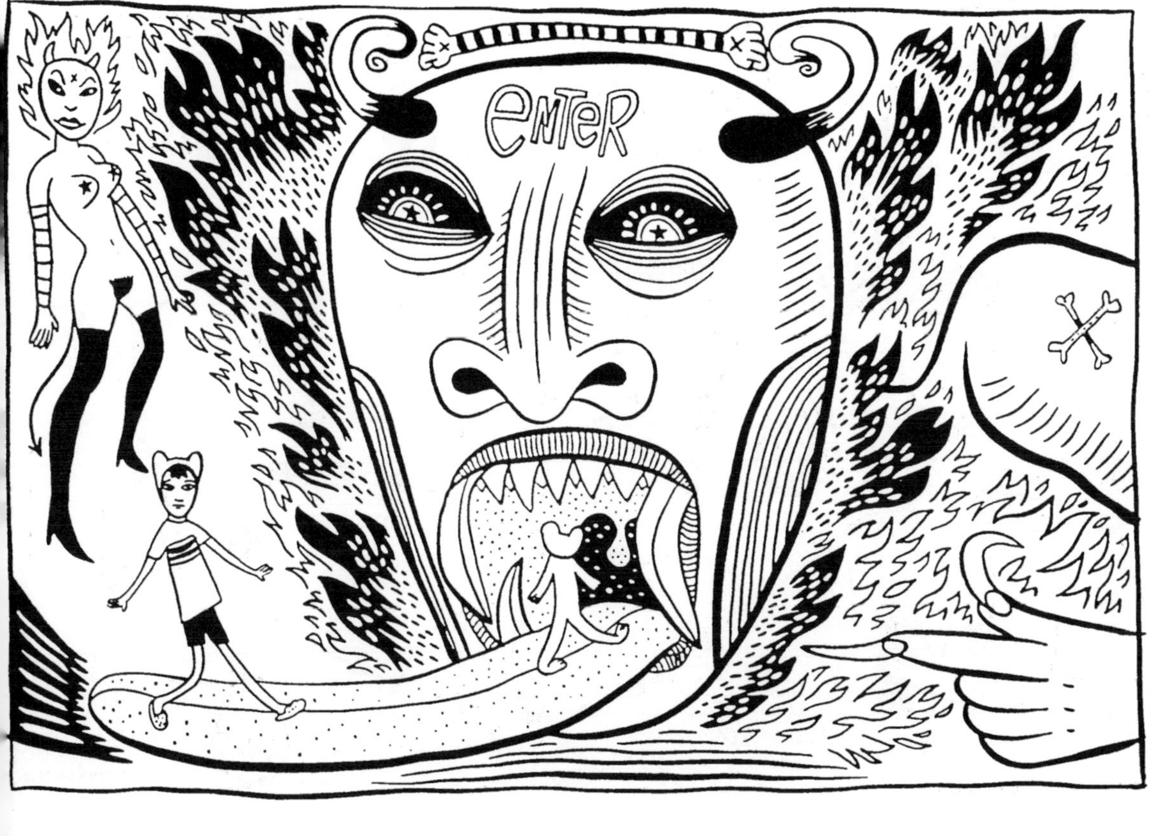
ENTER

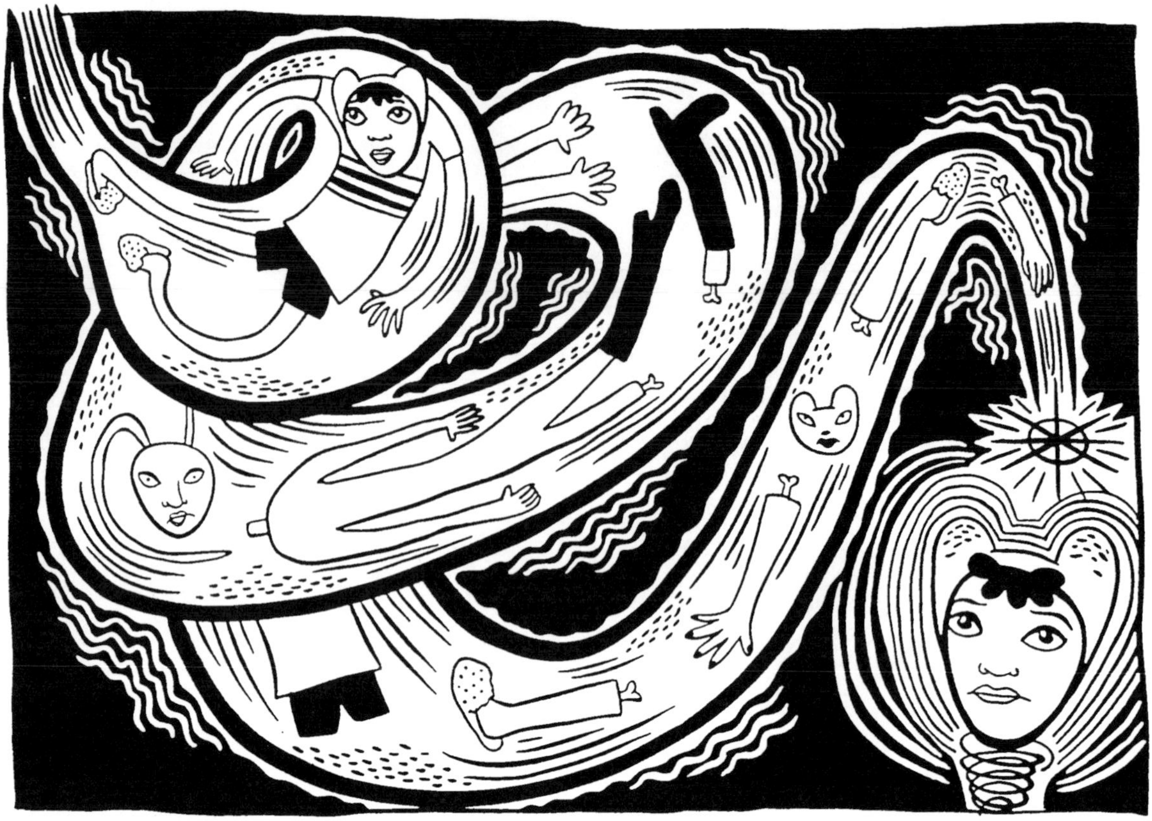

SIX

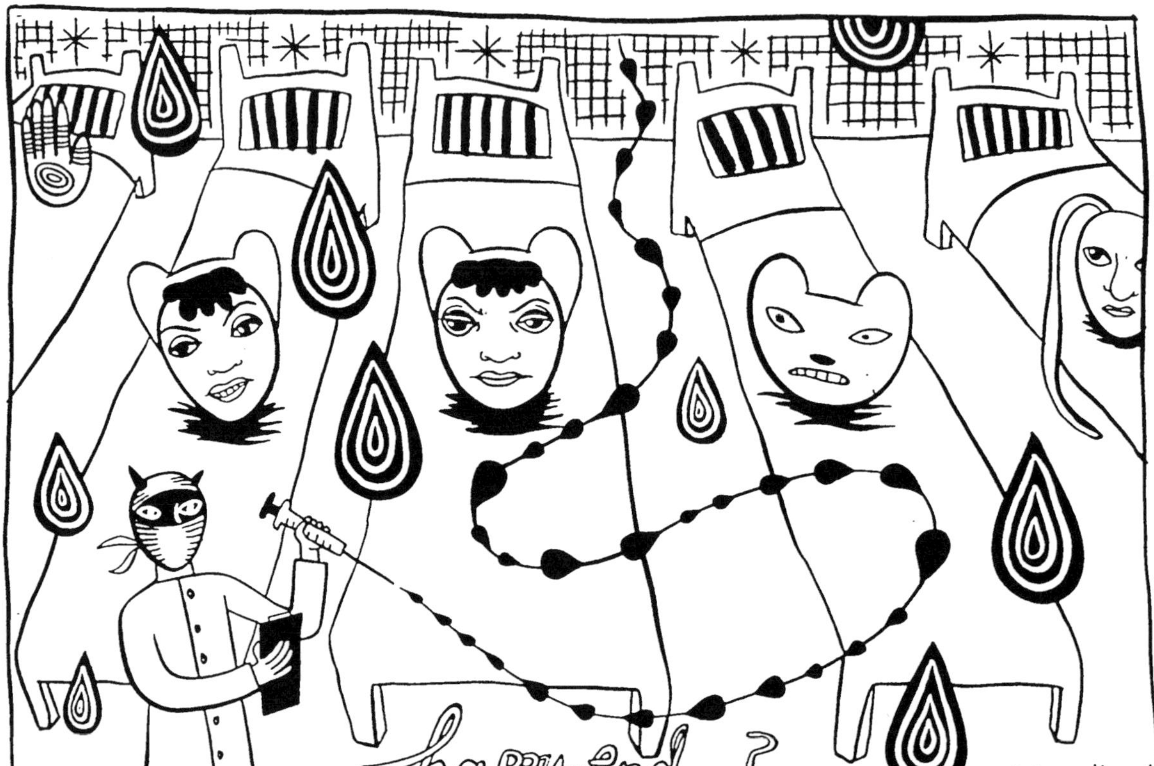
happy end?
to be continued

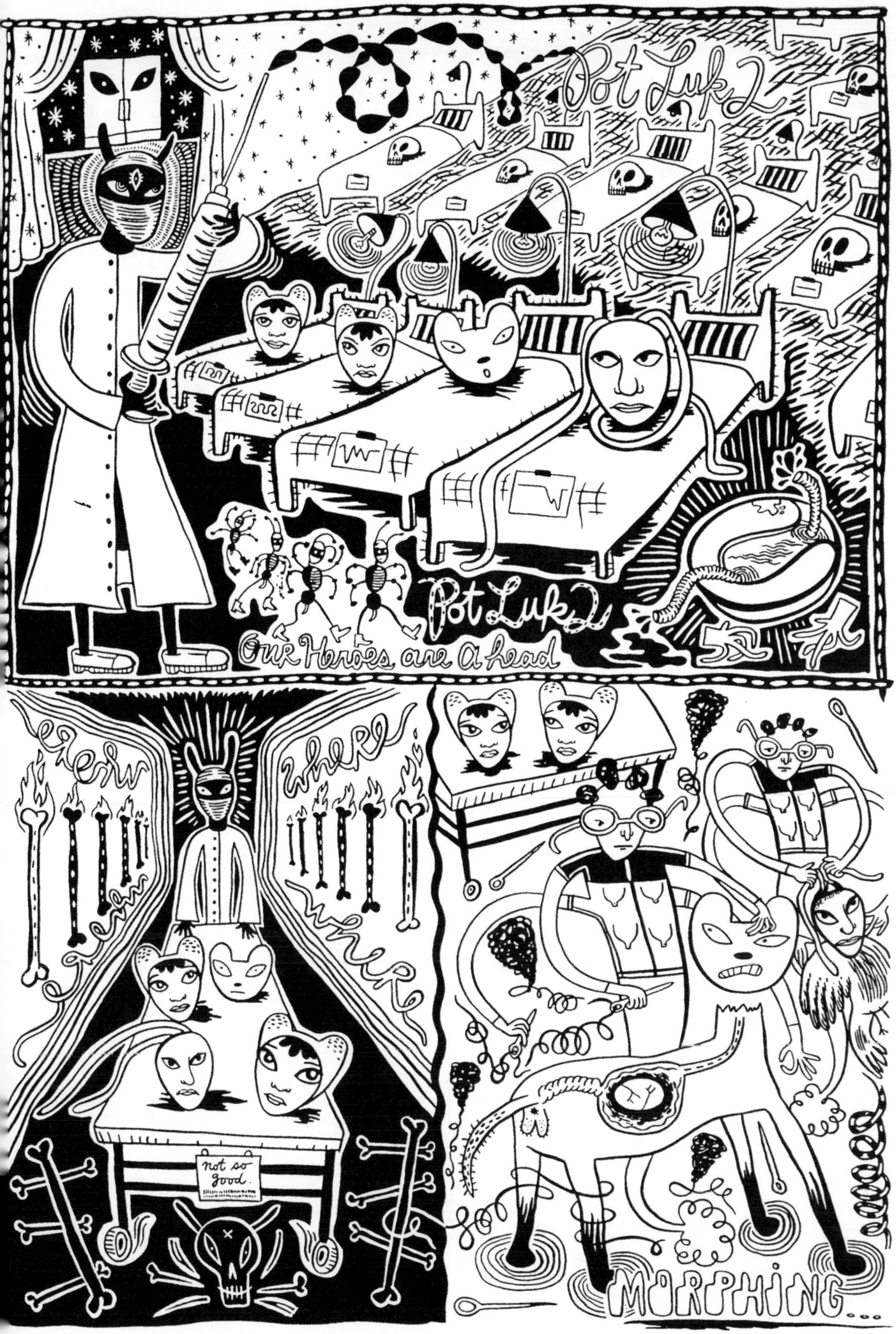
Pot Luk 2
Pot Luk 2
Our Heroes are a head
eeew
where
eeew
where
not so good.
MORPHING...

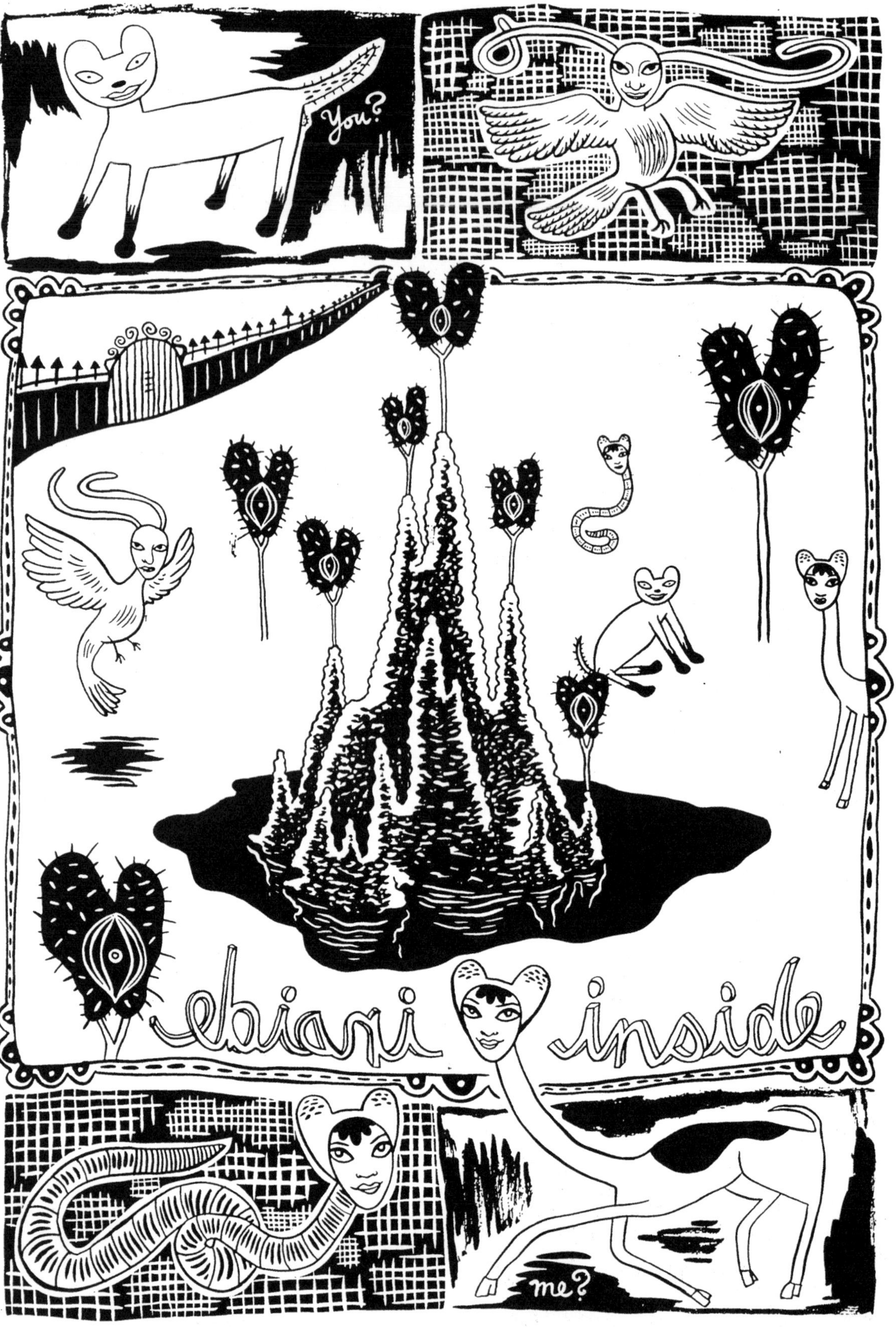

You?
ebiari inside
me?

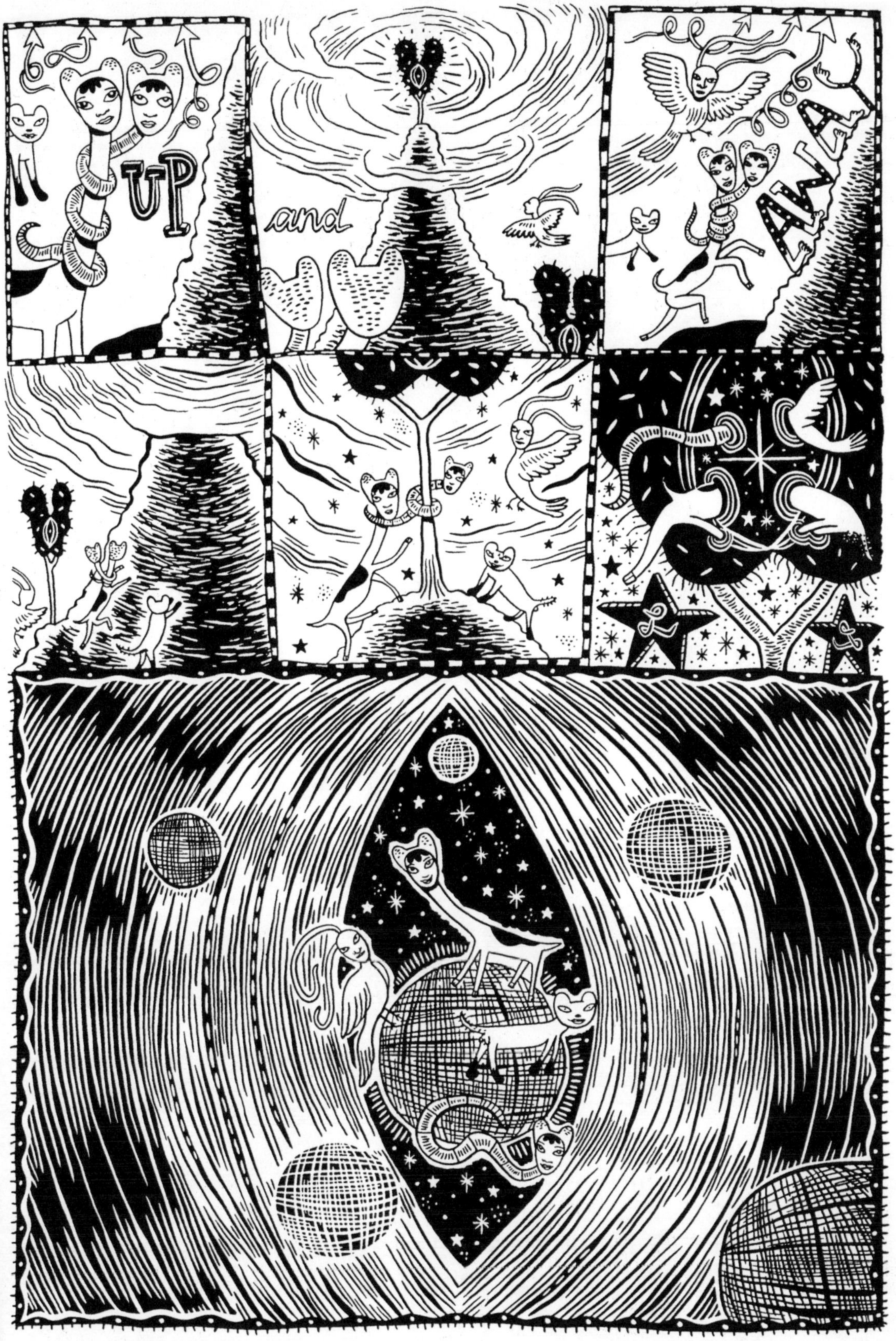
UP
and
AWAY

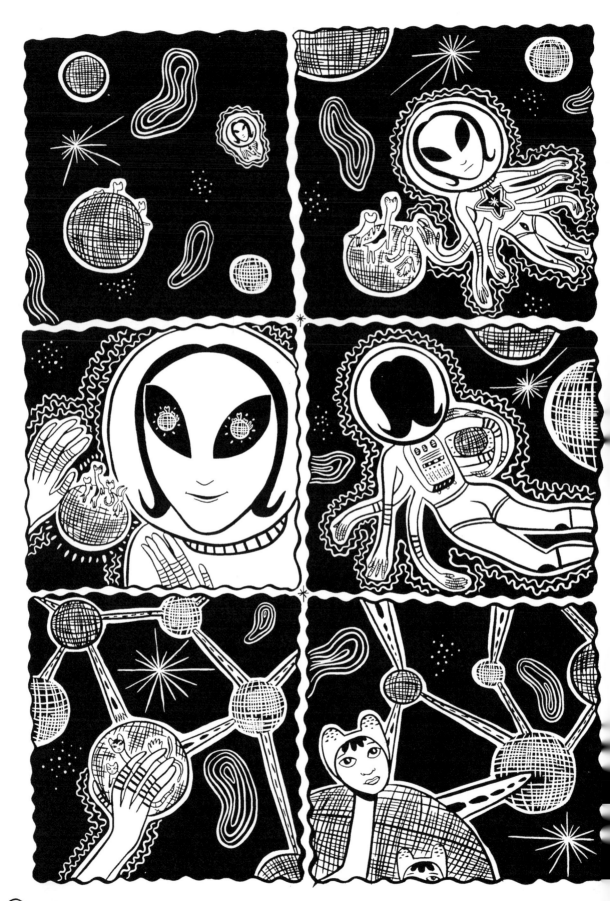

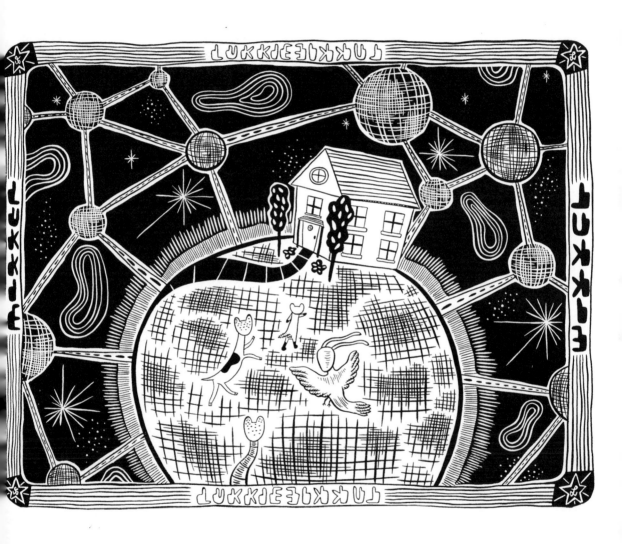

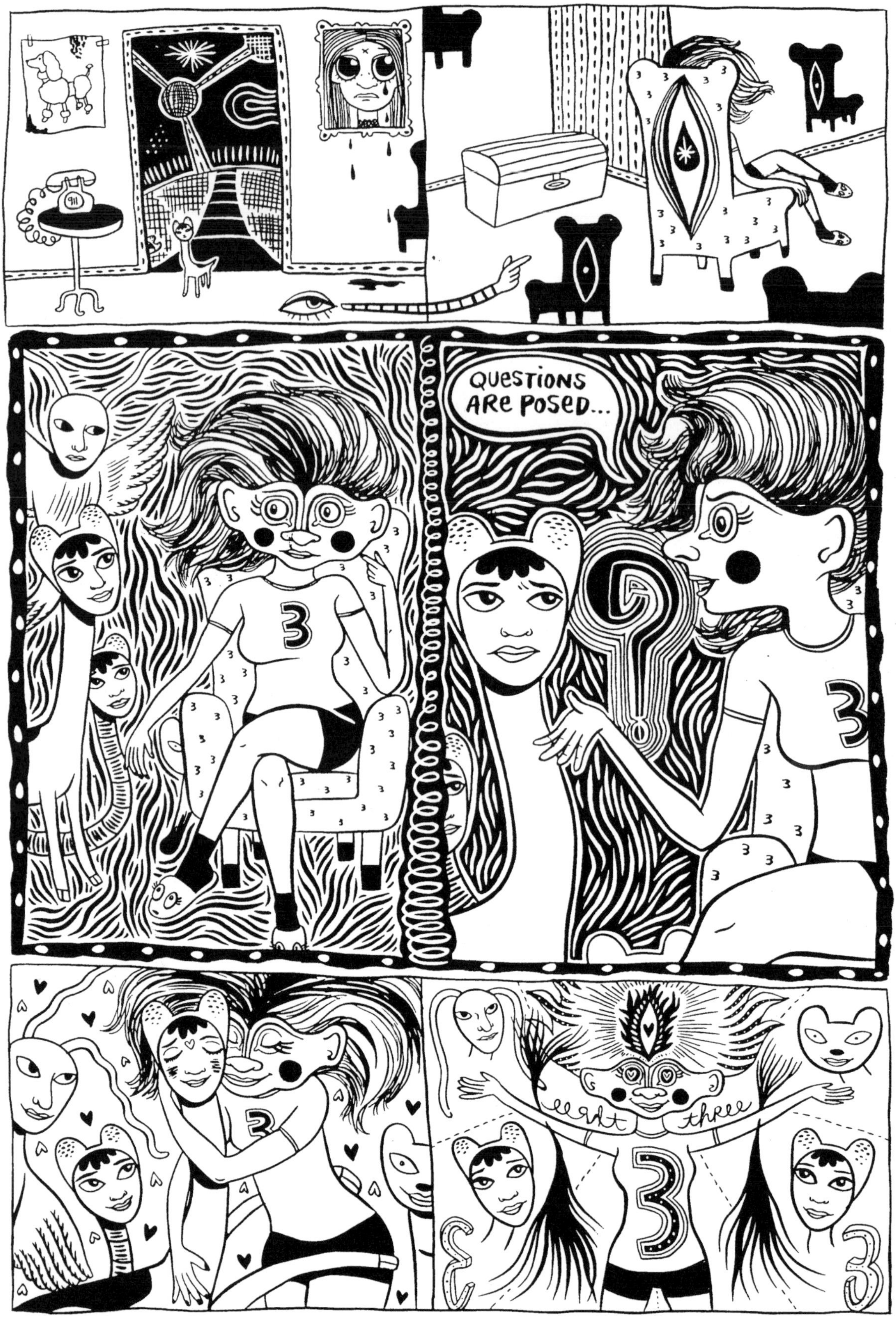

911
QUESTIONS ARE POSED...
three

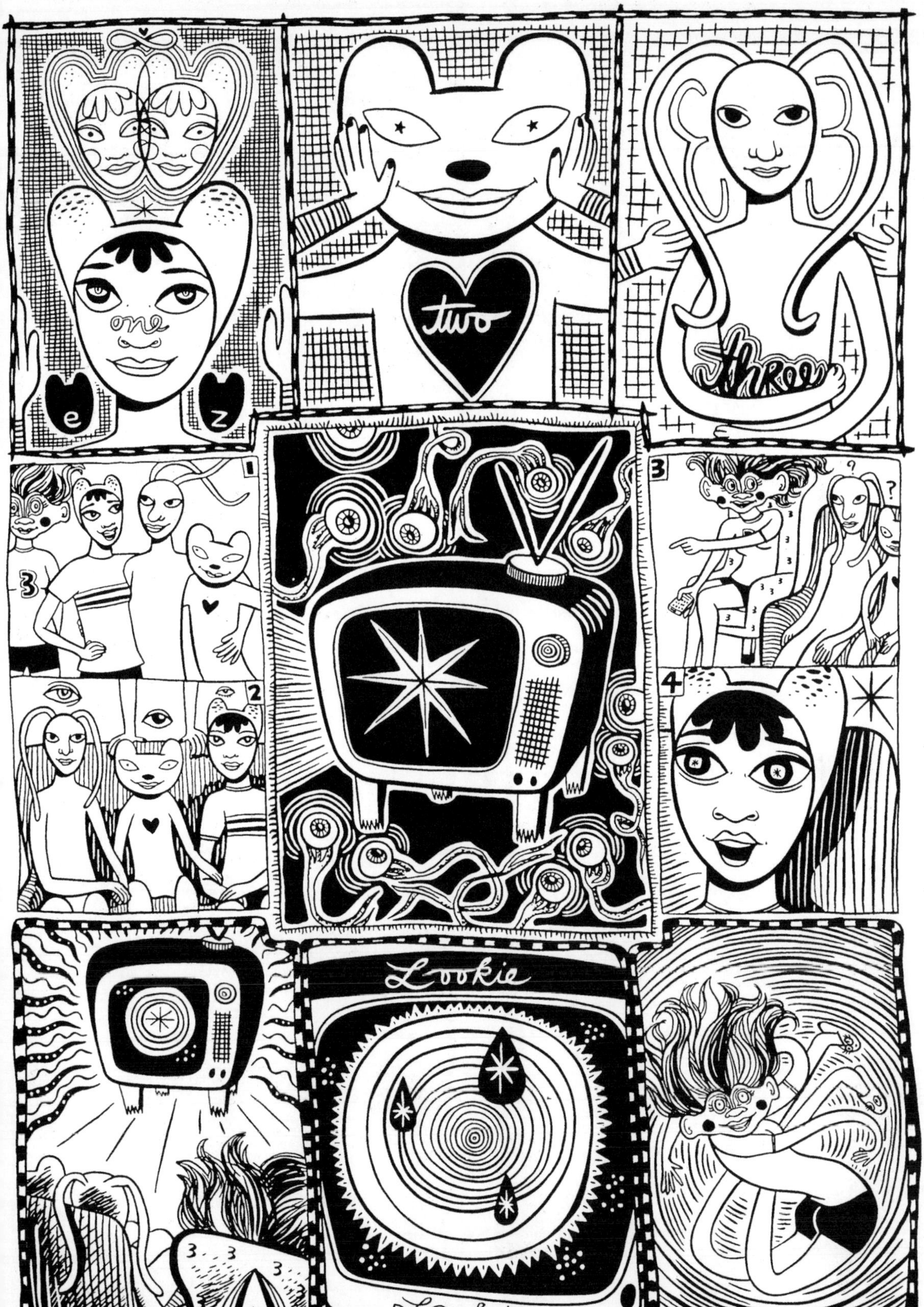
one
e
z
two
three
1
3
2
4
?
?
Lookie
Lookie

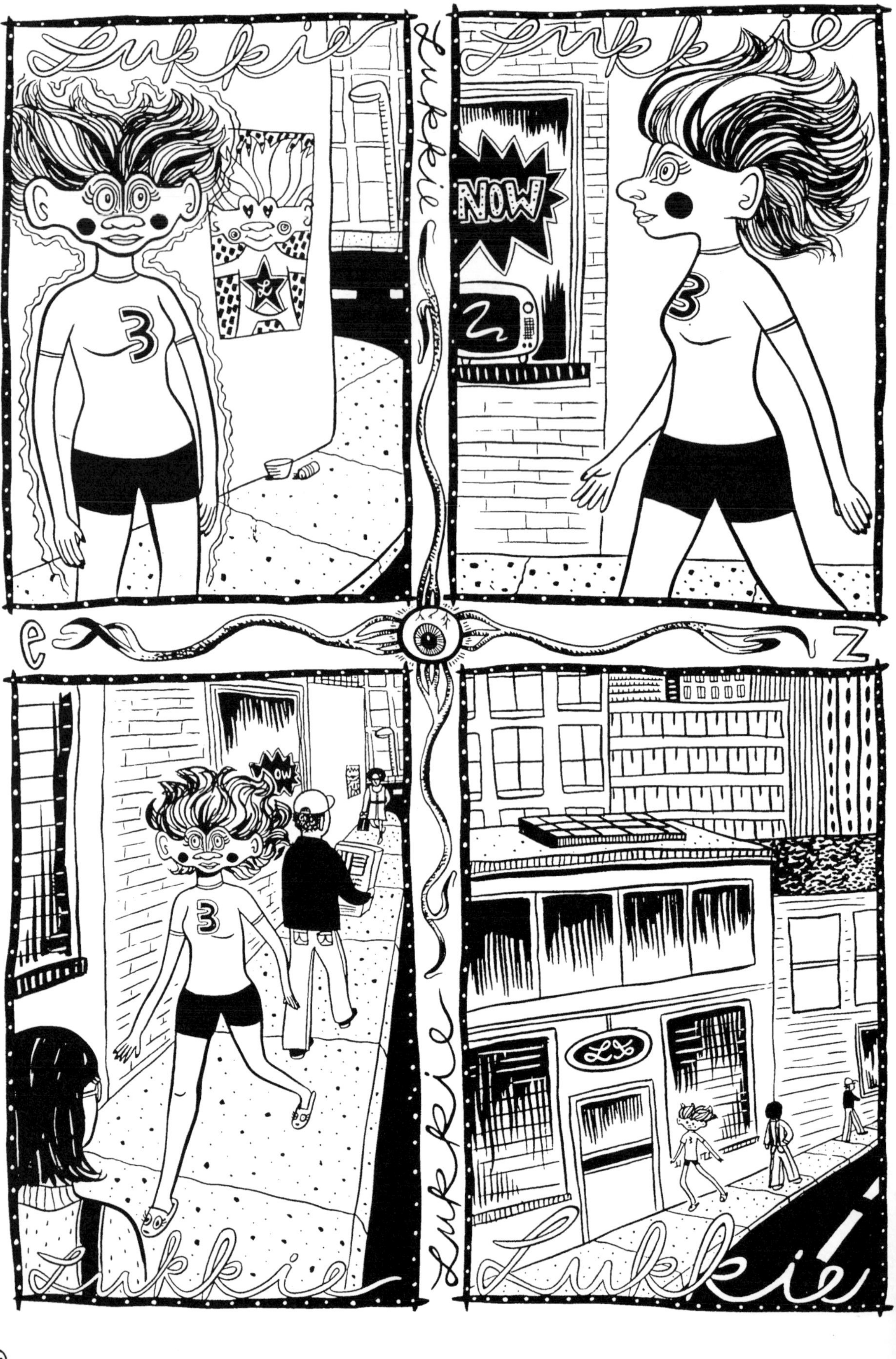
Lukkie
3
Lukkie
Lukkie
NOW
3
e
z
NOW
3
Lukkie
Lukkie
Lukkie

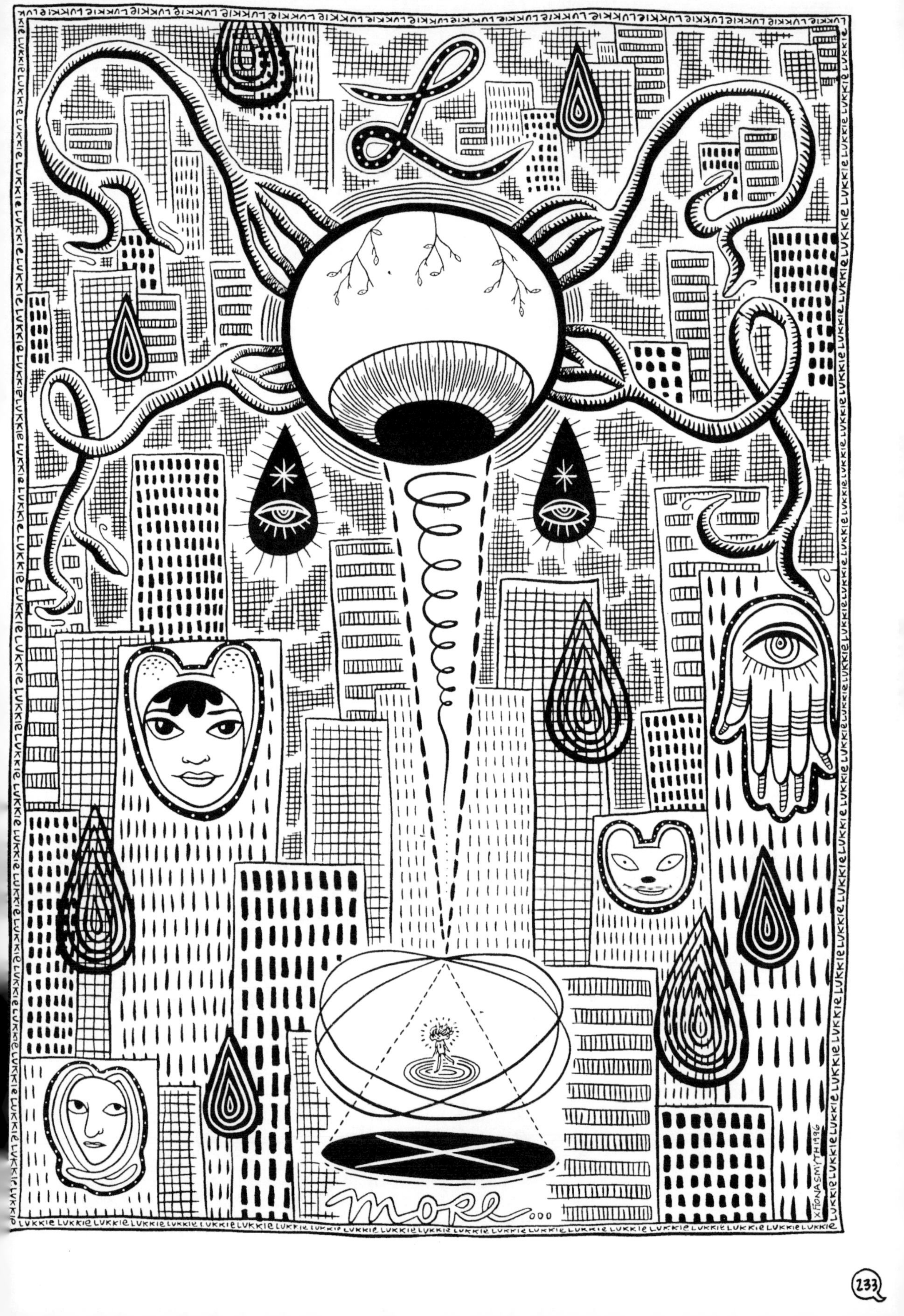
LUKKIE
L
more...
X FIONA SMYTH 1996

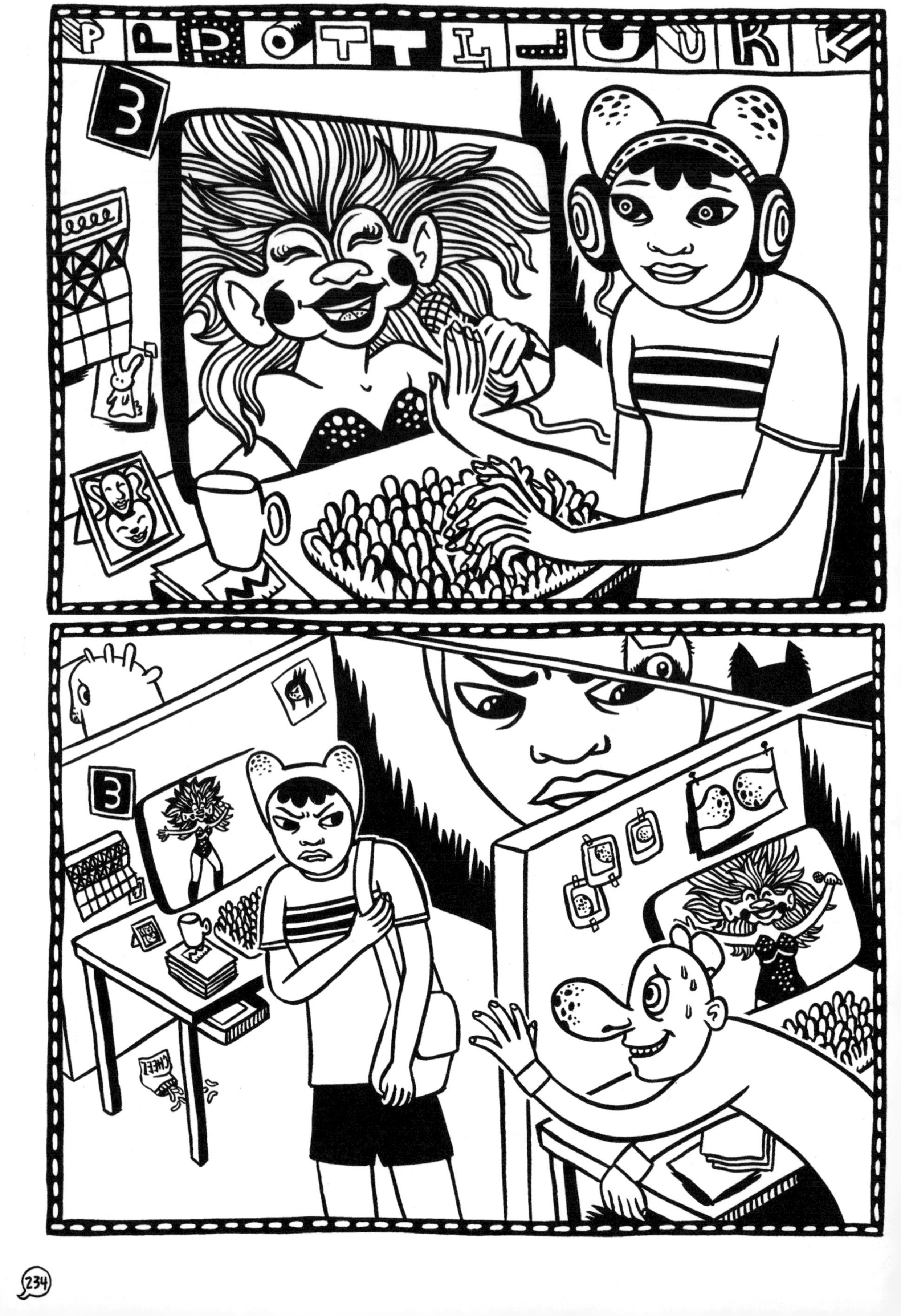
PLDOTTLJUUKK
3
3

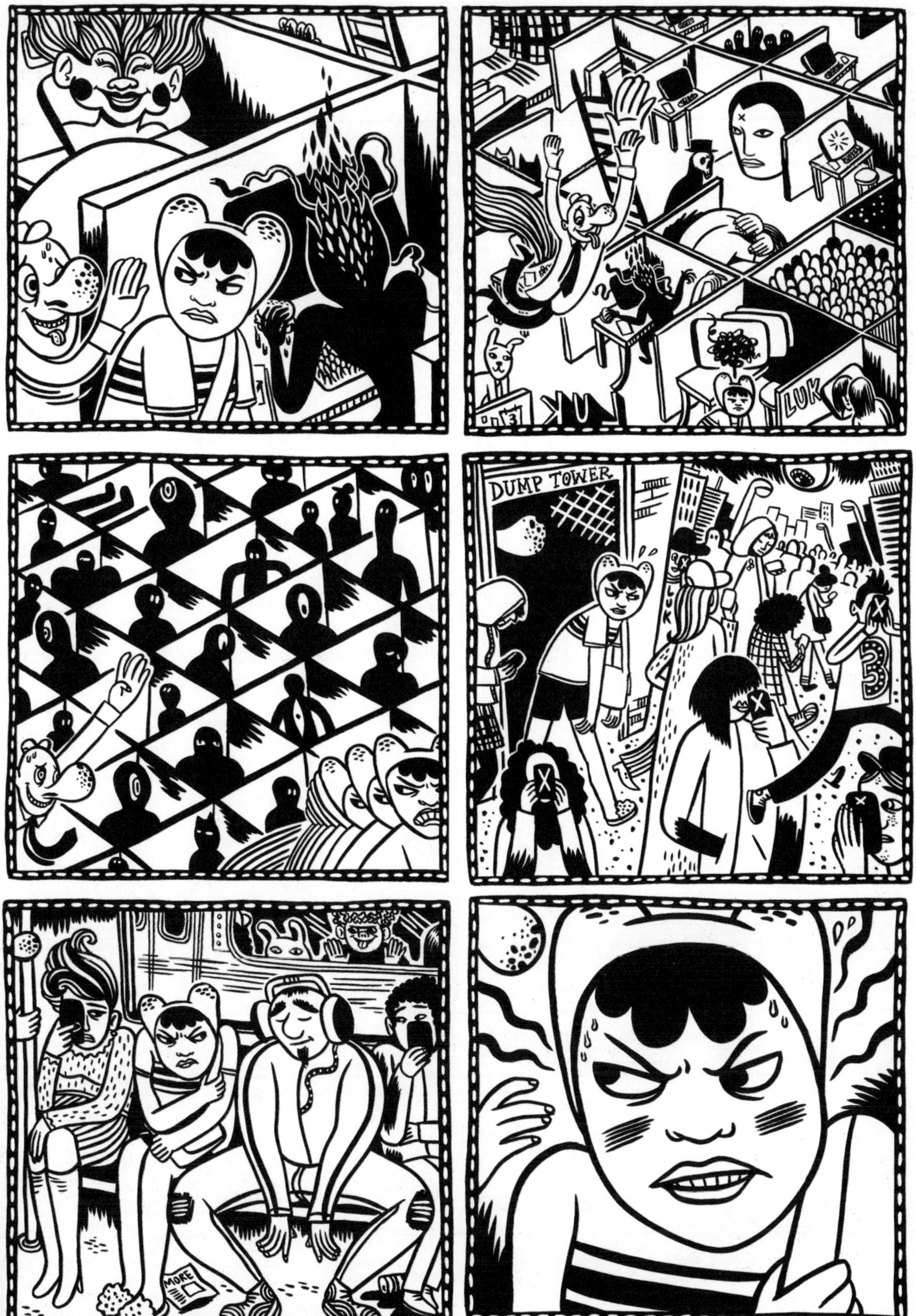
LUK
DUMP TOWER
LUK
MORE

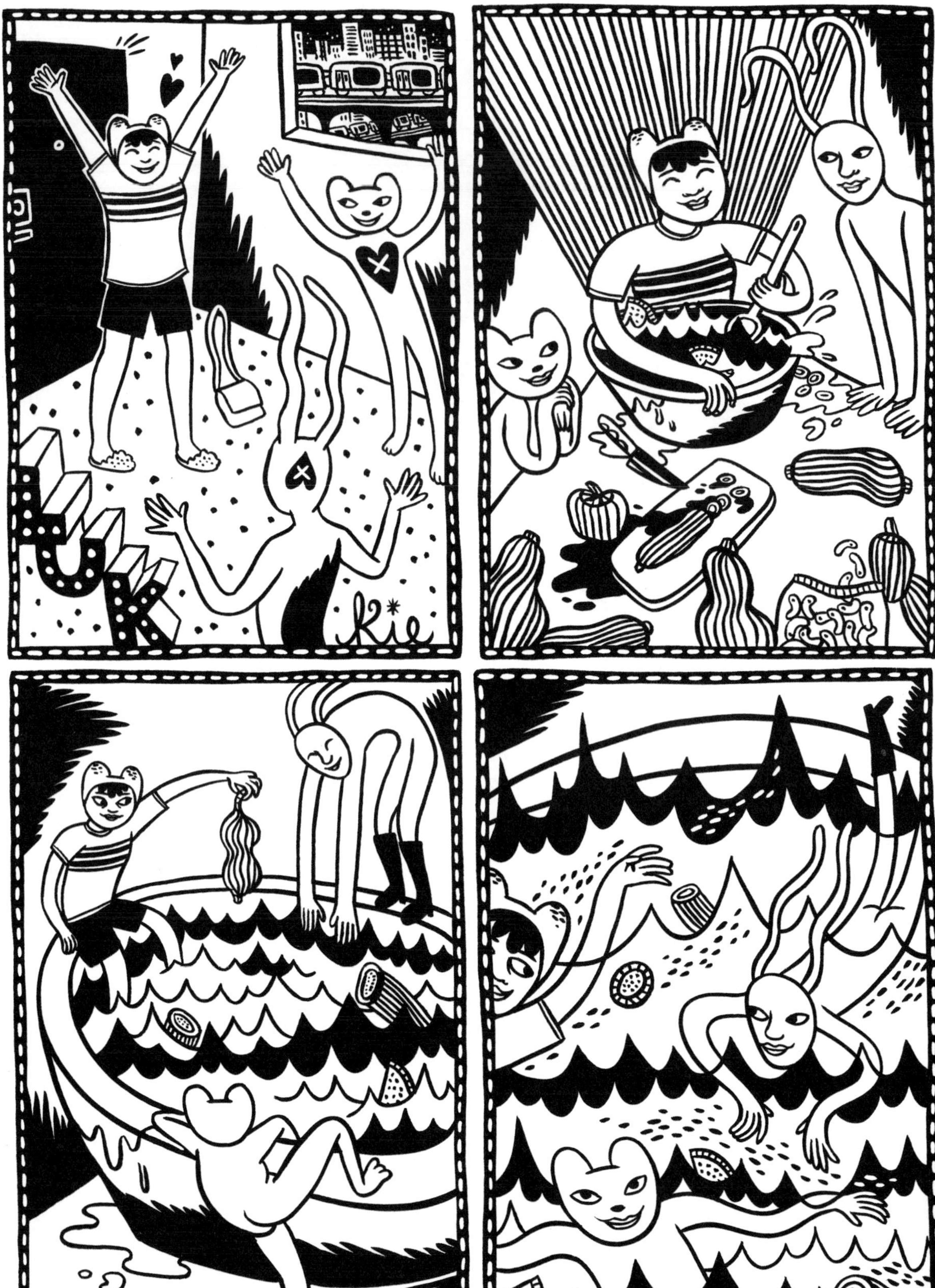
Kie

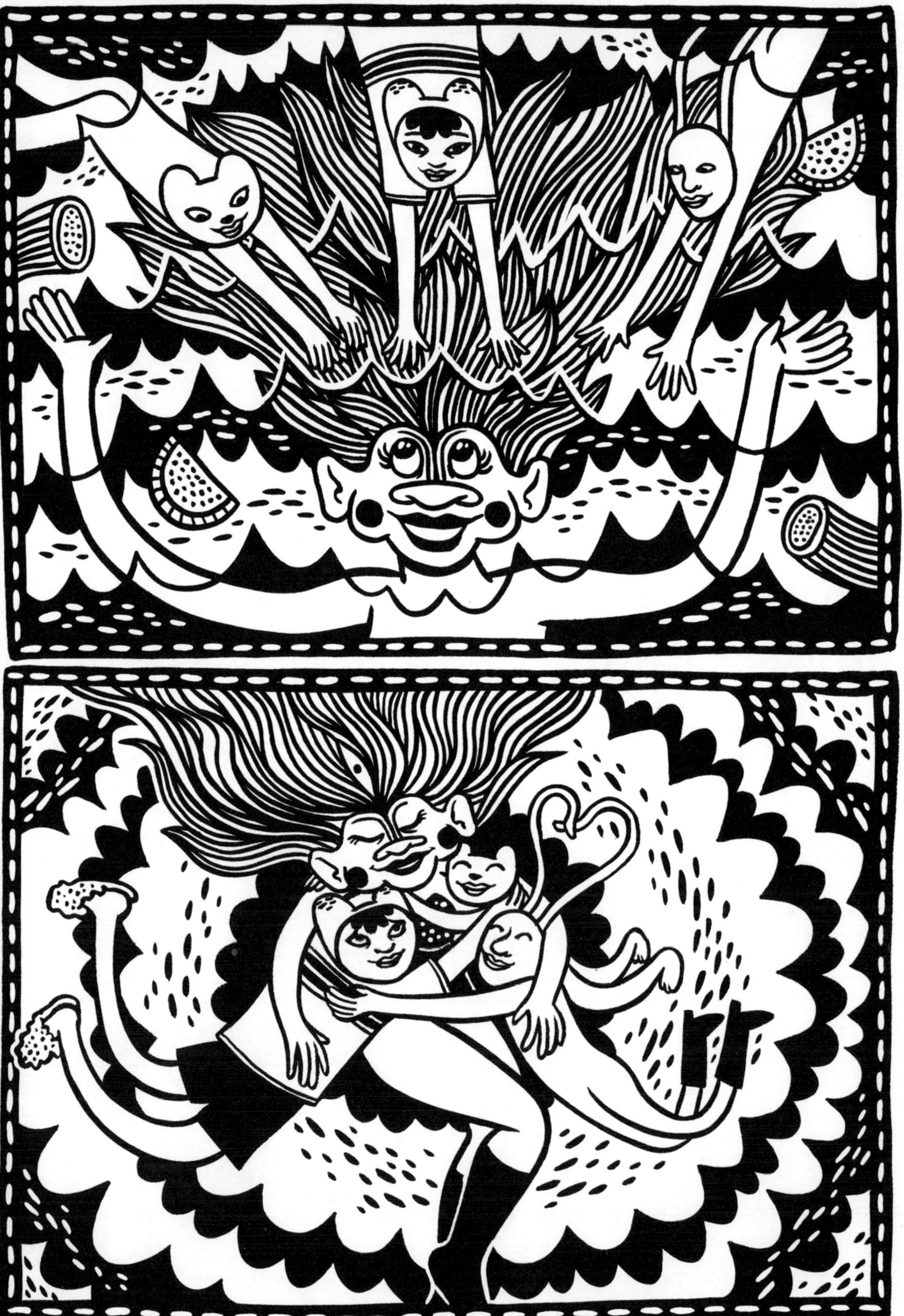

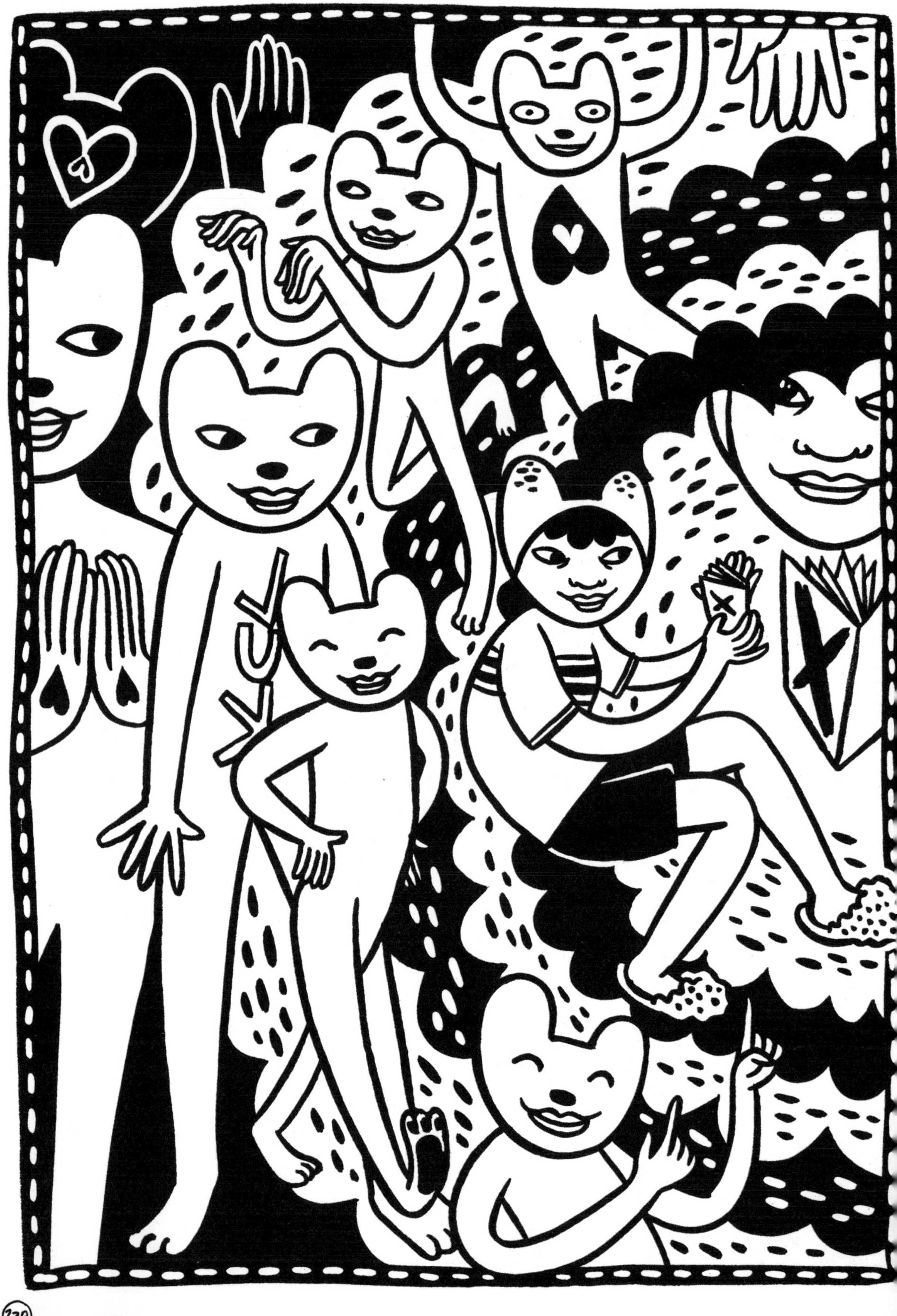

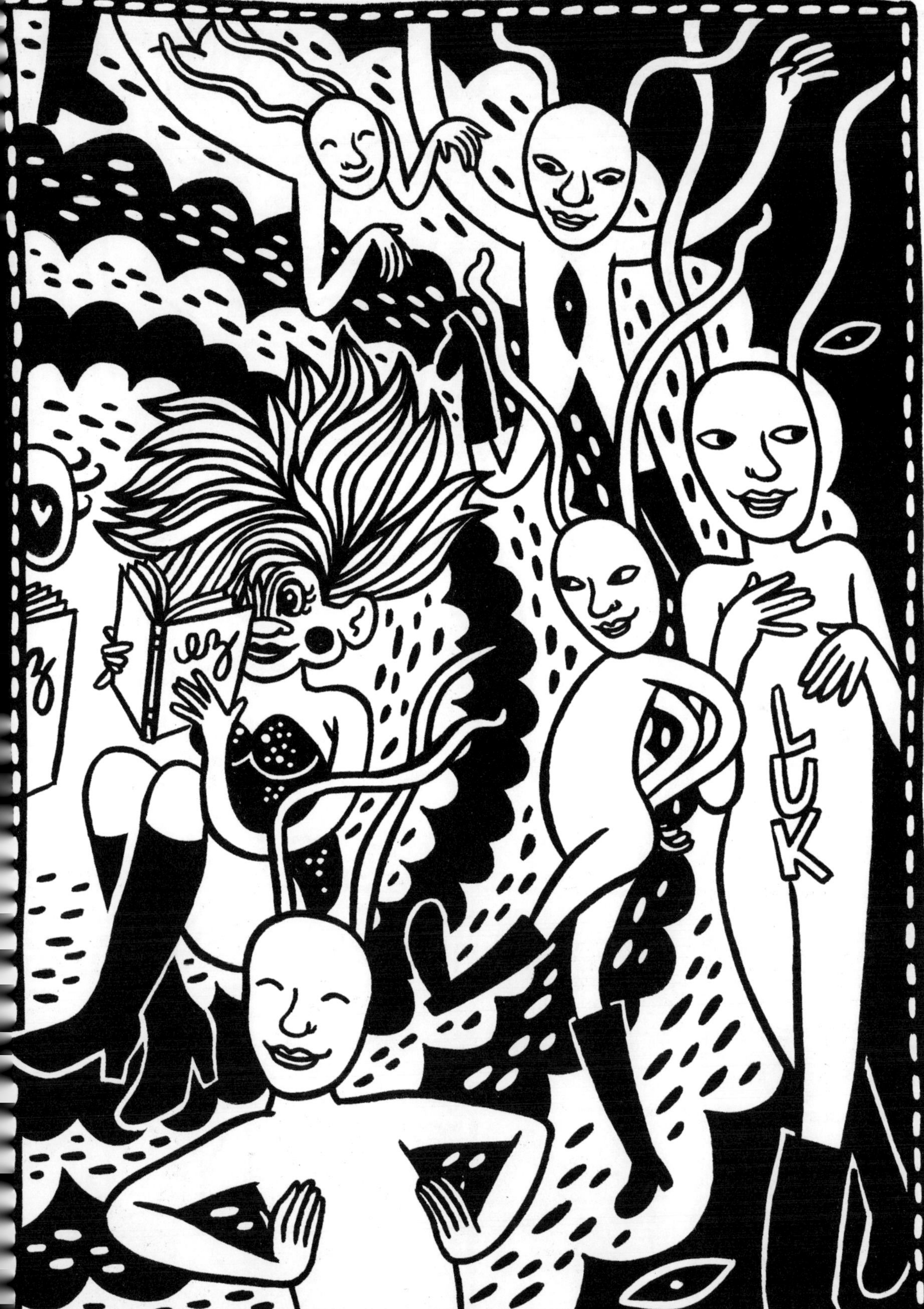
ez
LUCK

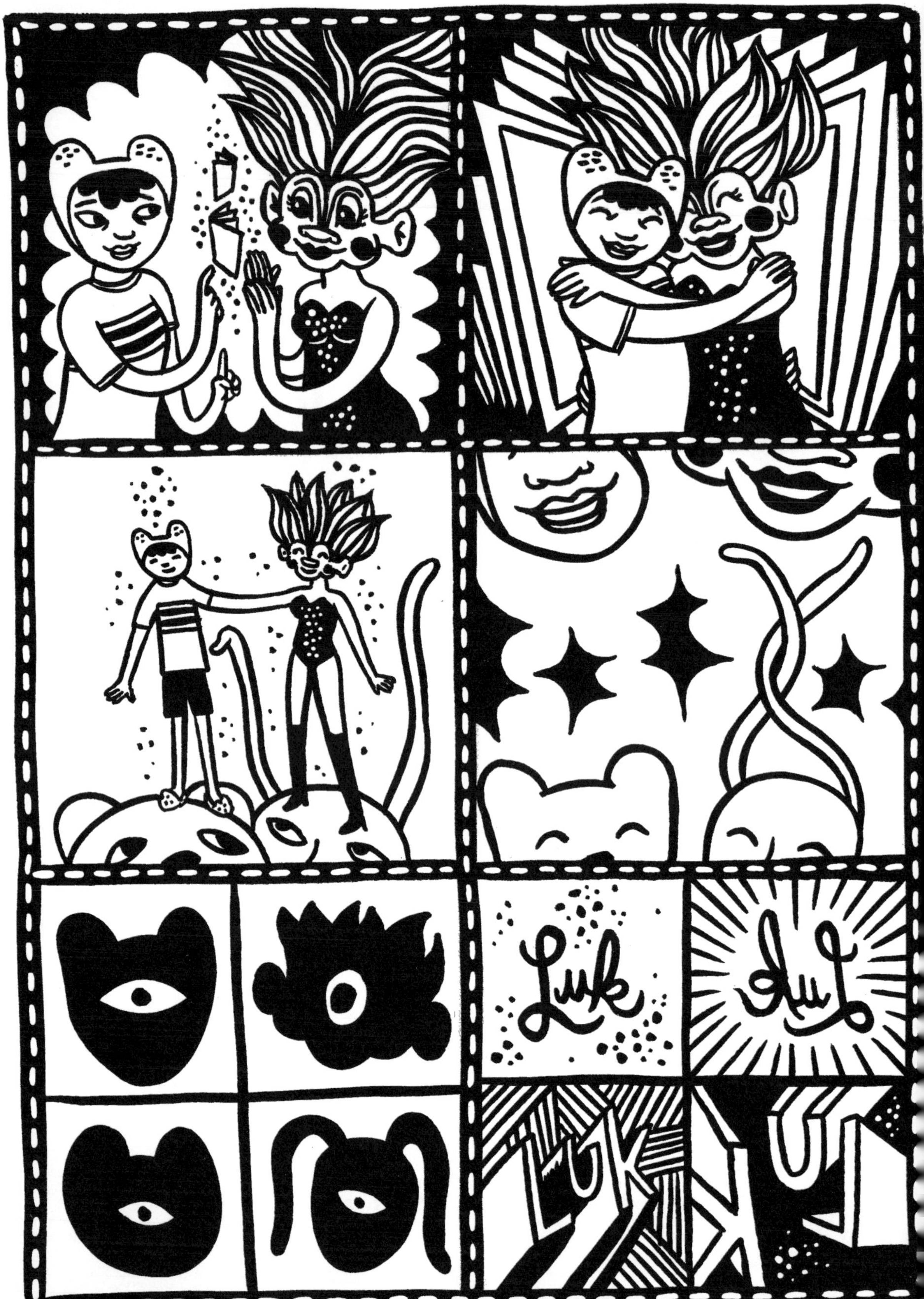
Luk
LUK

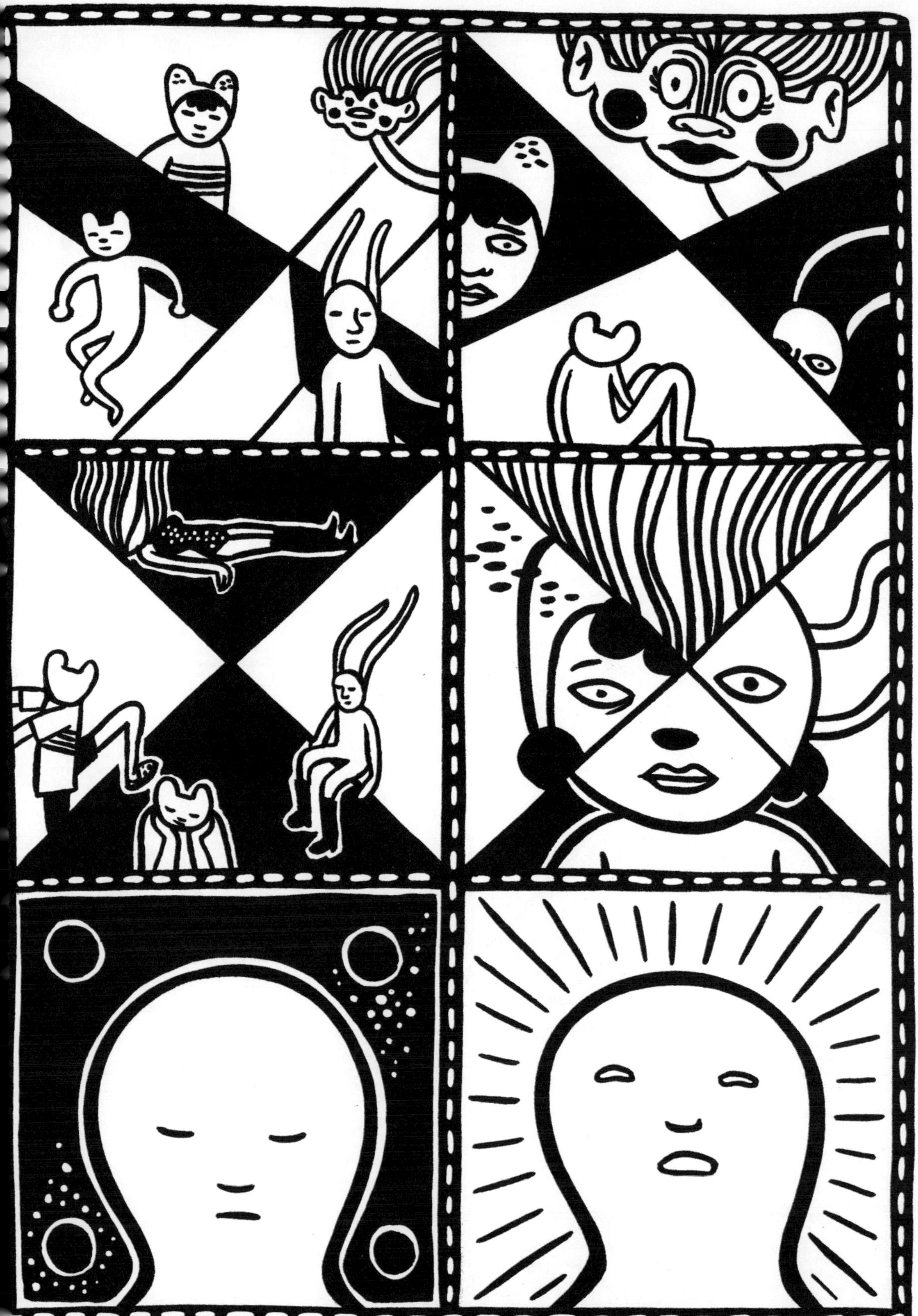

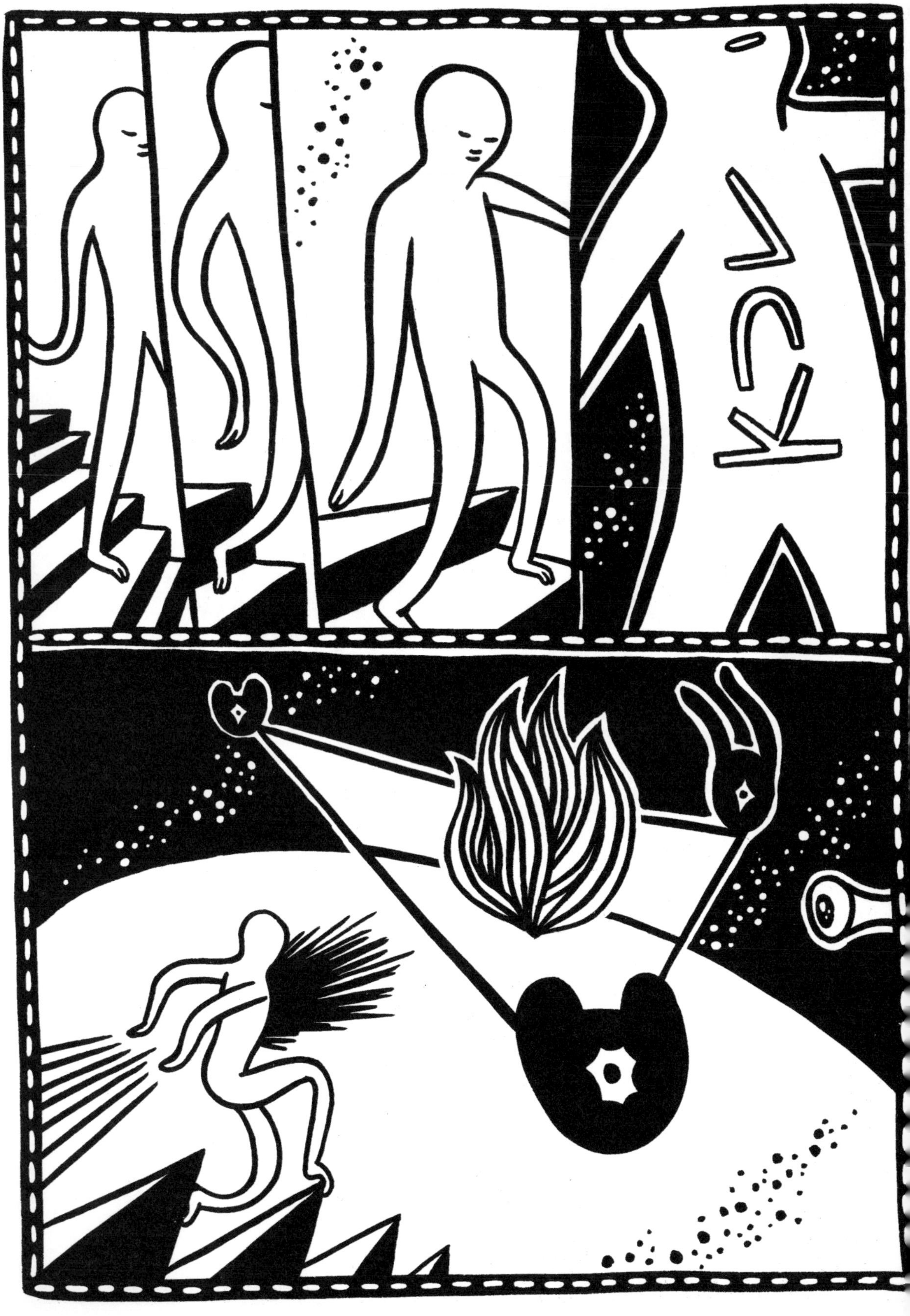

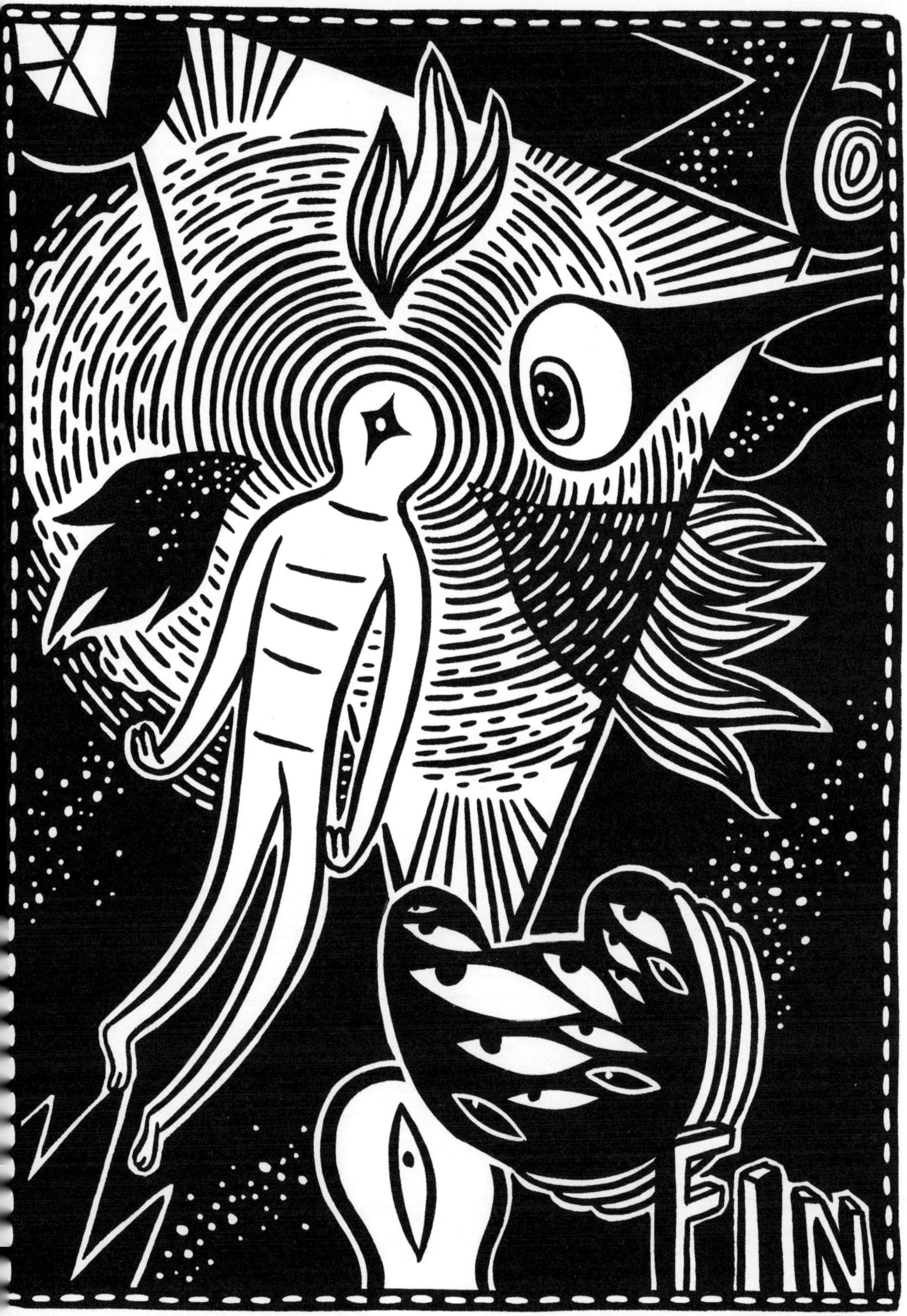
FIN

XFIONA SMYTH 2016

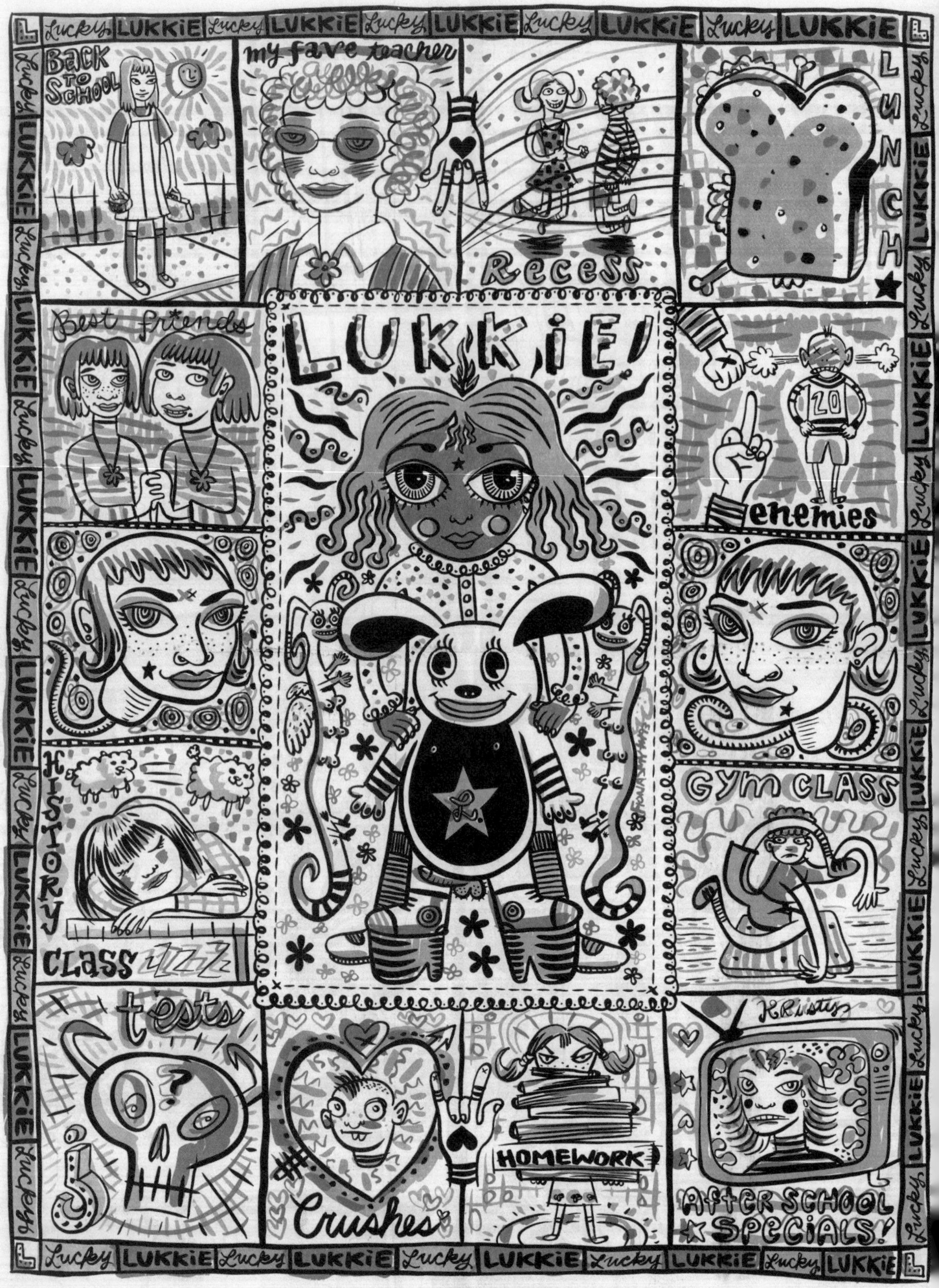

Lucky LUKKiE Lucky LUKKiE Lucky LUKKiE Lucky LUKKiE Lucky LUKKiE
Back to School
my fave teacher
Recess
LUNCH
Best friends
LUKKiE!
20
enemies
History Class zzz
Gym Class
tests
Crushes
HOMEWORK
Kristy
After School Specials!

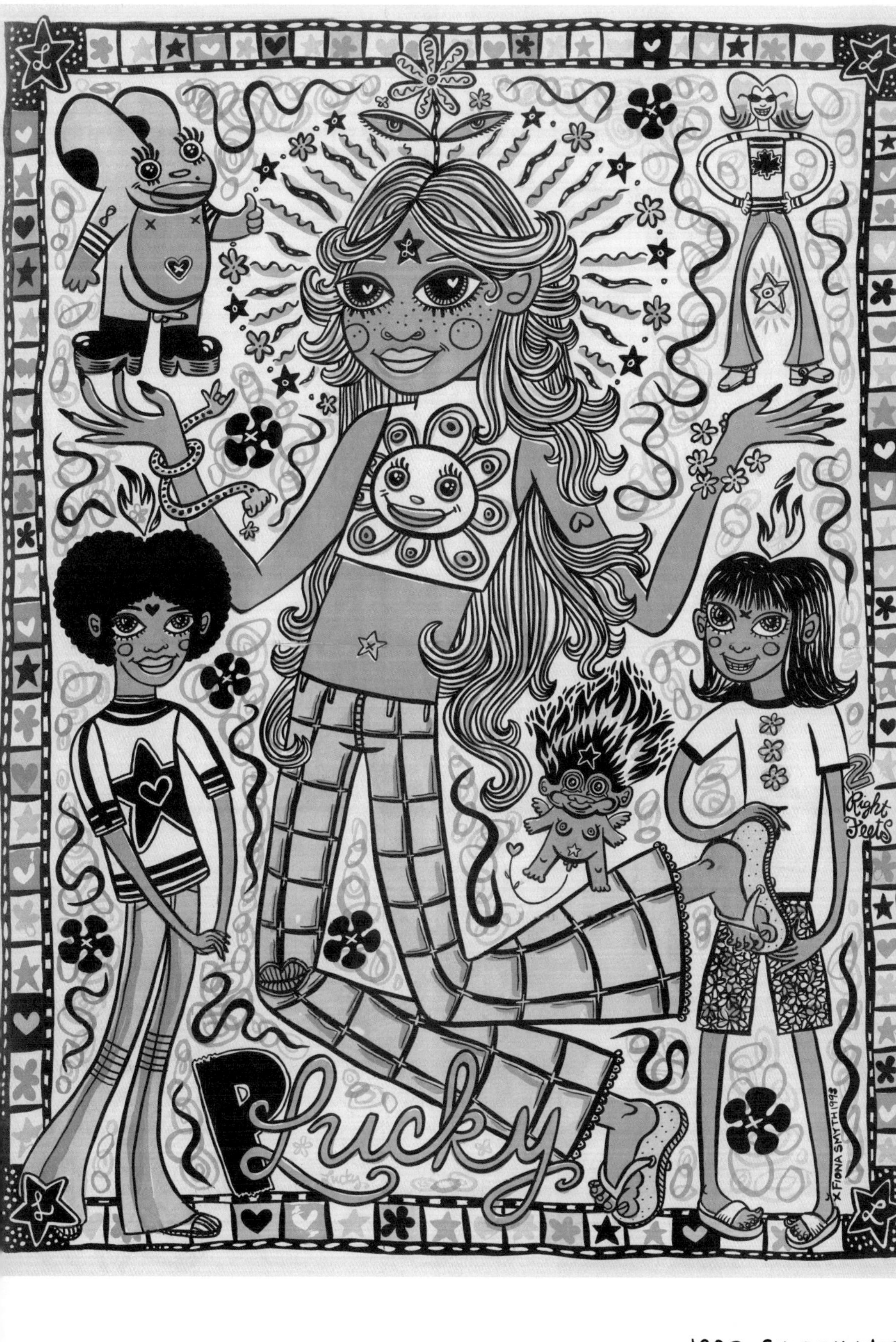
Plucky
2 Right Feets
FIONA SMYTH 1993

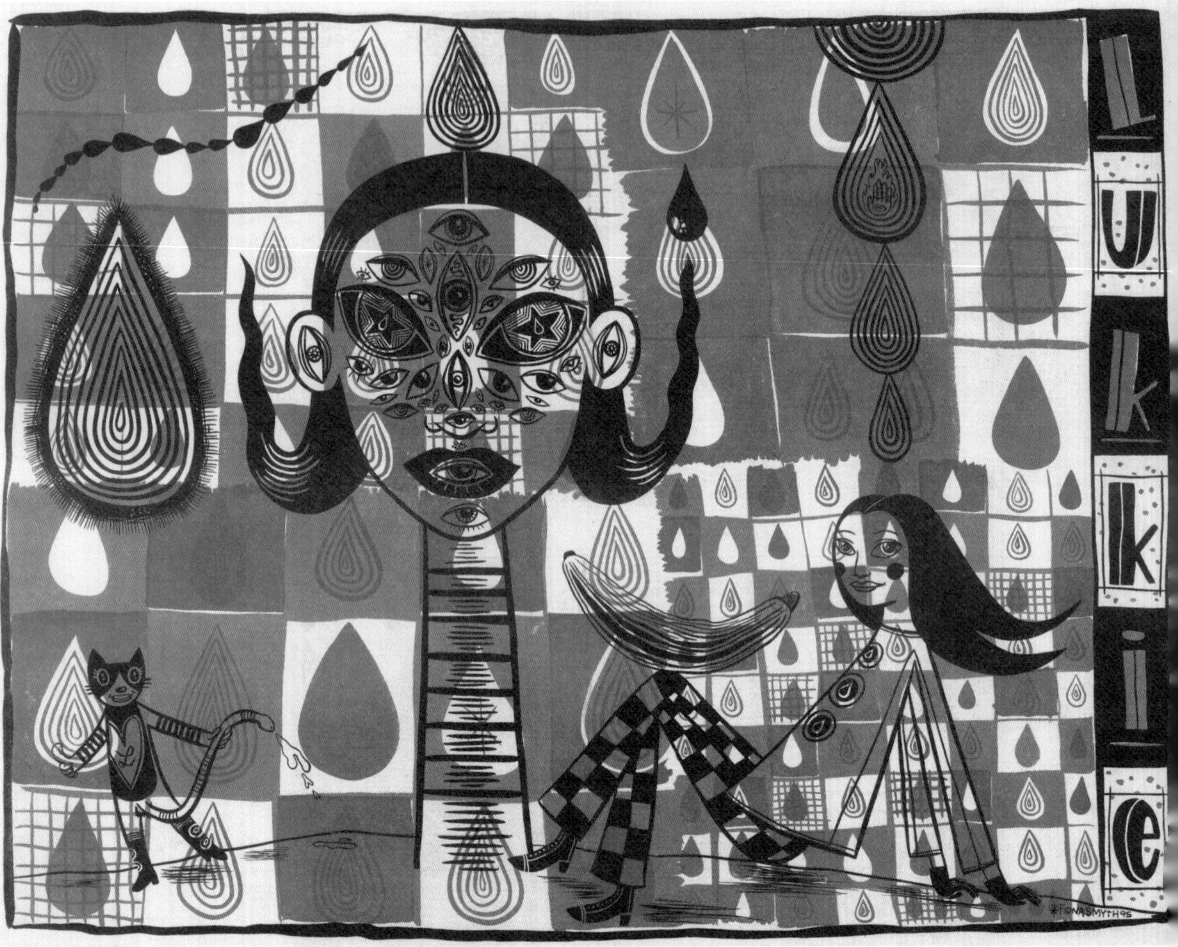
Lukkie
*FIONASMYTH95

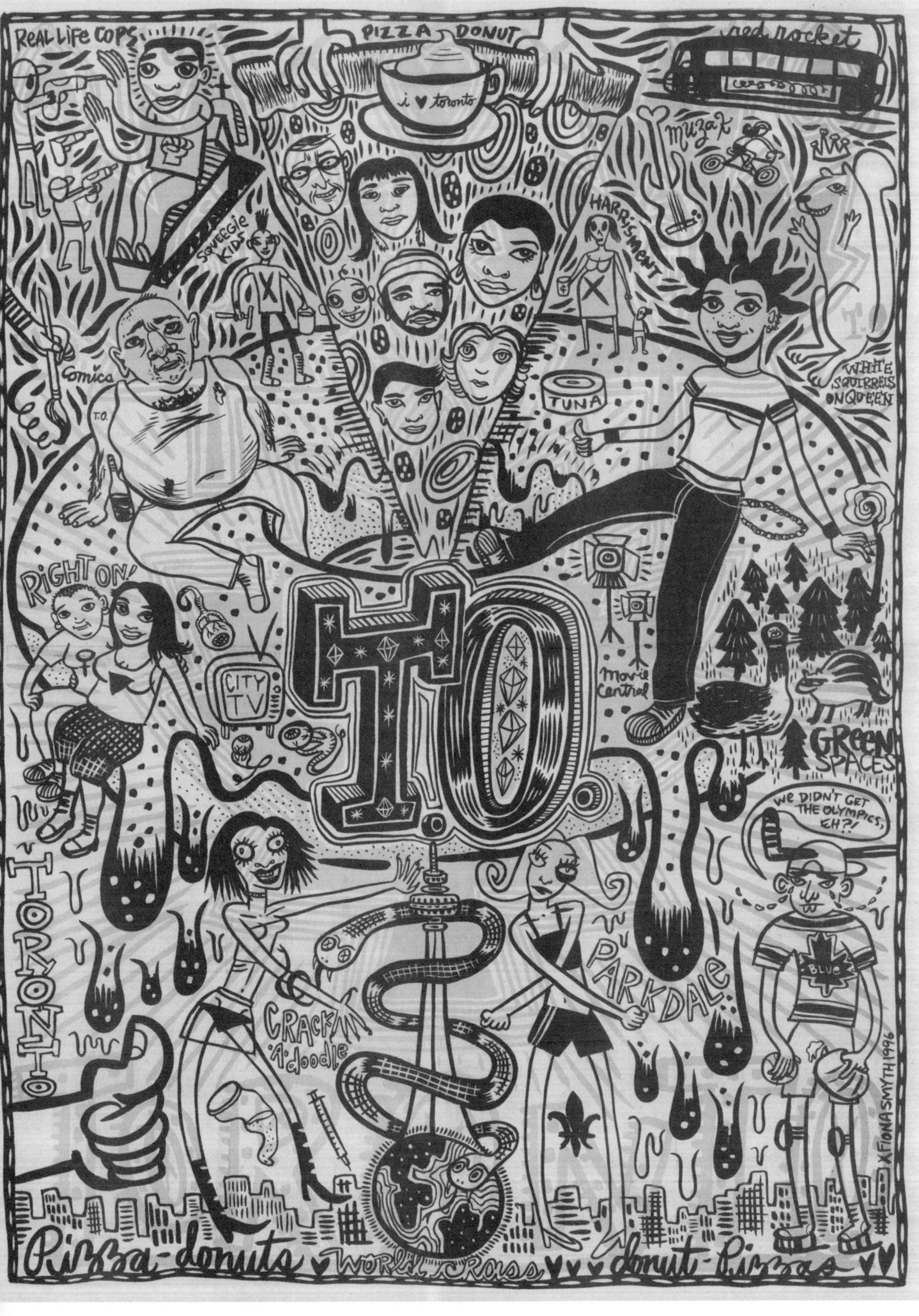
REAL LIFE COPS
PIZZA DONUT
red rocket
i ♥ toronto
muzak
HARRIS-MENT
SQUEEGIE KIDS
Comics
T.O.
TUNA
WHITE SQUIRRELS ON QUEEN
RIGHT ON!
CITY TV
T.O
movie Central
GREEN SPACES
WE DIDN'T GET THE OLYMPICS, EH?!
TORONTO
CRACK-A-doodle
PARKDALE
BLUE
XFIONASMYTH1996
Pizza-donuts
World Class
donut-Pizzas

1996 URBAN OUTFITTERS' SLANT MAGAZINE

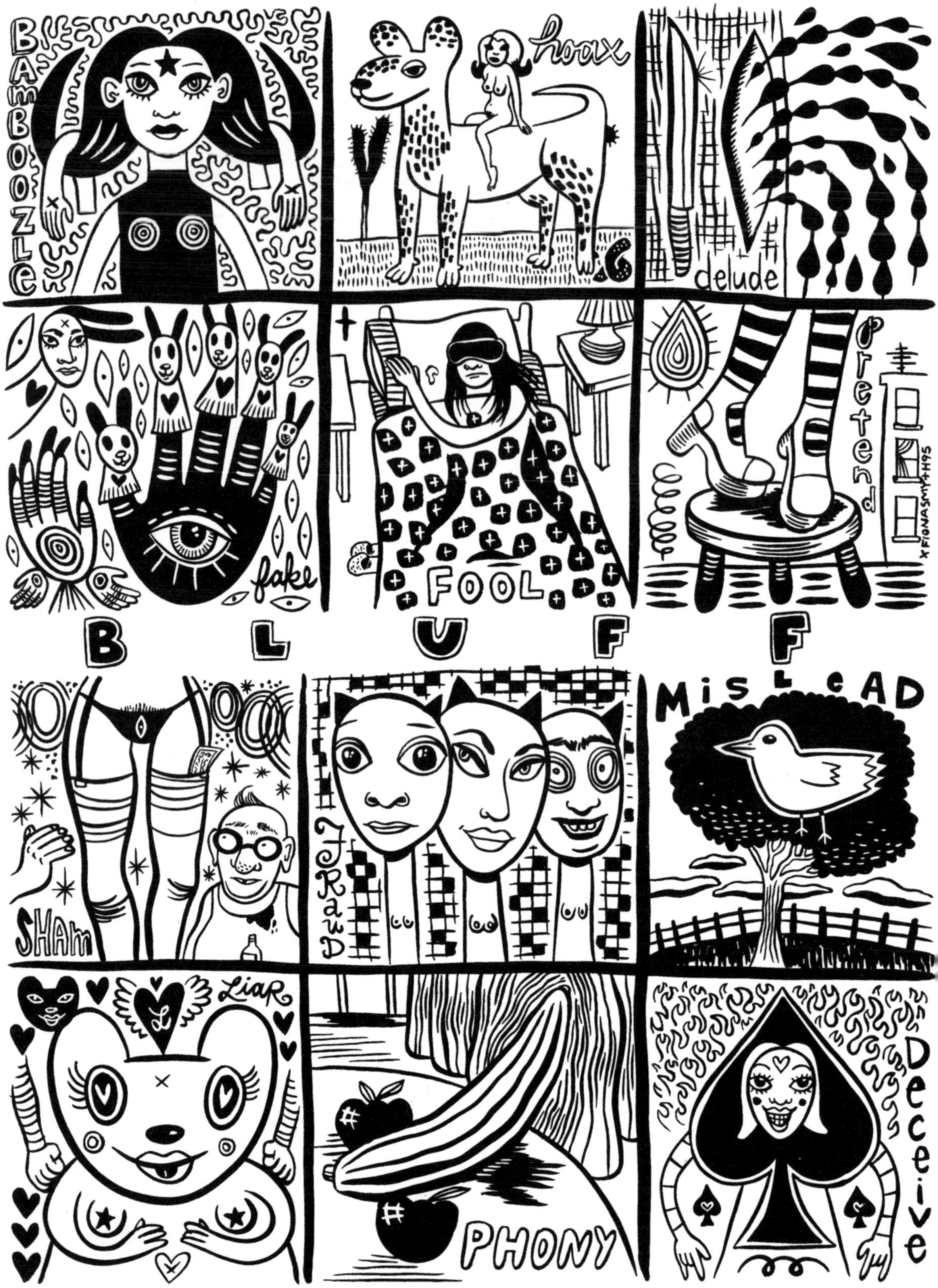
BAMBOOZLE
hoax
delude
fake
FOOL
pretend
xFIONASMYTH95
B L U F F
SHAM
FRAUD
MISLEAD
LIAR
PHONY
Deceive

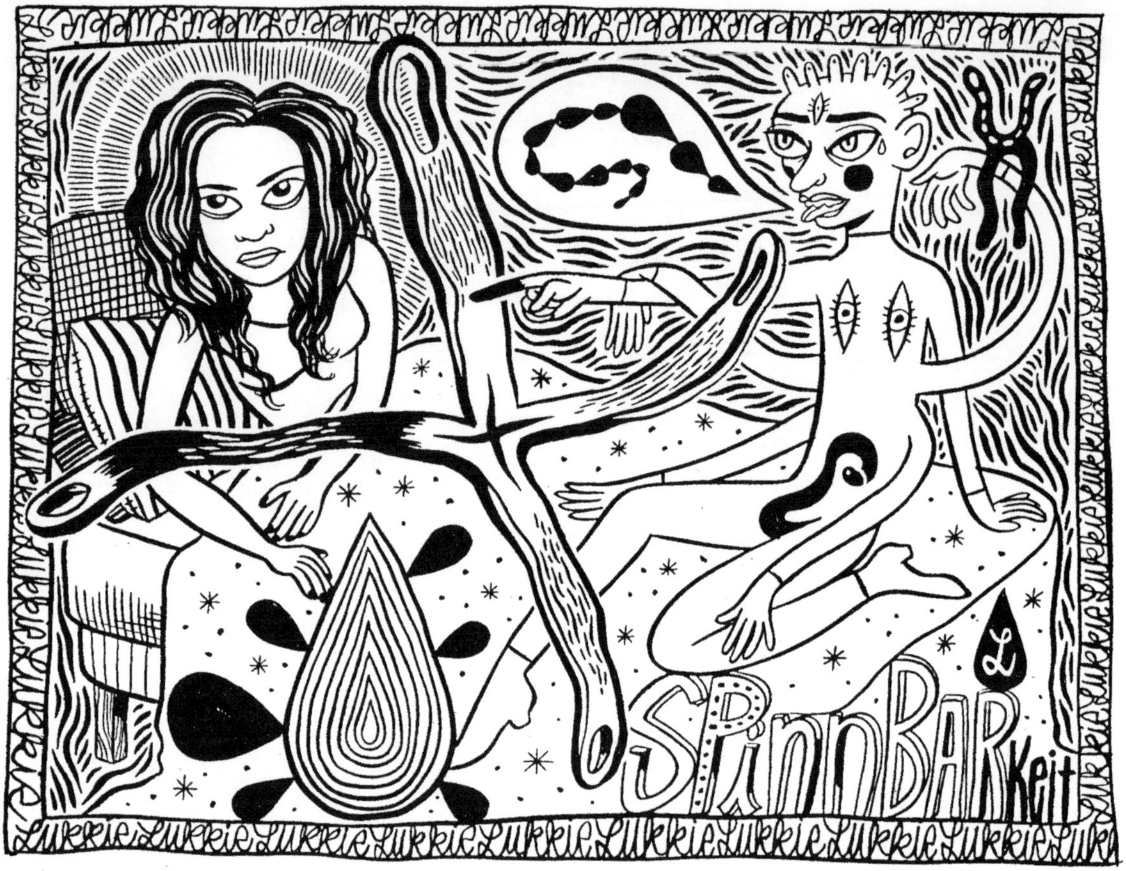
SPinnBAR
Keit
L

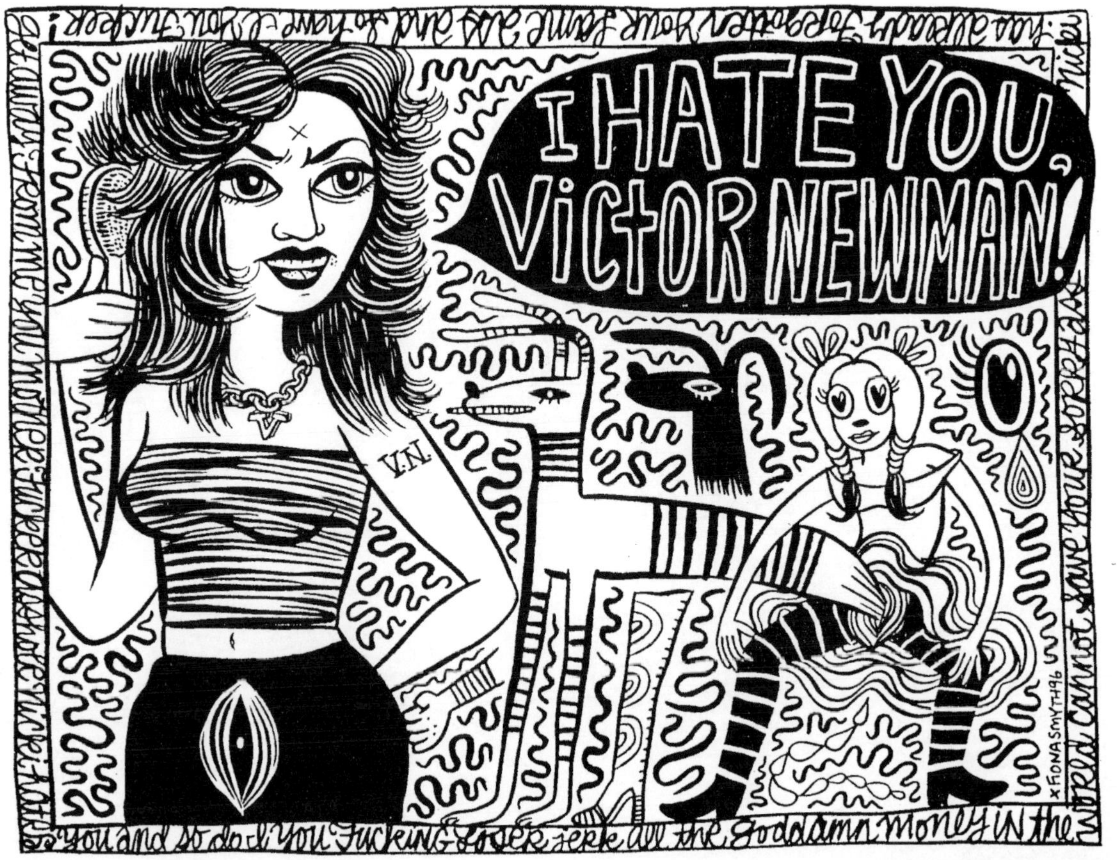
I HATE YOU, Victor NEWMAN!
V.N.
xFIONASMYTH96

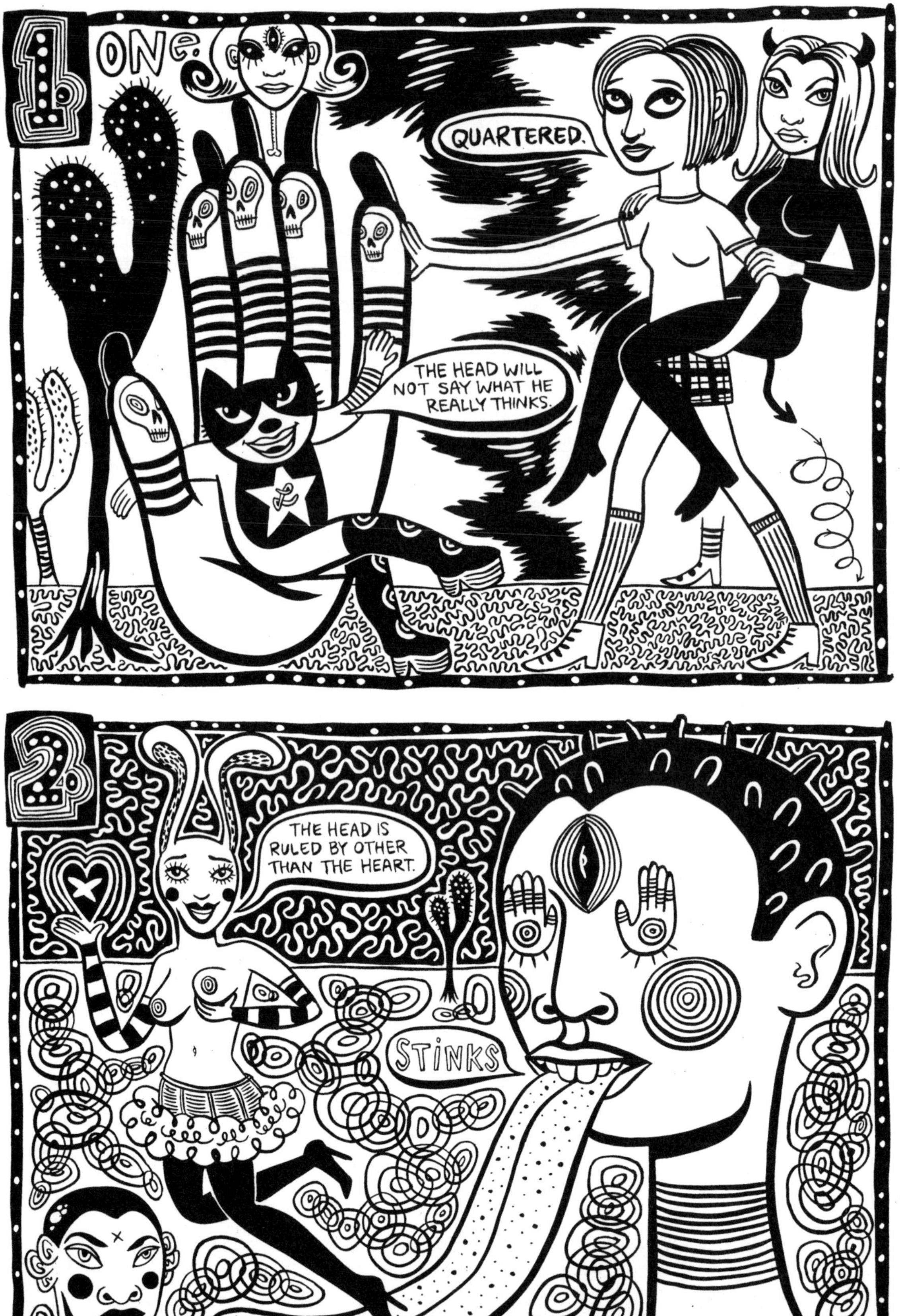
1
ONE.
QUARTERED.
THE HEAD WILL NOT SAY WHAT HE REALLY THINKS.
2
THE HEAD IS RULED BY OTHER THAN THE HEART.
STINKS

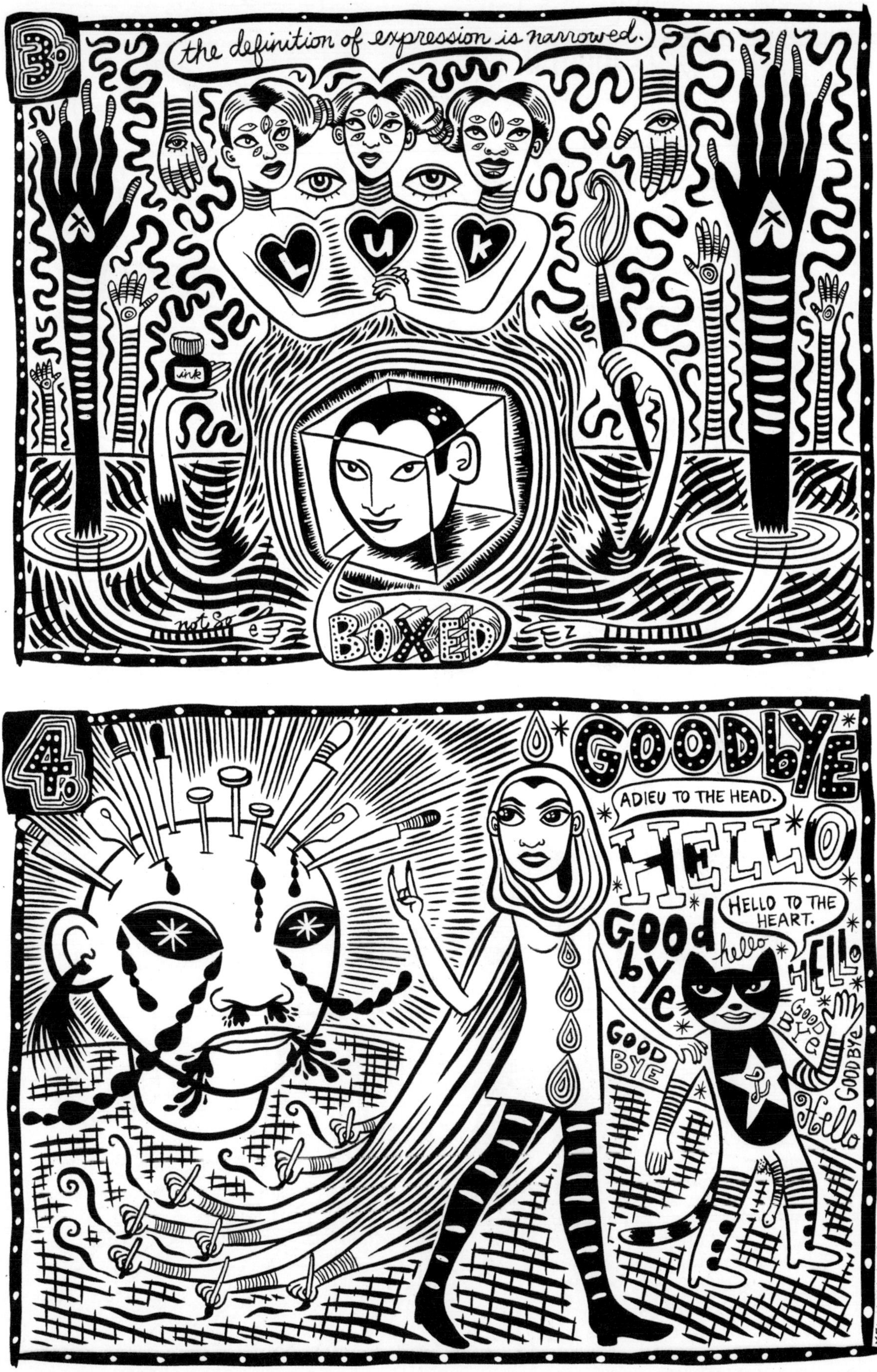
3
the definition of expression is narrowed.
ink
L
U
K
not so
BOXED
4
GOODbYE
ADIEU TO THE HEAD.
HELLO
HELLO TO THE HEART.
Good bye
hello
HELLO
GOOD BYE
GOOD BYE
GOODBYE
Hello
XFIONASMYTH1995

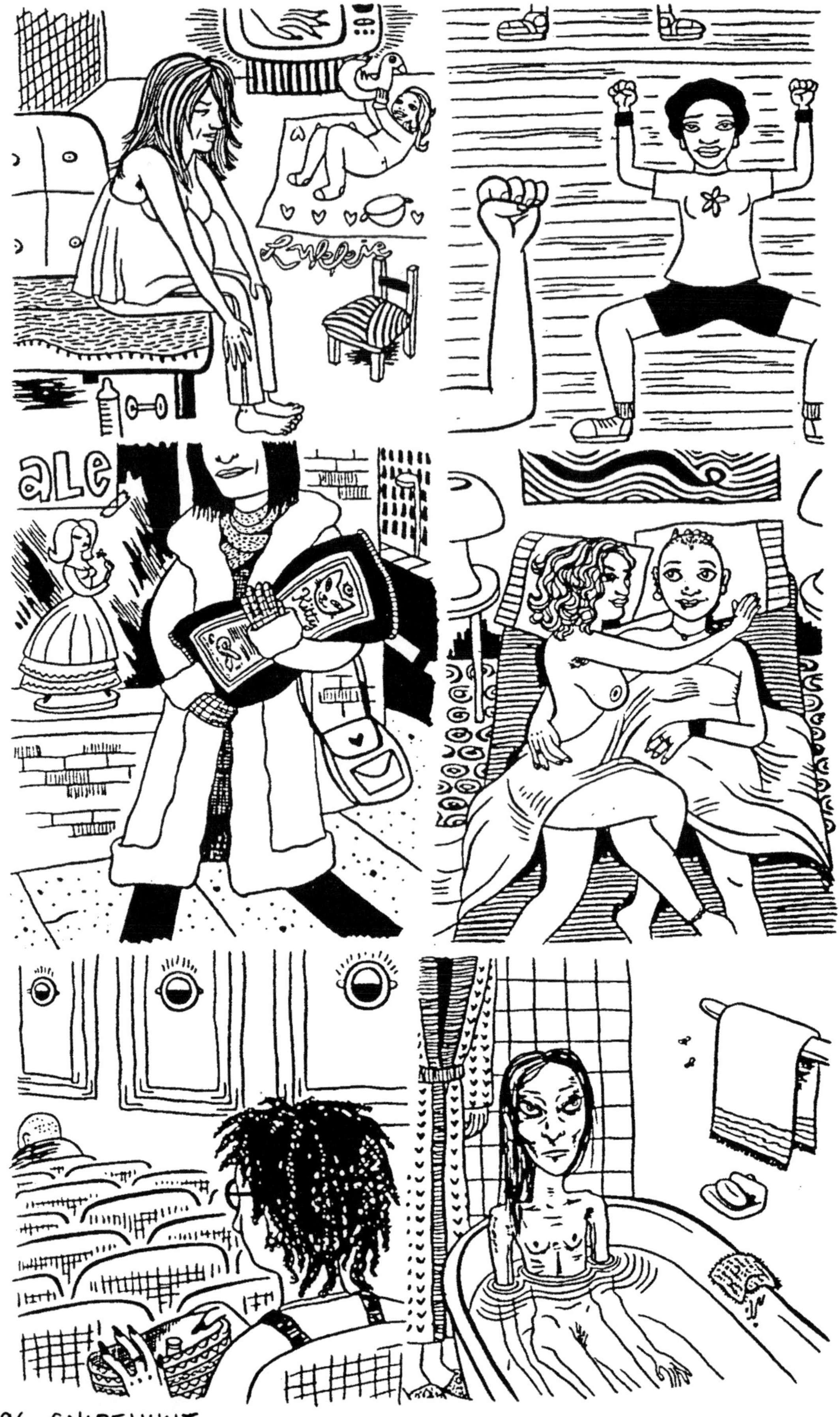

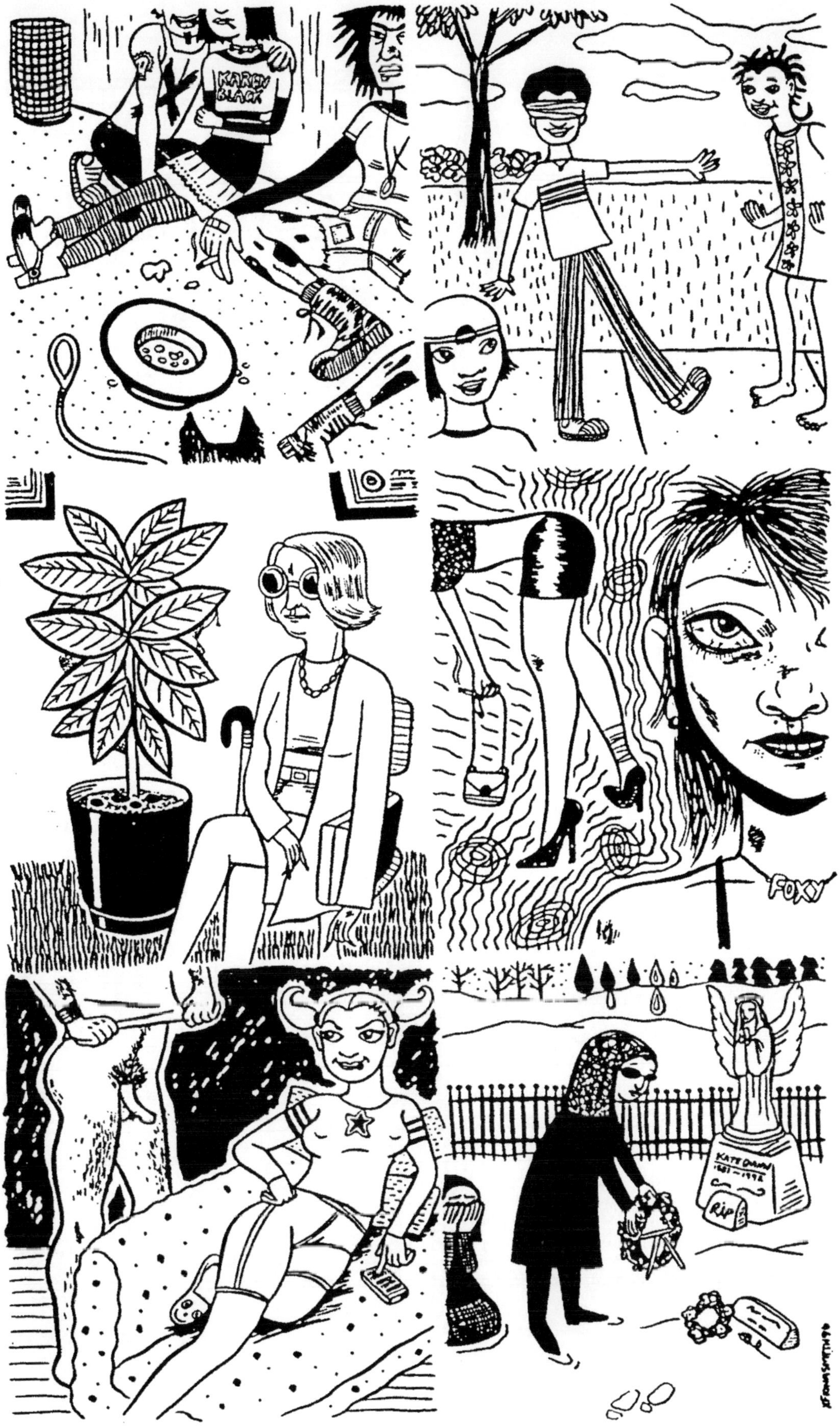
KAREN BLACK
FOXY
KATE DAWN
RIP

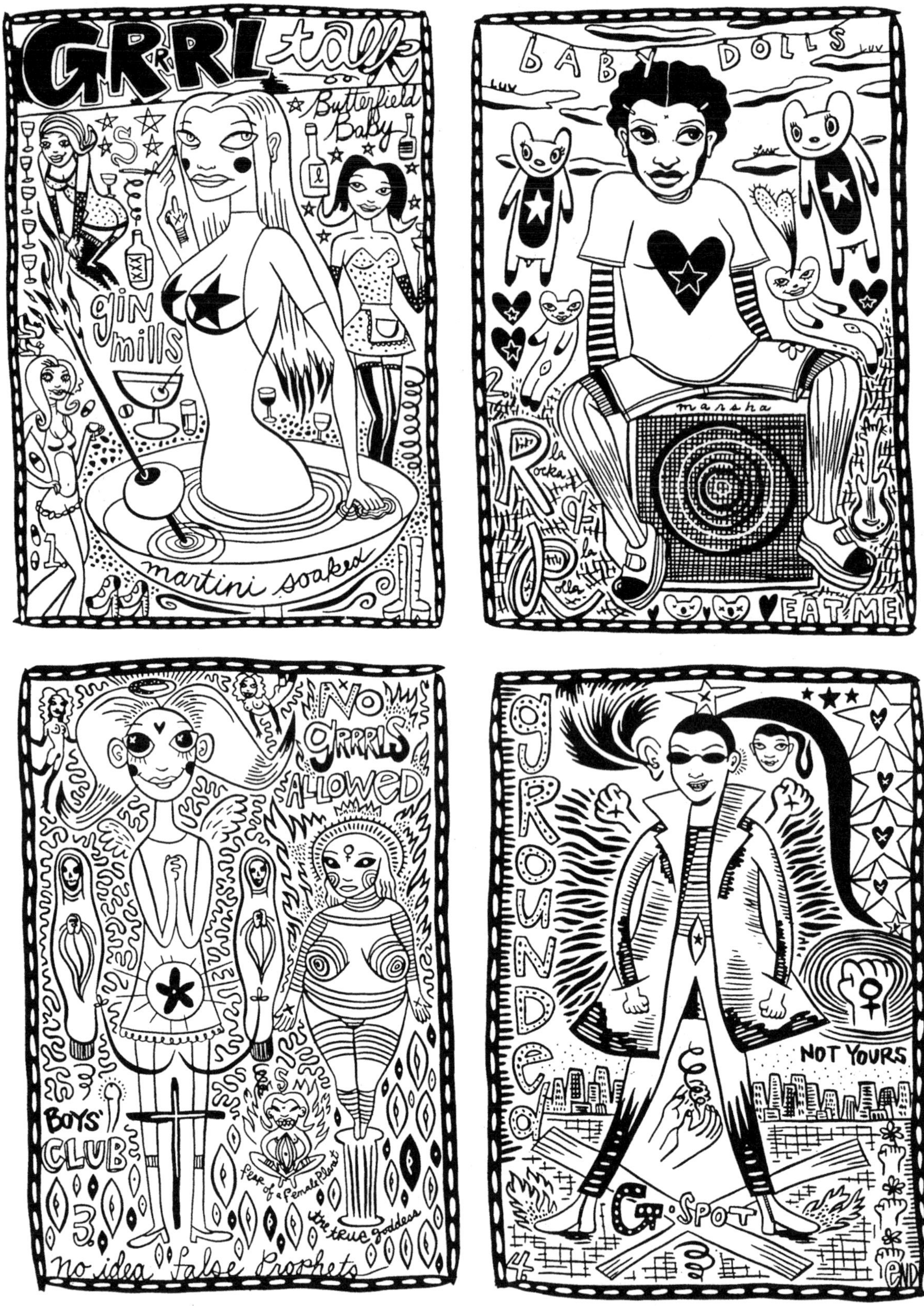
GRRRL talk
Butterfield Baby
XXX
gin mills
martini soaked
1
BABY DOLLS
LUV
LUV
2.
marsha
Rocka
la Rolla
EAT ME
NO GRRRLS ALLOWED
BOYS' CLUB
3.
fear of a female planet
the true goddess
no idea false prophets
NOT YOURS
G-SPOT
4
END

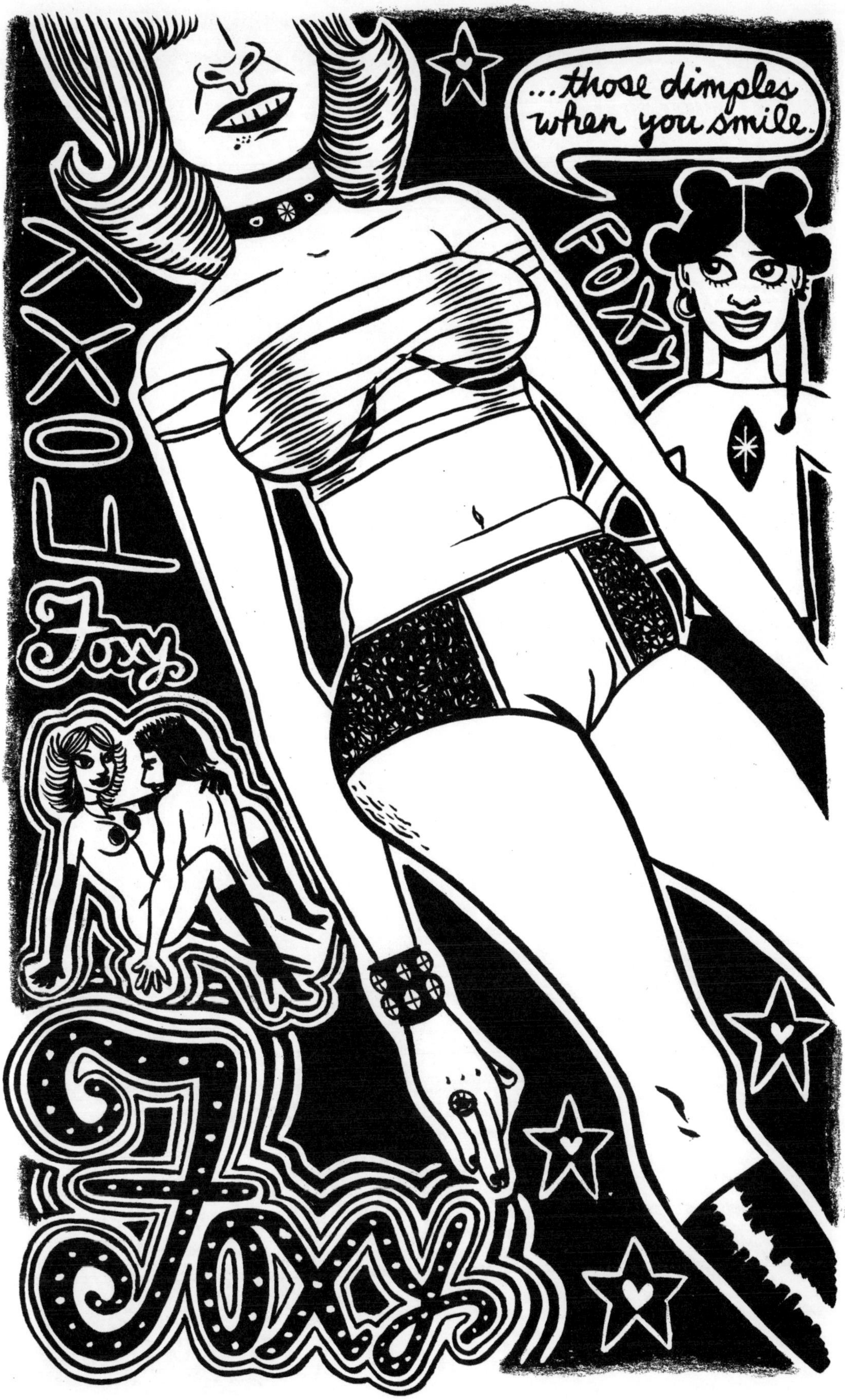
...those dimples when you smile.
FOXY
Foxy
FOXY
Foxy

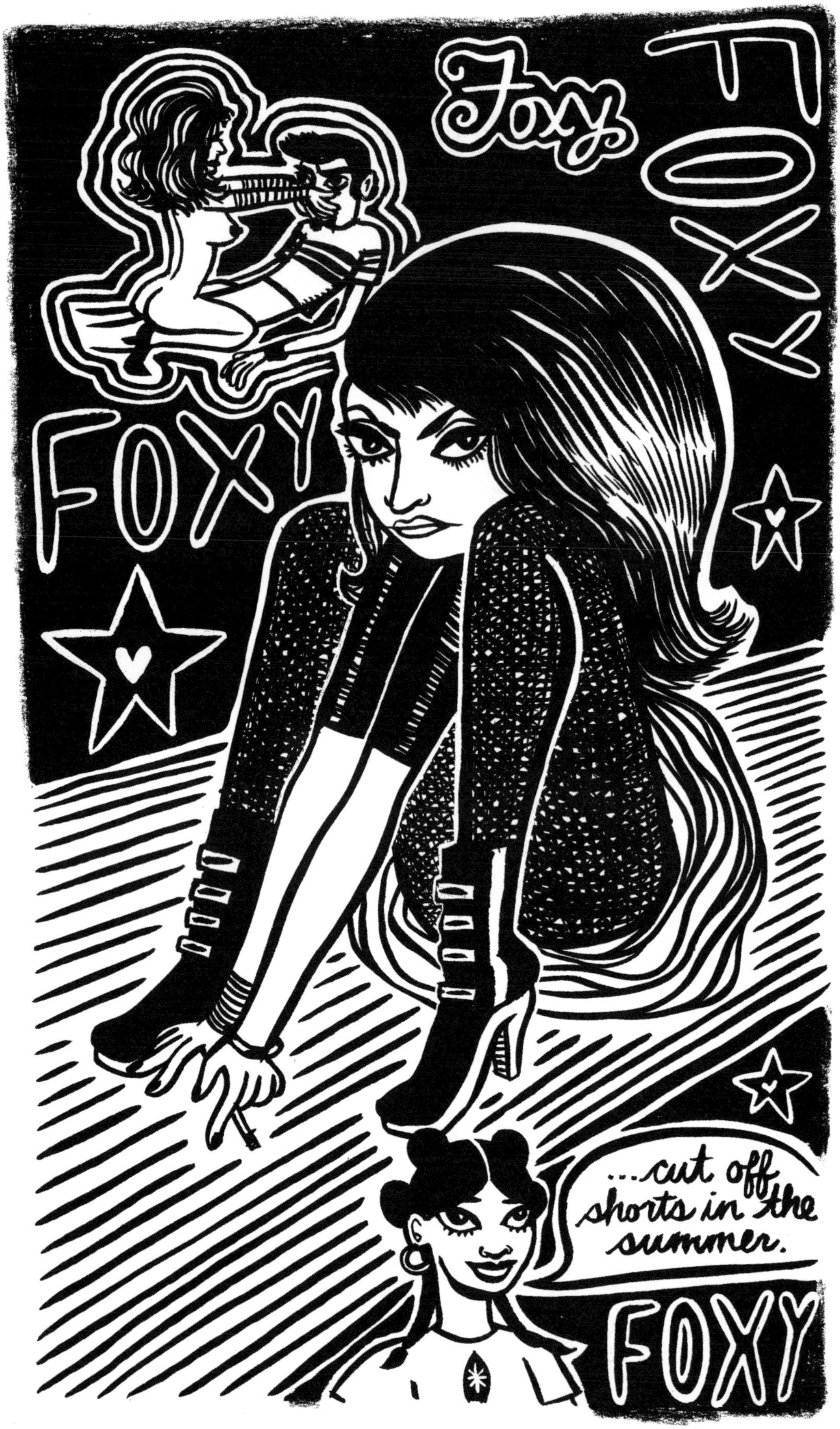
Foxy
FOXY
FOXY
...cut off shorts in the summer.
FOXY

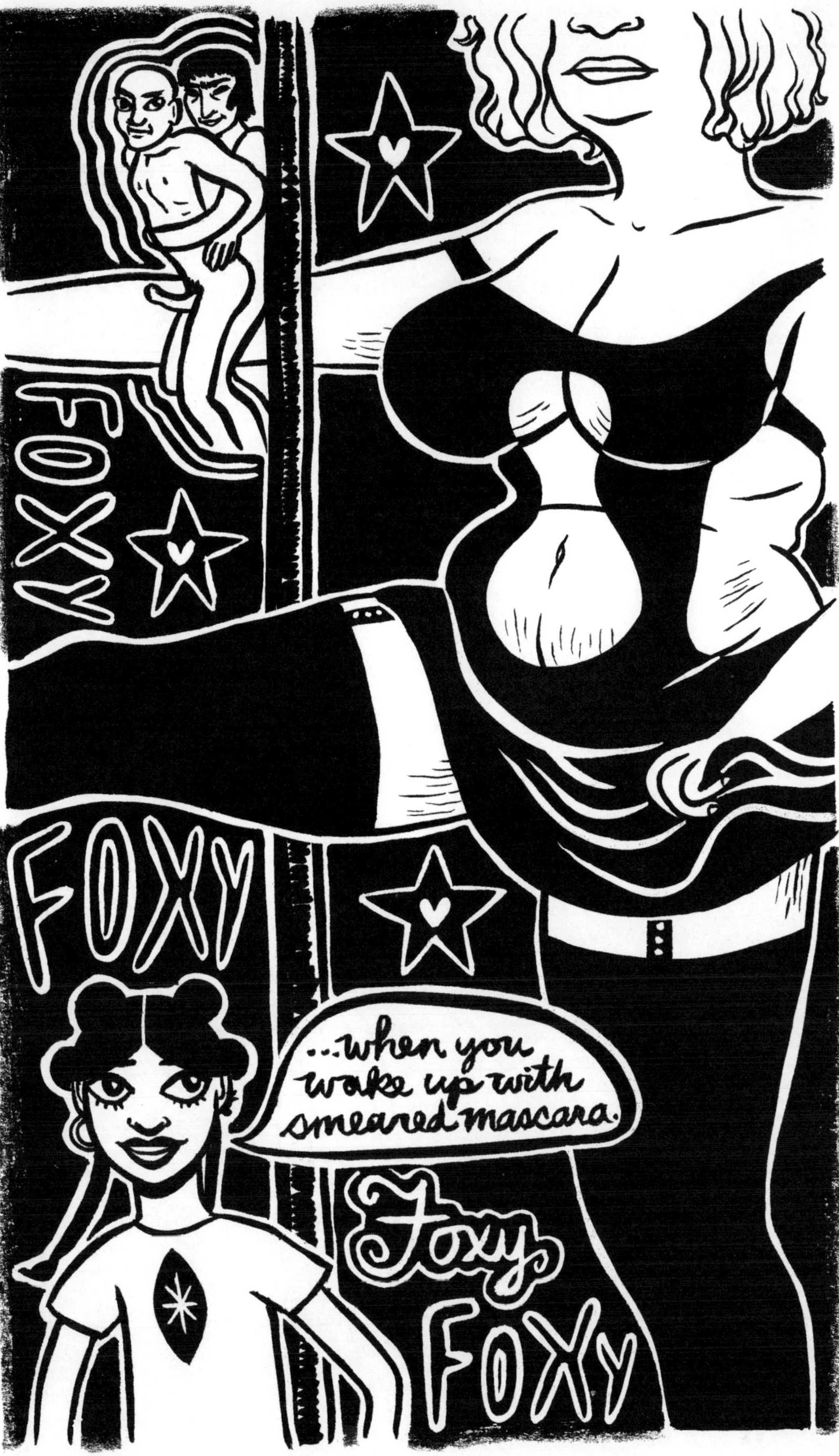
FOXY
FOXY
...when you wake up with smeared mascara.
Foxy
FOXY

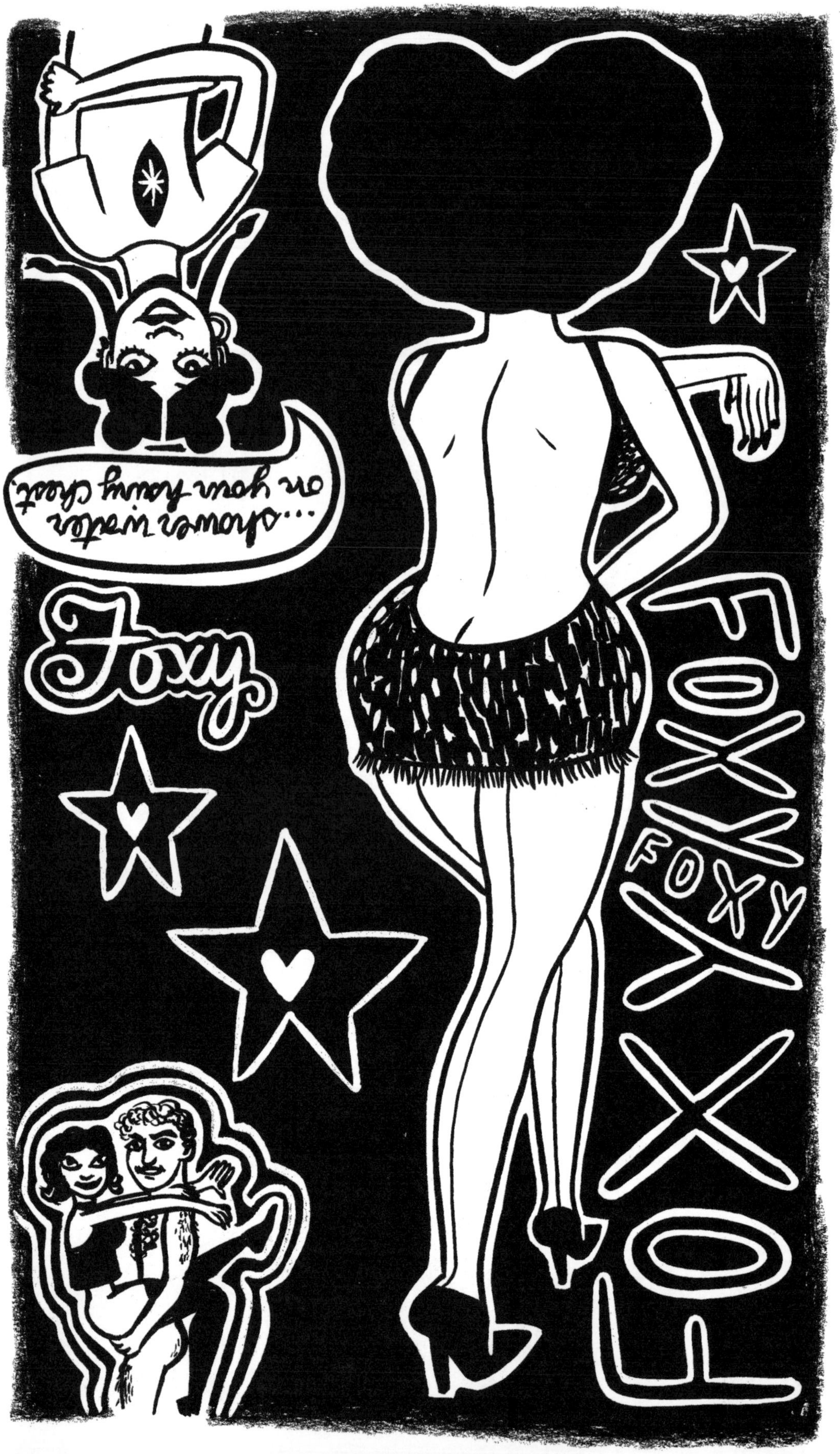
...shower water
on your hairy chest.
Foxy
FOXY
FOXY
FOXY
FOXY

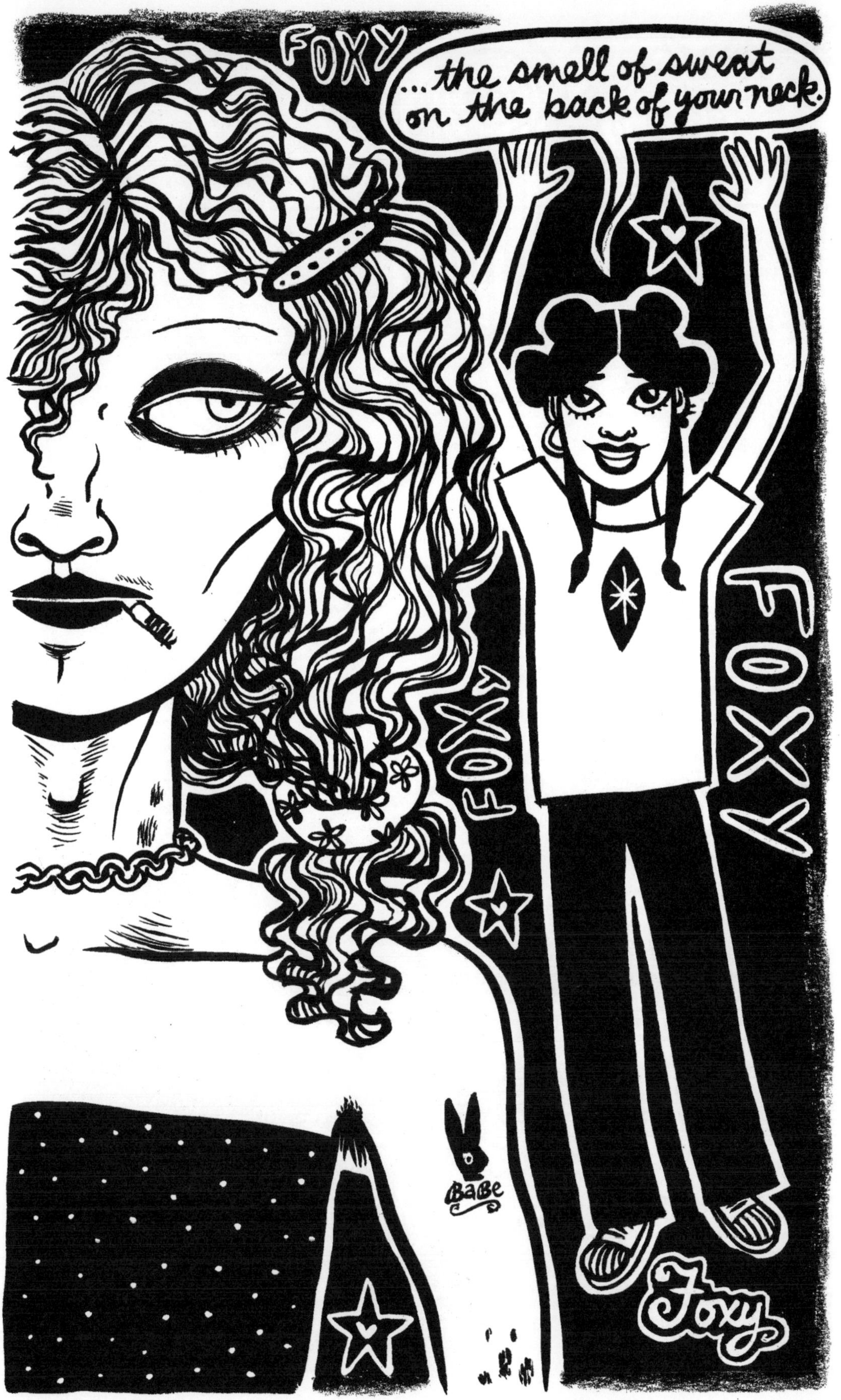
FOXY
...the smell of sweat on the back of your neck.
FOXY
FOXY
BaBe
Foxy

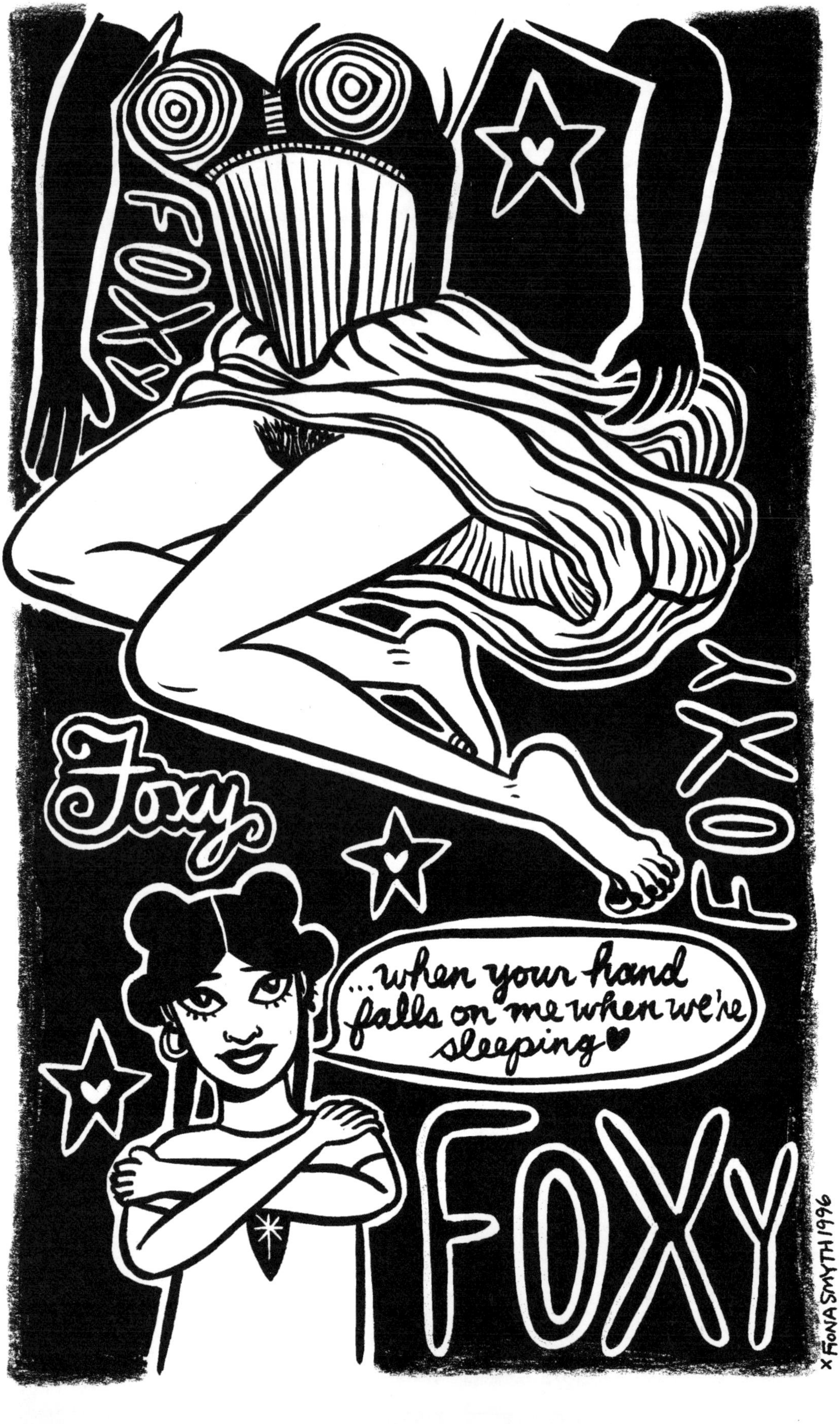
FOXY
FOXY
Foxy
...when your hand falls on me when we're sleeping♥
FOXY
x FIONA SMYTH 1996

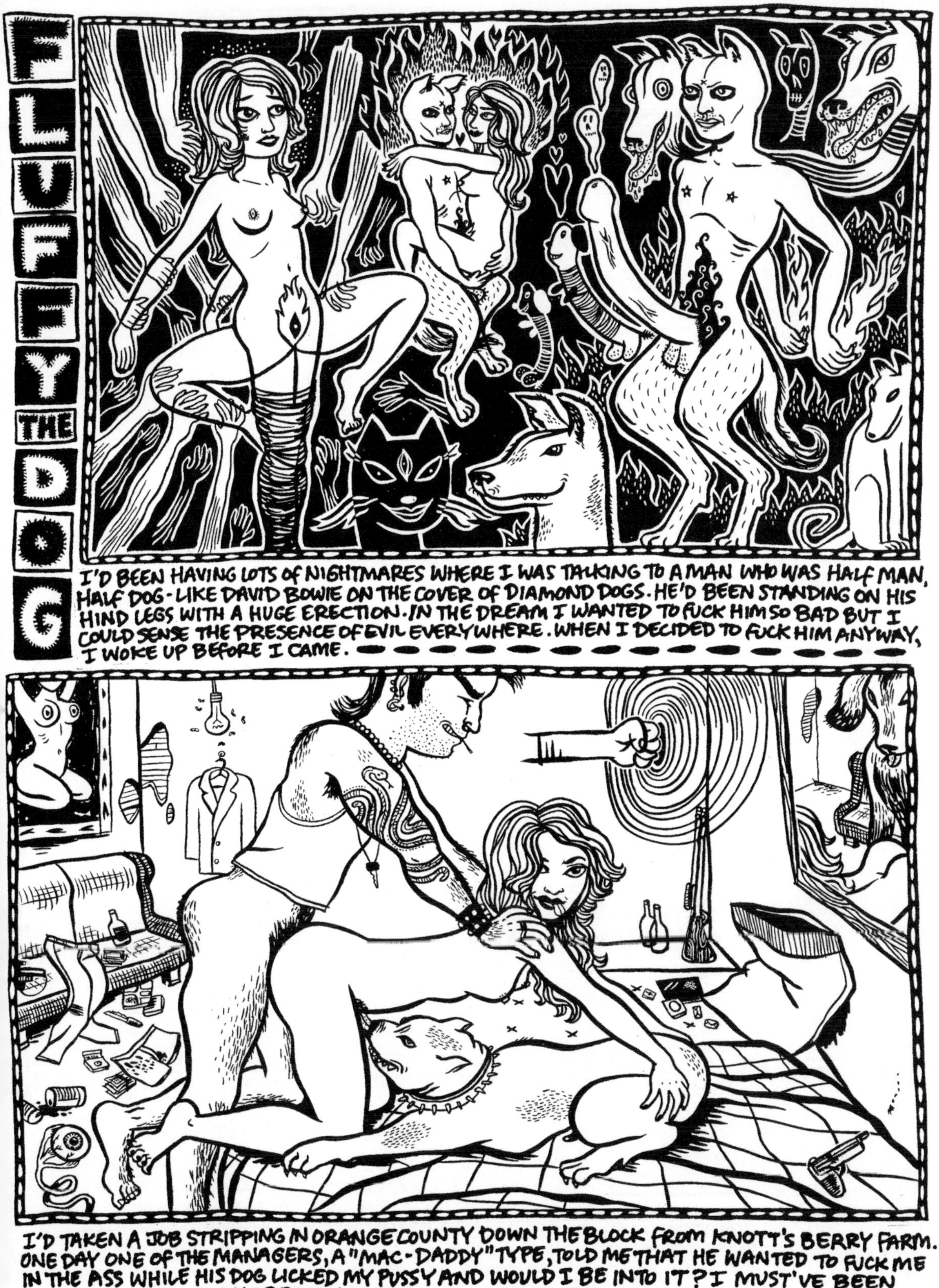
FLUFFY THE DOG
I'D BEEN HAVING LOTS OF NIGHTMARES WHERE I WAS TALKING TO A MAN WHO WAS HALF MAN, HALF DOG - LIKE DAVID BOWIE ON THE COVER OF DIAMOND DOGS. HE'D BEEN STANDING ON HIS HIND LEGS WITH A HUGE ERECTION. IN THE DREAM I WANTED TO FUCK HIM SO BAD BUT I COULD SENSE THE PRESENCE OF EVIL EVERYWHERE. WHEN I DECIDED TO FUCK HIM ANYWAY, I WOKE UP BEFORE I CAME.
I'D TAKEN A JOB STRIPPING IN ORANGE COUNTY DOWN THE BLOCK FROM KNOTT'S BERRY FARM. ONE DAY ONE OF THE MANAGERS, A "MAC-DADDY" TYPE, TOLD ME THAT HE WANTED TO FUCK ME IN THE ASS WHILE HIS DOG LICKED MY PUSSY AND WOULD I BE INTO IT? I MUST'VE BEEN TELLING HIM ABOUT MY DREAM. ANYWAY - IT WAS FOOD FOR THOUGHT.

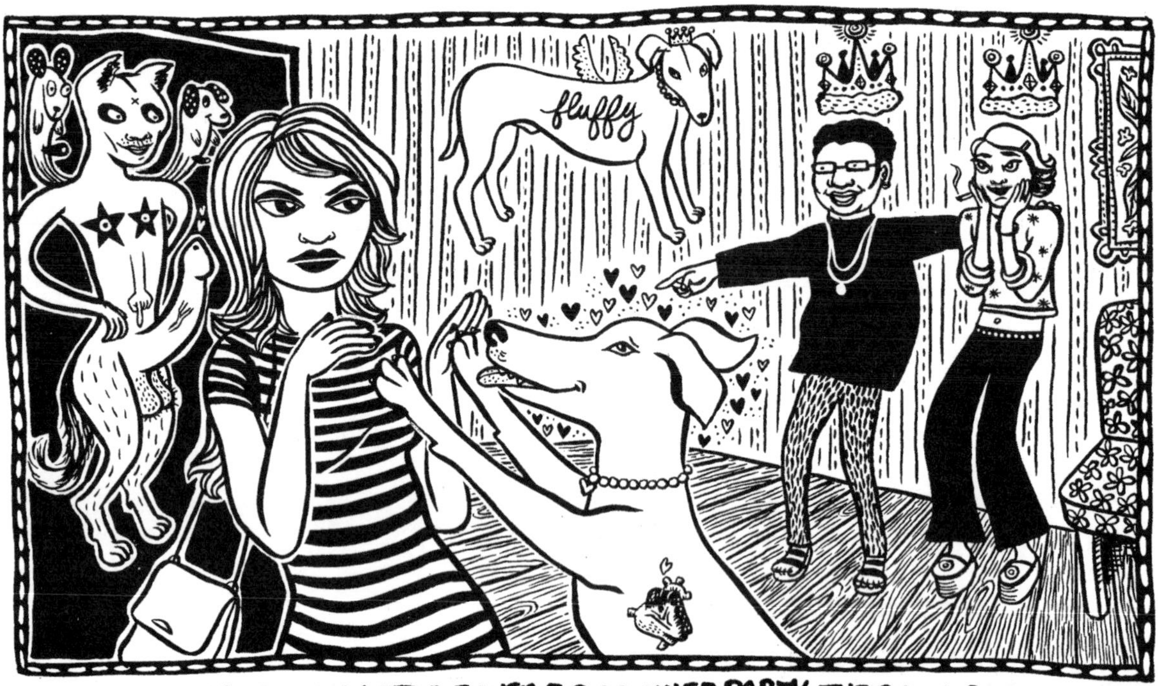
fluffy

THAT NIGHT MY FRIENDS INVITED ME OVER FOR A DINNER PARTY. THEIR DOG FLUFFY POUNCED ON ME WHEN I WALKED IN THE DOOR. FLUFFY IS ONE OF THOSE DOGS WITH PALE BLUE EYES, FLOPPY EARS AND A GREYHOUND'S BODY. HIS FUR LOOKED LIKE GREY VELVET. BUT HIS OWNERS ARE A COUPLE OF QUEENS - HENCE THE NAME FLUFFY.

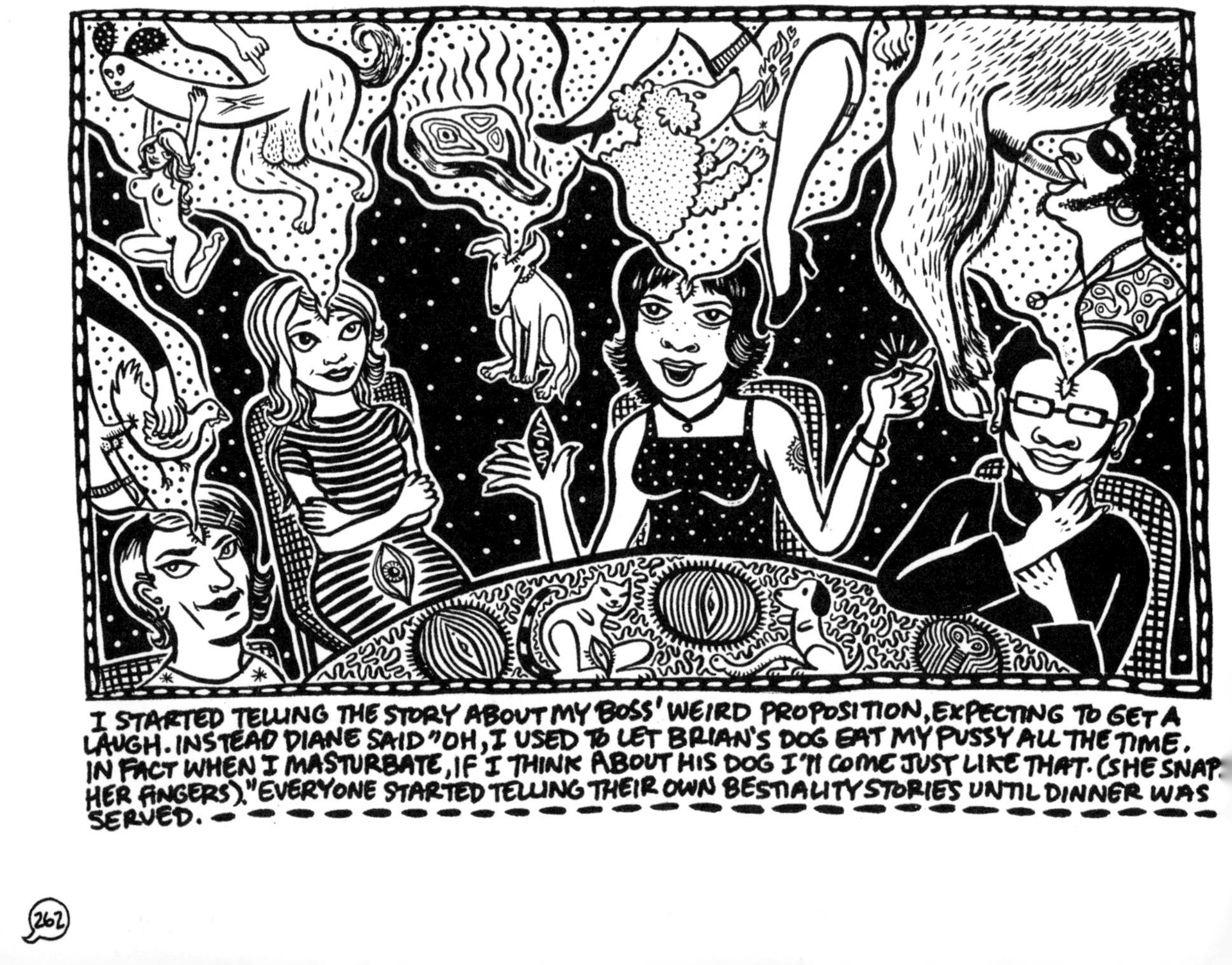

I STARTED TELLING THE STORY ABOUT MY 'BOSS' WEIRD PROPOSITION, EXPECTING TO GET A LAUGH. INSTEAD DIANE SAID "OH, I USED TO LET BRIAN'S DOG EAT MY PUSSY ALL THE TIME. IN FACT WHEN I MASTURBATE, IF I THINK ABOUT HIS DOG I'LL COME JUST LIKE THAT. (SHE SNAP HER FINGERS)." EVERYONE STARTED TELLING THEIR OWN BESTIALITY STORIES UNTIL DINNER WAS SERVED.

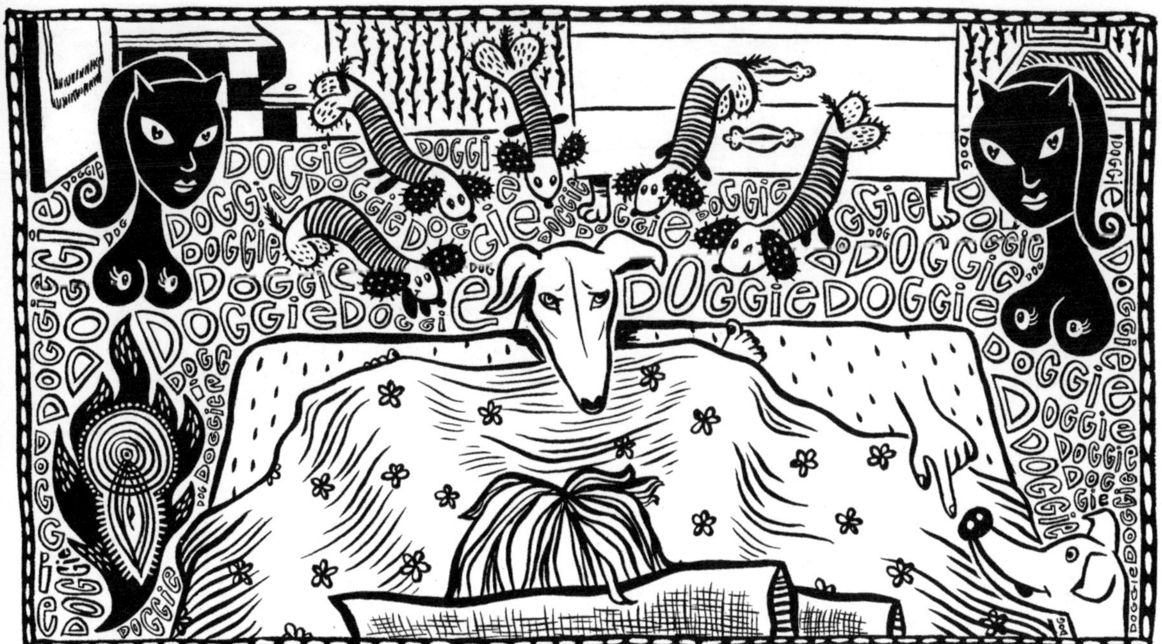
DOGGIE
DOGGIEDOGGIE

BY FOUR IN THE MORNING EVERYONE HAD EITHER LEFT OR FALLEN ASLEEP. I WAS TOO TIRED TO DRIVE SO I SLEPT IN THE GUEST ROOM. IN THE MIDDLE OF THE NIGHT, I WOKE UP FEELING SO HORNY I ALMOST FELT NAUSEOUS. (YOU KNOW HOW MAYBE ONCE A YEAR YOU WAKE UP LIKE THAT, WHERE IT'S SO INTENSE THAT YOU ALMOST GET PHYSICALLY SICK?) SO I STARTED TO MASTURBATE. I LOOKED DOWN AT THE FOOT OF THE BED AND FLUFFY LOOKED BACK AT ME. I WONDERED HOW YOU GET A DOG TO LICK YOUR PUSSY, SO I STUCK MY FINGERS INSIDE MYSELF AND PUT THEM IN FRONT OF FLUFFY'S NOSE. HE SNIFFED AND GAVE THEM A LICK. I DID IT AGAIN.

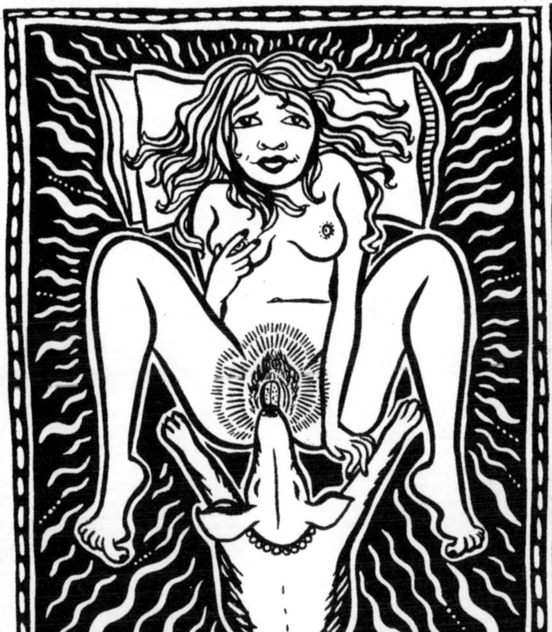

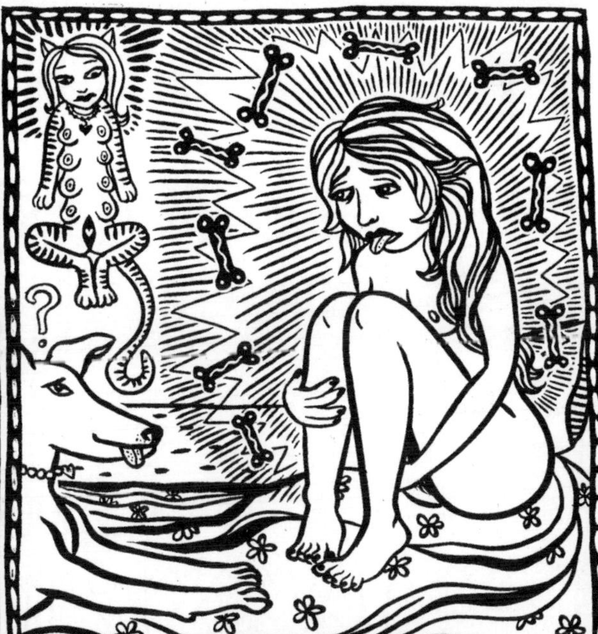
?

NEXT I SORT OF STEERED MY FINGERS AND HIS NOSE TOWARDS THE SOURCE. FOR ABOUT A MINUTE I WAS INTO IT, THEN I LOOKED AT THIS DOG MAKING THOSE DOG SOUNDS (LIKE WHEN THEY LICK THEIR BALLS) AND I FELT AN INTENSE BODY REPULSION I'D NEVER EXPERIENCED BEFORE.

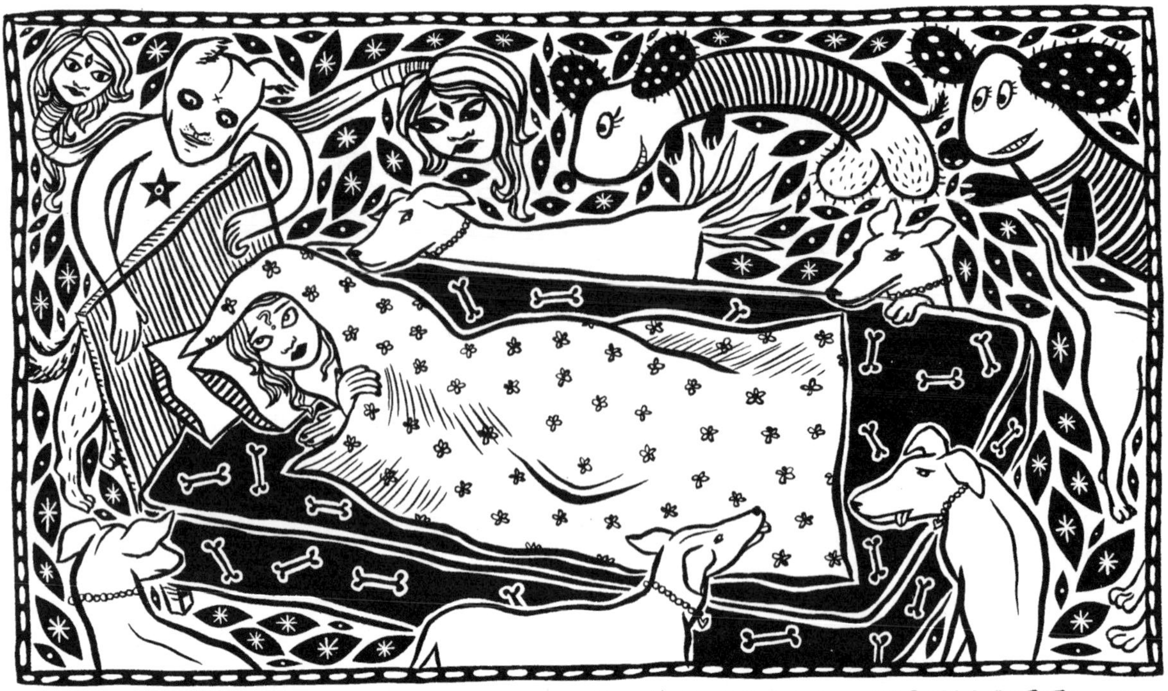

I WENT BACK UNDER THE COVERS, AND WONDERED WHETHER I WAS DRIVEN TO THIS BY CURIOSITY, DESIRE OR IF I WAS JUST DESPERATE. FLUFFY WAS ALL EXCITED NOW, AND PANTING, WALKING AROUND THE BED. I WAS FRIGHTENED THAT HE WAS GOING TO TRY TO FUCK ME. HIS PALE BLUE EYES LOOKED AS FREAKED OUT AS MINE DID. I GOT UP TO WASH MYSELF OFF IN THE BATHROOM AND FLUFFY RAN ALONG SIDE OF ME, EXCITED & CONFUSED. I BEGAN TO FEEL REMORSEFUL...

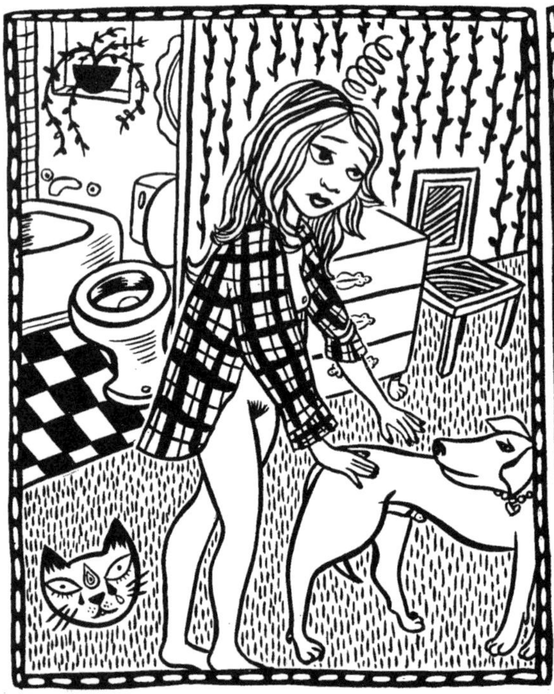

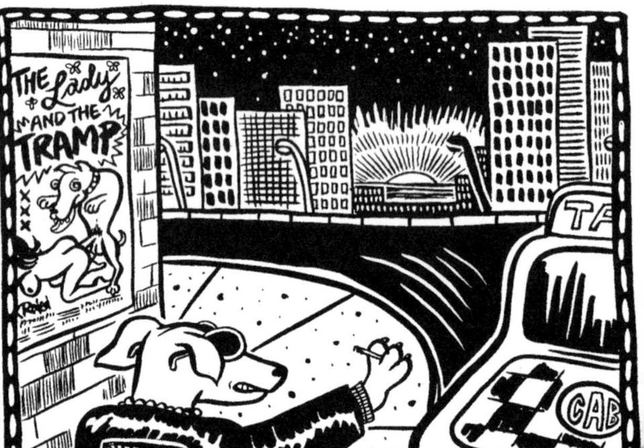
THE Lady AND THE TRAMP
XXX
TA
CAB

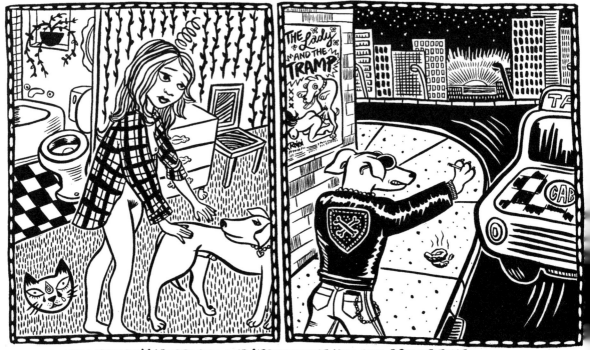

...LIKE I HAD SEXUALLY ABUSED HIM AND KEPT PATTING HIM AND APOLOGIZING. I COULDN'T SHAKE THAT BODY REPULSION THOUGH AND SORT OF WISHED FLUFFY HAD HIS OWN APARTMENT TO GO TO SO I COULD BE ALONE, AND NOT REMINDED OF HIM. (AT LEAST WITH MEN, YOU CAN SEND THEM AWAY AFTERWARDS IF YOU'RE NOT INTO THEM.)

WHEN I CRAWLED BACK INTO BED, FLUFFY TOOK HIS PLACE AT MY SIDE. I REALIZED THAT WE PROBABLY BOTH HAD THE SAME EXPRESSION ON OUR FACES. WE WERE BOTH HORNY AND CONFUSED. AND WE WERE PROBABLY THINKING THE SAME THING "WRONG SPECIES." *fin*

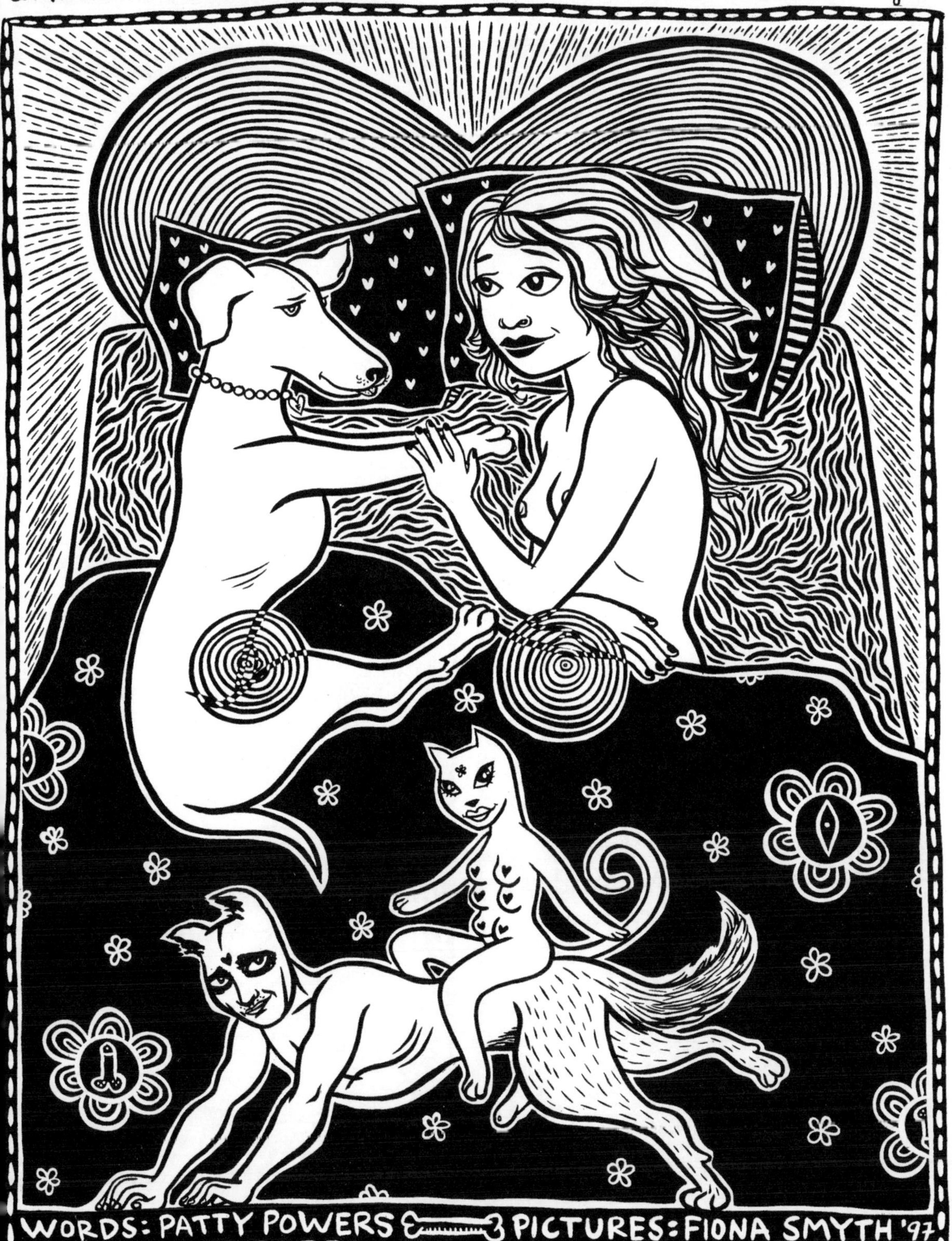
WORDS: PATTY POWERS
PICTURES: FIONA SMYTH '97

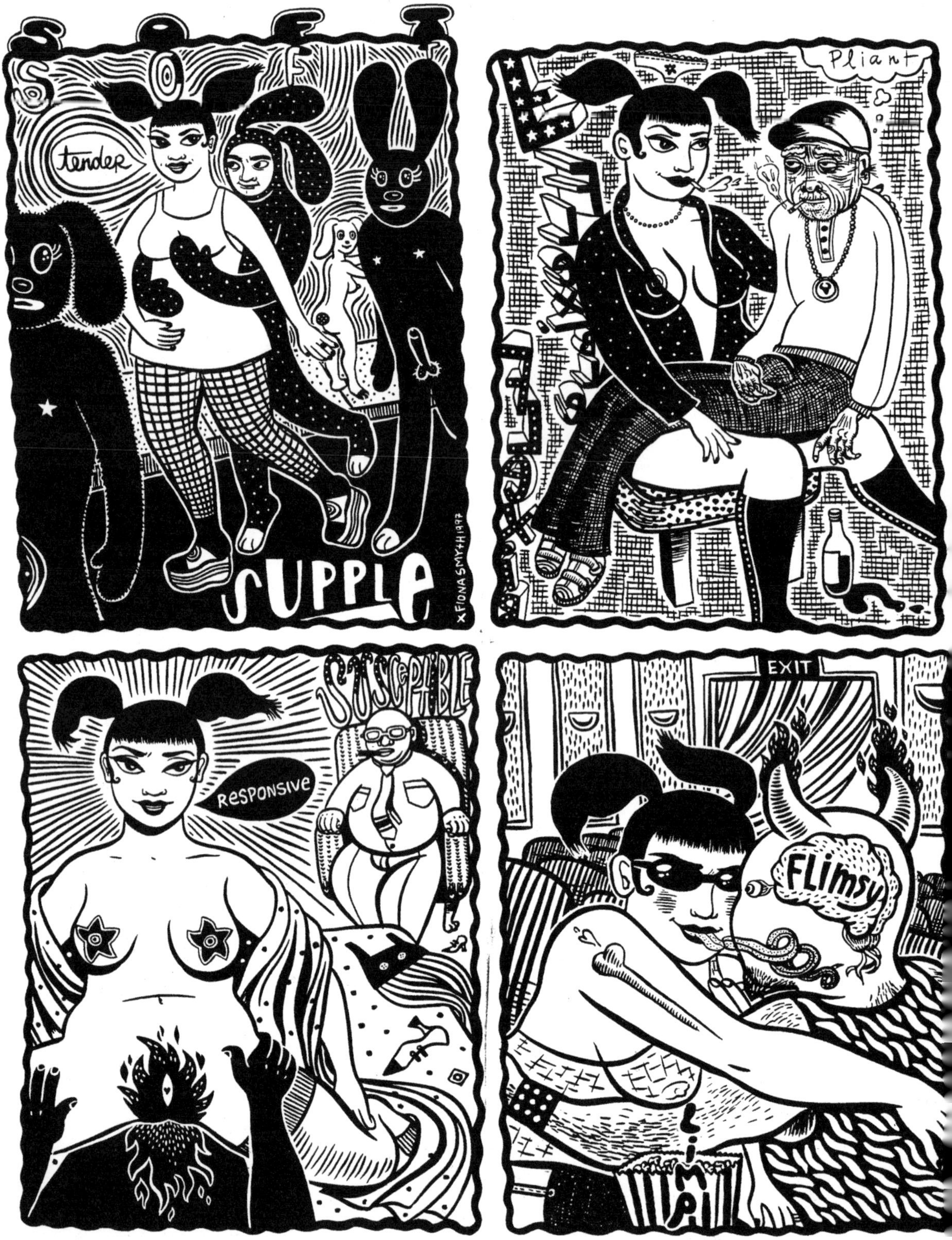
SOFT
tender
SUPPLE
x FIONA SMYTH 1997
Pliant
SUSCEPTIBLE
responsive
EXIT
Flimsy
LIMP

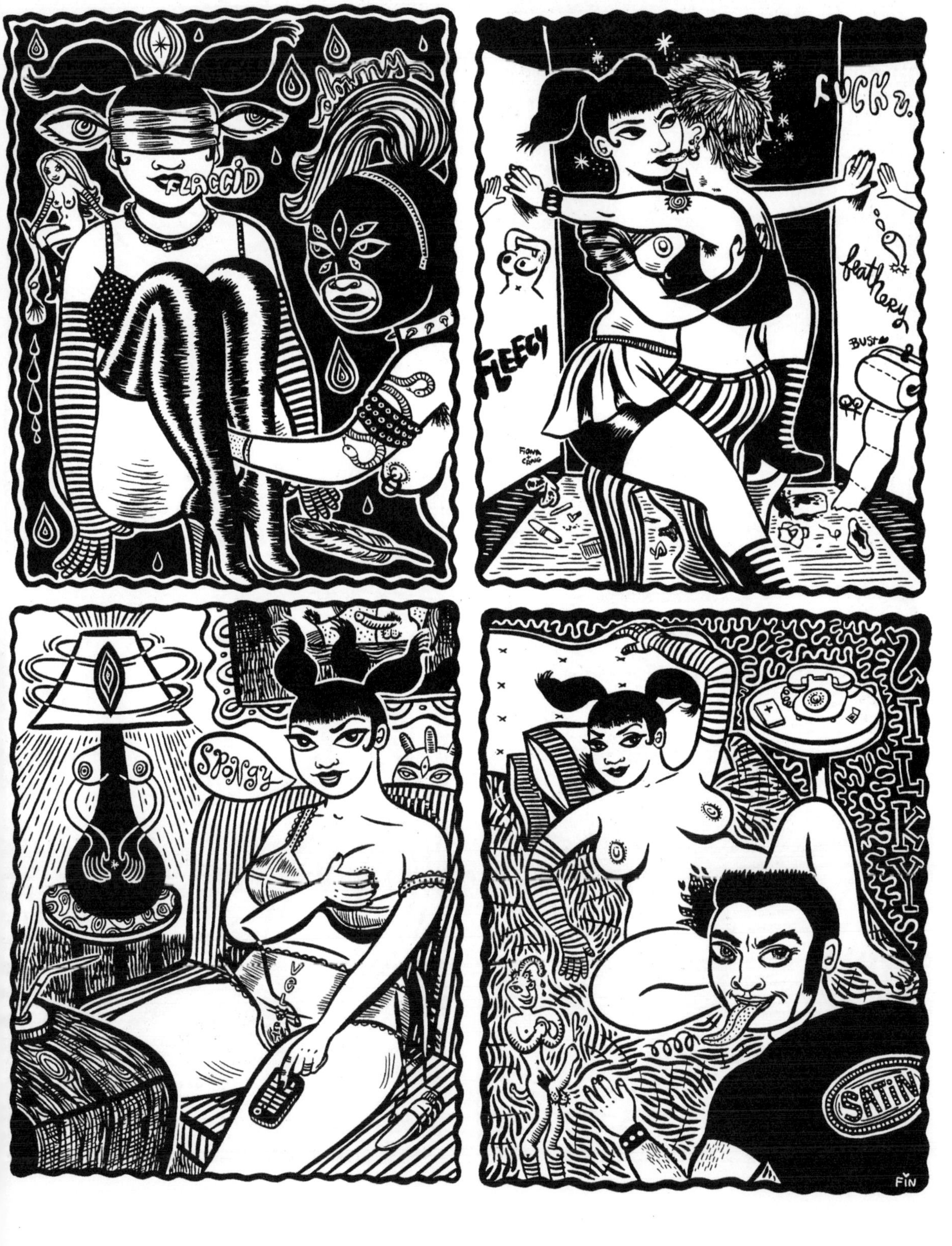

downy
FLACCID
FUCK U.
feathery
FLEECY
SPONGY
SILKY
SATIN
FIN

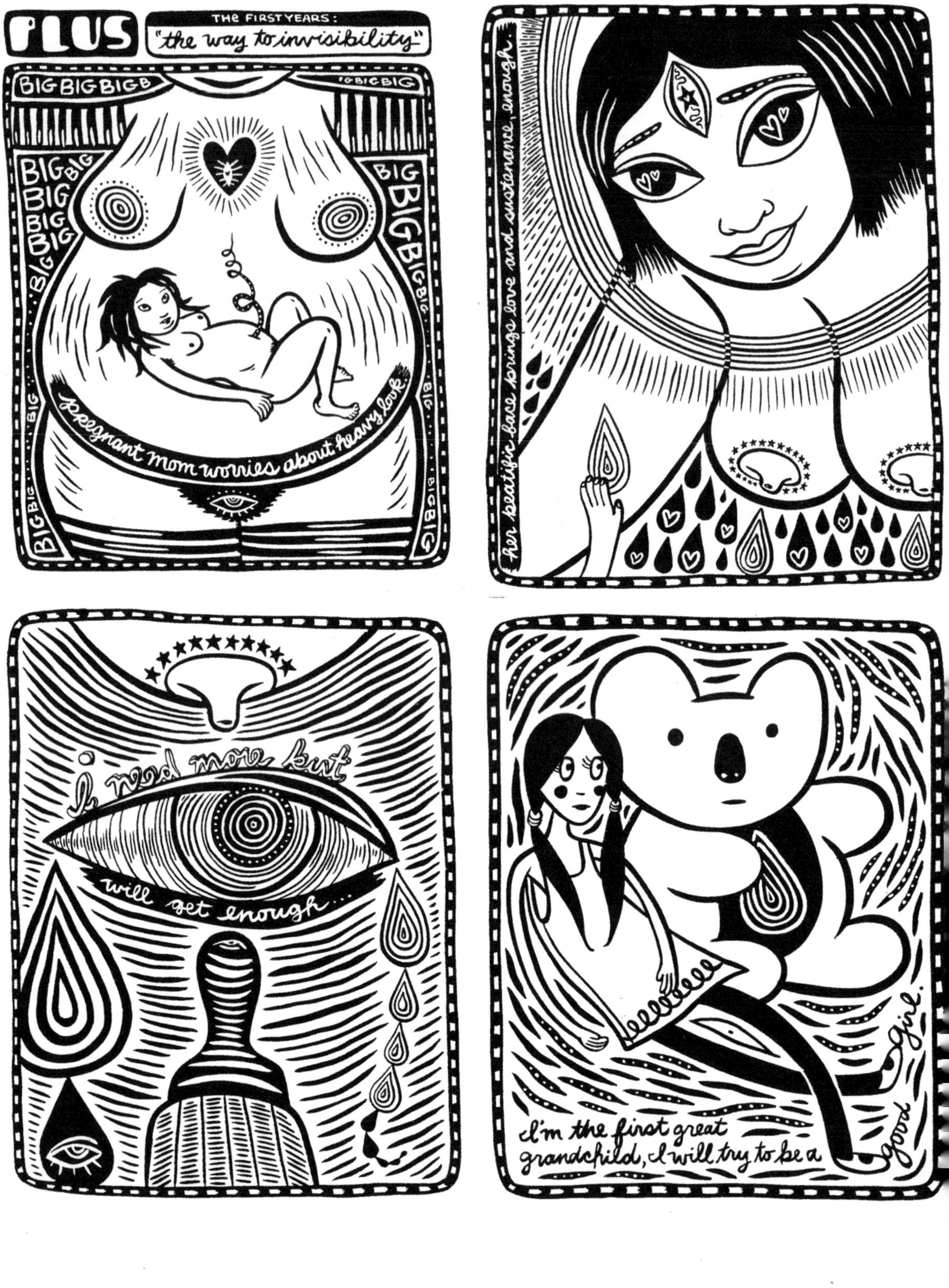
PLUS
THE FIRST YEARS:
"the way to invisibility"
BIG BIG BIG
pregnant mom worries about heavy look.
her beatific face brings love and sustenance, enough.
i need more but
will get enough
i'm the first great grandchild, i will try to be a good girl.

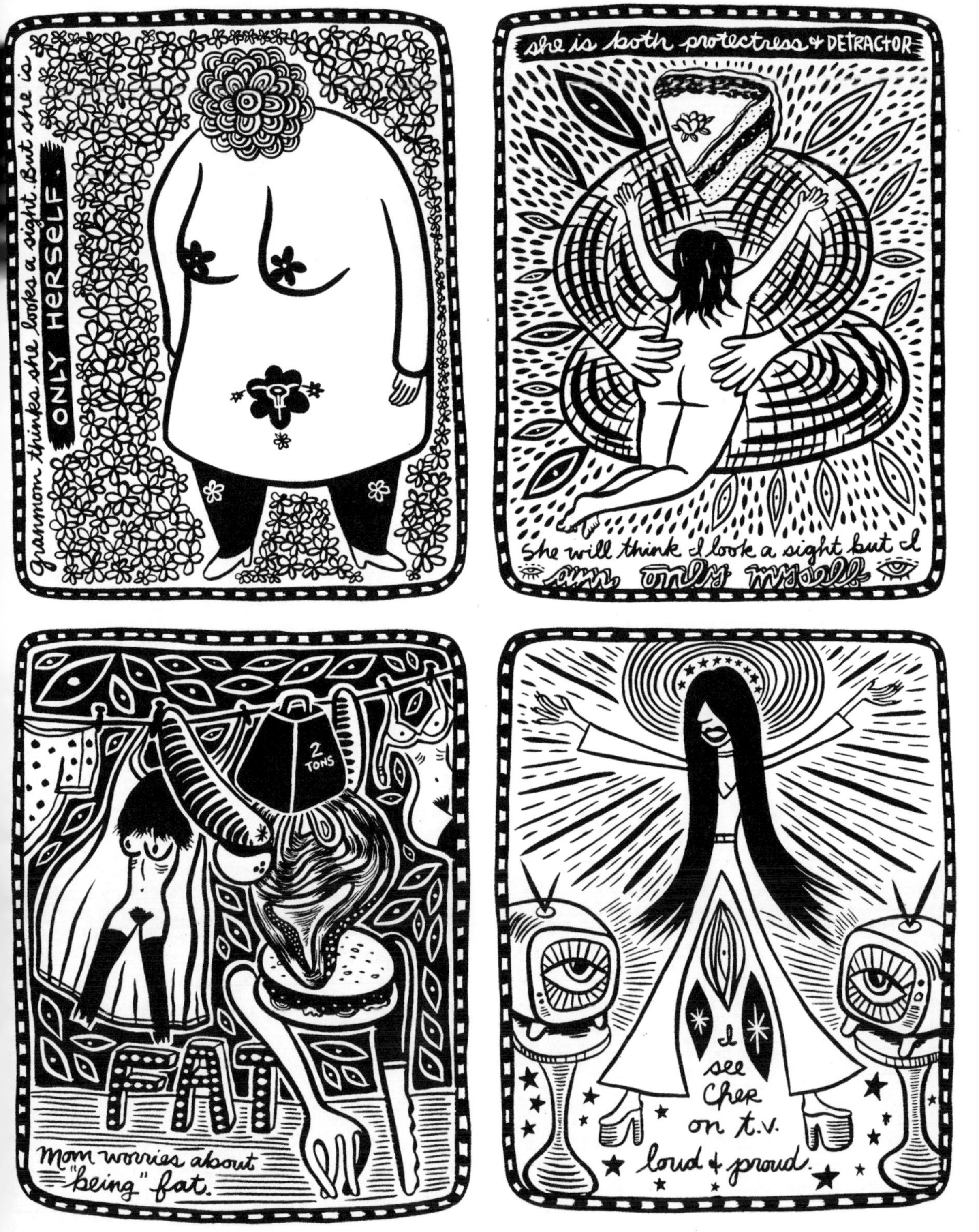
granmom thinks she looks a sight. But she is
ONLY HERSELF
she is both protectress & DETRACTOR
she will think I look a sight but I
am only myself
2 TONS
FAT
Mom worries about "being" fat.
I see Cher on t.v. loud & proud.

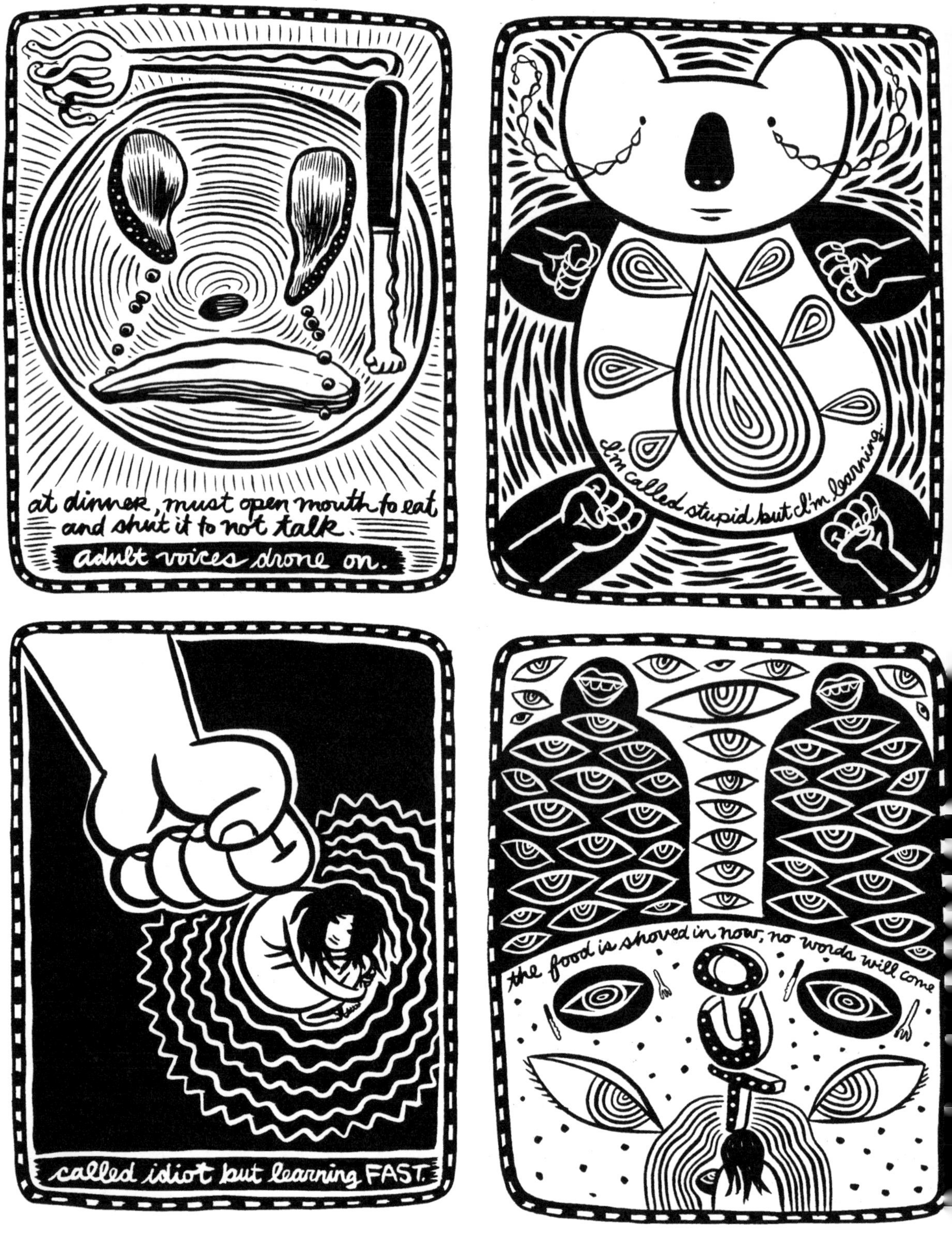
at dinner, must open mouth to eat and shut it to not talk
adult voices drone on.
I'm called stupid but I'm learning.
called idiot but learning FAST.
the food is shoved in now, no words will come

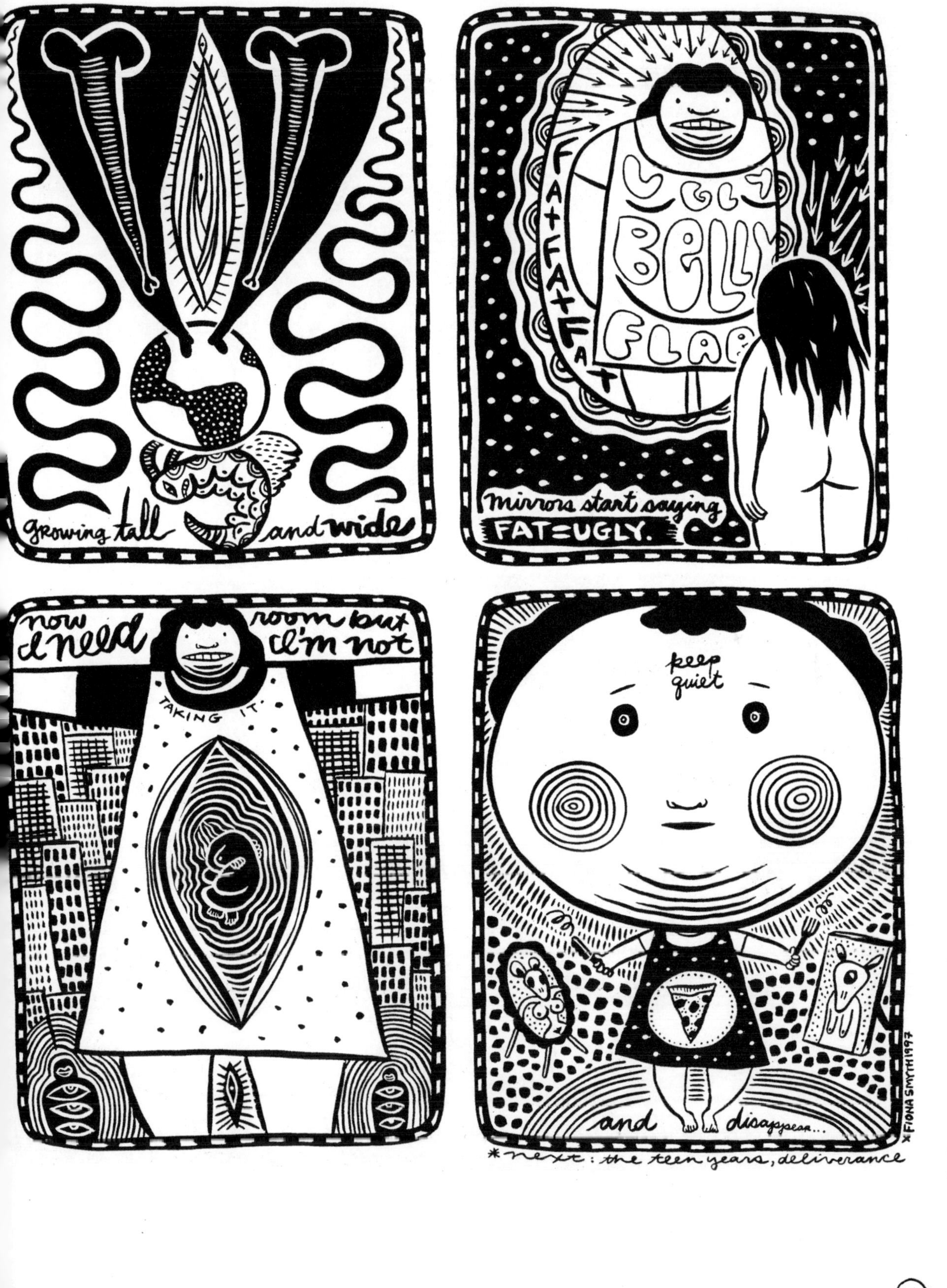
growing tall and wide
FAT FAT FAT
UGLY BELLY FLAP
mirrors start saying
FAT=UGLY.
now I need room but I'm not
TAKING IT.
keep quiet
and disappear...
FIONA SMYTH 1997
*next: the teen years, deliverance

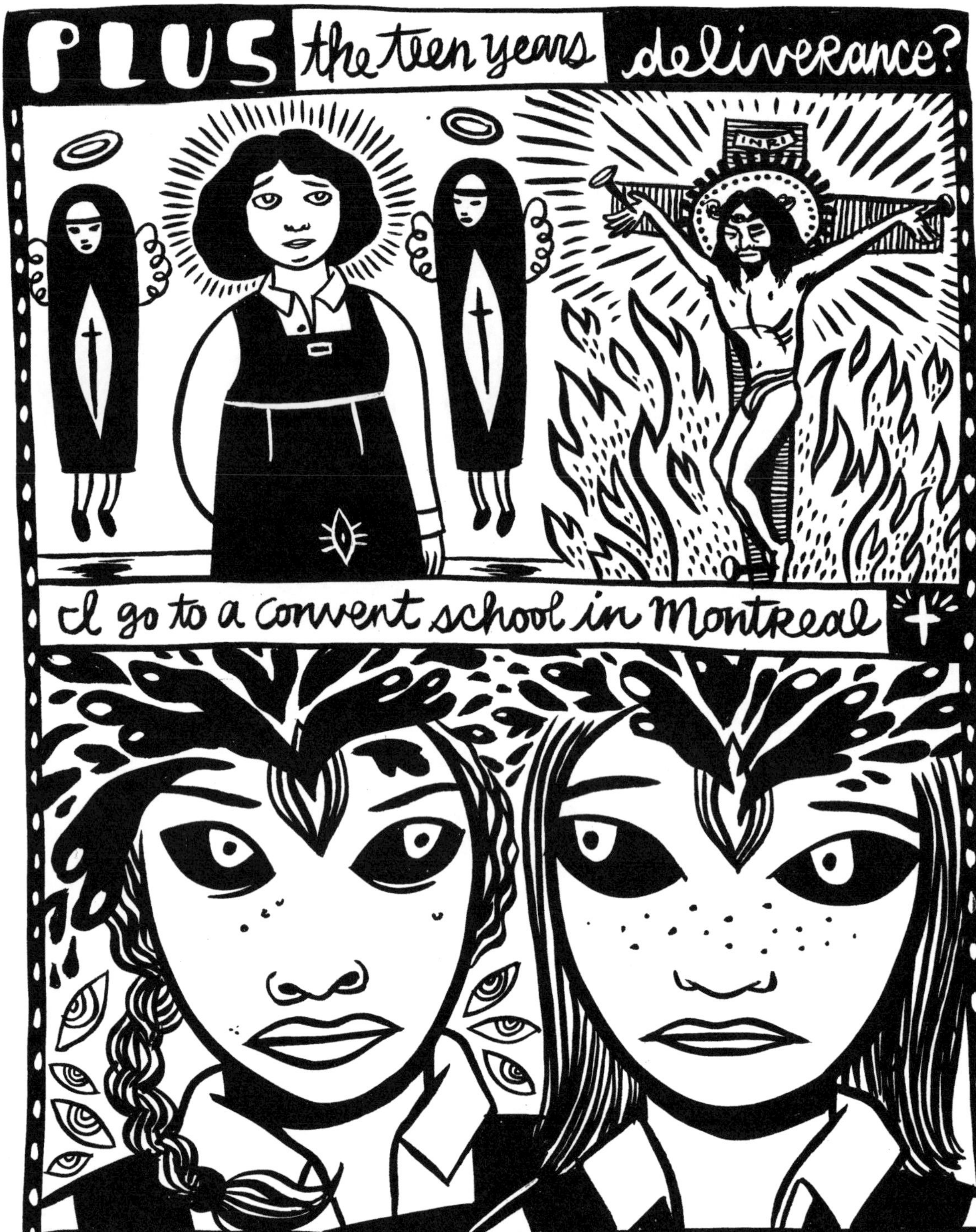
PLUS
the teen years
deliverance?
INRI
I go to a convent school in Montreal
a girls' school where no-one talks about periods

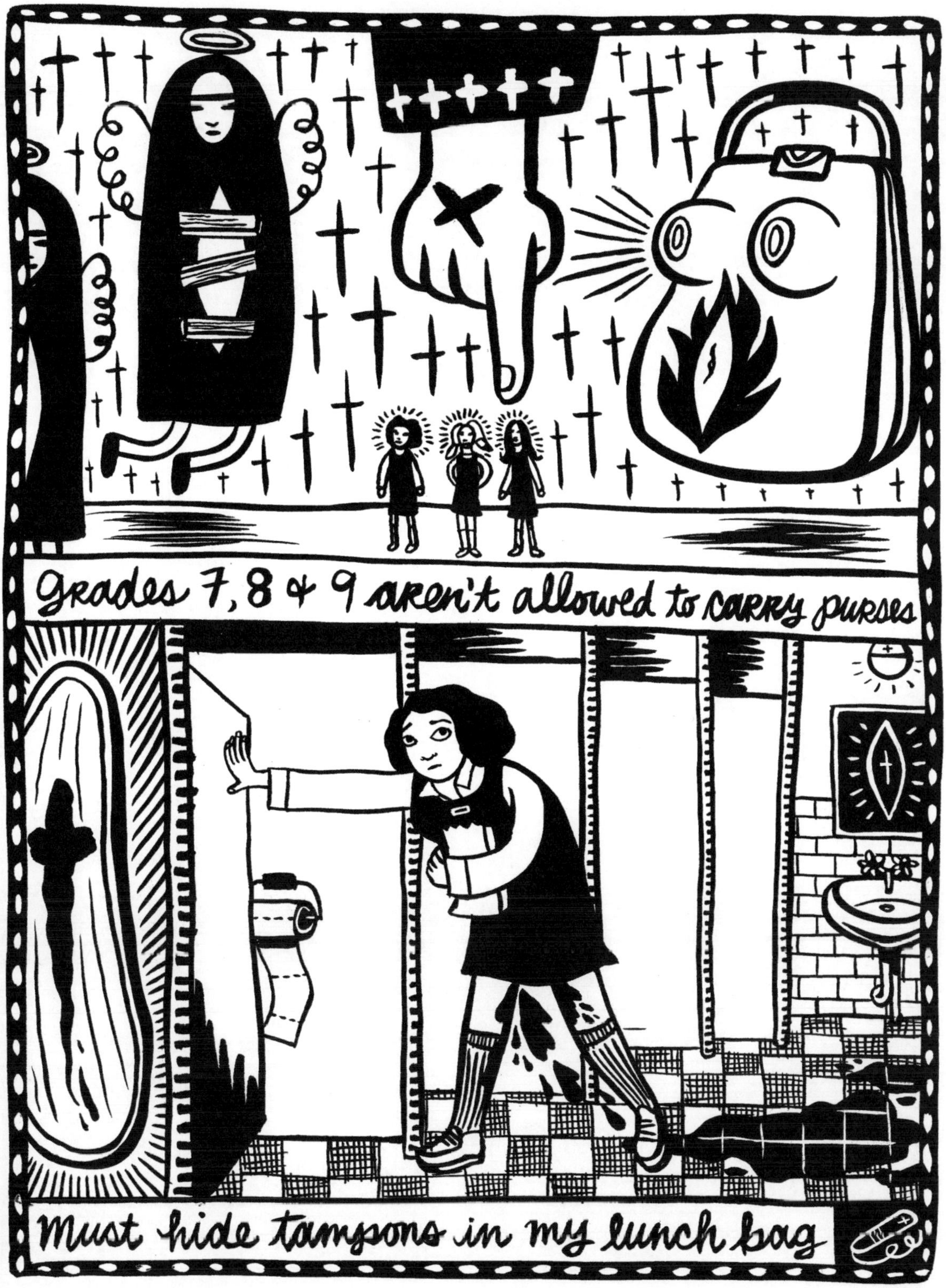
grades 7, 8 & 9 aren't allowed to carry purses
Must hide tampons in my lunch bag

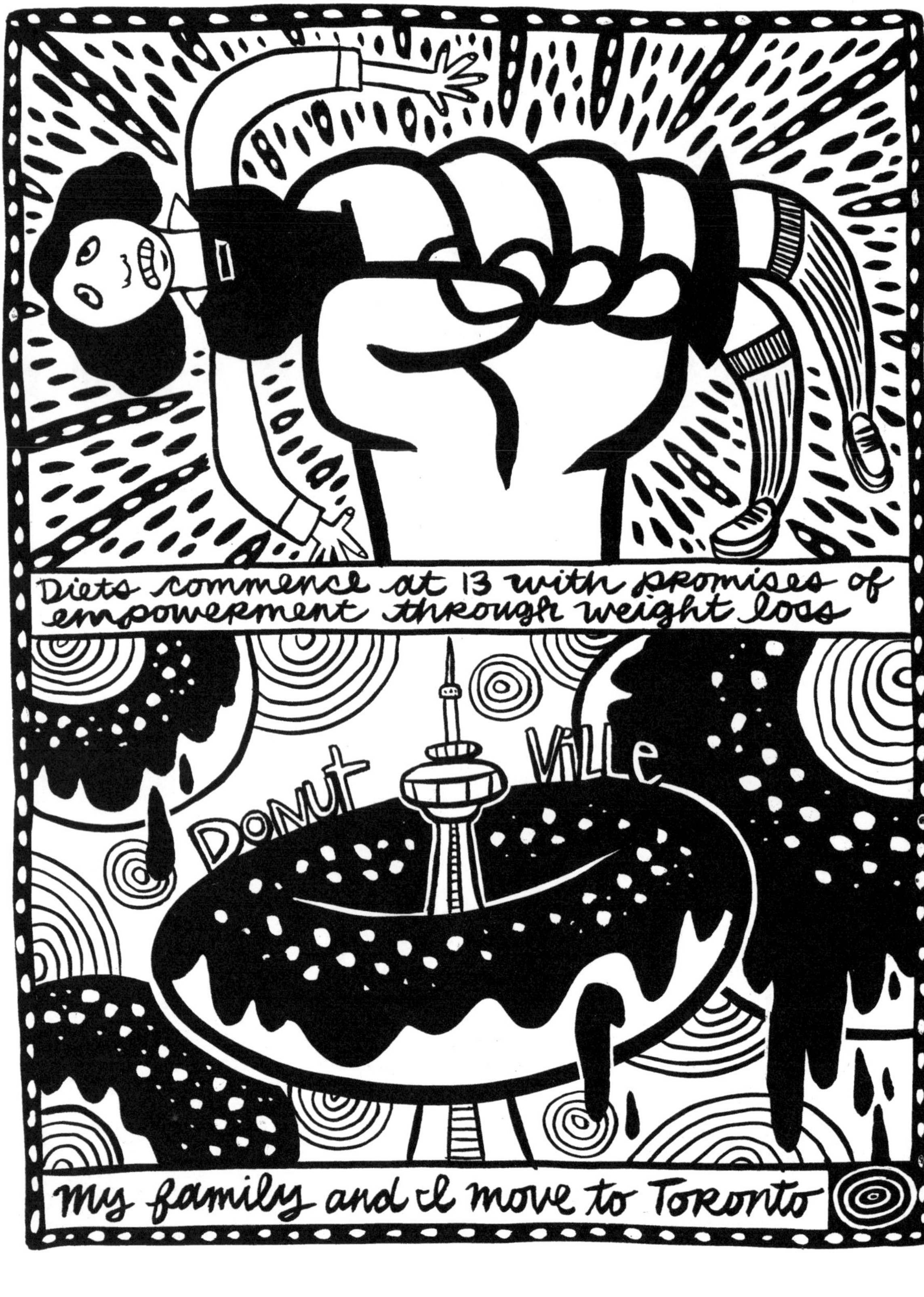
Diets commence at 13 with promises of empowerment through weight loss
DONUT VILLE
My family and I move to Toronto

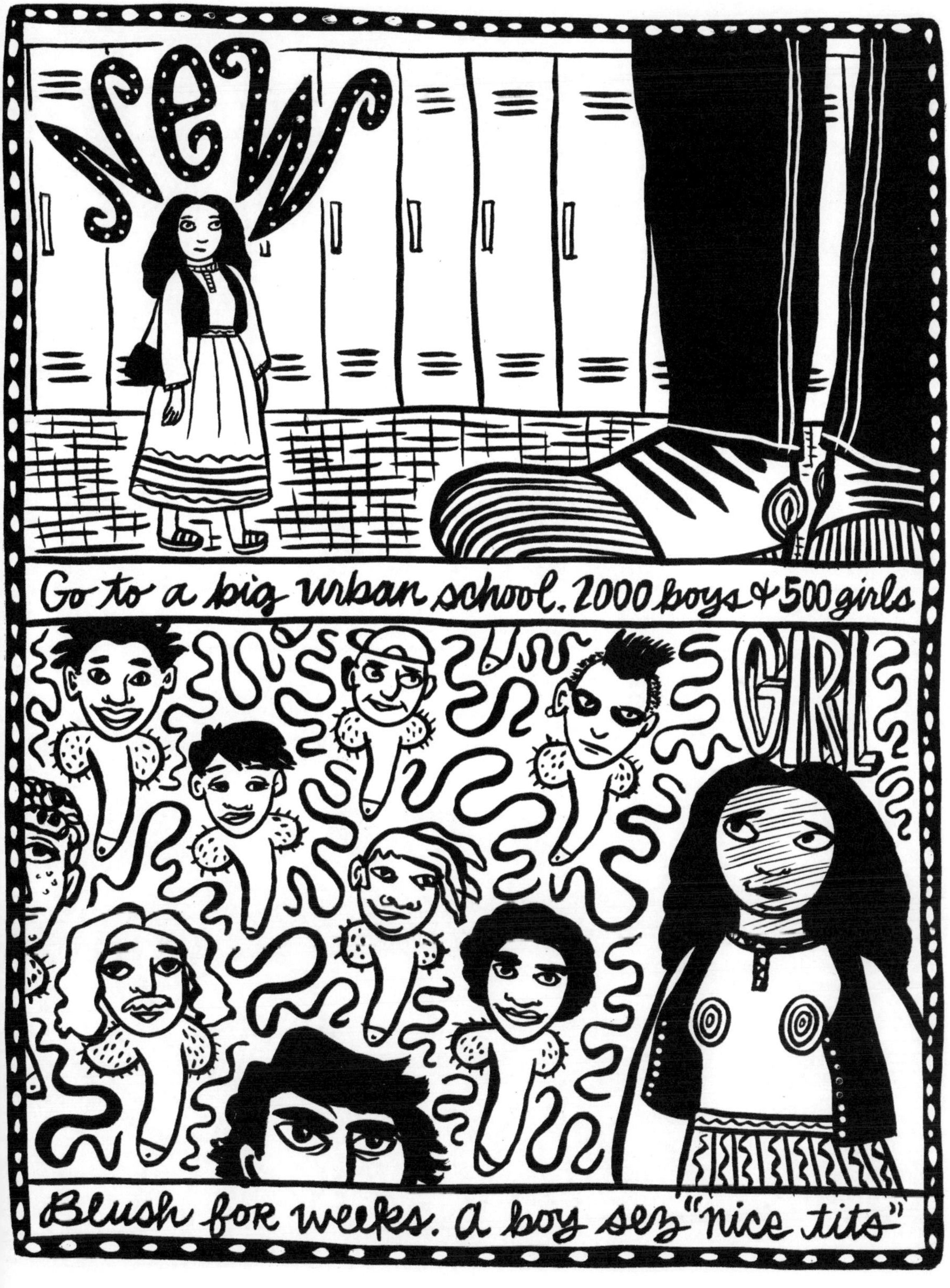
NEW
Go to a big urban school. 2000 boys & 500 girls
GIRL
Blush for weeks. a boy sez "nice tits"

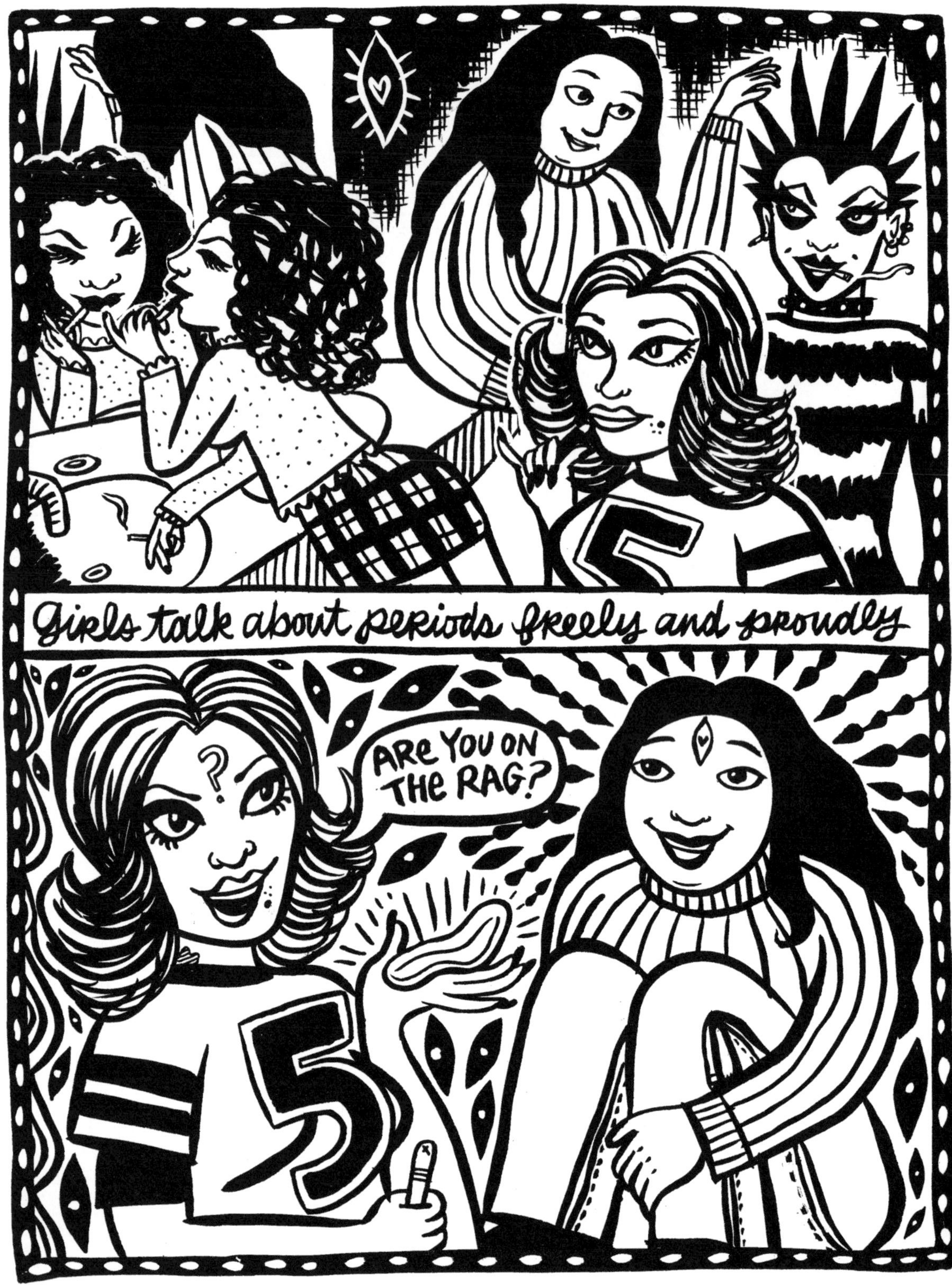
Girls talk about periods freely and proudly
ARE YOU ON THE RAG?

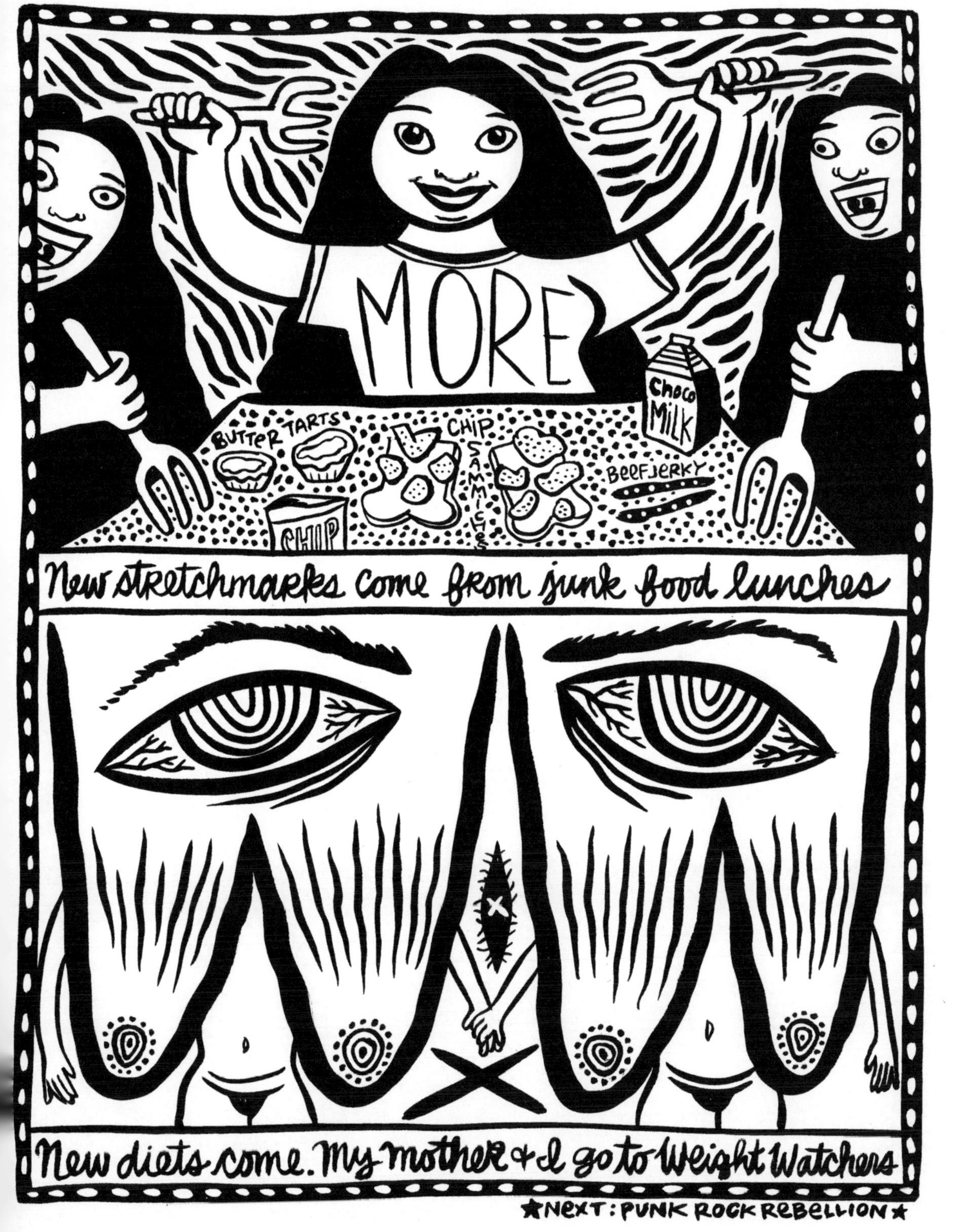
MORE
BUTTER TARTS
CHIP SAMMICHES
CHOCO MILK
BEEF JERKY
CHIP
New stretchmarks come from junk food lunches
New diets come. My mother & I go to Weight Watchers
★NEXT: PUNK ROCK REBELLION★

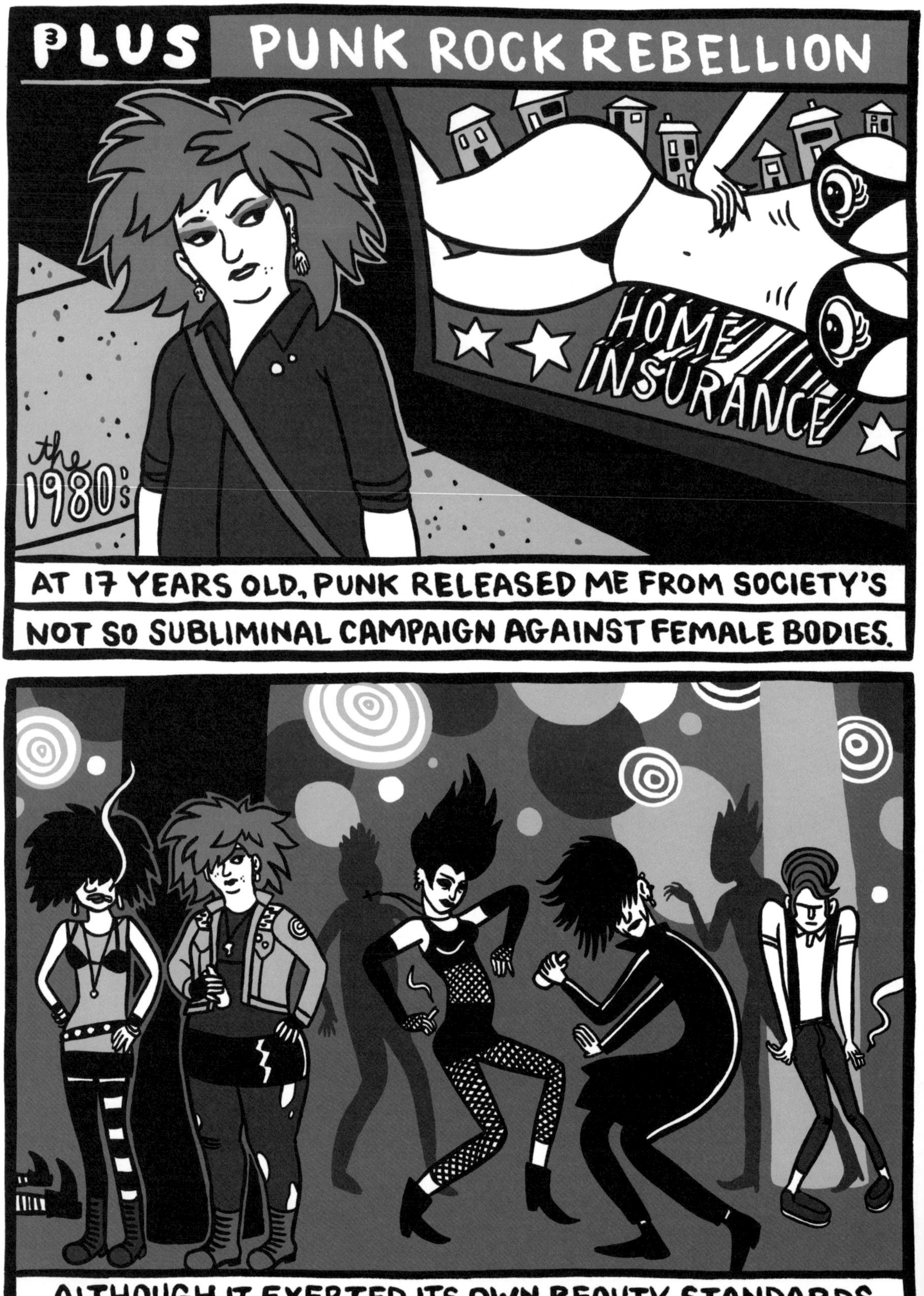
3 PLUS PUNK ROCK REBELLION
HOME INSURANCE
the 1980's
AT 17 YEARS OLD, PUNK RELEASED ME FROM SOCIETY'S NOT SO SUBLIMINAL CAMPAIGN AGAINST FEMALE BODIES.
ALTHOUGH IT EXERTED ITS OWN BEAUTY STANDARDS.

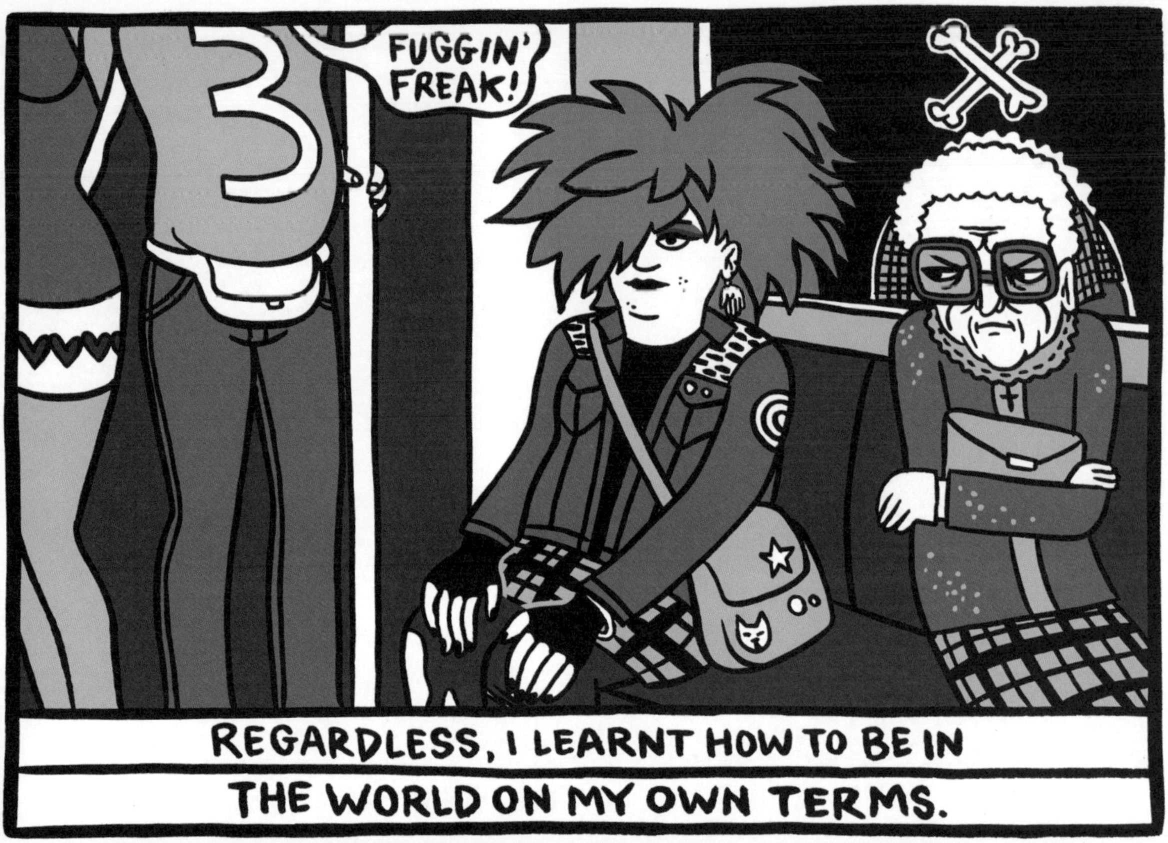
FUGGIN' FREAK!
REGARDLESS, I LEARNT HOW TO BE IN THE WORLD ON MY OWN TERMS.

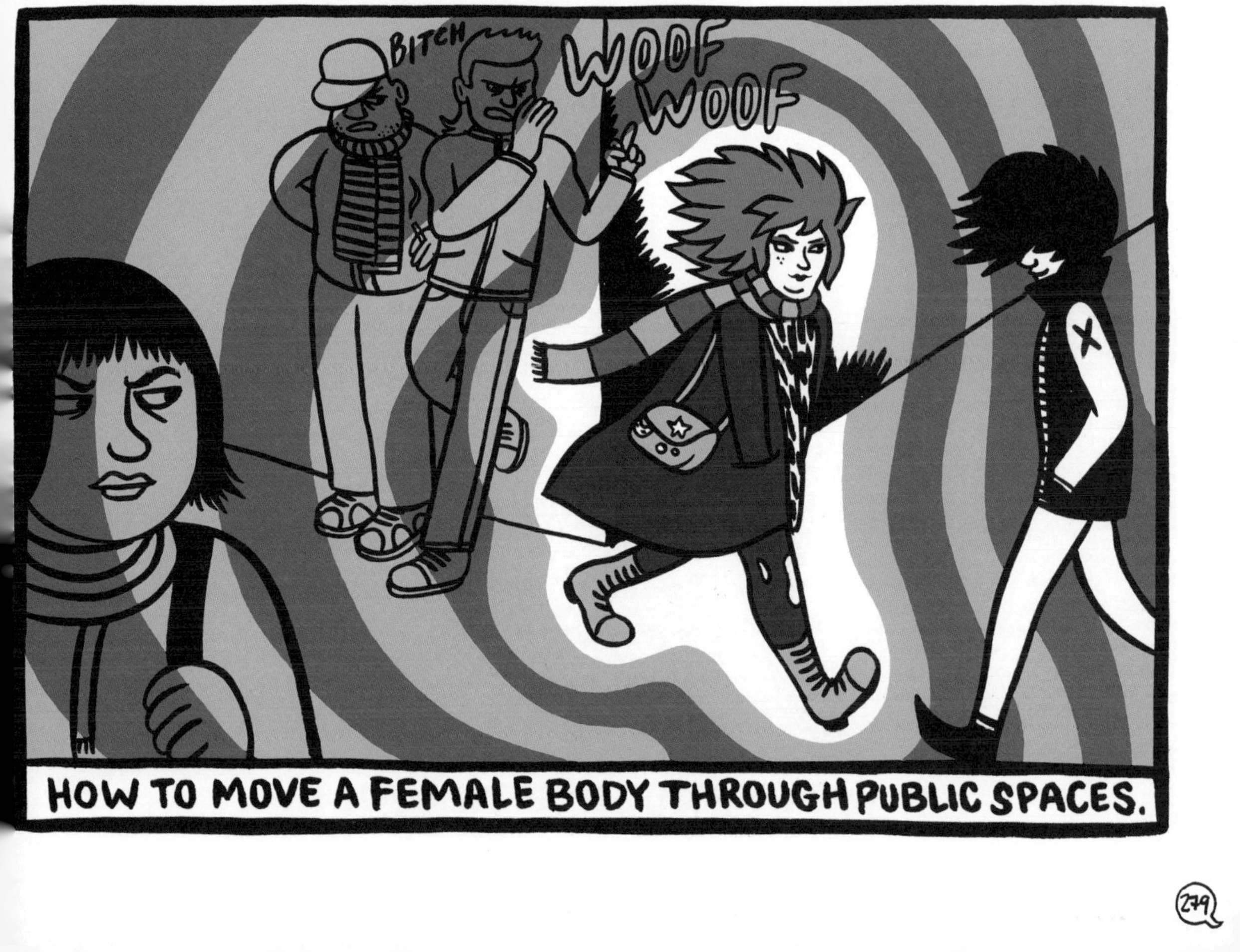
BITCH
WOOF WOOF
HOW TO MOVE A FEMALE BODY THROUGH PUBLIC SPACES.

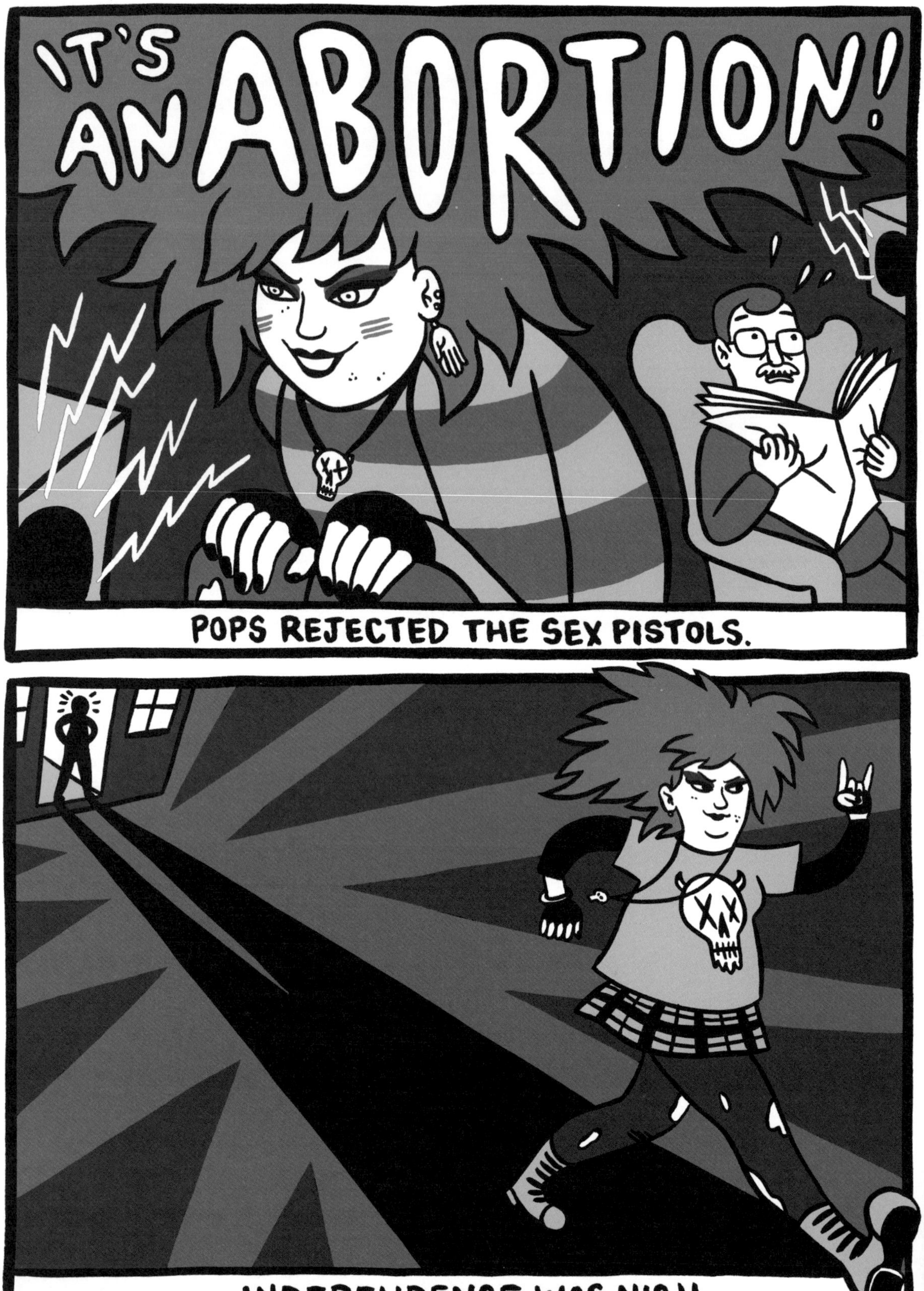
IT'S AN ABORTION!
POPS REJECTED THE SEX PISTOLS.
INDEPENDENCE WAS NIGH.

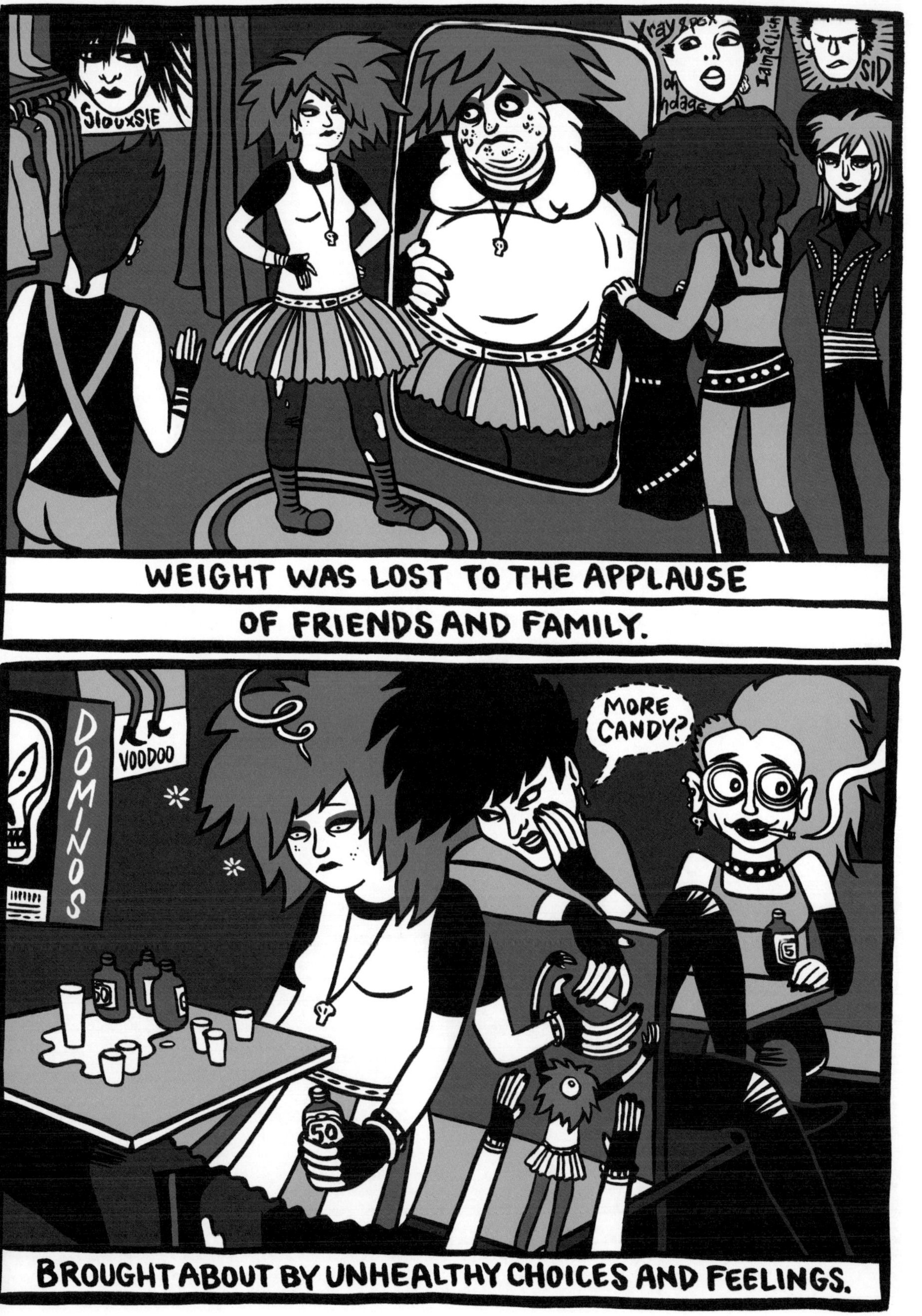
SIOUXSIE
Xray Spex
SID
WEIGHT WAS LOST TO THE APPLAUSE OF FRIENDS AND FAMILY.
VOODOO
DOMINOS
MORE CANDY?
BROUGHT ABOUT BY UNHEALTHY CHOICES AND FEELINGS.

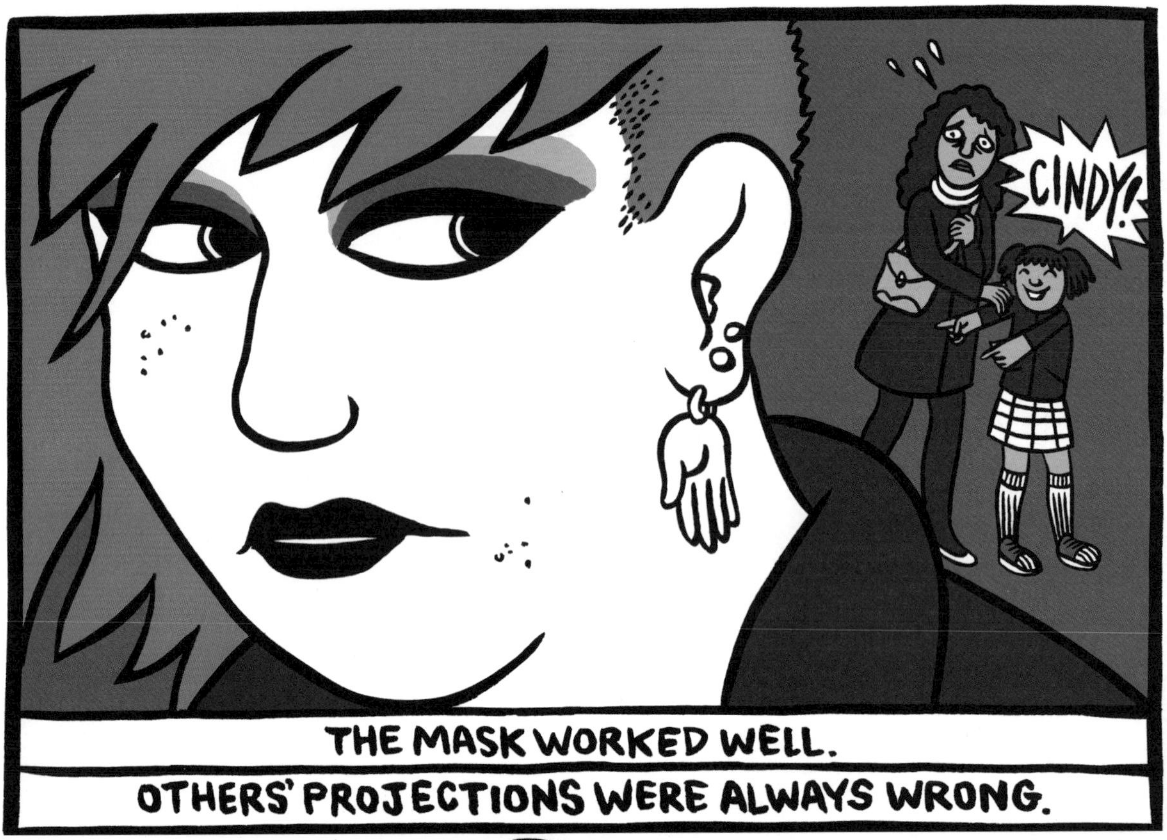
CINDY!
THE MASK WORKED WELL.
OTHERS' PROJECTIONS WERE ALWAYS WRONG.

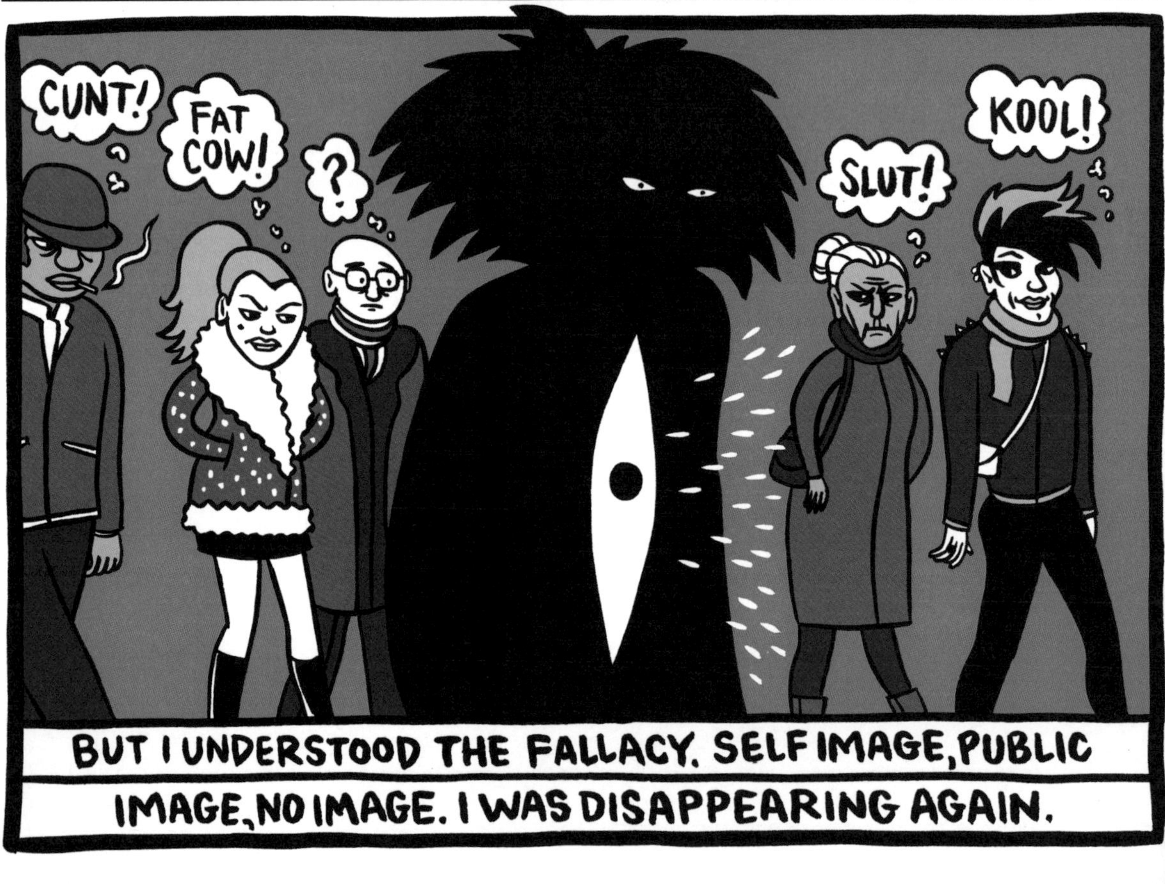
CUNT!
FAT COW!
?
SLUT!
KOOL!
BUT I UNDERSTOOD THE FALLACY. SELF IMAGE, PUBLIC
IMAGE, NO IMAGE. I WAS DISAPPEARING AGAIN.

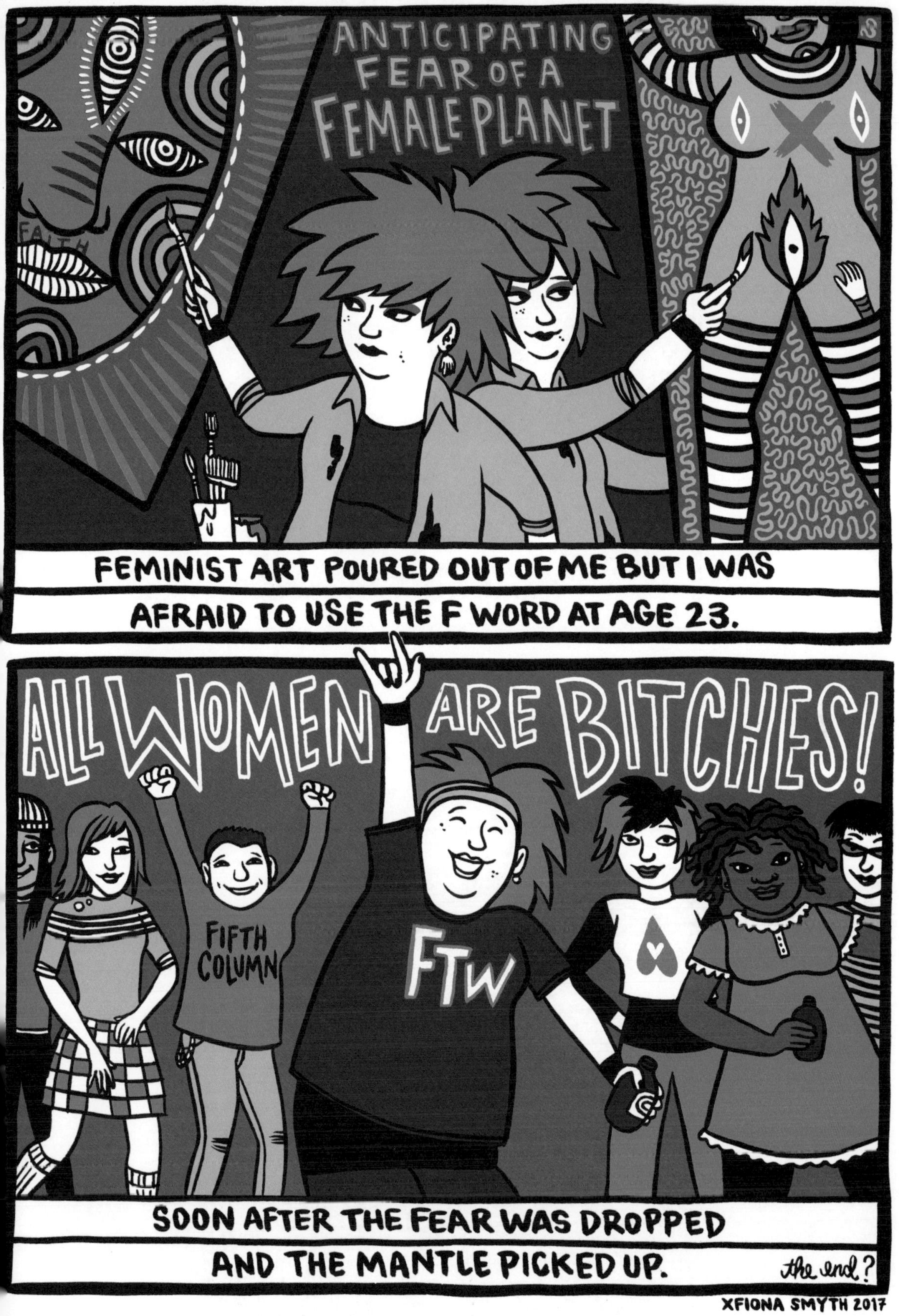
ANTICIPATING FEAR OF A FEMALE PLANET
FAITH
FEMINIST ART POURED OUT OF ME BUT I WAS AFRAID TO USE THE F WORD AT AGE 23.
ALL WOMEN ARE BITCHES!
FIFTH COLUMN
FTW
SOON AFTER THE FEAR WAS DROPPED AND THE MANTLE PICKED UP.
the end?

XFIONA SMYTH 2017

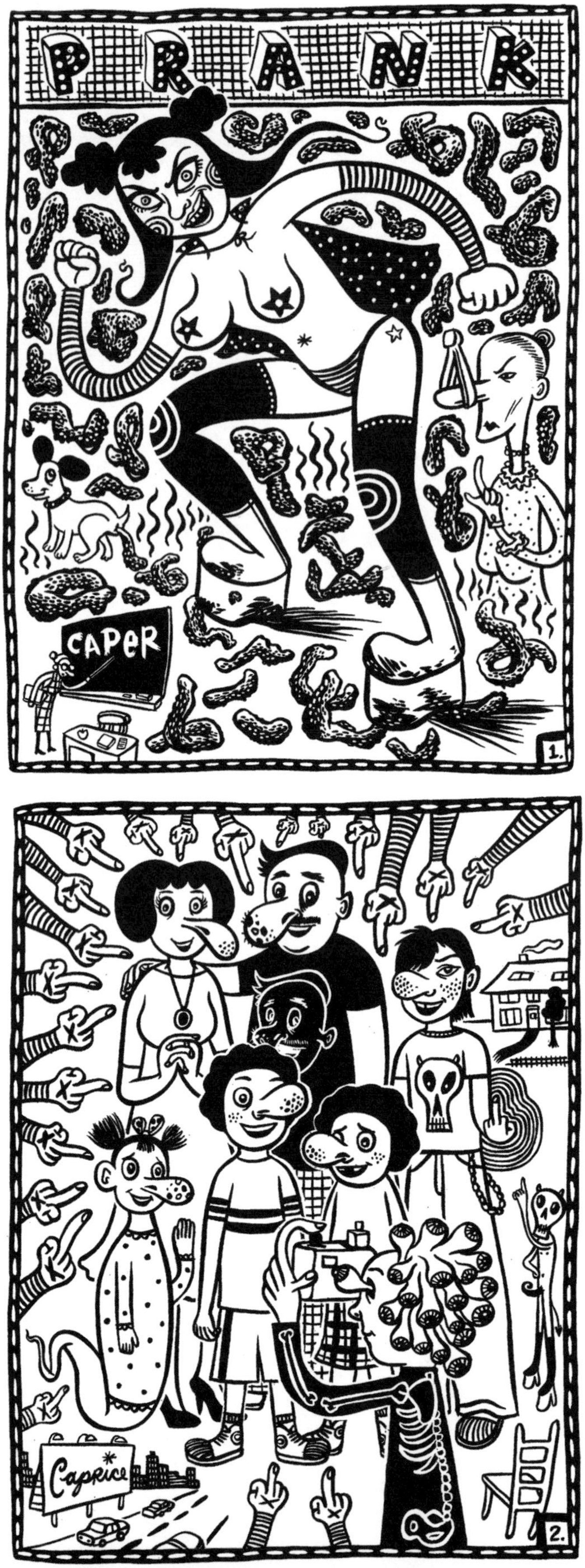
PRANK
CAPER
1.
Caprice
2.

ESCAPADE
3.
FROLIC
4.

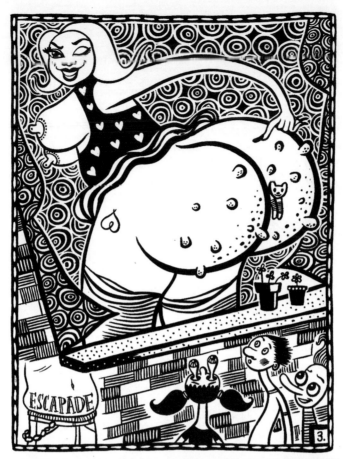

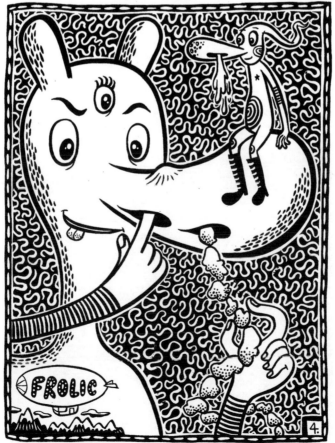

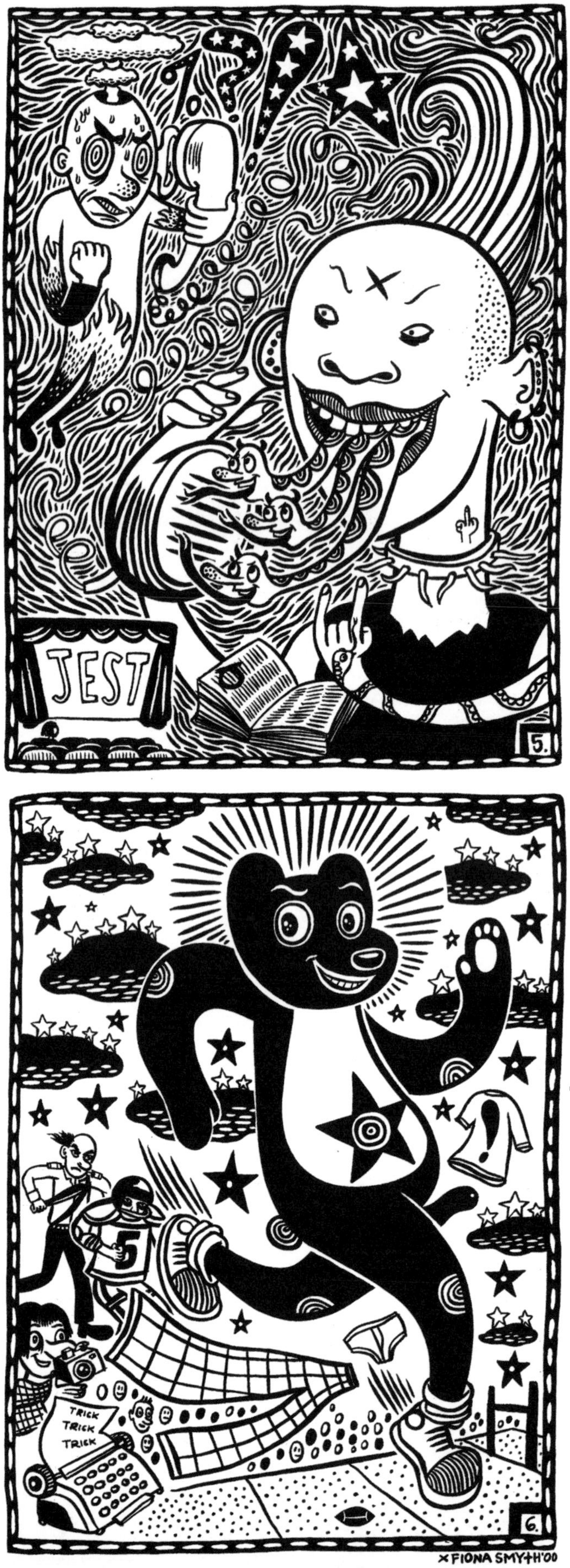
JEST
5.
TRICK
TRICK
TRICK
5
6.

×FIONA SMYTH'00

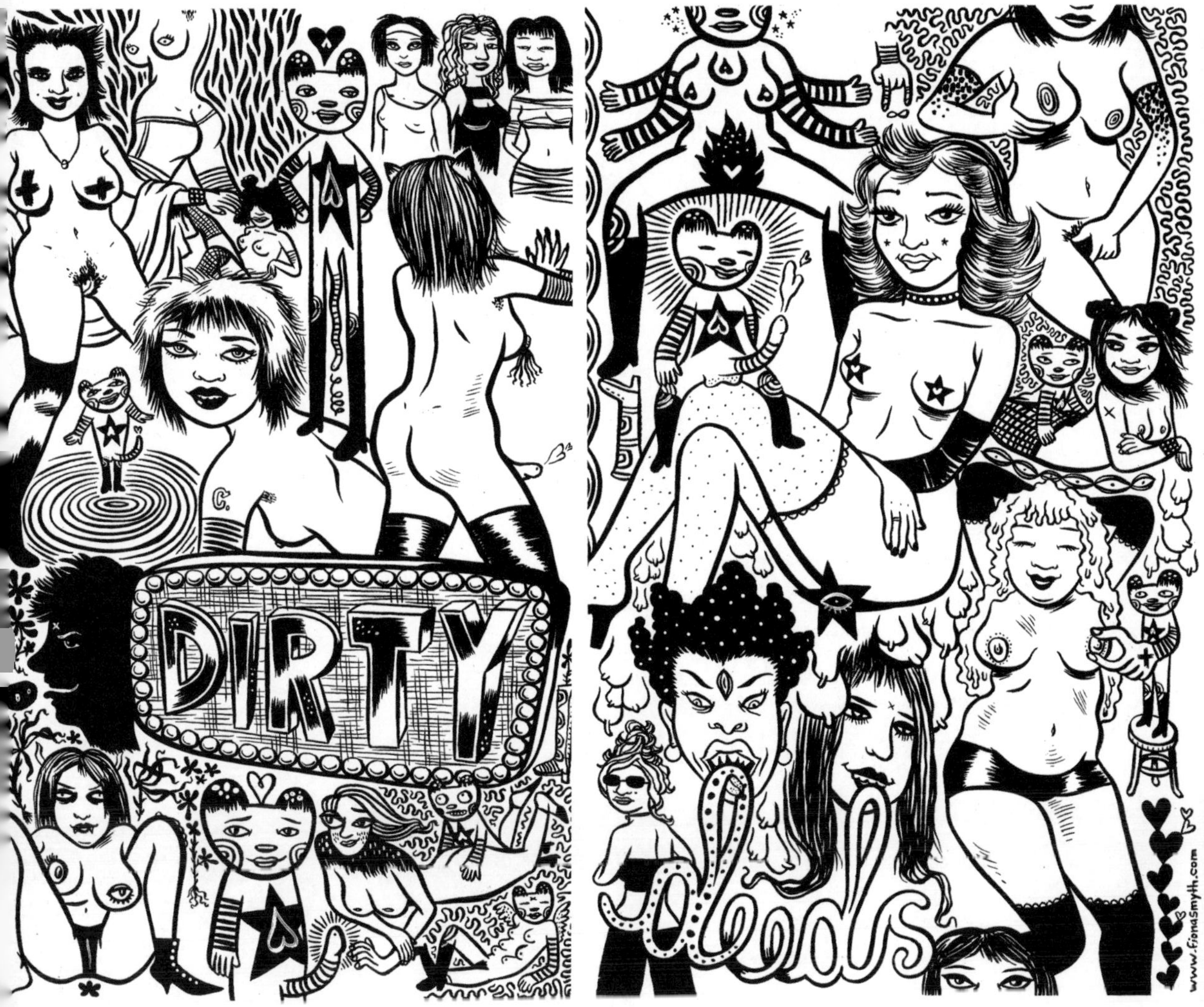
DIRTY
www.fionasmyth.com

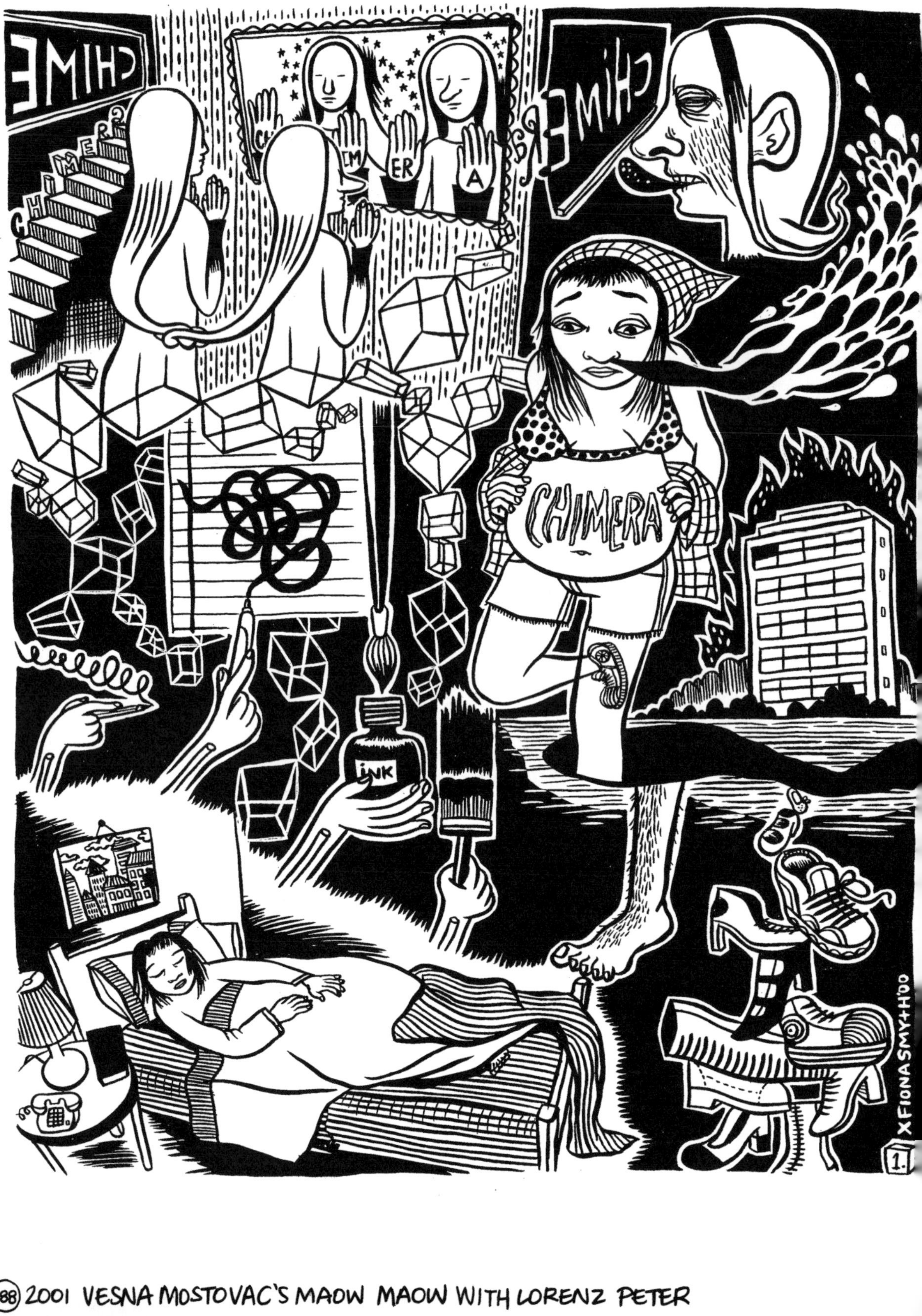
CHIME
CHIMER
ER
A
CHIMER
CHIMERA
INK
XFIONASMY+H'00
1.

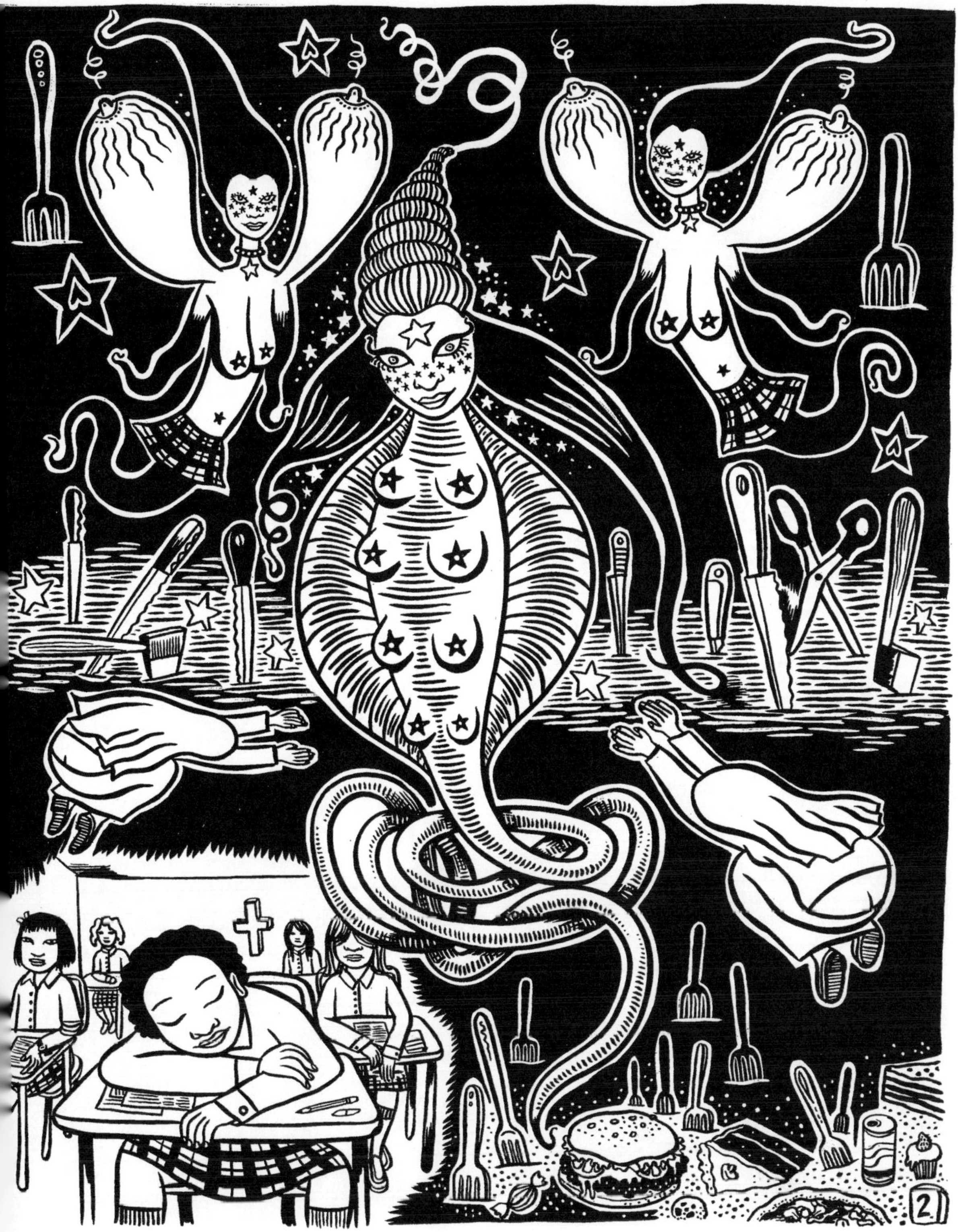
2

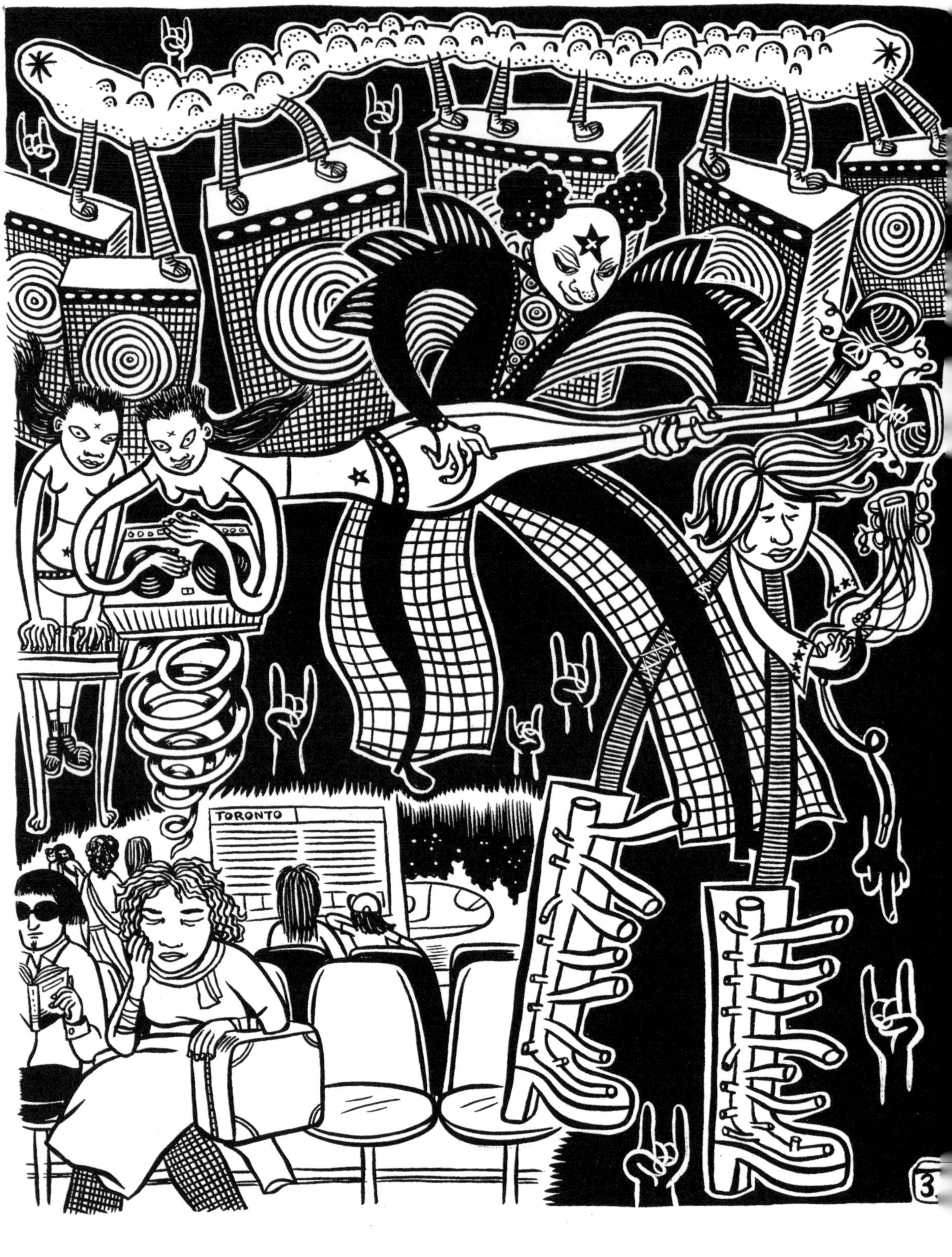
TORONTO
3

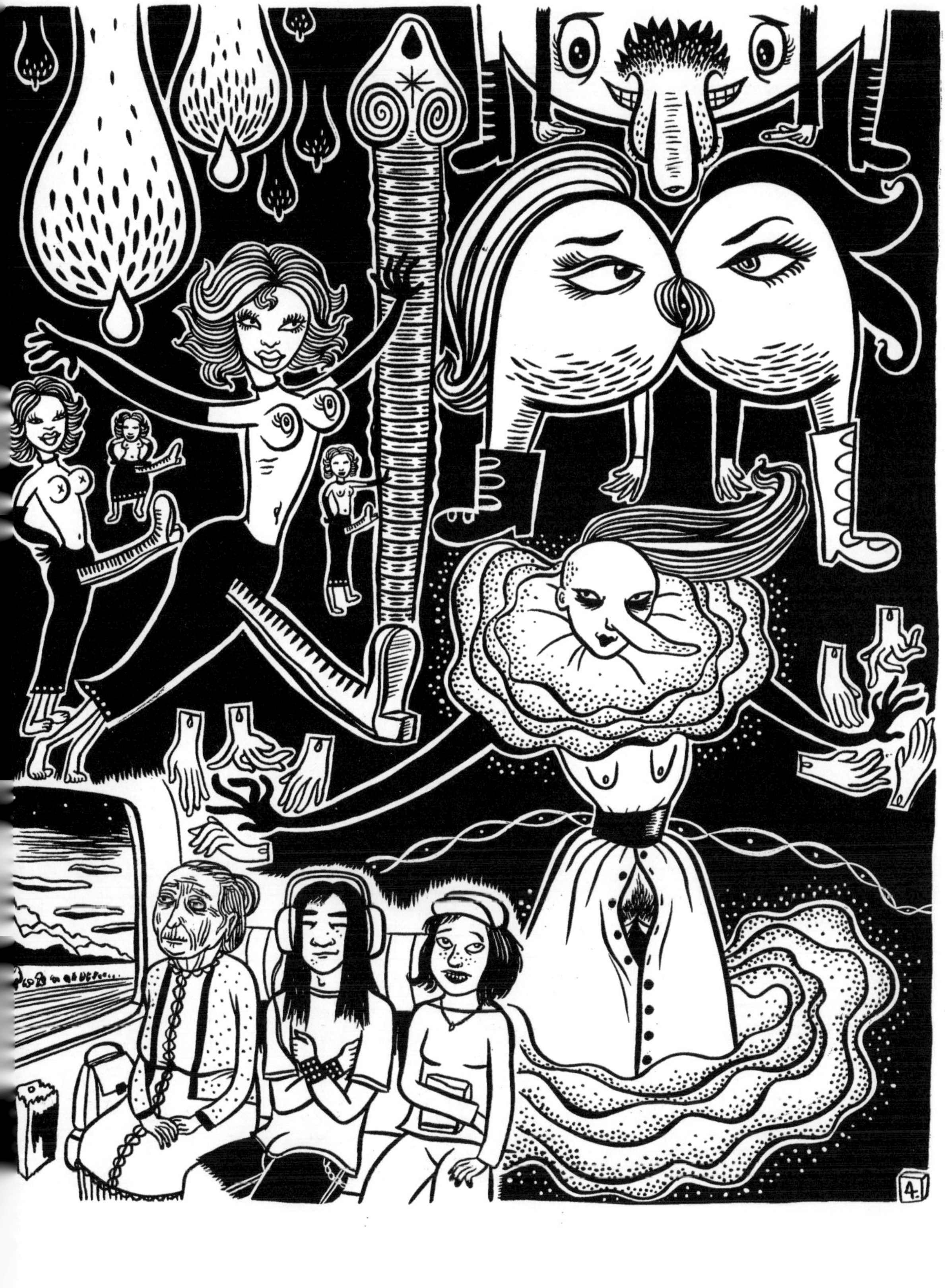
4.

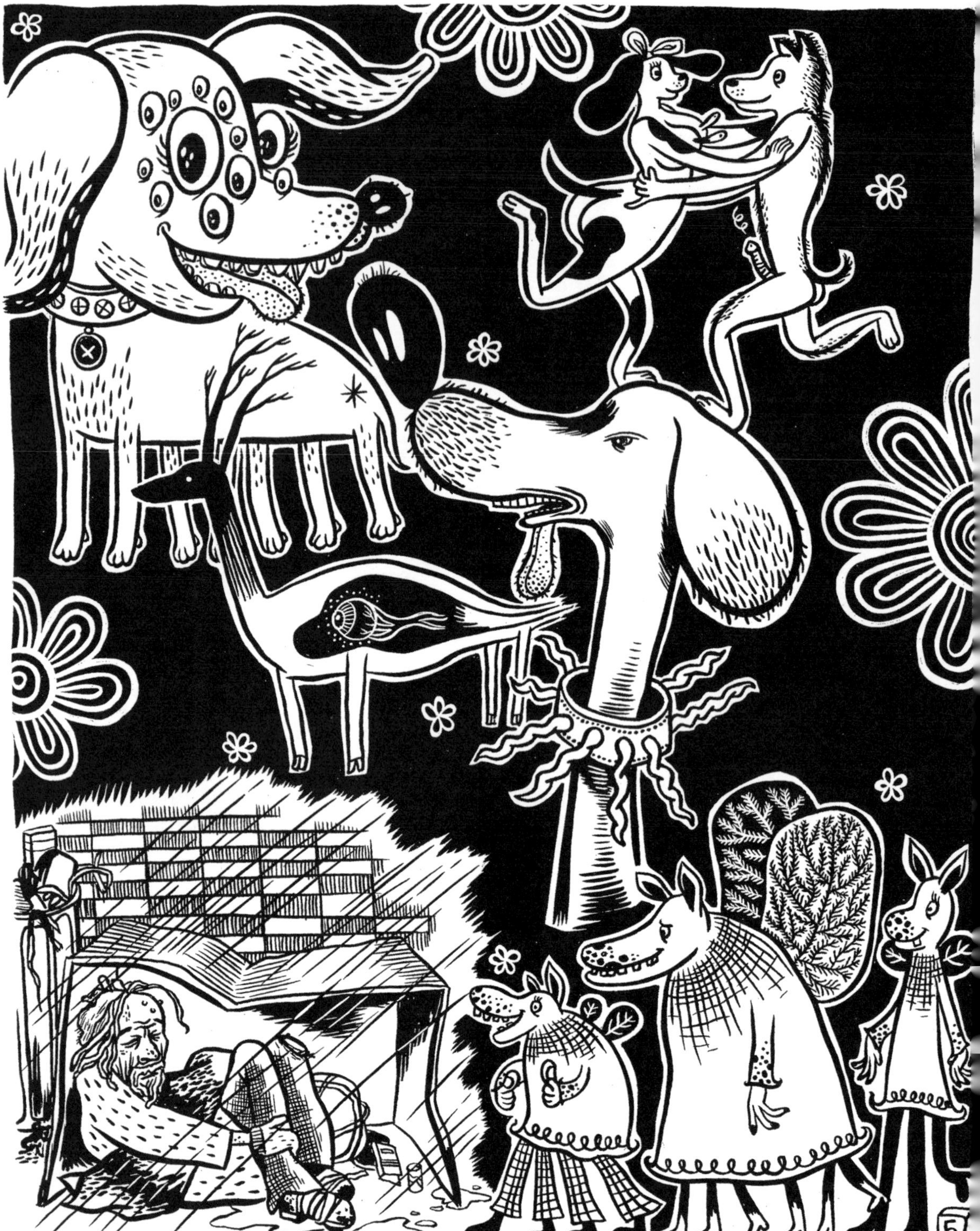
5.

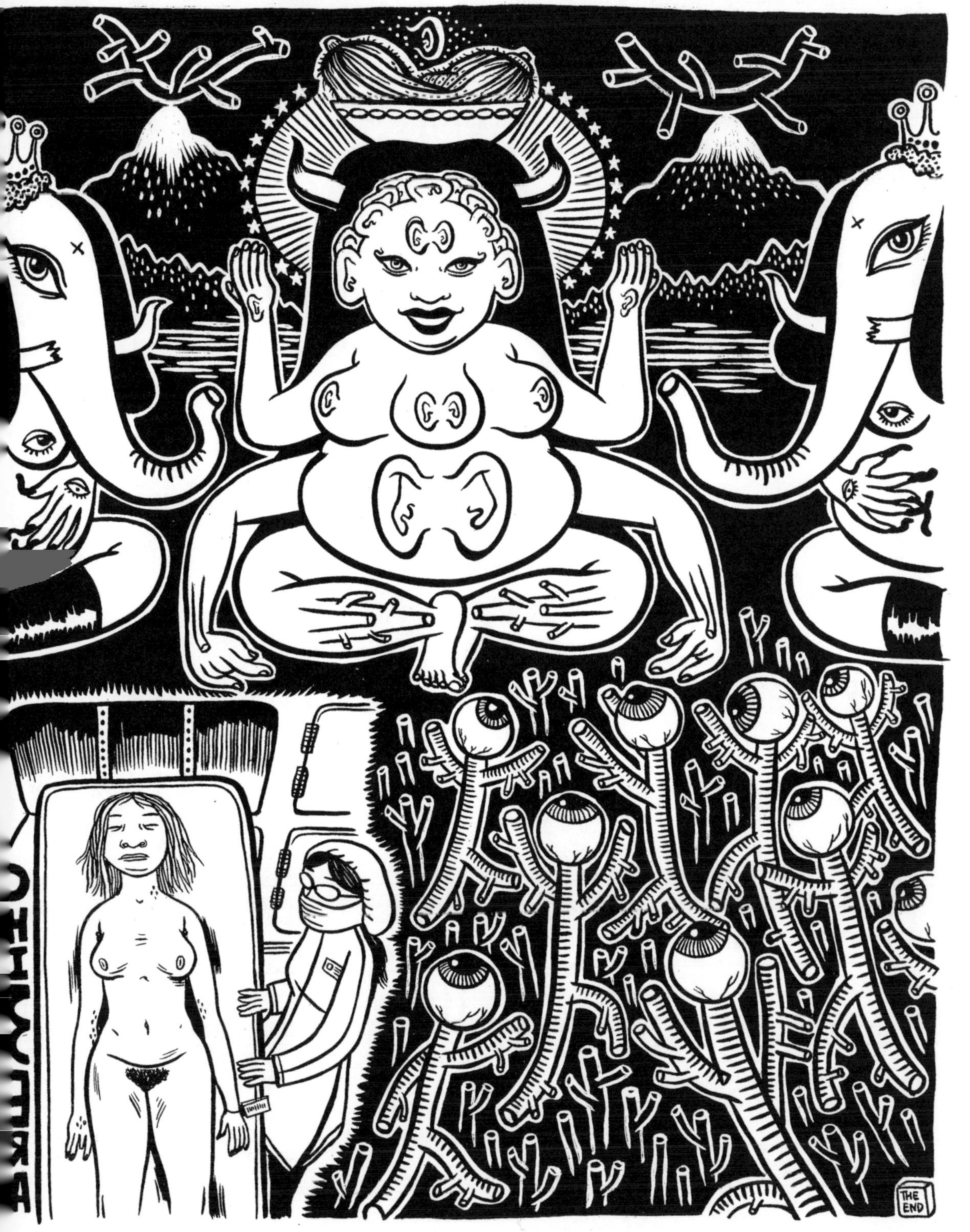
THE END

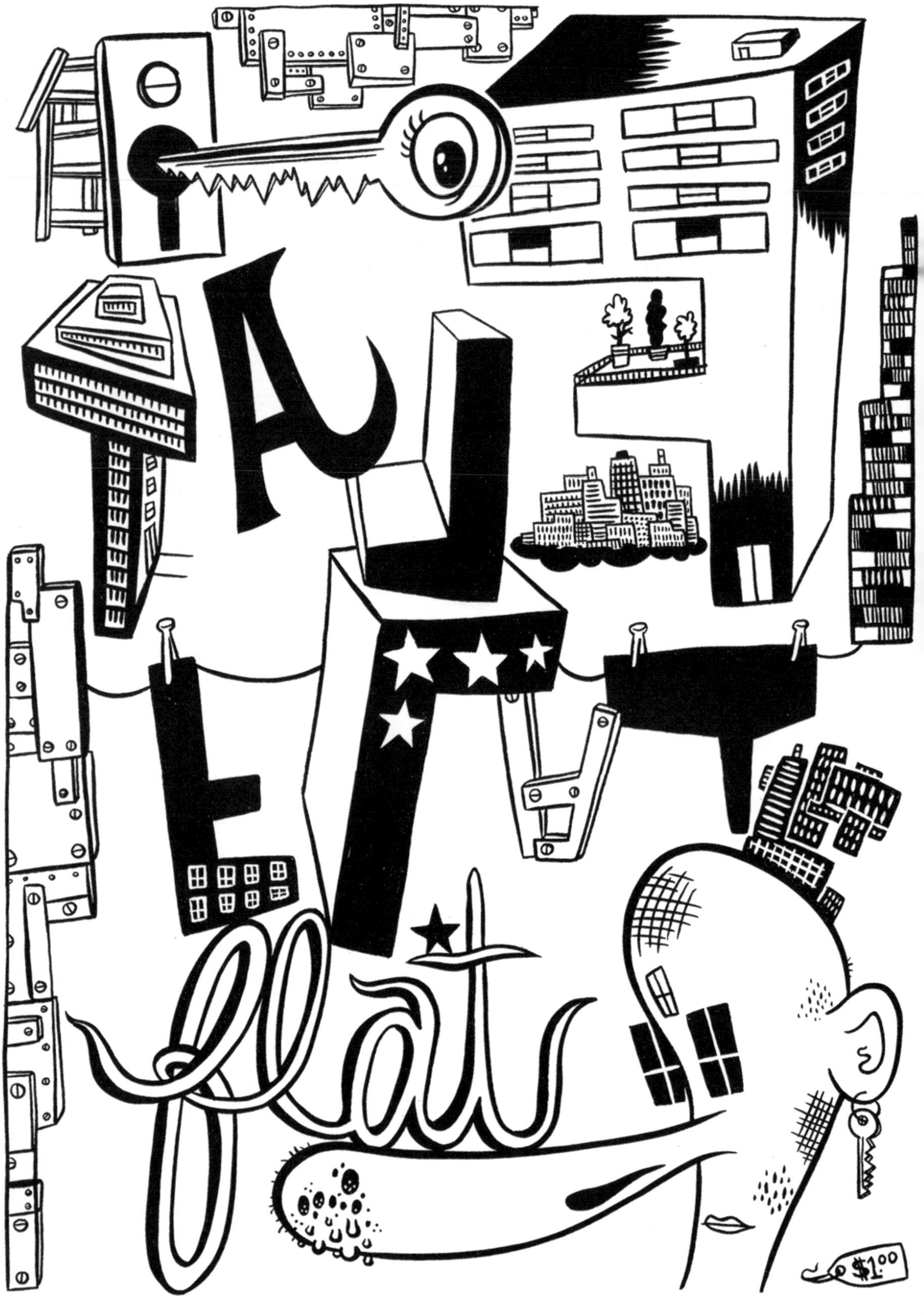
flat
$1.00

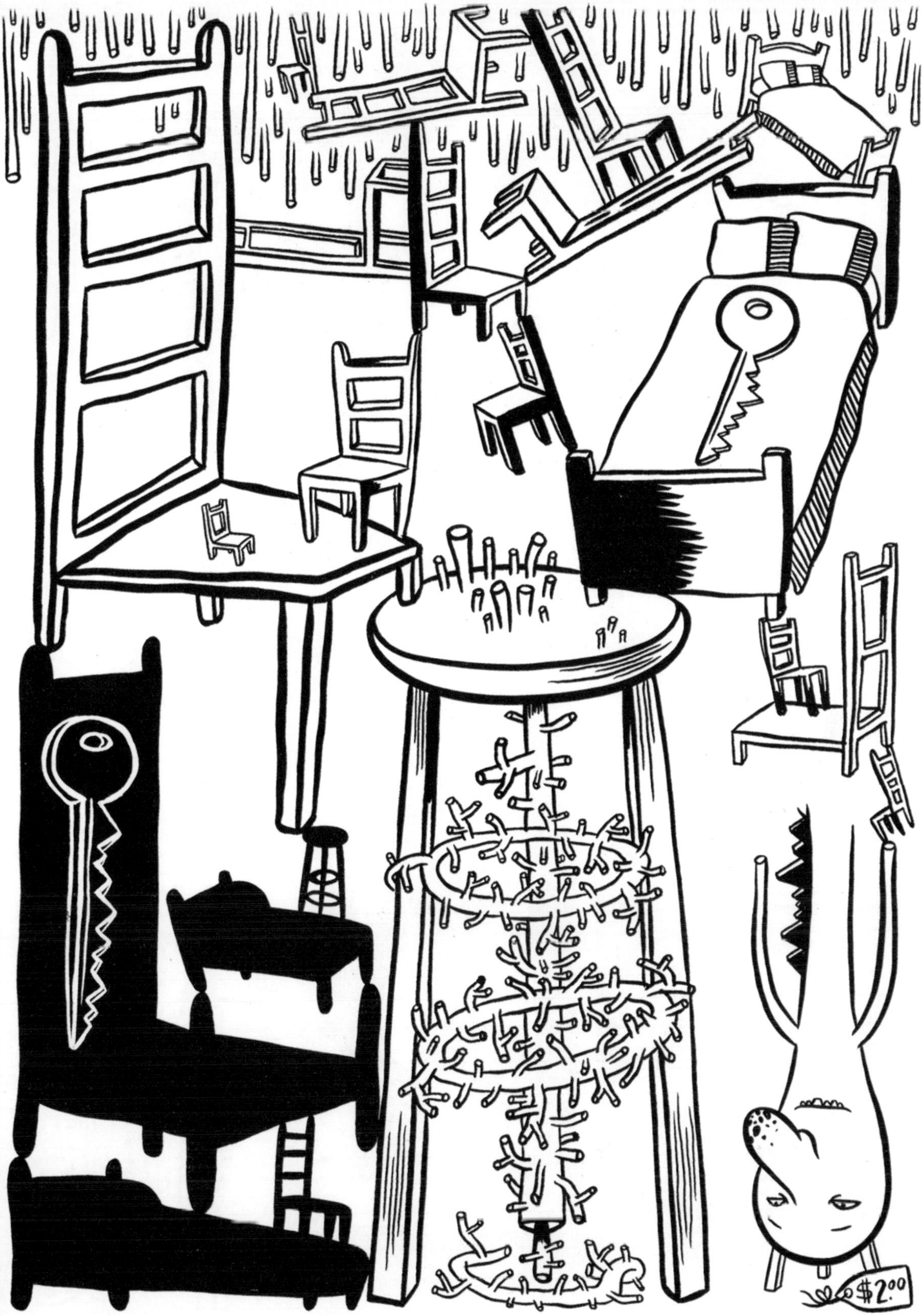
$2.00

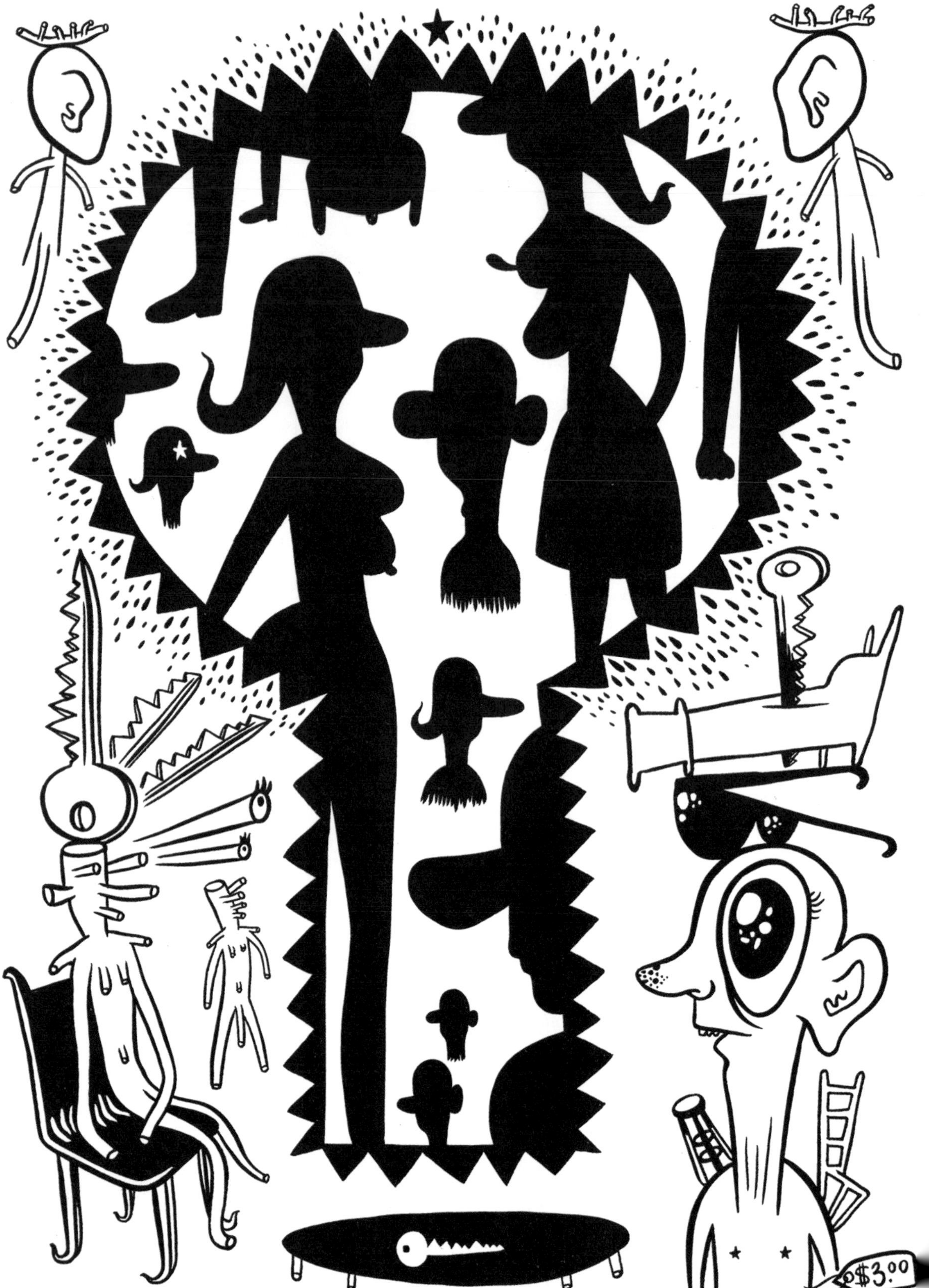
$3.00

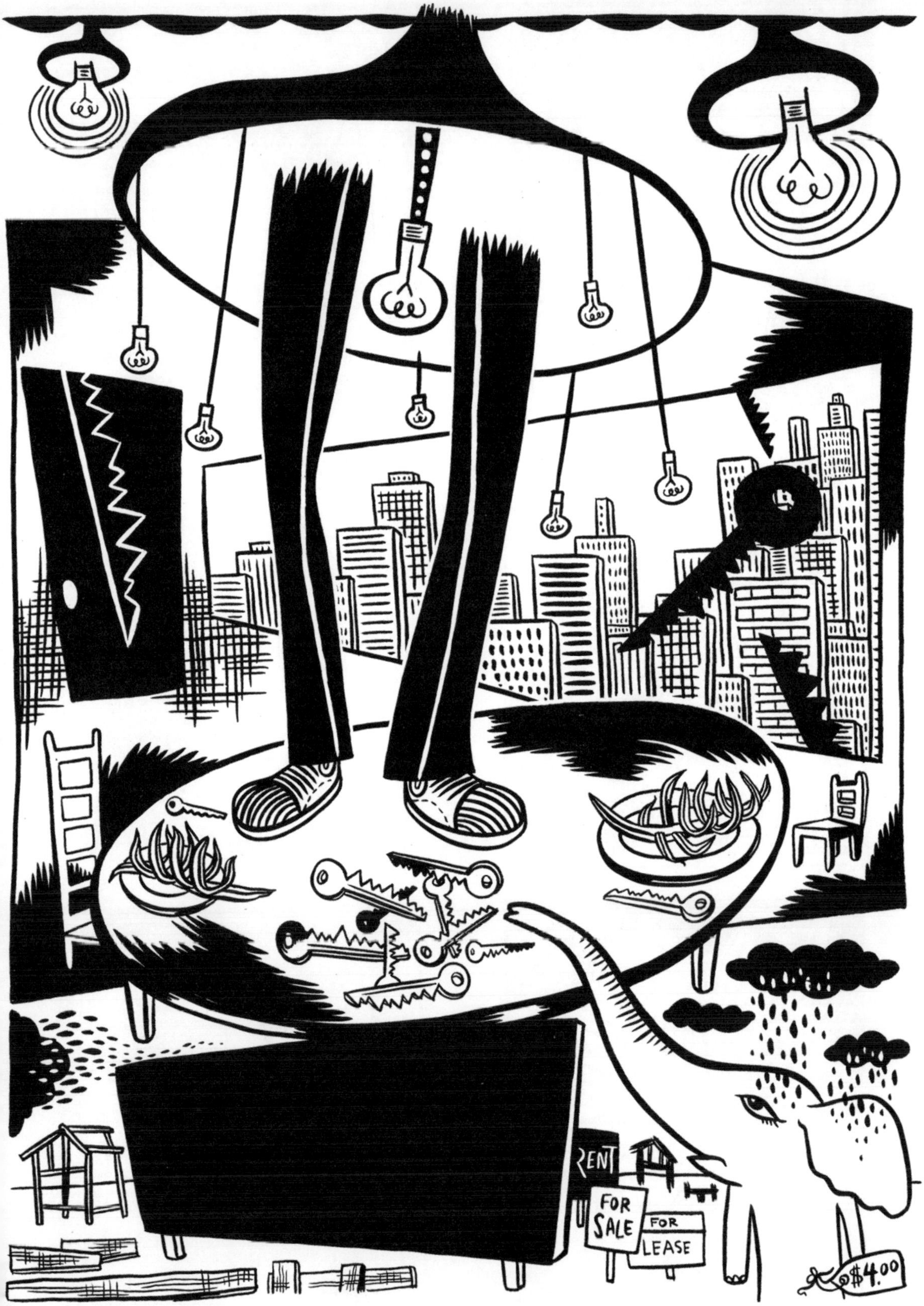
RENT
FOR SALE
FOR LEASE
$4.00

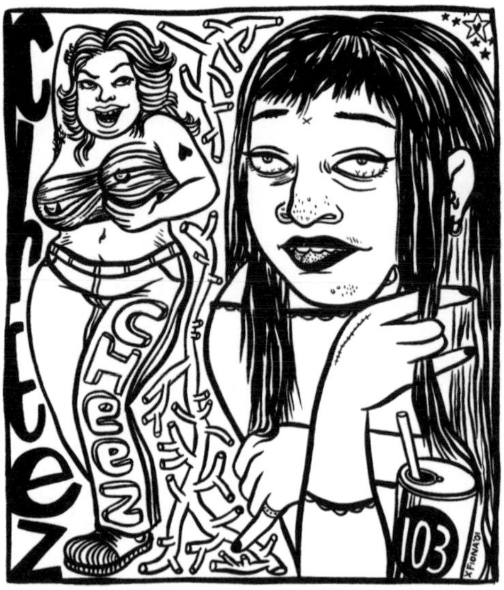
Cheez
CHEEZ
103

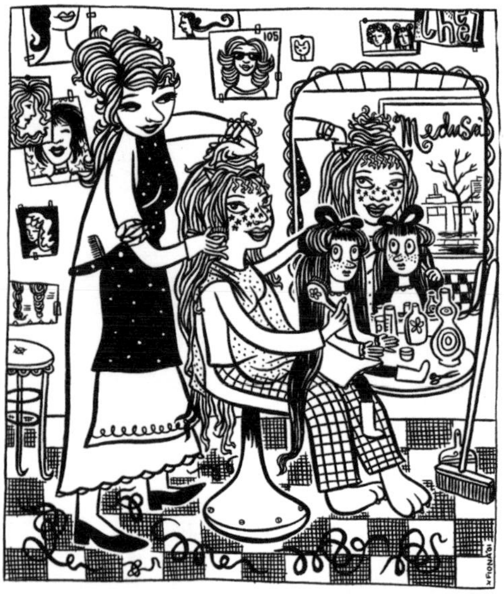
Medusa
105

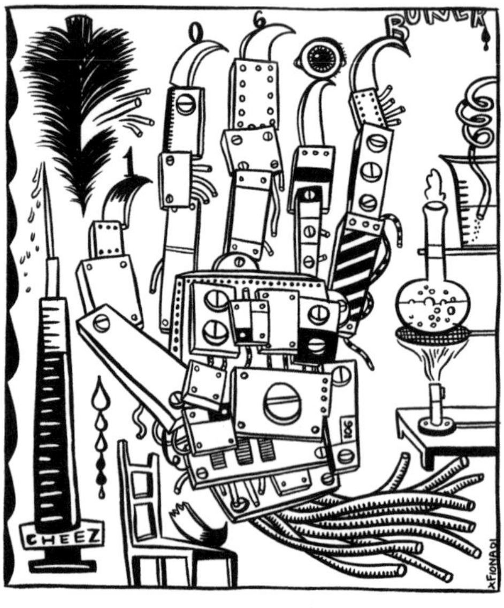
CHEEZ
106

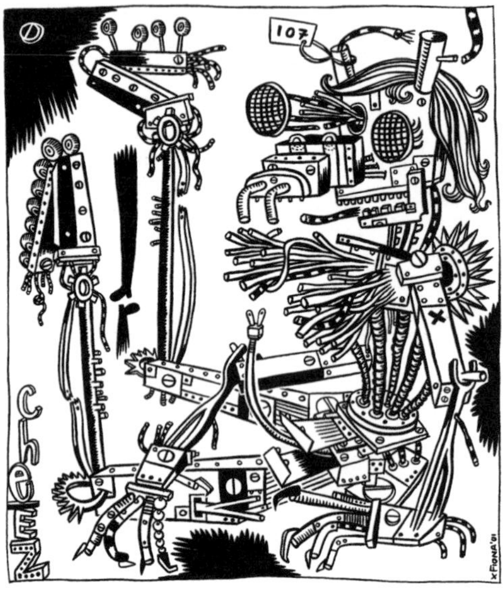
107
Cheez

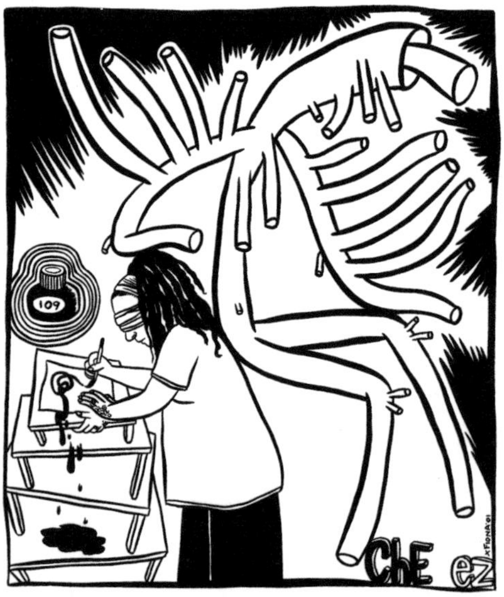
109
ChE ez

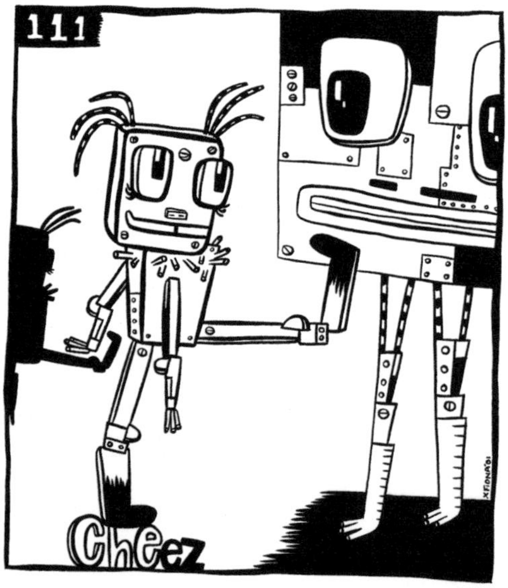
111
Cheez

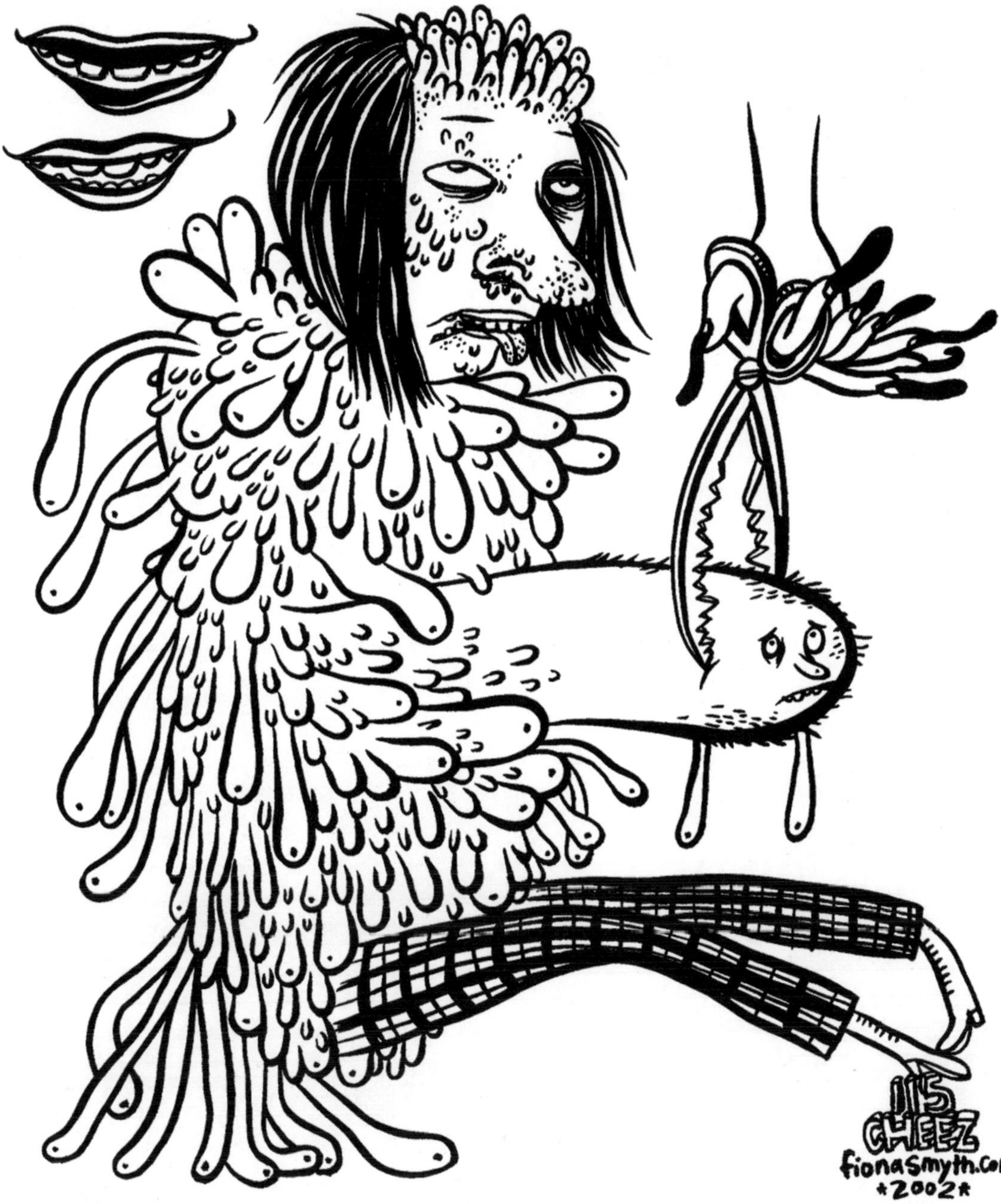
ITS CHEEZ
fionasmyth.com
2002

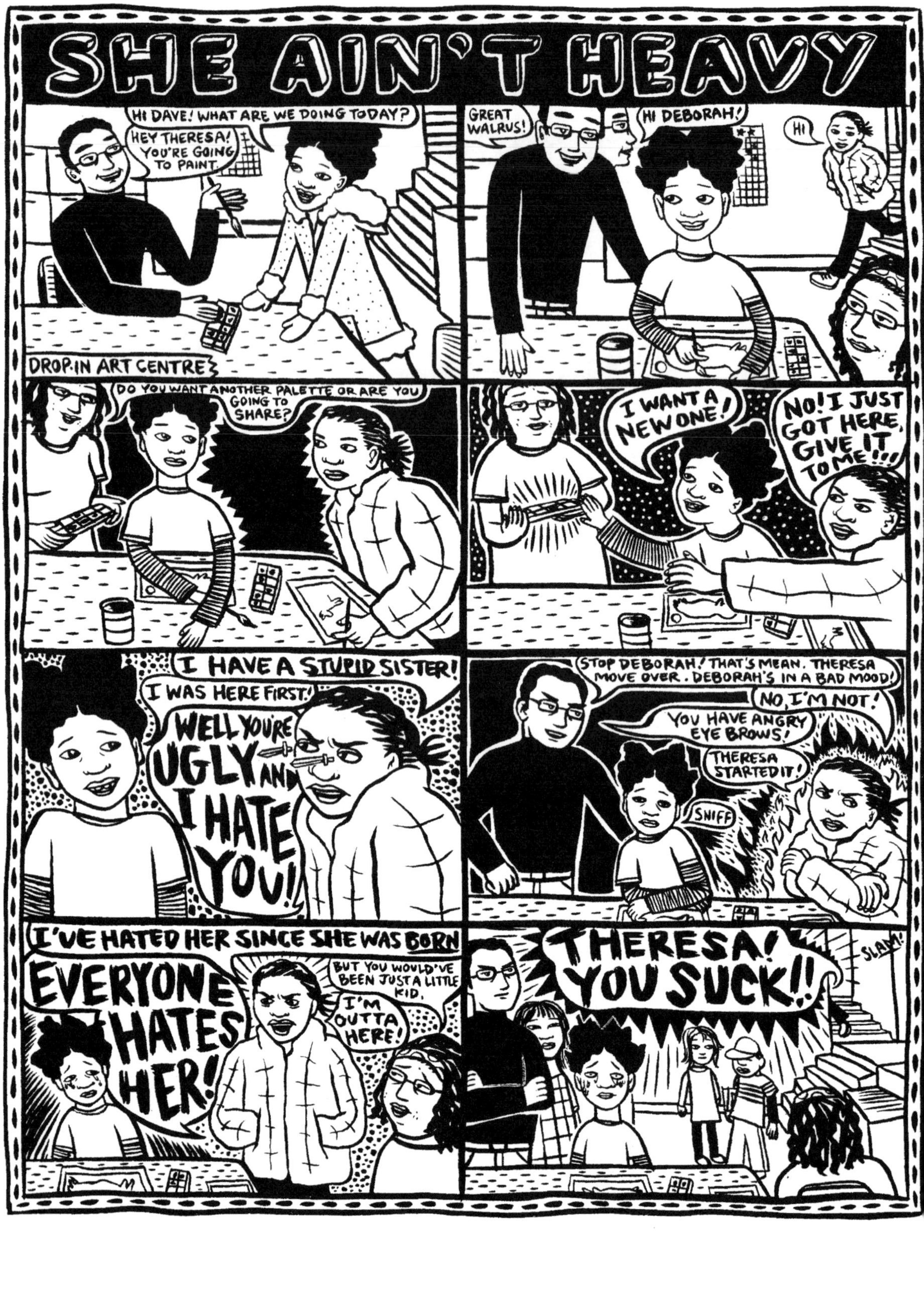
SHE AIN'T HEAVY
HI DAVE! WHAT ARE WE DOING TODAY?
HEY THERESA! YOU'RE GOING TO PAINT.
DROP-IN ART CENTRE
GREAT WALRUS!
HI DEBORAH!
HI
DO YOU WANT ANOTHER PALETTE OR ARE YOU GOING TO SHARE?
I WANT A NEW ONE!
NO! I JUST GOT HERE, GIVE IT TO ME!!!
I HAVE A STUPID SISTER!
I WAS HERE FIRST!
WELL YOU'RE UGLY AND I HATE YOU!
STOP DEBORAH! THAT'S MEAN. THERESA MOVE OVER. DEBORAH'S IN A BAD MOOD!
NO, I'M NOT!
YOU HAVE ANGRY EYE BROWS!
THERESA STARTED IT!
SNIFF
I'VE HATED HER SINCE SHE WAS BORN
EVERYONE HATES HER!
BUT YOU WOULD'VE BEEN JUST A LITTLE KID.
I'M OUTTA HERE!
THERESA! YOU SUCK!!
SLAM!

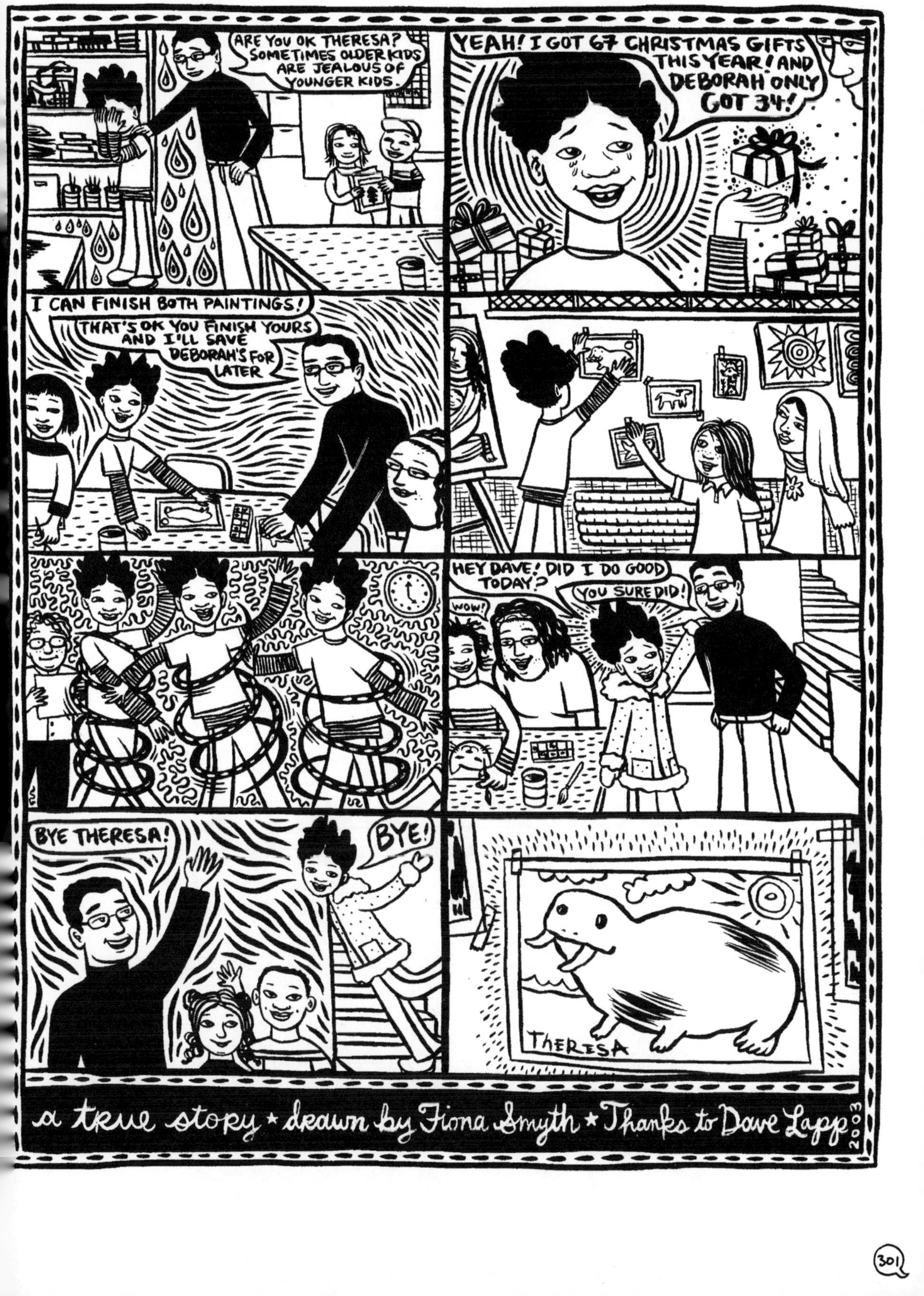

ARE YOU OK THERESA? SOMETIMES OLDER KIDS ARE JEALOUS OF YOUNGER KIDS.
YEAH! I GOT 67 CHRISTMAS GIFTS THIS YEAR! AND DEBORAH ONLY GOT 34!
I CAN FINISH BOTH PAINTINGS!
THAT'S OK YOU FINISH YOURS AND I'LL SAVE DEBORAH'S FOR LATER
HEY DAVE! DID I DO GOOD TODAY?
YOU SURE DID!
WOW!
BYE THERESA!
BYE!
THERESA
a true story ★ drawn by Fiona Smyth ★ Thanks to Dave Lapp
2003

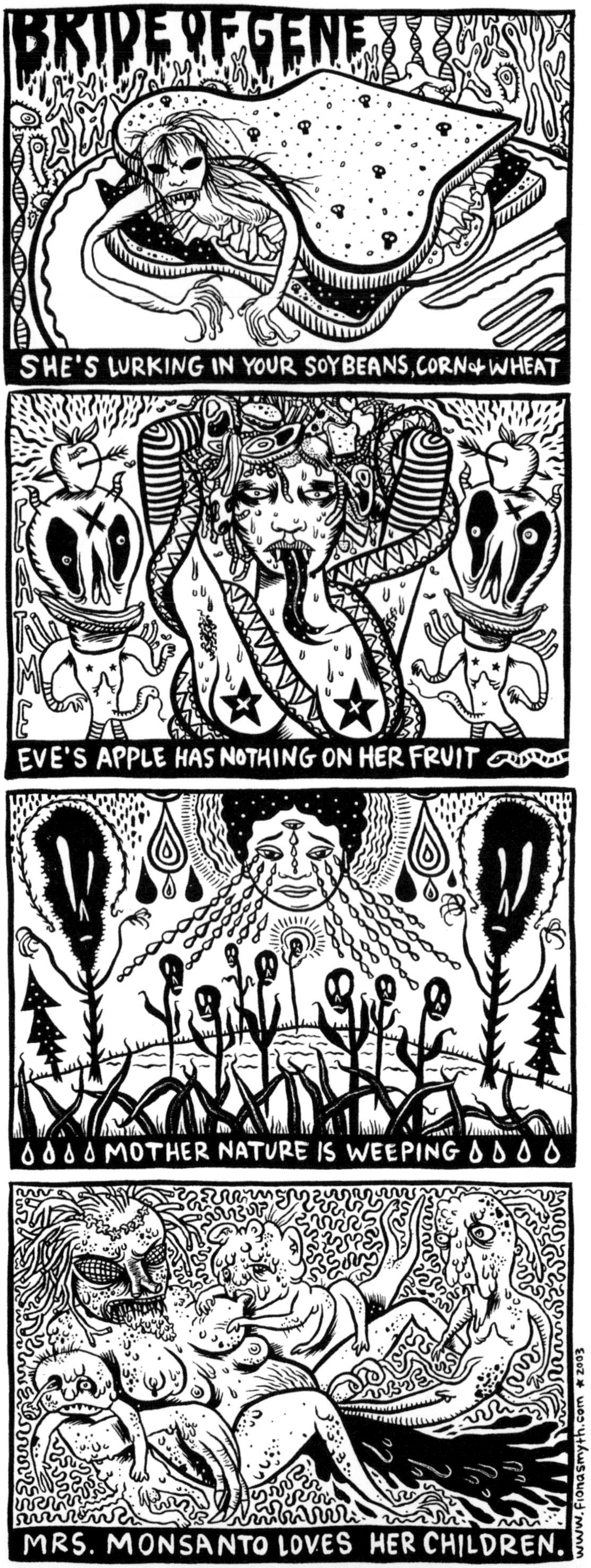
BRIDE OF GENE
SHE'S LURKING IN YOUR SOYBEANS, CORN & WHEAT
EAT ME
EVE'S APPLE HAS NOTHING ON HER FRUIT
MOTHER NATURE IS WEEPING
MRS. MONSANTO LOVES HER CHILDREN.
www.fionasmyth.com * 2003

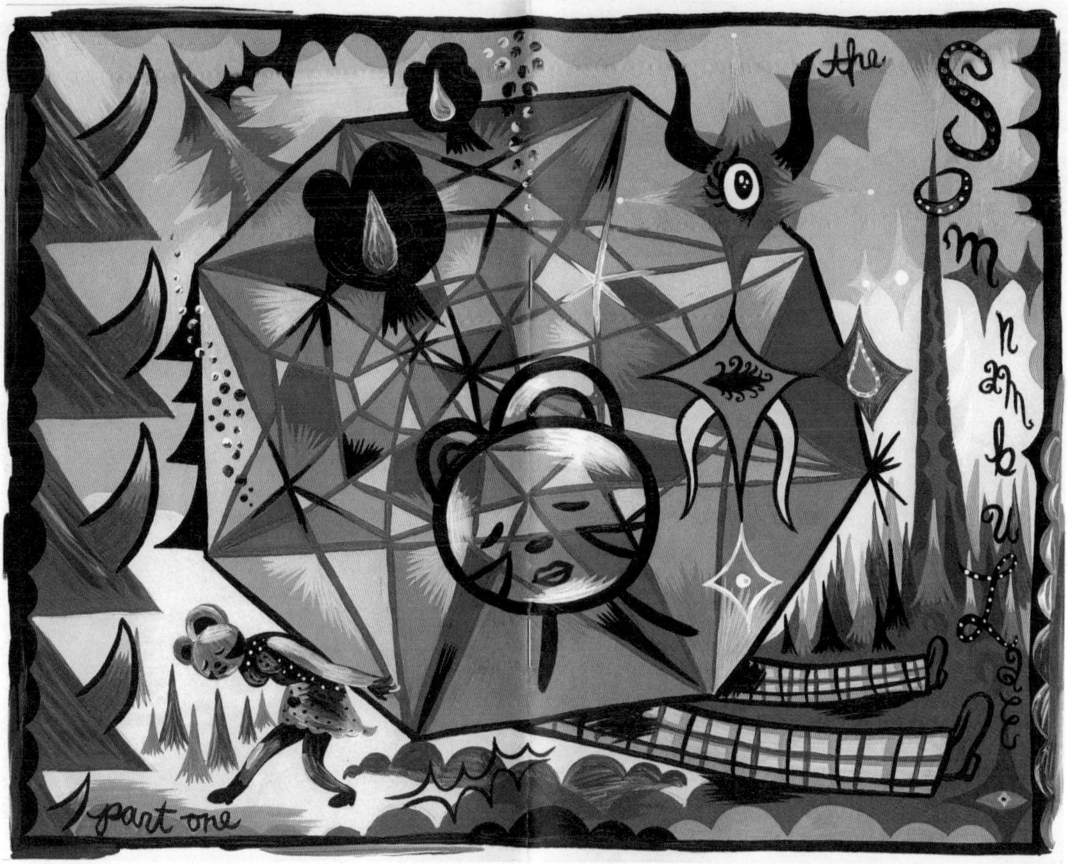
the Somnambule
part one

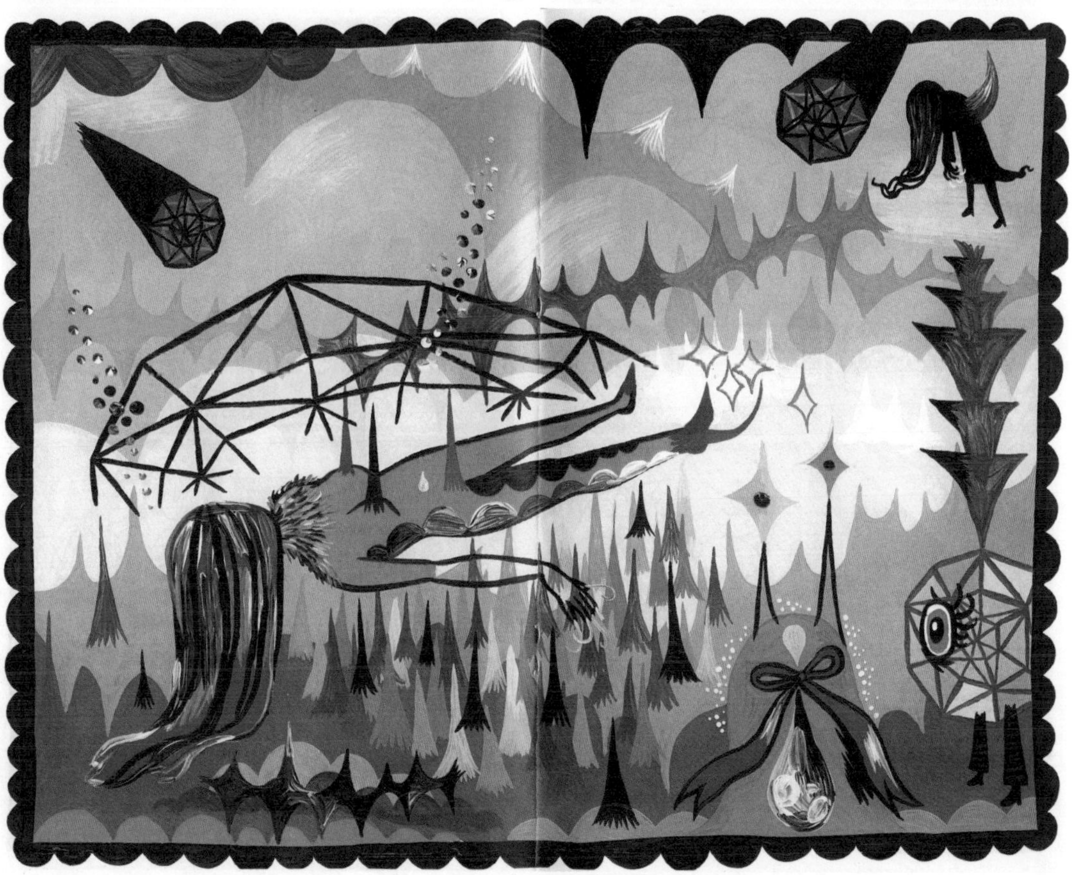

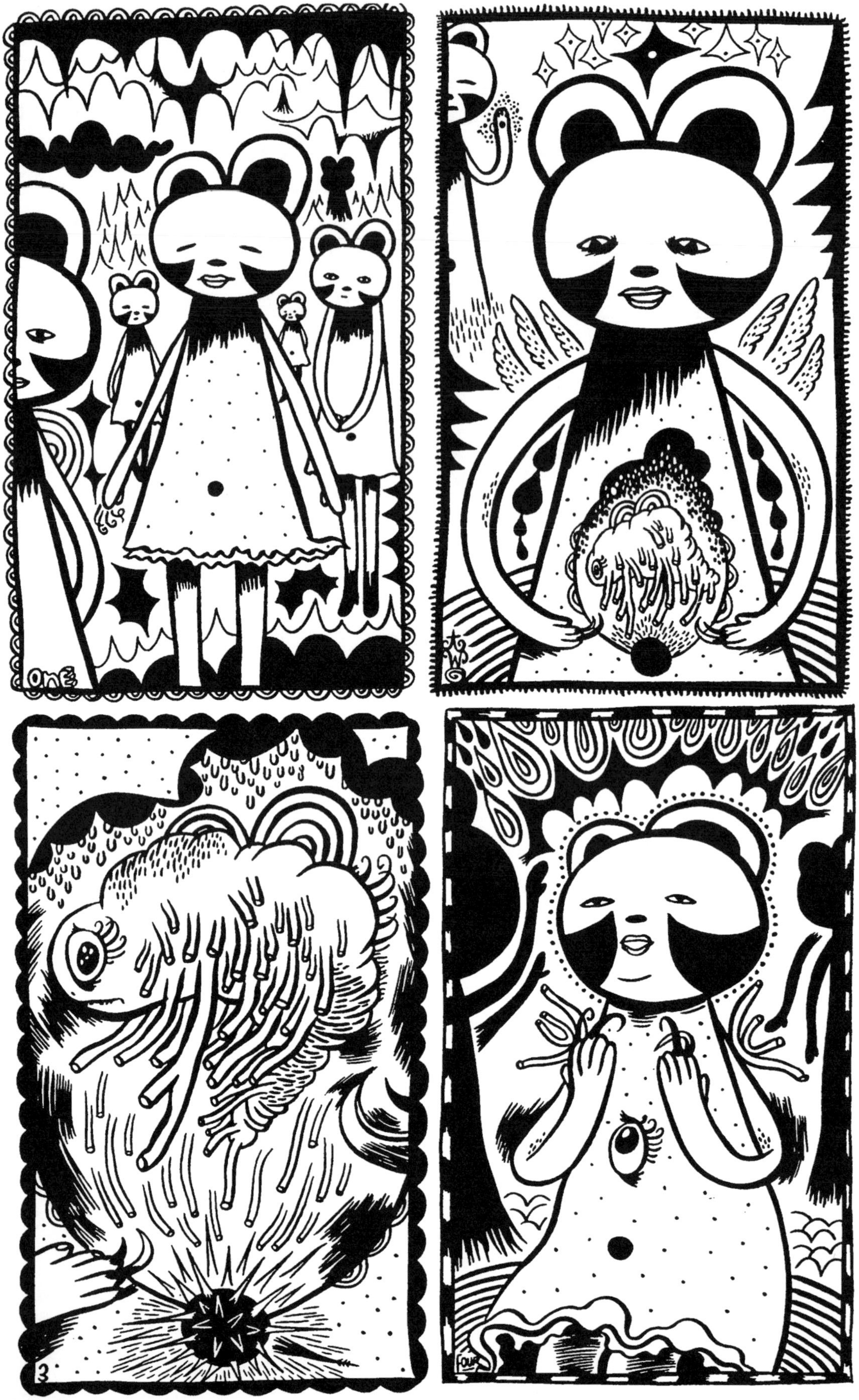
One
3

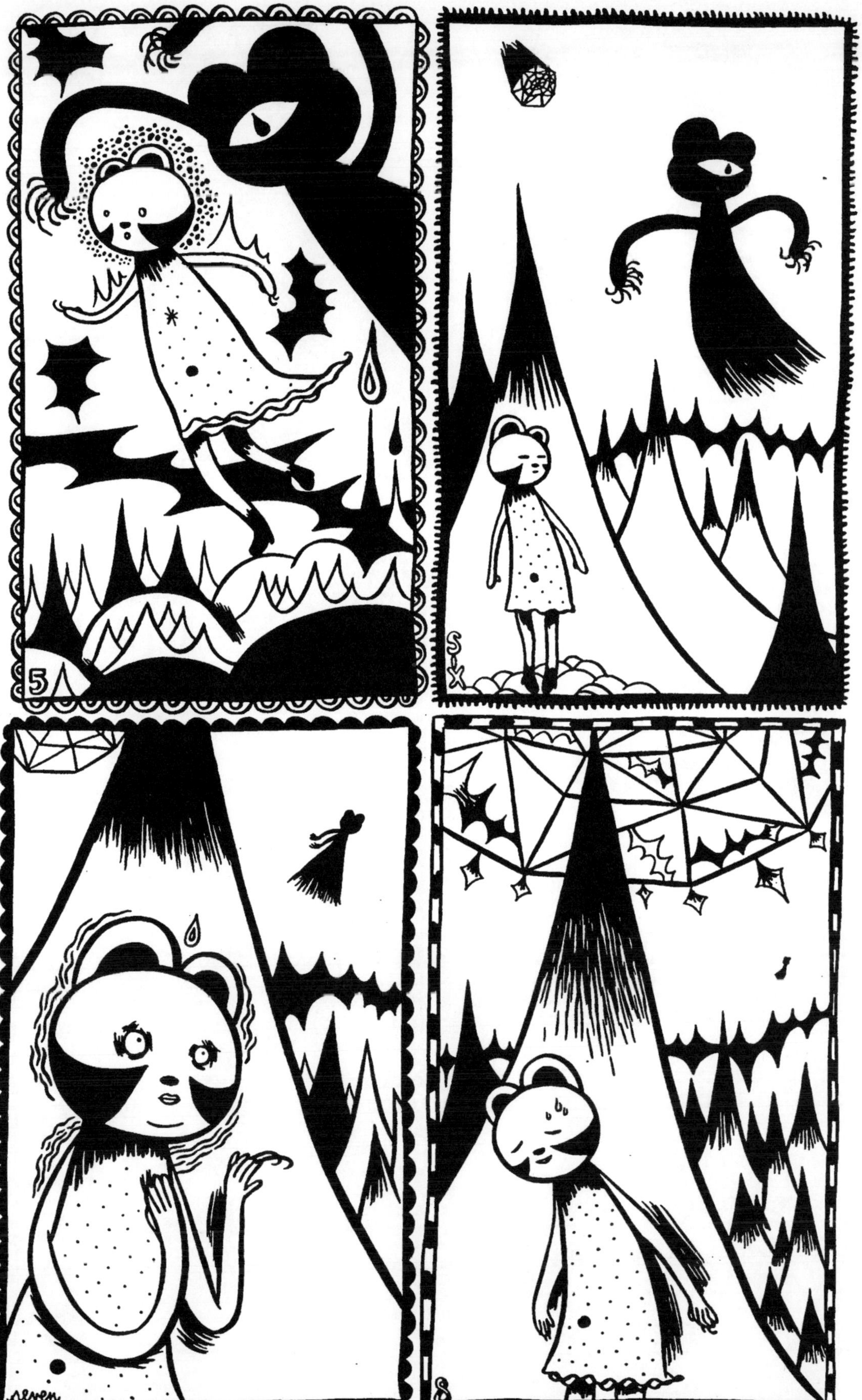
5
SIX
seven
8

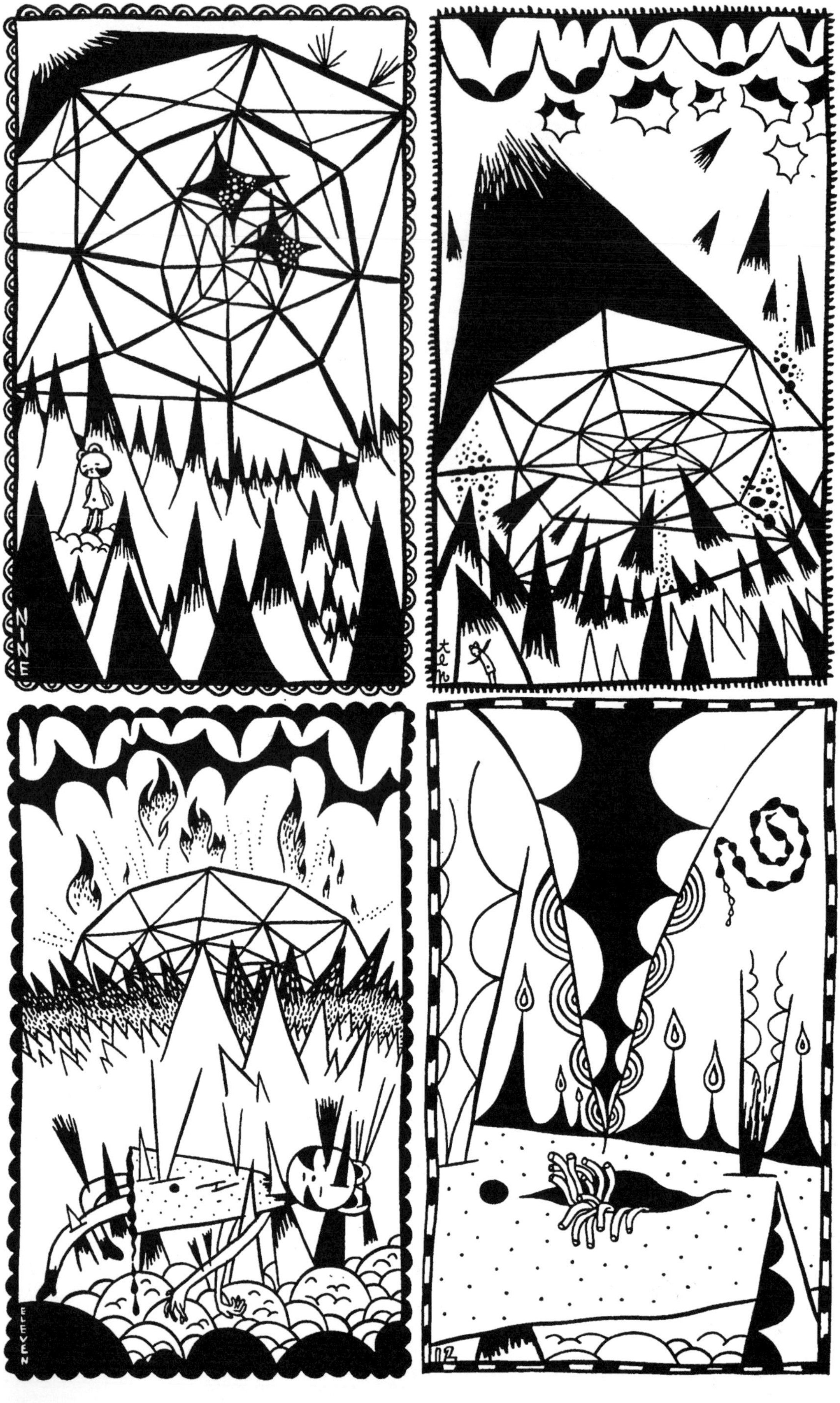
NINE
ten
ELEVEN
12

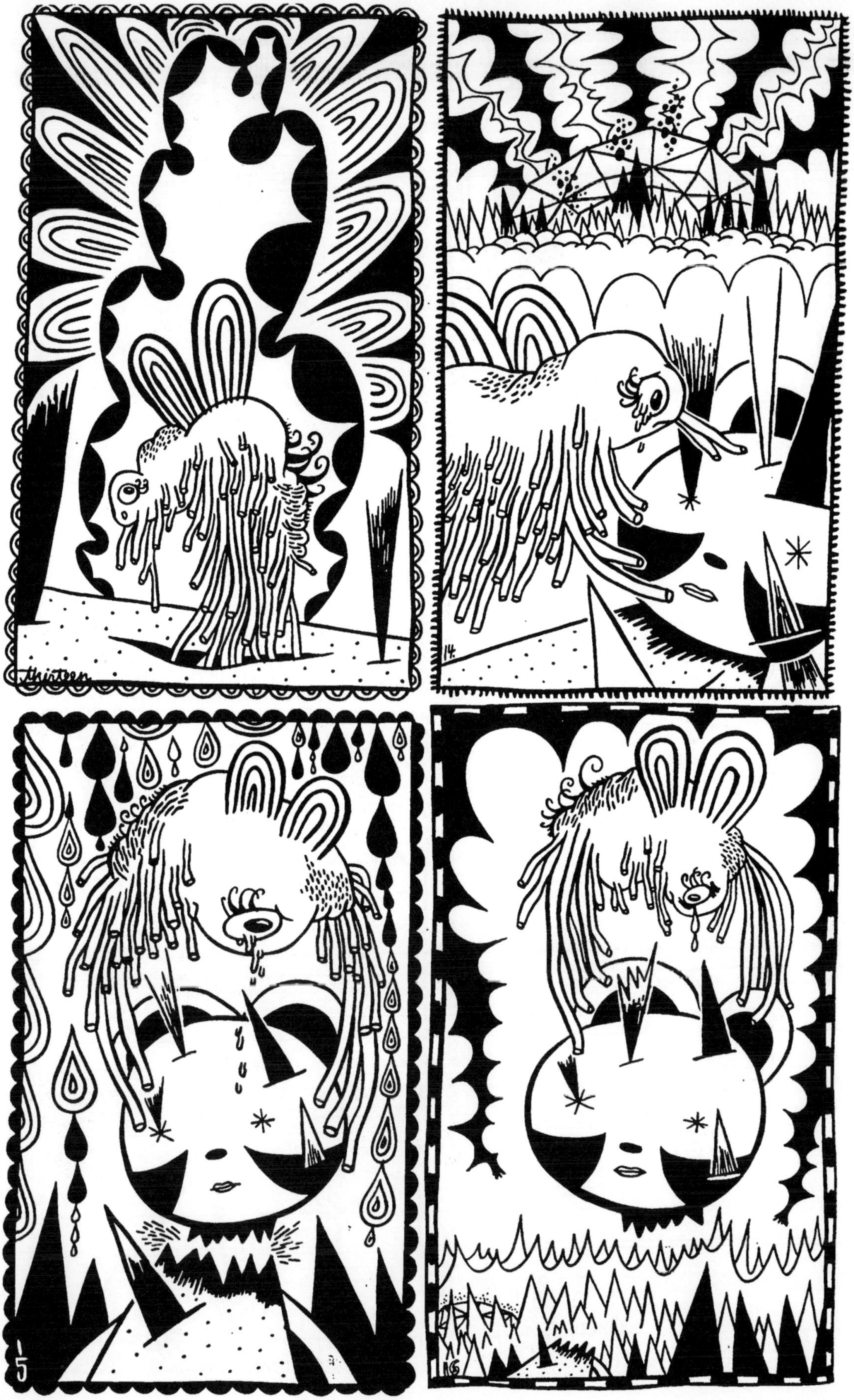
thirteen
14.
15
16

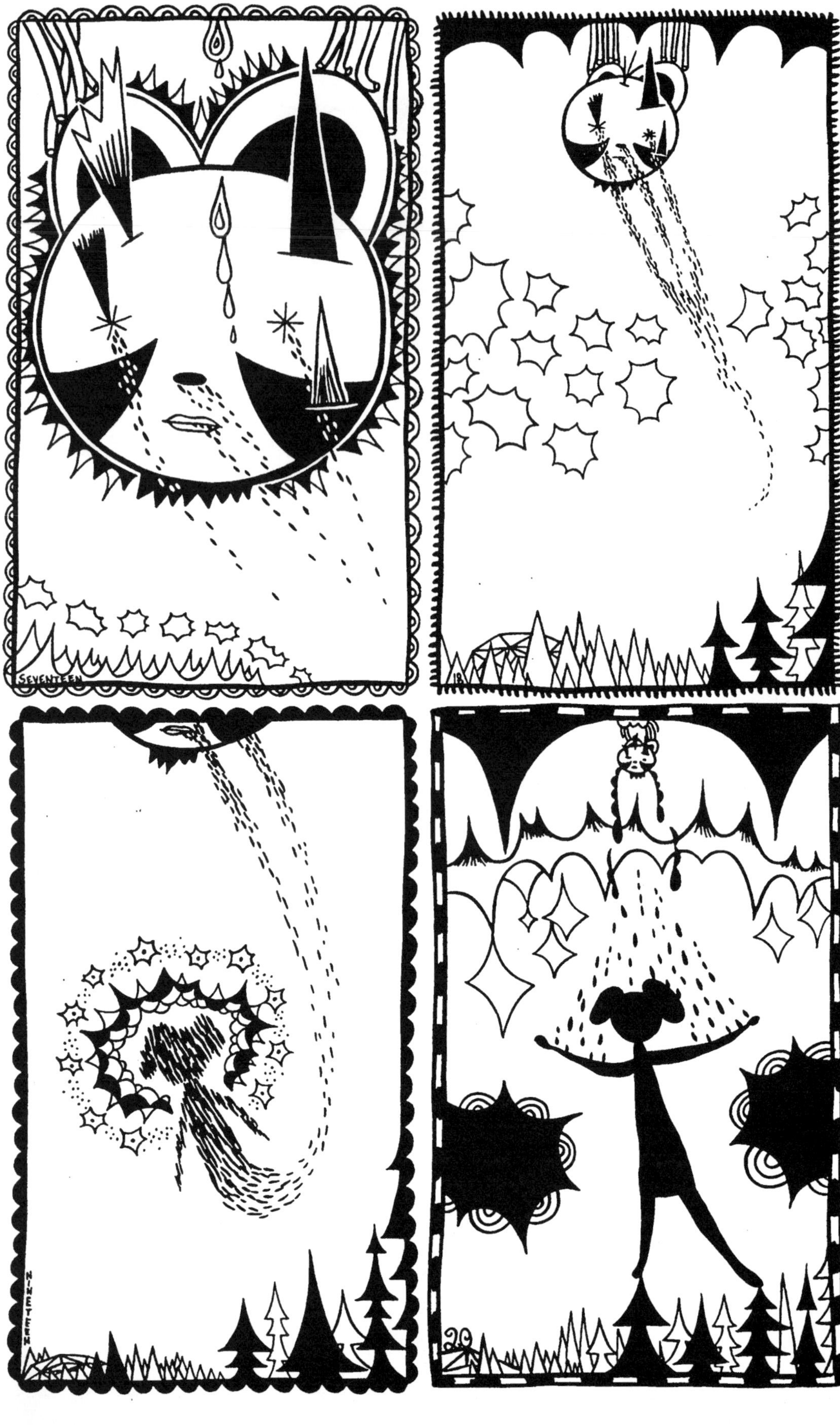
SEVENTEEN
18
NINETEEN
20

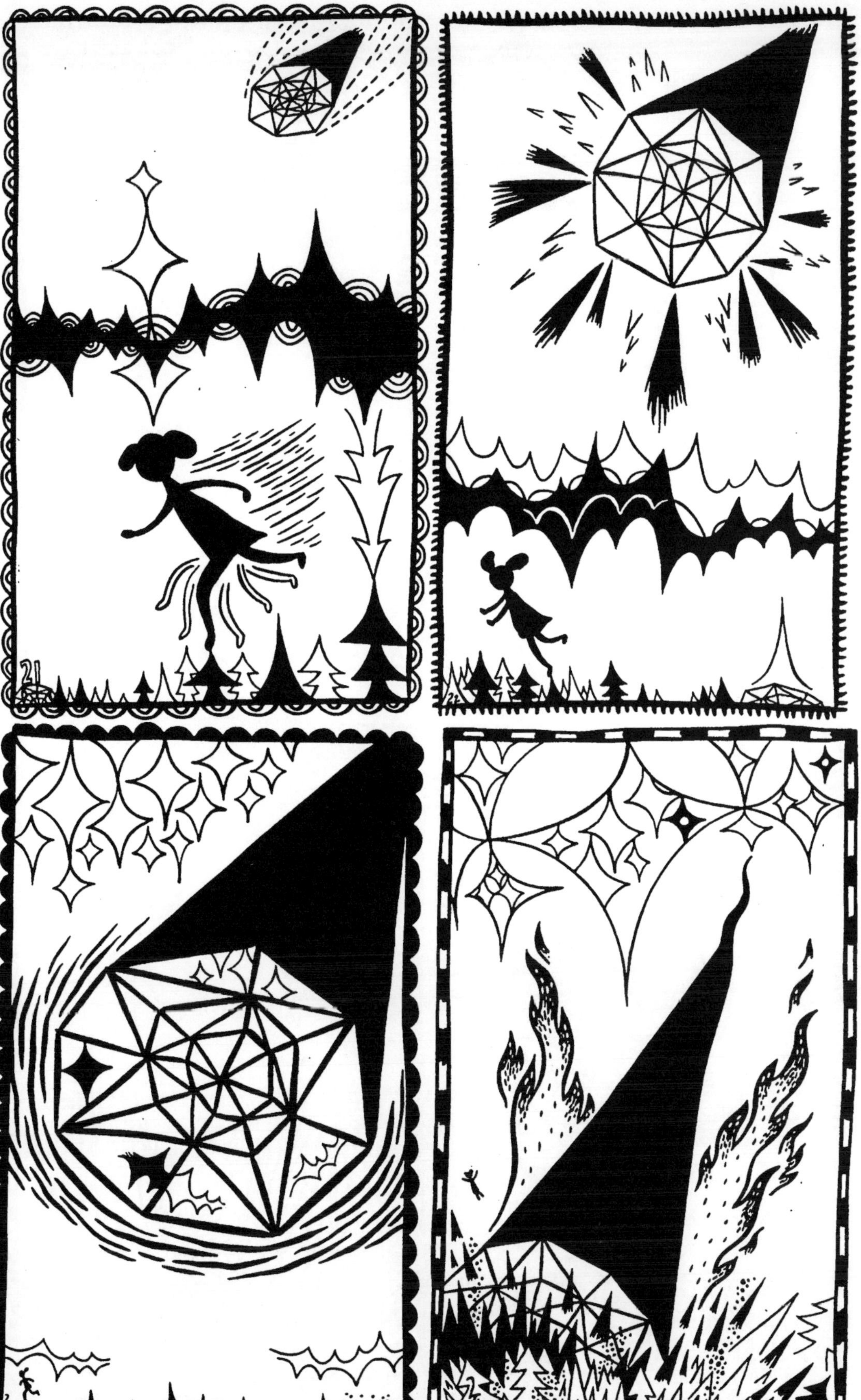
21
24

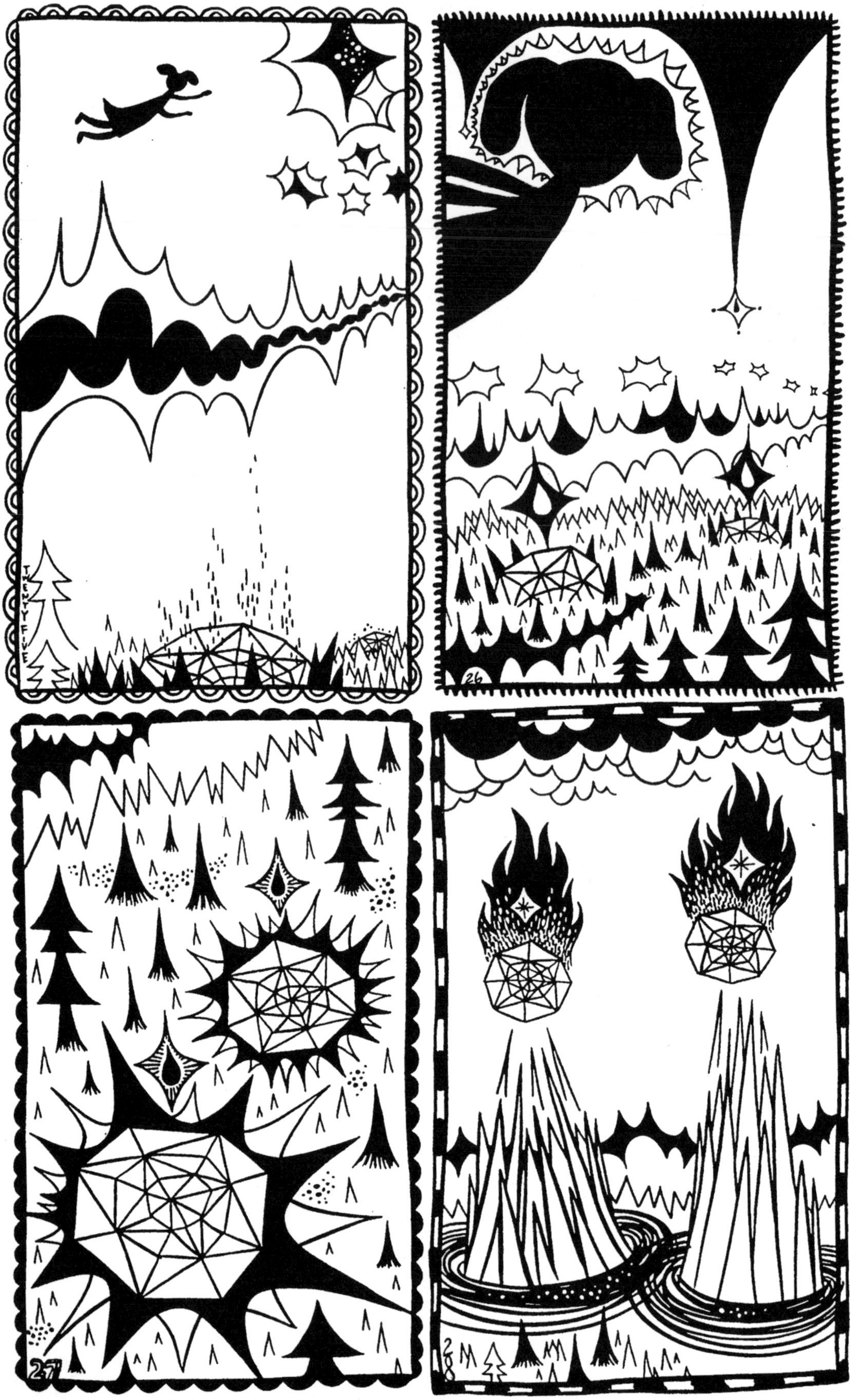
TWENTY FIVE
26
27
28

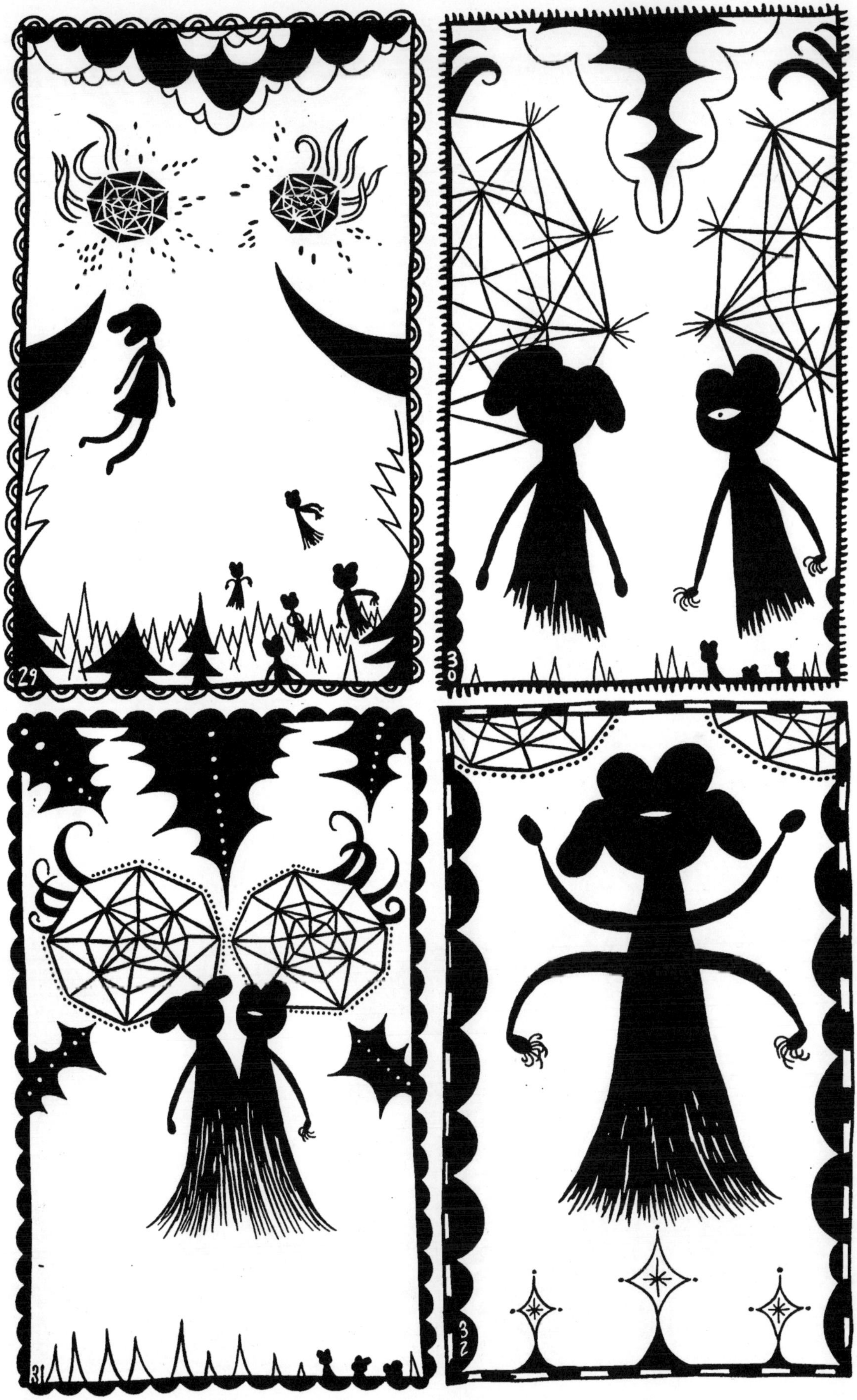
29
30
31
32

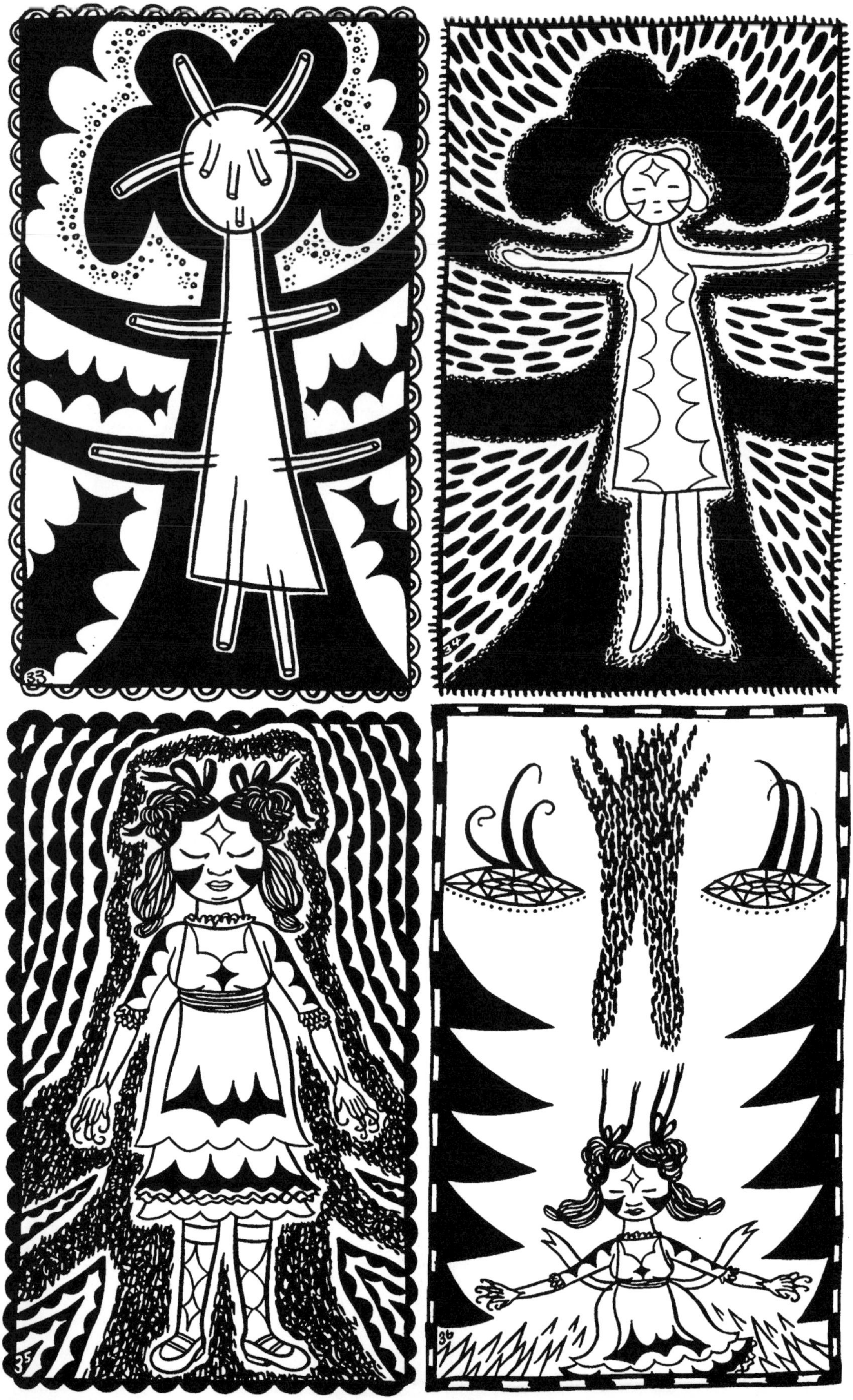
33
34
35
36

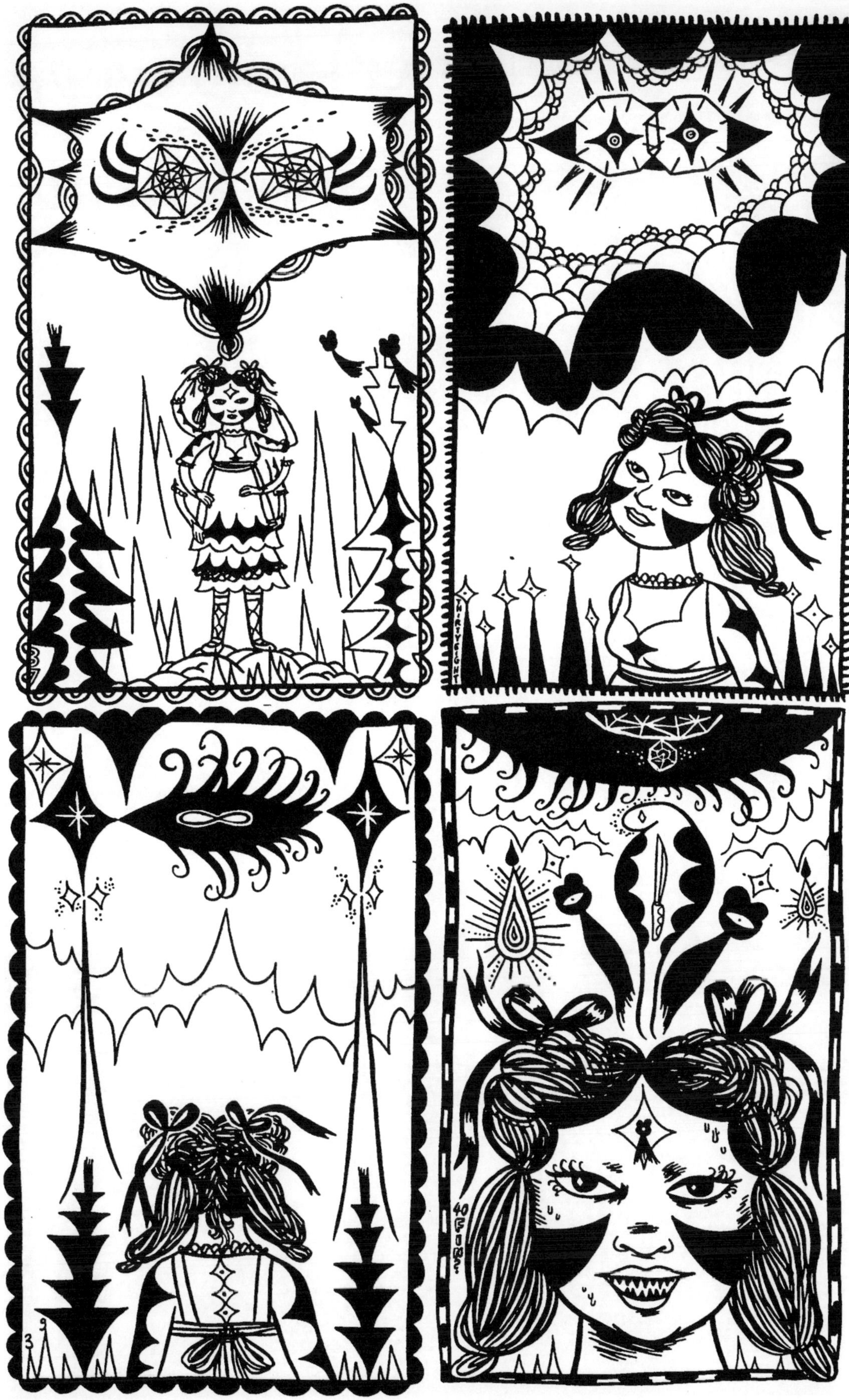

37
THIRTYEIGHT
39
40 FIN?

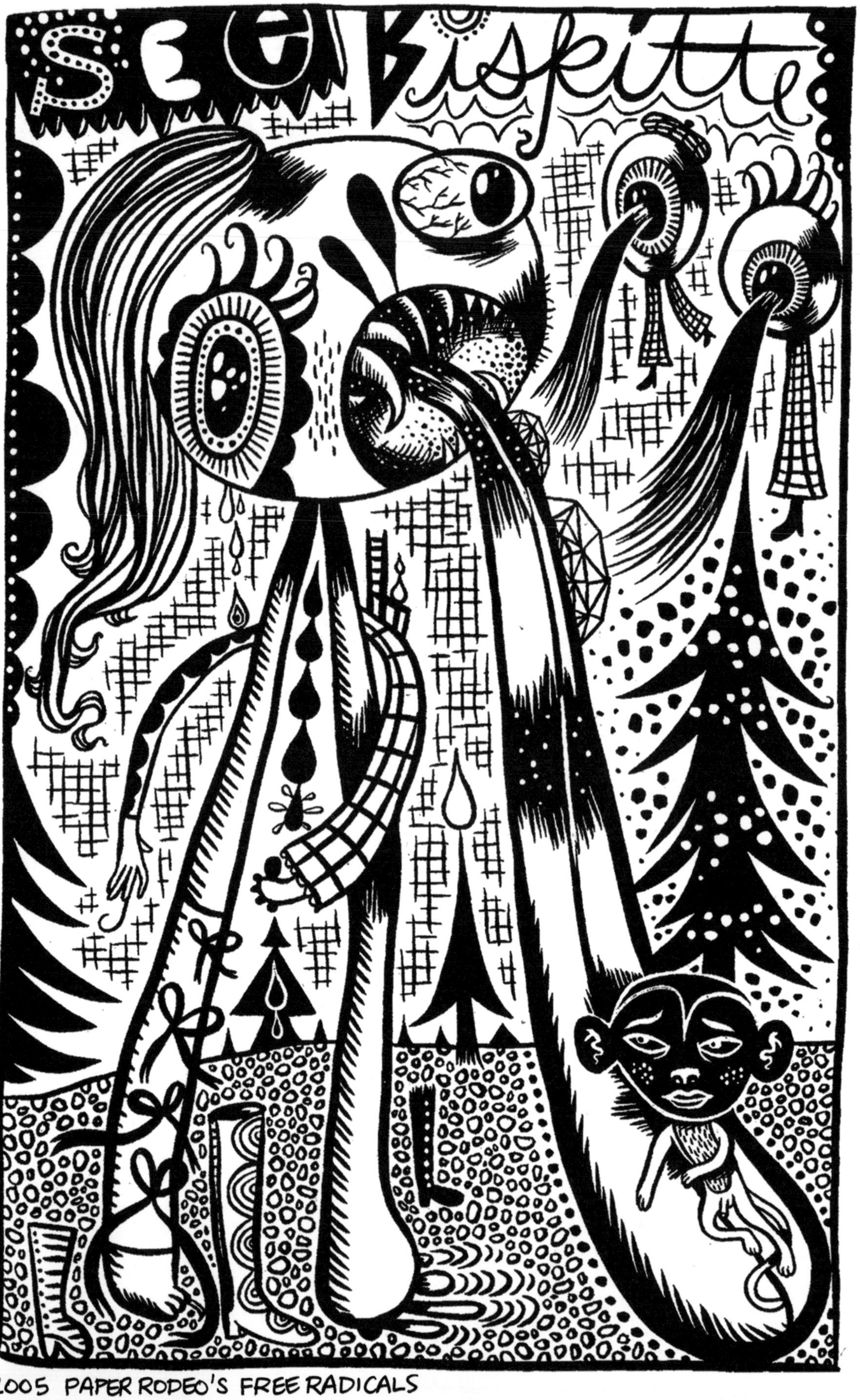
SEE BISKITTE

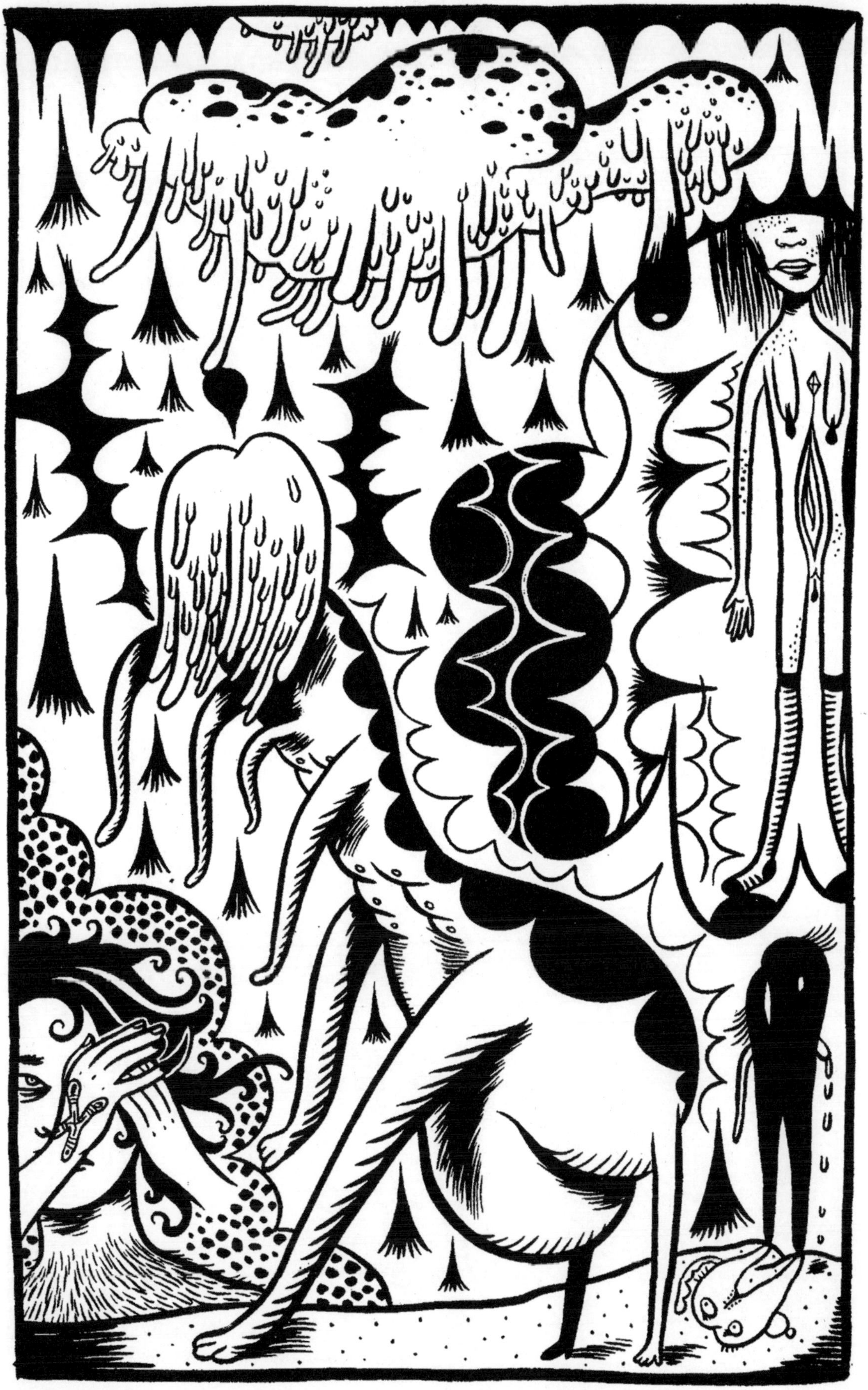

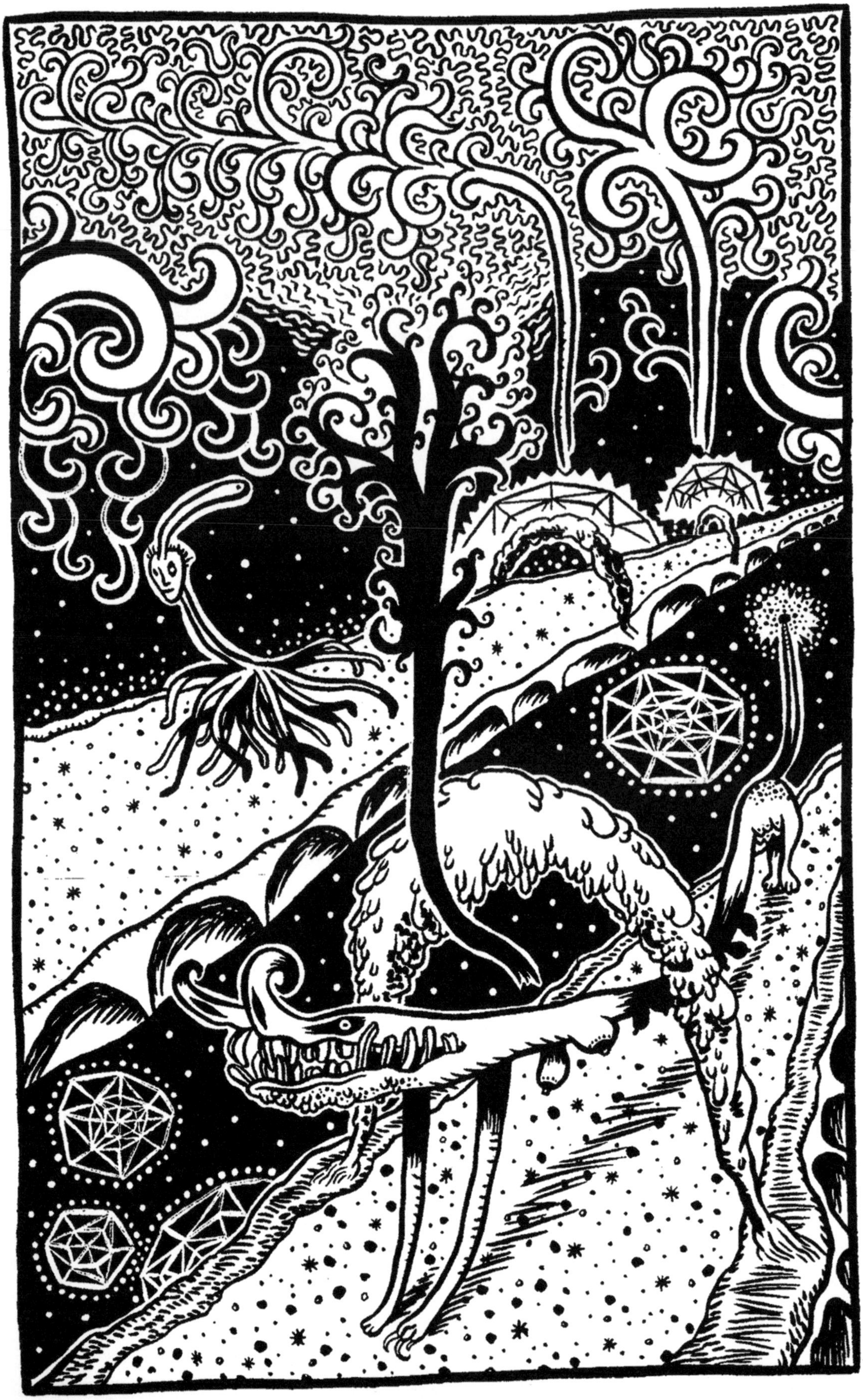

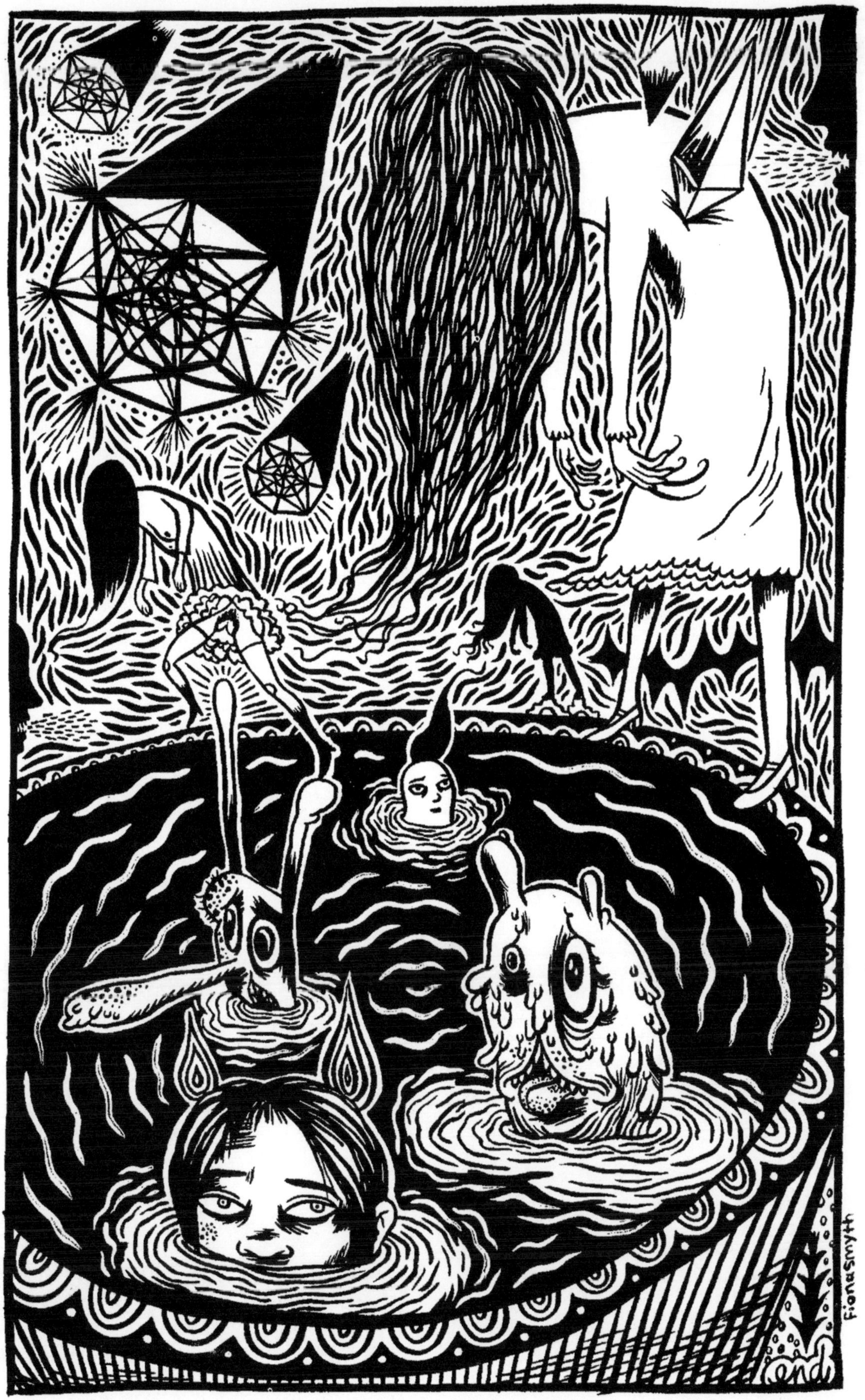
FionaSmyth
end

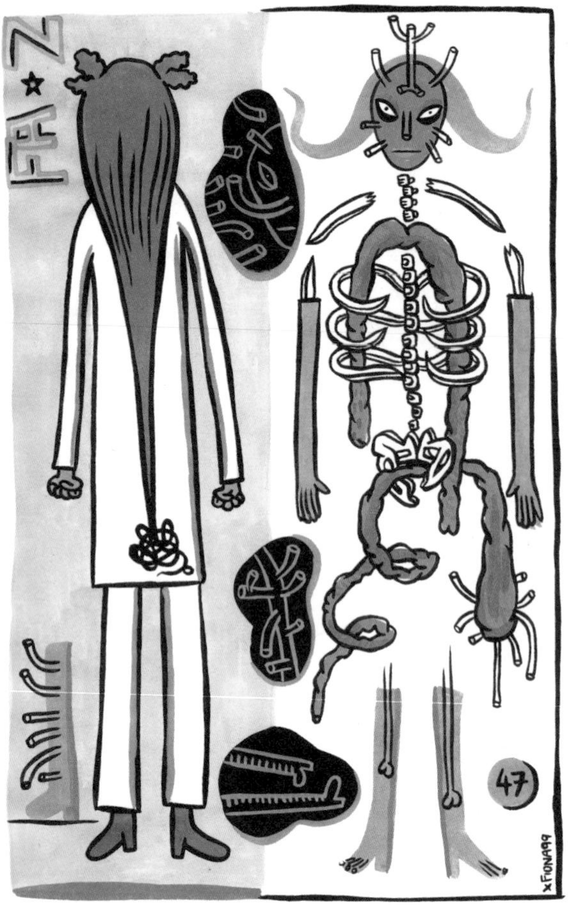
FA☆Z
47
xFIONA99

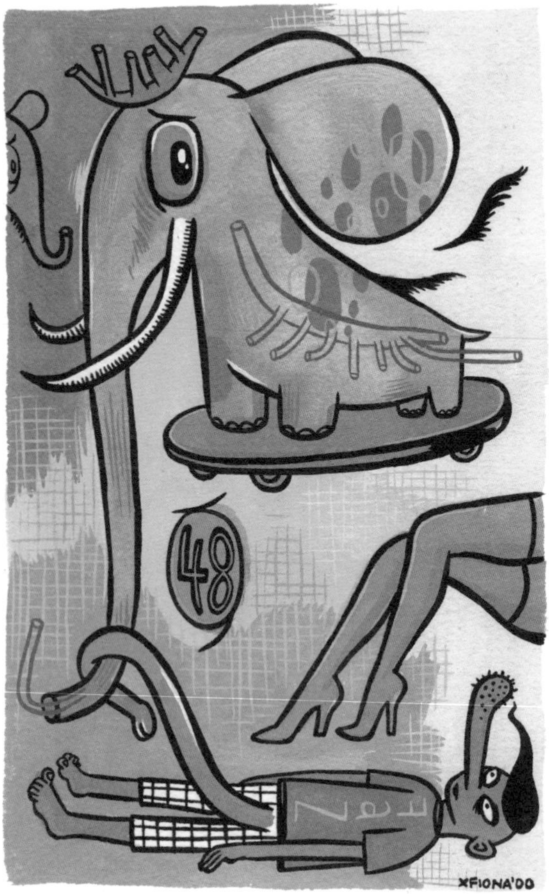
48
xFIONA'00

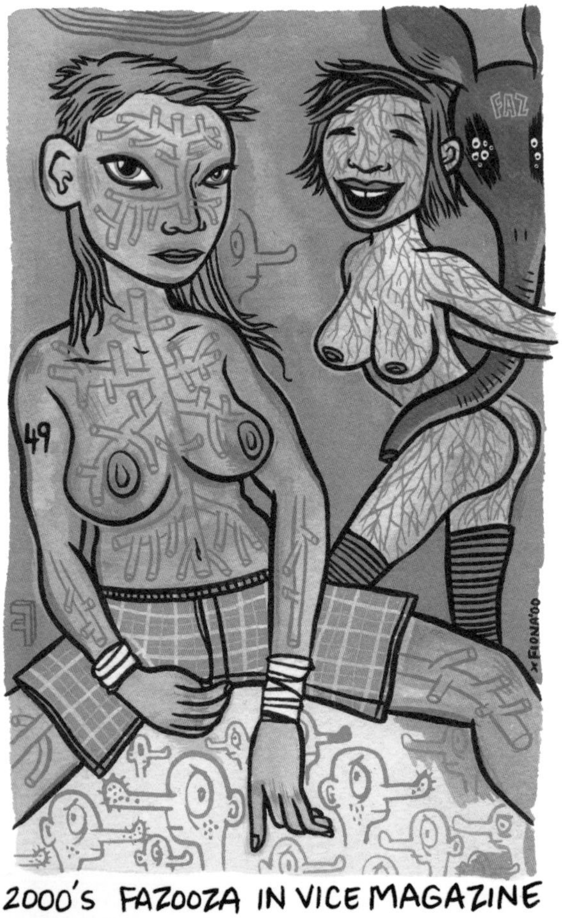
FAZ
49
xFIONA'00

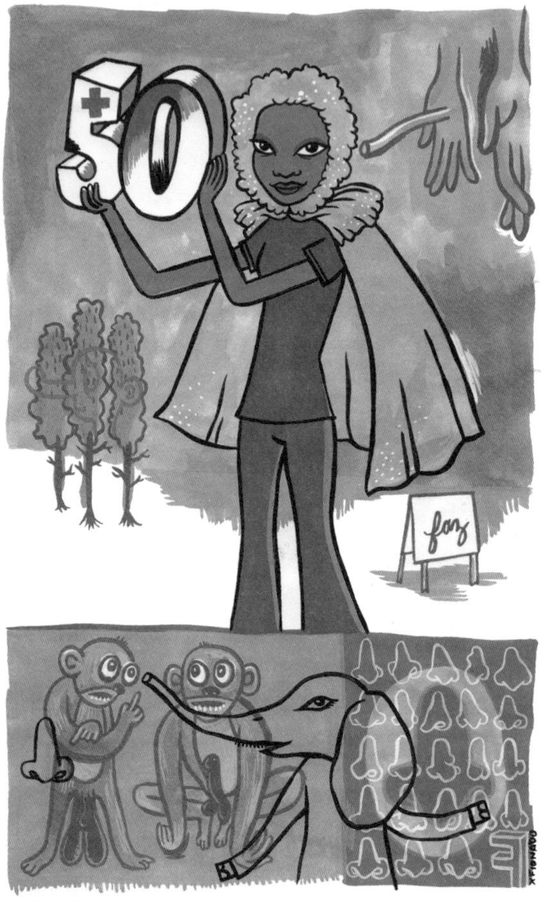
50
faz
xFIONA'00

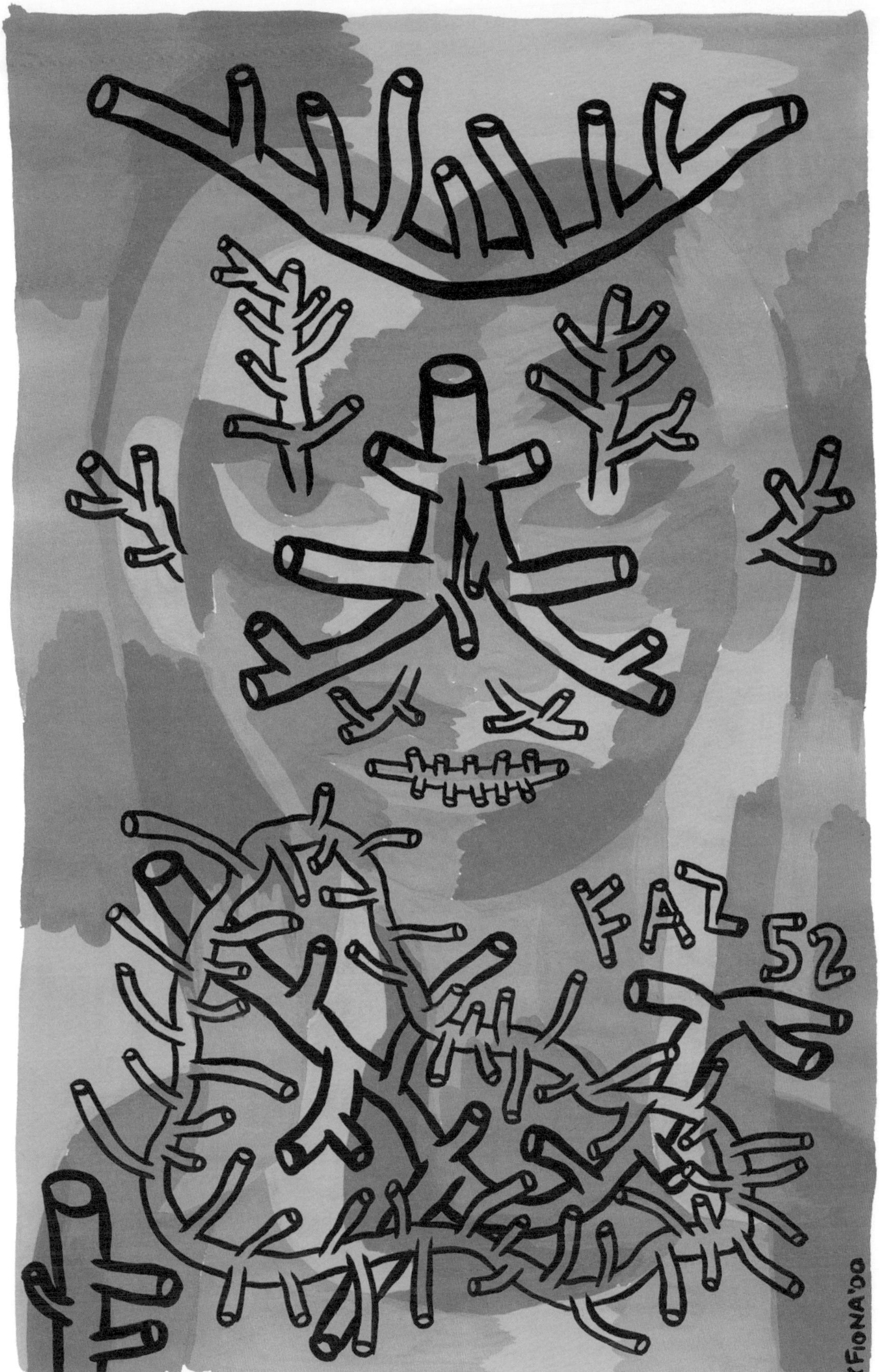
FAZ 52
FIONA'00

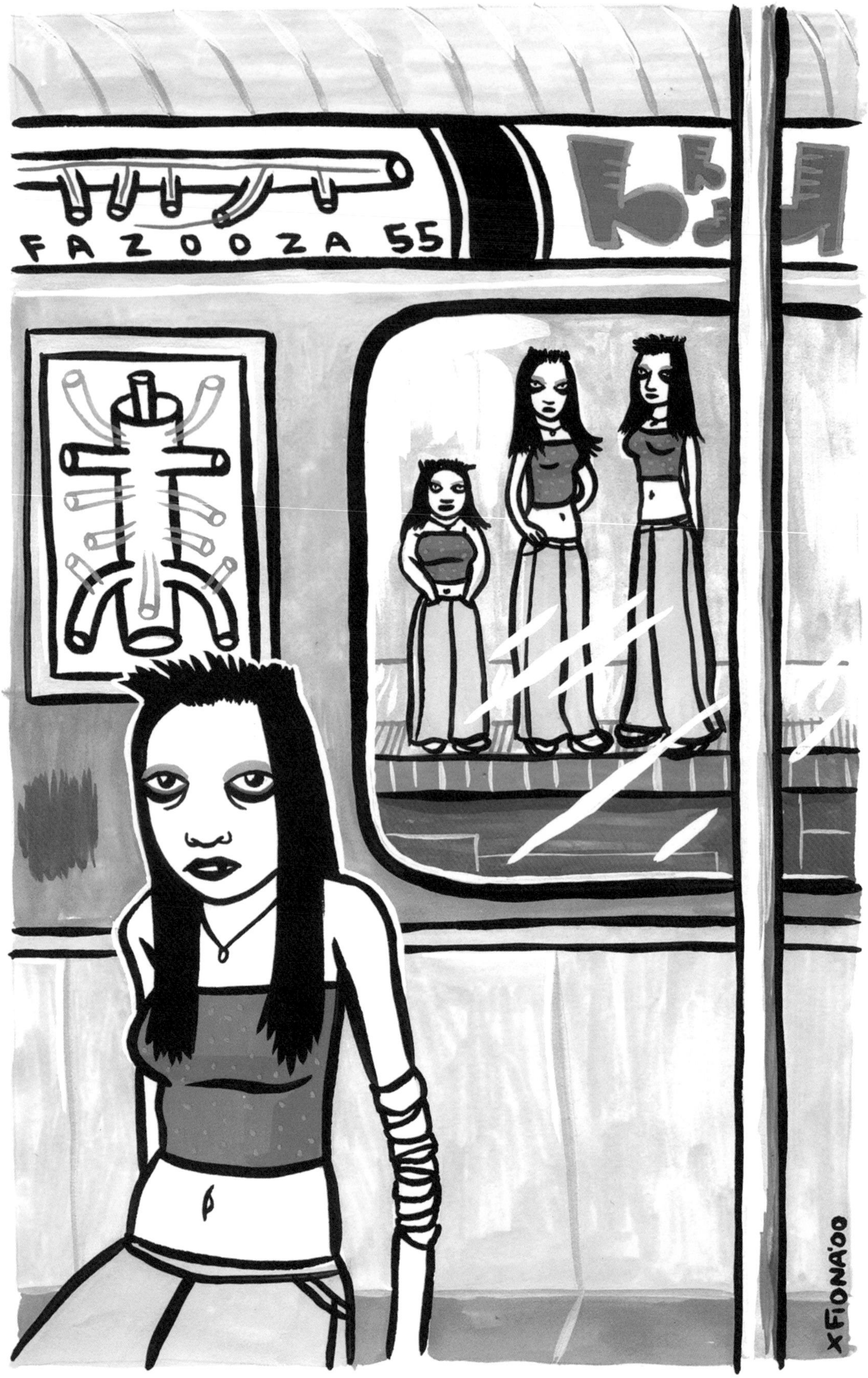
FAZOOZA 55
xFIONA'00

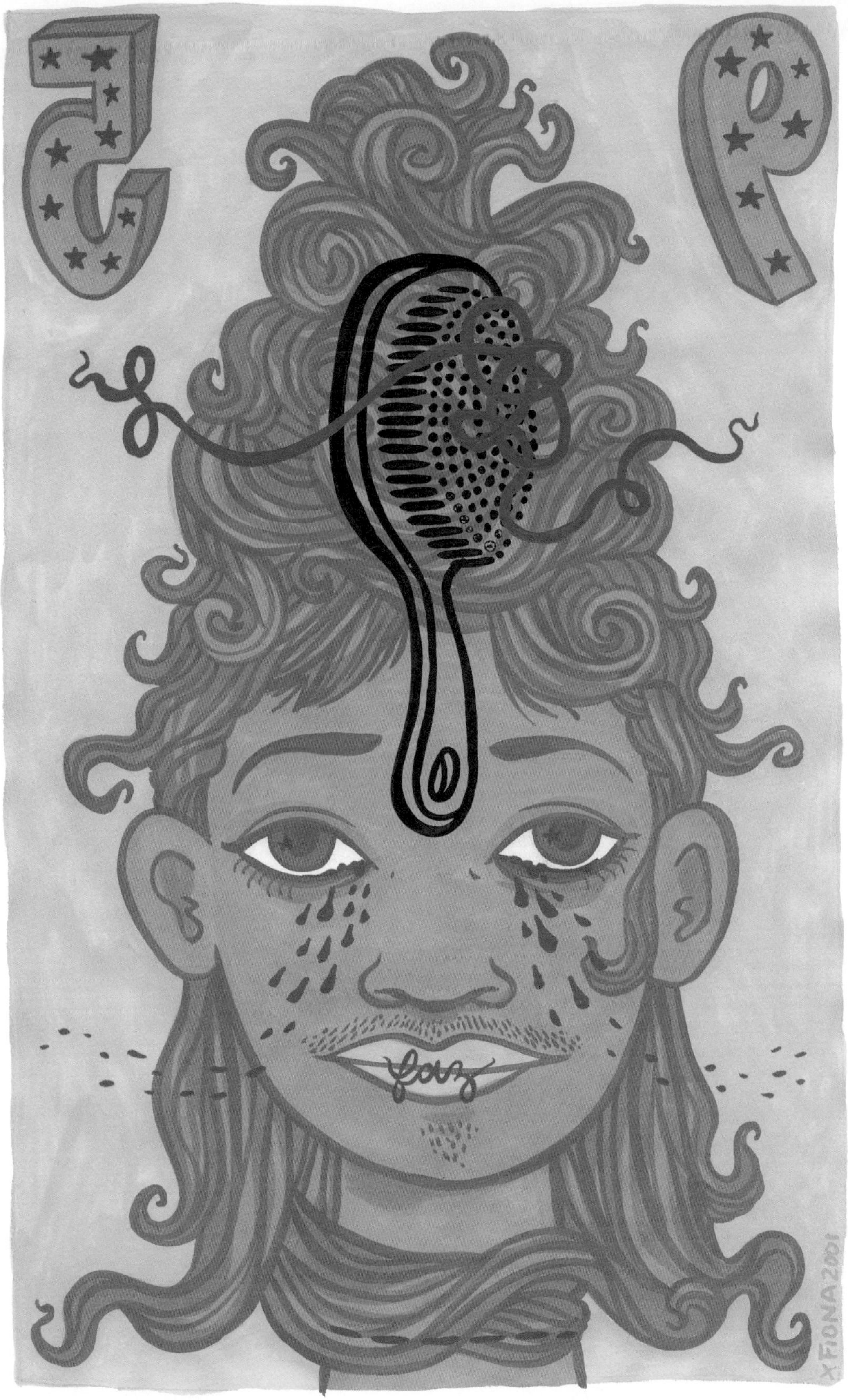
xFIONA2001

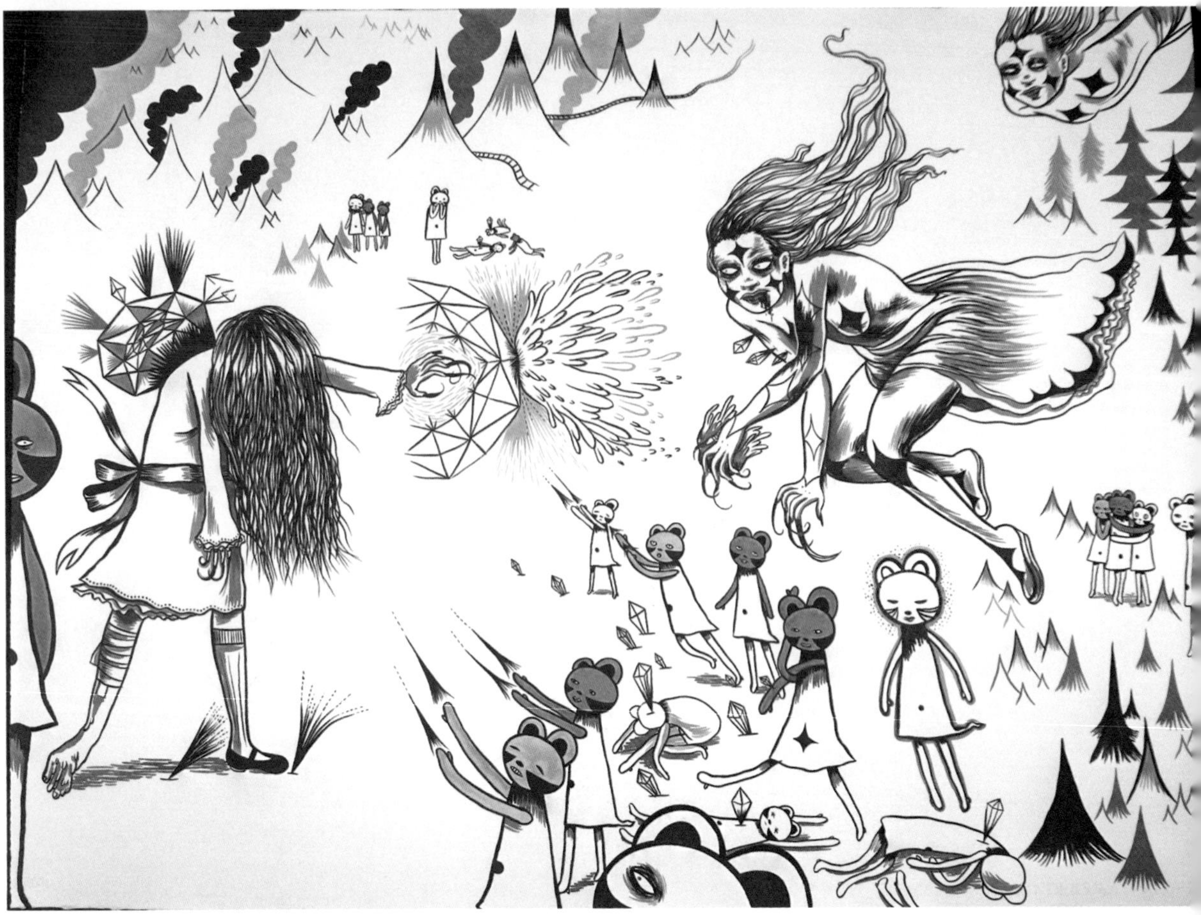

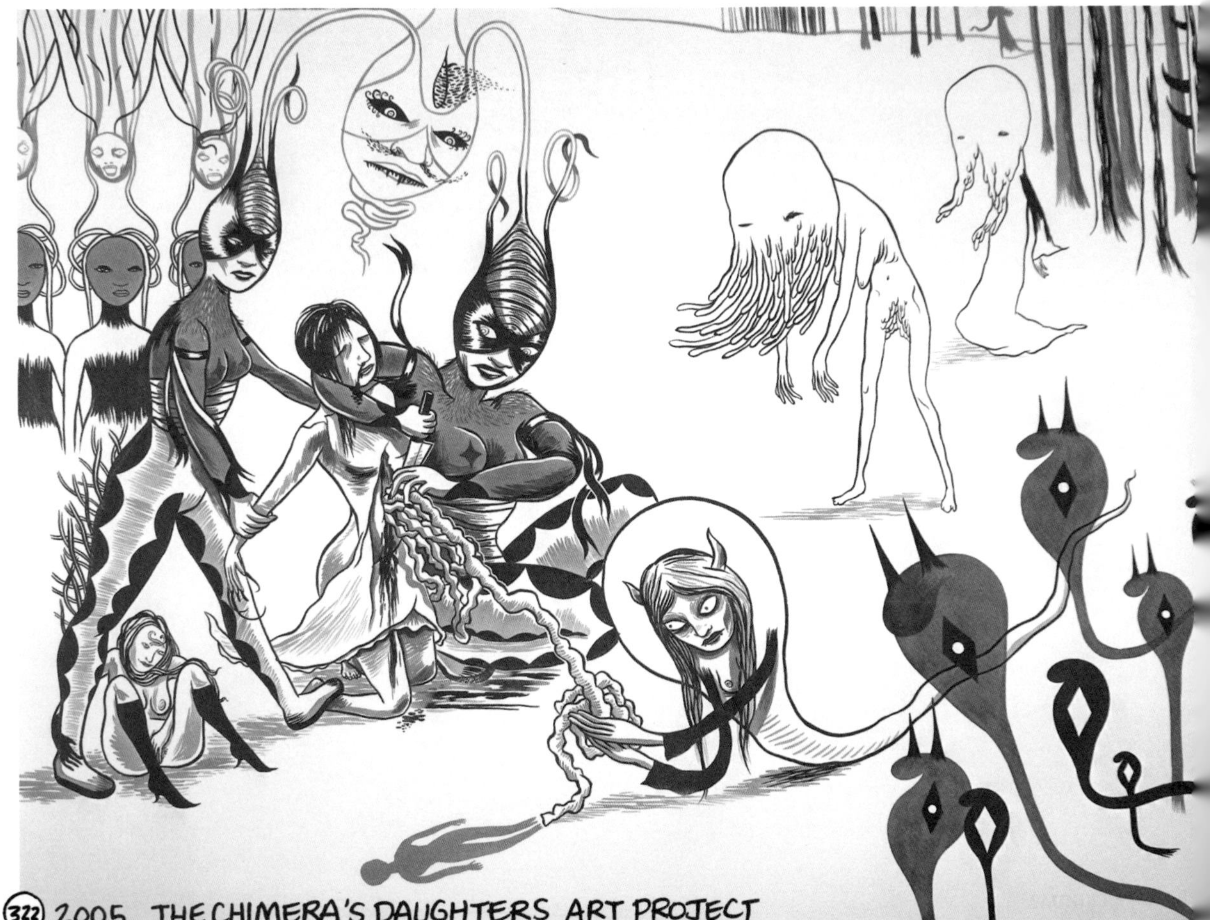

 2005 THE CHIMERA'S DAUGHTERS ART PROJECT

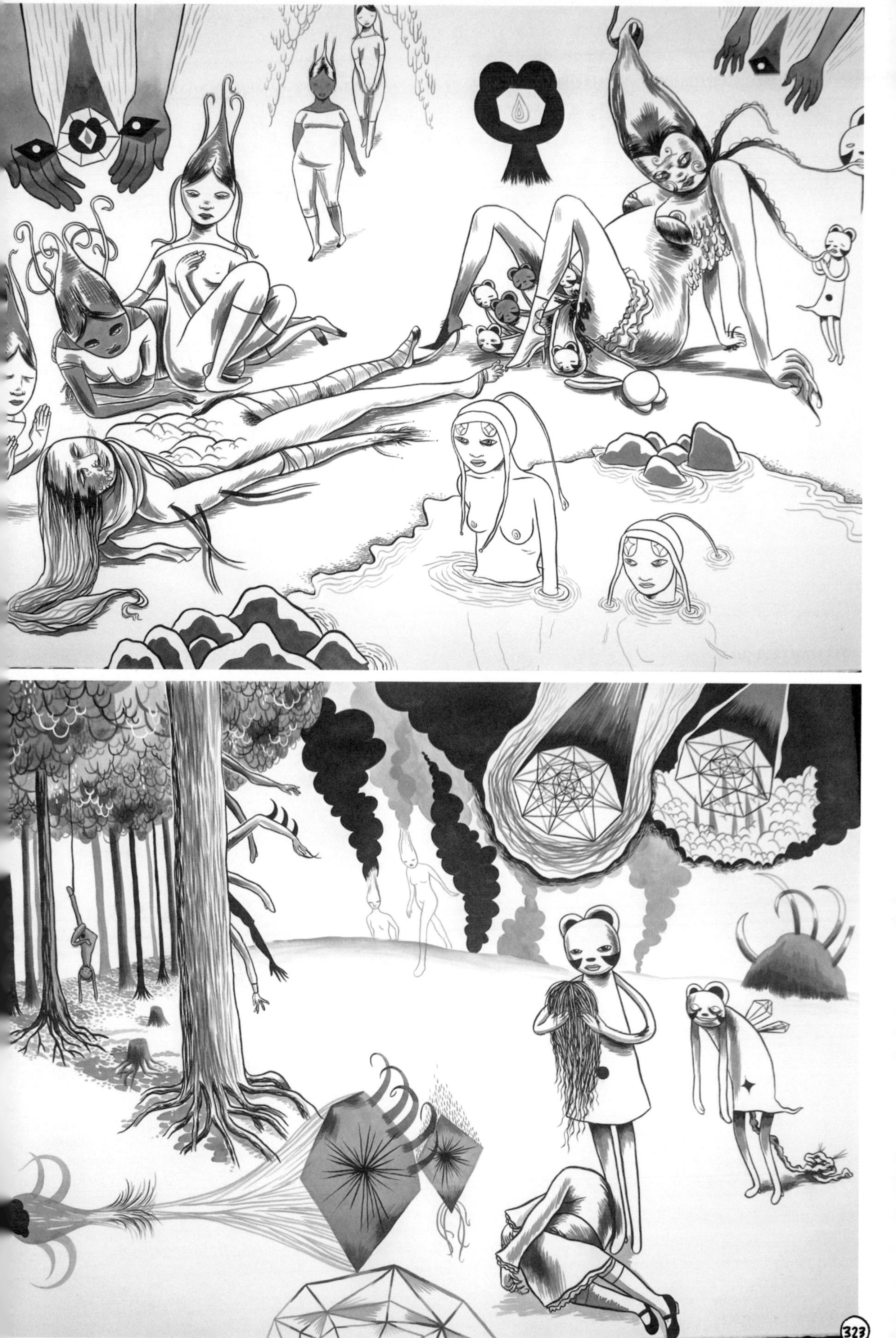

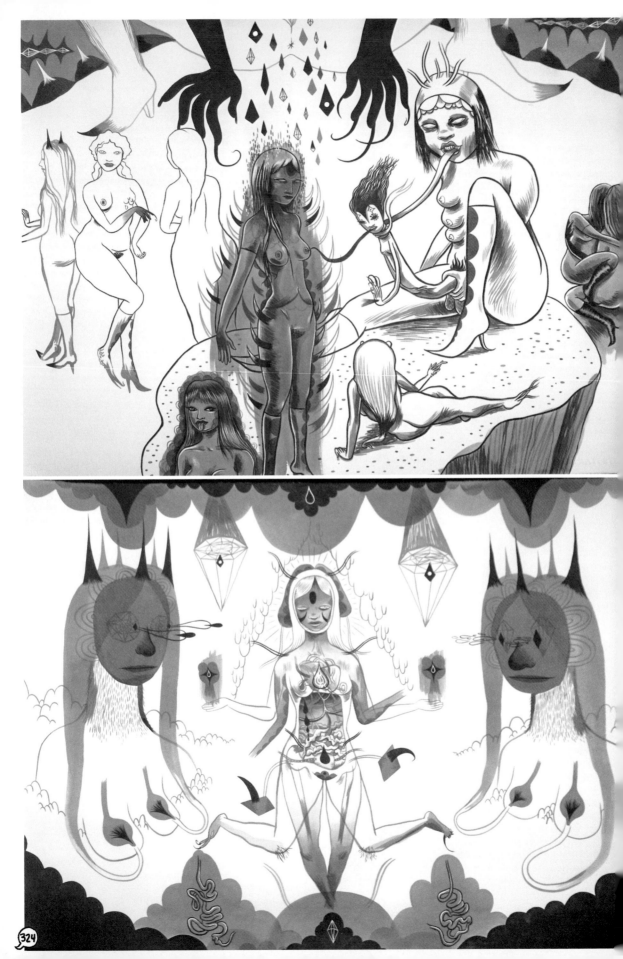

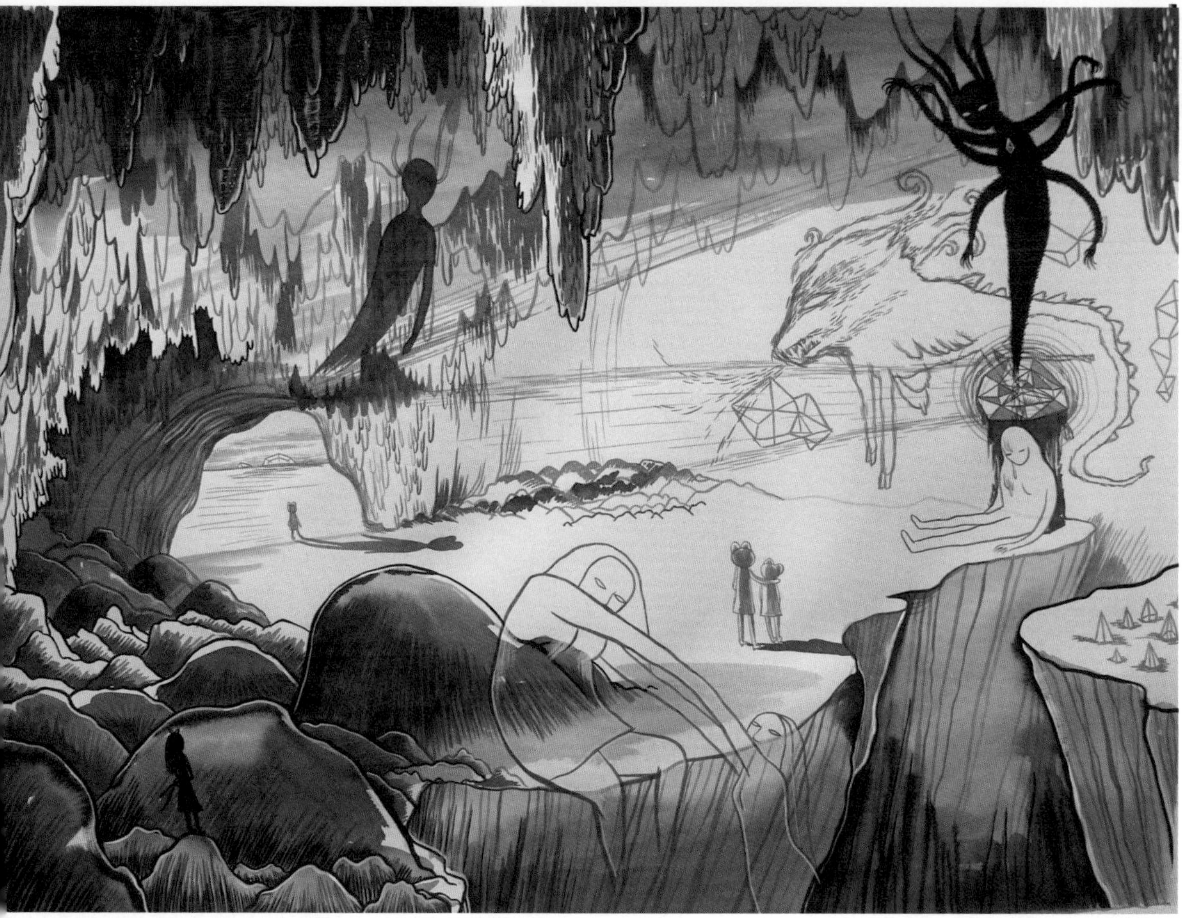

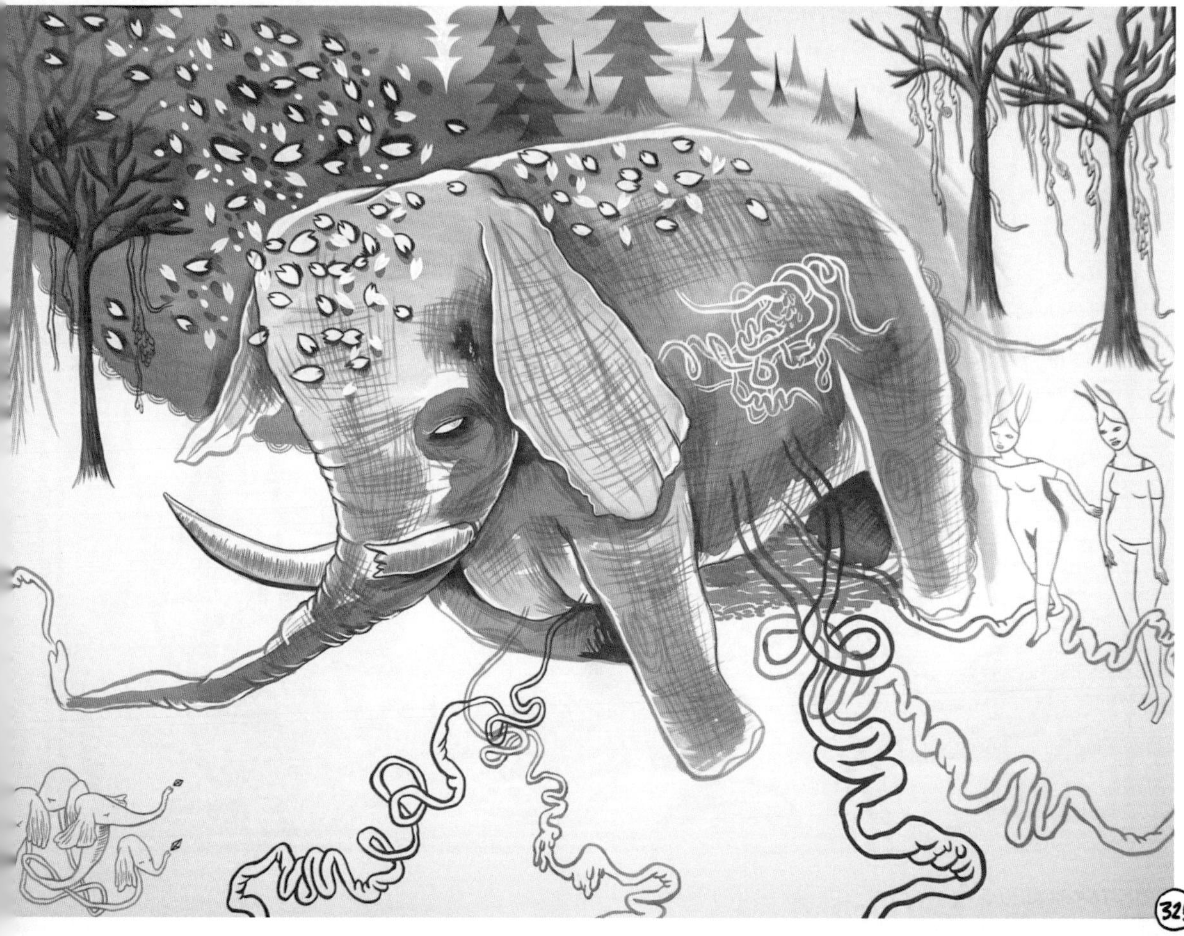

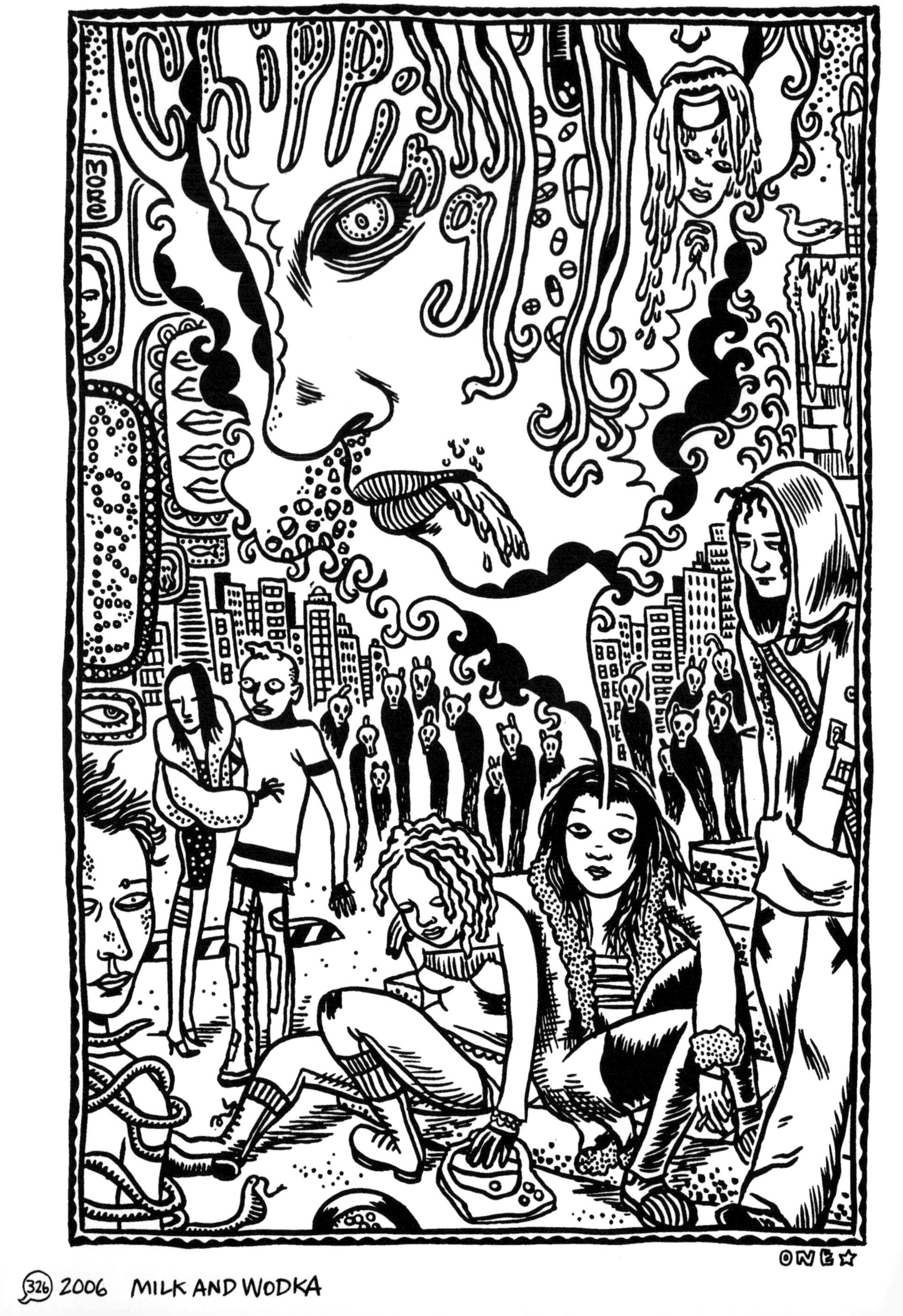
more

ONE☆

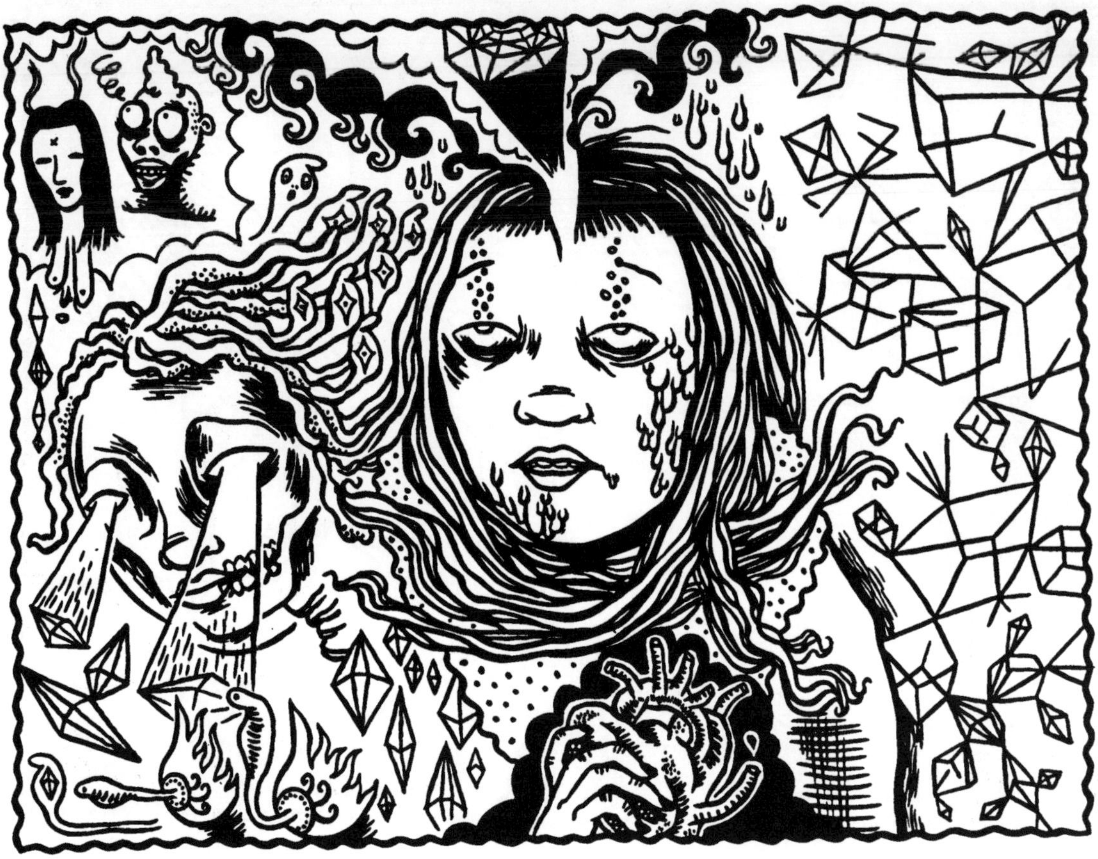

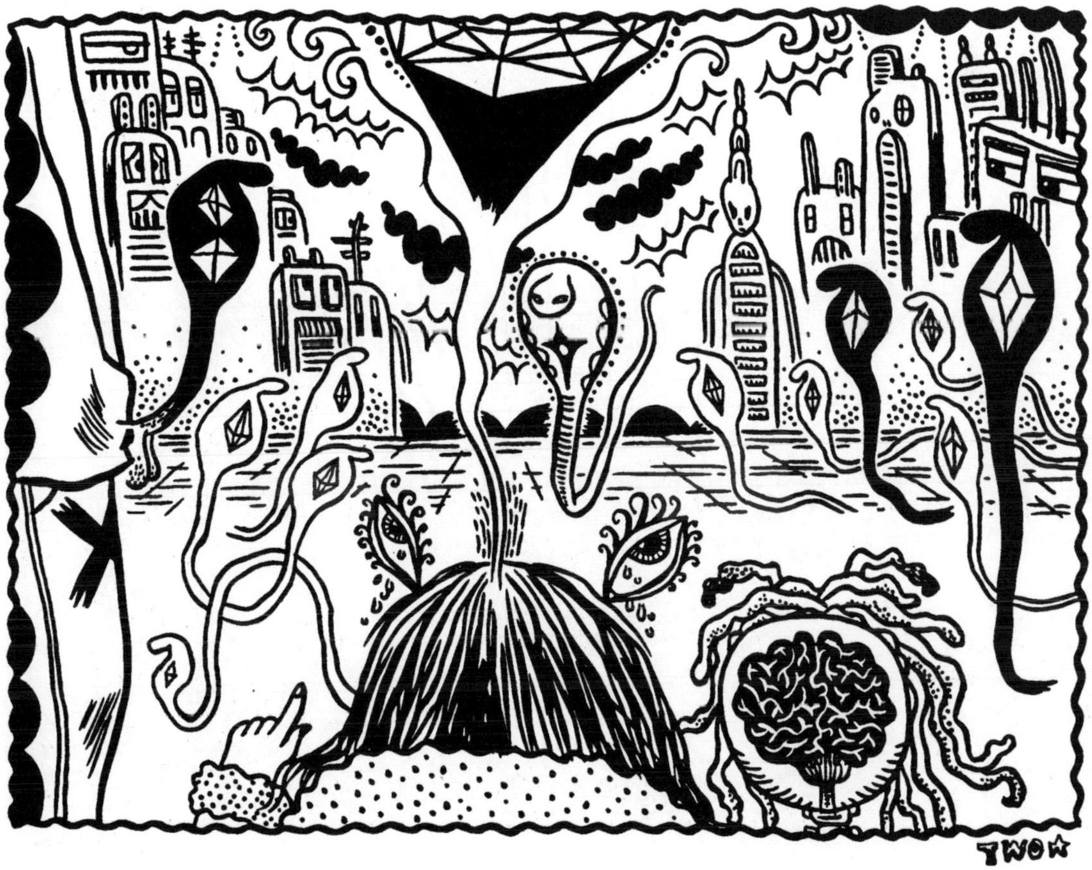

TWO★

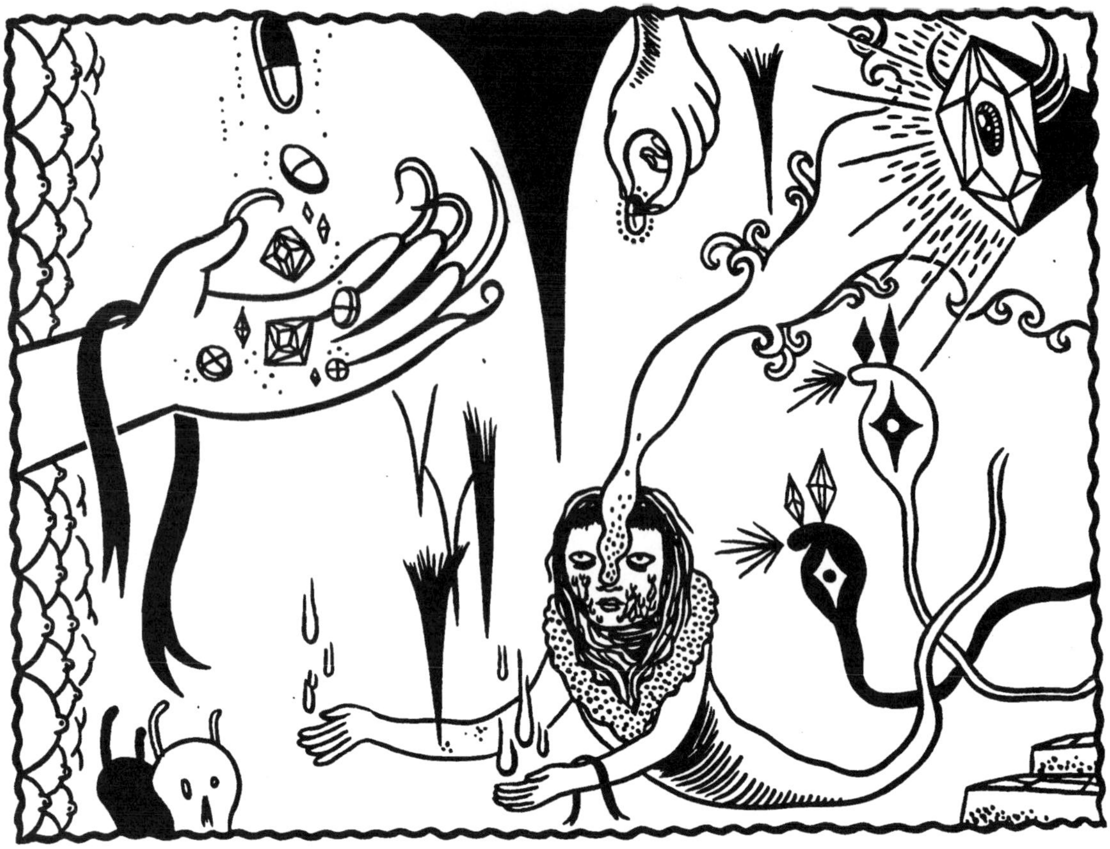

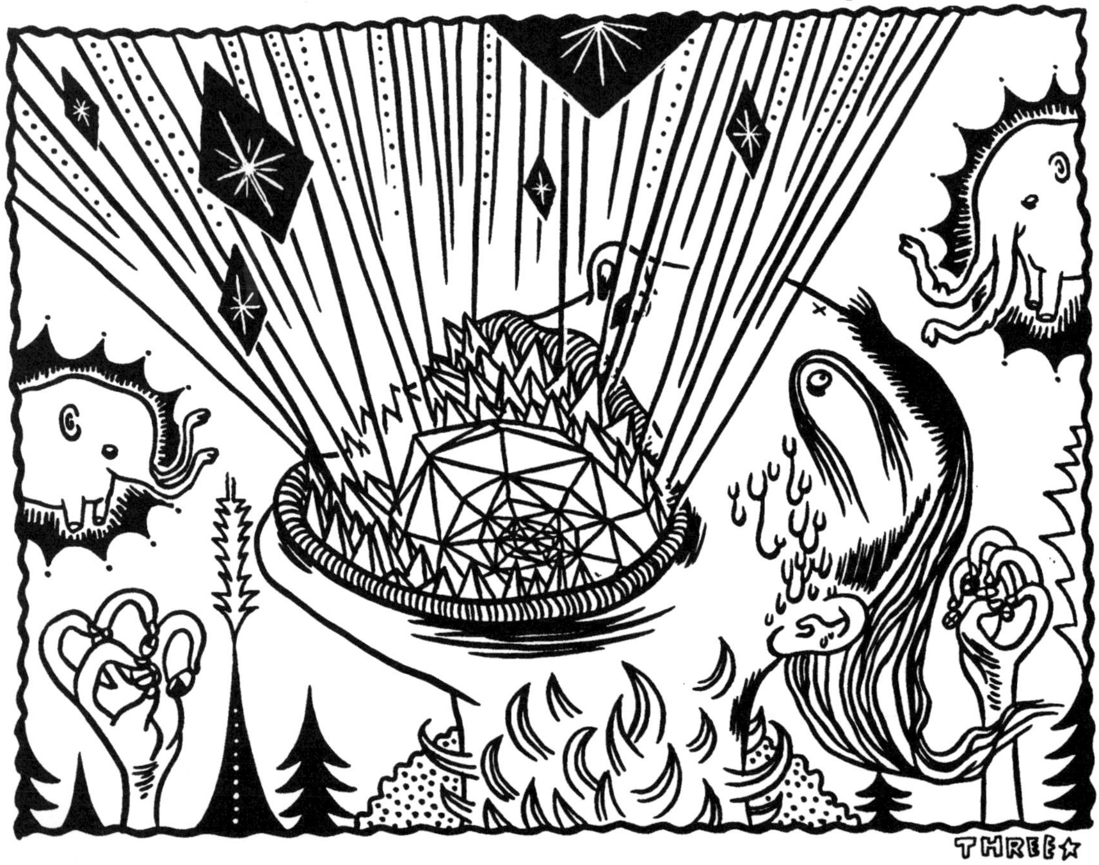

THREE☆

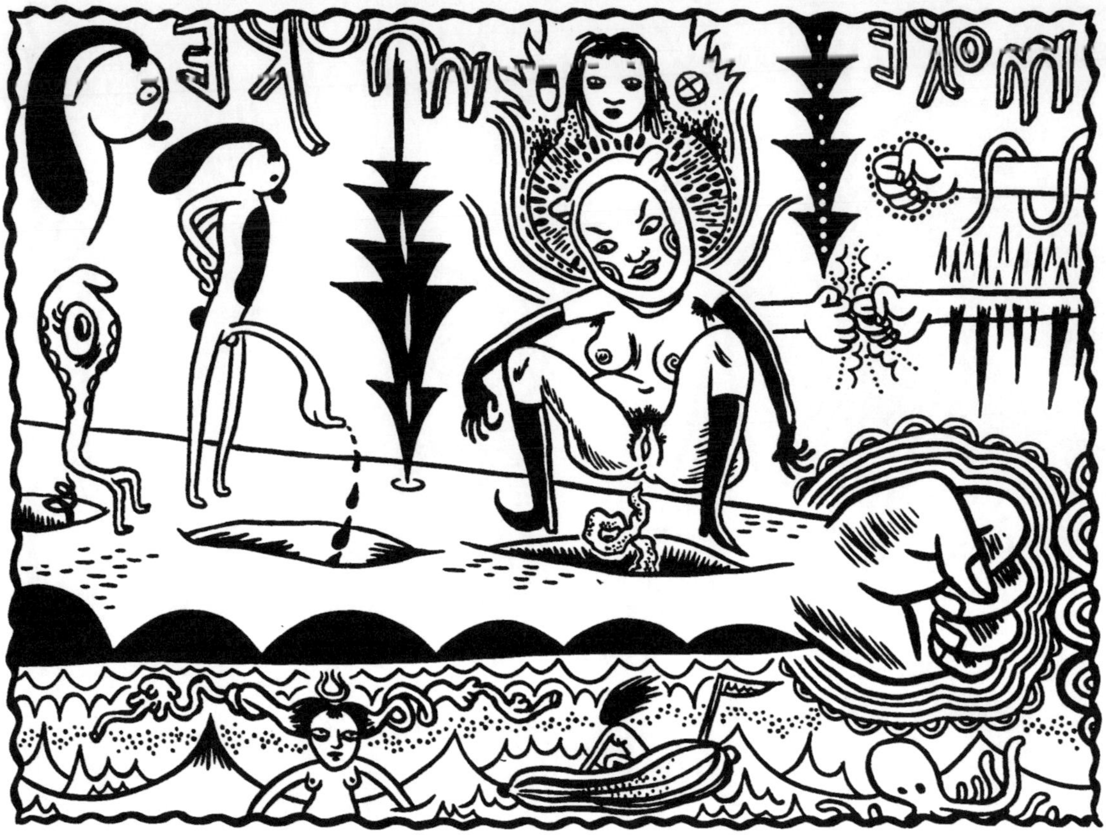

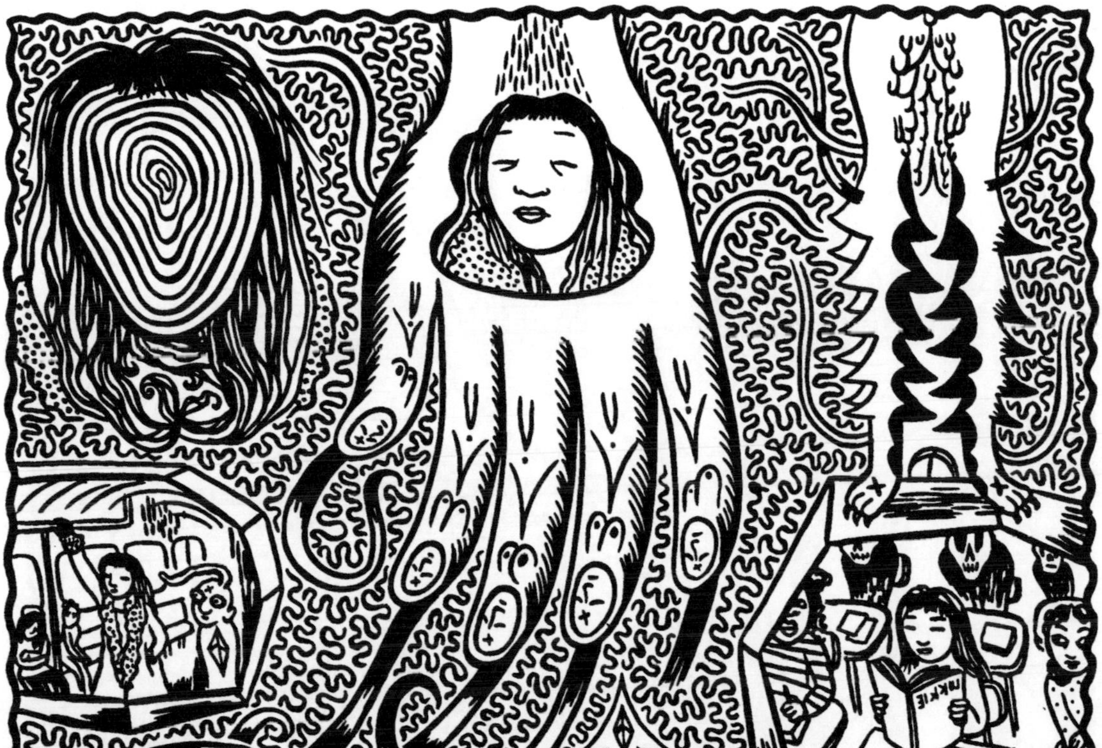

FOUR☆

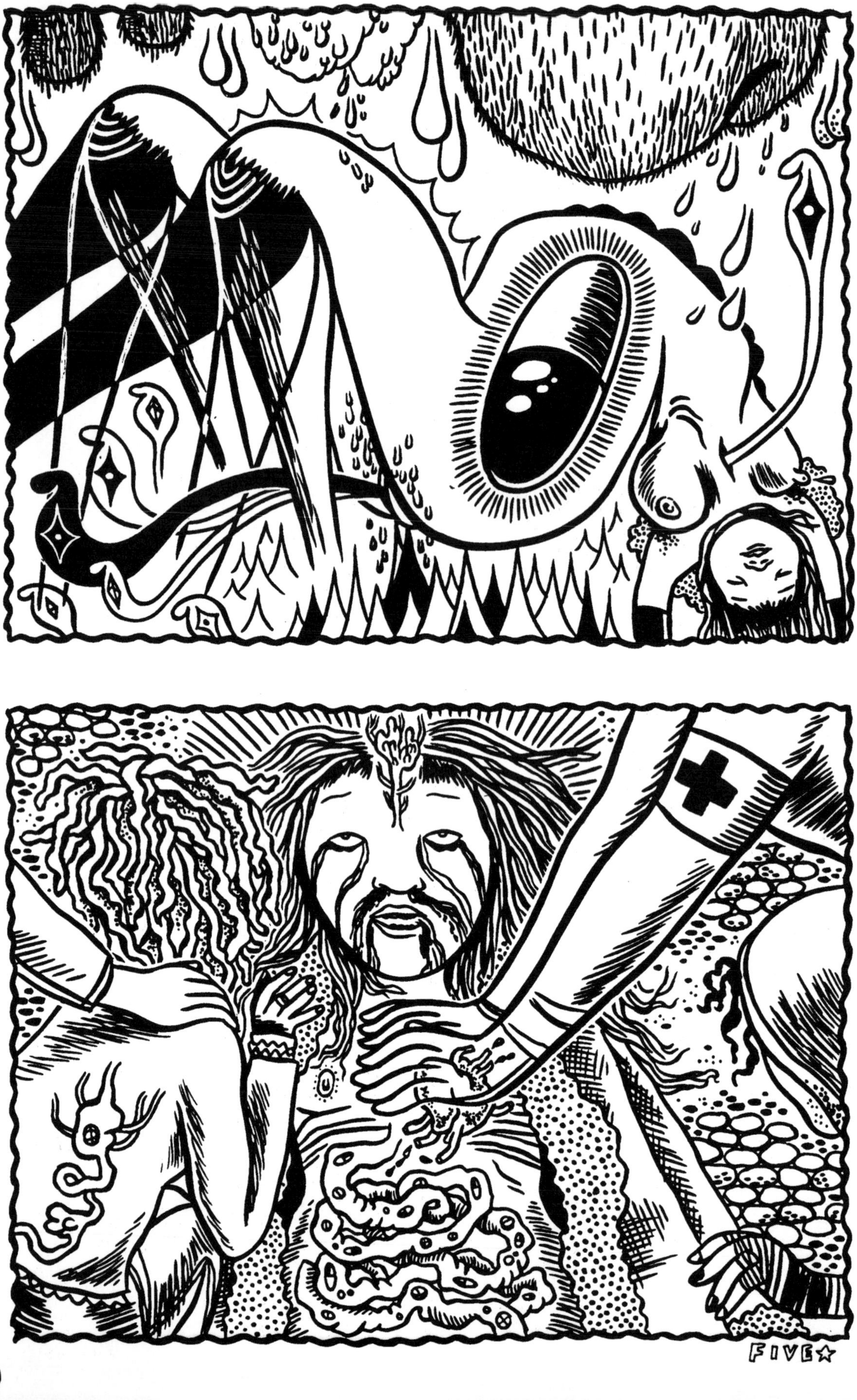
FIVE☆

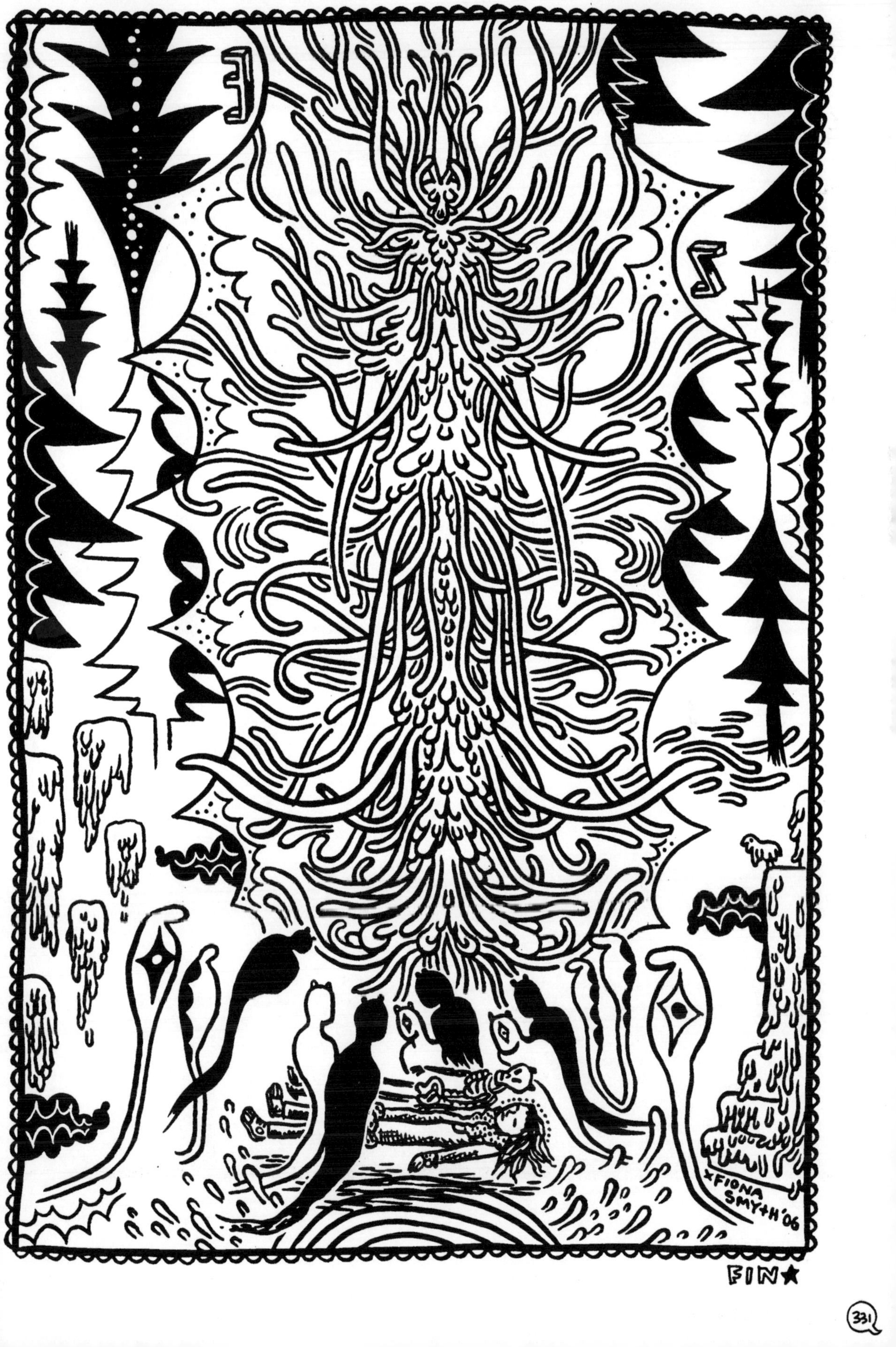
FIONA SMYTH '06

FIN★

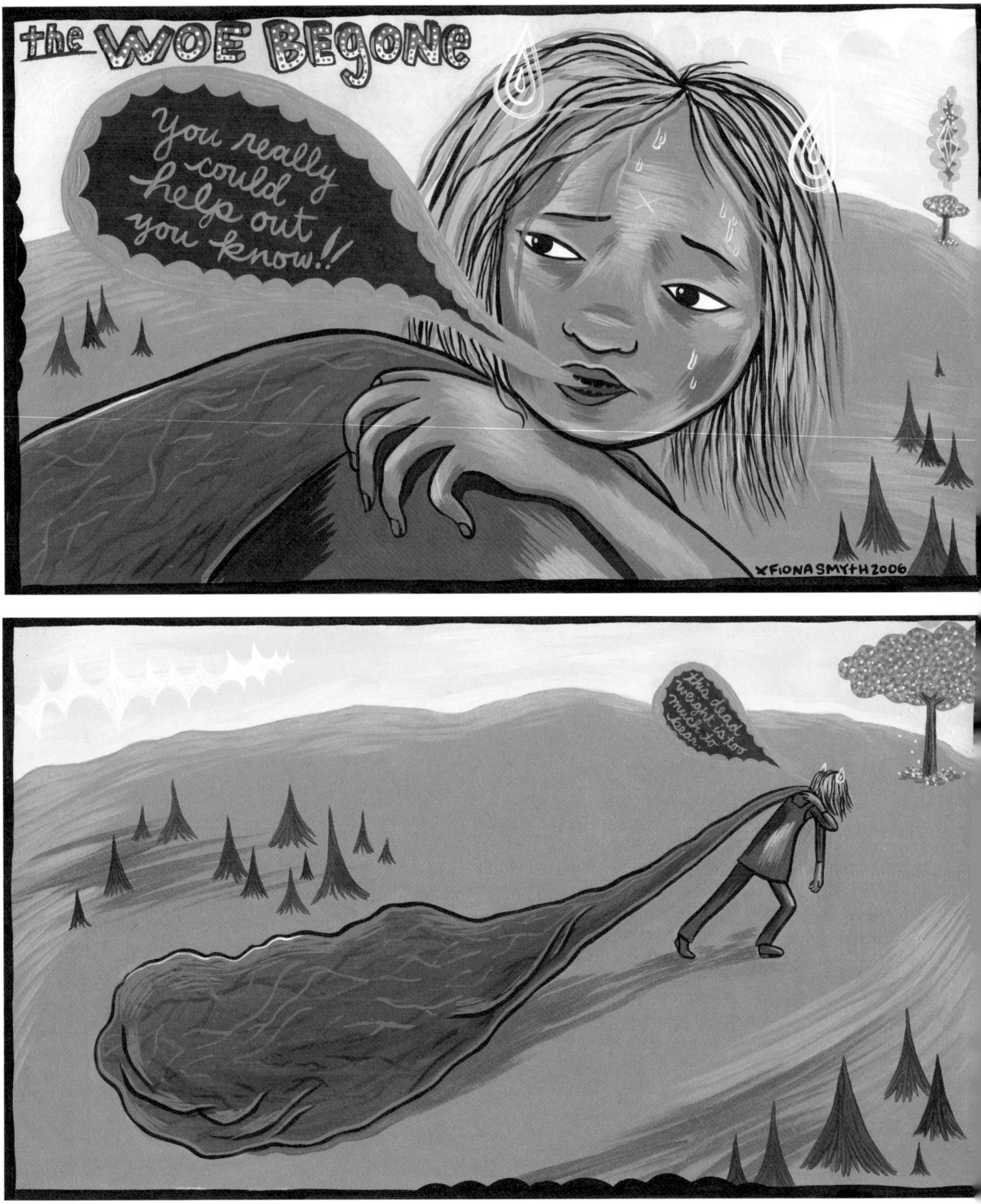
the WOE BEGONE
You really could help out you know!!
XFIONA SMYTH 2006
this dead weight is too much to bear.

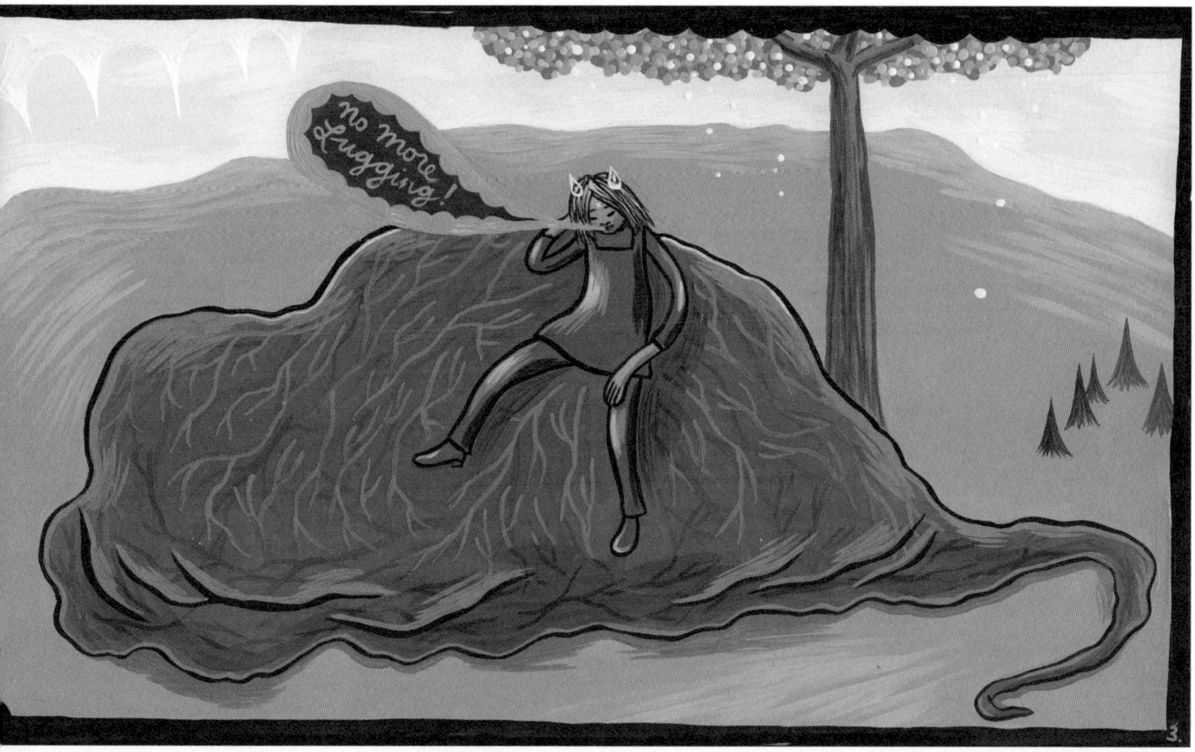
no more Lugging!
3.

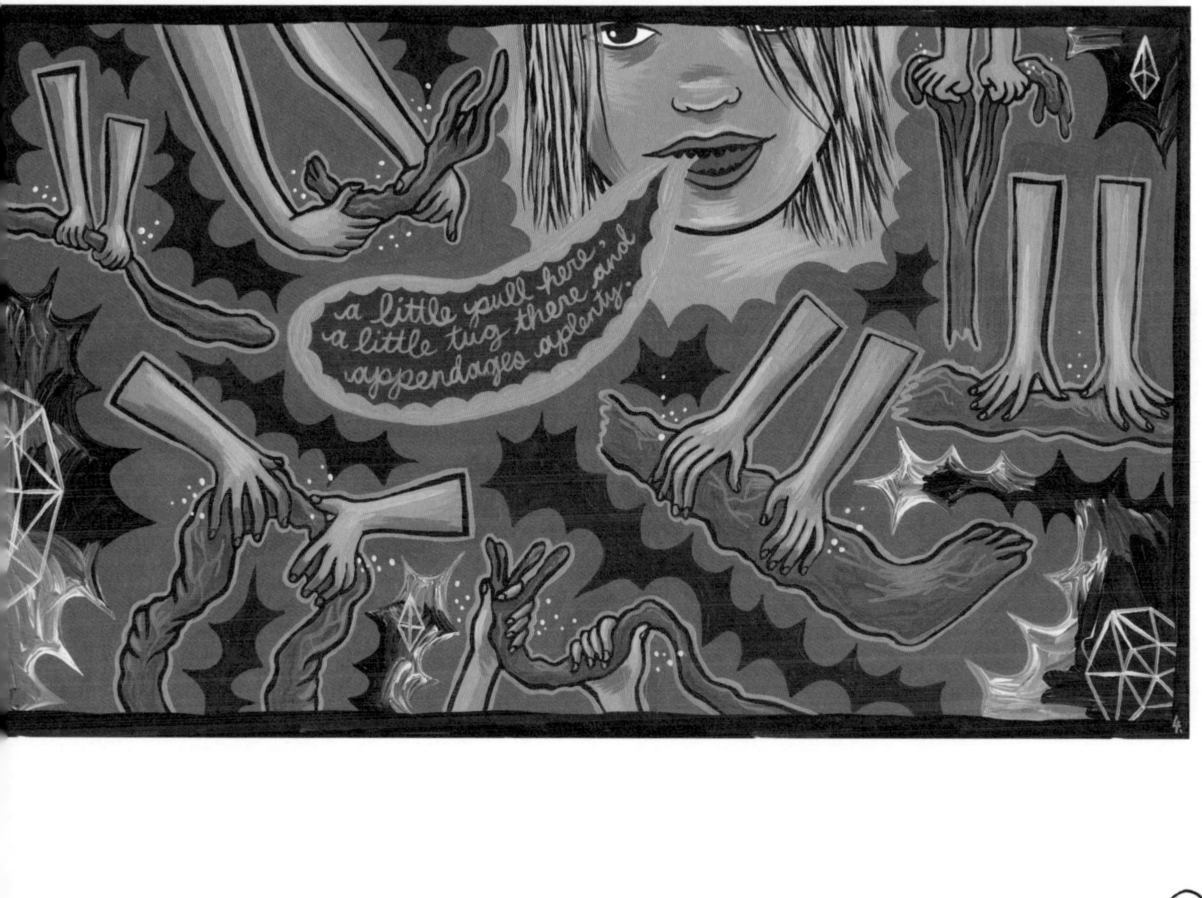
a little pull here, a little tug there and appendages aplenty.
4.

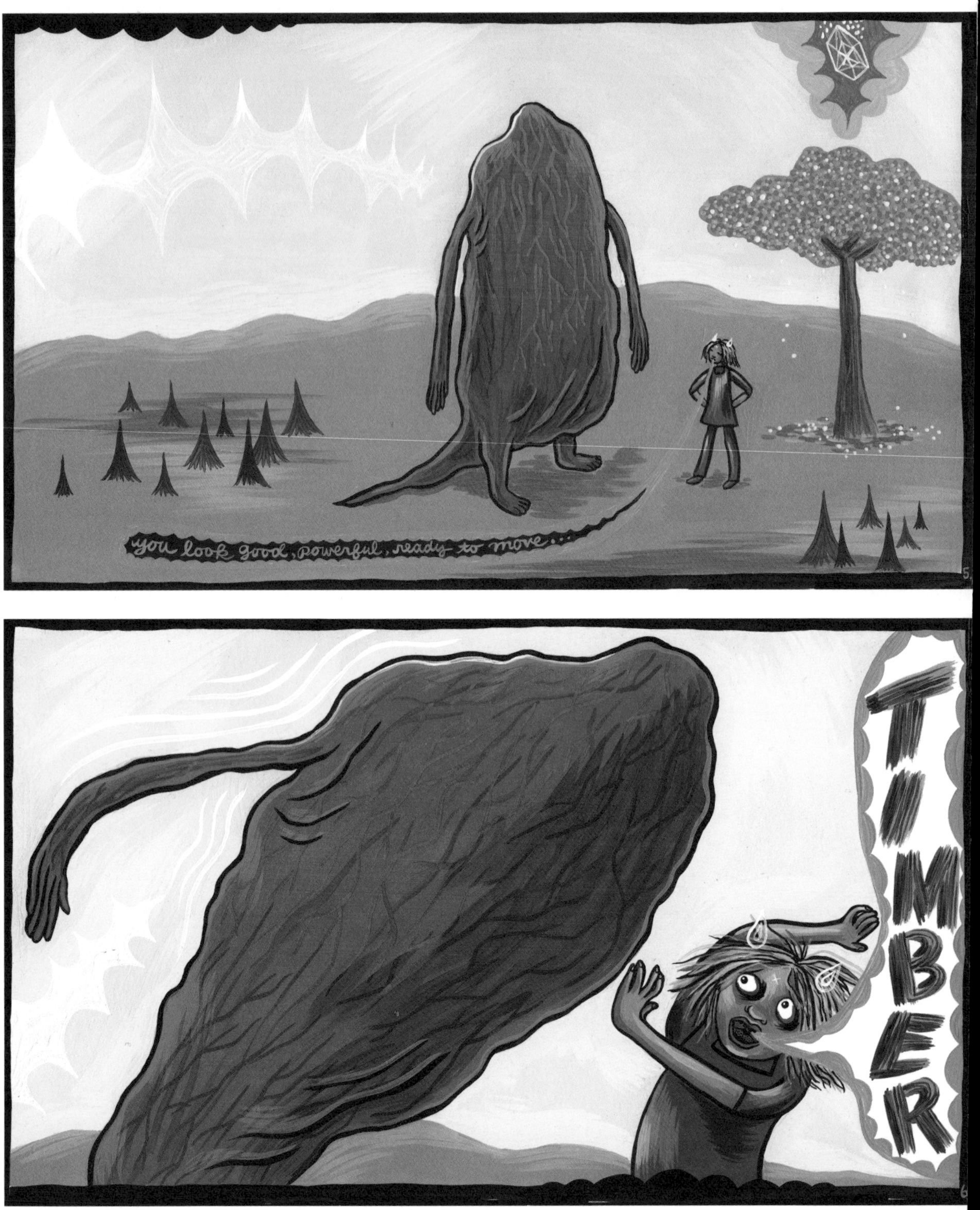
you look good, powerful, ready to move...
TIMBER

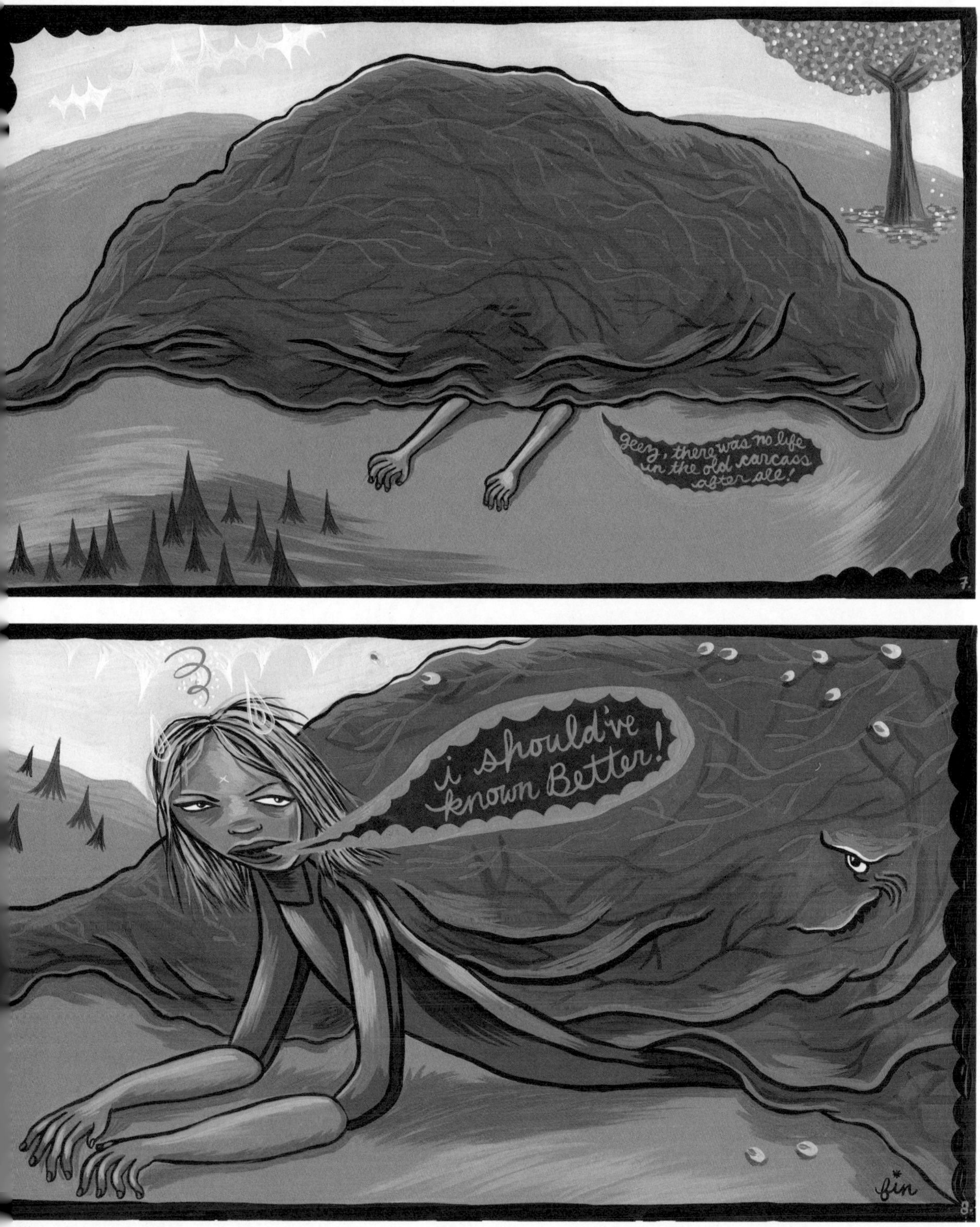
geez, there was no life in the old carcass after all!
7.
i should've known Better!
fin
8.

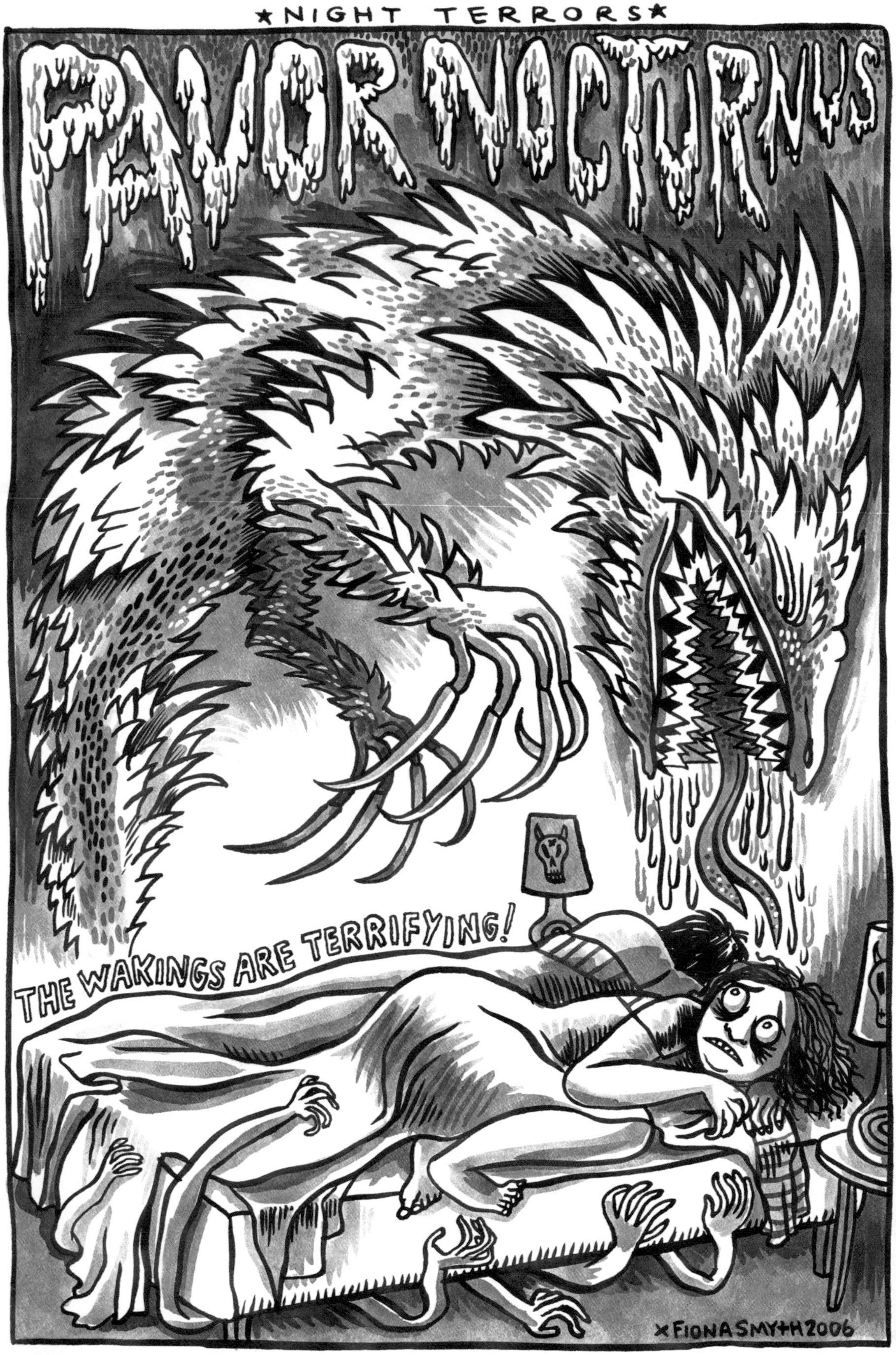
NIGHT TERRORS
PAVOR NOCTURNUS
THE WAKINGS ARE TERRIFYING!
*FIONA SMYTH 2006

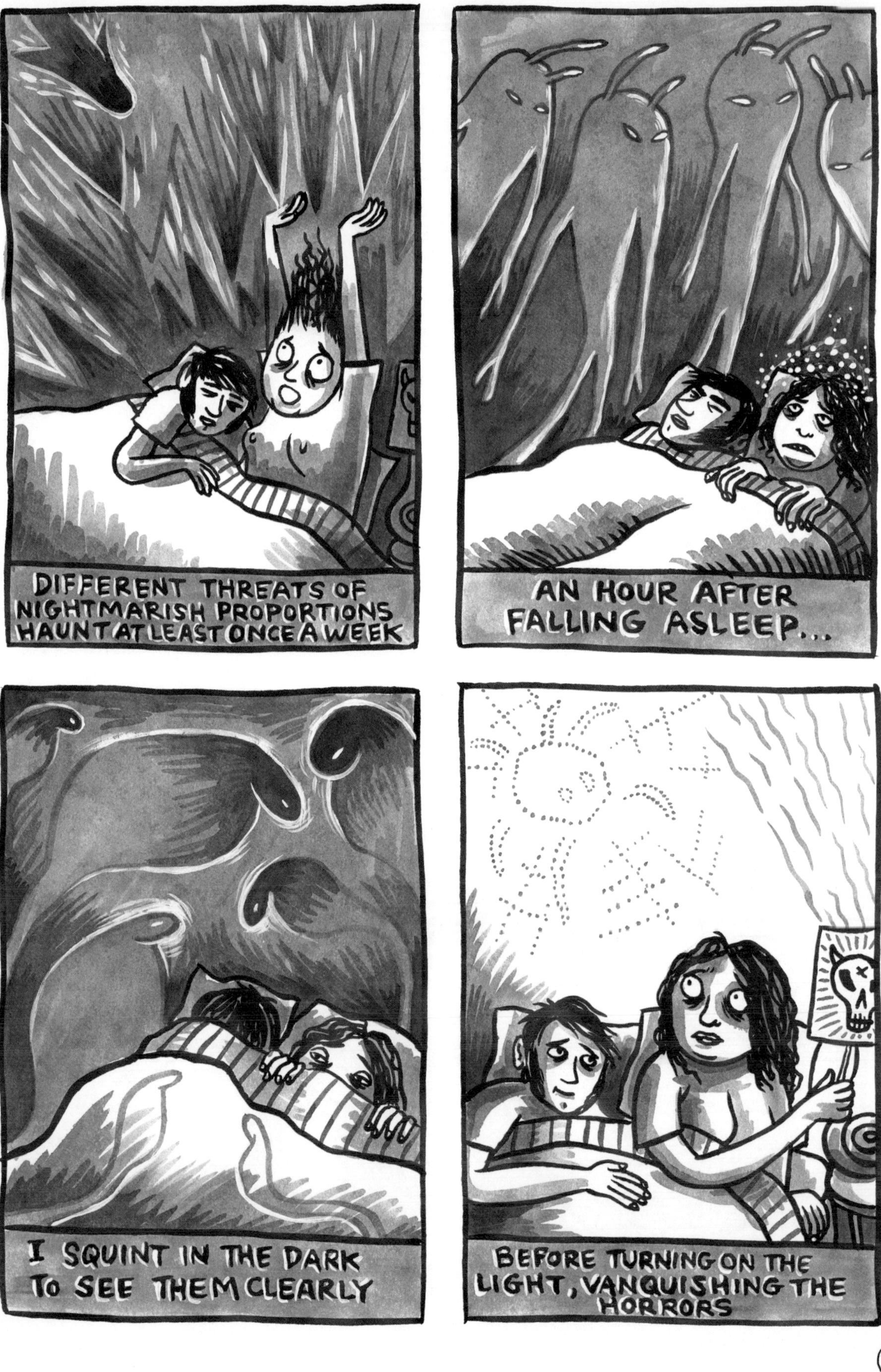
DIFFERENT THREATS OF NIGHTMARISH PROPORTIONS HAUNT AT LEAST ONCE A WEEK
AN HOUR AFTER FALLING ASLEEP...
I SQUINT IN THE DARK TO SEE THEM CLEARLY
BEFORE TURNING ON THE LIGHT, VANQUISHING THE HORRORS

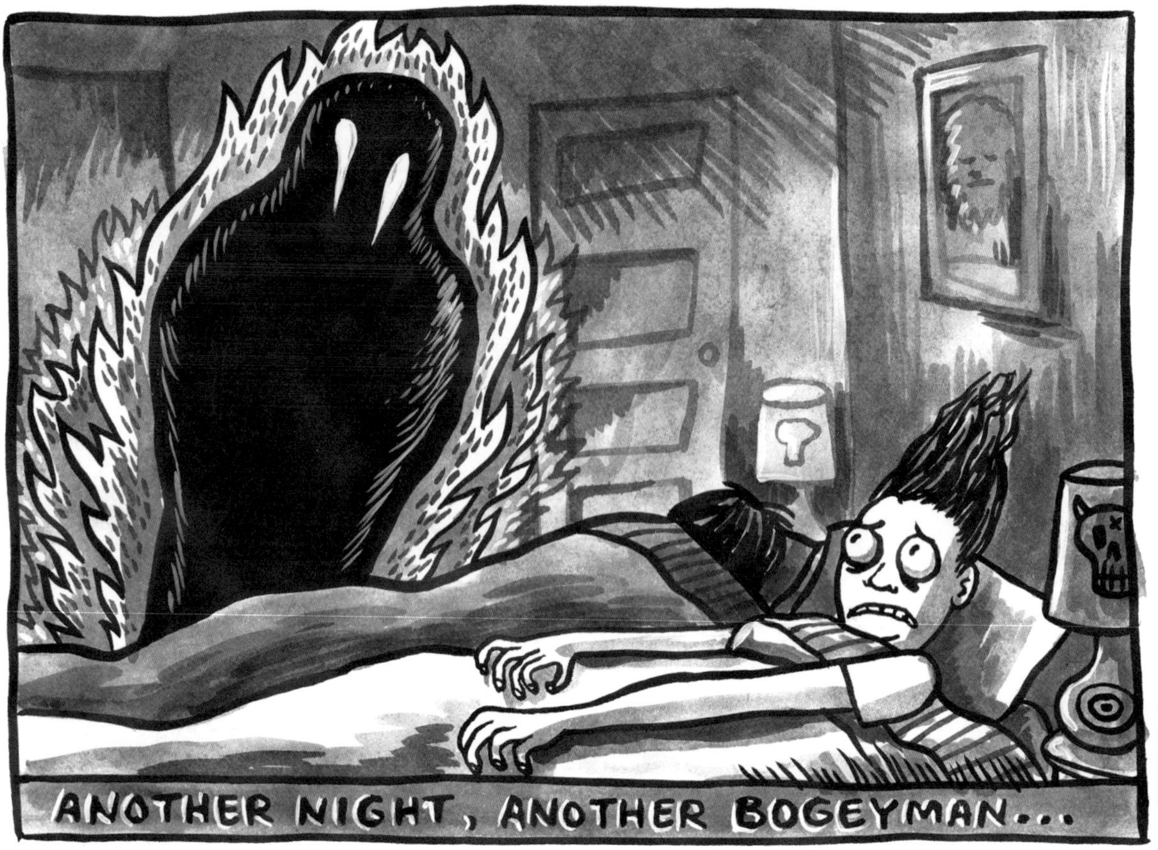
ANOTHER NIGHT, ANOTHER BOGEYMAN...

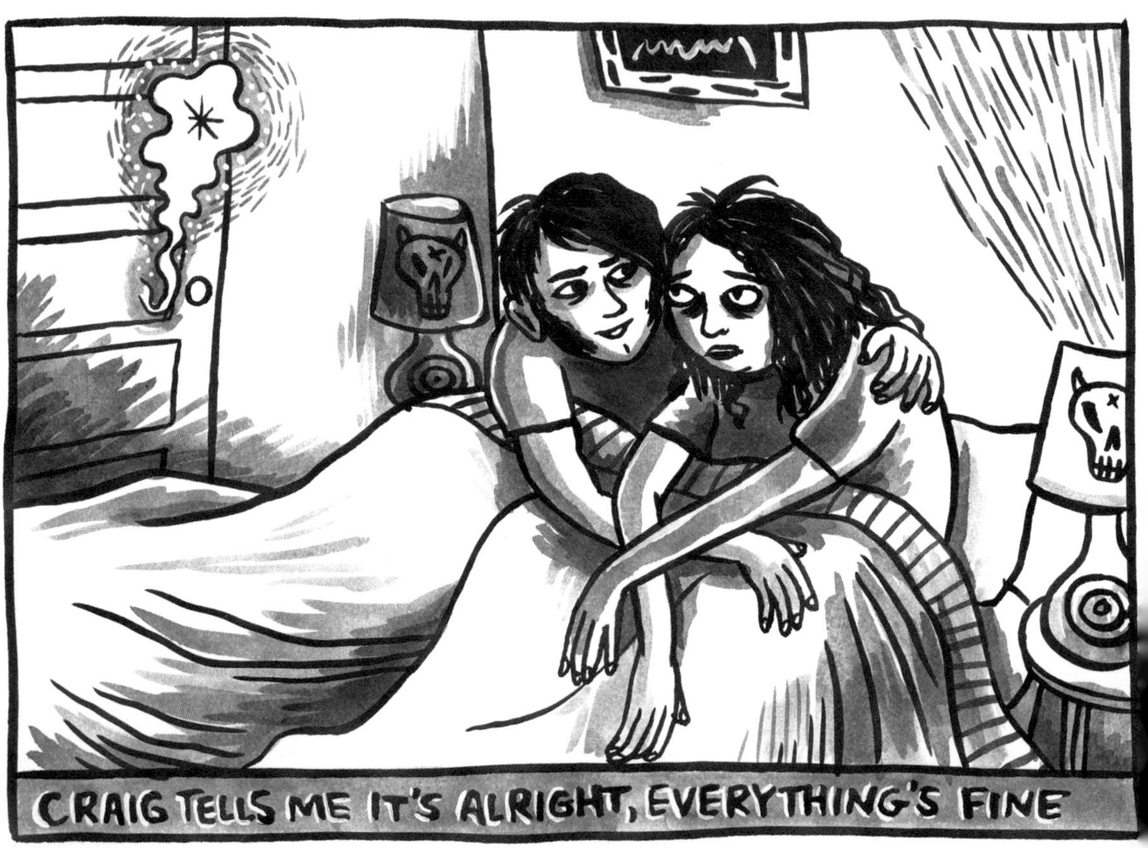
CRAIG TELLS ME IT'S ALRIGHT, EVERYTHING'S FINE

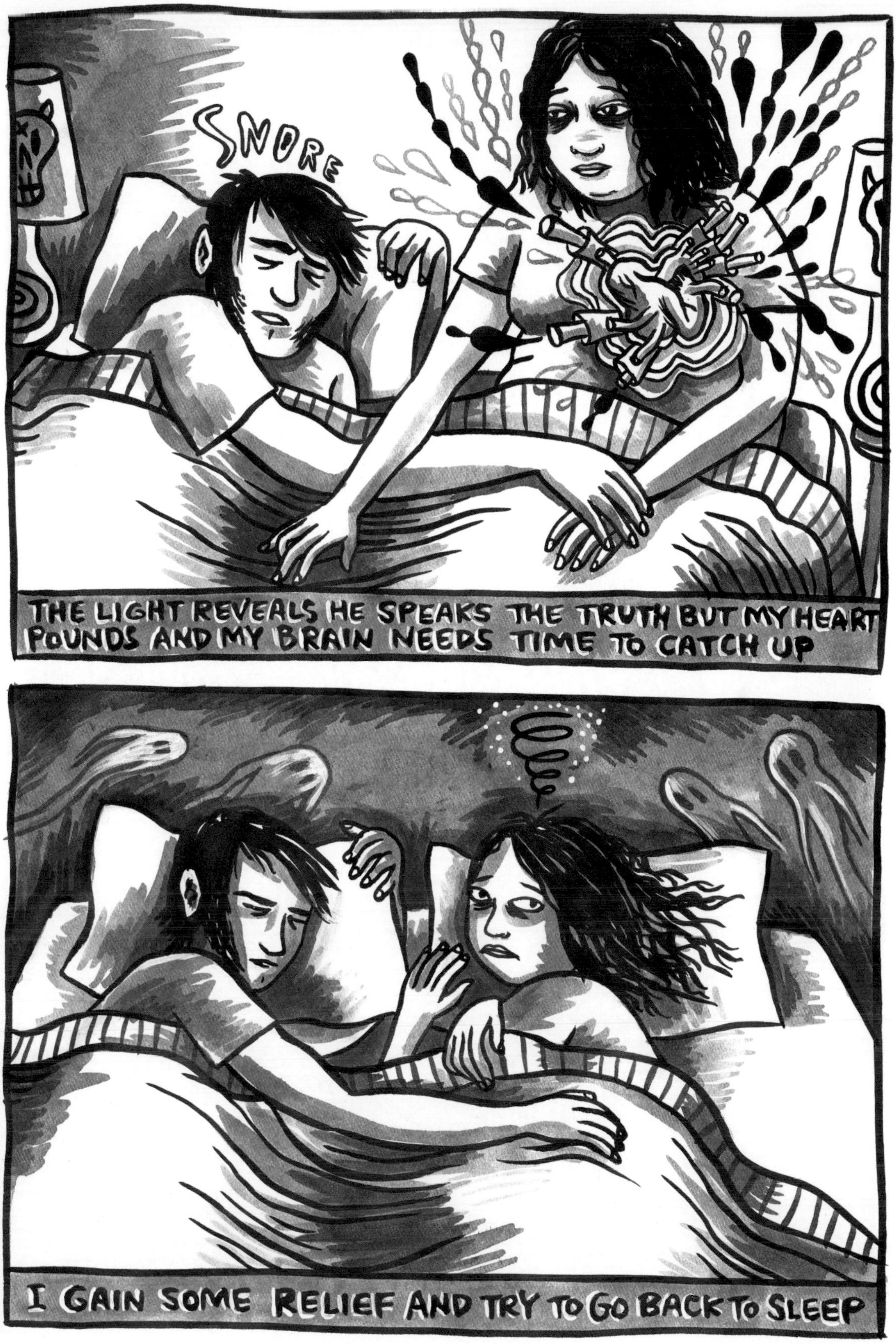
SNORE
THE LIGHT REVEALS HE SPEAKS THE TRUTH BUT MY HEART POUNDS AND MY BRAIN NEEDS TIME TO CATCH UP
I GAIN SOME RELIEF AND TRY TO GO BACK TO SLEEP

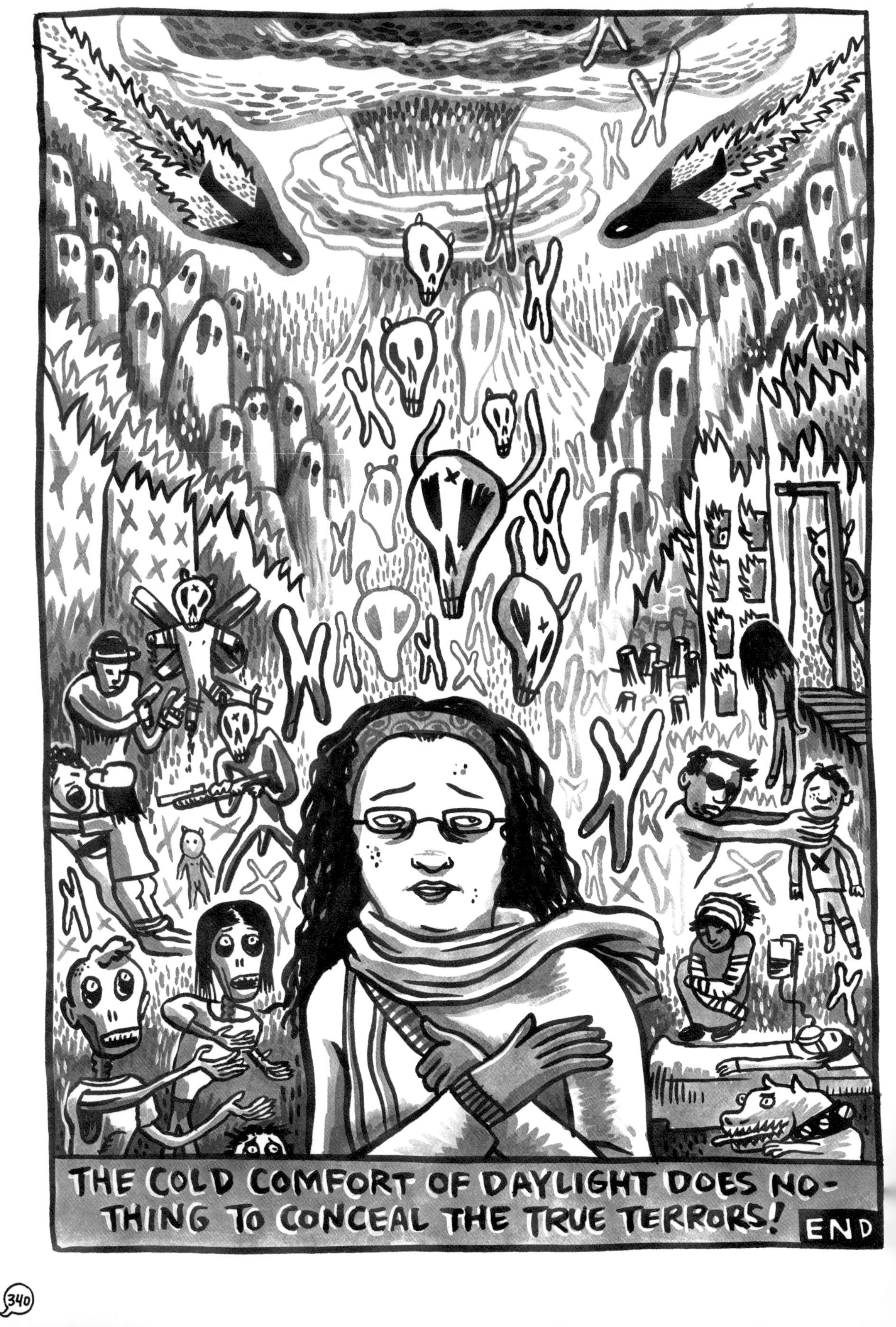
THE COLD COMFORT OF DAYLIGHT DOES NOTHING TO CONCEAL THE TRUE TERRORS!
END

KNOWS
THE
NOSE
KNOWS

SWONK
MAKES
SCENTS

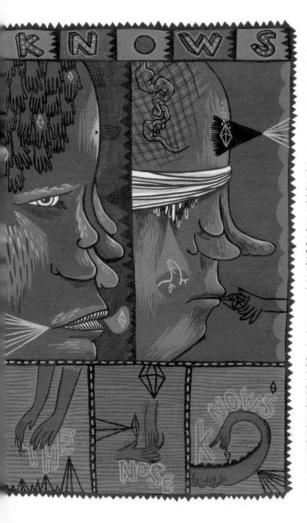

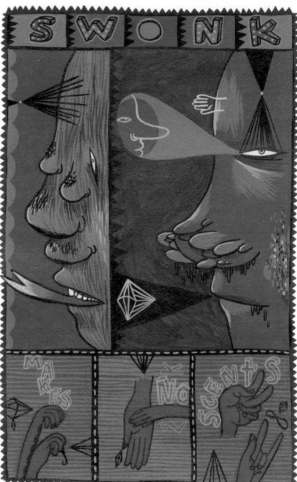

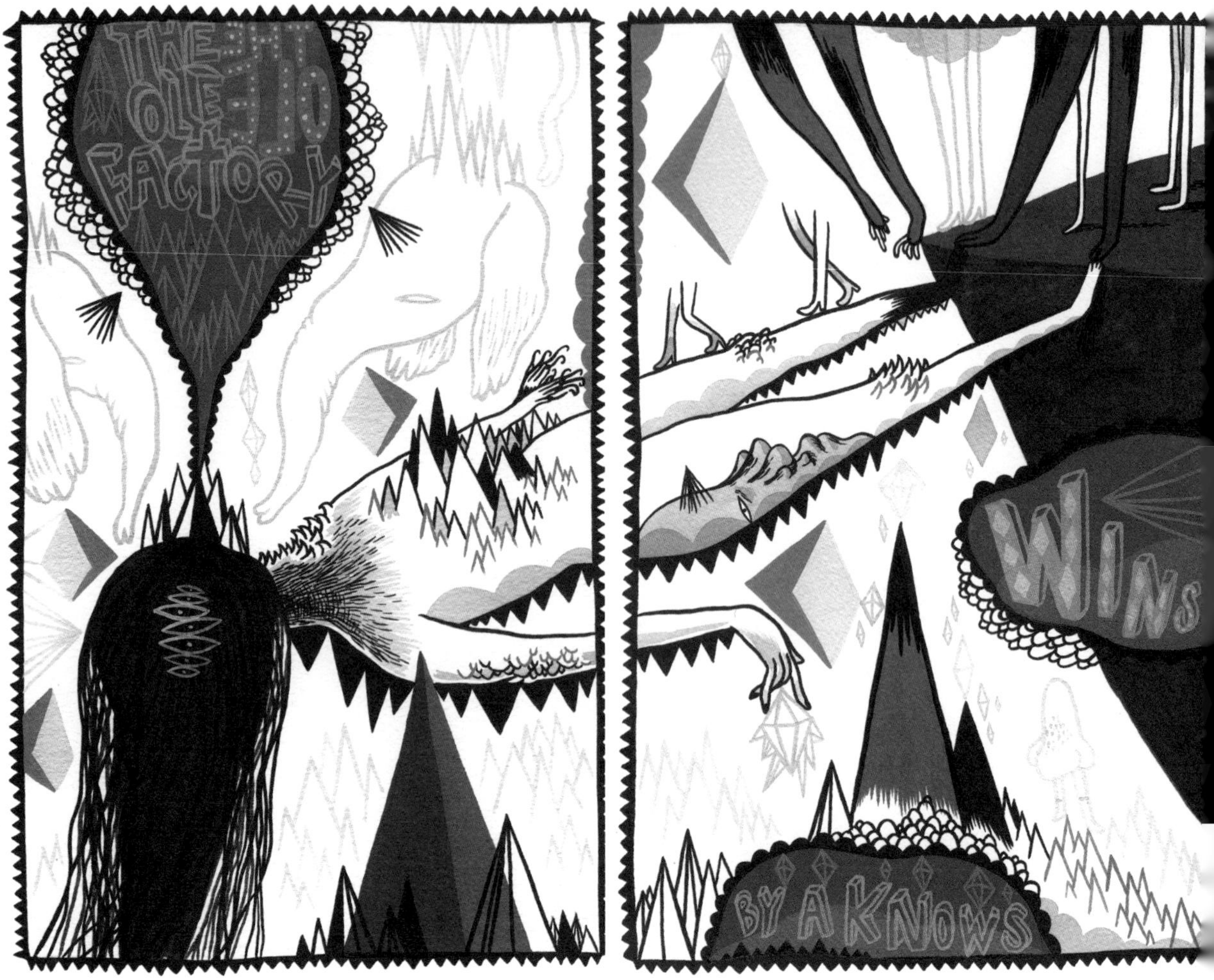
THE OLFACTORY
WINS
BY A KNOWS

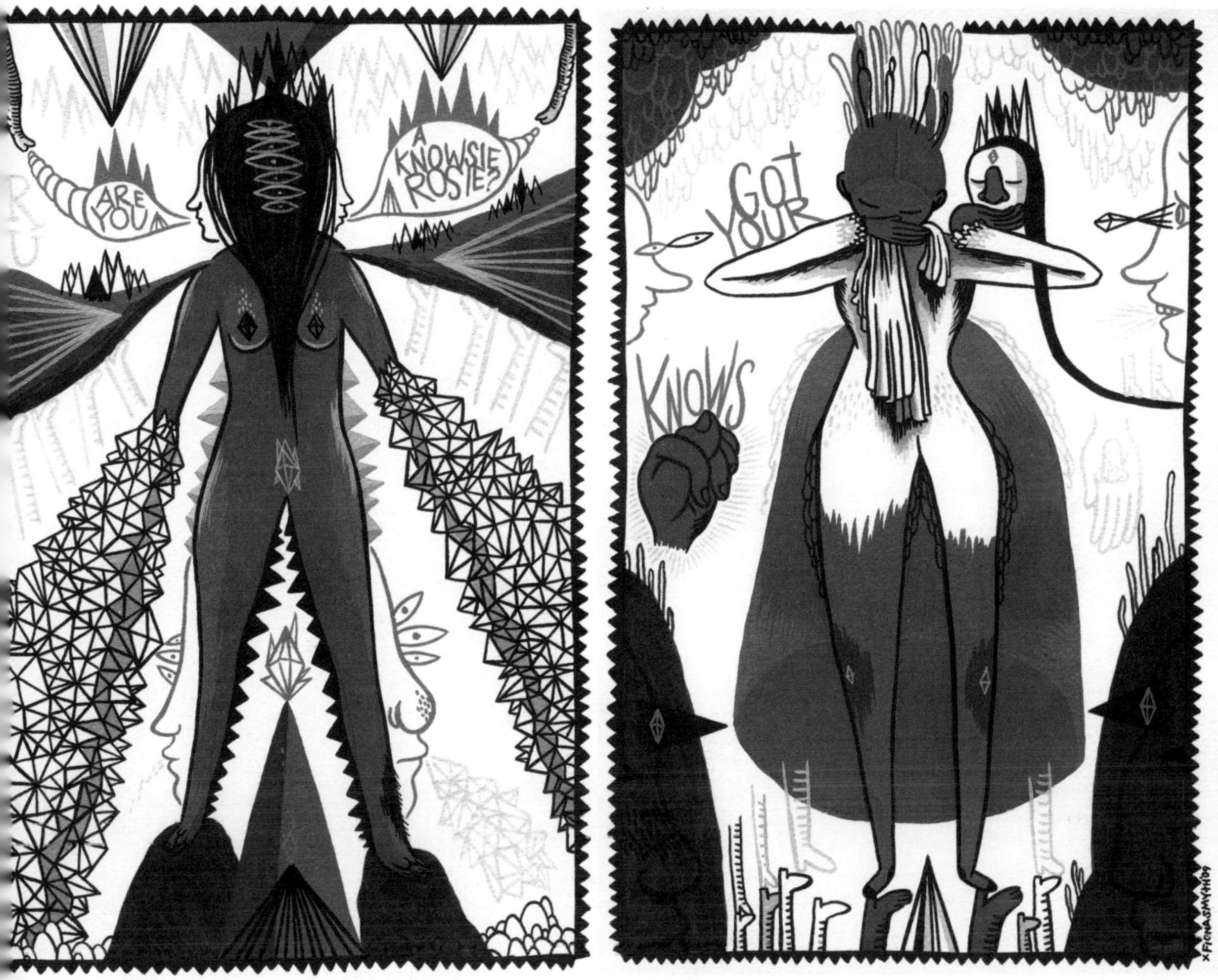
ARE YOU
A KNOWSIE ROSIE?
GOT YOUR
KNOWS

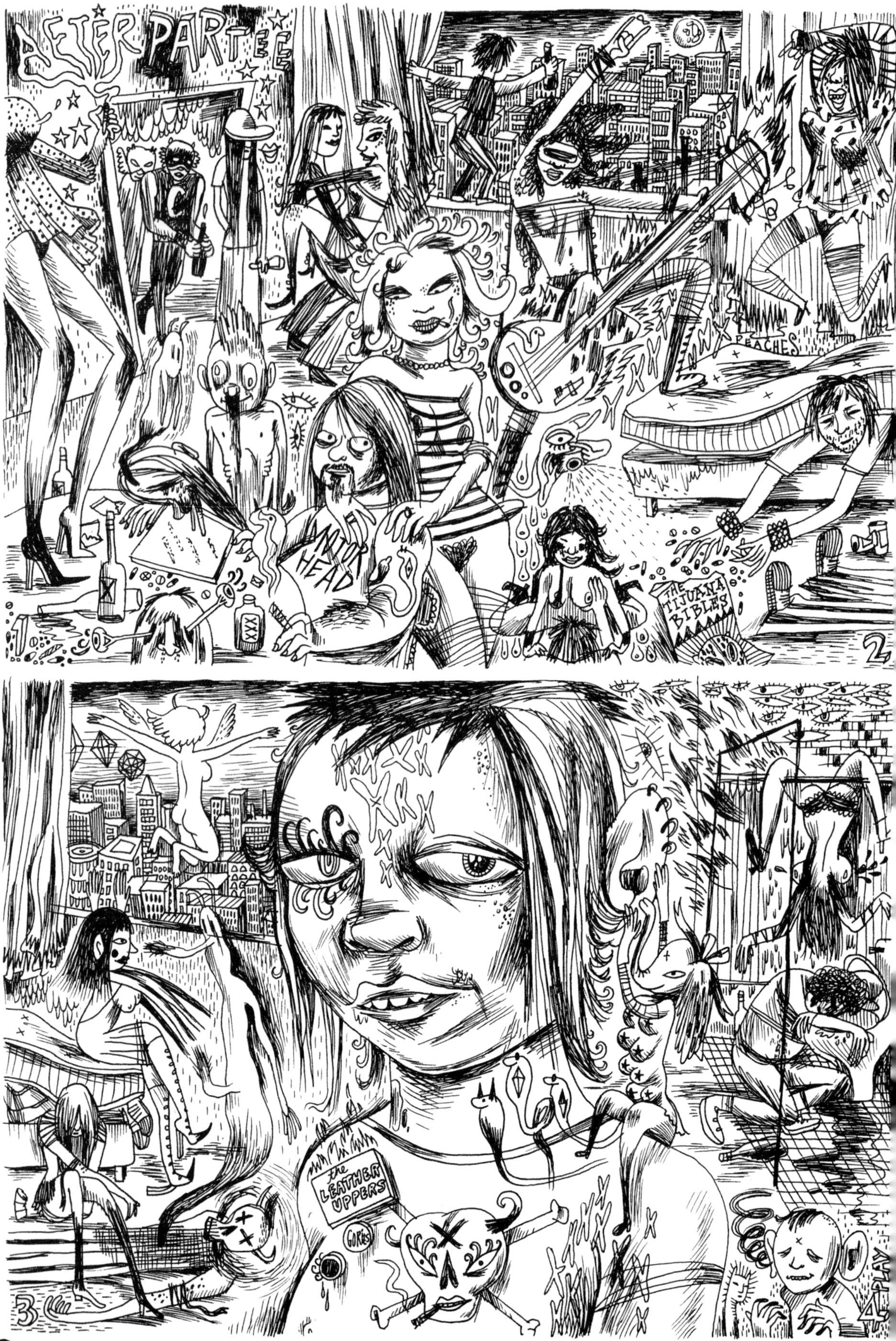
AFTER PARTEE
1
PEACHES
NTOR HEAD
THE TIJUANA BIBLES
2
the LEATHER UPPERS
GORÉES
3
4 PLAY

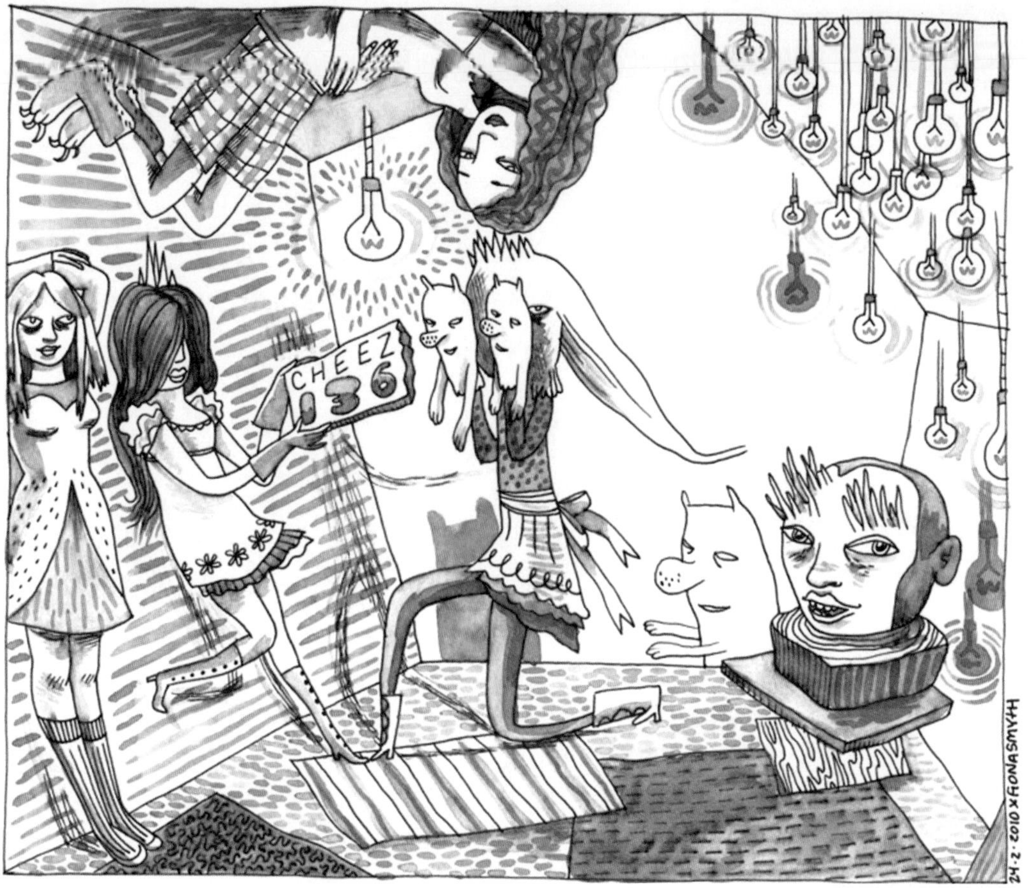
CHEEZ 136
24.2.2010 x FIONASMYTH

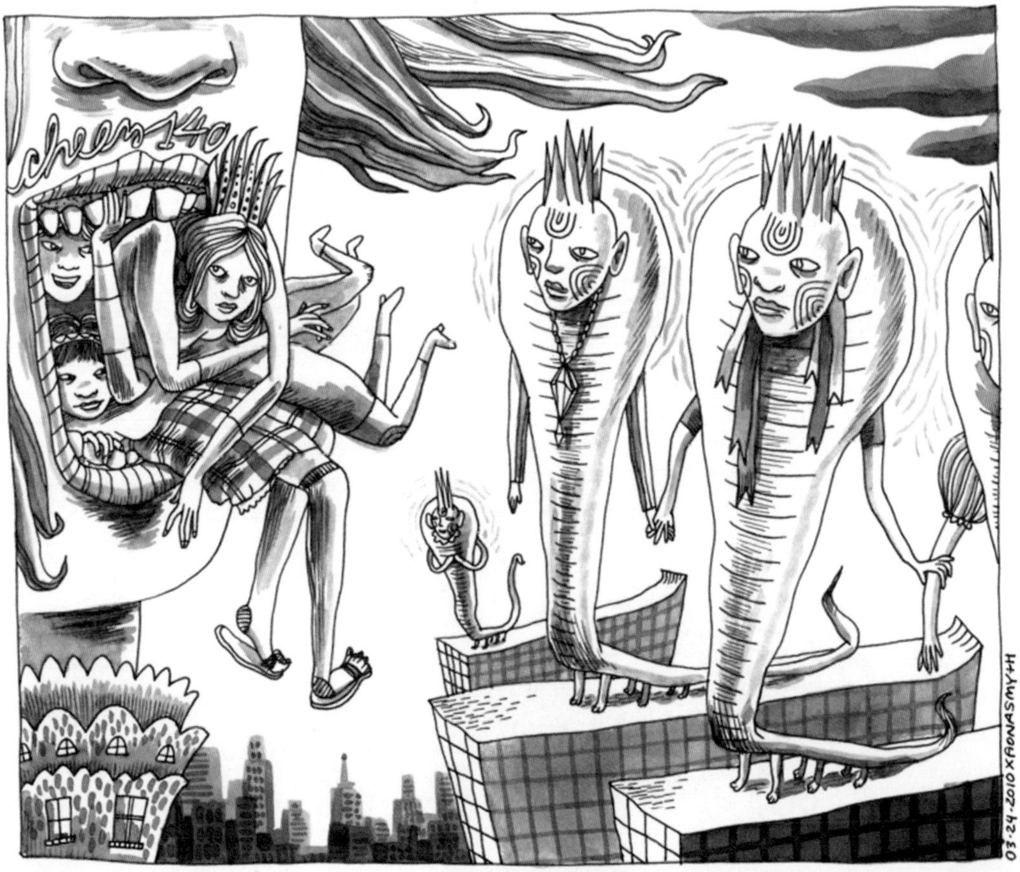
cheez 140
03.24.2010 x FIONASMYTH

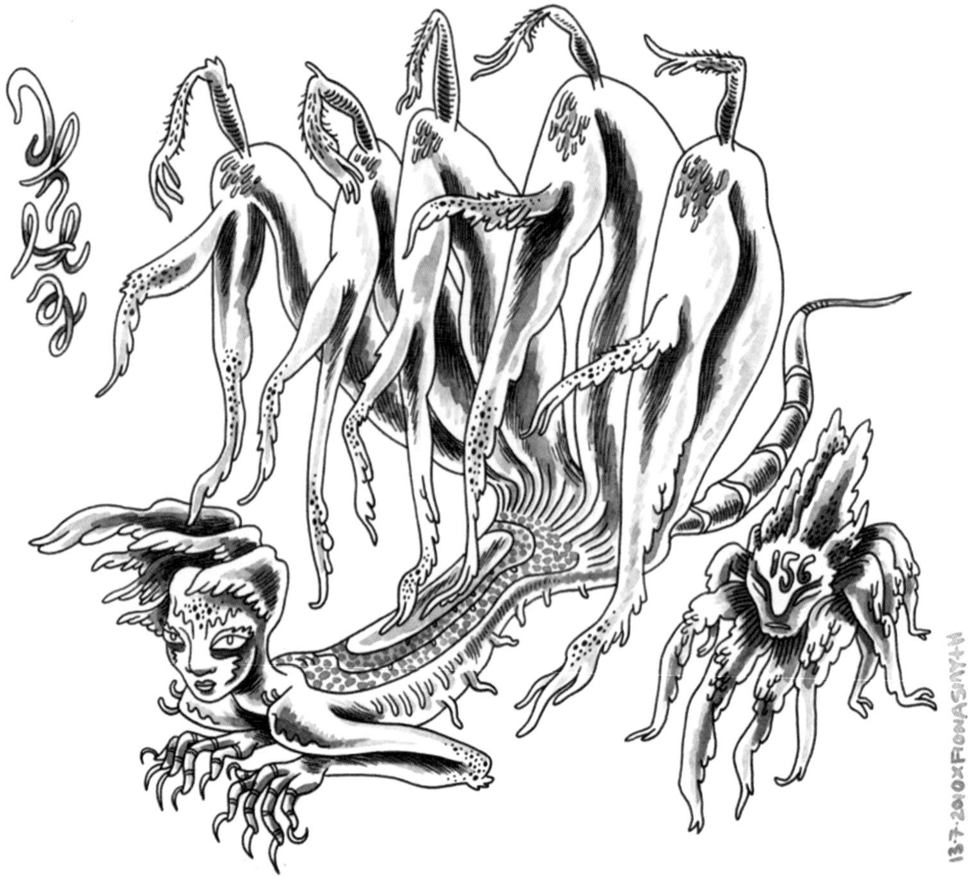
156
13·7·2010 x FIONASMYTH

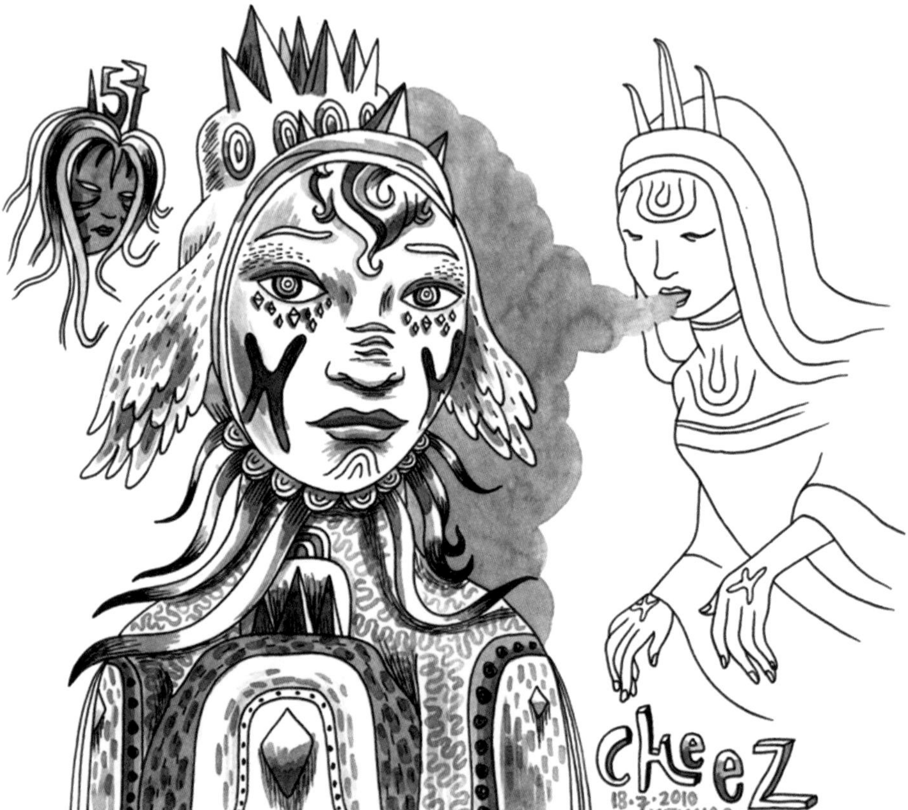
157
Cheez
18·7·2010 x FIONASMYTH

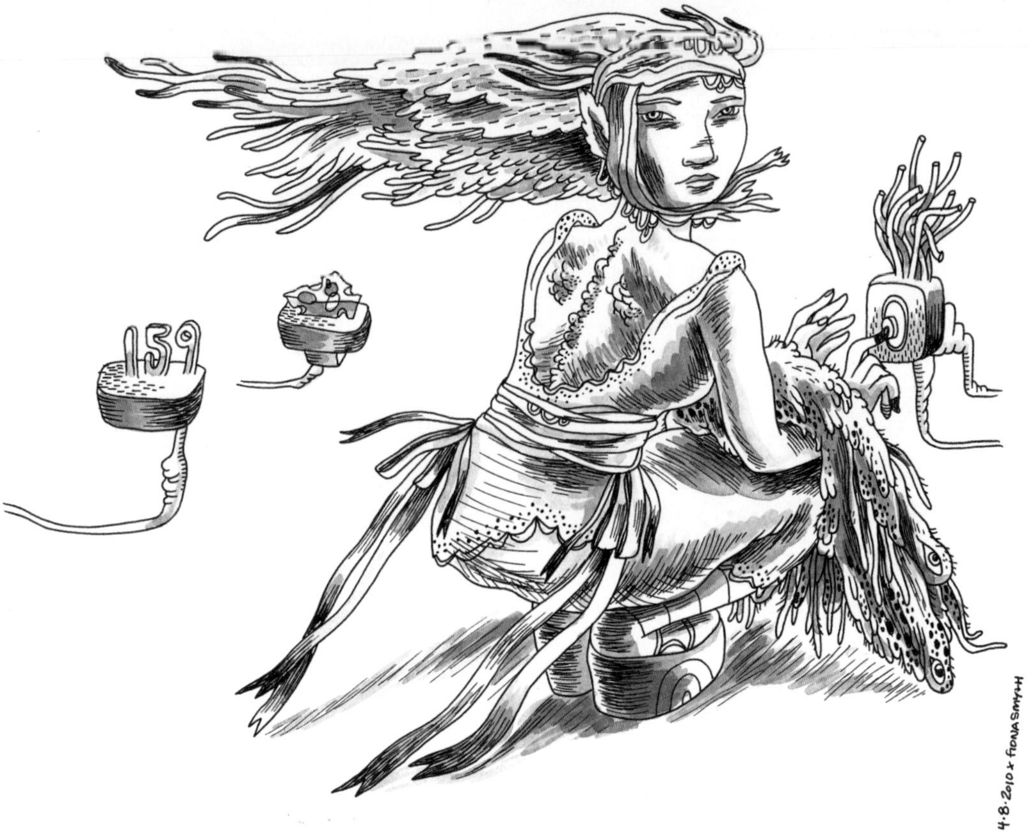
159
4.8.2010 x fionasmyth

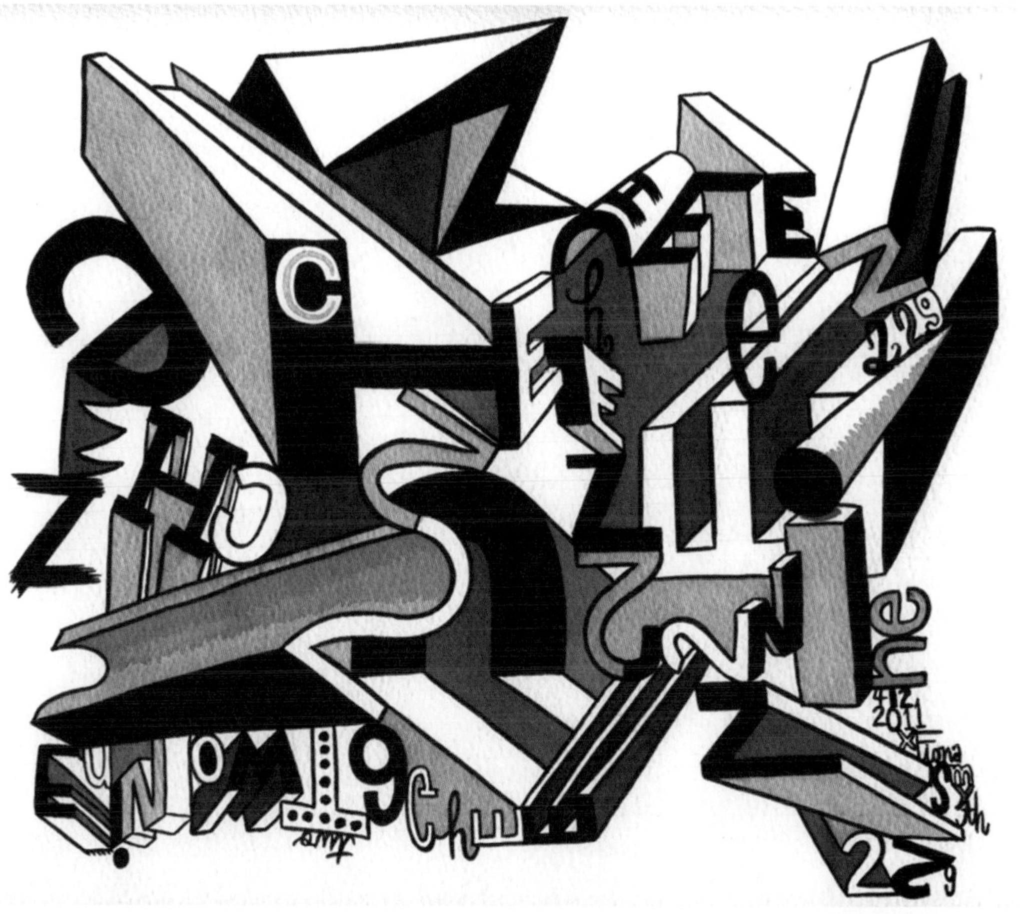

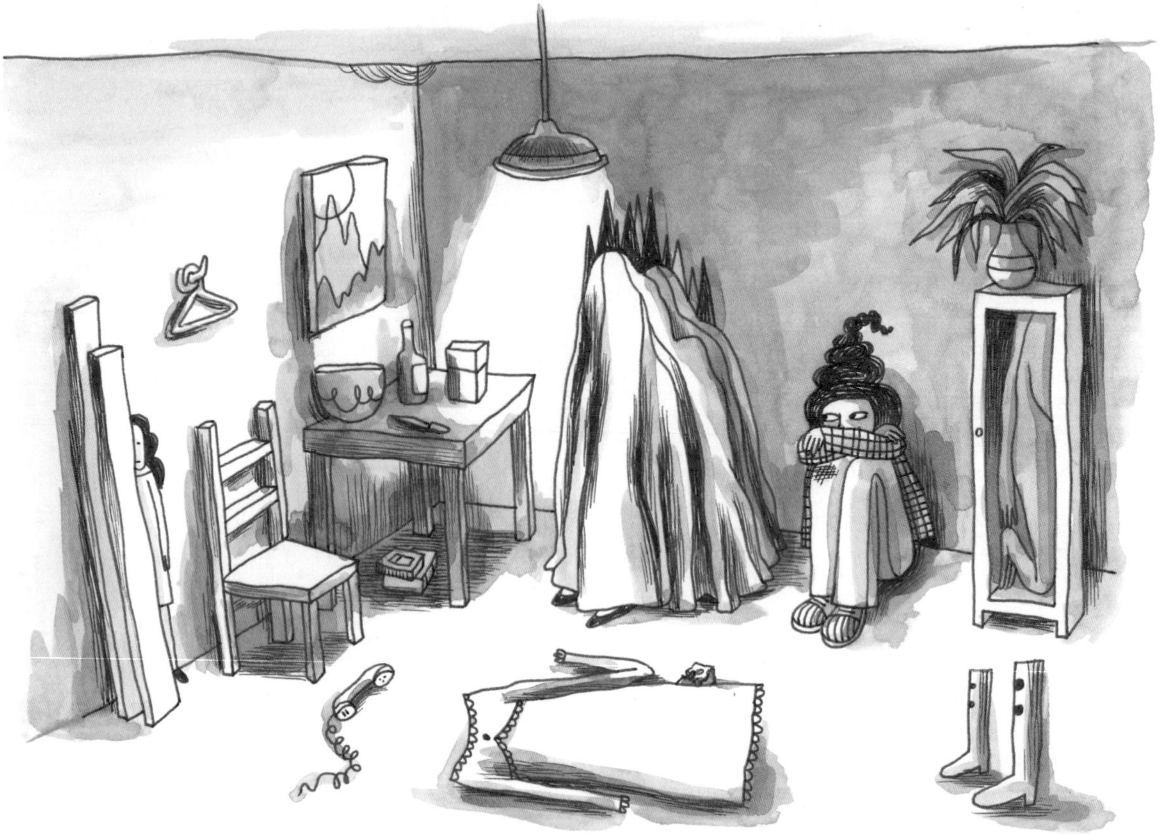
FOUR HUNDRED
17·3·2015
×FIONA
SMYTH

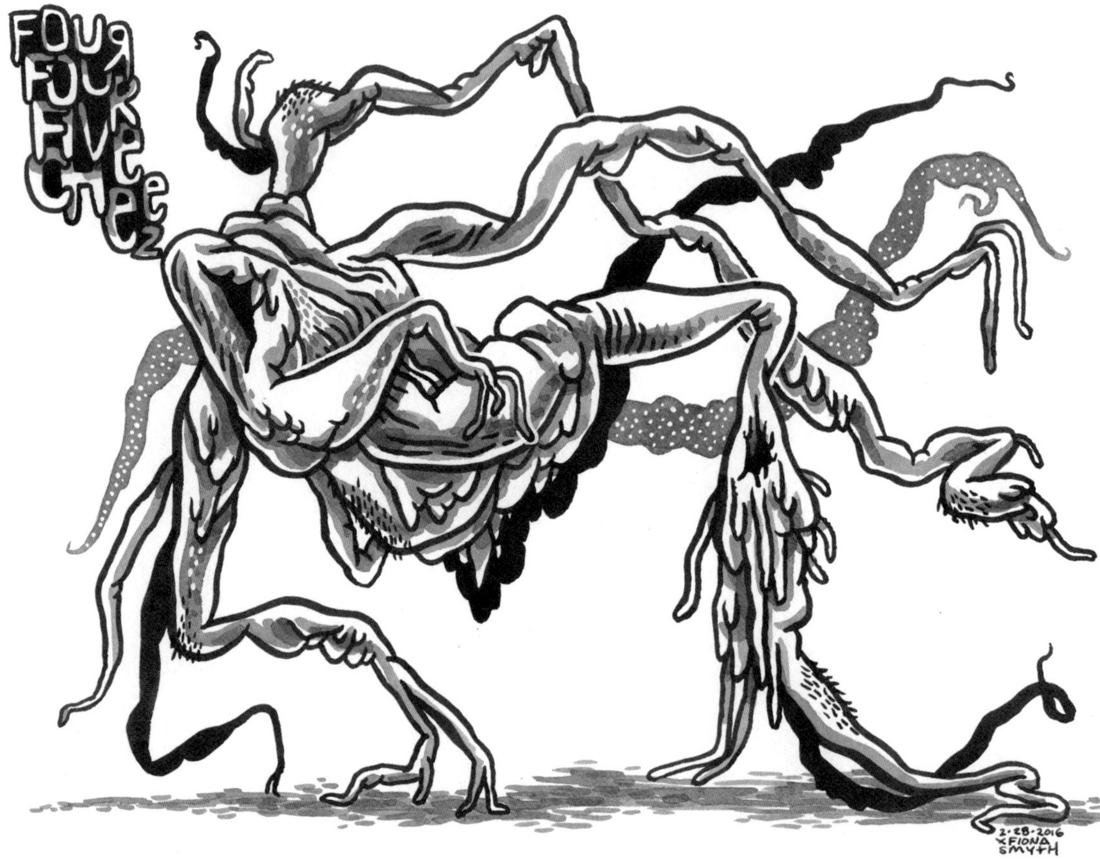
FOUR
FOUR
FIVE
Cheez
2·28·2016
×FIONA
SMYTH

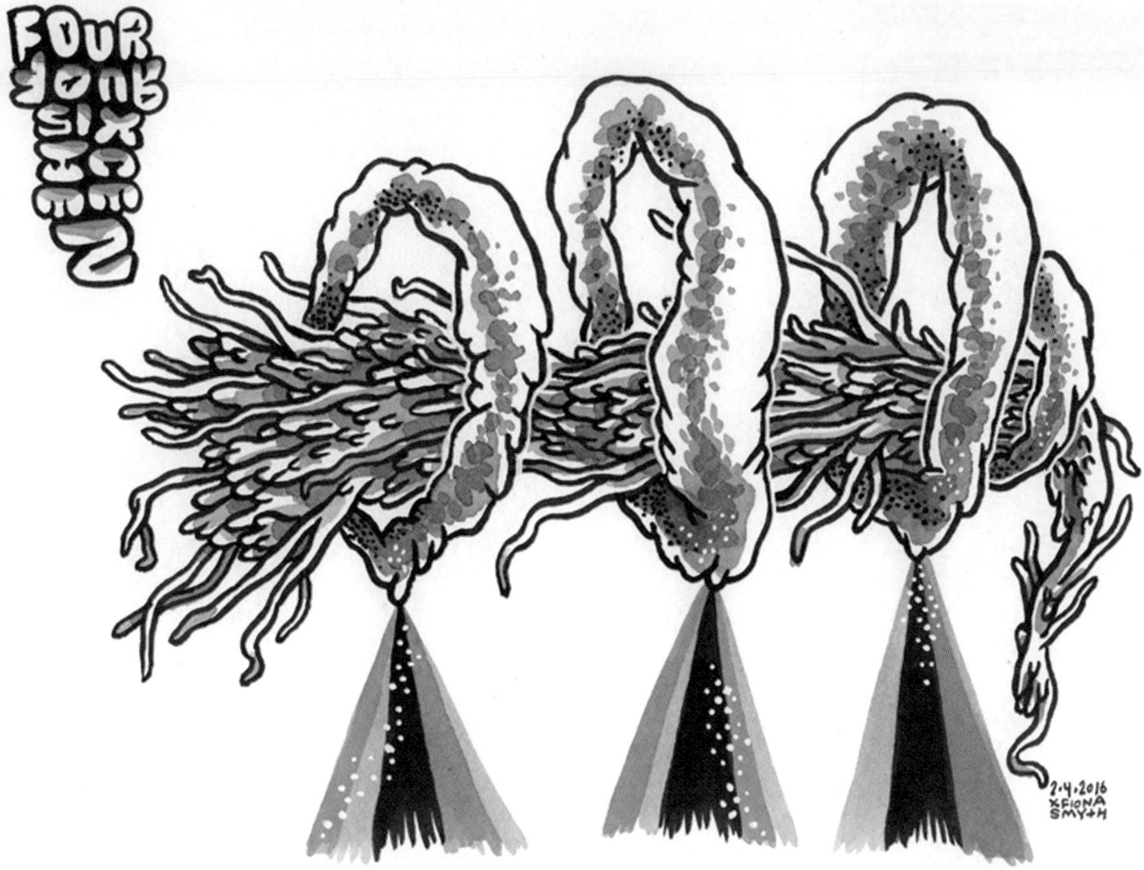
FOUR
SIX
2.4.2016 xFIONA SMYTH

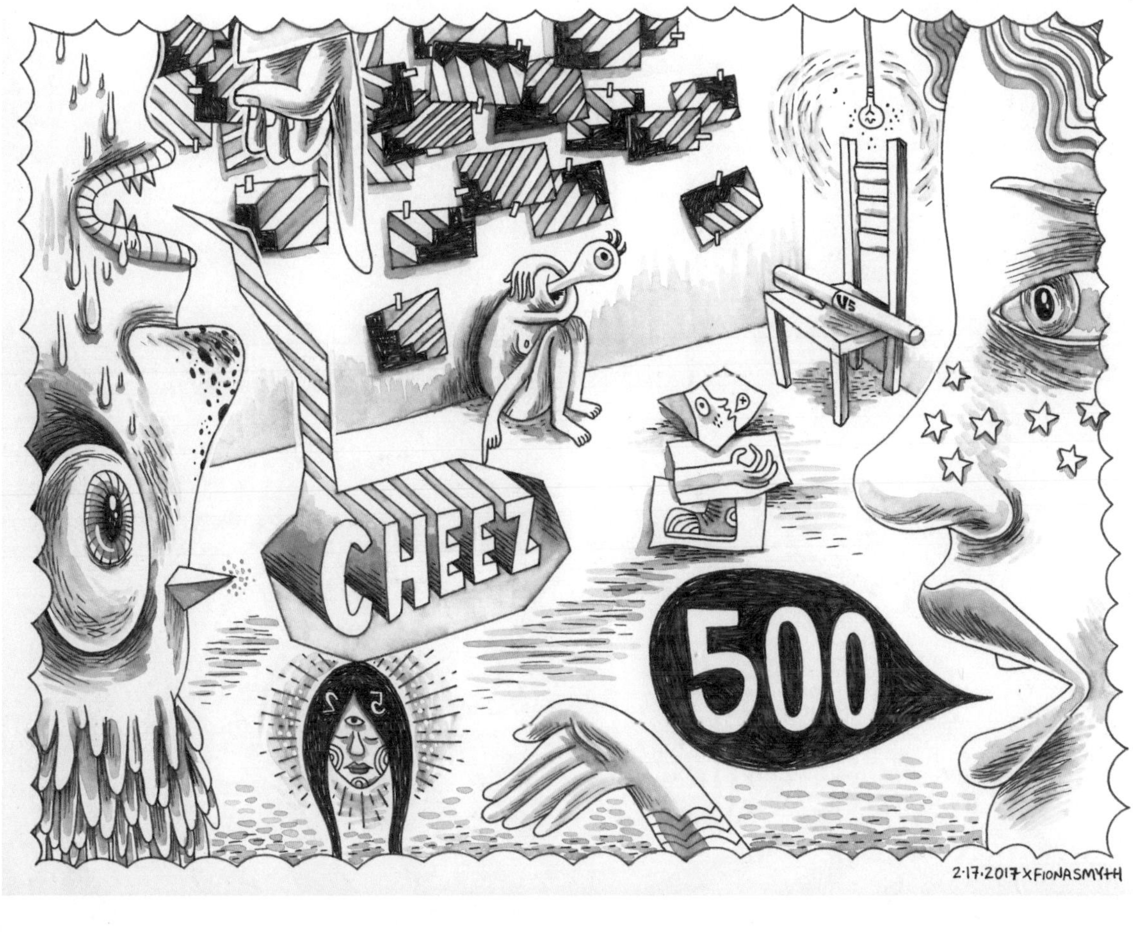
CHEEZ
500
2.17.2017 xFIONASMYTH

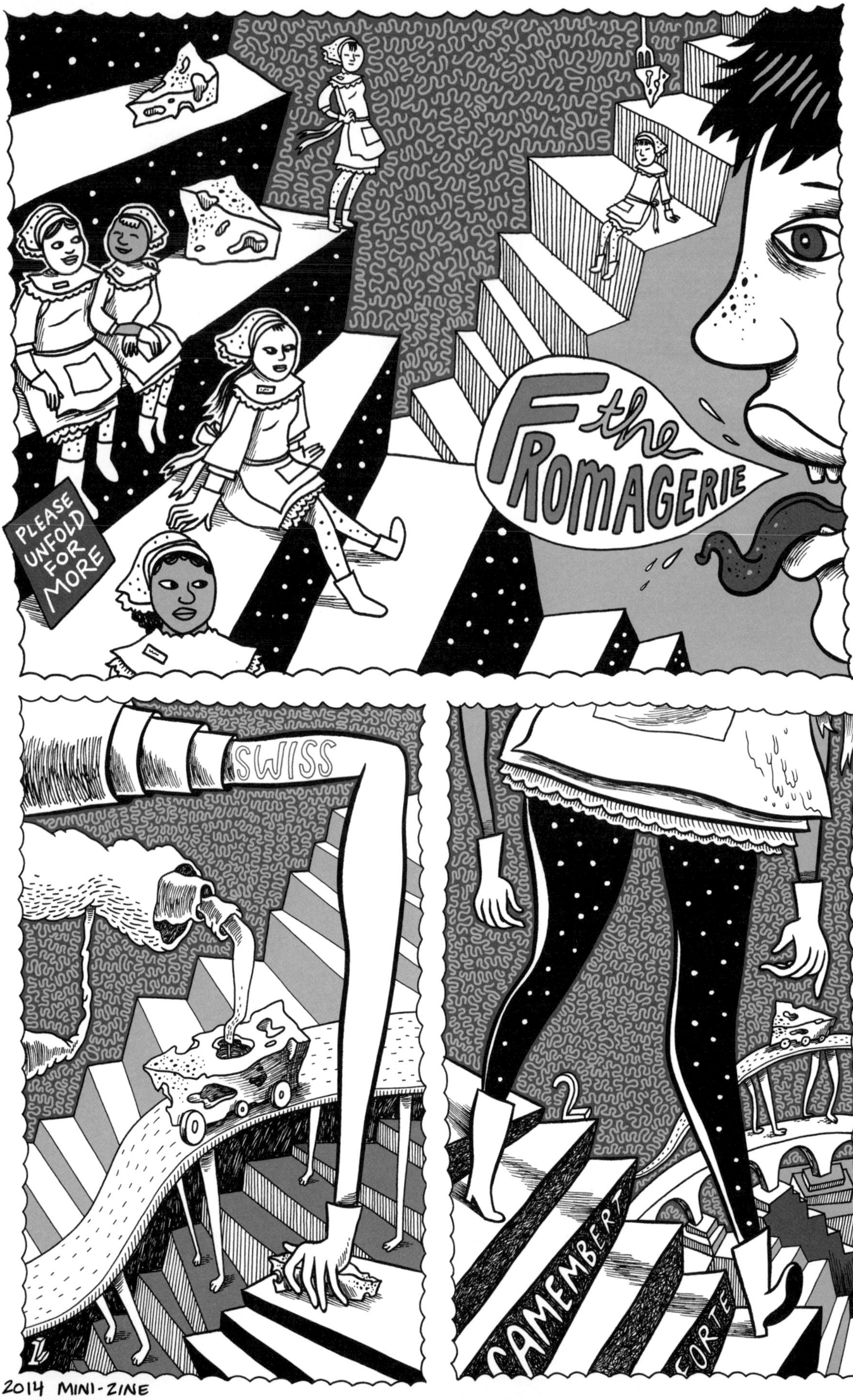

PLEASE UNFOLD FOR MORE
F the FROMAGERIE
SWISS
1
2
CAMEMBERT
FORTE

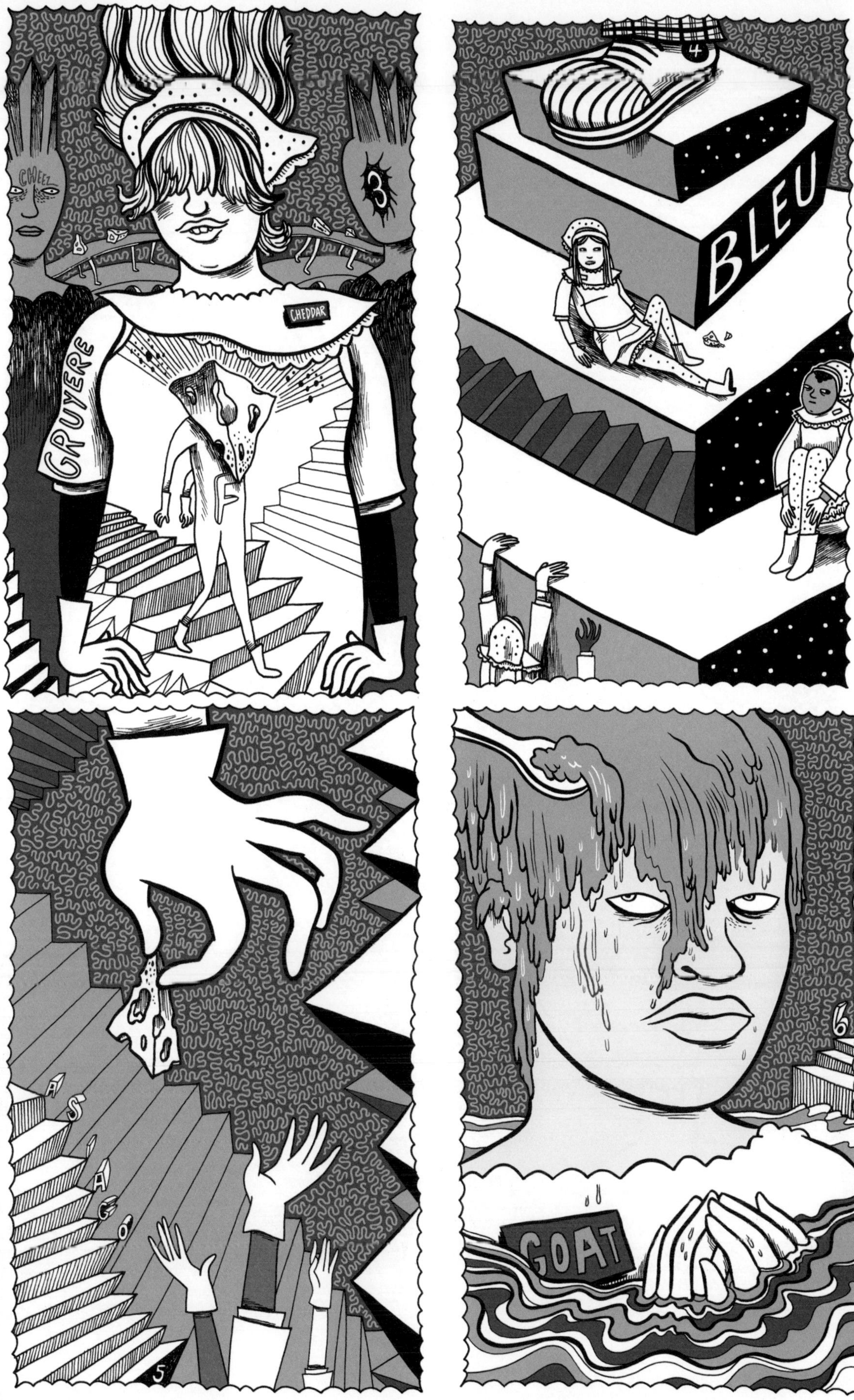

CHEEZ
3
CHEDDAR
GRUYERE
4
BLEU
ASIAGO
5
6
GOAT

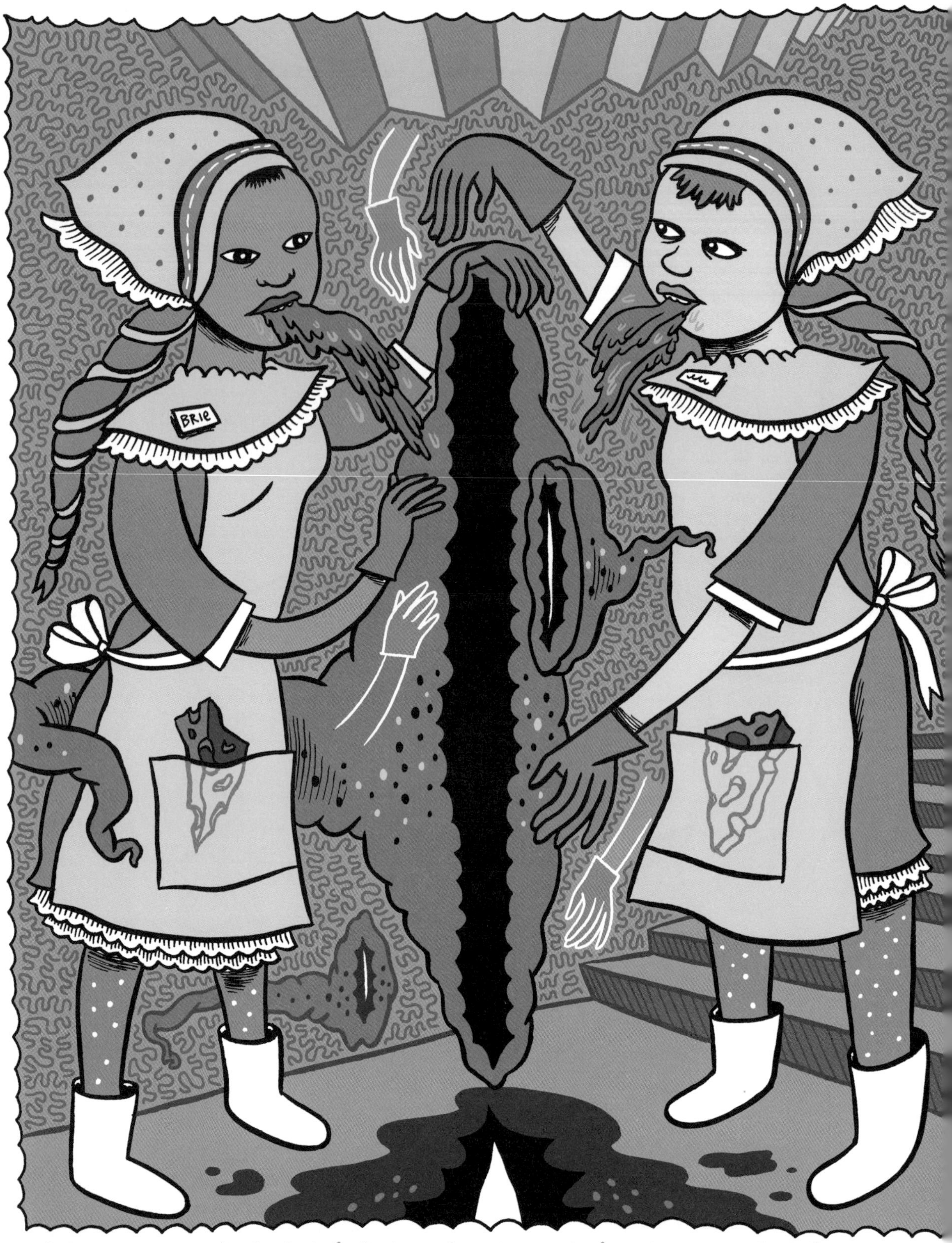
BRIE

fionacheez@gmail.com fiona-smyth.blogspot.ca

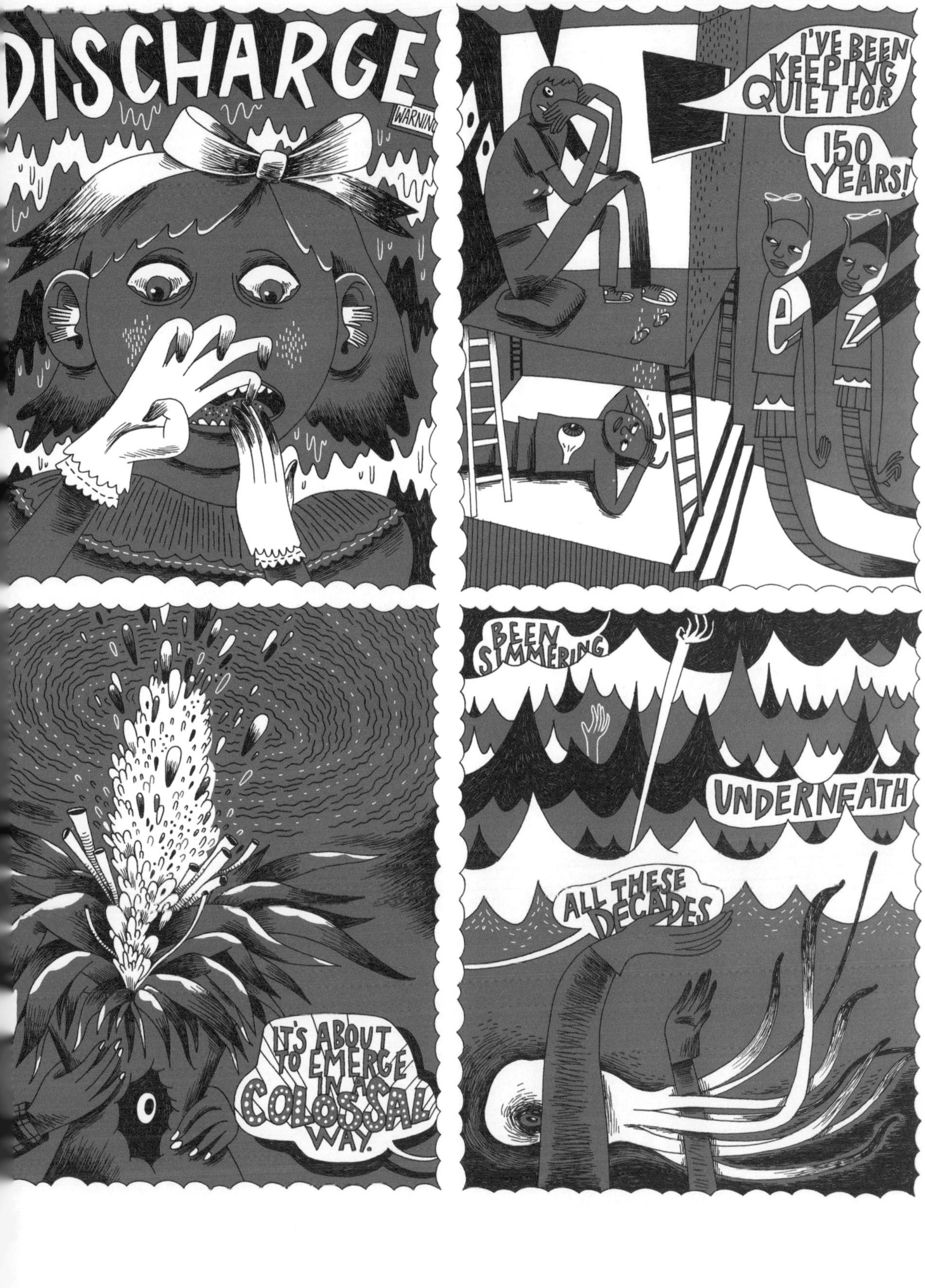
DISCHARGE
WARNING
I'VE BEEN KEEPING QUIET FOR
150 YEARS!
IT'S ABOUT TO EMERGE IN A COLOSSAL WAY.
BEEN SIMMERING
UNDERNEATH
ALL THESE DECADES

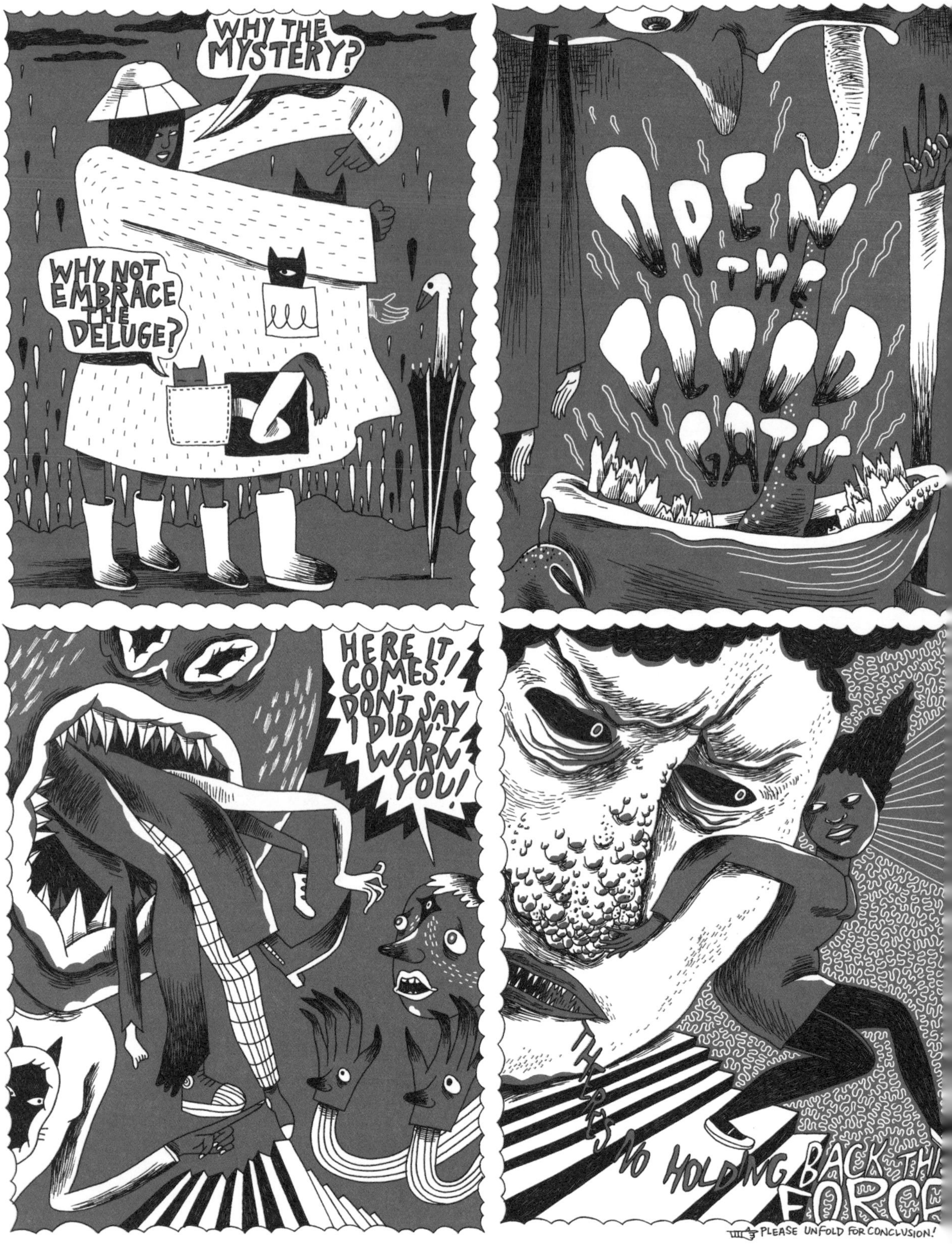
WHY THE MYSTERY?
WHY NOT EMBRACE THE DELUGE?
OPEN THE FLOOD GATES
HERE IT COMES! DON'T SAY I DIDN'T WARN YOU!
THERE'S NO HOLDING BACK THE FORCE

PLEASE UNFOLD FOR CONCLUSION!

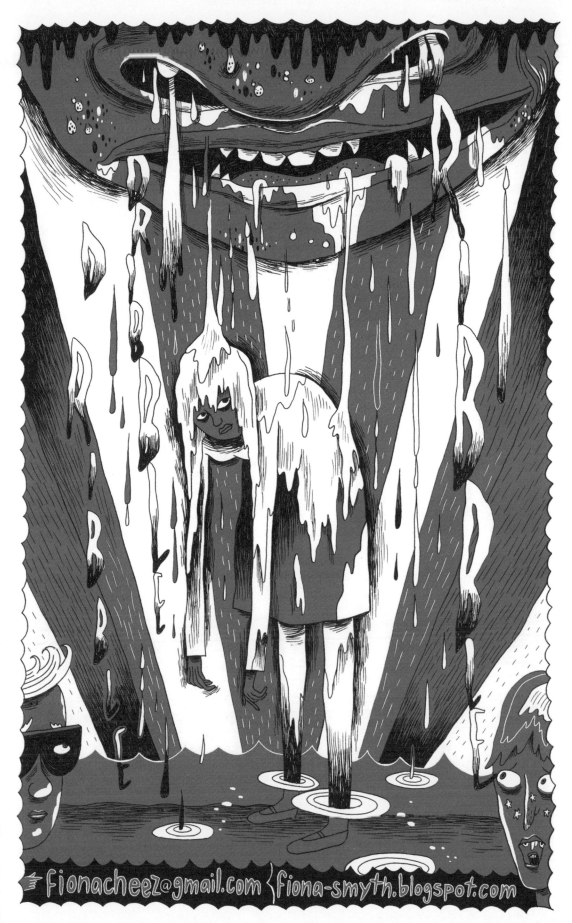

fionacheez@gmail.com fiona-smyth.blogspot.com

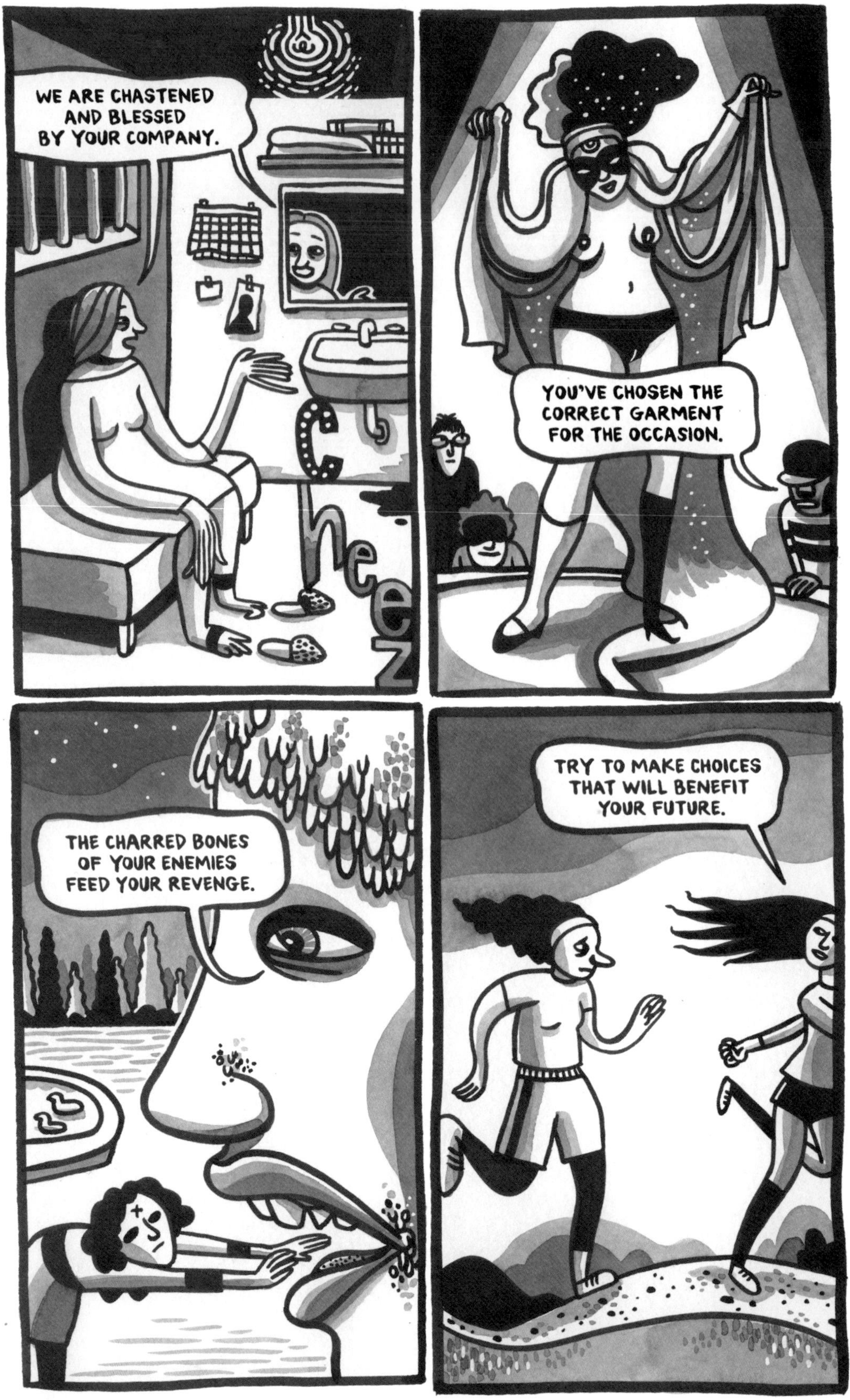
WE ARE CHASTENED AND BLESSED BY YOUR COMPANY.
Cheez
YOU'VE CHOSEN THE CORRECT GARMENT FOR THE OCCASION.
THE CHARRED BONES OF YOUR ENEMIES FEED YOUR REVENGE.
TRY TO MAKE CHOICES THAT WILL BENEFIT YOUR FUTURE.

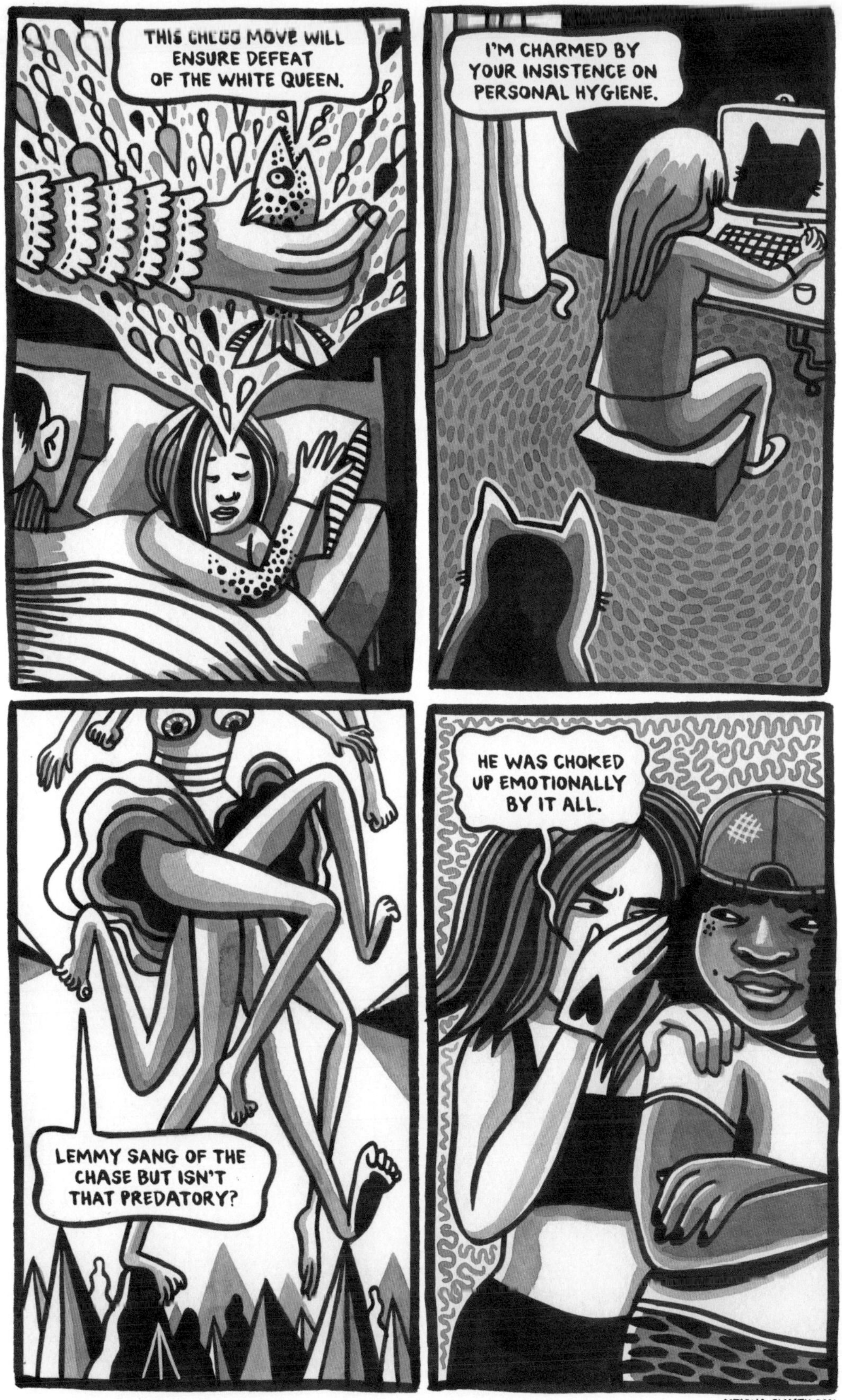

THIS CHESS MOVE WILL ENSURE DEFEAT OF THE WHITE QUEEN.
I'M CHARMED BY YOUR INSISTENCE ON PERSONAL HYGIENE.
LEMMY SANG OF THE CHASE BUT ISN'T THAT PREDATORY?
HE WAS CHOKED UP EMOTIONALLY BY IT ALL.

XFIONA SMYTH 2016

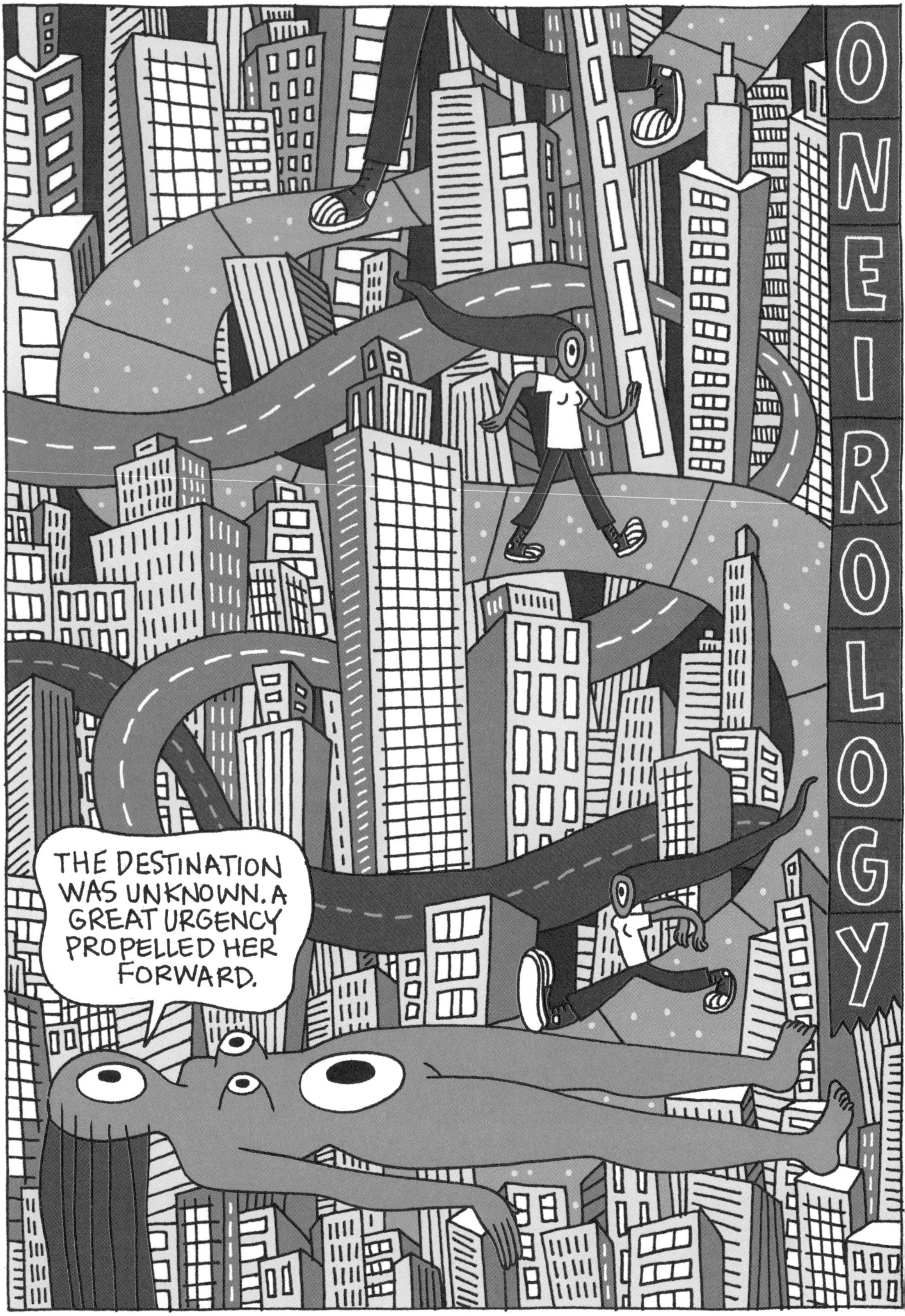
ONEIROLOGY
THE DESTINATION WAS UNKNOWN. A GREAT URGENCY PROPELLED HER FORWARD.

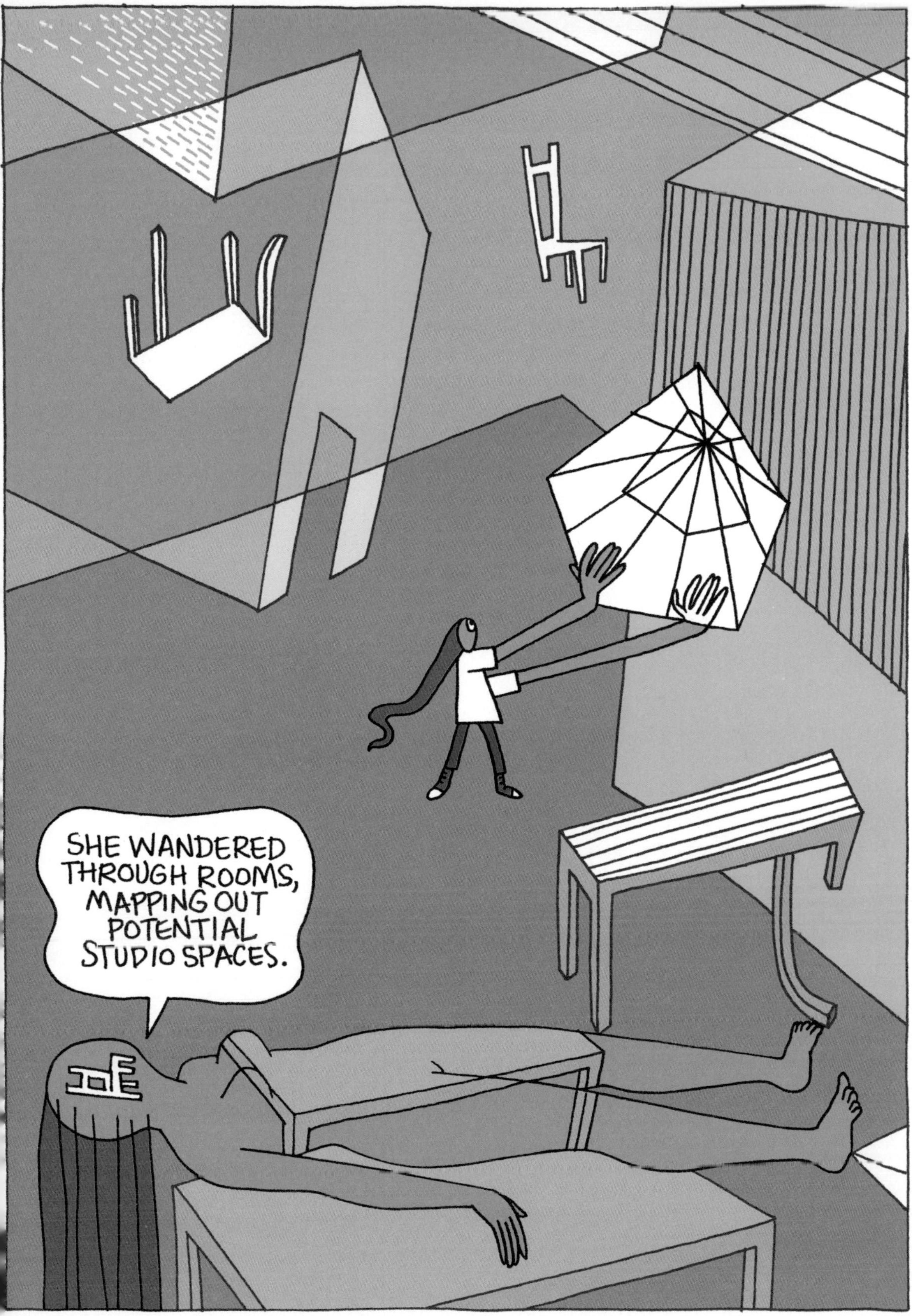
SHE WANDERED THROUGH ROOMS, MAPPING OUT POTENTIAL STUDIO SPACES.

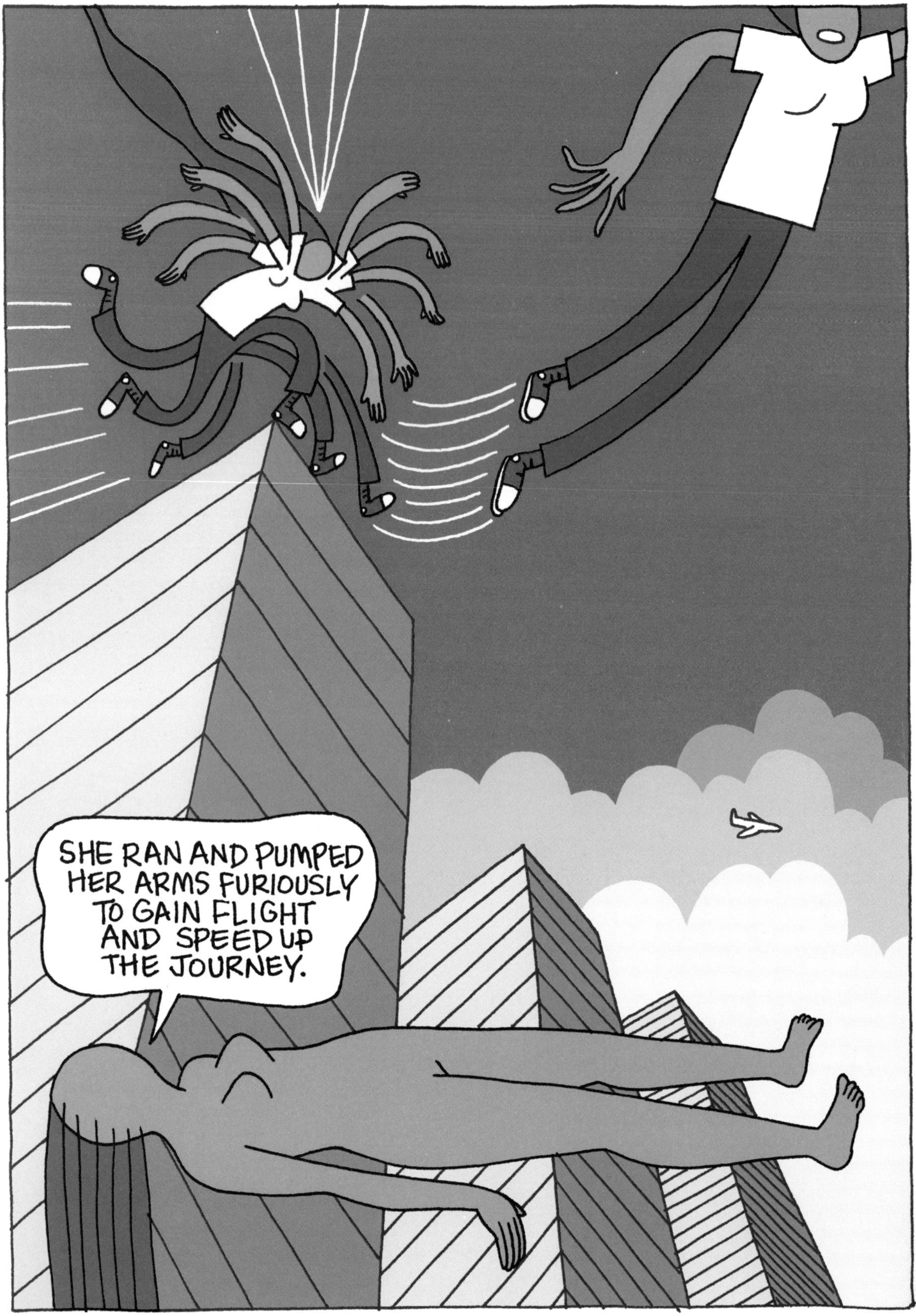
SHE RAN AND PUMPED HER ARMS FURIOUSLY TO GAIN FLIGHT AND SPEED UP THE JOURNEY.

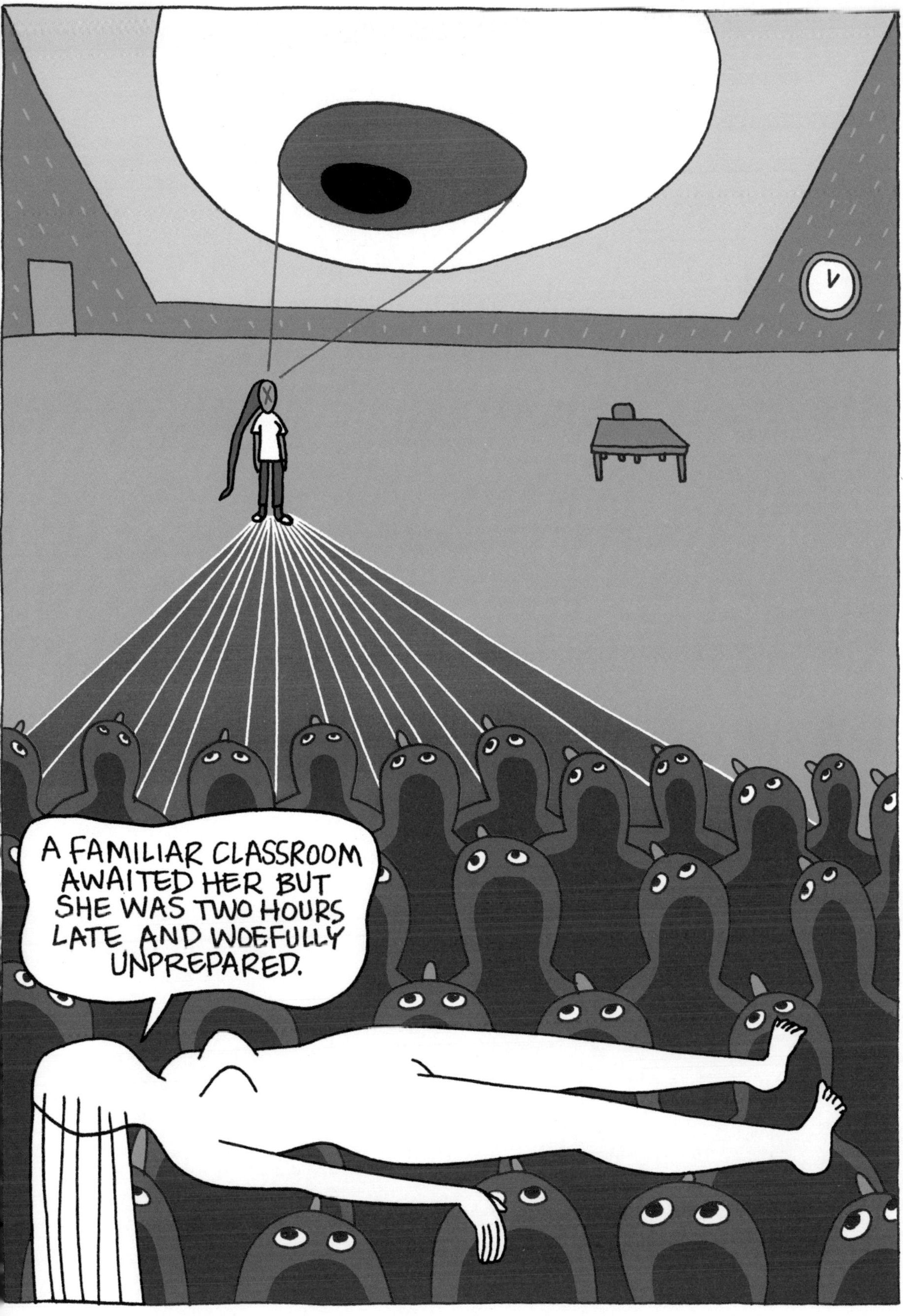
A FAMILIAR CLASSROOM AWAITED HER BUT SHE WAS TWO HOURS LATE AND WOEFULLY UNPREPARED.

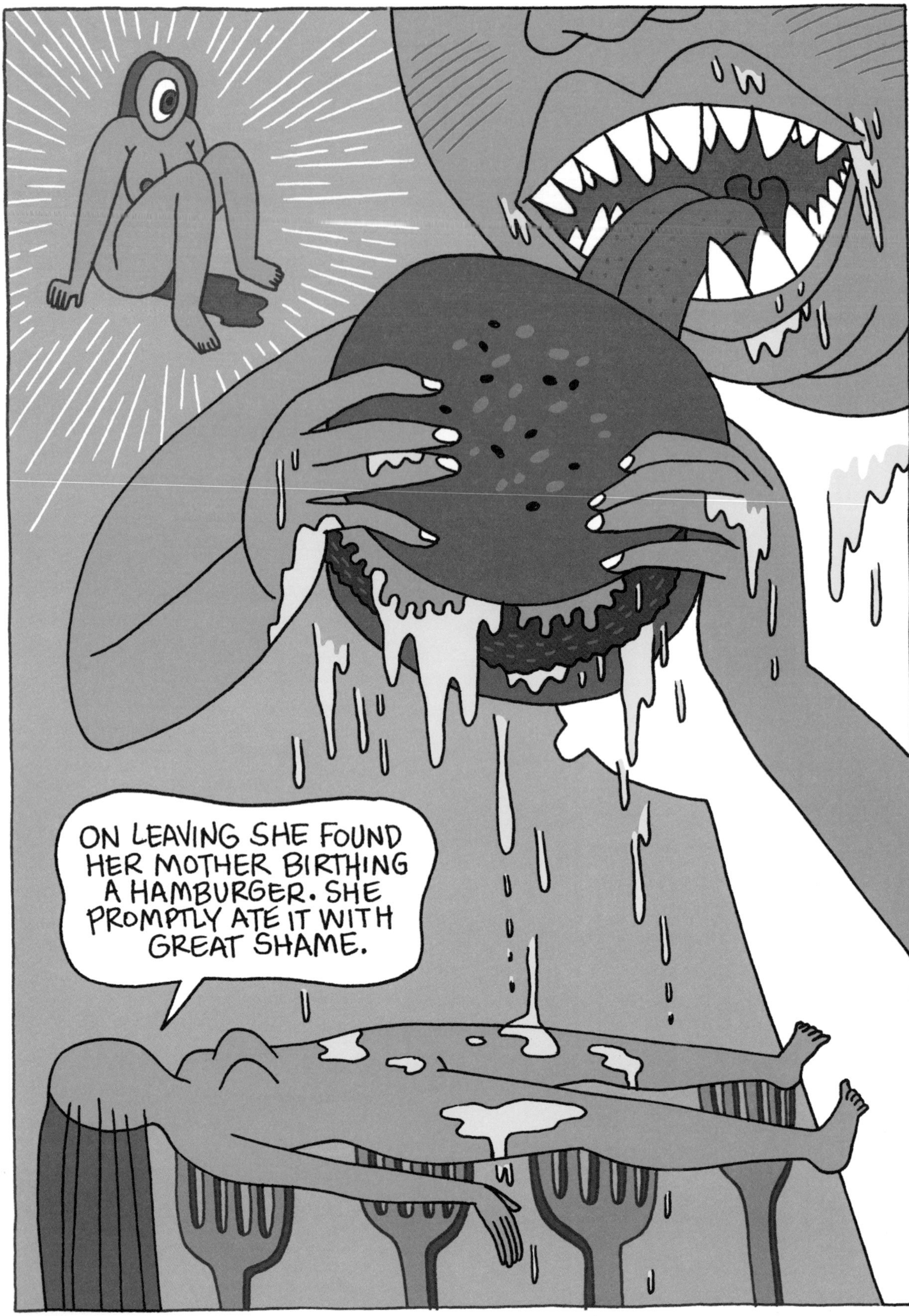
ON LEAVING SHE FOUND HER MOTHER BIRTHING A HAMBURGER. SHE PROMPTLY ATE IT WITH GREAT SHAME.

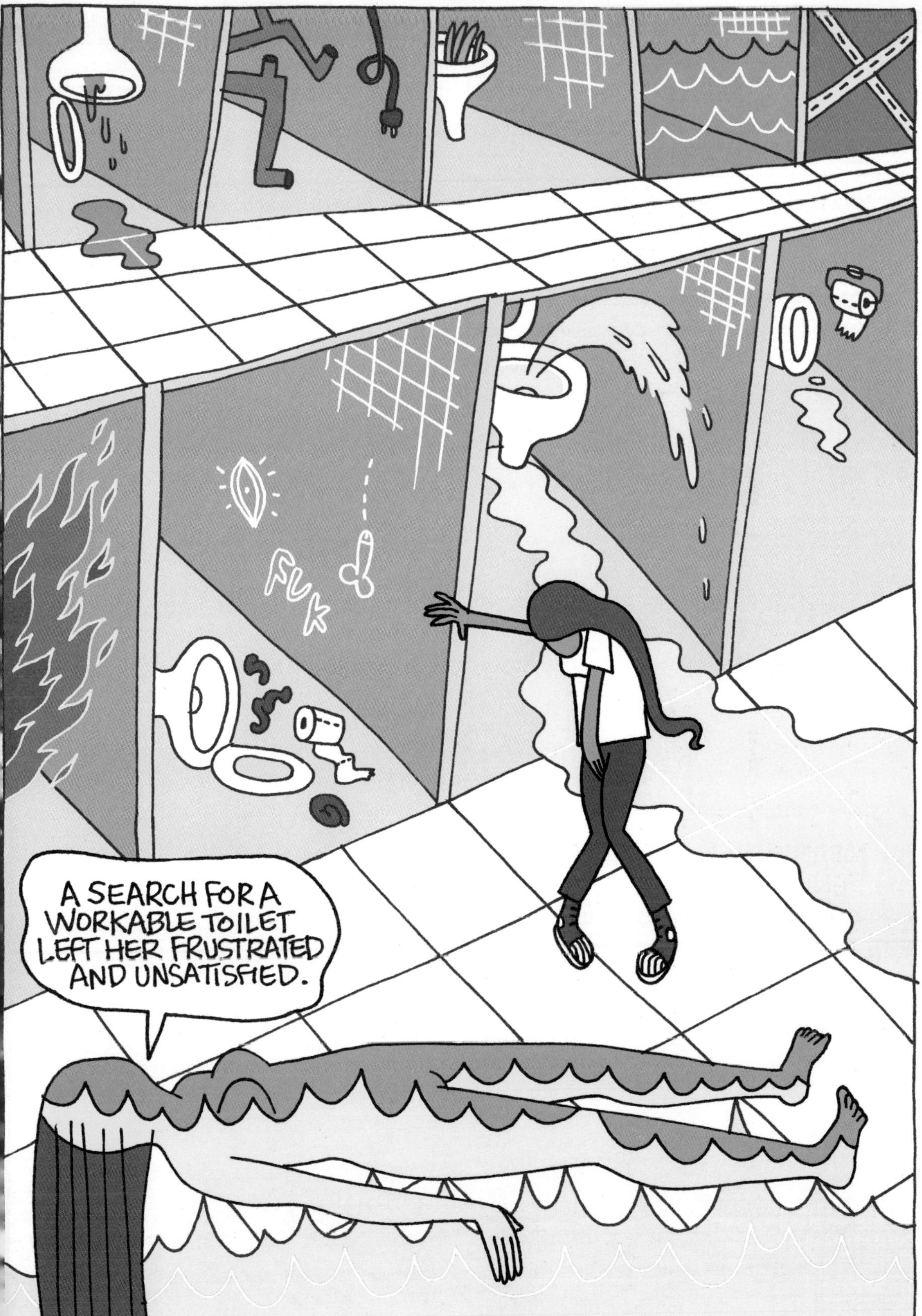
FUK
A SEARCH FOR A WORKABLE TOILET LEFT HER FRUSTRATED AND UNSATISFIED.

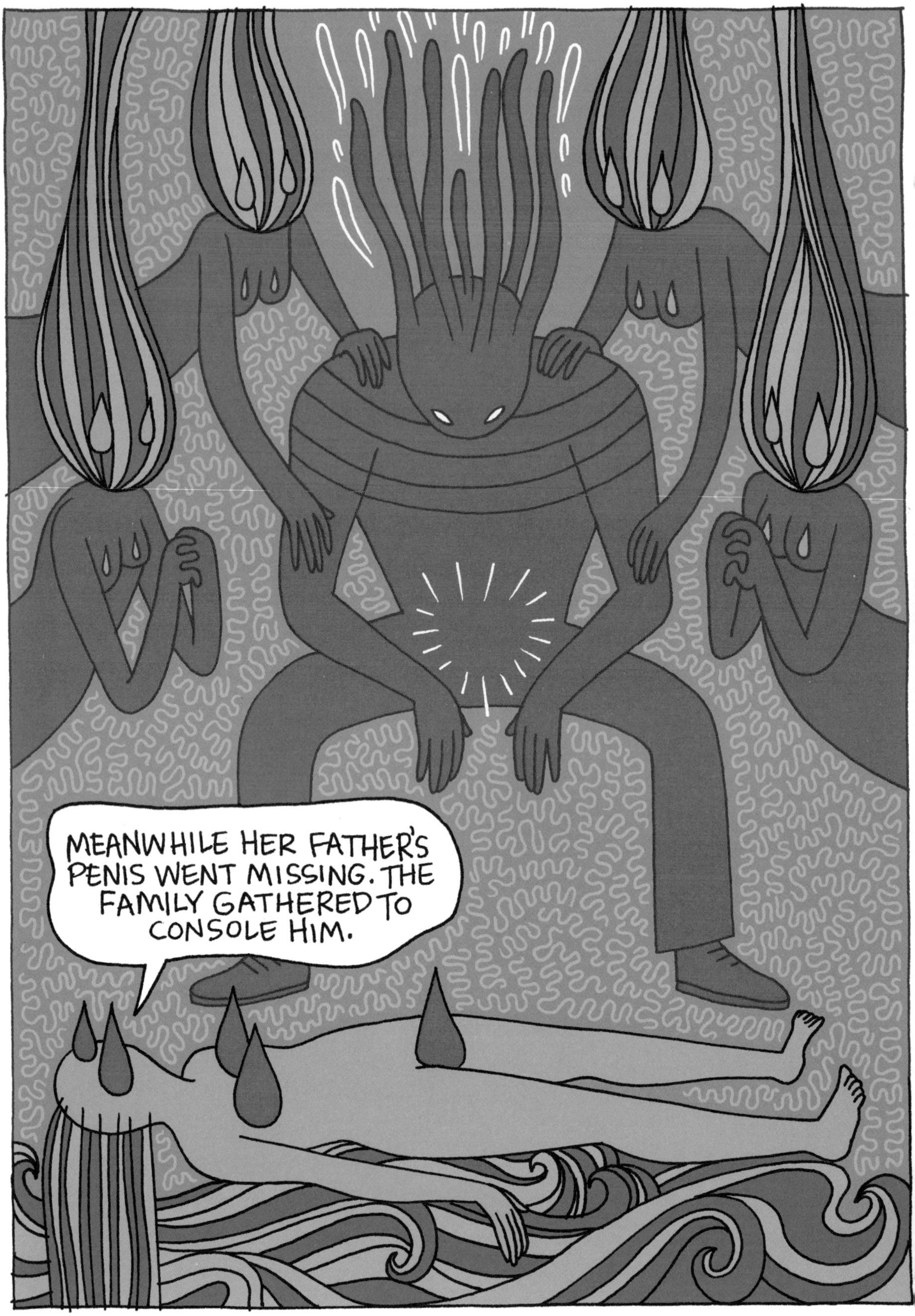
MEANWHILE HER FATHER'S PENIS WENT MISSING. THE FAMILY GATHERED TO CONSOLE HIM.

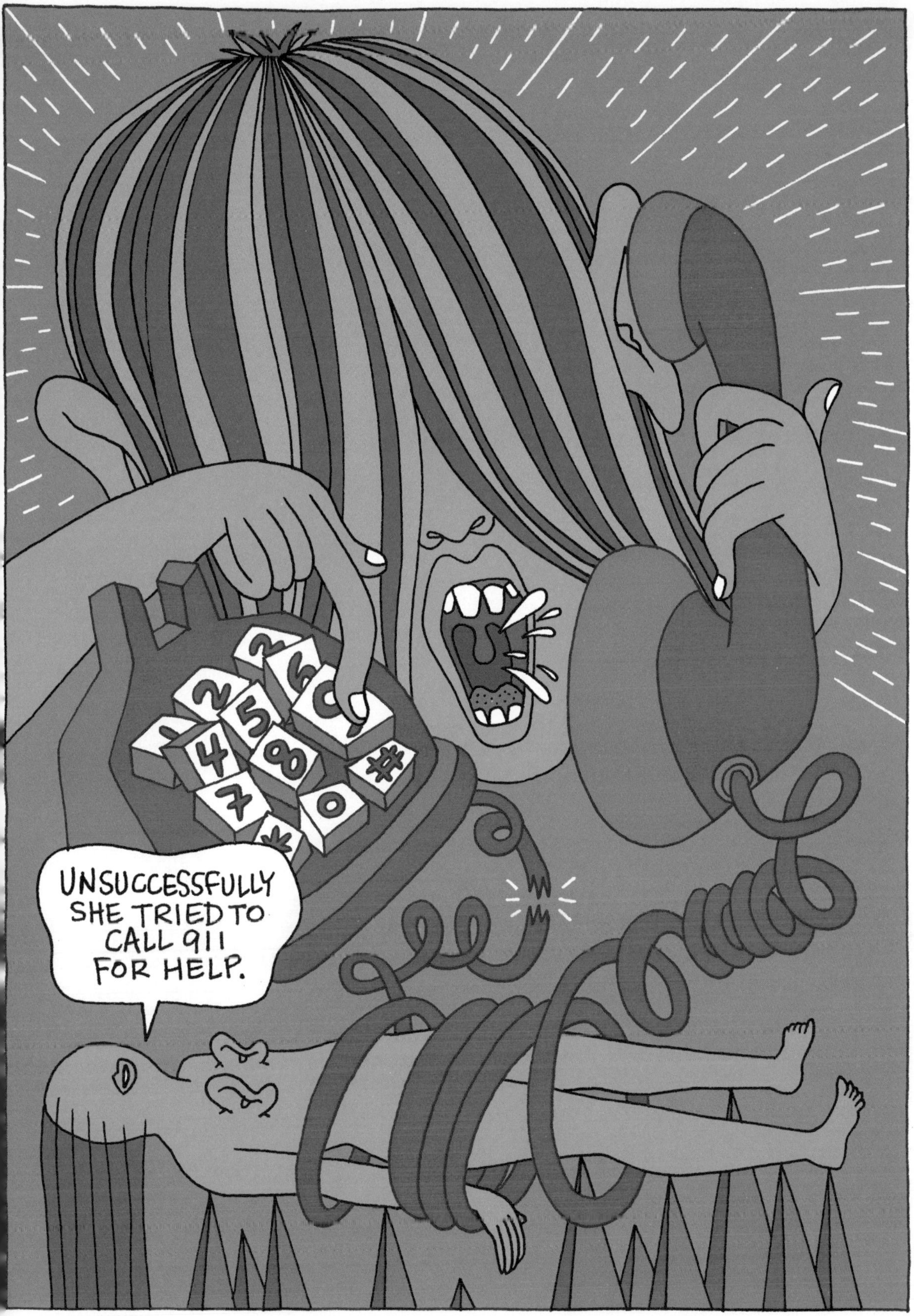
UNSUCCESSFULLY SHE TRIED TO CALL 911 FOR HELP.

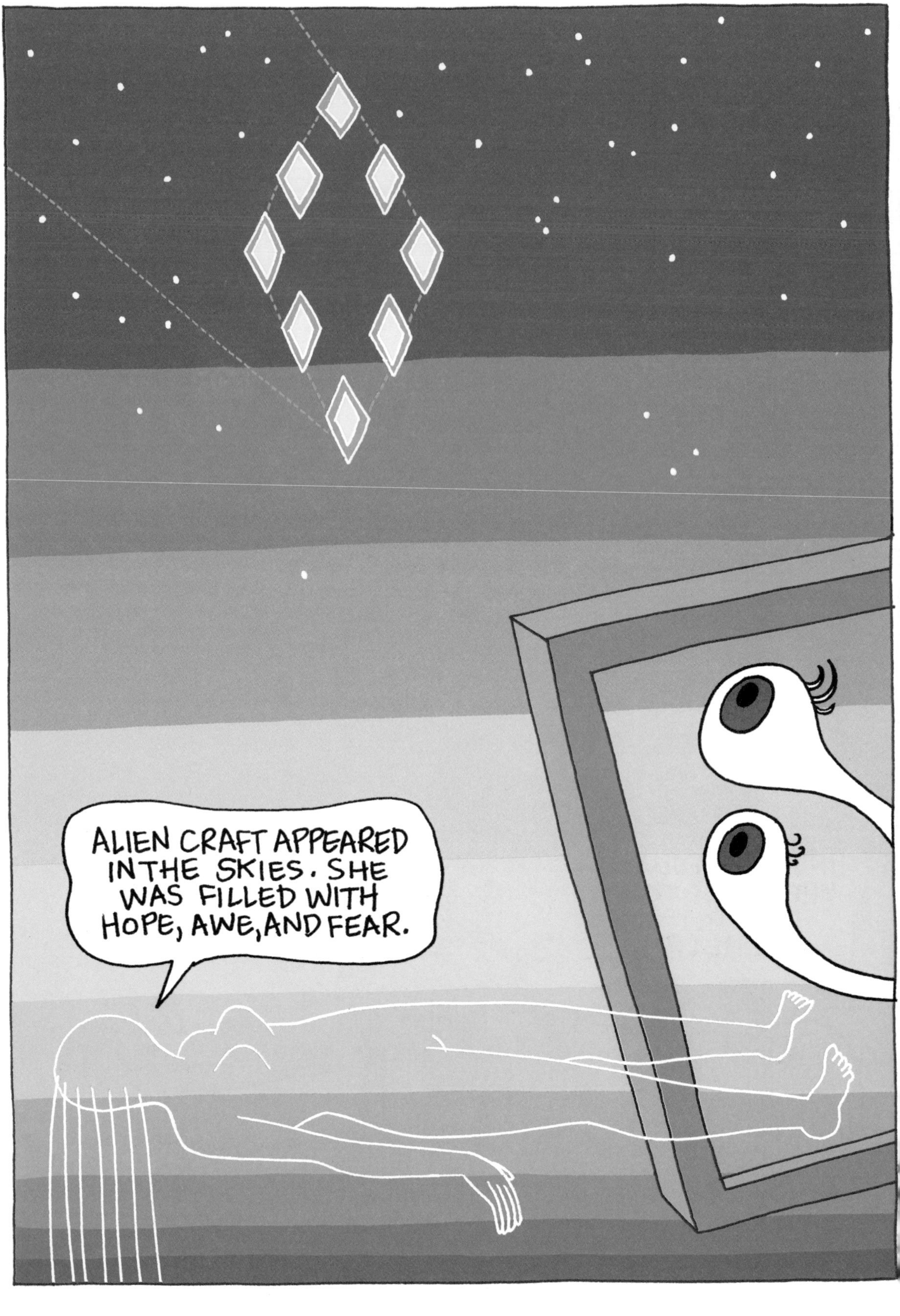
ALIEN CRAFT APPEARED IN THE SKIES. SHE WAS FILLED WITH HOPE, AWE, AND FEAR.

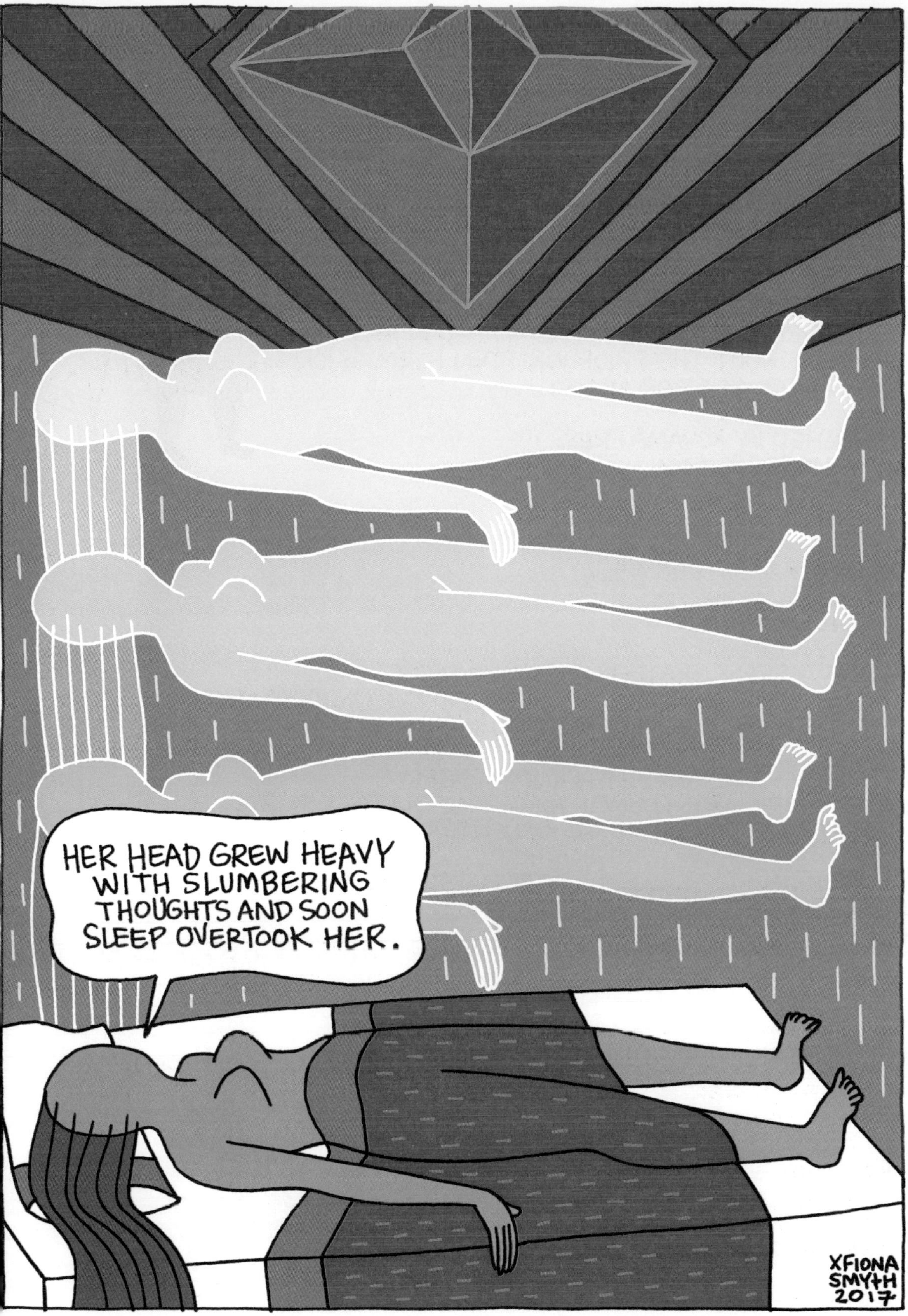
HER HEAD GREW HEAVY WITH SLUMBERING THOUGHTS AND SOON SLEEP OVERTOOK HER.
XFIONA SMYTH 2017

INDICIA

PUBLISHED BY KOYAMA PRESS
KOYAMAPRESS.COM

FIRST EDITION: MAY 2018

ISBN: 978-1-927668-54-2

PRINTED IN CHINA

KOYAMA PRESS GRATEFULLY ACKNOWLEDGES
THE CANADA COUNCIL FOR THE ARTS AND THE ONTARIO ARTS COUNCIL
FOR THEIR SUPPORT OF OUR PUBLISHING PROGRAM.

FIONA SMYTH GRATEFULLY ACKNOWLEDGES
THE ONTARIO ARTS COUNCIL FOR GRANT SUPPORT IN THE
CREATION OF THE CHIMERA'S DAUGHTERS, 2005

NOCTURNAL EMISSIONS #1 INTRODUCTION REPRINTED WITH
THE KIND PERMISSION OF SETH ©1991

"NIGHT OF THE OH-SO-VERY DEAD" WRITTEN BY DENNIS P. EICHHORN ©1992
"FLUFFY THE DOG" WRITTEN BY PATTY POWERS ©1998

THANKS AND LOVE TO:
• ANNIE KOYAMA FOR LEADING THE WAY, THEE PATRON SAINT OF COMICS
• RMV FOR NEVER-ENDING SUPPORT
• THE KOYAMA PRESS GANG
• T.O. COMICS FRIENDS AND SUPPORTERS
• MY COMICS STUDENTS
• FAMILY
• CORY SILVERBERG
• ANIQUE ROSENBAUM

DEDICATED TO CLASSY CRAIG DANIELS ♡♡♡